América del Sur

ANNOTATED INSTRUCTOR'S EDITION

¡Anda!

CURSO ELEMENTAL

AUDREY L. HEINING-BOYNTON
GLYNIS S. COWELL
The University of North Carolina at Chapel Hill

WITH

Jean LeLoup
María del Carmen Caña Jiménez
Sonia Torres-Quiñones

PEARSON
Prentice Hall

world Languages

UPPER SADDLE RIVER, NJ 07458

Executive Editor: *Bob Hemmer*
Editorial Assistant: *Katie Spiegel*
Director of Marketing: *Kristine Suárez*
Senior Marketing Manager: *Denise Miller*
Marketing Coordinator: *Bill Bliss*
Director of Editorial Development: *Julia Caballero*
Development Editor: *Janet García-Levitas; Guadalupe Parras-Serradilla*
Development Editor for Assessment: *Melissa Marolla Brown*
Senior Managing Editor (Production): *Mary Rottino*
Associate Managing Editor (Production): *Janice Stangel*
Senior Production Editor: *Nancy Stevenson*
Composition/Full-Service Project Management: *Natalie Hansen and Sandra Reinhard, Black Dot Group*
Media/Supplements Editor: *Meriel Martínez*
Editorial Coordinator/Assistant Developmental Editor: *Jennifer Murphy*
Senior Media Editor: *Samantha Alducin*

Senior Operations Supervisor: *Brian Mackey*
Operations Specialist: *Cathleen Petersen*
Interior and Cover Design: *Lisa Delgado, Delgado and Company, Inc.*
Art Manager: *Maria Piper*
Illustrators: *Eric Larsen; Andrew Lange*
Electronic Art: *Siren Design*
Maps: *Peter Bull Art Studio*
Director, Image Resource Center: *Melinda Reo*
Manager, Rights & Permissions IRC: *Zina Arabia*
Manager, Visual Research: *Beth Brenzel*
Image Permissions Coordinator: *Richard Rodrigues*
Photo Researcher: *Diane Austin*
Publisher: *Phil Miller*
Cover image: *Donald Nausbaum, Getty Images Inc. – Stone Allstock*
Printer/Binder: *Courier Kendallville*
Typeface: *10/12 Janson*

Credits and acknowledgments borrowed from other sources and reproduced, with permission, in this textbook appear on page A49.

DEDICATION

To David
— Audrey

To John, Jack, and Kate
— Glynis

PEARSON
Prentice
Hall

10 9 8 7 6 5 4 3 2 1
ISBNs: 0-13-118213-7 / 978-0-13-118213-4

BRIEF CONTENTS

CAPÍTULO PRELIMINAR A

This preliminary chapter is meant to jump-start learning. In some cases, students may have studied some Spanish previously and may already be familiar with this material. The vocabulary in this chapter is high frequency, high usage. Encourage students to refer to this chapter if they forget certain words and expressions.

CAPÍTULO 1

Verb presentations such as *tener* are done *deductively*, in which students are given the rules/forms and go directly to practice, to streamline presentation time. All grammar presentations in this chapter are deductive.

CAPÍTULO 2

We have made the conscious decision to present a very brief introduction to *gustar*. In order to practice vocabulary in complete sentences, we have decided to introduce the *I, you, s/he, it* forms with *gustar*. Indirect object pronouns and a more in-depth explanation of *gustar* will appear in *Capítulo 8*.

(The numbers next to the grammar and vocabulary sections indicate their location within the chapter.)

FIRST

	Capítulo Preliminar A Para empezar	Capítulo 1 ¿Quiénes somos?	Capítulo 2 La vida universitaria
Vocabulary sections	1 Saludos, despedidas y presentaciones 2 Expresiones útiles para la clase 4 Los cognados 7 Los adjetivos de nacionalidad 8 Los números 0–30 9 La hora 10 Los días, los meses y las estaciones 11 El tiempo	1 La familia 6 Gente 9 Los números 31–100	1 Las materias y las especialidades 2 La sala de clase 5 Los números 100–1.000 6 En la universidad 8 Emociones y estados 10 Los deportes y los pasatiempos
Grammar sections	3 El alfabeto 5 Los pronombres personales 6 El verbo **ser** 12 **Gustar**	2 El verbo **tener** 3 El singular y el plural 4 El masculino y el femenino 5 Los artículos definidos e indefinidos 7 Los adjetivos posesivos 8 Los adjetivos descriptivos	3 Presente indicativo de verbos regulares 4 La formación de preguntas y las palabras interrogativas 7 El verbo **estar** 9 El verbo **gustar**
Pronunciation		Spanish vowels	Word stress and accent marks
Cultural readings and country focus	● Cómo se saluda la gente ● ¿Tú o usted? ● ¿Quién habla español?	● Los nombres en el mundo hispano ● El español, lengua diversa **LOS ESTADOS UNIDOS**	● Los estereotipos ● Los deportes en el mundo hispano **MÉXICO**
Escucha		**Estrategia:** Determining the topic and listening for words you know	**Estrategia:** Listening for the gist
Escribe		Un poema	Una descripción
Ambiciones siniestras		**Lectura:** *Conexiones* **Estrategia:** Recognizing cognates **Video:** *¿Quiénes son?*	**Lectura:** *Las solicitudes* **Estrategia:** Skimming **Video:** *La aventura comienza*

SEMESTER

Capítulo 3 Estamos en casa	Capítulo 4 Nuestra comunidad	Capítulo 5 ¡A divertirse! La música y el cine	Capítulo 6 ¡Sí, lo sé!
1 La casa 3 Los muebles y otros objetos de la casa 4 Los quehaceres de la casa 5 Los colores 7 Los números 1.000–100.000.000	1 Los lugares 3 ¿Qué tienen que hacer? ¿Qué pasa? 7 Trabajos y servicios voluntarios	1 El mundo de la música 6 El mundo del cine	**Reviewing strategies**
2 Algunos verbos irregulares 6 Unas expresiones con **tener** 8 **Hay**	2 **Saber** y **conocer** 4 Los verbos con cambio de raíz 5 El verbo **ir** 6 **Ir + a +** infinitivo 8 Las expresiones afirmativas y negativas 9 Un repaso de **ser** y **estar**	2 Los adjetivos demostrativos 3 Los pronombres demostrativos 4 Los adverbios 5 El presente progresivo 7 Los números ordinales 8 **Hay que +** infinitivo 9 Los pronombres de complemento directo y la "a" personal	**Comunicación** Recycling of Capítulo Preliminar A to Capítulo 5
The letters **h**, **j**, and **g**	The letters **c** and **z**	Diphthongs and linking	
● ¿Dónde viven los españoles? ● Las mujeres del mundo hispano	● Actividades cotidianas: Las compras y el paseo ● La conciencia social	● La música latina en los Estados Unidos ● La influencia hispana en el cine norteamericano	
ESPAÑA	**HONDURAS, GUATEMALA Y EL SALVADOR**	**NICARAGUA, COSTA RICA Y PANAMÁ**	**Cultura**
Estrategia: Listening for specific information	**Estrategia:** Paraphrasing what you hear	**Estrategia:** Anticipating content	
Un anuncio (*flyer*)	Una tarjeta postal	Una reseña	
Lectura: *El concurso* **Estrategia:** Scanning **Video:** *¡Tienes una gran oportunidad!*	**Lectura:** *Las cosas no son siempre lo que parecen* **Estrategia:** Skimming and Scanning (II) **Video:** *¿Quiénes son en realidad?*	**Lectura:** *La búsqueda de Eduardo* **Estrategia:** Anticipating content **Video:** *Se conocen*	**Ambiciones siniestras** **Y por fin, ¿cómo andas?**

CAPÍTULO 3

We have chosen to introduce *conocer* in *Capítulo 3* as an irregular verb and to focus on the meaning "to be acquainted with." In *Capítulo 4* we present *saber* and contrast it with *conocer*.

CAPÍTULO 4

We have chosen to briefly introduce the *personal "a"* here in *Capítulo 4* with *conocer*, and then reintroduce/recycle it in *Capítulo 5* with direct object pronouns. The focus in *Capítulo 4* is to make students aware of the concept. In *Capítulo 5* there will be further practice with direct object pronouns as well as recycling of the *personal "a"* with *conocer*.

CAPÍTULO 5

Although a complete grammatical explanation of adverbs would include the fact that students can also modify verbs, whole phrases, clauses, or sentences, we have chosen to simplify the presentation. Also note that we have chosen to use the word *describe* rather than *modify* in the presentation. Although both words are grammatically acceptable, *describe* is a bit more casual and user-friendly.

CAPÍTULO 6

In this chapter we have synthesized the main points of the first five chapters in a recycled format for students to practice the new skills they are learning. You will note that all of these activities have the students *put it all together*—in other words, *all of the activities in Capítulo 6 are communicative.*

CAPÍTULO PRELIMINAR B

The intention of *Capítulo Preliminar B* is to methodically *review* and guide all students to begin at a similar point. You will notice that *Capítulo Preliminar B* moves more by small chunks of material than *Capítulo 6* does. *Capítulo Preliminar B* assumes that students need more step-by-step guidance and remediation so they can all arrive at a more common starting point.

CAPÍTULO 7

We have chosen to present both regular and irregular preterits in the same chapter to allow for greater focus on form and practice. You will note that this is the primary grammatical focus for *Capítulo 7*. In *Capítulos 8–11*, the preterit will be continually recycled (along with the present tense) for additional practice and reinforcement.

CAPÍTULO 8

Preferences for presenting the preterit and imperfect tenses can be highly personal. *¡Anda!* breaks down the use of the imperfect into four categories; you may prefer to combine them in a different way. The goal is to reach the learning styles of as many students as possible.

(The numbers next to the grammar and vocabulary sections indicate their location within the chapter.)

SECOND

	Capítulo Preliminar B **Introducciones y repasos**	Capítulo 7 **¡A comer!**	Capítulo 8 **¿Qué te pones?**
Vocabulary sections	**Capítulo Preliminar A** **Capítulo 1** **Capítulo 2** **Capítulo 3** **Capítulo 4** **Capítulo 5**	1 La comida 4 La preparación de las comidas 6 En el restaurante	1 La ropa
Grammar sections		2 Repaso del complemento directo 3 El pretérito 5 Unos verbos irregulares en el pretérito	2 Los pronombres de complemento indirecto 3 **Gustar** y verbos como **gustar** 4 Los pronombres de complemento directo e indirecto usados juntos 5 Las construcciones reflexivas 6 El imperfecto
Pronunciation		The letters **r** and **rr**	The letters **ll** and **ñ**
Cultural readings and country focus	**Cultura**	● Las comidas en el mundo hispano ● La comida hispana	● Zara: la moda internacional ● Los centros comerciales en Latinoamérica
		CHILE Y PARAGUAY	**ARGENTINA Y URUGUAY**
Escucha		**Estrategia:** Combining strategies	**Estrategia:** Guessing meaning from context
Escribe		Un recuerdo (*memory*) (I)	Un recuerdo (II)
Ambiciones siniestras	**Ambiciones siniestras** **Y por fin, ¿cómo andas?**	**Lectura:** *El rompecabezas* **Estrategia:** Predicting **Video:** *¡Qué rico está el pisco!*	**Lectura:** *¿Quién fue?* **Estrategia:** Guessing meaning from context **Video:** *El misterio crece*

SEMESTER

Capítulo 9 Estamos en forma	Capítulo 10 ¡Viajemos!	Capítulo 11 El mundo actual	Capítulo 12 Y por fin, ¡lo sé!
1 El cuerpo humano 3 Unas enfermedades y tratamientos médicos	1 Los medios de transporte 4 El viaje	1 Los animales 2 El medio ambiente 4 La política	**Reviewing strategies**
2 Un resumen de los pronombres de complemento directo, indirecto y reflexivos 4 **¡Qué!** y **¡cuánto!** 5 El pretérito y el imperfecto 6 Expresiones con **hacer**	2 Los mandatos informales 3 Los mandatos formales 5 Otras formas del posesivo 6 El comparativo y el superlativo	3 El subjuntivo 5 **Por** y **para** 6 Las preposiciones y los pronombres preposicionales 7 El infinitivo después de preposiciones	**Comunicación** Recycling of Capítulo Preliminar B to Capítulo 11
The letters **d** and **t**	The letters **b** and **v**	Review of word stress and accent marks	
● El agua y la buena salud ● Las farmacias en el mundo hispanohablante	● ¿Cómo nos movemos? ● Venezuela, país de aventuras	● El Yunque: tesoro tropical ● La política en el mundo hispano	
PERÚ, BOLIVIA Y ECUADOR	**COLOMBIA Y VENEZUELA**	**EL CARIBE: CUBA, PUERTO RICO Y LA REPÚBLICA DOMINICANA**	**Cultura**
Estrategia: Asking yourself questions	**Estrategia:** Listening for linguistic cues	**Estrategia:** Using visual organizers	
Un resumen	Un reportaje de un lugar turístico	Un anuncio	
Lectura: *¡Qué mentira!* **Estrategia:** Asking yourself questions **Video:** *No llores por mí*	**Lectura:** *¿Qué sabía?* **Estrategia:** Skipping words **Video:** *Falsas apariencias*	**Lectura:** *Celia* **Estrategia:** Using visual organizers **Video:** *El desenlace*	**Ambiciones siniestras** **Y por fin, ¿cómo andas?**

vii

CAPÍTULO 9

The presentation of pronouns, which began in *Capítulo 6*, concludes in this chapter with a review of all pronouns. Students have learned the difference between the form and functions of all the sets of pronouns and in *Capítulo 9* are able to analyze their uses through comparison and context.

CAPÍTULO 10

There are several approaches to teaching the commands. In *¡Anda!* we made the conscious decision to chunk the material; the authors have chosen to present the familiar commands first for several reasons. First, they are the commands that students will tend to use the most among themselves. Next, the affirmative commands are very easy to form. Finally, the negative familiar commands prepare the students for the formal commands to follow, and ultimately for the subjunctive.

CAPÍTULO 11

You will note that, yet again, we are taking a complex concept, the subjunctive, and breaking it down into "bite-size" chunks that make learning the concept possible. Also, you may have taught these fixed expressions as impersonal expressions with *ser*. In *¡Anda!*, we have chosen to simply call them fixed expressions, under the headings of opinion, doubt, probability, wishes, desires, and hopes. This eliminates any confusion between "personal" and "impersonal", because these expressions can be used regardless of the relationship to the speaker.

CAPÍTULO 12

After giving students strategies on how to conduct an overall review, this chapter is organized by beginning with communicative and engaging activities that focus on grammar and vocabulary from *Capítulo 7*. The recycling continues to move through the chapters, ending with *Capítulo 11*. This is followed by a more comprehensive review, truly *putting all the chapters together*. Finally, there is a recycling of countries, presented in *Capítulos 7–11*.

Why ¡Anda! ?

> andar *vi* to walk; to move; to travel around; **¡Anda!** *excl* Come on! That's it!

In survey after survey, and focus group after focus group, Spanish instructors tell us that they are finding it increasingly difficult to accomplish everything they want in their elementary Spanish courses. Contact hours are decreasing. Class sizes are increasing. And students' lives are busier than ever. At the same time, course goals have become more and more ambitious. Instead of focusing only on grammar and vocabulary, instructors have made it clear that they want to give their students a thorough exposure to Hispanic culture and an opportunity to develop and practice communication skills. But there simply isn't enough time to do all of this as well as most would like, and the available elementary Spanish texts do little to address the problem. As a result, some instructors end up galloping through their text in order to cover all the grammar and vocabulary, omitting interesting cultural topics and limiting student speaking time. Others have made the awkward choice to use a text designed for first-year Spanish over three or even four semesters.

Based on this extensive research, you now have another option: *¡Anda!*

¡Anda! has been developed to provide a practical response to the challenges today's Spanish instructors are facing. Its innovations center around three key areas:

1 Realistic goals with a realistic approach
2 Focus on student motivation
3 Tools to promote success

¡Anda! is ready to go! More of what you need ... less of what you don't!

Realistic goals with a realistic approach

¡Anda! is the first college-level Spanish program conceived from the outset as a four-semester sequence of materials. The *¡Anda!* program is divided into two halves, *¡Anda! Curso elemental* and *¡Anda! Curso intermedio*, each of which can be completed in one academic year.

Each volume's scope and sequence has been carefully designed, based on advice from hundreds of instructors at a wide variety of schools. Each volume introduces a realistic number of new vocabulary words, and the traditional first-year grammar sequence has been spread over two volumes so that it can be presented in four semesters rather than two. As a result, students have adequate time throughout the course to focus on communication, culture, and skills development, and to master the vocabulary and grammar concepts to which they are introduced.

Each volume of *¡Anda!* has been structured to foster preparation, recycling, and review within the context of a multi-semester sequence of courses. The ten regular chapters in each volume are complemented by *two preliminary* chapters and *two recycling* chapters.

Capítulo Preliminar A	Capítulo Preliminar B
Capítulo 1	Capítulo 7
Capítulo 2	Capítulo 8
Capítulo 3	Capítulo 9
Capítulo 4	Capítulo 10
Capítulo 5	Capítulo 11
Capítulo 6 (recycling)	Capítulo 12 (recycling)

- *Preliminary Chapter A* is designed with **ample vocabulary** to get students up and running and to give them a **sense of accomplishment** quickly. Many students will already be familiar with some of this vocabulary. It also has students reflect on the question "why study Spanish?".
- *Preliminary Chapter B* is a **review** of Preliminary A through Chapter 5 and allows those who join the class midyear or those who need a refresher to get up to speed at the beginning of the second half of the book.
- *Chapters 1–5* and *7–11* are **regular** chapters.
- *Chapters 6 and 12* are **recycling** chapters. No new material is presented. Designed for in-class use, these chapters recycle and recombine previously presented vocabulary, grammar, and culture, giving students more time to practice communication without the burden of learning new grammar or vocabulary.

Each regular chapter of *¡Anda!* has also been developed with the goal of providing a realistic approach for the achievement of realistic goals.

- New material is presented in manageable amounts, or **chunks,** allowing students to assimilate and practice without feeling overwhelmed.
- Each chapter contains a **realistic** number of new vocabulary words.
- Vocabulary and grammar explanations are interspersed, each **introduced at the point of need.**
- Grammar explanations are clear and concise with many supporting examples, followed by practice exercises and activities.
- Practice begins with **mechanical** exercises, for which there are correct answers, progresses through more **meaningful,** structured activities in which the student is guided but has some flexibility in determining the appropriate response, and ends with **communicative** activities in which students are manipulating language to create personalized responses.

Focus on student motivation

Many of the innovative features of *¡Anda!* have been designed to help instructors generate and sustain interest on the part of their students, whether they be of traditional college age or adult learners:

- Chapters are organized around themes that reflect **student interests** and tap into students' **real-life experiences.**
- Basic **vocabulary** has been selected and tested through *¡Anda!'s* development for its relevance and support, while additional words and phrases are offered so

that **students can personalize** their responses and acquire the vocabulary that is most meaningful to them. Additional vocabulary items are found in *Vocabulario útil* boxes throughout the chapters as well as in Appendix 3 (*También se dice...*).

- Exercises and activities have been designed to foster active participation by students. The focus throughout is on giving students opportunities to speak and on allowing instructors to **increase the amount of student "talk time"** in each class period. The majority of activities **elicit students' ideas and opinions,** engaging them to respond to each other on a variety of levels. Abundant pair and group activities encourage peer editing and help to create a comfortable arena for language learning.

- **No assumptions** are made concerning previous experience with Spanish or with language learning in general.

- Each exercise is designed to begin with **what the student already knows.**

- A **high-interest mystery story** runs through each chapter. Two episodes are presented in each regular chapter, one as the chapter's reading selection, the other in a corresponding video segment. Characters from the story are also integrated in the *Escucha* boxes.

- Both **"high"** and **"popular" culture** are woven throughout the chapters to enable students to learn to recognize and appreciate cultural diversity as they explore behaviors and values of the Spanish-speaking world. They are encouraged to think critically about these cultural practices and gifts to society.

Tools to promote success

The *¡Anda!* program includes many unique features and components designed to help students succeed at language learning and their instructors at language teaching.

Student learning support

- A **"walking tour"** of the *¡Anda! text and supplements* helps students understand their language program materials and the language of language learning before they use them.

- Explicit, systematic **recycling boxes with page references** help students link current learning to previously studied material in earlier chapters or sections.

- **Periodic review and self-assessment** boxes (*¿Cómo andas?*) help students gauge their understanding and retention of the material presented. A final assessment in each chapter (*Y por fin, ¿cómo andas?*) offers a comprehensive review.

- **Student notes** provide additional explanations and guidance in the learning process. Some of these contain cross-references to the English Grammar Guide and other student supplements. Others offer learning strategies (*Estrategia*) and additional information (*Fíjate*).

- An **English Grammar Guide,** available separately, explains the grammatical concepts students need in order to understand the Spanish grammar presentations in the text. Animated English grammar tutorials are also available within *MySpanishLab.*

- *MySpanishLab*™ offers students a wealth of online resources and a supportive environment for completing homework assignments. When enabled by the instructor, a "Need Help" box appears as students are doing online homework activities, providing links to English and Spanish grammar tutorials, e-book sections, and additional practice activities—all directly relevant to the task at hand. Hints, verb charts, a glossary, and many other resources are available as well.

- A **Workbooklet,** available separately, allows student to complete the activities that involve writing without having to write in their copy of the textbook itself.

Instructor teaching support

One of the most important keys to student success is instructor success. The *¡Anda!* program has all of the support that you have come to expect and, based on our research, it offers many other enhancements!

- The **Annotated Instructor's Edition** of *¡Anda!* offers a wealth of materials designed to help instructors teach effectively and efficiently. Strategically placed annotations explain the text's methodology and function as **a built-in course in language teaching methods.**
- **Estimated time indicators** for presentational materials and practice activities help instructors create class plans.
- Other annotations provide additional activities and suggested answers.
- **The annotations are color-coded** and labeled for ready reference and ease of use.
- A treasure trove of **extra activities,** known as the **Activity Cache,** allows instructors to choose additional materials for in-class use.

The authors' approach

Learning a language is an exciting, enriching, and sometimes life changing experience. The development of the *¡Anda!* program is the result of many years of teaching and research that guided the authors independently to make important discoveries about language learning, the most important of which center on the student. Research-based and pedagogically sound, *¡Anda!* is also the product of extensive information gathered firsthand from numerous focus group sessions with students, graduate instructors, adjunct faculty, full-time professors, and administrators in an effort to determine the learning and instructional needs of each of these groups.

The Importance of the National Foreign Language Standards in *¡ANDA!*

The *¡Anda!* program is based on the *National Foreign Language Standards.* The five organizing principles (the 5C's) of the Standards for language teaching and learning are at the core of *¡Anda!*: **Communication, Cultures, Connections, Comparisons,** and **Communities.** Each chapter opener identifies for the instructor where and in what capacity each of the 5C's are addressed. The **Weave of Curricular Elements** of the *National Foreign Language Standards* provide additional organizational structure for *¡Anda!* Those components of the **Curricular Weave** are: **Language System, Cultural Knowledge, Communication Strategies, Critical Thinking Skills, Learning Strategies, Other Subject Areas,** and **Technology.** Each of the Curricular Weave elements is omnipresent and, like the 5C's, permeates all aspects of each chapter of *¡Anda!*

- The *Language System*, which is comprised of components such as grammar, vocabulary, and phonetics, is at the heart of each chapter.
- The *Comunicación* sections of each chapter present vocabulary, grammar, and pronunciation at the point of need and maximum usage. Streamlined presentations are utilized that allow the learner to be immediately successful in employing the new concepts.

- *Cultural Knowledge* is approached thematically, making use of the chapter's vocabulary and grammar. Cultural presentations begin with the two-page chapter openers and always start with what the students already know about the cultural theme/concept from their home, local, regional, or national cultural perspective.
- *Communication and Learning Strategies* are abundant with tips for both students and instructors on how to maximize studying and in-class learning of Spanish, as well as how to utilize the language outside of the classroom.
- *Critical Thinking Skills* take center stage in *¡Anda!* Questions throughout the chapters, in particular tied to the cultural presentations, provide students with the opportunities to answer more than discrete point questions. The answers students are able to provide do indeed require higher-order thinking, but at a linguistic level completely appropriate for a beginning language learner.
- With regard to *Other Subject Areas*, *¡Anda!* is diligent with regard to incorporating **Connections** to other disciplines via vocabulary, discussion topics, and suggested activities.
- Finally, *Technology* is taken to an entirely new level with *MySpanishLab*™ and the *Ambiciones siniestras* DVD. The authors and Prentice Hall believe that technology is a means to the end, not the end in and of itself, and so the focus is not on the technology *per se*, but on how that technology can deliver great content in better, more efficient, more interactive, and more meaningful ways.

By embracing the *National Foreign Language Standards* and as a result of decades of experience teaching Spanish, the authors believe that:

- A **student-centered classroom** is the best learning environment.
- Instruction must **begin where the learner is,** and all students come to the learning experience with prior knowledge that needs to be tapped.
- All students can learn in a **supportive environment** where they are encouraged to take risks when learning another language.
- **Critical thinking** is an important skill that must constantly be encouraged, practiced, and nurtured.
- **Learners** need to **make connections** with other disciplines in the Spanish classroom.

With these beliefs in mind, the authors have developed hundreds of creative and meaningful language-learning activities for the text and supporting components that employ students' imagination and engage the senses. For both students and instructors, they have created an instructional program that is **manageable, motivating,** and **clear.**

The Authors

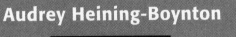

Audrey Heining-Boynton

Audrey Heining-Boynton has been a Professor of Education and Spanish at The University of North Carolina at Chapel Hill, where she has taught Spanish and education courses for many years. She has won many teaching awards including the prestigious ACTFL Anthony Papalia Award for Excellence in Teacher Education, the Foreign Language of North Carolina Teacher of the Year Award, and The UNC ACCESS Award for Excellence in Working with LD and ADHD Students. Dr. Heining-Boynton is a frequent presenter at national and international conferences; has published more than seventy articles, curricula, textbooks, and manuals; and has won nearly $4 million in grants to help create language programs in North Carolina and South Carolina. Dr. Heining-Boynton has also held many important positions: President of the American Council on the Teaching of Foreign Languages (ACTFL 2005, The Year of Languages), President of the National Network for Early Language Learning, Vice President of the Michigan Foreign Language Association, board member of the Foreign Language Association of North Carolina, committee chair for Foreign Language in the Elementary School (FLES) for the American Association of Teachers of Spanish and Portuguese (AATSP), and an elected Executive Council member of ACTFL.

Glynis Cowell

Glynis Cowell is the Director of the Spanish Language Program in the Department of Romance Languages and Literatures and an Assistant Dean in Academic Advising, General College and Arts and Sciences, at The University of North Carolina at Chapel Hill. She has taught first-year seminars, honors courses, numerous Spanish language courses, and team-teaches a graduate course on the theories and techniques of teaching foreign languages. Dr. Cowell received her M.A. in Spanish Literature and her Ph.D. in Curriculum and Instruction, with a concentration in Foreign Language Education, from The University of North Carolina at Chapel Hill. Prior to joining the faculty at UNC-CH in August 1994, she coordinated the Spanish Language Program in the Department of Romance Studies at Duke University. She has also taught Spanish at Davidson Community College in North Carolina. At UNC-CH she has received the university Students' Award for Excellence in Undergraduate Teaching as well as the Graduate Student Mentor Award for the Department of Romance Languages and Literatures.

Dr. Cowell has directed teacher workshops on Spanish language and cultures and has presented papers and written articles on the teaching of language and literature, the incorporation of information technology in language teaching, and teaching across the curriculum. She is the co-author of two other college textbooks.

The Development Story

At the beginning of the 21st century, it was clear that things had changed in language classes all across the country. At most institutions, there were more students per classroom than ever before. There were more schools where language classes met three or fewer times per week than there were with classes meeting four or five times per week. More students were working than ever before: The American Council on Education reported that 78% of students worked while they were enrolled in college, and that the average time worked was nearly thirty hours a week. At the same time, research shows that language instructors were clearly trying to do a better job of exposing students to the target culture, to spend more time practicing communication skills, and to establish a balance of four-skills practice. In short, with less time and fewer resources on the one hand and a desire to broaden the scope of language study on the other, something had to give. But what?

In 2004, 2005, and 2006, the authors and their editors surveyed hundreds of Spanish instructors. This is what we learned:

- When asked about the grammatical scope and sequence, 85% of instructors said that the most important thing to them was to have a text that had realistic goals about what students could accomplish in one year.
- When asked about the basis they used for making text decisions, 77% said that the text should be "based on good pedagogical practices."
- When asked if they would like to slow down the pace of grammar instruction to allow more time for communicative practice and coverage of cultural topics, 74% said yes.
- When asked if they would like to spread the traditional grammar syllabus over four semesters of instruction, 65% said yes.

With this information in hand, we developed a plan for a textbook series and supplements package that would address these salient preferences issues. To refine the plan, we enlisted the help of hundreds of instructors at a wide variety of schools (their names are listed on the following page). They gave us feedback on the plan through online surveys and traditional manuscript reviews. They attended focus groups on their local campuses or in other locations. Nine instructors attended a two-day reviewer conference in New Orleans to help us make decisions on issues where consensus had not yet been reached. The scope and sequence, the chapter structure, the mystery story, the page design, even the cover and the title—all benefited greatly from the many valuable suggestions made by these instructors.

Along the way, we also consulted students. Some 359 of them gave us feedback on their preference for art styles.

The results are for you to judge, but of one thing we are sure: The entire development of *¡Anda!* was driven by instructors and students and dedicated to providing contemporary solutions for the needs of today's language students and teachers.

To the many instructors and coordinators who dedicated countless hours helping us understand their and their students' needs, we are grateful. You will see your comments and suggestions reflected throughout the text. Thanks to you all!

Faculty Reviewers

James Abraham, *Glendale Community College*
Martha Aguilar, *Bronx Community College*
Pilar Alcalde, *University of Memphis*
Renee Andrade, *Mount San Antonio College*
Rafael Arias, *Los Angeles Valley College*
Mary Jo Arns-Radaj, *Normandale Community College*
Andrea Bacorn, *Montgomery College*
Angela Bagues, *Shippensburg University*
Amanda Baron, *Southeast Community College*
Roberto Batista, *Valencia Community College, East Campus*
Robert Baum, *Arkansas State University*
Rosa Bird, *University of Central Oklahoma*
Beatrice Bongiorno, *Bellevue Community College*
Mary Boutiette, *North Hennepin Community College*
Patrick Brady, *Tidewater Community College*
Cathy Briggs, *North Lake College*
Greg Briscoe, *Utah Valley State College*
Elaine Brooks, *University of New Orleans*
Karen Brunschwig, *University of La Verne*
Elizabeth Buckley Sánchez, *University of Tulsa*
Linda Burk, *Manchester Community College–Manchester Connecticut*
Isabel Bustamante-López, *California Polytechnic State University at Pomona*
Ana Caldero, *Valencia Community College (West Campus)*
Lisa Calvin, *Indiana State University*
Paul Cankar, *Austin Community College*
Karen Cárdenas, *South Dakota State University*
Morris Carson, *J. Sargent Reynolds Community College*
June Carter, *University of South Carolina Spartanburg*
Samira Chater, *Valencia Community College, East Campus*
Carmen Chávez, *Florida Atlantic University*
Robert Chierico, *Chicago State University*
Maritza Chinea-Thornberry, *University of South Florida*
Carrie Clay, *Anderson University*
Carmen Coracides, *Scottsdale Community College*
Steve Corbett, *Texas Tech University*
Manuel Cortes Castañeda, *Eastern Kentucky University*
José A. Cortes-Caballero, *Georgia Perimeter College*
Xuchitl Coso, *Georgia Perimeter College/Lawrenceville*
Judith Costello, *Northern Arizona University*
Dale Crandall, *Gainesville College*
José Cruz, *Fayetteville Technical Community College*
Julio de la Llata, *Austin Community College*
Aída Díaz, *Valencia Community College*
Héctor Enríquez, *University of Texas, El Paso*
Luz Escobar, *Southeastern Louisiana University*
Janan Fallon, *Georgia Perimeter College*
Mary Fatora-Tumbaga, *Kauai Community College*
Carmen Ferrero, *Moravian College*
Estelle Finley, *Spelman College*
Luz Font, *Florida Community College at Jacksonville*
Elizabeth Fouts, *Saint Anselm College*

Carmen García, *Texas Southern University*
José Manuel García, *Florida Southern College*
Rodolfo García, *Metropolitan State College of Denver*
José M. García Sánchez, *Eastern Washington University*
José García-Sánchez, *Eastern Washington University*
Pamela Gill, *Gaston College*
John Gladstein, *Howard College*
Julie Glosson, *Union University*
Olympia González, *Loyola University*
Yolanda L. González, *Valencia Community College*
Roberta Gordenstein, *Elms College*
Sergio Guzmán, *Community College of Southern Nevada*
Peggy Haas, *Kent State University*
Terry Hansen, *Pellissippi State Technical Community College*
Mary Harges, *Southwest Missouri State University*
Ana Lucy Hernández, *William Rainey Harper College*
Yanina Hernández, *Texas Southern University*
Ann Hills, *University of La Verne*
Kristi Hislope, *North Georgia College & State University*
Michelle Horner Grau, *Christopher Newport University*
Alexis Indenbaum, *Reading Area Community College*
Luis Jiménez, *Florida Southern College*
Valerie Job, *South Plains College*
Dimitrios Karayiannis, *Southern Illinois University at Carbondale*
Jacoba Koene, *Anderson University*
Ruth Konopka, *Grossmont College*
David Korn, *Anderson College*
Marianna Kunow, *Southeastern Louisiana University*
Andrea Labinger, *University of La Verne*
Edwin Lamboy, *Montclair State University*
Felipe Antonio Lapuente, *The University of Memphis*
Rebecca Leigh, *Williams Coastal Carolina University*
Jorge O. López R., *University of Tennessee at Martin*
José López-Marrón, *Bronx Community College–CUNY*
Margaret Lyman, *Bakersfield College*
Domenico Maceri, *Allan Hancock College*
Carlos Madan, *SUNY Plattsburgh*
Anne-Marie Martin, *Portland Community College*
Janie McNutt, *South Plains College*
Joseph Menig, *Valencia Community College*
Sandra Merrill, *Central Missouri State University*
Silvia Milosevich, *Butte College*
Deborah Mistron, *Middle Tennessee State University*
Libardo Mitchell, *Portland Community College, Sylvania*
Joshua Mora, *Wayland Baptist University*
Daniel Nappo, *University of Tennessee at Martin*
William Nowak, *University of Houston–Downtown*
Marcela Ochoa-Shivapour, *Cornell College*
Cecilia Ojeda, *Northern Arizona University*
Milagros Ojermark, *Diablo Valley College*
Dale Omundson, *Anoka-Ramsey Community College*
Ann Ortiz, *Campbell University*
Ruth Owens, *Arkansas State University*
Hannah Padilla, *Normandale Community College*

Diane Parmeter, *Clinton Community College*
Edward Pasko, *Purdue University Calumet*
Peggy Patterson, *Rice University*
Inmaculada Pertusa, *Western Kentucky University*
Todd Phillips, *Austin Community College*
Mirta Pimentel, *Moravian College*
Joyce Pinkard, *Fresno City College*
Harriet Poole, *Lake City Community College*
Enrique Porrua, *University of North Carolina at Pembroke*
Comfort Pratt, *Texas Tech University*
Marcie Pratt, *Black Hills State University*
Cheryl Reagan, *Sussex County Community College*
Claire Reetz, *Florida Community College-Jacksonville*
Marilyn Reit, *Shasta Tehama Joint Comm. College*
Robert Rice, *Austin Community College*
John T. Riley, *Fordham University*
Jennifer Robertson, *Valencia Community College*
Karen Robinson, *University of Nebraska at Omaha*
Vicki Roman-Lagunas, *Northeastern Illinois University*
Ana Romero, *Arkansas State University*
Francisco Ronquillo, *Albuquerque–TVI*
Sandra Rosenstiel, *University of Dallas*
Cecil J. Roth, Jr., *Jamestown College*
Linda Roy, *Tarrant County College–South*
Cecilia Ryan, *McNeese State University*
Carmen Salazar, *Los Angeles Valley College*
Elizabeth Sánchez, *University of Tulsa*
Edgard Sankara, *LaGrange College*
Robert Shell, *Missouri Western State College*
Virginia Shen, *Chicago State University*
Gregory Shepherd, *William Paterson University*
Eugenia Simien, *Southeastern Louisiana University*
Roger Simpson, *Clemson University*
Victor Slesinger, *Palm Beach Community College (Central Campus)*
Anita Smith, *Pitt Community College*
Ruth Smith, *University of Louisiana at Monroe*
Oscar U. Somoza, *University of Denver*
Irena Stefanova, *Santa Clara University*
Melissa Stewart, *Western Kentucky University*
Stuart Stewart, *Southeastern Louisiana University*
Jonathan Stowers, *Salt Lake Community College-Redwood*
Michael Tallon, *University of the Incarnate Word*
Pam Taylor, *University of North Carolina–Greensboro*
Mercedes Thompson, *El Camino College*
Sue Ann Thompson, *Butler University*
Richard Tooke, *South Dakota State University*
Stephanie Traynor, *Widener University*
Rene Vacchio, *Austin Community College*
Irma Valdez, *Blinn College*
Salvador Valdivia, *Shasta College*
Gloria Vélez-Rendón, *Purdue University Calumet*
Kathy Vestal, *Rowan-Cabarrus Community College*
Olga Vilella, *St. Xavier University*
Carlos Villacís, *Houston Community College*

Francisco Vivar, *The University of Memphis*
Geoffrey Voght, *Eastern Michigan University*
Gloria F. Waldman, *York College–CUNY*
Chris Weimer, *Oklahoma State University at Stillwater*
Bruce Williams, *William Paterson University*
Helga Winkler, *Moorpark College*
Gloria Yampey-Jorg, *Houston Community College*
Francisco Zermeno, *Chabot College*
Theresa Zmurkewycz, *Saint Joseph's University*

Faculty Focus Groups

Claudia Acosta, *College of the Canyons*
Clementina R. Adams, *Clemson University*
Sara Aguirre, *Reedley College*
Karin Alfaro, *Northeastern Illinois University*
Carlos Arce, *Cerritos College*
Rafael Arias, *Los Angeles Valley College*
Norma A. Arizpe, *Blinn College*
Rosalind Arthur, *Georgia Perimeter College*
Letvia M. Arza, *Georgia Perimeter College*
Jennifer Austin, *Rutgers University–Newark*
Marisol Ballester, *Broward Community College–North*
Enrique Barquinero, *Florida Community College, Jacksonville*
Erika Barragán, *Tarrant County College–NE*
Roberto Batista, *Valencia Community College*
Paul Begin, *Pepperdine University*
Tracy Bishop, *Hofstra University*
Julián Bueno, *Southern Illinois University–Edwardsville*
Susan Byrne, *SUNY–Oneonta*
Froylán Cabuto, *Cerritos College*
Alejandro Cáceres, *Southern Illinois University, Carbondale*
Ana Caldero, *Valencia Community College*
Marla A. Calico, *Georgia Perimeter College*
José A. Caraballo, *Blinn College*
Beth B. Cardon, *Georgia Perimeter College*
Dinora Cardoso, *Pepperdine University*
Norma I. Carrero Román, *Blinn College*
Samira Chater, *Valencia Community College*
Carmen Chávez, *Florida Atlantic University*
Robert J. Chierico, *Chicago State University*
Kathy Chonez, *Southern Illinois University, Carbondale*
Alicia Class, *El Camino College*
Daria Cohen, *Rider University*
Mary Cooley Lorenzo, *Blinn College*
Al L. Cooper, *Pima Community College, East*
José A. Cortes, *Georgia Perimeter College*
Mayra Cortés-Torres, *Pima Community College, East*
Xuchitl N. Coso, *Georgia Perimeter College*
Darren Crasto, *Houston Community College*
Patricia Crespo-Martin, *Foothill College*
Ivana Cuvalo, *South Suburban College–Cook Co.*
Aleta Davis, *El Camino College*
Susann M. Davis, *Western Kentucky University*

Ana María de Barling, *West Valley College*

Elizabeth Dowdy, *Manatee Community College*

James P. Dowdy, *Manatee Community College*

Kyle Echols, *Florida Community College, Jacksonville*

Nilsa O. Ehresman, *Blinn College*

Rhonda Eisner, *Los Angeles Valley College*

Margaret Eomurian, *Houston Community College*

Nora Erro-Peralta, *Florida Atlantic University*

Dina Fabery, *Valencia Community College*

Janan Fallon, *Georgia Perimeter College*

Ronna Feit, *SUNY–Nassau Community College*

Marino Fernández, *Valencia Community College*

Ruth E. Fernández, *Broward Community College*

María Rosa Fernández de Bell, *Southern Illinois University, Carbondale*

Patricia Figueroa, *Pima Community College, East*

Luz Font, *Florida Community College, Jacksonville*

Tom Fonte, *El Camino College*

Deborah Foote, *Columbia College–Chicago*

María Elena Francés-Benítez, *Los Angeles Valley College*

Ronald A. García, *Nova Southeastern University*

Luisa García-Conde, *CUNY–Queensborough Community College*

Nereyda Garza-Lozano, *Fresno City College*

Eddy H. Gaytán, *Chicago State University*

John S. Geary, *Northeastern Illinois University*

Robert Geraldi, *Palm Beach Community College-Boca Raton*

Beatrice Giannandrea, *Valencia Community College*

Scott Gibby, *Austin Community College*

Yolanda L. González, *Valencia Community College*

Esther Greenstein, *Broward Community College*

Mercedes Guadalupe, *Valencia Community College*

Scott Harris, *Clemson University*

Hiltrud A. Heller, *El Camino College*

Librada Hernández, *Los Angeles Valley College*

Julio F. Hernando, *Indiana University-South Bend*

Ana M. Hnat, *Houston Community College*

Michael Horswell, *Florida Atlantic University*

Patricia Houston, *Pima Community College, East*

Dimitrios H. Karayiannis, *Southern Illinois University, Carbondale*

Caroline Kreide, *Merced College*

Todd Lakin, *City Colleges of Chicago–Richard J. Daley College*

Jeffrey N. Lamb, *Solano Community College*

Stephanie Langston, *Georgia Perimeter College*

Carlos A. Lebrón, *Northeastern Illinois University*

Sonia Lenk, *Western Kentucky University*

Susana Liso, *The University of Virginia at Wise*

Susan Lister, *De Anza College*

Eder F. Maestre, *Western Kentucky University*

April Marshall, *Pepperdine University*

Delmarie Martínez, *Nova Southeastern University*

Linda Martínez, *Chicago State University*

Renato Martínez, *Fresno City College*

Sergio Martínez, *San Antonio College*

Melissa McClennen-Davis, *Blinn College*

Natasha J. McClure, *Western Kentucky University*

Mary Yetta McKelva, *Grayson County College*

Nancy Membrez, *University of Texas at San Antonio*

Joseph A. Menig, *Valencia Community College*

Dora Cecilia Mezzich Kress, *Florida Community College, Jacksonville*

Iván Miño, *Tarrant County College–SE*

Natasa Momcilovic, *Southern Illinois University, Carbondale*

Mónica Montalvo, *Valencia Community College*

Lizette S. Moon, *Houston Community College*

RoseAnna Mueller, *Columbia College–Chicago*

Araceli Muñoz, *Chicago State University*

Sonia Navarro-Milano, *Valencia Community College*

Ofélia R. Nikolova, *Southern Illinois University, Carbondale*

Gustavo Obeso, *Western Kentucky University*

Milagros Ojermark, *Diablo Valley College*

Carmel O'Kane, *Northeastern Illinois University*

Elma Orozco-Félix, *Fresno City College*

José J. Osorio, *CUNY–Queensborough Community College*

Mercedes Palomino, *Florida Atlantic University*

Isaías Paz S., *Fresno City College*

Carolina Pérez, *El Camino College*

Inmaculada Pertusa, *Western Kentucky University*

Joyce P. Pinkard, *Fresno City College*

Ramona Rendón, *Florida Atlantic University*

Sheila Rivera, *Valencia Community College*

Patricio Rizzo-Vast, *Northeastern Illinois University*

Anthony Robb, *Rowan University*

Cathy A. Robison, *Clemson University*

María T. Rocha, *Houston Community College*

Mónica Rojas, *Clemson University*

Amalia Ruiz, *Florida Atlantic University*

Daniel L. Russo, Jr., *Pima Community College, East*

Carmen Salazar, *Los Angeles Valley College*

Elena Sánchez, *Florida Atlantic University*

Rafael Sánchez-Alonso, *The University of Southern Mississippi*

Rhoda Segur, *Blinn College*

Virginia Shen, *Chicago State University*

Roger K. Simpson, *Clemson University*

Victor E. Slesinger, *Palm Beach Community College–Central*

Maggie Smallwood, *Clemson University*

María Jiménez Smith, *Tarrant County College–NE*

Eva Solano, *Florida Community College, Jacksonville*

Marguerite Solari, *Oakton College*

Lidia C. Stahl, *Southern Illinois University, Carbondale*

Edward Stering, *City College of San Francisco*

Melissa A. Stewart, *Western Kentucky University*

Greg Taylor, *Southern Illinois University, Carbondale*

Silvina Trica-Flores, *Nassau Community College*

Cristóbal Trillo, *Joliet Junior College*

Irma O. Valdez, *Blinn College*

María Gladys Vallieres, *Villanova University*

Fernando Vidal, *Valencia Community College*

Carlos Villacís, *Houston Community College*
Lisa M. Volle, *Central Texas College*
Luz E. Wright, *Georgia Perimeter College*
Gloria Yampey-Jorg, *Houston Community College*

Student Reviewers

We asked students to give us comprehensive feedback on the art that is used in Spanish textbooks. A total of 359 students from the following 21 colleges and universities responded to questions about the kinds of art they like, what they dislike, and what they find useful for each of the major sections of the text (e.g., grammar, vocabulary, and culture). The results are what you see in ¡*Anda!*

Colleges and Universities
Citrus College
Clemson University
Coastal Carolina Community College
Florida Atlantic University
Florida Community College at Jacksonville
Georgia Perimeter College
Harper College
Rowan Cabarrus Community College
South Plains College
The University of North Carolina at Chapel Hill
The University of Texas at Austin
Tidewater Community College
University of Cincinnati
The University of California, Los Angeles
University of Evansville
University of Central Florida
University of Florida
University of Louisiana at Monroe
University of Nevada, Reno
University of Texas at El Paso
Western Kentucky University

Students
Brenna, Kacy Cunningham, Grace M. Lear, Elyse Magdule, Jay Jacobson, Katey Jayne, Jenny Russo, Tabitha Potter, Alex Luft, Manuel Hernandez, Kelly De Stefano, Griselda Luna, Shaun Davis, Lamore Hanchard, Tiffany Lumpkin, James Shelton, Ryan Furkin, Yonel Roche, Nicole Holman, Riley O'Connell, Zenyth Propst, Katie Tucker, Jason L. Seward, Carolyn Buck, Brian Dunne, Jessica Hatter, Samantha Williams, Mike Williams, Elizabeth Clary Jocys, Kellie Shanahan, Tiffany Mills , Kate Lepley, Tara Schmidt, Danielle King, Jared Anderson, Josh Beasley , Kelli Clements, John Ponce, Miso Jang, Casey Cowan, Amiee, Jesse Belcher, Michael Lynch, Tim Falconbury, Ryan Cremeans, Latonya Sholar, Christopher

Campbell, Beard, Erik Belford, Ashley Skinner, Dylan Nielson, Michael Dickson, Tim Powers, Morgan Crosby, Saera Kim, Nathaniel Baker, Jade Wallace, Kristen Moore, Armando Delima, Traci Bird, Megan Guffee, Michelle, Erin Hunter, Lindsey Wheeler, Emmalyn Cochran, Julia Young, Crystal Washington, Trevor Seigler, Nick Johnson, Griselda Luna, Paul Loiodice, Kelly Dwight, Kristian Morales, Kristian Morales, Warren Giese, Lauren Johnson, Jacklyn Johns, Haneen Sayyad, Brittney Green, Randall Lee, Andy Robling, Ashley, Felicia Blackwood, Venessa Chandra, Jon Tuminski, Andrea Newsome, Jessica Collins, Thomas Russell, Everet Macias, Carrie Gray, Tamara Clarke, Sarah Harrington, Susie, Grace Aaron, Shelley Lewis, Margie, Haley, Joseph Fisher, Kelley Daoust, Rebecca Brown, Eric Dean, Anna Woodlock, Audrey Clark, Travis Greene, Emily Schultz, Jessica D. Taylor, Douglas Glenn, Ashley Pate, Anna Browning, Melisa Gonzales, Kara Murphy, Natalie Hood-Kramer, Jessica Johnson, Jayson Vignola, Gretchen Pegram, Tanya Aboul-Hosn, Brittney Martin, Matt Harlow, Leah Gibson, Leah Gibson, Clint Darter, Nkechinyere Nwoko, John H. Gagnon, Bernadette, Rachel, Larry James Reeder II, Ny'Sheria Sims, Nicholas Robino, Deanna Caniff, Michael Baker, Elizabeth Morgan, Brooke Swinson, Ian King, Seaqn Kaye, Mekisha F. Smith, David Hahn, Susan, Keri Britcher, Jean Henn, Bonnie Swift, Lisa Carrizales, Cori, April Michaud, Gailen Field, Stephanie Hoock, Nicole Rivera, Kristin Durant, Maria Melanie Meyer, Mallory Erford, Chris Banks, Sam Srour, Kate Glover, Madison Dunn, Jillian Murphy, Jose Quintanilla, Stephanie Lenk, Matthew Hoag, Femi, Laura Anderson, Jared Zirkle, Laura Yoder, Genna Offerman, Leigh Cash, Amy Creighton, Susannah Federowicz, Candice Mccarty, Mary Beth Whitmire, Annie Quach, Robert Burnside, Bryttne Lowden, Emily Hankinson, Sarah Gerald, Sarah Baber, Lawrence Lander, Amanda Carrington, Mariah Jimenez, Jordana Fyne, Thomas Giannini, Pamela Okeke, Dominique Brown, John Norton, Patrick S. Lockett, Jill Meinrath, Jenny Seifert, Jennifer Pritchett, Christine Reppa, Joshua Gorney, Vishal, Joseph Marker, June Clark, Jenny Forwark, Tara Hush, Whitney Schlotman, Daniel Zainfeld, Matthew Cross, Katiria Robles, Magdalena J. Semrau, Neal Ward, Barry Lacina, Katie K, Shawntavia Smith, Kati Payne, Brian Carter, Deanne Grantham, Sarah Hendrix, Kira Seward, Christin Huether, Chelsea Harp, Meaghan Jones, Rachel Blakely, Nicholas Emerick, Ramiro Tey, Rebecca Adams, Danielle King, Martina Blatterspiel, Greg Longstreth, Sarah Longtin, Jessica Torres, Sarah, Kimberly Deuble, Rachel Hopkins, Sara Tapia, Katherine Chudy, Sarah Kopp, Carmen Gilbert, Lynn Greco, Jen Robinson, Laura Busch, Mandie K. Rios, Sean Santoscoy-Mckillip, Lindsay Dewitt, Raquel Krauss, John Stroud, Stephanie Humphrey, Elaine Ellis, Carrie Ziegenmeyer, Bryan J Sykes, Tracy Delzeith, Matt Cherry, Yadira Anglin, Filipp Lassman, Lauren Barker, Terrilyon, Angela Schuch, Betsy Ortiz, Heinz

Landeck, Nash T. Bermudez, Curt Neichter, Arielle Goldberg, Kelli Walker, Yeong Oh, Brandon Cody Goehring, Jessica Irving, Alfonso Ontiveros, Jessica Davis, Marcus Donahue, Ashley Moeller, Kyle Milos, Toni Mcnair, Candace Lau, Jenifer, Jenessa Cottrell, Jessica Pollock, Ronni Rancich, Charla Mcdaniel, Laura Scullin, David Emery, Alex Montgomery, Kelly Mccafferty, Michael Lara, Angela Sehon, Alleene Strickland, Erika Maldeney, Jessica Elizondo, Jason Boone, Kellen Voss, Jessica Elley, Sara Bochiardy, Stephen Hopper, Garrett George, Mistoria Brown, Ian Singer, Christine Yau, Victoria Ng, Racquel Rolle, Jeremy Jacob, Matthew Korte, Josh Duran

Teacher Annotations

The teacher annotations in *¡Anda! Curso elemental* fall into several categories:

- **Methodology:** A deep and broad set of methods notes designed for the novice instructor.
- **Section Goals:** Set of student objectives for each section.
- **National Standards:** Information containing the correlation between each section with the National Standards as well as tips for increasing student performance.
- **Warm-up:** Suggestions for setting up an activity or how to activate students' prior knowledge relating to the task at hand.
- **Suggestion:** Teaching tips that provide ideas that will help with the implementation of activities and sections.
- **Note:** Additional information that instructors may wish to share with students beyond what is presented in the text.
- **Expansion:** Ideas for variations of a topic that may serve as wrap-up activities.
- **Cultural Background:** Information on people, places, and things that aid in the completion of activities and sections by providing background knowledge.
- **Additional Activity:** Independent activities related to the ones in the text that provide further practice than those supplied in the text.
- **Alternate Activity:** Variations of activities provided to suit each individual classroom and preferences.
- **Heritage Language Learners:** Suggestions for the Heritage language learners in the classroom that provide alternatives and expansions for sections and activities based on prior knowledge and skills.
- **Recap of *Ambiciones siniestras:*** A synopsis of the both the *Lectura* and *Video* sections for each episode of *Ambiciones siniestras.*

A guide to instructor icons

 This icon indicates approximately how many minutes instructors should allow to present a chunk of new material or to complete an exercise or activity. Obviously, these are meant only as a guide, to help instructors plan their classes.

 This icon indicates that there are additional activities in the Activity Cache, the online supplementary activities, which may be downloaded, copied, and distributed in class.

 This icon indicates that there is a PowerPoint presentation available on the topic under discussion.

 This icon indicates that there is relevant material in the Instructor's Resource Manual. The text below the icon tells you where to find it.

 This icon indicates that there is a transparency available for your use. The text below gives the transparency number for easy location.

 This icon refers to the supplement called the Testing Program. It includes the ready-made tests (Tests A and B) and the modules available for that chapter if you prefer to create your own tests.

ACKNOWLEDGMENTS

The first edition of *¡Anda! Curso elemental* is the result of careful planning between ourselves and our publisher and ongoing collaboration with students and you, our colleagues. We look forward to continuing this dialogue and sincerely appreciate your input. We owe special thanks to the many members of the Spanish-teaching community whose comments and suggestions helped shape the pages of every chapter—you will see yourselves everywhere. We gratefully acknowledge and thank in particular our reviewers for this first edition.

We are especially grateful to those who have collaborated with us in the writing of *¡Anda!* In addition to contributors such as Jean LeLoup, María del Carmen Caña Jiménez, and Sonia Torres-Quiñones, there are others whom we wish to recognize and thank.

We thank Josefa Lindquist for her work on the *También se dice...* appendix. We also thank Taryn Ferch for bringing her experience and contributing to the instructor annotations, as well as to both Taryn and Douglas Jensen for writing some of the student notes. We owe many thanks to Megan Echevarría for her superb work on the Student Activities Manual. Thank you also to Sharon D. Robinson for the Service Learning and Experiential Learning Activities and to Dolores Durán-Cerda for the Heritage language learners materials. Special thanks are also due to Luz Font, Cheryl McDonough, Patrick Brady, and María Mónica Montalvo for all of their work on the Testing Program, to Patricia Moore-Martínez for writing many of the activities in the Electronic Activities Cache, to Ignacio Pérez-Ibáñez for his work on the Instructor's Resource Manual, and to Virginia Shen for the Sample Syllabi and Lesson Plans. Additional thanks to the many talented contributors for the development of the web site materials to accompany the first edition.

All of the previously mentioned contributors have played an important part in this program, but equally important are the contributions of the highly talented individuals at Pearson Prentice Hall. We wish to express our gratitude and deep appreciation to the many people at Prentice Hall who contributed their ideas, tireless efforts, and publishing experience to the first edition of *¡Anda! Curso elemental*. First of all, a very special thank you to Bob Hemmer, Executive Editor, who has guided and supported us through every aspect of this exciting project. His intelligence, talent, and complete commitment to *¡Anda!* have helped us to realize our vision. Additionally, we are especially indebted to Janet García-Levitas, our Development Editor, for all of her hard work, suggestions, attention to detail, and dedication to the text. Her tireless efforts, support, and cheerful spirit helped us to achieve the final product we had envisioned.

Special thanks are due to Samantha Alducin, Senior Media Editor, for helping us produce such a superb video and for managing the creation of *¡Anda!* materials for MySpanishLab™ and the Companion Website. Thanks also to a/t Media Productions for their work on *Ambiciones siniestras*. We would also like to thank Melissa Marolla Brown, Development Editor for Assessment, for the diligent coordination between the text, Student Activities Manual, and Testing Program; and Meriel Martínez, Media Editor, and Jenn Murphy, Assistant Development Editor, for their efficient and meticulous work in managing the preparation of the other supplements. Thanks to Debbie King, Assistant Development Editor, and Katie Spiegel, Editorial Assistant, for their hard work and efficiency in obtaining reviews and attending to many administrative details.

We are very grateful to Kristine Suárez, Director of Marketing, who led the market development efforts for *¡Anda!* Her terrific work helped to connect us to the needs of students and instructors. Thanks too to Denise Miller, Senior Marketing Manager, and Bill Bliss, Marketing Coordinator, for their creativity and efforts in coordinating all marketing and promotion for this first edition. Many thanks are also due to Nancy Stevenson, Senior Production Editor, who guided *¡Anda!* through the many stages of production; to our Art Managers, Maria Piper and Gail Cocker-Bogusz; and to Siren Design for the creative reproductions of realia. We are particularly indebted to Andrew Lange and Eric Larsen for the amazing illustrations that translate our vision. All students will enjoy their artwork as they learn. Thanks to Lisa Delgado for her gorgeous interior and cover designs. We thank our partners at Black Dot Group for their careful and professional editing and production services.

We would like to sincerely thank Phil Miller, Publisher; Julia Caballero, Director of Editorial Development; Mary Rottino, Senior Managing Editor; and Janice Stangel, Associate Managing Editor; for their support and commitment to the success of *¡Anda!* We are also very grateful to Glen and Meg Burrston of Burrston House for the special care and attention they gave our project during the development stage.

We also thank our colleagues and students from across the country who inspire us and from whom we learn.

And finally, our love and deepest appreciation to our families for all of their support during this journey: David; John, Jack, and Kate.

Audrey L. Heining-Boynton

Glynis S. Cowell

A Walking Tour

¡Hola!
¡Bienvenidos!

I'm Audrey Heining-Boynton

and I'm Glynis Cowell

We are the authors of ¡ANDA! and we were thinking that when you visit a new place, one of the best ways to get to know your new environment quickly is to consult your guidebook before you take the trip! We thought it would be a good idea for you to join us on a "walking tour" of your new Spanish textbook and supplementary materials because we know from experience that language texts have a unique organization that is different from other textbooks… They use terminology that you might not be familiar with, and lots of the material is written in the language you don't know yet. So let's get on with the tour!

Here it is!

The doorway to **¡ANDA!** What does the cover tell you about what you'll find inside? No, it's not a spring break brochure to a Spanish-speaking country!

Think about it.

Check out the "map" of your book!

Scope and Sequence. You can think of the Scope and Sequence as the roadmap of the book. The scope tells you what is covered, and the sequence shows you the order of those topics. In other words, the Scope and Sequence tells you where everything is! It's a very useful tool for navigating ¡Anda!

Semester 1
Preliminary A
This chapter gets you up and running quickly. You will learn many easy-to-learn words that will allow you to begin speaking in Spanish very quickly. You should feel good about how much Spanish you can use after studying the preliminary chapter.

Chapters 1–5
These are the main textbook chapters. Each chapter has an overall theme—like food, for example—and teaches you the words to use (vocabulary) and how to put them together in a sentence (grammar) so that you can talk about that subject. You'll also focus on the four skills (speaking, listening, reading, and writing) as well as culture.

Semester 2
Preliminary B
This chapter reviews the basic vocabulary and grammar from the first half of the book. Maybe you need this; maybe you don't. Maybe you are joining this class from another school or from high school and you need a little refresher. That's what this chapter is for!

Chapters 7–11
These are typical chapters, just like Chapters 1–5 above.

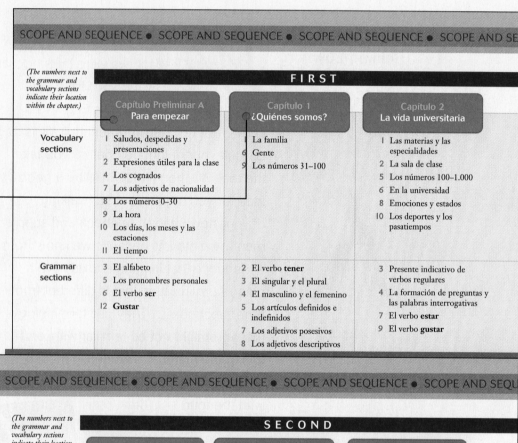

SCOPE AND SEQUENCE ● SCOPE AND SEQUENCE ● SCOPE AND SEQUENCE ● SCOPE AND SE

(The numbers next to the grammar and vocabulary sections indicate their location within the chapter.)

FIRST

	Capítulo Preliminar A Para empezar	Capítulo 1 ¿Quiénes somos?	Capítulo 2 La vida universitaria
Vocabulary sections	1 Saludos, despedidas y presentaciones 2 Expresiones útiles para la clase 4 Los cognados 7 Los adjetivos de nacionalidad 8 Los números 0–30 9 La hora 10 Los días, los meses y las estaciones 11 El tiempo	1 La familia 6 Gente 9 Los números 31–100	1 Las materias y las especialidades 2 La sala de clase 5 Los números 100–1.000 6 En la universidad 8 Emociones y estados 10 Los deportes y los pasatiempos
Grammar sections	3 El alfabeto 5 Los pronombres personales 6 El verbo **ser** 12 **Gustar**	2 El verbo **tener** 3 El singular y el plural 4 El masculino y el femenino 5 Los artículos definidos e indefinidos 7 Los adjetivos posesivos 8 Los adjetivos descriptivos	3 Presente indicativo de verbos regulares 4 La formación de preguntas y las palabras interrogativas 7 El verbo **estar** 9 El verbo **gustar**

SCOPE AND SEQUENCE ● SCOPE AND SEQUENCE ● SCOPE AND SEQUENCE ● SCOPE AND SEQU

(The numbers next to the grammar and vocabulary sections indicate their location within the chapter.)

SECOND

	Capítulo Preliminar B Introducciones y repasos	Capítulo 7 ¡A comer!	Capítulo 8 ¿Qué te pones?
Vocabulary sections	**Capítulo Preliminar A** **Capítulo 1** **Capítulo 2** **Capítulo 3** **Capítulo 4** **Capítulo 5**	1 La comida 4 La preparación de las comidas 6 En el restaurante	1 La ropa
Grammar sections		2 Repaso del complemento directo 3 El pretérito 5 Unos verbos irregulares en el pretérito	2 Los pronombres de complemento indirecto 3 **Gustar** y verbos como **gustar** 4 Los pronombres de complemento directo e indirecto usados juntos 5 Las construcciones reflexivas 6 El imperfecto

Chapter 6
We call this a recycling chapter. This means that you will be given the opportunity to reuse everything that you learned from Preliminary A through Chapter 5. No new information is presented in this chapter so that you can get some time to practice and internalize Spanish. It also helps you prepare for the final exam!

Chapter 12
This is another recycling chapter, just like Chapter 6 above.

Appendices
Yes, we know these are at the end of the book, but you might want to look at them now—not at the end of the semester when it's too late! Notice that there are five appendices and what each one is for:

Appendix 1
Inductive Grammar Answers

Appendix 2
Verb Charts

Appendix 3
También se dice... *You can also say...*

Appendix 4
Spanish–English Glossary

Appendix 5
English–Spanish Glossary

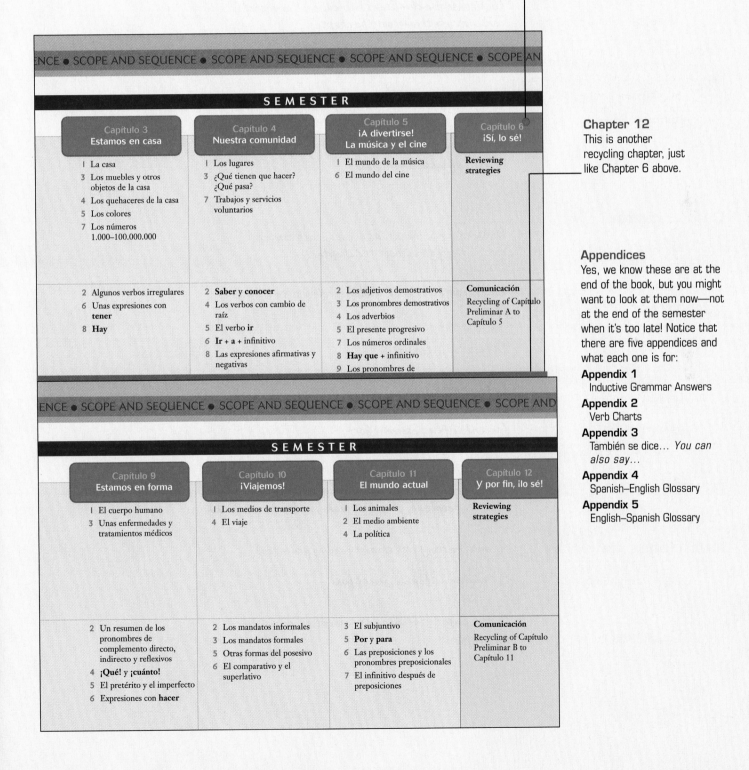

SCOPE AND SEQUENCE ● SCOPE AND SEQUENCE ● SCOPE AND SEQUENCE ● SCOPE AND SEQUENCE ● SCOPE AN

SEMESTER

Capítulo 3 Estamos en casa	Capítulo 4 Nuestra comunidad	Capítulo 5 ¡A divertirse! La música y el cine	Capítulo 6 ¡Sí, lo sé!
1 La casa 3 Los muebles y otros objetos de la casa 4 Los quehaceres de la casa 5 Los colores 7 Los números 1.000–100.000.000	1 Los lugares 3 ¿Qué tienen que hacer? ¿Qué pasa? 7 Trabajos y servicios voluntarios	1 El mundo de la música 6 El mundo del cine	**Reviewing strategies**
2 Algunos verbos irregulares 6 Unas expresiones con **tener** 8 **Hay**	2 **Saber** y **conocer** 4 Los verbos con cambio de raíz 5 El verbo **ir** 6 **Ir + a** + infinitivo 8 Las expresiones afirmativas y negativas	2 Los adjetivos demostrativos 3 Los pronombres demostrativos 4 Los adverbios 5 El presente progresivo 7 Los números ordinales 8 **Hay que** + infinitivo 9 Los pronombres de	**Comunicación** Recycling of Capítulo Preliminar A to Capítulo 5

SCOPE AND SEQUENCE ● SCOPE AND SEQUENCE ● SCOPE AND SEQUENCE ● SCOPE AND SEQUENCE ● SCOPE AND

SEMESTER

Capítulo 9 Estamos en forma	Capítulo 10 ¡Viajemos!	Capítulo 11 El mundo actual	Capítulo 12 y por fin, ¡lo sé!
1 El cuerpo humano 3 Unas enfermedades y tratamientos médicos	1 Los medios de transporte 4 El viaje	1 Los animales 2 El medio ambiente 4 La política	**Reviewing strategies**
2 Un resumen de los pronombres de complemento directo, indirecto y reflexivos 4 **¡Qué!** y **¡cuánto!** 5 El pretérito y el imperfecto 6 Expresiones con **hacer**	2 Los mandatos informales 3 Los mandatos formales 5 Otras formas del posesivo 6 El comparativo y el superlativo	3 El subjuntivo 5 **Por** y **para** 6 Las preposiciones y los pronombres preposicionales 7 El infinitivo después de preposiciones	**Comunicación** Recycling of Capítulo Preliminar B to Capítulo 11

Have you ever used a Spanish textbook before? Do you know what each section is about? Do you know what you're being asked to read, memorize, practice, and why? Here's an outline of a typical chapter in **¡ANDA!**, followed by some actual chapter sections so that you can see what they look like. And we couldn't resist… we made lots of notes for you!

Comunicación

Vocabulary and grammar — *(in manageable chunks, as needed, each numbered consecutively throughout the chapter)*

Pronunciation practice — *(after first vocabulary list)*

Cultural box — *(brief, contextualized readings, relevant to chapter theme)*

¿Cómo andas? — *(first self-assessment box)*

Comunicación

Vocabulary and grammar — *(in manageable chunks, as needed, each numbered consecutively throughout the chapter)*

Cultural box — *(brief, contextualized readings, relevant to chapter theme)*

Escucha — *(a focus on listening)*

Escribe — *(a focus on writing)*

¿Cómo andas? — *(second self-assessment box)*

Cultura

(a focus on one or more Spanish-speaking countries— what the people do, what they make, and how they think)

Ambiciones siniestras
(a mystery story told through reading and video)

Y por fin, ¿cómo andas? — *(cumulative self-assessment box)*

Vocabulario activo — *(a two-page list of all of the essential vocabulary of the chapter)*

Chapter opener

STOP 2

The chapter title announces the theme of the chapter, which is reflected in the visual on the right.

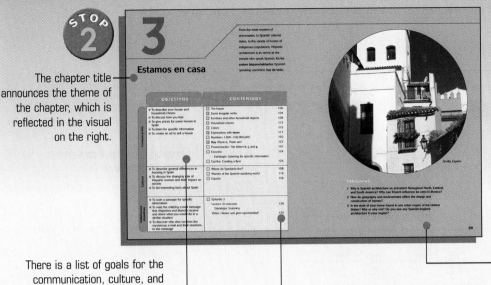

The questions are designed to get you to think about the topic for the chapter—not to get you to search for THE right answer. Bringing the topic to the forefront of your mind will help you make educated guesses about the meaning of Spanish words. Remember the topic as you work your way through the chapter.

There is a list of goals for the communication, culture, and mystery story sections under *Objetivos*. Notice how the goals relate to the chapter theme!

The content related to the goals is listed under *Contenidos*, with page numbers. It's in English so that you can understand it clearly!

Comunicación

STOP 3

Comunicación is divided into manageable chunks of what you need to learn: vocabulary (the words you need) and grammar (the structures that you use to put the words together). Vocabulary and grammar are two of the most important tools for communication! By the way, we didn't invent this—research indicates that the best presentation of language separates vocabulary and grammar for a manageable progression especially when combined with recycling and reintroduction of previously studied material—more on that later.

Communicative goals are listed for each *Comunicación* section.

The vocabulary sections are numbered consecutively throughout the chapter.

Pronunciación indicates the right way to make the sounds of the language. Pronunciation practice and activities, with new and recycled vocabulary, follow the first vocabulary chunk.

The vocabulary chunks introduce new vocabulary through art.

A lot of the vocabulary is presented without translations so that you can try to figure out the meaning of the Spanish word.

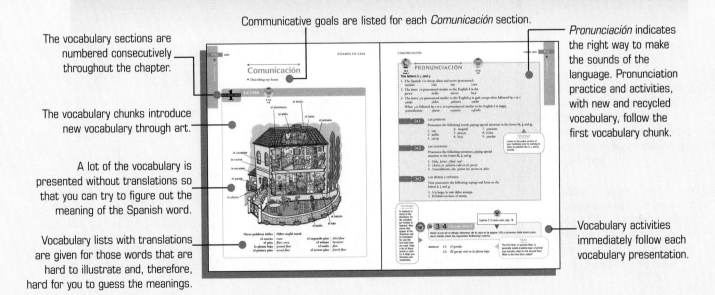

Vocabulary activities immediately follow each vocabulary presentation.

Vocabulary lists with translations are given for those words that are hard to illustrate and, therefore, hard for you to guess the meanings.

Grammar

The grammar sections introduce new grammar concepts.

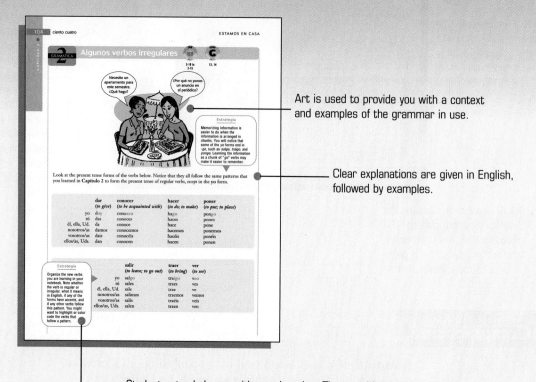

Art is used to provide you with a context and examples of the grammar in use.

Clear explanations are given in English, followed by examples.

Student notes help you with your learning. They provide additional background information, interesting facts, and strategies that help you learn!

Icons indicate when to work in pairs or groups, and also refer you to other resources (e.g., CD tracks for audio, corresponding activity numbers in the Student Activities Manual) when you need them.

Recycling boxes also point out when we have deliberately reused materials from a previous chapter—or from earlier in the same chapter—to help you build upon what you have already studied. Page references are provided so that you can return to that section of the book if you need and/or want to.

You'll find a blend of activities that practice individual words and verb forms, as well as activities in which you focus on putting everything together to use the language for purposes of communication.

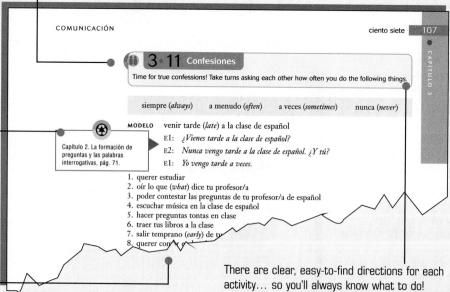

There are clear, easy-to-find directions for each activity... so you'll always know what to do!

Listening, writing, and self-assessment

STOP 5

The second **Comunicación** provides listening comprehension (**Escucha**) and writing activities (**Escribe**) prior to the self-assessment check (**¿Cómo andas?**).

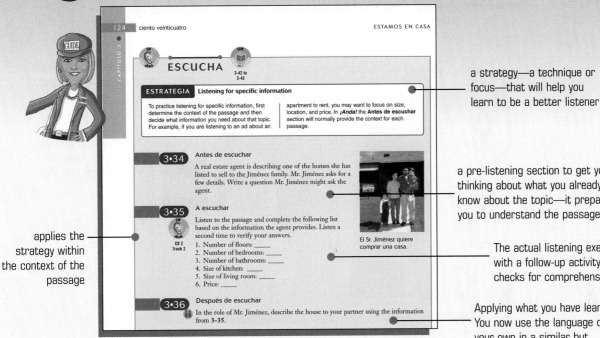

a strategy—a technique or focus—that will help you learn to be a better listener

a pre-listening section to get you thinking about what you already know about the topic—it prepares you to understand the passage.

applies the strategy within the context of the passage

The actual listening exercise with a follow-up activity checks for comprehension.

Applying what you have learned. You now use the language on your own in a similar but different context.

Like *Escucha, Escribe* is related to the chapter theme and walks you through the writing process with pre-writing and post-writing activities.

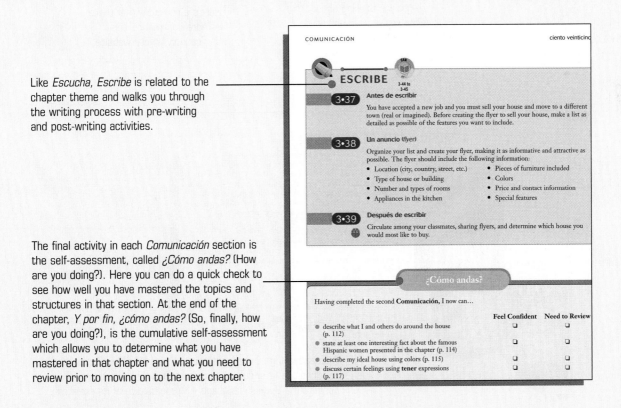

The final activity in each *Comunicación* section is the self-assessment, called *¿Cómo andas?* (How are you doing?). Here you can do a quick check to see how well you have mastered the topics and structures in that section. At the end of the chapter, *Y por fin, ¿cómo andas?* (So, finally, how are you doing?), is the cumulative self-assessment which allows you to determine what you have mastered in that chapter and what you need to review prior to moving on to the next chapter.

Time for a break to grab a cup of **café con leche**?

Between the second **Comunicación** and **Ambiciones siniestras** (the ongoing mystery story) is **Cultura**, designed to provide key facts and high interest information concerning Spanish-speaking countries and peoples.

A map gives you an idea about the geography of the country.

You'll find lots of photos with short captions in Spanish.

Read/listen to a native speaker explain a little bit about his or her country... what folks do there, what they think, and what they like. We hope you'll want to learn more about these countries and maybe even visit some of them.

An almanac of country statistics is given for each country presented.

We give some interesting facts about each country.

Here are some questions to get you thinking about what you've seen and read.

Here's a reminder that there is more information about this country on our website.

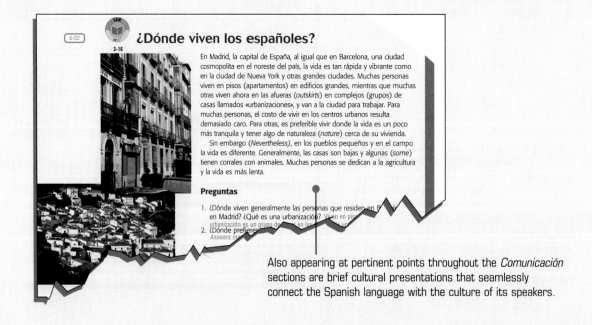

Also appearing at pertinent points throughout the *Comunicación* sections are brief cultural presentations that seamlessly connect the Spanish language with the culture of its speakers.

Reading and video

STOP 7

A mystery story called **Ambiciones siniestras** is presented through readings and videos. It re-uses many of the grammar structures and vocabulary words presented in the chapter.

The pre-reading activity helps you prepare for what you are about to read. It gets you thinking about topics that will be presented in the story so that the context will help you figure out what is going on.

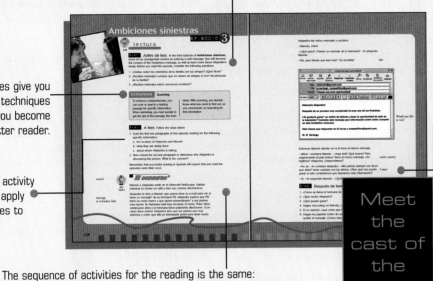

Strategies give you ideas and techniques to help you become a better reader.

The post-reading activity helps you check your comprehension.

The reading activity asks you to apply the strategies to the reading.

The sequence of activities for the reading is the same: pre-, during, and post-. The story that was started in the reading is continued in the video. To understand the story, you'll have to read first and then watch the video.

Meet the cast of the video:

Alejandra

Vocab summaries

STOP 8

The **Vocabulario activo** section at the end of each chapter is where you have all the new vocabulary from the chapter in one place. The words and phrases are organized by topic, in alphabetical order.

Cisco

Manolo

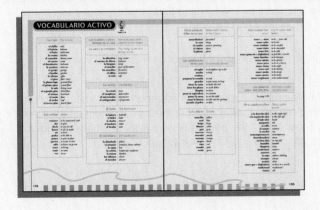

Eduardo

Marisol

Lupe

Sr. Verdugo

Supplementary materials

 STOP 9 Before we finish our walking tour, we want to walk through the many supplements that we provide. Your instructor may have selected some of them to be used in your course.

Student Activities Manual (paper)	The *Student Activities Manual* (SAM for short) contains practice activities that were designed as homework to reinforce what you learn in class. Although instructors may use the SAM in different ways, one thing is constant; the SAM is assigned as homework. So we make no assumptions… we know you probably won't have an instructor around to answer any questions when you're doing your homework at 2:00 A.M.!
Answer Key to Accompany the Student Activities Manual	Some instructors want their students to have this answer key; other instructors don't. We'll sell you the answer key only if your instructor requests it.
Workbooklet	We know that most students don't want to write in their textbooks, but we also know that writing is a great method for helping you to learn Spanish! So, we've created a *Workbooklet*, in which we have reproduced all of the activities in ¡Anda! where writing is an important part of the activity (e.g., you need to gather information in writing from classmates and then report back to the class orally).
Ambiciones siniestras DVD	The DVD of *Ambiciones siniestras* allows you to watch or rewatch the video at any point during your busy 24/7 life. This is a great tool for helping you practice your comprehension and listening skills!
Audio CD to Accompany the student text	This audio CD contains the listening passages that correlate with sections of your textbook. A listening icon appears in your text with a cross-reference to help you locate the audio.
Audio CDs to Accompany the Student Activities Manual	These audio CDs contain the listening passages you'll need for some of the activities in the SAM.
English Grammar Guide	After taking a Spanish class, most students say they learned as much about English grammar as they did about Spanish grammar. Here's a helpful pocket book that explains the English grammar points that will be helpful when studying Spanish. An icon cross-references the necessary grammar points in the guide for each of the Spanish grammar concepts presented in the text.
Vistas culturales DVD	If you want to listen to native speakers of Spanish and learn more about each of the Spanish-speaking countries, this is the DVD for you!
Companion Website	Extra practice available for free: you can find it online at www.prenhall.com/anda.
MySpanishLab™	*MySpanishLab™* contains all of the above supplements and more. It's a state-of-the-art learning management system, designed specifically for language learners and teachers. You'll need an access code to get in, but the price is very reasonable, considering how much stuff you get. For more information, go to www.myspanishlab.com.

When traveling, it's always helpful to watch out for the signposts. Here is a list of signposts that we've used in **¡Anda!**

 Accompanying the activity instructions, this pair icon indicates that the activity is designed to be completed in groups of two.

 This group icon indicates that an activity is designed to be completed in groups of three or more.

 The ear indicates that an activity involves listening and that the audio is provided for you either on the Companion Website (CW) or, if you are using *MySpanishLab*™, in the eBook.

 Activities that ask you to write have been duplicated in a separate *Workbooklet* so that you don't have to write in your text if you don't want to. This icon indicates that an activity has been reproduced in the *Workbooklet*.

 The activity references below this icon tell you which activities in the *Student Activities Manual* (SAM) are related to that particular section of the textbook. You may have the printed SAM or the electronic version in *MySpanishLab*™.

 One of two video icons, this icon tells you where to find the *Ambiciones siniestras* video: on DVD, VHS (instructors only), or *MySpanishLab*™.

 The other video icon, this one tells you where to find the *Vistas culturales* video: on DVD, VHS (instructors only), or *MySpanishLab*™.

 This icon means that the activity that it accompanies requires you to use the Internet.

 The numbers accompanying this icon indicate which English grammar points are related to the Spanish grammar topic that you are studying. The *English Grammar Guide* is available to users of **¡Anda!**

Back to the cover

So what do you think the cover image represents? We see those footsteps on a clear path, heading toward the horizon... to clear goals, a clear path, a bright and sunny future, blue skies, and clear sailing! **¡Anda!** was designed to keep you motivated and on a stress-free learning path.

¡Que disfruten! **Enjoy!**

INTRODUCTION TO
Chapter Opener

Each chapter has a two-page chapter opener. These pages help to orient your students regarding the content of the chapter and access any prior knowledge they may have regarding the theme. The intention is for the instructor to spend no more than five to seven minutes on these openers.

SECTION GOALS FOR
Chapter Opener

By the end of the chapter opener section, students will be able to:

- discuss the importance of speaking Spanish as participants in the global village.
- contrast the numbers of speakers of Chinese, English, Hindustani, Spanish, and Russian.
- identify characteristics of a successful language learner.

Preliminar

Para empezar

The top five world languages	
Chinese	1,075 billion
English	514 million
Hindustani	496 million
✓ Spanish	425 million
Russian	275 million

You are about to begin the exciting journey of studying the Spanish language and learning about Hispanic culture. Learning a language is a skill much like learning to ski or playing an instrument. Developing these skills takes practice and in the beginning, perfection is not expected. Research has shown that successful language learners are willing to take risks and experiment with the language. What

OBJETIVOS / CONTENIDOS

Comunicación

- To greet, take leave of, and introduce people
- To understand and respond appropriately to basic classroom expressions and requests
- To spell your name in Spanish
- To identify cognates
- To name the subject pronouns in Spanish
- To state your nationality
- To say the numbers 0–30
- To tell the time and date, and state weather conditions
- To state basic likes and dislikes

Cultura

- To give at least two reasons why it is important to study and be able to communicate in Spanish
- To compare and contrast greetings in the Spanish-speaking world and in the United States
- To explain when to use the familiar and formal "you" in Spanish
- To name the continents and countries where Spanish is spoken

NOTE FOR *The top five most-spoken languages*

The specific placement varies according to the source, but Spanish is consistently ranked among the top five most-spoken languages in the world by most reporting agencies. Chinese (Mandarin), English, Hindustani, Russian, and Arabic are the other languages most often found on the lists.

RECURSOS

Lesson Plan

is essential in learning Spanish is to keep trying and be willing to risk making mistakes, knowing that the practice will garner results. *¡Anda!* will be your guide and provide you with key essentials for becoming a successful language learner.

Why should you study Spanish, or for that matter, any language other than English? For some of you, the answer may be quite frankly, "because it is a graduation requirement!" Bear in mind, however, that Spanish is one of the most widely spoken languages in the world. You may find that knowledge of the Spanish language is a useful professional and personal tool.

If you have never studied Spanish before, this preliminary chapter will provide you with some basic words and expressions you will need to begin to use the language in meaningful ways. If you have already learned or studied some Spanish, this preliminary chapter can serve as a quick review.

PREGUNTAS

1 Why is it important to study Spanish?

2 How might Spanish play a role in your future?

3

NOTE ON
Capítulo Preliminar A

This preliminary chapter is meant to jump-start learning. In some cases, students may have studied some Spanish previously and may be familiar with this material already. The vocabulary in this chapter is high-frequency, high-usage. Encourage students to refer to this chapter if they forget certain words and expressions. The amount of time that you spend on this chapter will depend on the number of true beginners in your class.

THE NATIONAL STANDARDS

National Standards: *Standards for Foreign Language Learning in the 21st Century*

¡Anda! is committed to and based on the *Standards for Foreign Language Learning in the 21st Century*. These national foreign language standards are sometimes referred to as *the 5C's*, and they represent five goal areas: Communication, Cultures, Connections, Comparisons, and Communities. Each goal area has corresponding standards, which in turn, promote attainment of the specific goal. The beginning of each chapter will highlight how the standards underlying each of the 5C's will be addressed in that chapter. In particular, the standards and goals highlighted throughout the textbook are taken from the *Standards for Learning Spanish*. These are language-specific standards that reflect the goals as they relate to the teaching and learning of Spanish. Throughout the rest of *¡Anda!*, we will refer to the standards as the National Standards.

INTRODUCTION TO
Objetivos

The chapter objectives are an organizational tool for you and your students. They allow you to see the main points of the chapter at a glance, and they serve as a way for you to assess whether your students have mastered the main ideas and skills from every chapter. You can use the chapter objectives to preview what the students will be learning in a particular chapter and to review what you taught. Encourage your students to preview the chapter by reading the objectives, and to use the objectives from each chapter when they prepare for a test.

Comunicación

VOCABULARIO 1 Saludos, despedidas y presentaciones

A-1 to A-3

Los saludos	*Greetings*
¡Hola!	*Hi!; Hello!*
Buenos días.	*Good morning.*
Buenas tardes.	*Good afternoon.*
Buenas noches.	*Good evening; Good night.*
¿Cómo estás?	*How are you?* (familiar)
¿Cómo está usted?	*How are you?* (formal)
¿Qué tal?	*How's it going?*
Más o menos.	*So-so.*
Regular.	*Okay.*
Bien, gracias.	*Fine, thanks.*

Bastante bien.	*Just fine.*
Muy bien.	*Really well.*
¿Y tú?	*And you?* (familiar)
¿Y usted?	*And you?* (formal)

Las despedidas	*Farewells*
Adiós.	*Good-bye.*
Chao.	*Bye.*
Hasta luego.	*See you later.*
Hasta mañana.	*See you tomorrow.*
Hasta pronto.	*See you soon.*

—¿Qué tal?
—Bien.

—¿Cómo estás?
—Bien, gracias.

—Hasta mañana.
—Adiós.

Las presentaciones	*Introductions*
¿Cómo te llamas?	*What is your name?* (familiar)
¿Cómo se llama usted?	*What is your name?* (formal)
Me llamo…	*My name is…*
Soy…	*I am…*
Mucho gusto.	*Nice to meet you.*
Encantado/Encantada.	*Pleased to meet you.*
Igualmente.	*Likewise.*
Quiero presentarte a…	*I would like to introduce you to…* (familiar)
Quiero presentarle a…	*I would like to introduce you to…* (formal)

- The expressions **¿Cómo te llamas?** and **¿Cómo se llama usted?** both mean *What is your name?*, but the former is used among students and other peers (referred to as *familiar*). You will learn about the differences between these *familiar* and *formal* forms later in this chapter. Note that **Encantado** is said by a male, and **Encantada** is said by a female.

- Spanish uses special punctuation to signal a question or an exclamation. An upside-down question mark begins a question and an upside-down exclamation mark begins an exclamation, as in **¿Cómo te llamas?** and **¡Hola!**

1:00 **A·1** Saludos y despedidas

Match each greeting or farewell with its logical response. Compare your answers with a classmate.

1. __b__ ¿Qué tal?
2. __d__ Hasta luego.
3. __a__ ¿Cómo te llamas?
4. __c__ Que lo pases bien.

a. Me llamo Julia.
b. Bastante bien.
c. Igualmente.
d. Hasta pronto.

METHODOLOGY • Lesson Planning

We have provided suggested amounts of time for you to devote to each activity. These time estimates include: pairing up students, giving your students time to read the directions with their partner, performing the activity, and a brief follow-up. The follow-up should only include a spot check of some pairs and only some of the items. It is not appropriate to redo all of the activities that students have completed with a partner. Explain to students that they need to help each other and to self-correct within their small groups.

METHODOLOGY • Pair Work

¡Anda! strongly believes in the research that says "students learn best from students." Hence, there are an abundance of pair and group activities in *¡Anda!* For this chapter, simply have students turn to a partner. In subsequent chapters, ideas will be provided so that you can vary partners, preferably on a daily basis.

Suggestion for A-3 to A-5 Have students stand and circulate around the class. Many students will be shy about introducing themselves to classmates they do not know. Therefore, please encourage them to circulate.

Suggestion for A-5 If time permits, do this activity several times, changing the groups each time. This gives students an opportunity to get to know others in the class and builds community within the classroom.

A•2 ¡Hola! ¿Qué tal?

[2:00]

Greet five classmates and ask how each is doing. After you are comfortable with one greeting, try a different one.

MODELO

E1: *¡Hola! ¿Cómo estás?*

E2: *Bien, gracias. ¿Y tú?*

E1: *Bastante bien.*

A•3 ¿Cómo te llamas?

[1:00]

Introduce yourself to three classmates.

MODELO

E1: *¡Hola! Soy… ¿Cómo te llamas?*

E2: *Mucho gusto. Me llamo…*

E1: *Encantado/a.*

E2: *Igualmente.*

A•4 Quiero presentarte a…

[1:00]

Now, introduce one person you have just met to another classmate.

MODELO

E1: *John, quiero presentarte a Mike.*

MIKE: *Mucho gusto.*

JOHN: *Igualmente.*

A•5 Una fiesta [2:00]

Imagine that you are at a party. In groups of five, introduce yourselves to each other. Use the model as a guide.

MODELO

AMY: *Hola, ¿qué tal? Soy Amy.*

ORLANDO: *Hola Amy. Soy Orlando. ¿Cómo estás?*

AMY: *Muy bien, Orlando. ¿Y tú?*

ORLANDO: *Bien, gracias. Amy, quiero presentarte a Tom.*

TOM: *Encantado.*

E4: *…*

A-4 to
A-5

Cómo se saluda la gente

How do you generally greet acquaintances? Do you use different greetings for different people?

When native speakers of Spanish meet, they greet each other, ask each other how they are doing, and respond using phrases like the ones you just learned. In most of the Spanish-speaking world, men usually shake hands when greeting each other, although close male friends may greet each other with an **abrazo** (*hug*). Between female friends, the usual greeting is a **besito** (*little kiss*) on one or both cheeks (depending on the country) and a gentle hug. The **besito** is a gentle air kiss. When men and women greet each other, depending on their ages, how well they know each other, and what country they are in, they either simply shake hands and/or greet with a **besito.** While conversing, Spanish speakers may stand quite close to each other.

Preguntas

1. How do your male friends generally greet each other? And your female friends?

2. In general, how much distance is there between you and the person(s) with whom you are speaking?

INTRODUCTION TO
Cultural boxes

Each chapter has two cultural boxes, one in each *Comunicación* section. They are meant to be brief and are always contextualized and relevant to the theme of the chapter.

METHODOLOGY • Planning Ahead

We recommend assigning *all* culture sections to be read in advance. We also recommend assigning students to read *all* the grammar explanations before class since they are written in a very clear, concise fashion. The instructor's role then becomes that of clarifying or reviewing any points that the students read in advance.

Expansion for *¿Cómo se saluda la gente?* Some additional questions to ask your students are:

1. How do your male friends greet your female friends?
2. How do your parents greet their friends?
3. How do you greet your family members?

INTRODUCTION TO
Chunks / Chunking

The concept of *chunks* of material and *chunking* of material is a major notion that drove the development of *¡Anda!* Learning theory and the subsequent research of literally thousand of studies on general learning of any and all subject areas confirm that students learn best when information is grouped into smaller chunks. Giving students *all* of the rules and *all* of the ways to express an idea can be overwhelming. When information is not chunked, learners tend to shut down since they find the amount of information that needs to be learned to be overwhelming. Hence, chunking is the best way to insure that students see success and progress and are motivated to learn more.

METHODOLOGY • Teaching Commands

It is intentional that we have introduced lexically only the *Ud./Uds.* commands. The similarity in their endings makes it a more streamlined choice since the goal at this stage is to simplify language and to jump start your students, which aids greatly in motivation.

TPR Activity for *Expresiones útiles para la clase* You can use Total Physical Response (TPR) with some of the classroom expressions, e.g., *abra el libro, cierre el libro*. Students can also act out expressions such as *escuchen, escriban, lean, vaya(n) a la pizarra*.

VOCABULARIO 2 — Expresiones útiles para la clase

A-6 to A-8

2:00

The following list provides useful expressions that you and your instructor will use frequently.

Preguntas y respuestas	*Questions and answers*	Expresiones de cortesía	*Polite expressions*
¿Cómo?	*What?; How?*	De nada.	*You're welcome.*
¿Cómo se dice... en español?	*How do you say... in Spanish?*	Gracias.	*Thank you.*
¿Cómo se escribe... en español?	*How do you write... in Spanish?*	Por favor.	*Please.*
¿Qué significa?	*What does it mean?*	**Mandatos para la clase**	***Classroom instructions (commands)***
¿Quién?	*Who?*		
¿Qué es esto?	*What is this?*	Abra(n) el libro en la página...	*Open your book to page...*
Comprendo.	*I understand.*	Cierre(n) el/los libro/s.	*Close your book/s.*
No comprendo.	*I don't understand.*	Conteste(n).	*Answer.*
Lo sé.	*I know.*	Escriba(n).	*Write.*
No lo sé.	*I don't know.*	Escuche(n).	*Listen.*
Sí.	*Yes.*	Lea(n).	*Read.*
No.	*No.*	Repita(n).	*Repeat.*
		Vaya(n) a la pizarra.	*Go to the board.*

In Spanish, commands can have two forms. The singular form (**abra, cierre, conteste,** etc.) is directed to one person, while the plural form (those ending in **-n: abran, cierren, contesten,** etc.) is used with more than one person.

Suggestion for A-7 You, as the instructor, can also play your own role and practice with some students as well as with the class as a whole.

NOTE ON *El alfabeto*

We have included *ch* and *ll* in the alphabet in accordance with the standards of La Real Academia Española, which state:

"La variante española del alfabeto latino antes expuesta fue la utilizada por la Academia desde 1803 (cuarta edición del Diccionario académico) en la confección de todas sus listas alfabéticas. Pero en el X Congreso de la Asociación de Academias de la Lengua Española, celebrado en 1994, se acordó adoptar el orden alfabético latino universal, en el que la *ch* y la *ll* no se consideran letras independientes. En consecuencia, las palabras que comienzan por estas dos letras, o que las contienen, pasan a alfabetizarse en los lugares que les corresponden dentro de la *c* y de la *l*, respectivamente. Esta reforma afecta únicamente al proceso de ordenación alfabética de las palabras, no a la composición del abecedario, del que los dígrafos *ch* y *ll* siguen formando parte."

Suggestion for *El alfabeto* Make flashcards for each letter of the alphabet. Read the alphabet aloud and have the students repeat each letter. Have the students recite the alphabet without your assistance. Then have your students form a circle. Pass out a letter to each member of the class, and have them practice pronouncing each letter A–Z. As they do, they hold up the card for the class to see. Then practice Z–A (reverse alphabetical order). This requires them to pay attention, and they learn the sounds at the same time.

Estrategia

When working with a partner, always listen carefully. If your partner gives an incorrect response, help your partner achieve a correct response.

 A·6 Práctica `1:00`

Take turns saying which expressions or commands would be used in the following situations.

1. You don't know the Spanish word for something. No lo sé; ¿Cómo se dice/escribe… en español?
2. Your teacher wants everyone to listen. Escuchen.
3. You need your teacher to repeat what he/she has said. Repita por favor.
4. You don't know what something means. ¿Qué significa?
5. Your teacher wants students to turn to a certain page. Abran el libro en la página…
6. You don't understand something. No comprendo.

`2:00` **A·7** Más práctica

Play the roles of instructor (**I**) and student (**E**). The instructor either tells the student to do something or asks a question; the student responds appropriately. Practice with at least **five** sentences or questions, using the expressions that you have just learned; then change roles.

MODELO
    I: *Abra el libro.*
    E: (Student opens the book.)
    I: *¿Cómo se dice* "hello"?
    E: *Se dice "hola".*

Estrategia

To learn Spanish faster, you should attempt to speak only Spanish in the classroom.

GRAMÁTICA 3 — El alfabeto

A-9 to A-12   CD 1 Track 1

`2:00`

The Spanish alphabet is quite similar to the English alphabet except in the ways the letters are pronounced. Learning the proper pronunciation of the individual letters in Spanish will help you pronounce new words and phrases.

LETTER	LETTER NAME	EXAMPLES	LETTER	LETTER NAME	EXAMPLES
a	a	adiós	n	ene	noche
b	be	buenos	ñ	eñe	mañana
c	ce	clase	o	o	cómo
ch	che	Chile	p	pe	por favor
d	de	día	q	cu	qué
e	e	español	r	ere o erre	señora, carro
f	efe	por favor	s	ese	saludos
g	ge	luego	t	te	tarde
h	hache	hola	u	u	usted
i	i	señorita	v	ve o uve	nueve
j	jota	julio	w	doble ve o uve doble	Washington
k	ka	kilómetro	x	equis	examen
l	ele	luego	y	i griega	yo
ll	elle	Sevilla	z	zeta	pizarra
m	eme	madre			

A·8 En español · 2:00

Take turns saying the following abbreviations in Spanish, helping each other with pronunciation if necessary.

1. CD-RW	3. CNN	5. MCI	7. WWW	9. CBS
2. IBM	4. MTV	6. UPS	8. QVC	10. ABC

3:00 · A·9 ¿Qué es esto?

Complete the following steps.

Paso 1 Take turns spelling these words for a partner, who will write what you spelled. Then pronounce each word.

1. hola   2. mañana   3. usted   4. igualmente   5. que   6. noches

Paso 2 Now spell your name for your partner as he/she writes it down. Your partner will pronounce your name, based on your spelling.

MODELO   E1:   *de, a, ve, i, de; ese, eme, i, te, hache*

E2:   (escribe y repite) *D-a-v-i-d S-m-i-t-h*

VOCABULARIO 4 — Los cognados

A-13 to A-16   CD 1 Track 2

1:00 **Cognados,** or *cognates*, are words that are similar in form and meaning to their English equivalents. As you learn Spanish you will discover many cognates. Can you guess the meaning of the words below?

inteligente	septiembre	familia	universidad

A·10 Práctica · 2:00

Take turns giving the English equivalents for the following words.

1. importante	3. programa	5. atractivo	7. especial	9. famoso
2. animal	4. mapa	6. favorito	8. fantástico	10. diferente

A·11 ¿Hablas español? · 2:00

Read the classified ad and make a list of all of the cognates; then answer the following questions.

1. What job is advertised?
2. What are the requirements?
3. How much does it pay?
4. How can you get further information?

Cognates: administrator, department, service, public, hospital, general, experience, necessary, fluidity, English, telephone.
1. Administrator in hospital's Public Service Department
2. Experience and fluency in English and Spanish
3. $45,000 to $60,000
4. Call 480-555-2347

Administrador/a
Departamento de Servicio Público.
Hospital General de Mesa Grande, AR.
Experiencia necesaria.
Fluidez en inglés y español.
$45,000–$60,000.
Teléfono: 480-555-2347

GRAMÁTICA 5 — Los pronombres personales

SAM A-17 to A-18

Guide G 6, 7

4:00

Can you list the subject pronouns in English? When are they used? The chart below lists the subject pronouns in Spanish and their equivalents in English. As you will note, Spanish has several equivalents for *you*.

yo	*I*	**nosotros/as**	*we*
tú	*you* (familiar)	**vosotros/as**	*you* (plural, Spain)
usted	*you* (formal)	**ustedes**	*you* (plural)
él	*he*	**ellos**	*they* (masculine)
ella	*she*	**ellas**	*they* (feminine)

Tú

Usted

Generally speaking, **tú** (you, singular) is used for people with whom you are on a first-name basis, such as family members and friends.

Usted, abbreviated **Ud.,** is used with people you do not know well, or with people with whom you are not on a first-name basis. **Usted** is also used with older people, or with those to whom you want to show respect.

Spanish shows gender more clearly than English. **Nosotros** and **ellos** are used to refer to either all males or to a mixed group of males and females. **Nosotras** and **ellas** refer to an all-female group.

INTRODUCTION TO *Gramática* Presentations

Grammar is introduced, as is vocabulary, in *chunks*: small, manageable amounts of information. The presentations are always in English, and employ either deductive or inductive approaches. A very conscious effort has been made to present only the most basic information on each topic and not to burden beginning Spanish students with exceptions to the rules. The more sophisticated nuances of the language are reserved for intermediate levels and beyond. The goal is to build learners' confidence that Spanish is manageable and that they can communicate in the language.

NOTE FOR *Los pronombres personales*

¡Anda! will present, but not actively practice, the *vosotros* forms. If you wish to practice these forms, please add them to your classroom drills or to any of the exercises in this program.

METHODOLOGY • Teaching Concepts at the Point of Need

Our philosophy is to provide students with grammatical information they need to be successful at the moment, and not to overburden them. Hence, we delay the explanation of *it* until gender is introduced and they have noun subjects (in addition to people) to practice. E.g., *El libro es aburrido. No, es interesante.*

¿Tú o usted?

3:00   A-19 to A-22

Languages are constantly evolving. Words are added and deleted, they change in meaning, and the use of language in certain situations may change as well. For example, the use of **tú** and **usted (Ud.)** is changing dramatically in Spanish. **Tú** may now be used more freely in situations where **Ud.** was previously used. In some Spanish-speaking countries, it has become acceptable for a shopper to address a young store clerk with **tú.** Just a few years ago, only **Ud.** would have been appropriate in that context. Nevertheless, the traditional use of **tú** and **Ud.** still exists. Regarding your choice between **tú** or **Ud.**, a good rule of thumb is: *When in doubt, be more formal.*

There are a few regional differences in the use of pronouns. Spanish speakers in Spain use **vosotros** ("you all") when addressing more than one person with whom they are on a first-name basis. Elsewhere in the Spanish-speaking world, **ustedes,** abbreviated **Uds.,** is used when addressing more than one person on a formal or informal basis. In Costa Rica, Argentina, and other parts of Latin America, **vos** replaces **tú,** but **tú** would be perfectly understood in these countries.

Preguntas

To understand how Spanish is changing, consider what has happened to English over the years.

1. What new words have been added to the English language in the past twenty years?
   Possible answers include: technological terms such as virtual reality, cellular, digital, compact disc, etc.
2. What are some words and expressions that we do not use in English anymore?
   Possible answers include: groovy, icebox, buggy

1:00   **A·12 ¿Cómo se dice?**

Take turns expressing the following in Spanish.

1. we (all men)	nosotros	6. you (speaking to a professor)	usted
2. I	yo	7. they (just men)	ellos
3. you (speaking to a friend)	tú	8. they (fifty women and one man)	ellos
4. they (just women)	ellas	9. we (men and women)	nosotros
5. we (all women)	nosotras	10. they (men or women)	ellos/ellas

---

2:00   **A·13 ¿Tú o Ud.?**

Determine whether you would most likely address the following people with **tú** or **Ud.** State your reason, using the categories below.

A respect	**C** someone with whom you are on a first-name basis
B family member	**D** someone you do not know well

1. your sister	B: tú	6. a clerk in a department store	D: Ud.
2. your mom	B: tú	7. your doctor	A/D: Ud.
3. your Spanish professor	A: Ud.	8. someone you've just met who is older	A/D: Ud.
4. your grandfather	A/B: tú *or* Ud.	9. someone you've just met who is your age	C: tú
5. your best friend's father	A/D: Ud.	10. a child you've just met	C: tú

GRAMÁTICA 6 · El verbo *ser*

A-23 to A-26 | 7, 11, 12, 15

3:00

You have already learned the subject pronouns in Spanish. It is time to put them together with a verb. Consider first the verb *to be* in English. The *to* form of a verb, as in *to be* or *to see* is called an *infinitive*. Note that *to be* has different forms for different subjects.

to be

I	**am**	we	**are**
you	**are**	you (all)	**are**
he, she, it	**is**	they	**are**

Fíjate

The subject pronoun *it* does not have an equivalent in Spanish.

Verbs in Spanish also have different forms for different subjects.

ser (*to be*)

Singular			Plural		
yo	**soy**	*I am*	nosotros/as	**somos**	*we are*
tú	**eres**	*you are*	vosotros/as	**sois**	*you are*
él, ella, Ud.	**es**	*he/she is, you are*	ellos/as, Uds.	**son**	*they are, you are*

- In Spanish, subject pronouns are not required but rather used for clarification or emphasis. Pronouns are indicated by the verb ending. For example:

  Soy means *I am*.

  Es means either *he is*, *she is*, or *you* (formal) *are*.

- If you are using a subject pronoun, it will appear first, followed by the form of the verb that corresponds to the subject pronoun, and then the rest of the sentence, as in the examples:

  Yo **soy** Mark. **Soy** Mark.

  Él **es** inteligente. **Es** inteligente.

As you continue to progress in *¡Anda!*, you will learn to form and respond to questions, both orally and in writing, as well as have the opportunity to create longer sentences.

1:00

A·14 Vamos a practicar

Take turns saying the forms of the verb **ser** that you would use with the following pronouns. Correct your partner's answers as necessary.

1. nosotras somos
2. Ud. es
3. yo soy
4. él es
5. ellas son
6. tú eres
7. Uds. son
8. ella es

NOTE FOR *El verbo ser*

The verb *ser* is the first verb presented in this chapter. Accordingly, the verb "to be" is presented in English with its corresponding subject pronouns. You will notice in the verb chart of "to be," that the authors have used the words *you (all)* in the translation of *vosotros* and *vosotras* to indicate that this is the plural of the word *you*. In the Spanish verb chart for *ser*, however, the word *all* has been omitted, and just the word *you* is presented. At this point in the textbook, you can explain the use of *you all* as a way to express the plural of *you*. Because regional usage of *you* in the plural may vary, as the instructor you have the discretion to explain the plural *you* in the way that your students will best understand.

CAPÍTULO PRELIMINAR A

METHODOLOGY • Beginning Language Learning

The philosophy of ¡Anda! is to have beginning language learners speak meaningfully as soon as possible. The adjectives of nationality should provide an overview of the nationalities represented in your classes so that students can say *Soy. . .* or so that they can speak about their friends. Please adapt this list as needed.

NATIONAL STANDARDS
Connections

Goal Three of the National Standards is Connections. The Standards for Learning Spanish defines this goal as "Connect with Other Disciplines and Acquire Information." There are two standards that define this goal: Standards 3.1 and 3.2. Standard 3.1 states that "Students reinforce and further their knowledge of other disciplines through Spanish." Standard 3.2 states that "Students acquire information and recognize distinctive viewpoints that are only available through the Spanish language and its cultures." In ¡Anda!, we will provide opportunities for including other disciplines and showing your students how language can be combined with any life aspiration.

Suggestion for *Los adjetivos de nacionalidad* You may wish to share other adjectives of nationality from other Spanish-speaking countries. Or perhaps you have a diverse group of international students and you could introduce their nationalities. Also share with students others that they want to know that aren't listed. You will find additional adjectives of nationality in the *También se dice. . .* section in Appendix 3.

[1:00] **A•15** "Ser o no ser..."

Take turns changing these forms of **ser** to the plural if they are singular, and vice versa. Listen to your partner for accuracy and help him/her if necessary.

MODELO E1: yo soy
E2: *nosotros somos*

1. usted es ustedes son
2. nosotros somos yo soy
3. ella es ellas son
4. ellos son él es
5. tú eres ustedes son

VOCABULARIO 7 Los adjetivos de nacionalidad

[2:00] A-27 to A-28

Nacionalidad	Estudiantes				
alemán	Hans	español	Rodrigo	mexicano	Manuel
alemana	Ingrid	española	Guadalupe	mexicana	Milagros
canadiense	Jacques/Alice	francés	Jean-Paul	nigeriano	Yena
chino	Tsong	francesa	Brigitte	nigeriana	Ngidaha
china	Xue Lan	inglés	James	estadounidense	John/Kate
cubano	Javier	inglesa	Diana	(norteamericano/a)	
cubana	Pilar	japonés	Tabo	puertorriqueño	Ernesto
		japonesa	Yasu	puertorriqueña	Sonia

In Spanish:

- adjectives of nationality are not capitalized unless they are the first word in a sentence.
- most adjectives of nationality have a form for males, and a slightly different one for females. (You will learn more about this in **Capítulo 1.** For now, simply note the differences.)
- when referring to more than one individual, you make the adjectives plural by adding either an **-s** or an **-es.** (Again, in **Capítulo 1** you will formally learn more about forming plural words.)
- some adjectives of nationality have a written accent mark in the masculine form, but not in the feminine, like **inglés/inglesa** and **francés/francesa.** For example: **Mi papá es** *inglés* **y mi mamá es** *francesa.*

NOTE FOR *Los adjetivos de nacionalidad*

Adjective agreement and making words plural are presented in detail in *Capítulo 1.* Word stress and rules on written accents will be presented in *Capítulo 2.*

Expansion of A-17 If you have a diverse student population, you may wish to practice having students say *Me llamo. . . Soy* (nationality). *¿Y tú? Yo soy. . .* or bring in a map of the world and have students mark their countries of origin on the map. The class can take turns guessing: *¿Quién es de. . .?* And answering _____ *es de. . .*

3:00 **A·16** ¿Cuál es tu nacionalidad?

Describe the nationalities of the students listed on page 14. Form complete sentences using either **es** or **son** following the model. Then practice spelling the nationalities in Spanish with your partner.

MODELO
E1: china
E2: *Xue Lan es china.*
E1: chinos
E2: *Xue Lan y Tsong son chinos.*

1. francesa   Brigitte es francesa.
2. japonés   Tabo es japonés.
3. estadounidenses   John y Kate son estadounidenses.

4. canadiense   Alice/Jacques es canadiense.
5. mexicanos   Manuel y Milagros son mexicanos.
6. alemán   Hans es alemán.

2:00 **A·17** ¿Qué son?

Take turns naming the nationalities of the people listed. Make sure you use the correct form of **ser** in your sentence. Follow the model.

MODELO
E1: Yena
E2: *Yena es nigeriana.*
E1: Yena y Ngidaha
E2: *Yena y Ngidaha son nigerianos.*

1. Jacques   Jacques es canadiense.
2. Xue Lan y Tsong   Xue Lan y Tsong son chinos.
3. Ingrid   Ingrid es alemana.
4. Brigitte   Brigitte es francesa.
5. Kate   Kate es estadounidense.

6. Hans   Hans es alemán.
7. Javier y Pilar   Javier y Pilar son cubanos.
8. Jean-Paul   Jean-Paul es francés.
9. yo   Answers will vary.
10. mi familia y yo   Answers will vary.

VOCABULARIO 8   Los números 0–30

1:00   A-29 to A-32

0 cero	7 siete	13 trece	19 diecinueve	25 veinticinco
1 uno	8 ocho	14 catorce	20 veinte	26 veintiséis
2 dos	9 nueve	15 quince	21 veintiuno	27 veintisiete
3 tres	10 diez	16 dieciséis	22 veintidós	28 veintiocho
4 cuatro	11 once	17 diecisiete	23 veintitrés	29 veintinueve
5 cinco	12 doce	18 dieciocho	24 veinticuatro	30 treinta
6 seis				

2:00   **A·18 ¿Qué número?**

Take turns saying what number comes before and after those below. Your partner will check your accuracy.

1. 2 1/3   3. 8 7/9   5. 15 14/16   7. 20 19/21   9. 24 23/25
2. 5 4/6   4. 11 10/12   6. 17 16/18   8. 23 22/24   10. 26 25/27

2:00   **A·19 ¿Cuál es la secuencia?**

Take turns reading the number patterns aloud while filling in the missing numbers.

1. 1, 3, 5, __7__, 9, __11__, 13, __15__, 17
2. 2, 4, __6__, 8, __10__, 12, __14__, 16, __18__, 20, __22__
3. 3, __6__, 9, __12__, 15, __18__, 21, __24__, 27, __30__
4. 1, 3, 6, __10__, 15, __21__, 28

El mundo hispano

¿Sabías que...?

- Spanish is an official language of the European Union. Approximately 15% of the EU population speaks Spanish. It is the third-most-taught foreign language in the EU.
- The United States is the fifth-largest "Spanish-speaking country."
- There is no official language written into the U.S. Constitution.

PAÍS	POBLACIÓN
ARGENTINA	39.921.833
BOLIVIA	8.989.046
CHILE	16.134.219
COLOMBIA	43.593.035
COSTA RICA	4.075.261
CUBA	11.382.820
ECUADOR	13.547.510
EL SALVADOR	6.822.378
ESPAÑA	40.397.842
LOS ESTADOS UNIDOS	31.933.531
GUATEMALA	12.293.545
GUINEA ECUATORIAL	300.000
HONDURAS	7.326.496
MÉXICO	107.449.525
NICARAGUA	5.570.129
PANAMÁ	3.191.319
PARAGUAY	6.506.464
PERÚ	28.302.603
PUERTO RICO	3.927.188
LA REPÚBLICA DOMINICANA	9.183.984
URUGUAY	3.431.932
VENEZUELA	25.730.435

*CIA Fact Book, July 2006

Fíjate

When you see numbers or statistics presented in Spanish, the decimal point (.) represents a comma. In English, commas (,) are used to separate numbers.

A-33

¿Quién habla español?

Jennifer López es actriz, cantante y compositora puertorriqueña.

Omar Sosa es un músico cubano.

Rigoberta Menchú Tum es una activista maya guatemalteca.

Óscar Arias es un Nobel Laureate y presidente costarricense.

Many terms are associated with people from the Spanish-speaking world, most commonly *Hispanic* and *Latino*. While there is some controversy around the use of these terms, typically *Hispanic* refers to all people who come from a Spanish-speaking background. *Latino*, on the other hand, implies a specific connection to Latin America. Whichever term is used, the people denoted are far from homogeneous. Some are racially diverse, most are culturally diverse, and some do not even speak Spanish.

A·20 El mundo hispano `3:00`

Use the map and chart of the Spanish-speaking world on pp. 16–17 to answer the following questions in Spanish. Compare your answers with your partner.

1. Fill in the chart with the names of the Spanish-speaking countries in the appropriate column. How many countries are there in each of these areas? How many are there in the world?

AMÉRICA DEL NORTE	CENTROAMÉRICA	EL CARIBE	AMÉRICA DEL SUR	EUROPA	ÁFRICA

2. How many continents contain Spanish-speaking countries? What are they?
3. How many countries have a Spanish-speaking population of 25,000,000 or more? Name them and their continent.

Answers to A-20.
1. América del Norte: 2 (México y Estados Unidos); Centroamérica: 6 (Costa Rica, El Salvador, Guatemala, Honduras, Nicaragua y Panamá); El Caribe: 3 (Cuba, Puerto Rico y La República Dominicana); América del Sur: 9 (Argentina, Bolivia, Chile, Colombia, Ecuador, Paraguay, Perú, Uruguay y Venezuela); Europa: 1 (España); África: 1 (Guinea Ecuatorial); en total, 21 países
2. 4: América del Norte, América del Sur, Europa y África
3. 7: Argentina, Colombia, Perú, Venezuela—Suramérica; España—Europa; Estados Unidos, México—Norteamérica.

9 VOCABULARIO La hora

SAM
MSL

A-34 to
A-36

`3:00`

Es (la) medianoche.   Es (el) mediodía.   Es la una.   Son las diez y cinco.

Son las tres y cuarto.   Son las seis y media.   Son las nueve menos cuarto.   Son las diez menos veinticinco.

La hora	*Telling time*	¿A qué hora...?	*At what time...?*
¿Qué hora es?	*What time is it?*	... de la mañana	*... in the morning*
Es la una./Son las...	*It's one o'clock. It's...o'clock.*	... de la tarde	*... in the afternoon*
A la.../A las...	*At...o'clock.*	... de la noche	*... in the evening*

When telling time in Spanish:

- use **Es la...** to say times between 1:00 and 1:30.
- use **Son las...** with all times after 1:30.
- use **A la...** or **A las...** to say *at* what time.
- use the expressions **mediodía** and **medianoche** to say *noon* and *midnight*.
- use **la** with **una** (**a la una**) and **las** for hours greater than *one* (**a las ocho**).
- **de la tarde** tends to mean from noon until 7:00 or 8:00 P.M.
- **cuarto** and **media** are equivalent to the English expressions *quarter* (fifteen minutes) and *half* (thirty minutes). **Cuarto** and **media** are interchangeable with the numbers **quince** and **treinta**.

Suggestion for *La hora* You may wish to tell your students that in some countries, a typical way to ask for the time is: *¿Qué hora tienes?* A typical response could be: *Faltan. . . para las siete.* You may also wish to mention the use of 24-hour time in airports, train and bus stations, and schedules for movie, musical, and theater productions.

 A·21 ¿Qué hora es?

Look at the clocks and take turns asking and responding to **¿Qué hora es?**

MODELO

E1: *¿Qué hora es?*
E2: *Son las nueve de la mañana.*

1.

Son las once de la mañana.

2.

Es (el) mediodía.

3.

Es la una y media/treinta de la tarde.

4.

Son las ocho menos tres (minutos) de la noche.

5.

Son las dos y veintiséis de la mañana.

6.

Es (la) medianoche.

7.

Son las nueve menos cuarto/quince de la noche.

8.

Son las seis y diez de la mañana.

CAPÍTULO PRELIMINAR A

NOTE FOR A-22

Note that we suggest having Student 1 simply ask, *¿A qué hora?* There is no need to translate to English. Student 1's question is used as a prompt for Student 2 and gives your students practice with asking the time.

`2:00`

A·22 Tu horario

Think about your daily schedule. Then take turns asking and telling your partner at what times you do the following activities.

MODELO   go to sleep
E1: *¿A qué hora?*
E2: *a la una y media*

1. wake up
2. eat breakfast
3. attend your first class
4. eat lunch
5. finish classes for the day
6. study
7. eat dinner
8. exercise
9. go to bed

`2:00`

A·23 ¿Y el fin de semana?

What is your schedule for the weekend? Take turns telling your partner at what times you plan to do the activities from **A-22** this coming weekend.

VOCABULARIO 10   Los días, los meses y las estaciones

A-37 to A-43

Los meses y las estaciones (*Months and seasons*)

`2:00`

la primavera

marzo, abril y mayo

el verano

junio, julio y agosto

el otoño

septiembre, octubre y noviembre

el invierno

diciembre, enero y febrero

Los días de la semana	Days of the week	Expresiones útiles	Useful expressions
lunes	Monday	¿Qué día es hoy?	What day is today?
martes	Tuesday	¿Cuál es la fecha de hoy?	What is today's date?
miércoles	Wednesday	Hoy es lunes.	Today is Monday.
jueves	Thursday	Hoy es el 1 (primero)	Today is September first.
viernes	Friday	de septiembre.	
sábado	Saturday	Mañana es el 2 (dos)	Tomorrow is September second.
domingo	Sunday	de septiembre.	

Unlike in English, the days of the week and the months of the year are not capitalized in Spanish. Also, in the Spanish-speaking world, Monday is considered the first day of the week. On calendars the days are listed from Monday through Sunday.

1:00

A·24 Antes y después

Which days come directly before and after the ones listed? Take turns saying the days in Spanish.

1. sábado   viernes/domingo
2. lunes   domingo/martes
3. viernes   jueves/sábado
4. domingo   sábado/lunes
5. jueves   miércoles/viernes
6. miércoles   martes/jueves

1:00

A·25 Y los meses

Now do the same activity as A-24 with the months listed here.

1. octubre   septiembre/noviembre
2. febrero   enero/marzo
3. mayo   abril/junio
4. agosto   julio/septiembre
5. diciembre   noviembre/enero
6. junio   mayo/julio
7. septiembre   agosto/octubre
8. enero   diciembre/febrero
9. octubre   septiembre/noviembre
10. marzo   febrero/abril

Suggestion for A-24 and A-25 Have students play Ping-Pong with the days and months. This fast-paced game consists of partners taking turns saying the days and months quickly (back and forth) in order.

MODELO
E1: *lunes*
E2: *martes*
E1: *miércoles*

3:00 ⅱ **A·26** ¿Cuándo es?

Look at the activities included in the **Guía del ocio.** Take turns determining what activity takes place and at what time on the following days.

GUÍA DEL OCIO MADRID

MÚSICA

Sábado 4

• **XVI Festival de Jazz:**
Joe Henderson
La Riviera. 21 h.

• **Alonso y Williams**
La Madriguera. 24 h.

Domingo 5

• **Pedro Iturralde**
Clamores. Pases: 22.45 y 0.45 h. Libre.

Lunes 6

• **Moreiras Jazztet**
Café Central. 22 h.

CINE
Las vidas de Celia
(2005, España)****
Género: Drama
Director: Antonio Chavarrías
Interpretación: Najwa Nimri, Luis Tosar…
Najwa Nimri da vida a una mujer que intenta suicidarse la misma noche que otra joven es asesinada.

Mujeres en el parque
(2006, España)*****
Género: Drama
Director: Felipe Vega
Interpretación: Adolfo Fernández, Blanca Apilánez…
Una película llena de pequeños misterios, donde los personajes se enfrentan a lo difícil de las relaciones personales.

Volver (2006, España)*****
Género: Comedia dramática
Director: Pedro Almodóvar
Interpretación: Penélope Cruz, Carmen Maura…
Se basa en la vida y los recuerdos del director sobre su madre y el lugar donde se crió.

EXPOSICIONES
• **Museo Nacional Centro de Arte Reina Sofía**
Santa Isabel, 52.
Metro Atocha
Tel. 91 4675062
Horario: de 10 a 21 h. Domingo de 10 a 14.30 h. Martes cerrado.

Un recorrido del arte del siglo XX, desde Picasso. Salas dedicadas a los comienzos de la vanguardia. Además, exposiciones temporales.

• **Museo del Prado**
Paseo del Prado, s/n. Metro Banco de España.
Tel. 91 420 36 62 y 91 420 37 68
Horario: martes a sábado de 9 a 19 h. Domingo de 9 a 14 h. Lunes cerrado.

Todas las escuelas españolas, desde los frescos románicos hasta el siglo XVIII. Grandes colecciones de Velázquez, Goya, Murillo, etc. Importante representación de las escuelas europeas (Rubens, Tiziano, Durero, etc.). Escultura clásica griega y romana y Tesoro del Delfín.

Upper right: The Art Archive/Picture Desk, Inc./Kobal Collection.

MODELO   E1:   el lunes por la noche

E2:   *El Moreiras Jazztet es a las diez.*
El XVI Festival de Jazz de Madrid; El Museo Nacional es de 10 a 21 h.;

1. el sábado por la tarde   El Museo del Prado es de 9 a 19 h.
2. el miércoles por la mañana   El Museo Nacional es de 10 a 21 h.; El Museo del Prado es de 9 a 19 h.
3. el domingo   Pedro Iturralde
4. el sábado por la noche   El XVI Festival de Jazz y Alonso y Williams.
5. el martes por la tarde   El Museo del Prado es de 9 a 19 h.

VOCABULARIO 11 El tiempo

A-44 to
A-46

`1:00`

¿Qué tiempo hace? (*What's the weather like?*)

el sol
Hace sol. Hace buen tiempo.

la lluvia
Llueve. Hace mal tiempo.

la nube
Está nublado.

el viento
Hace viento.

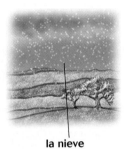

la nieve
Nieva.

la temperatura

99 °F/37 °C
Hace calor.

14 °F/210 °C
Hace frío.

`1:00` **A·27** ¿Qué tiempo hace?

Take turns asking and answering what the most typical weather is during the following seasons where you go to school.

MODELO E1: ¿Qué tiempo hace… en (el) otoño?

E2: *En (el) otoño hace sol.*

¿Qué tiempo hace…?

1. en (el) otoño
2. en (el) invierno
3. en (la) primavera
4. en (el) verano

Expansion for A-27 Ask students to create a weather log for where they live for the current week or for the previous week.

Suggestion for A-28 and A-29
Practice naming the countries and
their capitals with your students.

Expansion for A-28 and A-29
Physical map: Divide the class in
two teams. Make a set of cards with
the name of each Spanish-speaking
country on a different card. Give
each group a set. Groups are
instructed to place themselves
appropriately to create an accurate
physical map. The group that does
so first, or that is the most accurate,
wins. For the second round, the students must write the name of each
capital on the back of the card. The
group that gets the most capitals
correct wins.

`2:00` ## A·28 España

Take turns
answering the
question **¿Qué
tiempo hace?**
based on the map
of Spain.

Possible answers to A-28.
1. Hace sol.
2. Hace frío, nieva y hace viento.
3. Está nublado. No hace sol.
4. Está nublado, hace viento y hace frío.
5. Llueve.

MODELO   E1:   ¿Qué tiempo
hace en Sevilla?

          E2:   *Hace calor.*

1. ¿Qué tiempo hace en Mallorca?
2. ¿Qué tiempo hace en Pamplona?
3. ¿Qué tiempo hace en Barcelona?

4. ¿Qué tiempo hace en Madrid?
5. ¿Qué tiempo hace en Córdoba?

`2:00` ## A·29 y América del Sur

Take turns making
statements about
the weather based
on the map of
South America.
You can say what
the weather is like
and also what it is
not like. Follow the
model.

MODELO   E1:   *Llueve en
Bogotá.*

          E2:   *No hace
frío en
Venezuela.*

Fíjate

To make a negative
statement, simply place the
word *no* before the verb: *No
llueve en Caracas. No nieva
en Buenos Aires. No hace
calor en Punta Arenas.*

Possible answers to A-29.
1. Llueve en Bogotá.
2. Hace sol y hace calor en Caracas.
3. Hace viento en Buenos Aires.
4. Nieva en Punta Arenas.
5. Está nublado en Lima.

GRAMÁTICA 12 Gustar

A-47 to
A-49

2:00

To express likes and dislikes, you say the following:

Me gusta la primavera.

No me gusta el invierno.

Me gustan los viernes.

No **me gustan** los lunes.

1. To say you like or dislike one thing, what form of **gustar** do you use?
2. To say you like or dislike more than one thing, what form of **gustar** do you use?

Check your answers to the preceding questions in Appendix 1.

NOTE FOR *GUSTAR*

Gustar is introduced here in an abbreviated fashion with the goal of having students state their likes and dislikes. In this chapter *gustar* is presented lexically. Then, there is an expanded presentation in *Capítulo 2*. Finally, *gustar* is reviewed and then presented in a complete fashion along with verbs like *gustar* in *Capítulo 8*.

Suggestion for drawings for *Gustar*
Review the months and seasons with the class. Then discuss what the weather is like in your area for each season. Ask the students to describe the pictures in the text. What is the weather like in each picture? Using *gustar*, have students state why they like or dislike the weather in each picture. You might want to include some new verbs in the infinitives such as *tomar el sol*, *esquiar*, or *correr en el parque*. That way, students can explain why they like certain weather patterns.

RECURSOS

A-G12 | Electronic Activity Cache

Suggestion for A-31 You may wish to point out the number of words that look like their English equivalents in this activity.

2:00

A-30 ¿Qué te gusta?

Ask your partner if he/she likes or dislikes the following things.

MODELO la primavera

E1: *¿Te gusta la primavera?*

E2: *Sí, me gusta la primavera.*

1. el otoño
2. el invierno
3. el verano
4. los lunes
5. los sábados
6. los domingos
7. los viernes
8. la clase de español

2:00

A-31 ¿Qué más te gusta?

Take turns asking your partner about the following places and things.

MODELO las hamburguesas

E1: *¿Te gustan las hamburguesas?*

E2: *No, no me gustan las hamburguesas.*

1. Nevada
2. la guitarra
3. los autos Ford
4. la pizza de Domino's
5. Los Ángeles y San Francisco
6. San Antonio
7. los teléfonos celulares
8. el béisbol y el fútbol.

Y por fin, ¿cómo andas?

Each of the coming chapters of ¡*Anda!* will have three self-check sections for you to assess your progress. A **¿Cómo andas?** (*How are you doing?*) section will appear one third of the way through each chapter, another will appear at the two-thirds point, and a third and final one at the end of the chapter called **Y por fin, ¿cómo andas?** (*Finally, how are you doing?*). Use the checklists to measure what you have learned in the chapter. Place a check in the *Feel confident* column of the topics you feel you know, and a check in the *Need to Review* column of those that you need to practice more. Be sure to go back and practice because it is the key to your success!

Having completed this chapter, I now can…

	Feel Confident	Need to Review
Comunicación		
greet, say goodbye, and introduce someone (p. 4)	❑	❑
ask and respond to simple questions when meeting or greeting someone (p. 5)	❑	❑
understand and respond appropriately to basic classroom expressions, and requests (p. 8)	❑	❑
spell my name using the Spanish alphabet (p. 9)	❑	❑
identify cognates (p. 10)	❑	❑
state the subject pronouns (p. 11)	❑	❑
use the verb **ser** to say who I am and talk about some nationalities (p. 13, 14)	❑	❑
say the numbers 0–30 (p. 16)	❑	❑
tell time (p. 18)	❑	❑
say the months, days of the week, and seasons (p. 20)	❑	❑
talk about the weather (p. 23)	❑	❑
state some things that I like and dislike (p. 25)	❑	❑
Cultura		
state at least two reasons why it is important for me to study and be able to communicate in Spanish (p. 2)	❑	❑
state the similarities and differences in greetings between the Spanish-speaking world and the United States (p. 7)	❑	❑
know when to use **tú** and **Ud.** (p. 12)	❑	❑
name the continents and countries where Spanish is spoken (p. 16)	❑	❑

Estrategia

The *¿Cómo andas?* and *Por fin, ¿cómo andas?* sections are designed to help you assess your understanding of specific concepts. In the *Capítulo Preliminar,* there is one opportunity for you to reflect on how well you understand the concepts. Beginning with *Capítulo 1* there will be three opportunities for you to stop and reflect on what you have learned. These checklists help you become accountable for your own learning, and help you determine what you need to review. Also use the checklist as a way to communicate with your instructor about any concepts you still need to review. Additionally, you might also use your checklist as a way to study with a peer group or peer tutor. If you need to review a particular concept, more practice is available on your ¡*Anda!* web site, where you will find quizzes online.

INTRODUCTION TO
Y por fin, ¿cómo andas?
Throughout the textbook, you will encounter three sections per chapter that allow the students to self-assess. The first two sections are titled *¿Cómo andas?*, and the last section is titled *Y por fin, ¿cómo andas?* Each section has a chart listing the concepts from the chapter. For each concept, students can check off whether they feel confident about it or whether they need to review it. As students complete the *¿Cómo andas?* section, you can survey the class to see which areas students need to review. If the majority of students are having difficulties, you may want to review the concept in class. As an instructor, you can suggest that students make an appointment for extra help on any concept they need to review. This checklist is especially helpful if students have a peer tutor or study group, because they can keep a record of the concepts that are difficult. Peer tutors will appreciate having a checklist of concepts they should review for each tutoring session. Each chapter will normally have three self-checks, but since *Capítulo Preliminar A* is meant to be a quick introduction to Spanish, there is only one self-check in this chapter. Encourage students to use these self-checks, since they help them become accountable for their own learning and promote self-actualization.

Suggestion for *Y por fin, ¿cómo andas?* If you have time constraints, we recommend these self-assessments be completed by the students outside of class. You may want to spot-check some students and ask how they are doing (e.g., "How many of you feel confident with greeting, saying good-bye, and introducing someone?"). For those students who do not raise their hands, remind them that they need to consult the pages listed to review the material. If you have time to do them in class, one approach is to have students write short answers to the topics, then check in their textbook to verify their answers. Based on this verification, they can rate themselves on the concept and hand in their ratings to you at the end of class.

VOCABULARIO ACTIVO

CD 1
Tracks 3–16

Los saludos — *Greetings*

Bastante bien.	*Just fine.*
Bien, gracias.	*Fine, thanks.*
Buenos días.	*Good morning.*
Buenas noches.	*Good evening.; Good night.*
Buenas tardes.	*Good afternoon.*
¿Cómo está usted?	*How are you?* (formal)
¿Cómo estás?	*How are you?* (familiar)
¡Hola!	*Hi!; Hello!*
Más o menos.	*So-so.*
Muy bien.	*Really well.*
¿Qué tal?	*How's it going?*
Regular.	*Okay.*
¿Y tú?	*And you?* (familiar)
¿Y usted?	*And you?* (formal)

Las despedidas — *Farewells*

Adiós.	*Good-bye.*
Chao.	*Bye.*
Hasta luego.	*See you later.*
Hasta mañana.	*See you tomorrow.*
Hasta pronto.	*See you soon.*

Las presentaciones — *Introductions*

¿Cómo te llamas?	*What is your name?* (familiar)
¿Cómo se llama usted?	*What is your name?* (formal)
Encantado.	*Pleased to meet you.*
Encantada.	
Igualmente.	*Likewise.*
Me llamo…	*My name is…*
Mucho gusto.	*Nice to meet you.*
Quiero presentarte a…	*I would like to introduce you to…* (familiar)
Quiero presentarle a…	*I would like to introduce you to…* (formal)
Soy…	*I am…*

Expresiones útiles para la clase — *Useful classroom expressions*

Preguntas y respuestas — *Questions and answers*

¿Cómo?	*What?; How?*
¿Cómo se dice… en español?	*How do you say… in Spanish?*
¿Cómo se escribe… en español?	*How do you write… in Spanish?*
(No) comprendo.	*I (don't) understand.*
Lo sé.	*I know.*
No lo sé.	*I don't know.*
No.	*No.*
Sí.	*Yes.*
¿Qué es esto?	*What is this?*
¿Qué significa?	*What does it mean?*
¿Quién?	*Who?*

Expresiones de cortesía — *Polite expressions*

De nada.	*You're welcome.*
Gracias.	*Thank you.*
Por favor.	*Please.*

Mandatos para la clase — *Classroom instructions (commands)*

Abra(n) el libro en la página…	*Open your book to page…*
Cierre(n) el/los libros.	*Close your book/s.*
Conteste(n).	*Answer.*
Escriba(n).	*Write.*
Escuche(n).	*Listen.*
Lea(n).	*Read.*
Repita(n).	*Repeat.*
Vaya(n) a la pizarra.	*Go to the board.*

Las nacionalidades — *Nationalities*

alemán/alemana	*German*
canadiense	*Canadian*
chino/a	*Chinese*
cubano/a	*Cuban*
español/a	*Spanish*
francés/francesa	*French*
inglés/inglesa	*English*
japonés/japonesa	*Japanese*
mexicano/a	*Mexican*
nigeriano/a	*Nigerian*
estadounidense (norteamericano/a)	*American*
puertorriqueño/a	*Puerto Rican*

Los números 0–30 — *Numbers 0–30*

See page 16.

La hora — *Telling time*

A la…/A las…	*At… o'clock.*
¿A qué hora…?	*At what time…?*
… de la mañana	*… in the morning*
… de la noche	*… in the evening*
… de la tarde	*… in the afternoon*
¿Cuál es la fecha de hoy?	*What is today's date?*
Es la…/Son las…	*It's… o'clock.*
Hoy es…	*Today is…*
Mañana es…	*Tomorrow is…*
la medianoche	*midnight*
el mediodía	*noon*
¿Qué día es hoy?	*What day is today?*
¿Qué hora es?	*What time is it?*

Los días de la semana — *Days of the week*

lunes	*Monday*
martes	*Tuesday*
miércoles	*Wednesday*
jueves	*Thursday*
viernes	*Friday*
sábado	*Saturday*
domingo	*Sunday*

Los meses del año — *Months of the year*

enero	*January*
febrero	*February*
marzo	*March*
abril	*April*
mayo	*May*
junio	*June*
julio	*July*
agosto	*August*
septiembre	*September*
octubre	*October*
noviembre	*November*
diciembre	*December*

Las estaciones — *Seasons*

el invierno	*winter*
la primavera	*spring*
el otoño	*autumn; fall*
el verano	*summer*

Expresiones del tiempo — *Weather expressions*

Está nublado.	*It's cloudy.*
Hace buen tiempo.	*The weather is nice.*
Hace calor.	*It's hot.*
Hace frío.	*It's cold.*
Hace mal tiempo.	*The weather is bad.*
Hace sol.	*It's sunny.*
Hace viento.	*It's windy.*
Llueve.	*It's raining.*
la lluvia	*rain*
Nieva.	*It's snowing.*
la nieve	*snow*
la nube	*cloud*
¿Qué tiempo hace?	*What's the weather like?*
el sol	*sun*
la temperatura	*temperature*
el viento	*wind*

Unos verbos — *Some verbs*

gustar	*to like*
ser	*to be*

29

¿Quiénes somos?

What makes us who we are? What makes each of us unique? We may come from different geographical locations and represent different cultures, races, and religions, yet in many respects we are much the same. We have the same basic needs, share common likes and dislikes, and possess similar hopes and dreams.

NATIONAL STANDARDS

Comunicación
- To talk about your family (Communication)
- To describe yourself and others (Communication)
- To give telephone numbers in Spanish (Communication, Cultures)
- To write a poem in Spanish (Communication, Cultures)

Cultura
- To explain how Hispanic last names are formed (Cultures, Comparisons, Communities)
- To state several regional and national differences in both the English and Spanish languages (Communication, Comparisons, Communities)
- To discuss the size, location, and makeup of the Hispanic population in the United States (Cultures, Connections)

Ambiciones siniestras
- To meet the six protagonists in the continuing mystery story, *Ambiciones siniestras* (Communication, Cultures)
- To begin to recognize cognates in reading (Comparisons)
- To view the video to learn more about the classes the protagonists in *Ambiciones siniestras* are taking and more about their lives (Communication)

SECTION GOALS FOR
Chapter Opener

By the end of the chapter opener section, students will be able to:
- compare and contrast various cultures and nationalities.
- discuss what factors contribute to individual differences.
- analyze how the social environment affects the individual.

OBJETIVOS / CONTENIDOS

Comunicación

OBJETIVOS	CONTENIDOS	
• To talk about your family	① The family	32
• To describe yourself and others	② The verb **tener** (*to have*)	35
• To give telephone numbers in Spanish	③ Singular and plural nouns	37
• To write a poem in Spanish	④ Masculine and feminine nouns	38
	⑤ Definite (*the*) and indefinite (*a, an, some*) articles	39
	⑥ People	41
	⑦ Possessive adjectives (*my, your, our,* etc.)	42
	⑧ Adjectives	44
	⑨ Numbers 31–100	48
	☐ Pronunciación: Spanish vowels	33
	☐ Escucha:	50
	Estrategia: Determining the topic and listening for words you know	
	☐ Escribe: Writing a poem	51

Cultura

OBJETIVOS	CONTENIDOS	
• To explain how Hispanic last names are formed	☐ First and last names in the Spanish-speaking world	34
• To state several regional and national differences in both the English and Spanish languages	☐ The diversity of the Spanish language	48
• To discuss the size, location, and makeup of the Hispanic population in the United States	☐ Hispanics in the United States	52

Ambiciones siniestras

OBJETIVOS	CONTENIDOS	
• To meet the six protagonists in the continuing mystery story, *Ambiciones siniestras*	☐ Episodio 1	
• To begin to recognize cognates when reading	Lectura: *Conexiones*	54
• To view the video to learn more about the classes the protagonists in *Ambiciones siniestras* are taking and more about their lives	Estrategia: Recognizing cognates	
	Video: *¿Quiénes son?*	56

METHODOLOGY • The National Foreign Language Standards

The American Council on the Teaching of Foreign Languages, along with the American Association of Teachers of Spanish and Portuguese and other language organizations, created the National Foreign Language Standards. *¡Anda!* is based on the National Standards, and the Standards' 5C's (*Communication, Cultures, Connections, Comparisons, and Communities*) will always be identified with each chapter's objectives. For more information on the National Foreign Language Standards, please consult www.actfl.org.

RECURSOS

IRM

Lesson Plan

PREGUNTAS

1 List the personal characteristics that make you unique. Which of the characteristics do you share with members of your family? Whom do you resemble most in your family?

2 How does where you live affect who you are? What social factors have contributed to the development of the person you are today?

3 What are some different nationalities and cultures you encounter on a regular basis in the United States? What do you have in common with them?

31

METHODOLOGY • Starting Where the Learner Is

Beginning with what students themselves already know best helps to build interest in the chapter. Answer the questions in *Preguntas* in English in pairs or as a class activity. The philosophy of *¡Anda!* acknowledges the need to use English briefly at the beginning of each chapter during the first semester in order to access students' prior knowledge. John Dewey's philosophy encourages instructors to start where the learners are, which includes what they already know about the subject. Being able to share about what they already know helps to motivate the learners and to put them in an anticipatory state for the chapter's content.

Warm-up for *Chapter Opener* Ask students to give their impressions of the photo on this page. Have them silently read the chapter objectives. We suggest you spend no more than 5–7 minutes on chapter openers.

Expansion for *Preguntas* Ask your students: *In what ways will you be a different person in ten years? Why?* These questions should elicit responses based on the socio-anthropological fact that we are all products of our environments and that if in the future students are in a different place, they may find that they too have changed.

PLANNING AHEAD

To save time in class, assign actividad **1-5** as homework. Also, assign actividad **1-29** in advance so students bring in pictures. For the culture presentation, *Los nombres en el mundo hispano* on p. 34, have students bring in wedding announcements for an expansion activity in which they practice formulating names *a la española*.

We recommend assigning *all* culture sections to be read in advance. Also, assign students to read *all* grammar explanations before class since they are clear and concise. The instructor's role then is to clarify or review as necessary any points students read in advance. Finally, we suggest assigning the *Escribe* sections and the *Ambiciones siniestras* text and video episodes as homework.

NATIONAL STANDARDS
Communities

Ask students to identify areas in your community where large populations of Spanish speakers live. What types of services do these Spanish speakers need? What services could your students provide? Is there an activity that the students and the community members should share? Some ideas of service learning projects in your area might include: collections of food and clothing for shelters, educational services such as tutoring or after-school enrichment programs, music, reading to those who cannot, or simply keeping someone company. Remind students that everyone shares basic needs that need to be fulfilled, regardless of nationality or culture.

NOTE ON
Comunicación

There are two *Comunicación* sections in each chapter of *¡Anda!* Within each of these sections the new grammar and vocabulary are introduced, and all grammar and vocabulary (both new and recycled from previous chapters) are practiced. Also in each *Comunicación* are culture presentations that reinforce the chapter theme and/or focus country or countries. You and your students will know that you have reached the end of a *Comunicación* because there is a self-evaluation for your students entitled *¿Cómo andas?* Each *Comunicación* section is designed to be completed in about one week.

SECTION GOALS FOR
Comunicación

By the end of the *Comunicación* section, students will be able to:

• describe their family members.
• explain the relationships between members of the family.
• pronounce the vowels in Spanish.
• contrast the use of surnames in Spanish and English.
• express possession using the forms of the verb *tener*.
• narrate the characteristics of someone else's family using *tener* and vocabulary from *la familia*.
• form the plural of nouns and adjectives.
• distinguish between masculine and feminine endings of nouns and adjectives.
• practice identifying cognates.
• differentiate between the definite and indefinite articles.

NATIONAL STANDARDS
Communication

This series of activities uses oral communication to move from highly structured to more open-ended, personalized activities.

Standard 1.1 requires students to use Spanish by engaging in conversations and providing and obtaining information in an interpersonal mode. The *Preguntas* in *¿Quiénes somos?* allow students to work with a partner and exchange information about their heritage.

The students practice answering and asking questions, and they can share this information with other members of the class. You will find other interpersonal activities that

Comunicación

• Describing family members

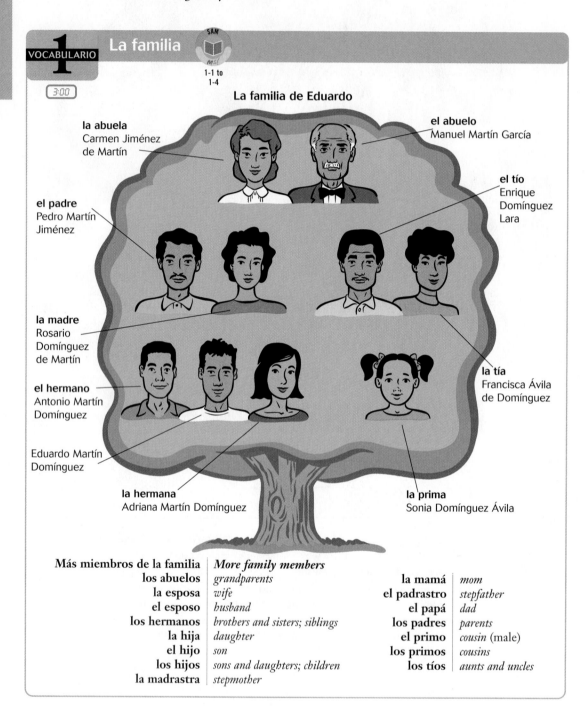

VOCABULARIO 1 La familia

SAM 1-1 to 1-4

3:00

La familia de Eduardo

la abuela
Carmen Jiménez de Martín

el abuelo
Manuel Martín García

el padre
Pedro Martín Jiménez

el tío
Enrique Domínguez Lara

la madre
Rosario Domínguez de Martín

el hermano
Antonio Martín Domínguez

la tía
Francisca Ávila de Domínguez

Eduardo Martín Domínguez

la hermana
Adriana Martín Domínguez

la prima
Sonia Domínguez Ávila

Más miembros de la familia	*More family members*		
los abuelos	*grandparents*	la mamá	*mom*
la esposa	*wife*	el padrastro	*stepfather*
el esposo	*husband*	el papá	*dad*
los hermanos	*brothers and sisters; siblings*	los padres	*parents*
la hija	*daughter*	el primo	*cousin (male)*
el hijo	*son*	los primos	*cousins*
los hijos	*sons and daughters; children*	los tíos	*aunts and uncles*
la madrastra	*stepmother*		

encourage your students to work in pairs to practice communicating in Spanish.

Note: Do not repeat in unison with your students since you will be unable to monitor their pronunciation.

METHODOLOGY • Introducing New Vocabulary

For new instructors (and as a reminder for those of us who have been teaching), whenever introducing new vocabulary, say the word, have students repeat after you, then say the word again, having them repeat once again. Even though the words are pronounced on the *¡Anda!* CD, reinforcement in class helps novice learners. Spend approximately 3 minutes introducing new vocabulary.

METHODOLOGY • *También se dice. . .* Appendix 3

The *También se dice. . .* appendix provides additional words that pertain to each topic. Words presented in introductory courses may not be the exact words that students wish to use; even native speakers sometimes search for additional vocabulary. *También se dice. . .* is meant to serve as an amplification of vocabulary for all students. The list should not be included on chapter assessments.

RECURSOS

C	P	Electronic
TI-1 to TI-2	TI-1 to TI-2	Electronic Activity Cache

PRONUNCIACIÓN [3:00]

CD 1
Track 17

SAM

1-5 to
1-7

Spanish vowels

The vowels, *a, e, i, o, u*, are nearly always pronounced the same way. Their pronunciation is crisp and shorter than in English. For example:

a like the "a" in *father* but shorter   o like the "o" in *zone* but shorter
e like the "e" in *hey* but shorter   u like the "u" in *rule* but shorter
i like the "ee" in *meet* but shorter

1·1 Las palabras

Practice pronouncing the following words and focus on the vowels.

1. la madrastra   4. el primo   7. el otoño
2. la hermana   5. inteligente   8. Uruguay
3. el esposo   6. los hijos   9. uno

1·2 Las oraciones

Pronounce the following sentences, paying special attention to the vowels.

1. Mi primo es mexicano. Es inteligente y simpático.
2. Me gusta la primavera y el otoño. No me gustan los lunes.
3. Mis hermanos son cómicos. Su música favorita es la música clásica.

1·3 Los dichos y refranes (*Sayings*)

Now pronounce the following saying (**dicho**), focusing on the vowels.

¡A, E, I, O, U, el burro eres tú!

Capítulo Preliminar A. El verbo *ser*, pág. 13.

1·4 La familia de Eduardo [3:00]

Look at Eduardo's family tree and state how the following people are related to him. Share your answers with a partner.

MODELO   E1: *¿Quién es* (Who is) *Antonio?*
          E2: *Es su* (his) *hermano.*

1. Francisca Francisca es su tía.
2. Carmen   Carmen es su abuela.
3. Enrique   Enrique es su tío.
4. Manuel   Manuel es su abuelo.

5. Pedro   Pedro es su padre.
6. Rosario   Rosario es su madre.
7. Sonia   Sonia es su prima.
8. Adriana   Adriana es su hermana.

Estrategia

¡Anda! has provided you with recycling references to help guide your continuous review of previously learned material. Make sure to consult the indicated pages if you need to refresh your memory about the topic.

INTRODUCTION TO
Pronunciación

Each chapter has a brief presentation on Spanish pronunciation after the initial vocabulary section. These presentations are concise, taking examples both from vocabulary just presented and previously learned, as well as from cognates. The presentations are brief so that students can focus on small portions of Spanish pronunciation without feeling overwhelmed.

SECTION GOALS FOR
Pronunciación

By the end of the *Pronunciación* section, students will be able to:
- pronounce the Spanish vowels *a, e, i, o, u.*
- practice pronouncing cognates and new vocabulary by sounding out each letter.

METHODOLOGY • Pronunciación

You may either pronounce the words for your students or have them listen to the CD. Encourage them to practice these sections outside of class with their CD.

METHODOLOGY • Using English in the Classroom

The philosophy of *¡Anda!* regarding the use of English is as follows:
1. Grammar explanations are brief and in English.
2. Critical-thinking questions or those tapping students' prior knowledge (such as those in this chapter opener) start in English due to the limited nature of the students' Spanish language capability. As the program progresses, these questions will be in Spanish.
3. Directions for activities are in English until *Capítulo 3*, when students are eased into Spanish and weaned away from English.

The use of Spanish in *¡Anda!* is based on Stephen Krashen's Input Hypothesis (*i* + 1), which states that students acquire more language when exposed to structures that are a little beyond (+1) what they completely comprehend (*i*).

1·5 Mi familia

6:00

Paso 1 Draw and label **three** generations of your own family tree, or create a fictitious one. Share your information with a partner, following the model. Please save your drawing! You will need it for actividad **1-10**.

MODELO   E1: *Mary es mi* (my) *hermana.*
　　　　　　　E2: *George es mi papá.*

Paso 2 Write **five** of the sentences that you shared orally with your partner, or **five** different sentences about your family members. Follow the **modelo** in **Paso 1.**

MODELO _____ _____ mi _____ .
　　　　　　 (Subject)　*(verb)*　　*(family member)*

> **Estrategia**
>
> For additional vocabulary choices, consult Appendix 3, *También se dice…*

5:00   SAM   1-8 to 1-9

Los nombres en el mundo hispano

In Spanish-speaking countries, it is customary for people to use both paternal and maternal last names (surnames). For example, Eduardo's father is **Pedro Martín Jiménez** and his mother's maiden name is **Rosario Domínguez Lara**. Eduardo's first last name would be his father's first last name (**Martín**); Eduardo's second last name would be his mother's first last name (**Domínguez**). Therefore, Eduardo's full name would be **Eduardo Martín Domínguez.** In most informal situations, though, Eduardo would use only his first last name, so he would call himself **Eduardo Martín.**

In most Hispanic countries, a woman usually retains the surname of her father upon marriage, while giving up her mother's surname. She takes her husband's last name, preceded by the preposition **de** (*of*). For example, when Eduardo's mother married his father, her name became **Rosario Domínguez de Martín.** Therefore, if a woman named **Carmen Torres López** married **Ricardo Colón Montoya,** her name would become **Carmen Torres de Colón.**

Preguntas

1. Hispanic last names may seem very long to you. Are there any equivalents in the United States or in other countries?
Hyphenated last names, double last names (e.g., Courteney Cox Arquette).
2. Can you think of any advantages to using both the mother's and the father's last names?
Some answers may include: less confusion in phone books with common names, family last names are not lost, and potentially easier reconstruction of a family's heritage.

> **Fíjate**
>
> Below are some common Spanish first names and nicknames.
>
> **Hombres**
> | | |
> |---|---|
> | Antonio | Toño, Toni |
> | Francisco | Paco, Pancho, Cisco |
> | Guillermo | Memo, Guillo, Guille |
> | Jesús | Chu, Chuito, Chucho, Chus |
> | José | Pepe |
> | Manuel | Manolo, Mani |
> | Ramón | Moncho, Monchi |
>
> **Mujeres**
> | | |
> |---|---|
> | Antonia | Toñín, Toña, Toñi(ta) |
> | Concepción | Concha, Conchita |
> | Guadalupe | Lupe, Lupita |
> | María Soledad | Marisol |
> | María Teresa | Maite, Marité, Maritere |
> | Pilar | Pili |
> | Rosario | Charo |

sometimes, for professional or personal reasons, married women in the United States keep their maiden name, while others hyphenate both last names, or use both names without a hyphen. When students understand how to address someone correctly, they are more likely to communicate effectively. Standard 5.1 encourages the use of Spanish skills beyond the school setting. Mastering the use of surnames in Spanish allows students to connect with Spanish speakers.

Expansion for *Los nombres en el mundo hispano*
Additional questions/ projects for your students:

1. What is your full name in the Spanish style? Write it out, then write the names of five family members or friends *a la española.* For example, Gail Parker's mother's maiden name is Smith. Her name *a la española* would be *Gail Parker Smith.*
2. Ask students to bring the wedding announcement page of a newspaper to class. Have them work in pairs to decide what the names of five new brides

would be *a la española* if they took their new husbands' last names.

GRAMÁTICA 2

El verbo *tener*

1-10 to 1-13   7, 11, 12, 15

1:00

Tengo una hermana y un hermano.

In **Capítulo Preliminar A** you learned the present tense of **ser.** Another very common verb in Spanish is **tener** (*to have*). The present tense forms of the verb **tener** follow.

tener (*to have*)					
Singular			**Plural**		
yo	**tengo**	*I have*	nosotros/as	**tenemos**	*we have*
tú	**tienes**	*you have*	vosotros/as	**tenéis**	*you have*
él, ella, Ud.	**tiene**	*he/she has, you have*	ellos/as, Uds.	**tienen**	*they have, you have*

1:00 **1·6 ¿Quiénes tienen?**

Take turns giving the correct form of the verb **tener** for each subject listed.

MODELO   E1: la prima

        E2: *tiene*

1. tú   tienes
2. los padres   tienen
3. nosotros   tenemos
4. Pedro, Carmen y Rosario   tienen
5. yo   tengo
6. el tío   tiene

3:00 **1·7 Practica conmigo**

Take turns saying the following subject pronouns with the corresponding forms of **tener.** Practice in random order until you can say them quickly with no errors.

1. tú   tienes
2. Uds.   tienen
3. yo   tengo
4. nosotros   tenemos
5. ella   tiene
6. ellas   tienen
7. él   tiene
8. ellos   tienen
9. Ud.   tiene
10. tú y yo   tenemos

METHODOLOGY • Student Accountability

When students are working in class, either with a partner or by themselves, always circulate around the room to ensure they are on task. We suggest giving a daily class participation grade for student accountability. Also, spot-check activity answers not only for comprehension, but also for accountability. It sends a strong message to students that they must stay on task, as does allotting a brief but appropriate time for each activity.

METHODOLOGY • Grammar Explanations
Grammar explanations are simple and concise so that students can read them before coming to class. You may wish to review the presentation *briefly* (e.g., pronounce verb forms, etc.), but then move directly into the activities.

METHODOLOGY • Deductive Presentations of Grammar

Verb presentations such as the one for *tener* are done *deductively* (give students the rules/forms and go directly to practice) to streamline presentation time. All grammar presentations in this chapter are deductive.

⏱ 3:00   **1•8** ¡Apúrate!

One person makes a ball out of a piece of paper, says a subject pronoun, and tosses the ball to someone in the group. That person catches it, gives the corresponding form of **tener**, then says another pronoun and tosses the ball to someone else. After finishing **tener**, repeat the game with **ser**.

MODELO   E1: *yo*
E2: *tengo; ellas*
E3: *tienen; Ud.*
E4: *tiene; …*

Capítulo Preliminar A. El verbo *ser*, pág. 13.

⏱ 3:00   **1•9** La familia de José

Complete the paragraph with the correct forms of **tener**. Then share your answers with a partner. Finally, based on what you learned in the previous culture presentation regarding last names, what is José's father's last name? What is José's mother's maiden name?   Olivo, Peralta

José Olivo Peralta y su familia

Yo soy el primo de José. Él (1) ___tiene___ una familia grande. (2) ___Tiene___ tres hermanos, Pepe, Alonso y Tina. Pepe está casado (*is married*) y (3) ___tiene___ dos hijos. También José y sus hermanos (4) ___tienen___ muchos tíos, siete en total. La madre de José (5) ___tiene___ tres hermanos y dos están casados. El padre de José (6) ___tiene___ una hermana y ella está casada con mi padre, ¡es mi madre! Nosotros (7) ___tenemos___ una familia grande. ¿Y tú?, ¿(8) ___tienes___ una familia grande?

1•10 De tal palo, tal astilla   ⏱ 3:00

Create **three** sentences with **tener** based on the family tree that you sketched for actividad **1-5**, page 34. Tell them to your partner, who will then share what you said with another classmate.

MODELO   E1 (ALICE): *Tengo un hermano, Scott. Tengo dos tíos, George y David. No tengo abuelos.*

E2 (JEFF): *Alice tiene un hermano, Scott. Tiene dos tíos, George y David. No tiene abuelos.*

Fíjate

The word *un* in the *modelo* for actividad **1-10** is the shortened form of the number *uno*. It is used before a masculine noun—a concept that will be explained later in this chapter.

GRAMÁTICA 3 — El singular y el plural

1-14 to 1-16   2, 3

3:00

Raúl tiene dos primas y Jorge tiene una prima.

To pluralize singular nouns and adjectives in Spanish, follow these simple guidelines.

1. If the word ends in a vowel, add **-s**.

hermana	→	hermanas	abuelo →	abuelos
día	→	días	mi →	mis

2. If the word ends in a consonant, add **-es**.

mes	→	meses	ciudad →	ciudades
televisión	→	televisiones	joven →	jóvenes

3. If the word ends in a **-z**, change the **z** to **c**, and add **-es**.

lápiz	→	lápices	feliz →	felices

> **Fíjate**
>
> Note that *televisión* loses its accent mark in the plural. Also note the plural of *joven* is *jóvenes*. You will learn about accent marks in *Capítulo 2*.

1·11 Te toca a ti 1:00

Take turns making the following singular nouns plural.

MODELO   E1:   primo
             E2:   *primos*

1. padre   padres
2. tía   tías
3. taxi   taxis
4. francés franceses
5. nieto   nietos
6. alemán   alemanes
7. abuela   abuelas
8. sol   soles
9. emoción   emociones
10. favor   favores

1·12 De nuevo 1:00

Now take turns making the following plural nouns singular.

MODELO   E1:   primos
             E2:   *primo*

1. hijos   hijo
2. días   día
3. discusiones   discusión
4. madres   madre
5. lápices   lápiz
6. jóvenes   joven

GRAMÁTICA 4 — El masculino y el femenino

1-17 to 1-18   4

5:00

El abuelo y las tías.

In Spanish, all nouns (people, places, and things) have a gender; they are either masculine or feminine. Use the following rules to help you determine the gender of nouns. If a noun does not belong to any of the following categories, you must memorize the gender as you learn that noun.

1. Most words ending in **-a** are feminine.

   la hermana, la hija, la mamá, la tía

   *Some exceptions: **el día, el papá,** and words of Greek origin ending in **-ma,** such as **el problema** and **el programa.**

2. Most words ending in **-o** are masculine.

   el abuelo, el hermano, el hijo, el nieto

   *Some exceptions: **la foto** (*photo*), **la mano** (*hand*), **la moto** (*motorcycle*)

   *Note: **la foto** and **la moto** are shortened forms for **la fotografía** and **la motocicleta.**

3. Words ending in **-ción** and **-sión** are feminine.

   la discusión, la recepción, la televisión

   *Note: The suffix **-ción** is equivalent to the English *-tion.*

4. Words ending in **-dad** or **-tad** are feminine.

   la ciudad (*city*), **la libertad, la universidad**

   *Note: these suffixes are equivalent to the English *-ty.*

> **Estrategia**
>
> Making educated guesses about the meaning of unknown words will help to make you a successful Spanish learner!

As you learned in **Capítulo Preliminar A,** words that look alike and have the same meaning in both English and Spanish, such as **discusión** and **universidad,** are known as *cognates.* Use them to help you decipher meaning and to form words. For example, **prosperidad** looks like what English word? What is its gender?

1·13 ¿Recuerdas?   2:00

Take turns determining which of the following nouns are masculine (**M**) and which are feminine (**F**). **¡OJO!** Some are exceptions!

1. __F__ hijas
2. __F__ discusión
3. __M__ mapa
4. __F__ nacionalidad
5. __M__ hermano
6. __F__ manos
7. __F__ mamá
8. __M__ abuelos

RECURSOS   I-G4   Electronic Activity Cache

1·14 Para practicar

Take turns deciding whether these cognates are masculine or feminine. Can you guess their English equivalents?

1. guitarra   F / guitar
2. teléfono   M / telephone
3. computadora   F / computer
4. drama   M / drama
5. cafetería   F / cafeteria
6. educación   F / education

GRAMÁTICA 5

Los artículos definidos e indefinidos

1-19 to 1-22   1

Eduardo tiene una hermana.
La hermana de Eduardo se
llama Adriana.

Like English, Spanish has two kinds of articles, definite and indefinite. The definite article in English is *the*; the indefinite articles are *a*, *an*, and *some*.

In Spanish, articles and other adjectives mirror the gender (masculine or feminine) and number (singular or plural) of the nouns to which they refer. For example, an article referring to a singular masculine noun must also be singular and masculine. Note the forms of the articles in the following charts.

Fíjate

Note that *el* means "the," and *él* means "he."

Los artículos definidos

el hermano	*the brother*	**los** hermanos	*the brothers/the brothers and sisters*
la hermana	*the sister*	**las** hermanas	*the sisters*

Los artículos indefinidos

un hermano	*a/one brother*	**unos** hermanos	*some brothers/some brothers and sisters*
una hermana	*a/one sister*	**unas** hermanas	*some sisters*

1. *Definite articles* are used to refer to **the** person, place, or thing.
2. *Indefinite articles* are used to refer to **a** or **some** person, place, or thing.

Adriana es **la** hermana de Eduardo y **los** abuelos de él se llaman Carmen y Manuel.

Jorge tiene **una** tía y **unos** tíos.

Adriana is Eduardo's sister, and his grandparents' names are Carmen and Manuel.

Jorge has an aunt and some uncles.

METHODOLOGY • Grammar for True Beginners

Based on decades of experience, the authors of *¡Anda!* believe that the initial presentation of grammar rules needs to be basic. Too many exceptions to the rule may confuse and frustrate true beginners. Hence, additional exceptions, such as *el agua*, are presented at the point of introduction of the vocabulary. If you have Heritage language learners or false beginners, you may expand the presentation to suit their needs.

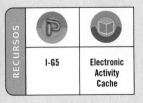

RECURSOS

I-G5 | Electronic Activity Cache

3:00 **1·15 Vamos a practicar**

Complete these steps.

Paso 1 Take turns giving the correct form of the *definite* article for each of the following nouns.

MODELO E1: tías
E2: *las tías*

1. tío el
2. padres los
3. mamá la
4. papá el
5. hermanas las
6. hijo el
7. abuela la
8. primo el

Paso 2 This time provide the correct form of the *indefinite* article.

MODELO E1: tías
E2: *unas tías*

1. un tío
2. unos padres
3. una mamá
4. un papá
5. unas hermanas
6. un hijo
7. una abuela
8. un primo

3:00 **1·16 Una concordancia**

Take turns matching the family members with the corresponding articles. Each family member will have **two** articles: one definite, one indefinite.

1. __a/e__ hijo
2. __d/h__ hermanas
3. __b/f__ tía
4. __d/h__ primas
5. __c/g__ abuelos
6. __b/f__ nieta

a. el
b. la
c. los
d. las
e. un
f. una
g. unos
h. unas

3:00 **1·17 ¿Quiénes son?**

Fill in the blanks with the correct form of either the definite or indefinite article. Then take turns sharing your answers and explaining your choice. Use the family tree on page 32.

MODELO Adriana es *la* hermana de Eduardo.

(1) __Los (the)__ abuelos se llaman Manuel y Carmen. Eduardo tiene (2) __un (a)__ tío. (3) __El (the)__ tío se llama Enrique. Eduardo tiene (4) __una (a)__ prima; se llama Sonia. (5) __El (the)__ hermano de Eduardo se llama Antonio.

Estrategia

To say "Eduardo's sister," or "Eduardo's grandparents," you add *de Eduardo* to each of your sentences: *Es la hermana de Eduardo. Son los abuelos de Eduardo.*

¿Cómo andas?

Each chapter has three places at which you will be asked to assess your progress. This first assessment comes as you have completed approximately one third of the chapter. How confident are you with your progress to date?

Having completed the first **Comunicación**, I now can...

	Feel Confident	Need to Review
● talk about my family using the verbs **ser** and **tener** (pp. 32, 35)	❑	❑
● pronounce the Spanish vowels correctly (p. 33)	❑	❑
● describe how Hispanic last names are formed (p. 34)	❑	❑
● pluralize singular words (p. 37)	❑	❑
● identify nouns as masculine or feminine (p. 38)	❑	❑
● say *the* and *a/an/some* in Spanish (p. 39)	❑	❑

Comunicación

- Describing yourself and others

Gente

1-23 to
1-25

2:00

Miguelito/Clarita

el niño/la niña

Daniel/Mariela

**el chico, el muchacho/
la chica, la muchacha**

Javier/Ana

el joven/la joven

Manolo/Pilar

el amigo/la amiga

Roberto/Pepita

el novio/la novia

Manuel/Manuela

el hombre/la mujer

el señor Martín/la señora
Torres/la señorita Sánchez

**el señor/la señora/
la señorita**

El hombre and **la mujer** are terms for *man* and *woman*. **Señor, señora,** and **señorita** are often used as titles of address; in that case, they may also be abbreviated as **Sr., Sra.,** and **Srta.,** respectively.

—Buenos días, **señor** Martín.   *Good morning, Mr. Martín.*
—¿Cómo está Ud., **Sra.** Sánchez?   *How are you, Mrs. Sánchez?*

> **Fíjate**
>
> The abbreviations *Sr.*, *Sra.*, and *Srta.* are always capitalized, just like their equivalents in English.

 1·18 Los opuestos   1:00

Take turns giving the gender opposites for the following words. Include the appropriate articles.

MODELO   E1:   el novio
             E2:   *la novia*

1. el chico   la chica
2. un hombre una mujer

3. la joven   el joven
4. un señor   una señora

5. una amiga   un amigo
6. la niña   el niño

1·19 ¿Cómo se llama?

[1:00]

Take turns
answering the
following
questions based
on the drawings
on page 41.

MODELO   E1:   ¿Cómo se llama el hombre?
          E2:   *El hombre se llama Manuel.*

1. ¿Cómo se llama la joven? La joven se llama Ana.
2. ¿Cómo se llama el niño? El niño se llama Miguelito.
3. ¿Cómo se llaman los novios? Los novios se llaman Roberto y Pepita.
4. ¿Cómo se llama la señora? La señora se llama Sra. Torres.

Capítulo Preliminar A.
Saludos, despedidas y
presentaciones pág. 4.

GRAMÁTICA 7 Los adjetivos posesivos

SAM 1-26 to 1-29   Guide G 4, 17

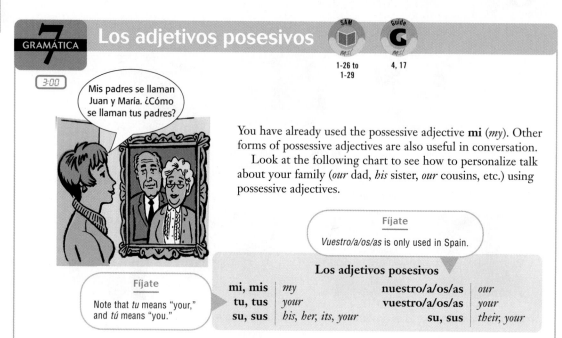

[3:00]

Mis padres se llaman
Juan y María. ¿Cómo
se llaman tus padres?

You have already used the possessive adjective **mi** (*my*). Other
forms of possessive adjectives are also useful in conversation.
    Look at the following chart to see how to personalize talk
about your family (*our* dad, *his* sister, *our* cousins, etc.) using
possessive adjectives.

Fíjate

Vuestro/a/os/as is only used in Spain.

Fíjate

Note that *tu* means "your,"
and *tú* means "you."

Los adjetivos posesivos

mi, mis	*my*	**nuestro/a/os/as**	*our*
tu, tus	*your*	**vuestro/a/os/as**	*your*
su, sus	*his, her, its, your*	**su, sus**	*their, your*

Please note:

1. Possessive adjectives agree in form with the person, place, or thing possessed, *not with the possessor.*

2. Possessive adjectives agree in number (singular or plural), and in addition, **nuestro** and **vuestro** indicate gender (masculine or feminine).

3. The possessive adjectives **tu/tus** (*your*) refer to someone with whom you are familiar and/or on a first name basis. **Su/sus** (*your*) is used when you are referring to people whom you refer to with *Uds.*, that is, more formally and perhaps not on a first-name basis. **Su/sus** (*your* plural or *their*) is used when referring to individuals whom you are addressing with *Uds.*, or when expressing possession with *ellos* and *ellas.*

mi hermano	*my brother*	**mis** hermanos	*my brothers/siblings*
tu primo	*your cousin*	**tus** primos	*your cousins*
su tía	*her/his/your/their aunt*	**sus** tías	*her/his/your/their aunts*
nuestra familia	*our family*	**nuestras** familias	*our families*
vuestra mamá	*your mom*	**vuestras** mamás	*your moms*
su hija	*your/their daughter*	**sus** hijas	*your (plural)/their daughters*

RECURSOS

I-G7 | Electronic
Activity
Cache

Eduardo tiene una novia.
Su novia se llama Julia.

Eduardo has a girlfriend.
His girlfriend's name is Julia.

Nuestros padres tienen dos amigos.
Sus amigos son Jorge y Marta.

Our parents have two friends.
Their friends are Jorge and Marta.

1·20 ¿Quién pertenece a quién?

1:00

Take turns supplying the correct possessive adjectives for the family members listed.

MODELO   E1:   (*our*) papás
             E2:   *nuestros papás*

1. (*your*/familiar) novia   tu novia
2. (*my*) hermanos   mis hermanos
3. (*our*) mamá   nuestra mamá
4. (*your*/formal) tío   su tío
5. (*her*) amiga   su amiga
6. (*his*) hermanas   sus hermanas

1·21 Relaciones familiares

2:00

Take turns completing the paragraph about Eduardo's family relationships, from Sonia's point of view. You may want to refer to the family tree on page 32.

Yo soy Sonia. Eduardo es (1) _____mi_____ primo. Antonio y Adriana son (2) _____mis_____ primos también (*also*). (3) _____Sus_____ padres, Pedro y Rosario, son (4) _____mis_____ tíos. (5) _____Mis_____ padres se llaman Enrique y Francisca. (6) Además (*Furthermore*), _____mi_____ amiga Pilar es como (*like*) parte de (7) (*our*) _____nuestra_____ familia.

Estrategia

Using your own friends and family will help you remember the vocabulary. Write the names of your immediate family or your best friends. Then write a description of how those people are connected to each other. E.g., *Karen es la madre de Brian* or *Brian es el hijo de Karen.*

1·22 Tu familia   *2:00*

Using at least **three** different possessive adjectives, talk to a partner about your family. You may want to refer to the family tree you drew for actividad **1-5**.

MODELO   *En mi familia somos cinco personas. Mi padre se llama John y mi madre es Marie. Sus amigos son Mary y Dennis. Tengo dos hermanos, Clark y Blake. Nuestros tíos son Alice y Ralph y nuestras primas se llaman Gina y Glynis.*

Expansion for 1-22 As a follow-up, have at least one student present his/her family to the entire class. Tell students that they will have to listen carefully. When s/he finishes, ask comprehension questions like, *¿Cúantos hermanos tiene? ¿Cómo se llama su hermana? ¿Cómo se llaman sus padres?* Holding students accountable for what others say helps them to become better listeners and keeps them actively engaged in class.

Additional Activity for *Los adjetivos posesivos* Tell the students you are going to play a game. You can bring in objects that are familiar to students or use the students' possessions (the textbook, a backpack, paper, pencils, etc.). "Rob" the students and move the possessions around the room to different students and have them act out whose possession it is. One student can be the police officer and the other students can "report" what's theirs, or simply "steal" the possessions back, stating, *No, ¡es MI libro!.*

GRAMÁTICA 8

Los adjetivos descriptivos

1-30 to 1-35   3, 4

3:00

Descriptive adjectives are words that describe people and things. In English, adjectives usually come before the words they describe (e.g., **red** car), but in Spanish, they usually follow the word (e.g., **coche** *rojo*).

1. Adjectives in Spanish agree with the noun they modify in number (singular or plural) and in gender (masculine or feminine).

Carlos es un **chico** simpático.	*Carlos is a nice boy.*
Adela es una **chica** simpática.	*Adela is a nice girl.*
Carlos y Adela son (unos) **chicos** simpáticos.	*Carlos and Adela are (some) nice children.*

2. A descriptive adjective can also follow the verb **ser** directly. When it does, it still agrees with the noun to which it refers, which is the subject in this case.

Carlos es simpático.	*Carlos is nice.*
Adela es simpática.	*Adela is nice.*
Carlos y Adela son simpáticos.	*Carlos and Adela are nice.*

> **Estrategia**
>
> Review *Los adjetivos de nacionalidad* in *Capítulo Preliminar A* in order to describe people in more detail.

Las características físicas, la personalidad y otros rasgos

alto   alta   bajo   baja

guapo   guapa

delgado
delgada

gordo
gorda

débil   fuerte

inteligente

joven   mayor

pobre   rico   rica

La personalidad	*Personality*
aburrido/a	*boring*
antipático/a	*unpleasant*
bueno/a	*good*
cómico/a	*funny; comical*
interesante	*interesting*
malo/a	*bad*
paciente	*patient*
perezoso/a	*lazy*
responsable	*responsible*
simpático/a	*nice*
tonto/a	*silly; dumb*
trabajador/a	*hard-working*

Las características físicas	*Physical characteristics*
bonito/a	*pretty*
feo/a	*ugly*
grande	*big; large*
pequeño/a	*small*

Otras palabras útiles	*Other useful words*
muy	*very*
(un) poco	*(a) little*

1:00

1·23 ¿Cómo son?

Take turns describing the following people to a classmate.

MODELO   E1:   Jorge
            E2:   *Jorge es débil.*

Jorge

1. Juan   Juan es fuerte.

2. María   María es alta y delgada.

3. Lupe y Marco   Lupe y Marco son ricos.

4. Eduardo   Eduardo es alto y delgado.

5. Adela   Adela es baja.

6. yo   Answers will vary.

Suggestion for *Los adjetivos descriptivos* Lead students in playing the association game with this list of new words, using movie and television characters, e.g., *¿Quién es cómico? ¿Homer Simpson?*

3:00   ## 1·24 ¿Cómo los describes?

Circulate among your classmates, asking for descriptions of the people listed below. Write what each person says, along with his or her name.

MODELO   E1: *¿Cómo es LeBron James?*

E2: *LeBron James es alto, fuerte, simpático, inteligente y muy rico.*

E1: *¿Cómo te llamas?*

E2: *Mi nombre es Rubén.*

PERSONA(S)	DESCRIPCIÓN	NOMBRE DEL ESTUDIANTE
Lebron James	*Es alto, fuerte, simpático, inteligente y muy rico.*	*Rubén*
1. Jennifer Aniston y Courteney Cox Arquette	Aniston y Cox son bajas, delgadas y bonitas.	
2. Kanye West	Kanye West es bajo, guapo y rico.	
3. Shakira	Shakira es bonita y rica.	
4. tus padres	*Answers will vary.*	
5. tu mejor (*best*) amigo/a y tú	*Answers will vary.*	
6. David Letterman	Letterman es cómico.	
7. Dwayne "The Rock" Johnson	The Rock es fuerte.	
8. Beyoncé	Beyoncé es bonita.	
9. Shaquille O'Neal	O'Neal es alto.	
10. yo	*Answers will vary.*	

2:00  ## 1·25 Al contrario

Student 1 creates a sentence using the cues provided, and Student 2 expresses the opposite. Pay special attention to adjective agreement.

MODELO   los hermanos González / guapo

E1: *Los hermanos González son guapos.*

E2: *¡Ay no, son muy feos!*

1. los abuelos / pobre
2. la señora López / muy antipático
3. Jaime / delgado
4. la tía Adela / mayor
5. Tomás y Antonia / alto
6. nosotros / perezoso

Capítulo Preliminar A. El verbo *ser*, pág. 13.

1·26 ¿Cómo eres? `5:00`

Imagine you are applying to a dating service.

Paso 1 Describe yourself to your partner using at least **three** adjectives, and then describe your ideal date.

MODELO *Me llamo Julie. Soy joven, muy inteligente y alta. Mi hombre ideal es inteligente, paciente y cómico.*

Paso 2 How similar are you and your partner's ideal mates?

MODELO *Rebeca y yo somos jóvenes, altas y muy inteligentes. Nuestros hombres ideales son cómicos y pacientes.*

Soy inteligente, cómico y responsable.
No soy muy rico pero soy trabajador.
¿Eres inteligente, simpática y cómica?
Contacta con matchideal.com/chucho.

Estrategia

Being an "active listener" is an important skill in any language. *Active listening* means that you hear and understand what someone is saying. Being able to repeat what someone says helps you practice and perfect the skill of active listening.

`5:00` 1·27 ¿Es cierto o falso?

Describe **five** famous (or infamous!) people or characters. Your partner can react by saying **Es verdad** (*It's true*) or **No es verdad** (*It's not true*). If your partner disagrees with you, he/she must correct your statement.

MODELO E1: *Garfield es gordo y un poco antipático.*

E2: *No es verdad. Sí, es gordo pero no es antipático. Es simpático.*

`5:00` 1·28 ¿Cuáles son sus cualidades?

Think of the qualities of your best friend and those of someone you do not particularly like (**una persona que no me gusta**). Using adjectives that you know in Spanish, write at least **three** sentences that describe each of these people. Share your list with a partner.

MODELO   MI MEJOR (*BEST*) AMIGO/A   UNA PERSONA QUE NO ME GUSTA

1. *Es trabajador/a.*   1. *Es antipático/a.*
2. *Es inteligente.*   2. *No es paciente.*
3. ...   3. ...

Capítulo Preliminar A. Los pronombres personales, pág. 11.

`3:00` 1·29 Describe una familia

Bring family photos (personal ones or some taken from the Internet or a magazine) to class and describe the family members to a classmate, using at least **five** sentences.

MODELO *Tengo dos hermanas, Kate y Ana. Ellas son simpáticas y bonitas. Mi papá no es aburrido y es muy trabajador. Tengo seis primos...*

METHODOLOGY • The Active Listener

Note that once again in actividad **1-27**, students are asked to be active listeners and to compare what they have heard each other say.

CAPÍTULO 1

NATIONAL STANDARDS

Communication, Comparisons, Communities

El español, lengua diversa offers insight into the many ways in which communication takes place. Communicating in Spanish is Goal One, and Standard 1.1 encourages students to engage in conversations. The fact that Spanish vocabulary varies by country reinforces the awareness of linguistic variations in English. Students are able to make comparisons, as defined in Standard 4.1, between regional and linguistic differences that occur in English and Spanish. Students can apply this knowledge when interacting with Hispanic people in the United States and abroad. Standard 5.1 encompasses using Spanish within and beyond an academic environment, and taking risks with the language by communicating with Spanish speakers from all over the world is part of being a successful language learner.

Suggestion for *Los números 31–100* Although all vocabulary is pronounced for your students on the accompanying *¡Anda!* CD, it can be helpful to pronounce the numbers in class and have students repeat after you. Additional practice can include having them count by twos or fives or counting backwards.

METHODOLOGY • Teaching Numbers

An easy way to introduce numbers is to have visuals with numbers that you can then take out of numerical order. Students need practice with numbers out of sequence. Using visuals helps to accommodate different learning styles.

El español, lengua diversa

Guagua, camión o autobús.

The title of this chapter, **¿Quiénes somos?**, suggests that we are all a varied combination of many factors, one of which is language. As you know, the English language is rich in state, regional, and national variations. For example, what word do you use when referring to soft drinks? Some people in the United States say *soda*, others say *pop*, and still others use *Coke* as a generic term for all brands and flavors of soft drinks.

The Spanish language also has many variations. For example, to describe someone as *funny* you could say **cómico/a** in many Latin American countries, but **divertido/a** or **gracioso/a** in Spain. Similarly, there are multiple ways to say the word *bus*: in Mexico, **camión;** in Puerto Rico and Cuba, **guagua;** in Spain, **autobús.** In *¡Anda!,* such variants will appear in **También se dice...**, Appendix 3.

The pronunciation of English also varies in different parts of the United States and throughout the rest of the English-speaking world, and so it is with Spanish across the Spanish-speaking world. Nevertheless, wherever you go you will find that Spanish is still Spanish, despite regional and national differences. You should have little trouble understanding native speakers from different countries or making yourself understood. You may have to attune your ears to local vocabulary or pronunciation, but that's part of the intrigue of communicating in another language.

Preguntas

1. What are some characteristics of the English spoken in other countries, such as Canada, Great Britain, Australia, and India? *Possible answers:* Accents and pronunciation. Different words such as *lift* for *elevator, flat* for *apartment, barbie* for *barbeque,* etc.
2. What are some English words that are used where you live that are not necessarily used in other parts of the country? *Possible answers: Bayou* in Texas and other places in the South; *arroyo* in the Southwest; *put up* versus *put away;* pronunciation differences for words like *roof, creek,* etc.

9 VOCABULARIO Los números 31–100

1-38 to 1-41

2:00

The numbers 31–100 function in much the same way as the numbers 0–30. Consider how the numbers 30–39 are formed. This pattern will repeat itself up to 100.

31	treinta y uno	37	treinta y siete	51	cincuenta y uno...
32	treinta y dos	38	treinta y ocho	60	sesenta
33	treinta y tres	39	treinta y nueve	70	setenta
34	treinta y cuatro	40	cuarenta	80	ochenta
35	treinta y cinco	41	cuarenta y uno...	90	noventa
36	treinta y seis	50	cincuenta	100	cien

Estrategia

Practice the numbers in Spanish by reading and pronouncing any numbers you see in your daily routine (e.g., highway signs, prices on your shopping receipts, room numbers on campus, or phone numbers).

RECURSOS

Electronic Activity Cache

1·30 Examen de matemáticas [3:00]

Are you ready to test your math skills? Take turns reading and solving the problems aloud. Then create your own math problems to test your partner.

Vocabulario útil

más	*plus*
menos	*minus*
son	*equals*
por	*times; by*
dividido por	*divided by*

MODELO   E1: $97 - 53 =$

E2:   *Noventa y siete menos cincuenta y tres son cuarenta y cuatro.*

1. $81 + 13 =$ 94
2. $65 - 26 =$ 39
3. $24 + 76 =$ 100
4. $99 - 52 =$ 47
5. $12 \times 8 =$ 96
6. $8 \times 7 =$ 56
7. $65 \div 5 =$ 13
8. $100 \div 2 =$ 50

1·31 ¿Qué número es? [2:00]

Look at the pages from the telephone book. Say **five** phone numbers and have your partner tell you whose numbers they are. Then switch roles.

MODELO   E1:   *Ochenta y ocho, sesenta y ocho, setenta y cinco*

E2:   *Adelaida Santoyo*

```
SANTOS JAIME-SIERRA 12I 12 SM 3 CP 77500....84-0661
SANTOS JAVIER L1 Y 12 M10 SM43 PEDREGAL CP
77500.................................................80-5138
SANTOS SEGOVIA FREDDY CALLE 45 NTE MANZ 34
LTE 3 COL 77528....................................80-2242
SANTOS SEGURA ALBA ROSA COL LEONA VICARIO
M 8 L SM 74 77500.................................80-0861
SANTOS SOLIS FELIPE CALLE 20 OTE NO 181 SM 68
M 12 L 28 CP 77500................................80-1330
SANTOS VELÁZQUEZ MARÍA JESÚS CALLE 3 NO 181
77537..................................................86-6949
SANTOS VILLANUEVA ARMINDA CALLE 46 PTE
MANZ 20 77510......................................88-3999
SANTOS JOSÉ E CALLE 33 OTE 171 L 14 M 25 CP
77500..................................................80-1175
SANTOSCOY LAGUNES ELIZABETH CERRADA FLAM-
BOYANES 2 SM23....................................87-6204
SANTOYO ADELAIDA CALLE 75 NTE DEPTO 7 EDIF 2
SM 92 CP 77500.....................................88-6875
SANTOYO BETANCOURT PEDRO ARIEL HDA NUM 12
NABZ 61 77517......................................88-7941
SANTOYO CORTEZ LIGIA EDIFICIO QUETZAL DEPTO
C-1 SM 32 77500....................................87-4676
SANTOYO MARTÍN AIDA MARÍA NANCE DEP 4 MZA
12 NUM 13............................................87-3799
```

1·32 ¿Quiere dejar un recado? [3:00]

Imagine that you work in a busy office. You take messages with the following phone numbers. Say the numbers to a partner who will write them down. Then switch roles, mixing the order of the numbers.

MODELO   E1:   223-7256

E2:   *dos, veintitrés, setenta y dos, cincuenta y seis*

1. 962-2136
2. 615-9563
3. 871-4954
4. 414-4415
5. 761-7920
6. 270-2325

1·33 Los hispanos en los EE.UU. [2:00]

Use the information from the pie chart on page 53 to answer the following questions in Spanish. Round the answers to the nearest whole number.

Fíjate

In most of the Spanish-speaking world, commas are used where we use decimal points, and vice versa. For example, in English one says "six point four percent," in Spanish, *seis coma cuatro por ciento.*

Capítulo Preliminar A. Los números 0–30, pág. 16.

Vocabulario útil

por ciento   *percent*

Answers to 1-33.
4. Either 6,4% if your students respond to *Otros países*; 20,4% if they add 14% of *Centroamérica* y *Suramérica*, and 6,4% *Otros países*
5. 9% + 4% + 14% + 6,4% = 33,4%

1. What percentage of U.S. Hispanics is from Cuba?   4%
2. What percentage of U.S. Hispanics is from Puerto Rico?   9%
3. What percentage of U.S. Hispanics is from Mexico?   66,1%
4. What percentage of Hispanics comes from other Spanish-speaking countries?
5. What percentage of U.S. Hispanics comes from countries other than Mexico?

NOTE FOR 1-31

Explain that when reading a long list of numbers, such as phone numbers or serial numbers, Spanish speakers often group the numbers in pairs. For example, in a seven-digit phone number, the first number is said alone and the remainder said as 3 two-digit numerals. Thus, the phone number 919-4827 in Mexico is said as *nueve, diecinueve, cuarenta y ocho, veintisiete.*

NATIONAL STANDARDS
Communication, Cultures

Actividades **1-31** and **1-32** allow students to provide and exchange information (Standard 1.1) in an interpersonal mode. Students are asked to work in pairs as they practice pronouncing the numbers and listening to whose number the partner is saying. Each person is responsible for the exchange of information.

ESCUCHA

Alejandra

Aural comprehension is critical in learning to communicate in Spanish. You are working on developing your listening skills every time your instructor speaks or when you work in pairs or groups in class. You will also practice this skill when you watch the video episodes of **Ambiciones siniestras,** the mystery story that accompanies *¡Anda!*

In *¡Anda!* you will have the opportunity to learn and practice strategies to assist you in developing listening skills in Spanish. Let's begin with listening for words you know, including cognates.

ESTRATEGIA   **Determining the topic and listening for words you know**

The first steps to becoming a successful listener are to determine the topic and then listen for words that you know. If you are in a social situation, you can determine the topic by looking for visual cues (body language, pictures, etc.) or by asking the speaker(s) for clarification. When listening to passages in *¡Anda!,* look at the activities or questions connected with the passage to help you determine the topic. Remember that words that you know include *cognates* which are words that look and sound like words in English.

1•34   **Antes de escuchar**

In the following segment, Alejandra, one of the characters from **Ambiciones siniestras,** introduces her family. Write down two things that you expect to hear.
Answers may vary. Some possibilities are: who her family members are, their names, what they are like.

1•35   **A escuchar**

CD 1
Track 18

Listen as Alejandra introduces her family. Use the following steps to help you.

a. First, look at the incomplete sentences in **c.** They will give you an idea about the topic of the passage.
b. Listen to the passage, concentrating on the words you know. Make a list of those words.   *Possible answers:* but will include: grande, hermanos, hermanas, dos.
c. Listen one more time and complete these sentences.
   1. La familia de Alejandra es _____grande_____.
   2. Los nombres de sus padres son _____Raúl y Pilar_____.
   3. Alejandra tiene _____dos_____ hermanos y _____tres_____ hermanas.

1•36   **Después de escuchar**

Take turns saying **three** sentences about you and your family to a partner. Your partner will tell you the words he/she knows.

INTRODUCTION TO
Escucha

A listening section entitled *Escucha* appears approximately two thirds of the way through each chapter. These presentations utilize examples from the vocabulary and grammar presented in the current, as well as previous, chapters. The passages are brief to help students focus on and practice one strategy at a time so that they will not feel overwhelmed.

SECTION GOALS FOR
Escucha

By the end of the *Escucha* section, students will be able to:
• identify cognates.
• report about Alejandra's family.
• discuss characteristics of their families.

NATIONAL STANDARDS
Communication

The strategy, listening for cognates, facilitates communication in the interpretive mode. Standard 1.2 requires that students understand and interpret spoken Spanish on a variety of topics. In *Capítulo 1,* students listen for a description of family members and they focus on cognate recognition. The short conversations that students have about their own families are interpersonal communication: Standard 1.1.

AUDIOSCRIPT FOR 1-35

Hola. Soy Alejandra. Mi familia es muy grande. Mis padres son Raúl y Pilar. Tengo dos hermanas y tres hermanos.

METHODOLOGY • *Escucha*

You may either read these sections aloud or have students listen to the CD. This can be done in class or assigned for homework. Encourage students to listen to the *Escucha* sections multiple times outside of class.

METHODOLOGY • Checking for Listening Comprehension in English

When checking listening comprehension with beginning students, it is always acceptable to check for comprehension in English. At this stage, many students can comprehend more than they can produce. Allowing students to respond to the comprehension questions in English is fine at this point. As they progress, they will be able and expected to respond in Spanish.

ESCRIBE

SAM
1-45 to
1-46

1•37 Antes de escribir

Write down all the Spanish nouns and adjectives you can think of that describe you. Start by reviewing the vocabulary lists for **Capítulo 1** and **También se dice…**, Appendix 3.

1•38 Un poema

Complete the following steps in order to write your first poem in Spanish.

Paso 1 Using either your first, middle, or last name, match a noun or descriptive adjective with each letter of that name. For example:

"*Sarah*": **S** = *simpática*, **a** = *alta*, **r** = *responsable*, **a** = *amiga*, **b** = *hermana*

With these words, create what is known as an *acrostic* poem.

Paso 2 Now build phrases or sentences around your letters, using **tener, ser,** possessive adjectives, and numbers.

MODELO

Simpática	*SARAH*
Alta	*es Simpática*
Responsable	*no es baja; es Alta*
Amiga	*no es Responsable*
Hermana	*tiene cien Amigos (¡es rica!)*
	es mi Hermana.

1•39 Después de escribir

Read your poem to a classmate.

¿Cómo andas?

This is your second self-assessment. You have now completed two thirds of the chapter. How confident are you with the following topics and concepts?

Having completed the second **Comunicación,** I now can…

	Feel Confident	Need to Review
● tell the difference between words like **niño** and **joven** as well as which titles (**Sr., Srta.,** etc.) to use when addressing someone (p. 41)	❏	❏
● use different types of adjectives: possessive (**mi, tus,** etc.) and descriptive (**inteligente, alto,** etc.) (p. 42, 44)	❏	❏
● describe myself and others in complete sentences (p. 44)	❏	❏
● state one fact about the diverse nature of the Spanish language (p. 48)	❏	❏
● count from 31 to 100 (p. 48)	❏	❏
● listen for words I know (p. 50)	❏	❏
● write a short poem (p. 51)	❏	❏

METHODOLOGY • Teaching Writing

Writing is a culminating, integrated activity in each chapter of *¡Anda!* Research suggests that students first focus on speaking, and then on writing because "if they can say it, they can write it."

Expansion activities for 1-38

Have students create an additional acrostic poem using the name of a friend or family member or a word they have learned, such as *estudiante.*

INTRODUCTION TO
Escribe

Escribe, a process writing section, appears at the end of each chapter. Students will be led to write step by step, using vocabulary and structures from the current chapter as well as previous ones.

SECTION GOALS FOR
Escribe

By the end of the *Escribe* section, students will be able to:

- compile a list of nouns and adjectives that define the students.
- write an acrostic poem.
- match letters with the beginning sounds of words.
- modify the poems to create sentences using *ser* and *tener.*

ALTERNATE ACTIVITY FOR
Escribe

As an alternate writing activity for this section, have your students describe their family or their favorite relative.

NATIONAL STANDARDS
Communication

Actividad **1-39** asks students to present their poems. Depending on how you implement the activity, it could satisfy Standards 1.1 or 1.3. Standard 1.1 asks students to express feelings and emotions and share opinions. They are reporting things about themselves to a classmate, and the classmate can offer opinions about the poem. This might include agreement or disagreement with the adjectives used, or what the classmate likes or dislikes about the poem. Implemented in this way, the activity becomes an interpersonal exchange. Conversely, Standard 1.3 requires students to present to an audience of readers or listeners. Students could write the poem and display it in a collection of class poems, or students could have a poetry reading, where they read their poem aloud to the class. This way of using the poem requires the presentational mode of communication.

Alberto Martínez Vergara

Los Estados Unidos

CD 1
Track 19

1-47

Vistas
culturales

Les presento mi país

Mi nombre es Alberto Martínez Vergara y soy de Paterson, Nueva Jersey. Soy bilingüe: hablo inglés y español. Soy estadounidense pero mi padre es de México y mi madre es de Puerto Rico. Hay muchos hispanohablantes (*Spanish speakers*) en los Estados Unidos. **¿Puedes (*Can you*) identificar otras cuatro o cinco ciudades en el mapa con grandes poblaciones hispanohablantes?** Hay hispanohablantes famosos de muchas carreras diferentes, como Jennifer López y Pedro Martínez. **¿Por qué son famosas estas personas?** También se nota la influencia hispana en los restaurantes y en los supermercados donde se ofrecen productos hispanos de compañías como Goya, Ortega, Corona, Marinela y Tecate. Mi restaurante favorito se llama *La Bodega*. **¿Cuál es tu restaurante favorito?**

Pedro Martínez es un beisbolista dominicano famoso.

St. Augustine es la primera ciudad europea en los EE.UU., fundada en 1535 por los españoles.

Cristina Saralegui tiene un programa de televisión.

Celebrando la herencia puertorriqueña en Nueva York.

Los productos Goya se encuentran en muchos supermercados.

RECURSOS | TI-6 | TI-6 | Cultural Background Notes

● ALMANAQUE ●

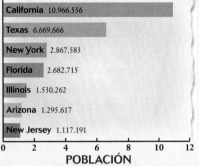

Nombre oficial:	Estados Unidos de América
Gobierno:	República constitucional y federal
Población:	299.209.430 (est., 2006)
Población de origen hispano:	41,3 millones (est., 2006)
Moneda:	el dólar ($)

PORCENTAJE DE POBLACIÓN HISPANA

Otros países 6.4%
Centroamérica y Suramérica 14%
Cuba 4%
Puerto Rico 9%
México 66.1%

Source: U.S. Census Bureau

ESTADO

California	10.966.556
Texas	6.669.666
New York	2.867.583
Florida	2.682.715
Illinois	1.530.262
Arizona	1.295.617
New Jersey	1.117.191

0 2 4 6 8 10 12
POBLACIÓN

Source: Frank Hobbs and Nicole Stoops, U.S. Census Bureau, Special Reports, Series

AUMENTO (Rise) EN LA POBLACIÓN HISPANA EN LOS ÚLTIMOS 20 AÑOS

Ciudad	Población	Porcentaje
Raleigh, NC	72.580	1180%
Atlanta, GA	268.851	995%
Greensboro, NC	62.210	962%
Charlotte, NC	77.092	932%
Orlando, FL	271.627	859%
Las Vegas, NV	322.038	753%
Nashville, TN	40.139	630%
Fort Lauderdale, FL	271.652	578%
Sarasota, FL	38.682	538%

Source: Brookings Institution

CIUDAD

Los Angeles	4.242.213
New York	2.339.836
Chicago	1.416.584
Miami	1.291.737
Houston	1.248.586
Riverside-San Bernardino	1.228.962
Orange County	875.579
Phoenix	817.012
San Antonio	816.037
Dallas	810.499

0 1 2 3 4 5
POBLACIÓN

Source: Brookings Institution

¿Sabías que...?

● Para el año 2050, una de cada cuatro personas en los Estados Unidos va a ser de origen hispano.

● En los Estados Unidos se celebra el mes de la herencia hispana entre el 15 de septiembre y el 15 de octubre.

PREGUNTAS

1. ¿Qué importancia tiene St. Augustine, Florida?
2. ¿Qué estados tienen la mayor (the largest) población hispana?
3. ¿Quiénes son algunos (some) hispanos famosos en los EE.UU.? ¿Cuál es tu favorito?

En la Red
Learn more about Hispanics in the United States on your *¡Anda!* web site.

53

HERITAGE LANGUAGE LEARNERS

Web-based activities that can benefit a variety of students will be provided for each chapter. For example, Heritage language learners, false beginners, more advanced students, students who need additional practice, or those who love the Internet can all benefit from the following activities. You may wish to give the directions in Spanish for Heritage language learners. Give them in English for the other students.

1. Busca en la Red cifras que indiquen la participación hispana en la sociedad estadounidense en los siguientes casos:
   a. Número de ciudadanos latinos que votaron en la última elección presidencial
   b. Número de latinos que sirven en las fuerzas armadas estadounidenses
   c. Número de negocios con propietarios hispanos
   Palabras clave: número o porcentaje de hispanos, fuerzas armadas, el voto presidencial, datos de participación, negocios.

2. Trata de encontrar cuál va a ser la población latina para el año 2050, cuando los hispanos van a constituir el 24 por ciento de la población estadounidense.
   Palabras clave: población latina, año 2050.

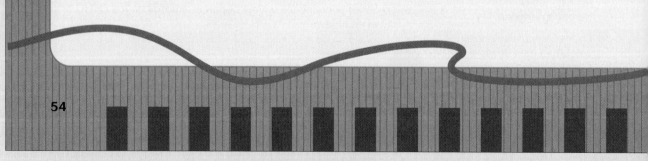

Ambiciones siniestras

EPISODIO 1

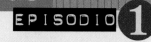

lectura

1-49

SAM
M.S.

Three students from different universities are writing e-mail messages to friends or family members. What can you learn about the three students from their e-mails? What can you learn about the person to whom or about whom each one is writing?

1-40   Antes de leer. You are about to discover what happens to a group of college students as they unwittingly become involved in a sinister international plot. Before you read the first episode of **Ambiciones siniestras,** answer these questions.

1. How much time do you spend on the computer composing, reading, and answering e-mails?
2. To whom do you write most frequently? For what purpose(s)?
3. With a partner, list as many reasons as you can for sending e-mails.

ESTRATEGIA   **Recognizing Cognates**

When you read something for the first time, you are not expected to understand every word. In addition to focusing on the words that you *do* know, look for words similar to those you know in English, *cognates*. Cognates are an excellent way to help you understand what you are reading. Make sure that you complete the **Antes de leer** activities to practice this strategy.

1-41   A leer. Read through the messages quickly, underlining all cognates. Share your list with a classmate. Then answer these questions.

1. How many messages are there?
2. Who wrote each message?
3. To whom or for whom were the messages written?

Estrategia

When writing or reading e-mails, note what parts are common to all of them. Usually you find the following information: who sent the message and the address from where it came, the subject line that indicates what the e-mail is about, a list of other people who might have received it, etc. Use your knowledge of writing and receiving e-mails in English to see if you can understand the additional information presented in *Ambiciones siniestras*.

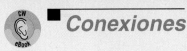

Conexiones

CD 1
Track 20

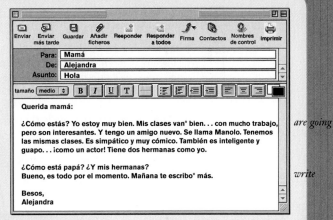

Para: Mamá
De: Alejandra
Asunto: Hola

tamaño medio ♦ B I U T

Querida mamá:

¿Cómo estás? Yo estoy muy bien. Mis clases van° bien. . . con mucho trabajo, *are going*
pero son interesantes. Y tengo un amigo nuevo. Se llama Manolo. Tenemos
las mismas clases. Es simpático y muy cómico. También es inteligente y
guapo. . . ¡como un actor! Tiene dos hermanas como yo.

¿Cómo está papá? ¿Y mis hermanas?
Bueno, es todo por el momento. Mañana te escribo° más. *write*

Besos,
Alejandra

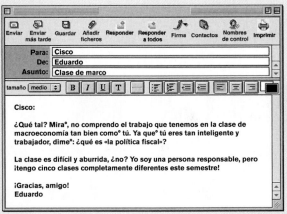

Para: Cisco
De: Eduardo
Asunto: Clase de marco

tamaño medio ♦ B I U T

Cisco:

¿Qué tal? Mira°, no comprendo el trabajo que tenemos en la clase de   *Look*
macroeconomía tan bien como° tú. Ya que° tú eres tan inteligente y   *as well as/Since*
trabajador, dime°: ¿qué es «la política fiscal»?   *tell me*

La clase es difícil y aburrida, ¿no? Yo soy una persona responsable, pero
¡tengo cinco clases completamente diferentes este semestre!

¡Gracias, amigo!
Eduardo

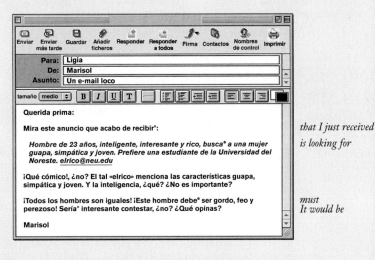

Para: Ligia
De: Marisol
Asunto: Un e-mail loco

tamaño medio ♦ B I U T

Querida prima:

Mira este anuncio que acabo de recibir°:   *that I just received*

Hombre de 23 años, inteligente, interesante y rico, busca° a una mujer *is looking for*
guapa, simpática y joven. Prefiere una estudiante de la Universidad del
Noreste. elrico@neu.edu

¡Qué cómico!, ¿no? El tal «elrico» menciona las características guapa,
simpática y joven. Y la inteligencia, ¿qué? ¿No es importante?

¡Todos los hombres son iguales! ¡Este hombre debe° ser gordo, feo y   *must*
perezoso! Sería° interesante contestar, ¿no? ¿Qué opinas?   *It would be*

Marisol

1-42 **Después de leer.** Answer the following questions.

1. What was the purpose of each message? Was it friendly communication?
   Did the person need something from someone else?

2. Of the senders, recipients, and others mentioned in the messages, which
   person is most like you? Which one would you most like to meet? Why?

55

NATIONAL STANDARDS
Comparisons

The reading from *Ambiciones siniestras* contains many cognates. Students of Spanish should recognize that there are many cognates between English and Spanish. Students use Standard 4.1 when they understand the nature of Spanish by making comparisons between Spanish and their own language. By scanning any reading passage to find cognates, students are focusing on how much they already know in Spanish instead of what they have yet to learn.

METHODOLOGY • Teaching Reading

After completing the pre-reading activities, ask students to read the first paragraph of the first e-mail message. Ask if there are any words they do not understand. If so, other students may know or be able to infer the meanings quickly. Then read the second paragraph together (an overhead transparency works well here). Have students pick out and discuss words they know before talking them through discovering the meaning of unfamiliar words. Repeat this process for the remainder of the text. Here is an example for guiding students toward discovering meaning from context.

Take a look at the last two sentences of the e-mail message:
Bueno, es todo por el momento. Mañana te escribo más.

1. Explain that in addition to "good," *bueno* can mean "Well, . . . "
2. Ask what students think *por el momento* means, pointing out, if necessary, that *momento* is a cognate.
3. Next ask what *es todo* means, especially given its location in the sentence and the message "Well, . . . for the moment . . . " If the meaning is not readily clear move on to the last sentence, asking them to decipher it.
4. Finally, based on all the other pieces of the puzzle, the meaning for *es todo* should become clear to at least some.
5. After guiding students through the passage, go immediately to the post-reading activities.

METHODOLOGY • Checking for Reading Comprehension

Again, for this first reading we recommend checking comprehension in English. This is a non-threatening, confidence-building way for students to demonstrate that they understood. If you have false beginners or Heritage language learners, you may ask brief questions in Spanish about the episode.

Expansion for *Después de leer* Ask your students the following questions regarding the e-mails they have just read:

* *Questions for the first e-mail:* What is the name of Alejandra's new friend? Describe him. How many sisters does he have?
* *Questions for the second e-mail:* What class is Eduardo struggling with? Do you think Eduardo likes the class? Why or why not? How many classes does Eduardo have?

* *Questions for the third e-mail:* What kind of person is "el rico" looking for? How does Marisol imagine "el rico" to be?

video

1-50 to 1-54

In the first reading episode you were introduced briefly to some of the characters of the mystery story **Ambiciones siniestras.** The next episode in video format will provide a further glimpse into the lives of the characters on their respective campuses.

1-43 **Antes del video.** Let's think about you and your campus experiences for a minute. Do you take classes on a traditional college campus? What courses are you currently taking? Are your classes large or small? Are you friends with any of your classmates? What are your professors like?

Cisco y Eduardo en su clase de macroeconomía.

La familia de Lupe es hispana y la familia de Marisol es hispana también.

Alejandra y Manolo en su clase de literatura española.

Episodio 1

¿Quiénes son?

Relax and watch the video, more than once if you choose, then complete the activity that follows.

1-44 **Después del video.** Identify the person(s) who fit(s) each description below.

Lupe   Cisco   Eduardo   Marisol   Manolo   Alejandra

This character...

1. has grandparents who are Hispanic and speaks Spanish with siblings.
2. seems to like Phillip Jones and introduces him to her friend.
3. has a class every Tuesday and Thursday at 2 P.M.
4. helps Eduardo prepare for class.
5. is a student in a Spanish literature class.

Estrategia.

In this video episode, you get to place the names of the characters with their faces. Using the information in your textbook, focus on the specific items you will need to answer after watching the video. For actividad **1-44** (*Después del video*), you see the characters' names. While you are listening and watching, jot down the name of each character that fits the description.

56

Y por fin, ¿cómo andas?

Each chapter will end with a checklist like the one that follows. This is the third time in the chapter that you are given the opportunity to check your progress. Use the checklist to measure what you have learned in the chapter. Place a check in the *Feel confident* column of the topics you feel you know, and a check in the *Need to Review* column for the topics that you need to practice more.

Having completed this chapter, I now can…

	Feel Confident	Need to Review
Comunicación		
● talk about my family using the verbs **ser** and **tener** (pp. 32, 35)	❏	❏
● pronounce the Spanish vowels correctly (p. 33)	❏	❏
● pluralize singular words (p. 37)	❏	❏
● identify nouns as masculine or feminine (p. 38)	❏	❏
● use *the* and *a/an/some* appropriately in Spanish (p. 39)	❏	❏
● know the difference between words like **niño** and **joven** as well as which titles (**Sr., Srta.,** etc.) to use when addressing someone (p. 41)	❏	❏
● use different types of adjectives: possessive (**mi, tus,** etc.) and descriptive (**inteligente, alto,** etc.) (p. 42, 44)	❏	❏
● describe myself and others in complete sentences (p. 44)	❏	❏
● count from 31 to 100 (p. 48)	❏	❏
● listen for words I know (p. 50)	❏	❏
● write a short poem (p. 51)	❏	❏
Cultura		
● describe how Hispanic last names are formed (p. 34)	❏	❏
● state one fact about the diverse nature of the Spanish language (p. 48)	❏	❏
● state three facts about Hispanics in the United States (p. 52)	❏	❏
Ambiciones siniestras		
● recognize cognates when I read (p. 54)	❏	❏
● describe three of the protagonists in **Ambiciones siniestras** briefly (p. 56)	❏	❏

METHODOLOGY • Student Self-Assessment with *Y por fin, ¿cómo andas?*

This is the chapter's third and final self-assessment. It is cumulative for the entire chapter. These self-assessments help students determine where they are with regard to their learning, and what individual remediation might be needed. Research contends that instructors have to make students ultimately responsible for their own learning, and one of the ways to do this is by having them self-assess. Research also finds that students tend to be overly critical of what they do and do not know, and periodic self-assessments help them to self-evaluate realistically.

Suggestions for *Y por fin, ¿cómo andas?* Spot-check and ask how they are doing (e.g., "How many of you feel confident greeting, saying goodbye, and introducing someone?"). Remind students who do not raise their hands that they need to review the topics they don't feel confident with on their own by consulting the pages listed. If you have time to do the assessments in class, one approach is to have students write short answers to the topics, then check in their textbook to verify answers. Based on this verification, they can rate themselves on the concept and hand in their ratings to you at the end of class. If you have time constraints, students can complete these self-assessments outside of class.

VOCABULARIO ACTIVO

La familia	Family
el/la abuelo/a	grandfather/grandmother
los abuelos	grandparents
el/la esposo/a	husband/wife
el/la hermano/a	brother/sister
los hermanos	brothers and sisters; siblings
el/la hijo/a	son/daughter
los hijos	sons and daughters; children
la madrastra	stepmother
la madre/la mamá	mother/mom
el padrastro	stepfather
el padre/el papá	father/dad
los padres	parents
el/la primo/a	cousin
los primos	cousins
el/la tío/a	uncle/aunt
los tíos	aunts and uncles

La gente	People
el/la amigo/a	friend
el/la chico/a	boy/girl
el hombre	man
el/la joven	young man/young woman
el/la muchacho/a	boy/girl
la mujer	woman
el/la niño/a	little boy/little girl
el/la novio/a	boyfriend/girlfriend
el señor (Sr.)	man; gentleman; Mr.
la señora (Sra.)	woman; lady; Mrs.
la señorita (Srta.)	young woman; Miss

Las características físicas	Physical characteristics
alto/a	tall
bajo/a	short
bonito/a	pretty
débil	weak
delgado/a	thin
feo/a	ugly
fuerte	strong
gordo/a	fat
grande	big; large
guapo/a	handsome/pretty
joven	young
mayor	old
pequeño/a	small

Los adjetivos	Adjectives
La personalidad y otros rasgos	*Personality and other characteristics*
aburrido/a	*boring*
antipático/a	*unpleasant*
bueno/a	*good*
cómico/a	*funny; comical*
inteligente	*intelligent*
interesante	*interesting*
malo/a	*bad*
paciente	*patient*
perezoso/a	*lazy*
pobre	*poor*
responsable	*responsible*
rico/a	*rich*
simpático/a	*nice*
tonto/a	*silly; dumb*
trabajador/a	*hard-working*

Los números 31–100	Numbers 31–100
treinta y uno	*thirty-one*
treinta y dos	*thirty-two*
treinta y tres	*thirty-three*
treinta y cuatro	*thirty-four*
treinta y cinco	*thirty-five*
treinta y seis	*thirty-six*
treinta y siete	*thirty-seven*
treinta y ocho	*thirty-eight*
treinta y nueve	*thirty-nine*
cuarenta	*forty*
cuarenta y uno	*forty-one*
cincuenta	*fifty*
cincuenta y uno	*fifty-one*
sesenta	*sixty*
setenta	*seventy*
ochenta	*eighty*
noventa	*ninety*
cien	*one hundred*

Los verbos	Verbs
tener	*to have*

Otras palabras útiles	Other useful words
muy	*very*
(un) poco	*(a) little*

Vocabulario útil	Useful vocabulary
más	*plus*
menos	*minus*
son	*equals*
por ciento	*percent*
por	*times; by*
dividido por	*divided by*

If you are interested in discovering additional vocabulary for the topics studied in each chapter, consult Appendix 3, **También se dice…,** for additional words. It contains expanded vocabulary that you may need for your own personal expression, including regionally used words and slang. Enjoy!

59

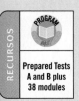

2

La vida universitaria

The majority of universities throughout the Spanish-speaking world tend to be public, charging minimal tuition, if any. Students must pass rigorous admission exams in order to attend. In many countries, the exams they take or the scores they receive determine the career they may choose. In their first year, college students begin to take courses in their major area. Public universities generally have vast numbers of students.

OBJETIVOS

Comunicación

- To talk about your school and your life as a student
- To create questions
- To utilize numbers 100-1,000
- To express feelings and emotions
- To mention the sports and pastimes you like and dislike
- To write a brief personal statement that could be used for a job application

Cultura

- To discuss stereotypes
- To compare sports and some other aspects of university life in Spanish-speaking countries and the United States
- To explore the diverse and colorful world of our southern neighbor, Mexico

Ambiciones siniestras

- To learn how to skim a story
- To learn more about the protagonists and their lives in *Ambiciones siniestras*

CONTENIDOS

La biblioteca de la
*Universidad Nacional
Autónoma de México
(UNAM)*

PREGUNTAS

1 How large is your college or university? What are the advantages of studying at a college or university of this size? Are there any disadvantages?

2 What are some possible advantages and disadvantages of the large universities of some Spanish-speaking countries?

3 Why do many colleges and universities require general education courses prior to entering courses for the major? Why do many colleges and universities have a language requirement?

61

Answers to *Preguntas*

1. *Possible advantages of a larger university:* greater number of course offerings, more potential majors/specialties, more extracurricular opportunities including sporting events; *Possible disadvantages:* less personal attention from administration and faculty. *Possible advantages of a smaller university:* smaller classes, more interaction among students and faculty; *Possible disadvantages:* fewer course offerings, fewer extracurricular opportunities.

2. *Possible advantages:* larger number of course offerings, more possible majors, more students have the opportunity to attend, more economical to maintain. Possible disadvantages: large class size, less personal attention.

3. Possible answers: General education courses provide a basic knowledge base on which to build, and many entering students have not yet chosen a major/profession. Knowing a second (or multiple) language(s) better prepares individuals for an increasingly global community and may be necessary for some professions.

Expansion for *Preguntas* You may want to also discuss other academic settings: junior colleges, community colleges, technical schools, etc. Consider posing the following question for your students: In most Spanish-speaking countries, students take English as a required course in earlier levels of school. Should students in the United States study foreign languages throughout their school years rather than waiting until high school or college?

PLANNING AHEAD

For actividad **2-18** you will want to have current exchange rates taken from the newspaper or the Internet. Also, for actividad **2-19**, students should each bring at least five ads of items with prices. You may want to have extras in case some students forget.

METHODOLOGY • Meaningful Learning

One purpose of the discussion questions is to begin a topic with what your students already know so they can see how major themes of the chapter relate to their lives more clearly. This facilitates learning by encouraging active mental participation in relating new material to existing knowledge, the basic tenet of Ausubel's "meaningful learning." (Ausubel, D. *Educational Psychology: A cognitive view.*

New York: Holt, Rinehart & Winston, 1968.) Initially, these questions are in English. As the program progresses, the questions will be in Spanish.

CAPÍTULO 2

Comunicación

- Talking about school

VOCABULARIO 1

Las materias y las especialidades

3:00

2-1 to 2-4

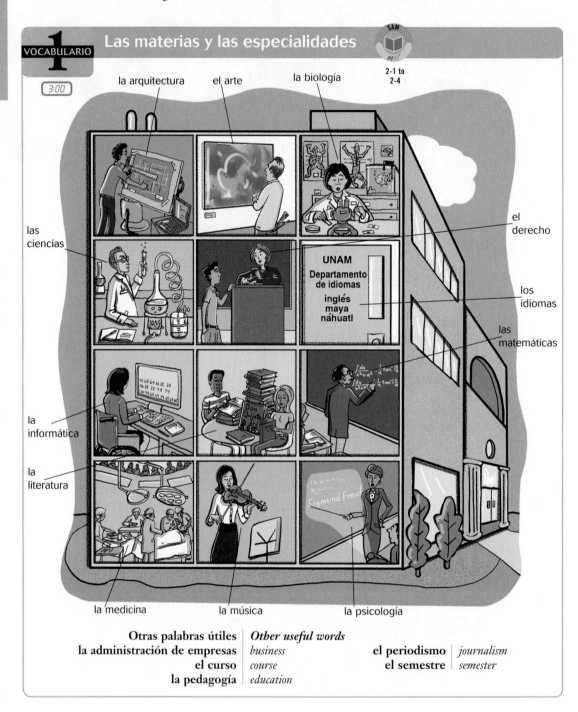

la arquitectura

el arte

la biología

las ciencias

UNAM
Departamento de idiomas

inglés
maya
náhuatl

el derecho

los idiomas

las matemáticas

la informática

la literatura

la medicina

la música

la psicología

Otras palabras útiles	Other useful words		
la administración de empresas	*business*	el periodismo	*journalism*
el curso	*course*	el semestre	*semester*
la pedagogía	*education*		

RECURSOS			
	T2-1	T2-1	Electronic Activity Cache

PRONUNCIACIÓN ⏱6:00

CD 1 Track 29

2-5 to 2-7

Word stress and accent marks

In Spanish, written accents are used to distinguish word meaning, or when a word is "breaking" a pronunciation rule. Here are the basic rules of Spanish pronunciation and accentuation.

1. Words ending in a vowel, or in the consonants **n** or **s** are stressed on the *next-to-last syllable*. Listen to and then pronounce the following words.
   medicina, derecho, grande, tienen, abuelos, nosotros, arte

2. Words ending in consonants other than **n** or **s** are stressed on the *last syllable*. Listen to and then pronounce the following words.
   tener, usted, Rafael, ciudad, Gabriel, feliz, llegar

3. All words "breaking" rules **#1** and **#2** above need a written accent on the stressed syllable. Listen to and then pronounce the following words.
   televisión, biología, informática, fácil, Ramón, música

4. Written accents are used on all *interrogative* and *exclamatory* words. Listen to and then pronounce the following words.
   ¿Cómo?, ¿Qué?, ¿Cuándo?, ¿Quién?, ¿Cuántos?, ¿Dónde?, ¡Qué bueno!

5. Written accents are also used to *differentiate meaning* of certain one-syllable words that are written and pronounced alike. Listen to and then pronounce the following words.

él (*he*)	**el** (*the*)
mí (*me*)	**mi** (*my*)
sí (*yes*)	**si** (*if*)
tú (*you*)	**tu** (*your*)

> **Fíjate**
>
> Accent marks appear only over vowels.

2•1 Las palabras

Practice pronouncing the following words, focusing on the stress.

1. abuelos
2. medicina
3. ¿Dónde?
4. música
5. tener
6. arte
7. usted
8. derecho
9. nosotros
10. biología

2•2 Las oraciones

Practice pronouncing the following sentences and pay special attention to the stress.

1. Estudio medicina. ¿Qué estudias tú?
2. La música jazz es muy interesante.
3. Mi abuelo se llama Manuel Ramón Jiménez.

2•3 Los dichos y refranes

Now pronounce the following saying and focus on the stress.

Dime con quién andas y te diré quién eres.

Suggestion for *Las materias y las especialidades* Get to know the students in your class. If the class is composed of mostly first-year students, secondary (high school) students, part-time students, or community members taking the course for fun, recognize that they might not have majors or they might not have declared a major yet. Ask them to report about which classes they are currently taking, and ask them to identify to what major those classes belong.

SECTION GOALS FOR
Pronunciación

By the end of the *Pronunciación* section, students will be able to:
- distinguish the differences in pronunciation between accented and non-accented words.
- emphasize the accented syllable.
- pronounce question words and emphasize the stress on the proper syllable.

Suggestion for *Pronunciación*
Students should be encouraged to practice pronunciation both in and out of the classroom. In class, the most effective way to practice is for the instructor to say the sound, word, or phrase, and then have the students repeat it. Then say the sound, word, or phrase again and have students repeat it once again. Not repeating with the students allows you to hear how well they are imitating the sounds of the words.

Suggestion for 2-1 You may wish to have your students underline the stressed vowel in addition to pronouncing the words.

Follow up to 2-3 Ask students if they know a similar *refrán* in English; or if they are from another country, ask if there is a similar proverb in their language. Once they have translated the *refrán*, ask the students if they think what the *refrán* says is true. If not, why?

CULTURAL BACKGROUND FOR
Los dichos y refranes

Dime con quién andas y te diré quién eres is a popular *refrán* used in Spanish-speaking countries. Some popular translations in English include: "Tell me with whom you walk and I will tell you who you are", "A man is known by the company he keeps", or "A man is known by his friends".

2·4 ¿Cuál es su especialidad? `4:00`

Complete the following steps.

Paso 1 Take turns matching the following famous people with the majors they may have studied in college.

1. ___b___ Pablo Picasso
2. ___e___ Maya Angelou
3. ___f___ Marie Curie
4. ___c___ Sigmund Freud
5. ___h___ el presidente de Coca-Cola
6. ___g___ former Supreme Court Justice Sandra Day O'Connor
7. ___a___ Shania Twain/Johann Sebastian Bach
8. ___d___ Bill Gates

a. música
b. arte
c. psicología
d. informática
e. literatura
f. ciencias
g. derecho
h. administración de empresas

Paso 2 Now, can you name the majors the following famous Hispanics may have studied in college?
Ellen Ochoa: ciencias; *Geraldo Rivera:* periodismo; *Isabel Allende:* literatura; *Carlos Santana:* música

Ellen Ochoa

Geraldo Rivera

Isabel Allende

Carlos Santana

`5:00` 📖 ## 2·5 ¿Qué clases tienes?

Complete the following chart, then share your schedule with a partner.

HORARIO DE CLASES

CLASES	DÍAS DE LA SEMANA	HORA
matemáticas	martes y jueves	1:30

Capítulo Preliminar A. La hora, pág. 18; Los días de la semana, pág. 20.

MODELO *Este semestre tengo cinco cursos. Tengo la clase de matemáticas los martes y jueves a la una y media… ¿Y tú?*

▼ **Estrategia**

If the meaning of any of the vocabulary words is not clear, verify the definition in the *Vocabulario activo* at the end of this chapter.

2 6 Unos estereotipos

8:00

Do you think stereotypes exist just at your university? In your opinion, the following characteristics are stereotypically associated with students majoring in which fields? Share your responses with your group of three or four students, then report the group findings to the class.

MODELO

Capítulo 1. El verbo *tener*, pág. 35; Los adjetivos descriptivos, pág. 44.

E1: *Tengo "Los estudiantes de administración de empresas son ricos". ¿Qué tienes tú?*

E2: *También tengo "Los estudiantes de administración de empresas son ricos".*

E3: *Tengo "Los estudiantes de informática son ricos".*

GRUPO: *Tenemos "Los estudiantes de administración de empresas y los estudiantes de informática son ricos".*

Los estudiantes de...
1. _____ son ricos.
2. _____ son simpáticos.
3. _____ son trabajadores.
4. _____ son cómicos.
5. _____ son responsables.
6. _____ son pacientes.
7. _____ son interesantes.
8. _____ son muy inteligentes.

Estrategia

Go to Appendix 3, *También se dice…*, for an expanded list of college majors. *También se dice…* includes additional vocabulary and regional expressions for all chapters. Although not exhaustive, the list will give you an idea of the variety and richness of the Spanish language.

Los estereotipos

5:00

2-8

The first definition that the American Heritage Dictionary lists for *stereotype* is "a conventional, formulaic, and usually oversimplified conception, opinion, or belief." While we all make generalizations in fun about our world, e.g., "the absent-minded professor," perpetuating stereotypes can be hurtful and mean-spirited.

As we learn about the Spanish-speaking world, remember that it is comprised of a vast group of individuals united by the same language. Making generalizations about the Spanish-speaking world is as problematic as making generalizations about the English-speaking world.

Preguntas

1. What are some stereotypes that foreigners hold about people from the United States?
   Possible answers: They are loud, rich, wasteful, overweight, dress poorly, etc.
2. What confusion would using the phrase "I am an American" create at a meeting with people from Central and South America?
   All people from North, Central, and South America are essentially "Americans" to the rest of the world.

NOTE FOR 2-6 and
Los estereotipos (box)

In actividad **2-6** students are reminded that stereotyping exists, even on college campuses. The purpose of the floating culture box that follows *Los estereotipos* is to make students aware that stereotyping can be hurtful. They are encouraged to explore how they themselves may be stereotyped by others and to consider that the Spanish-speaking world is as diverse as the world in which they live.

NATIONAL STANDARDS
Cultures, Connections

When learning a language and studying the culture, it is important to dispel any common stereotypes about the people whose language you are teaching. Standards 2.1 and 2.2 discuss the cultural behaviors within the Hispanic community and how those behaviors shape their practices and their products. Many students may consider some of the practices or products to be "backward," simply because they are different from those in the United States. Students may also have stereotypical ideas about some academic majors. As the instructor, you can point out that any major or minor discipline can be enhanced through the study of Spanish. Standard 3.1 states that knowledge of other disciplines is reinforced through Spanish. You might ask them to think of a job where knowing the Hispanic culture and Spanish language would not be useful (there will not be a job that they can argue) to highlight that Spanish can help them in whatever they decide to study.

Expansion for *Los estereotipos* You may want to ask these additional questions:

1. Are there any stereotypes about your college or university? Are there any stereotypes about your town?
2. Have you ever experienced any untrue, unkind stereotypes? How did you feel?
3. How do stereotypes begin? How can they be stopped?
4. What stereotypes do we hold about Hispanics, based on what we see in films and on TV?

VOCABULARIO 2 — La sala de clase

2-9 to 2-11

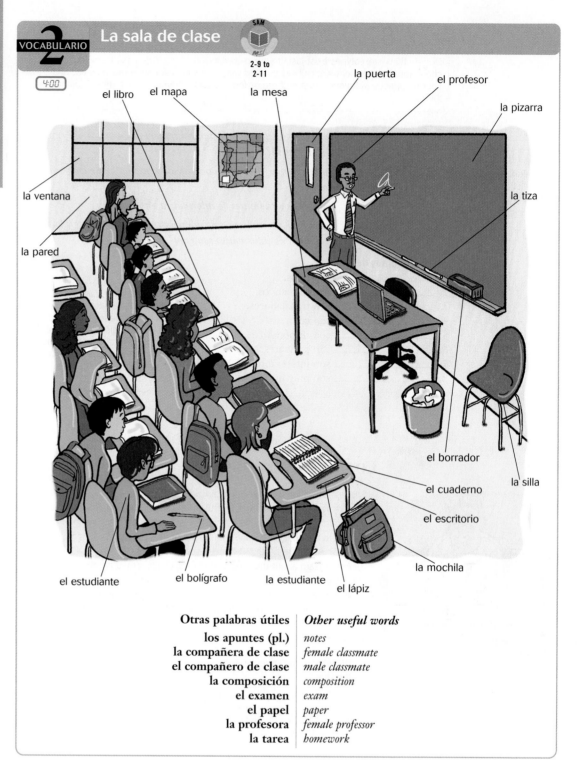

Otras palabras útiles	Other useful words
los apuntes (pl.)	*notes*
la compañera de clase	*female classmate*
el compañero de clase	*male classmate*
la composición	*composition*
el examen	*exam*
el papel	*paper*
la profesora	*female professor*
la tarea	*homework*

T-2 to T-3	T-2 to T-3	Electronic Activity Cache

2·7 ¿Cómo es tu sala de clase?

Using the numbers 0–30, take turns indicating how many there are in your classroom of each of the items presented in **La sala de clase.** You and your partner should each create at least **five** sentences following the model.

MODELO

E1: *Hay veinticinco mochilas y tres ventanas.*

E2: *Sí, y también hay diecinueve cuadernos.*

Capítulo Preliminar A. Los números 0–30, pág. 16.

Fíjate

Hay is a little word that carries a lot of meaning. It can be both singular and plural and it means both "there is" and "there are."

Vocabulario útil

hay	*there is; there are*
pero	*but*
también	*too; also*
y	*and*

 2·8 ¿Qué tiene Chucho?

Chucho is running late for class again. He has remembered some things and forgotten others. Make a list of **five** things he possibly has and does not have for class, using the verb **tener.** Share your list with a classmate.

MODELO *Chucho tiene los apuntes pero no tiene el libro de matemáticas. También tiene...*

Fíjate

To make a negative statement, simply place the word *no* before the verb: *Chucho tiene los apuntes. Chucho **no** tiene los apuntes.*

Expansion for 2-8 In groups of three or four, students should brainstorm a list of four things that each person in the group has brought to class and at least one thing no one brought.

CAPÍTULO 2

NOTE FOR 2-9

Activities like **2-9** require students to write. *¡Anda!* offers at least two of these activities per chapter. Some require recording personal information that will be shared; others require gathering information from others. Students do not need to write in their books. These activities are available in the Workbooklet, or they may write on a separate sheet of paper.

NATIONAL STANDARDS

Comparisons

Most grammar explanations in *¡Anda!* will encourage students to consider English grammar as the point of departure for understanding Spanish grammar.

NOTE FOR

Presente indicativo de verbos regulares

Preferences vary regarding the presentation of *-ar*, *-er*, and *-ir* verbs separately or together. We believe that presenting them at the same time, but in progression (first *-ar*, then *-er*, then *-ir*), allows students to learn the *-ar* conjugation and then build on that knowledge, substituting the changes for *-er* and then *-ir* conjugations.

Suggestion for *Presente indicativo de verbos regulares* You may want to use these drawings after you have reviewed the present tense conjugations. Have students describe Mario's schedule in more detail. You can also return to these drawings to practice question formation.

2·9 ¿Qué tienen tus compañeros?

Randomly choose three students and complete the chart below. Then take turns having your partner identify the classmates as you state **five** things each one has or does not have for class.

Fíjate

As in English, when listing a series of things, the word *y* (*and*) is placed just before the last item. In Spanish, however, note that you do not place a comma before *y*.

MODELO   E1: *La estudiante 1 tiene dos cuadernos, un libro, un bolígrafo y dos lápices. ¡No tiene la tarea!*

E2: *¿Es Sarah?*

E1: *Sí, es Sarah. / No, no es Sarah.*

ESTUDIANTE 1 _____	ESTUDIANTE 2 _____	ESTUDIANTE 3 _____
(NO) TIENE…	(NO) TIENE…	(NO) TIENE…
1.	1.	1.
2.	2.	2.
3.	3.	3.
4.	4.	4.
5.	5.	5.

GRAMÁTICA 3   **Presente indicativo de verbos regulares**

2-12 to 2-15   7, 11, 13, 14

Mario es un estudiante de derecho. ¿Qué hace (*does he do*) todos los días?

Llega a la clase a las nueve de la mañana.

Lee en la biblioteca.

Habla con sus compañeros.

Trabaja dos horas como tutor.

Come en la cafetería con amigos.

A las 6:30 **espera** el autobús y **regresa** a su apartamento.

RECURSOS   2-G3   Electronic Activity Cache

Spanish has three groups of verbs which are categorized by the ending of the infinitive. Remember that an infinitive is expressed in English by the word *to: to have, to be,* and *to speak* are all infinitive forms of English verbs. Spanish infinitives end in **-ar, -er,** or **-ir.** Look at the following infinitives.

Verbos que terminan en *-ar*

comprar	*to buy*	**pregunt**ar	*to ask (a question)*
contestar	*to answer*	**prepar**ar	*to prepare; to get ready*
enseñar	*to teach; to show*	**regres**ar	*to return*
esperar	*to wait for; to hope*	**termin**ar	*to finish; to end*
estudiar	*to study*	**tom**ar	*to take; to drink*
hablar	*to speak*	**trabaj**ar	*to work*
llegar	*to arrive*	**us**ar	*to use*
necesitar	*to need*		

Verbos que terminan en *-er*

aprender	*to learn*	**corr**er	*to run*
comer	*to eat*	**cre**er	*to believe*
comprender	*to understand*	**le**er	*to read*

Verbos que terminan en *-ir*

abrir	*to open*	**recib**ir	*to receive*
escribir	*to write*	**viv**ir	*to live*

To talk about daily or ongoing activities or actions, you need to use the present tense. You can also use the present tense to express future events.

Mario **lee** en la biblioteca. — *Mario reads in the library.* / *Mario is reading in the library.*

Mario **lee** en la biblioteca mañana. — *Mario will read in the library tomorrow.*

To form the present indicative, drop the **-ar, -er,** or **-ir** endings from the infinitive, and add the appropriate ending. The endings are highlighted in the following chart. Follow this simple pattern with all regular verbs.

> **Estrategia**
>
> If you would like to review the difference between the formal "you" and the informal "you," return to the cultural reading *¿Tú o usted?* on page 12 of *Capítulo Preliminar A.*

	hablar (*to speak*)	**comer** (*to eat*)	**vivir** (*to live*)
yo	habl**o**	com**o**	viv**o**
tú	habl**as**	com**es**	viv**es**
él, ella, Ud.	habl**a**	com**e**	viv**e**
nosotros/as	habl**amos**	com**emos**	viv**imos**
vosotros/as	habl**áis**	com**éis**	viv**ís**
ellos/as, Uds.	habl**an**	com**en**	viv**en**

HERITAGE LANGUAGE LEARNERS

Your Heritage language learners will most likely not understand the concept of "regular" and "irregular" verbs, much like the native English speakers do not recognize that the concept of conjugation exists in English. They probably have not had to conjugate verb forms in Spanish before, but they will be able to determine if something sounds right or not. They might substitute *usted* command forms for the present tense (e.g., *hable* instead of *habla*) because that is something they have heard at home.

Additional activity for *Presente indicativo de verbos regulares*

Have students practice the following verbs by quickly saying the correct forms using the following nouns and pronouns.

Verbs: *estudiar, hablar, comer, correr, escribir, vivir*

Subjects: *tú, nosotros, Marco, usted, ustedes, Juan y Eva, yo, ellas, Mariela, ella*

NOTE FOR 2-10

Remind students that sometimes, when working with pairs in class, there will be an odd number of students. Instead of using the *tú* form, you could ask the same questions of the other two students in your group in the *Ustedes* form.

Suggestion for 2-10 Encourage your students to select verbs that they need to practice more.

Expansion for 2-12 This can be expanded into a listening activity. Students take turns reading their sentences to a partner. While one student reads, the other student listens carefully and connects the items mentioned. Then they can check each other's work to see if the lines match what was read.

2·10 Vamos a practicar [8:00]

Take ten small pieces of paper and write a different noun or pronoun (**yo, tú, él,** etc.) on each one. On another five small pieces of paper write five infinitives, one on each piece of paper. Take turns drawing a paper from each pile. Give the correct form of the verb you selected to match the noun or pronoun you picked from the pile. Each person should say at least **five** verbs in a row correctly.

MODELO		
INFINITIVE:		*preguntar*
PRONOUN OR NOUN:		*mi madre*
E1:		*mi madre pregunta*

[6:00]

2·11 El *e-mail* de Carlos

Complete Carlos's e-mail message to his mother on a separate sheet of paper, using the correct form of the verbs.

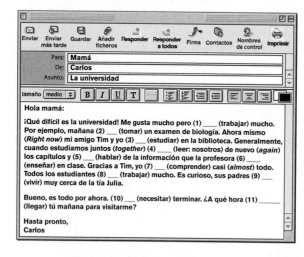

Carlos es estudiante de la UNAM. ¿Qué escribe?

Answers to 2-11.
1. trabajo	4. leemos	8. trabajan
2. tomo	5. hablamos	9. viven
3. estudiamos	6. enseña	10. Necesito
	7. comprendo	11. llegas

2·12 Dime quién, dónde y cuándo

[4:00]

Look at the three columns below. With a pen, connect a pronoun to an activity and then to a class to create **five** sentences. Share your answers with a classmate.

Fíjate

Remember that subject pronouns (*yo, tú, él, ella,* etc.) are used for emphasis or clarification, and therefore do not always need to be expressed.

MODELO
E1: nosotros / usar un microscopio / clase de ciencias
E2: *Usamos un microscopio en la clase de ciencias.*

PRONOMBRE	ACTIVIDAD	CLASE
yo	preparar una presentación	matemáticas
nosotros/as	leer mucho	inglés
ellos/as	necesitar una calculadora	español
ella	estudiar leyes (*laws*)	periodismo
tú	escribir muchas composiciones	historia
Uds.	contestar muchas preguntas	derecho
él	aprender mucho	ciencias políticas

HERITAGE LANGUAGE LEARNERS
Feel free to modify the directions of an activity for Heritage language learners in order for them to practice their writing and reading skills. In particular, the mechanical practice of writing out each question will alert them to the punctuation and accent marks used in questions.

2·13 ¿A quién conoces que…?

Who exhibits the following characteristics? Complete the questions below. Then take turns asking and answering in complete sentences to practice the new verbs.

MODELO ¿Quién _____ (hablar) mucho?

E1: *¿Quién habla mucho?*

E2: *Mi hermano Tom habla mucho. También mis hermanas hablan mucho.*

1. ¿Quién __corre__ (correr) mucho?
2. ¿Quién __estudia__ (estudiar) muy poco (*very little*)?
3. ¿Quién __escribe__ (escribir) muchos e-mails?
4. ¿Quién __llega__ (llegar) siempre tarde a la clase?
5. ¿Quién __abre__ (abrir) su mochila?
6. ¿Quién __usa__ (usar) los apuntes de sus amigos?
7. ¿Quién __comprende__ (comprender) todo (*everything*) cuando el/la profesor/a habla español?
8. ¿Quién __cree__ (creer) en Santa Claus?

GRAMÁTICA 4

La formación de preguntas y las palabras interrogativas

 SAM
2-16 to 2-19

 Guide G
8, 10

Asking yes/no questions

Yes/no questions in Spanish are formed in two different ways:

a. Adding question marks to the statement.

Antonio habla español. → ¿Antonio habla español?

Antonio speaks Spanish. *Does Antonio speak Spanish?* or *Antonio speaks Spanish?*

As in English, your voice goes up at the end of the sentence. Remember that written Spanish has an upside-down question mark at the beginning of a question.

b. Inverting the order of the subject and the verb.

Antonio habla español. → ¿Habla Antonio español?

SUBJECT + VERB → VERB + SUBJECT

Antonio speaks Spanish. *Does Antonio speak Spanish?*

Answering yes/no questions

Answering questions is also like English.

Antonio: ¿Cuántos idiomas hablas?
Silvia: Hablo dos, español y francés. ¿Y tú?
Antonio: Sólo hablo español pero mi loro habla cinco idiomas.

¿Habla Antonio español? *Does Antonio speak Spanish?*
Sí, habla español. *Yes, he speaks Spanish.*
No, no habla español. *No, he does not speak Spanish.*

Notice that in the negative response to the question above, both English and Spanish have two negative words.

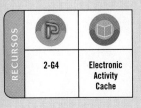

NOTE FOR

Las palabras interrogativas

Since the students are not familiar with the personal *a, whom* is not introduced at this point.

METHODOLOGY • The Natural Approach

This sequence of activities is a good example of the *Natural Approach* for language acquisition, taking students from simple yes/no questions to slightly longer sentence utterances.

Information questions

Information questions begin with interrogative words. Study the list of question words below and remember, accents are used on all interrogative words and also on exclamatory words: **¡Qué bueno!** (*That's great!*).

Las palabras interrogativas

¿Adónde?	*To where?*	**¿Adónde** va Antonio?	*(To) Where is Antonio going?*
¿Cómo?	*How?*	**¿Cómo** está Antonio?	*How is Antonio?*
¿Cuál?	*Which (one)?*	**¿Cuál** es su clase favorita?	*Which is his favorite class?*
¿Cuáles?	*Which (ones)?*	**¿Cuáles** son sus clases favoritas?	*Which are his favorite classes?*
¿Cuándo?	*When?*	**¿Cuándo** es la clase?	*When is the class?*
¿Cuánto/a?	*How much?*	**¿Cuánto** estudia Antonio para la clase?	*How much does he study for the class?*
¿Cuántos/as?	*How many?*	**¿Cuántos** idiomas habla Antonio?	*How many languages does he speak?*
¿Dónde?	*Where?*	**¿Dónde** vive Antonio?	*Where does Antonio live?*
¿Por qué?	*Why?*	**¿Por qué** no trabaja Antonio?	*Why doesn't Antonio work?*
¿Qué?	*What?*	**¿Qué** idioma habla Antonio?	*What language does Antonio speak?*
¿Quién?	*Who?*	**¿Quién** habla cinco idiomas?	*Who speaks five languages?*
¿Quiénes?	*Who?*	**¿Quiénes** hablan cinco idiomas?	*Who speaks five languages?*

Note that, although not always necessary, when the subject is included in the sentence it follows the verb.

[4:00] **2·14** **¿Sí o no?**

Take turns asking and answering the following yes/no questions.

MODELO E1: ¿Estudias francés?

E2: *Sí, estudio francés. / No, no estudio francés.*

1. ¿Hablas español?
2. ¿Estudias mucho?
3. ¿Aprendes mucho?
4. ¿Escribes mucho en clase?
5. ¿Es tu profesor/a cubano/a?
6. ¿Trabajas?
7. ¿Vives con tus padres?
8. ¿Lees muchas novelas?

`5:00` **2•15** Preguntas, más preguntas

Determine with a partner which interrogative word would elicit the following responses and create a complete question that would elicit each statement.

MODELO   E1:   Estudio **matemáticas.**

          E2:   *¿Qué estudias?*

Fíjate

Porque written as one word and without an accent mark means "because."

1. Martín estudia **en la sala de clase.**   ¿Dónde estudia Martín?
2. Estudiamos español **porque es interesante.**   ¿Por qué estudiamos español?
3. **Susana y Julia** estudian.   ¿Quiénes estudian?
4. Estudian **entre las 7:00 y las 10:00 de la noche.**   ¿Cuándo estudian?
5. Leen **rápidamente.**   ¿Cómo leen?
6. Leo **tres libros.**   ¿Cuántos libros lees?

`8:00` **2•16** ¿y tú?

Interview your classmates using the following questions about Spanish class.

MODELO   E1:   ¿Cuántas sillas hay en la clase?

          E2:   *Hay veinte sillas.*

Vocabulario útil	
difícil	*difficult*
fácil	*easy*

1. ¿Quién enseña la clase?
2. ¿Dónde enseña la clase?
3. ¿Quiénes hablan en la clase generalmente?
4. ¿Cuántos estudiantes hay?
5. ¿Qué libro(s) usas en la clase?
6. ¿Tomas muchos apuntes en la clase?
7. ¿Es la clase fácil o difícil?
8. ¿Trabajas mucho en la clase de español?

`8:00` **2•17** ¿y tu familia o amigos?

Write **five** questions you could ask classmates about their families or friends, then move around the room asking those questions of as many people as possible.

MODELO   E1:   *¿Cómo se llaman tus padres?*
                  ¿Dónde viven tus abuelos?

          E2:   *¿Cuántos hermanos tienes? ...*

Capítulo 1. La familia, pág. 32.

METHODOLOGY • Building and Creating Sentences

We are committed to helping students work toward building and creating sentences. These kinds of descriptions and activities help to move them in that direction.

Suggestion for 2-16 Encourage students to circulate around the classroom, interviewing as many different people as possible.

NOTE FOR 2-17

Actividad **2-17** allows students to create their own questions without cues.

Additional activity for *Las palabras interrogativas*
Split the class into groups made up of two or three students; then have them create and write six questions (two addressed to their best friend, two addressed to two of their professors, and two asking about any one or two of their classmates) using the verbs and vocabulary of the chapter. Once the questions are formulated, they are to exchange them with another group and have them answer the other group's questions. This drill should be performed several times per term.

NOTE FOR

Los números 100–1.000

Remind students that the numbers 16–19 and 21–29 are written as single words: *dieciséis, diecisiete, veintiuno, veintidós*, etc.

Suggestion for 2-18 Bring in a newspaper or printout from a web site with the current values of currency from different Spanish-speaking countries in comparison to the U.S. dollar. Then help students convert some of the amounts given into the foreign currencies of your choice.

VOCABULARIO 5 — Los números 100–1.000

2-20 to
2-22

100	cien	200	doscientos	600	seiscientos
101	ciento uno	201	doscientos uno	700	setecientos
102	ciento dos	300	trescientos	800	ochocientos
116	ciento dieciséis	400	cuatrocientos	900	novecientos
120	ciento veinte	500	quinientos	1.000	mil

1. The conjuction **y** is used to connect tens and ones only.

   32 = treinta **y** dos, 101 = ciento uno, 151 = ciento cincuenta **y** uno

2. **Ciento** is shortened to **cien** before any noun.

   cien hombres   **cien** mujeres

3. Multiples of **cientos** agree in number and gender with nouns they modify.

   doscientos hombres   **trescientas** mujeres

4. Note the use of a decimal instead of a comma in **1.000.**

4:00  **2 18** ¡Dinero!

Take turns saying the following amounts of money aloud, in the currencies listed below.

MODELO   E1:   325 USD

E2:   *trescientos veinticinco dólares*

U.S. dollar (dólares) = USD   Euro (euros) = EUR   Mexican peso (pesos) = MXN   Peruvian Nuevo Sol (soles) = PEN

1. 110 USD   ciento diez dólares
2. 415 MXN   cuatrocientos quince pesos
3. 376 PEN   trescientos setenta y seis soles
4. 822 EUR   ochocientos veintidós euros

5. 638 MXN   seiscientos treinta y ocho pesos
6. 544 USD   quinientos cuarenta y cuatro dólares
7. 763 PEN   setecientos sesenta y tres soles
8. 999 EUR   novecientos noventa y nueve euros

RECURSOS

Electronic Activity Cache

2·19 Vamos a adivinar

On a popular TV show, *The Price is Right,* contestants must guess the price of different items. Bring in **five** ads of items priced between $100 and $1,000 dollars and cover the prices. In groups of three or four, take turns guessing the prices in U.S. dollars. The person who comes closest without going over the price wins the item!

MODELO

E1: ¿*Cuesta* (It costs) *ciento cincuenta y cinco dólares?*

E2: *No.*

E1: *Cuesta ciento ochenta dólares.*

E2: *Sí.*

Fíjate

If the item you are pricing is plural, the verb form will be *cuestan.*

¿Cómo andas?

Having completed the first **Comunicación,** I now can...

	Feel Confident	Need to Review
• talk about school subjects and majors (p. 62)	❏	❏
• explain where the stress falls in Spanish words and when accents are used (p. 63)	❏	❏
• give an example of a stereotype (p. 65)	❏	❏
• describe a typical classroom (p. 66)	❏	❏
• form regular **-ar, -er,** and **-ir** verbs in the present tense, know their meanings, and use them in complete sentences (p. 68)	❏	❏
• create and answer questions (p. 71)	❏	❏
• use numbers 100–1,000 (p. 74)	❏	❏

PLANNING AHEAD

For actividad **2-19,** the students need to bring in at least five ads with prices for their classmates to guess. You may want to bring extras in the event some students forget.

METHODOLOGY • Small Group Work

¡Anda! is based on research. One important area of research deals with pair work and cooperative learning. The research states that students learn best from other students. Hence, this program has numerous pair and small group activities. Vary groups and partners on a regular basis. You can group students in numerous ways: the same birth months, physical characteristics, likes and dislikes, colors of clothing, simply by having students count off, etc.

SECTION GOALS FOR
Comunicación

By the end of the *Comunicación* section, students will be able to:

- describe common places and buildings on a campus.
- state the forms of *estar*.
- use *estar* for location, description of feelings, and changes from the norm.
- explain where certain cities are located.
- express how they and others are feeling.
- give opinions about their likes and dislikes using *gustar*.
- report about the sports and leisure activities they enjoy.

NATIONAL STANDARDS
Communication

The activities describing the university, daily routine, location, and feelings all require communication. The pair activities foster interpersonal communication (Standard 1.1), as students exchange information, opinions, and feelings about school. You can modify actividad **2-21** by asking students to draw, photograph, cut out pictures, or use clip art to show the items in their rooms and label those items in Spanish. If they prepare their inventory for an audience of readers and/or present it to an audience, they can satisfy Communication Standard 1.3.

Comunicación

- Describing student life, feelings, and where things are located

VOCABULARIO 6 En la universidad

Los lugares

2-23 to 2-26

5:00

el cuarto

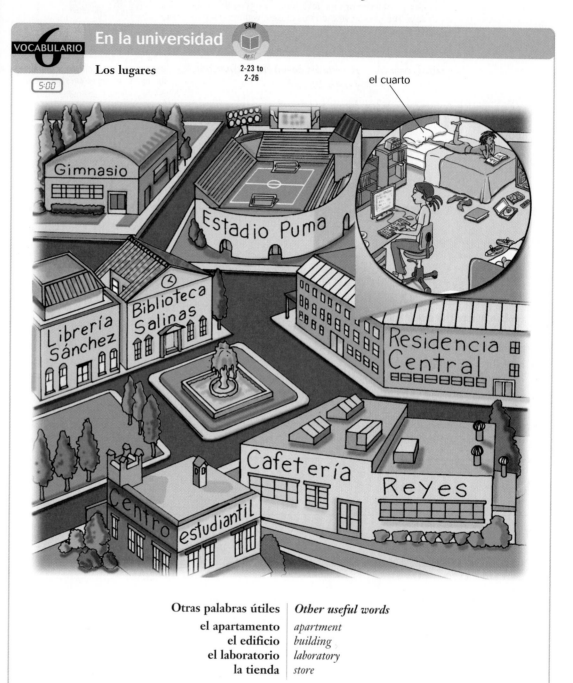

Otras palabras útiles	Other useful words
el apartamento	*apartment*
el edificio	*building*
el laboratorio	*laboratory*
la tienda	*store*

T2-4 to T2-5	T2-4 to T2-5	Electronic Activity Cache

RECURSOS

La residencia

Fíjate

El radio is the radio, *la radio* is the broadcast.

el radio/
la radio

el despertador

la compañera de cuarto

el reloj

el televisor

la computadora

los discos
compactos
(los CD)

el DVD

la calculadora

el dinero

Otras palabras útiles	*Other useful words*
el compañero de cuarto	*male roommate*
el horario (de clases)	*schedule (of classes)*
el reproductor de CD/DVD	*CD/DVD player*

Additional activity for *En la universidad* Have students give an actual name for these places found on your campus: 1. *el estadio*, 2. *la biblioteca*, 3. *una residencia estudiantil*, 4. *una tienda*, 5. *el centro estudiantil*, 6. *la cafetería*, 7. *un edificio*, 8. *una librería*. E.g., *el estadio* "John F. Kenan Memorial Stadium."

RECURSOS

T2-6   T2-6

2·20 ¡Lo sé!

Take turns choosing the word from the vocabulary list, **Los lugares,** that is associated with each of the words below.

MODELO E1: leer libros, estudiar
      E2: *la biblioteca*

1. pasta, pizza, café
2. libros para comprar
3. básquetbol
4. experimentos científicos
5. fútbol
6. Sears Tower, Chicago, IL
7. leer libros y estudiar
8. hablar con amigos

2·21 En mi cuarto…

Take turns telling your partner which items from the list **La residencia** you have in your room or where you live. Then say which items you do not have.

MODELO E1: *Tengo una calculadora, una computadora, un despertador…*
      E2: *No tengo un radio, un reproductor de DVD…*

2·22 Datos personales

You are a foreign exchange student in Mexico, living with a family. Your Mexican little "brother" wants to know all about you! Answer his questions, which follow, then ask a classmate these same questions.

1. ¿De dónde eres?
2. ¿Qué estudias?
3. ¿Dónde estudias?
4. ¿Dónde comes?
5. ¿Dónde compras tus libros?
6. ¿Dónde vives?
7. ¿Qué necesitas para tu clase de español?
8. ¿Qué necesitas para una clase de matemáticas?
9. ¿Qué tienes en tu mochila?

GRAMÁTICA 7 — El verbo *estar*

2-27 to 2-30   7, 11, 12, 15

¿Dónde está mi hijita?

Estoy aquí, papi, ¡en el armario!

Another verb that expresses *to be* in Spanish is **estar.** Like **tener** and **ser, estar** is not a regular verb; that is, you cannot simply drop the infinitive ending and add the usual **-ar** endings.

estar (*to be*)

Singular		Plural	
yo	**estoy**	nosotros/as	**estamos**
tú	**estás**	vosotros/as	**estáis**
él, ella, Ud.	**está**	ellos/as, Uds.	**están**

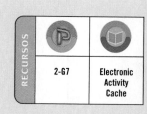
RECURSOS   2-G7   Electronic Activity Cache

Ser and estar are not interchangeable because they are used differently. Two uses of **estar** are:

1. To describe the location of someone or something.

Manuel **está** en la sala de clase. — *Manuel is in the classroom.*
Nuestros padres **están** en México. — *Our parents are in Mexico.*

2. To describe how someone is feeling or to express a change from the norm.

Estoy bien. ¿Y tú? — *I'm fine. And you?*
Estamos tristes hoy. — *We are sad today. (Normally we are upbeat and happy.)*

2·23 ¿Cuál es la palabra? `2:00`

Take turns giving the correct form of **estar** for each subject.

1. nosotras — estamos
2. el estudiante — está
3. tú — estás
4. la pizarra — está
5. yo — estoy
6. los profesores — están

2·24 Busco... `5:00`

Estrategia

You have noted that the majority of the classroom activities are with a partner. So that each person has equal opportunities, one of you should do the even numbered items in an activity, the other do the odd numbered items.

You are on campus and you want to know where you can find the following. Take turns creating questions to determine the location of each person or thing. Your partner provides a response using the correct form of **estar + en** (*in, on,* or *at*).

MODELO — el mapa/libro

E1: *¿Dónde está el mapa?*
E2: *El mapa está en el libro.*

1. las calculadoras/la mochila
2. los apuntes/el cuaderno
3. tú/el laboratorio
4. el despertador/la mesa
5. yo/la residencia
6. mi amigo y yo/el centro estudiantil

2·25 ¡Ahora mismo! `5:00`

Determine together what the following people may be doing, using the verbs listed below.

MODELO — E1: Marta está en la sala de clase.
E2: *Toma apuntes.*

aprender	comprar	comer	escribir	estudiar
hablar	leer	preparar	tomar	trabajar

1. Juan y Pepa están en la biblioteca.
2. Mi hermana está en la librería.
3. El profesor está en su casa.
4. Los estudiantes están en la cafetería.
5. María está en su apartamento.
6. Patricia está en el centro estudiantil.
7. Tú estás en el laboratorio.
8. Mi amiga y yo estamos en la clase de español.

METHODOLOGY • Pair Work

For actividades **2-23** through **2-26**, you may want Student 1 to do the even-numbered items while Student 2 does the odd items. It is important for you to overtly tell students to take turns when working in pairs. If not, one student may monopolize the pair work.

 Additional activity for *El verbo* estar Working in pairs, have students say whether the following places are *cerca* or *lejos*. For example: destination vs. where the student is now: *la biblioteca/la sala de clase de español; La biblioteca está lejos.*

1. *la biblioteca/la cafetería*
2. *la residencia estudiantil (o apartamento/casa)/la librería de la universidad*
3. *un laboratorio de computadoras/el centro estudiantil*
4. *el gimnasio/el estadio*
5. *un laboratorio de ciencias/la biblioteca*
6. *la casa de tu familia/tu residencia estudiantil (o el lugar donde vives)*
7. *el centro estudiantil/el estadio*

Suggestion for 2-26 If you have not yet modeled the pronunciation of the Spanish-speaking countries and capitals, this is a good opportunity to do so. You may wish to refer to the map on p. 16 of *Capítulo Preliminar A*.

Expansion for 2-26 You will notice that not all of the Hispanic countries are listed in actividad **2-26**. You can use a classroom map, project a map from the Internet, ask students to turn to the map in *Capítulo Preliminar A*, or project a transparency of a map to include other Hispanic countries such as Venezuela, Ecuador, Uruguay, Paraguay, Colombia, Guatemala, El Salvador, Nicaragua, Costa Rica, and Panama.

3:00

2·26 La clase de geografía

Take turns asking a partner in which countries the following capitals are located.

MODELO   E1:   *¿Dónde está Washington, D.C.?*

E2:   *Washington, D.C. está en los Estados Unidos.*

Fíjate

Knowledge of geography is increasingly important in our global community. Actividad **2-26** presents an opportunity to review the countries and capitals of the Spanish-speaking world.

1. Madrid
2. México, D.F.
3. Lima
4. San Juan
5. La Paz

6. Buenos Aires
7. Santiago
8. Tegucigalpa
9. Santo Domingo
10. La Habana

VOCABULARIO 8 — Emociones y estados

2-31 to 2-33

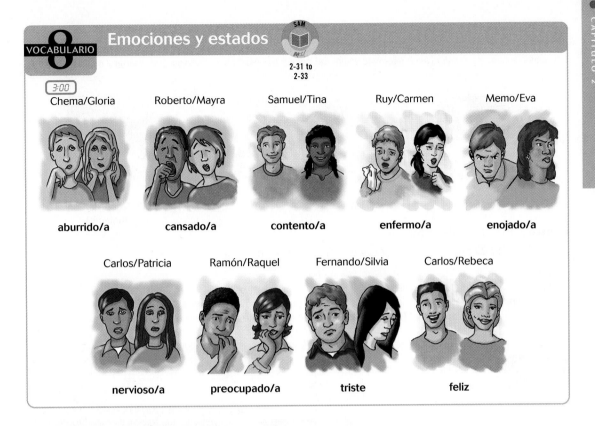

Chema/Gloria — **aburrido/a**

Roberto/Mayra — **cansado/a**

Samuel/Tina — **contento/a**

Ruy/Carmen — **enfermo/a**

Memo/Eva — **enojado/a**

Carlos/Patricia — **nervioso/a**

Ramón/Raquel — **preocupado/a**

Fernando/Silvia — **triste**

Carlos/Rebeca — **feliz**

Suggestion for *Emociones y estados* Poll students to see which ones are tired, sick, happy, nervous, worried, etc.

Expansion for 2-28 Have students create additional situations that illicit these emotions and states.

2·27 ¿Cómo están?

Look at the drawings above and take turns answering the following questions.

MODELO E1: ¿Cómo está Silvia?

E2: *Silvia está triste.*

1. ¿Cómo están Ruy y Carmen? Están enfermos.
2. ¿Cómo está Roberto? Está cansado.
3. ¿Quién está preocupada? Raquel está preocupada.
4. ¿Quiénes están nerviosos? Carlos y Patricia están nerviosos.
5. ¿Cómo están Chema y Gloria? Están aburridos.
6. ¿Cómo estás tú? Estoy. . .

2·28 ¿Qué pasa?

Which adjectives from the drawings above best describe how you might feel in each situation? Share your responses with a partner.

MODELO E1: recibes $1.000

E2: *Estoy contento/a.*

1. Estás en el hospital. Estoy enfermo/a.
2. Tienes un examen muy difícil hoy. Estoy nervioso/a.
3. Corres quince millas (*miles*). Estoy cansado/a.
4. Tu profesor de historia lee un libro por (*for*) una hora y quince minutos. Estoy aburrido/a.
5. Esperas y esperas pero tu amigo no llega (¡y no te llama por teléfono!). Estoy enojado/a / preocupado/a.
6. Sacas una "A" en tu examen de español. Estoy contento/a.

RECURSOS

| T2-7 | T2-7 | Electronic Activity Cache |

METHODOLOGY • Lexical
Presentations at the Point
of Need

In ¡Anda!, we have made the
conscious decision to teach *gustar*
in a very brief introduction.
Educational psychologists inform us
that all humans like to talk about
themselves. We love to express our
likes and dislikes early on in conversation. In order for your students to
express their personal feelings and
that of their friend or family member, it is important for them to be
able to say at the very least *I like . . .*
In order to practice vocabulary in
complete sentences. *In ¡Anda!* we
have decided to introduce the pronouns *I, you, s/he,* and *it* with *gustar.*
Indirect object pronouns and a more
in-depth explanation of *gustar* will
appear in *Capítulo 8.* You may also
choose to present "to please" as a
possible equivalent to *gustar.*

METHODOLOGY • Inductive
Presentation of Grammar

This presentation is done inductively,
where you give students a grammar
presentation and have them create
the rules.

2·29 ¿Dónde y cómo? `3:00`

Together, look at the drawings and determine where the people are, what they are doing, and how they might be feeling.

Tomás

Tina

Ana y Mirta

El Profesor Martín y
sus estudiantes.

MODELO   E1:   El profesor Martín

E2:   *El profesor Martín está en la clase. Enseña matemáticas. Está contento.*

1. Tomás   Tomás está en la biblioteca. Estudia/Lee. Está aburrido.
2. Tina   Tina está en su cuarto. Está enferma.
3. Ana y Mirta   Ana y Mirta están en una tienda. Compran un disco compacto (CD). Están contentas.
4. Los estudiantes del profesor Martín   Están en la clase. Aprenden matemáticas/Tienen un examen. Están nerviosos.

GRAMÁTICA 9   El verbo *gustar*

`3:00`   2-34 to 2-37

Fíjate

You can go back to
page 25 in *Capítulo
Preliminar A* for more
information on *gustar.*

¿Te gusta
el arte
abstracto?

To express likes and dislikes
you say the following:

Me gusta la profesora.
Me gustan las clases de idiomas.
¿**Te gust**an las novelas de Sandra Cisneros?
Te gusta el arte abstracto.
No **le gust**a estudiar.

I like the professor.
I like language classes.
Do you like Sandra Cisneros's novels?
You like abstract art.
He does not like to study.

Estrategia

You may have noticed that there are
two types of grammar presentations
in *¡Anda!:*

1. You are given the grammar rule.
2. You are given guiding questions to
help *you* construct the grammar
rule, and to state the rule in your
own words.

No matter which type of presentation,
educational researchers have found it
is *always* important for you to state
the rules orally. Correctly stating the
rules demonstrates that you are on
the road to using the grammar
concept(s) correctly in your speaking
and writing.

1. To say you like or dislike one thing, what form of **gustar** do you use?
2. To say you like or dislike more than one thing, what form of **gustar** do you use?
3. Which words in the examples mean *I? You? He/she?*
4. If a verb is needed after **gusta/gustan,** what form of the verb do you use?

To check your answers to the preceding questions, see Appendix 1.

[3:00] **2·30** ¿Qué te gusta?

Decide whether or not you like these items and share your opinions with a classmate.

MODELO   E1:   los lunes
             E2:   *(No) Me gustan los lunes.*

1. el centro estudiantil
2. los sábados
3. vivir en un apartamento
4. las matemáticas

5. aprender idiomas
6. la cafetería
7. correr
8. los libros de Harry Potter

Answers to 2-31.
1. ¿Te gusta el centro estudiantil?
2. ¿Te gustan los sábados?
3. ¿Te gusta vivir en un apartamento? [4:00]
4. ¿Te gustan las matemáticas?
5. ¿Te gusta aprender idiomas?
6. ¿Te gusta la cafetería?
7. ¿Te gusta correr?
8. ¿Te gustan los libros de Harry Potter?

2·31 Te toca a ti

Now change the cues from actividad **2-30** into questions, and ask a different classmate to answer.

MODELO   E1:   *¿Te gusta la informática?*
             E2:   *Sí, me gusta la informática.*
             E1:   *¿Te gustan los lunes?*
             E2:   *No, no me gustan los lunes.*

Estrategia

Remember, if you answer negatively, you will need to say *no* twice. If you need to review, check *La formación de preguntas* on page 71 of this chapter.

---

10 VOCABULARIO   Los deportes y los pasatiempos

[4:00]

The following are some sports and pastimes that Mexican students of the UNAM enjoy.

SAM
2-38 to
2-42

jugar al fútbol

ir de compras

hacer ejercicio

escuchar música

tomar el sol

jugar al tenis

METHODOLOGY • Presentation and Practice of Infinitives

To reinforce the presentation of *gustar*, the students will practice with the infinitives of *los deportes y los pasatiempos*. Feel free to practice the regular verbs with directed questions such as: *¿Bailas bien? ¿Cuándo nadas? ¿Quiénes montan en bicicleta?*, etc.

NOTE FOR

Los deportes y los pasatiempos

Remind students that they have already learned several *deportes y pasatiempos* such as *correr* and *leer*.

Suggestion for *Los deportes y los pasatiempos* Ask students to name the sport or activity depicted in each photo.

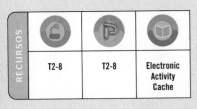

RECURSOS

| T2-8 | T2-8 | Electronic Activity Cache |

Más deportes y pasatiempos	More sports and pastimes
bailar	*to dance*
caminar	*to walk*
jugar al básquetbol	*to play basketball*
jugar al béisbol	*to play baseball*
jugar al fútbol americano	*to play football*
jugar al golf	*to play golf*
montar en bicicleta	*to ride a bike*

nadar	*to swim*
patinar	*to skate*
tocar un instrumento	*to play an instrument*
ver la televisión	*to watch television*

Otras palabras útiles	Other useful words
el equipo	*team*
la pelota	*ball*

Capítulo Preliminar A. Los días, los meses y las estaciones, pág. 20.

[4:00] **2·32** ¿En qué mes te gusta…?

As a fan or a participant, sports can be seasonal.

Paso 1   Make a list of the top **three** sports or pastimes you enjoy in the months listed below.

enero   mayo   julio   octubre

MODELO   enero

    1. patinar; 2. bailar; 3. tocar un instrumento

Paso 2   Circulate around the classroom and compare your preferences with those of your classmates. Do you see any trends?

MODELO   E1:   *¿Qué deportes y pasatiempos te gustan más en enero?*

        E2:   *Me gusta patinar, bailar y tocar un instrumento.*

[8:00] **2·33** ¿Cuánto te gusta?

What activities do you enjoy in your spare time? Write **ten** activities in the chart and rank the sports and pastimes by placing a mark in the column that best describes your feeling toward the sport or pastime. What do you suppose **¡Lo odio!** means? Share your answers, following the model.

MODELO   E1:   *Me gusta mucho bailar.*

        E2:   *No me gusta ver la televisión.*

	ME GUSTA MUCHO	ME GUSTA	NO ME GUSTA	¡LO ODIO!
1. el fútbol				
2. patinar				
3. …				

Los deportes en el mundo hispano

2-43

Los Juegos Panamericanos ocurren cada cuatro años.

Estrategia

Remember to use your reading strategy "*Recognizing cognates*" from *Capítulo 1* to assist you with this and all future reading passages.

El fútbol es el deporte más popular en el mundo hispanohablante. Sin embargo (*Nevertheless*), los hispanos participan en una gran variedad de actividades físicas y deportivas como el béisbol, el boxeo, el básquetbol (o baloncesto), el tenis, el vóleibol y el atletismo (*track and field*). España y los países latinoamericanos participan en los Juegos Olímpicos. Además, los países latinoamericanos, juntos con Canadá y los Estados Unidos, participan en los Juegos Panamericanos que tienen lugar (*take place*) cada cuatro años, siempre un año antes de los Juegos Olímpicos.

Los deportes forman una parte importante de la vida universitaria, especialmente en la Universidad Nacional Autónoma de México (la UNAM). Además (*Furthermore*) de contar con el equipo de fútbol Club Universidad Nacional, ofrecen (*they offer*) unas treinta y nueve disciplinas deportivas que incluyen los deportes mencionados y también el fútbol americano, el judo, el karate, el ciclismo, la natación, la lucha libre (*wrestling*) y más. Hay gimnasios, dos estadios, siete piscinas y muchas otras áreas para practicar estos deportes.

Preguntas

1. What is the most important sport in the Spanish-speaking world?
   soccer
2. Does your college/university offer the same sports as the UNAM? What are some differences?
   Answers may vary.

  8:00

2 34 ¿Eres activo/a?

Just how active are you? Complete the chart with activities that should, or do, occupy your time. Share your results with a partner. So… are you leading a well-balanced life?

Vocabulario útil

a menudo	*often*
a veces	*sometimes; from time to time*
nunca	*never*

A MENUDO	A VECES	NUNCA	NECESITO HACERLO (*DO IT*) MÁS
1.	1.	1.	1.
2.	2.	2.	2.
3.	3.	3.	3.
4.	4.	4.	4.
5.	5.	5.	5.

NATIONAL STANDARDS
Cultures, Comparisons

The cultural reading, *Los deportes en el mundo hispano*, focuses on the understanding between the products and perspectives of Hispanic cultures (Standard 2.2). The reading highlights the importance of *el fútbol* and *los Juegos Panamericanos* in Hispanic culture, but it also highlights what activities and sports the United States shares in common with Hispanic countries. Standard 4.2 embraces the cultural differences between Hispanic cultures and the students' cultures.

CULTURAL BACKGROUND FOR

Los deportes en el mundo hispano

Los Juegos Parapanamericanos is a sporting event for physically challenged athletes. The Games are held right after the Panamerican Games, making use of the same facilities.

Expansion for *Los deportes en el mundo hispano* Additional questions to ask your students are:

1. What is the most popular sport in the United States? Why do you think these sports became so popular in their respective cultures?
2. What sports do you think athletes compete in for the Panamerican Games? Guess first and then investigate and confirm your response on the Internet at the Panamerican Games site (*Palabras clave: juegos panamericanos*). What sports surprised you and why? Does this have anything to do with Latino stereotypes?
3. All kinds of sports are important in the Hispanic world. See how many Hispanic athletes and their sports you can name with a partner.

Answers: 1. football, then baseball, then basketball 2. *Answers may vary.* 3. e.g., Miguel Ángel Induráin, *el ciclismo*; Arantxa Sánchez–Vicario, *el tenis*; Sammy Sosa, *el béisbol*; Nancy López, *el golf*; Alberto Salazar, *el atletismo/el maratón*; Rodolfo «El Gato» González, *el boxeo*

CAPÍTULO 2

Expansion for 2-35 As a follow-up to activity **2-35**, determine the top three most popular and three least popular sports and pastimes of the class.

Additional activity for *Los deportes y los pasatiempos* Working in pairs, instruct students to make three lists, referring to the vocabulary for Los deportes y los pasatiempos. In the first list, they should write the names of activities that are normally done in teams. In the second list, they write the names of the activities that can be done alone, and in the third list, the names of the activities that work best with a partner. Have students determine which activities appear on more than one list.

2·35 Tus preferencias

Select your **three** favorite sports and/or pastimes (**que más me gustan**) and then select your **three** least favorite (**que menos me gustan**) from actividad **2-34.**

Paso 1   Write your choices in the chart. Then, create **two** sentences summarizing your choices.

LOS DEPORTES/PASATIEMPOS QUE MÁS ME GUSTAN	LOS DEPORTES/PASATIEMPOS QUE MENOS ME GUSTAN
1. *patinar*	1.
2. *bailar*	2.
3. *leer*	3.

MODELO   *Los deportes o pasatiempos que más me gustan son patinar, bailar y leer.*
Los deportes o pasatiempos que menos me gustan son...

Paso 2   Circulate around the classroom to find classmates with the same likes and dislikes as you. Follow the model. When you find someone with the same likes or dislikes, write his/her name in the chart that follows.

MODELO   E1:   *¿Qué deporte o pasatiempo te gusta más?*
E2:   *El deporte que me gusta más es jugar al tenis.*
E1:   *¿Qué deporte o pasatiempo te gusta menos?*
E2:   *El pasatiempo que me gusta menos es ir de compras.*

LOS/LAS COMPAÑEROS/AS	EL DEPORTE/PASATIEMPO QUE MÁS LES GUSTA
1.	
2.	
3.	
LOS/LAS COMPAÑEROS/AS	EL DEPORTE/PASATIEMPO QUE MENOS LES GUSTA
1.	
2.	
3.	

ESCUCHA

6:00

SAM
MSL
2-44 to
2-47

2·36 Antes de escuchar

In the following segment Eduardo, a university student and one of the characters from **Ambiciones siniestras,** is talking on the phone with his mother. Write a question you might possibly hear in their conversation.

ESTRATEGIA | Listening for the gist

When *listening for the gist,* you listen for the main idea(s). You do not focus on each word, but rather on the overall meaning. When you listen for the gist, you should be able to summarize what you heard in several words or a sentence.

2·37 A escuchar

CW
eBook

CD 1
Track 30

Listen as Eduardo and his mother converse.

1. The first time you listen, concentrate on the questions she asks. Also, jot down key words and ideas.
2. In the second listening, focus on Eduardo's answers. Jot down key words and ideas.
3. During the third listening determine if these sentences are true (**T**) or false (**F**).
   a. Eduardo's mother calls Eduardo to see how he is doing.   F
   b. Eduardo does not have classes on Tuesday.   F
   c. Eduardo's mother ends the conversation abruptly.   T
   d. Eduardo wants to ask his mother for something.   T
4. Now in one sentence, what is the gist of their conversation?   His mom wants to know why he's not in class and he wants to ask for money.

Eduardo habla con su madre.

2·38 Después de escuchar

With a partner, provide a different ending to the conversation. Then play the roles of Eduardo and his mother.

METHODOLOGY • Checking for Listening Comprehension in English

The comprehension questions in the *Escucha* section are simple enough so that most students should be able to respond to them in Spanish. Encourage those students who can to do so.

SECTION GOALS FOR
Escucha

By the end of the *Escucha* section, students will be able to:

- distinguish between speakers in a telephone conversation.
- listen for the main idea.
- recognize questions in a conversation.
- retell the main points of the conversation by role-playing.

NATIONAL STANDARDS
Communication

In *Capítulo 2*, students practice listening for the gist, or main idea, of a listening passage. Students must understand and interpret spoken Spanish (Standard 1.2) each time they complete the *Escucha* section. The follow-up activity, **2-38**, encompasses the interpersonal communicative mode and the presentational communicative mode. In small groups or pairs, students provide alternate endings to the conversation (Standard 1.1) and present the endings as if they were Eduardo and his mother. If they present the dialogue to the class they can also meet Standard 1.3.

AUDIOSCRIPT FOR 2-37

(*Sound of phone ringing*)
MAMÁ: (*mother answers*) Dígame.
EDUARDO: (*sleepily*) Hola, Mamá. ¿Cómo estás?
MAMÁ: (*lovingly*) Ay, Eduardo. Buenos días. Yo estoy muy bien, ¿y tú, mi vida?
EDUARDO: Bien, Mamá. Muy bien. Mira . . . (*mother interrupts*)
MAMÁ: Eduardo, son las nueve de la mañana. ¿No tienes clases hoy?
EDUARDO: (*uncertain*) Pues sí. A ver . . . hoy es martes . . . A las diez tengo psicología. Y a las dos tengo la clase de literatura inglesa . . . creo.
MAMÁ: (*excitedly*) Bueno hijo. Gracias por llamar, pero tú tienes clase. Hablamos luego. ¡Adiós!
EDUARDO: (*frustrated*) Pero, mamá, necesito dinero . . . (*click–call is ended*).

ESCRIBE

2-48 to
2-49

2•39 Antes de escribir

Have you ever tried to describe yourself to someone? Have you ever applied for a job for which describing yourself was a part of the application process? For some jobs it is important for the employer to know if you will indeed "fit in." Imagine that you are applying for a job on campus—either to work in the library, the student center, or the athletic department. Decide which department interests you most and determine the information you should share that would make you a viable applicant. Make a list of that information in Spanish.

MODELO   (athletic department)

LISTA:

✓ *me gustan los deportes; nado y corro muy bien*
✓ *soy buena estudiante, inteligente, creativa, organizada y trabajadora*
✓ *me gustan las cosas nuevas/las personas nuevas*
✓ *no tengo clases después de las dos.*

2•40 Una descripción

Using your list, create a short personal description following the model below.

MODELO   *Tengo veinte años y soy buena estudiante. Soy inteligente, creativa, organizada y trabajadora. Me gustan mucho los deportes. Me gusta aprender cosas nuevas y trabajar con personas diferentes. No tengo clases después de las dos de la tarde y tengo los fines de semana libres (free) también.*

2•41 Después de escribir

Your instructor will collect the descriptions and read some of them to the class. She/He may ask you to guess who wrote each one.

¿Cómo andas?

Having completed the second **Comunicación,** I now can…

	Feel Confident	Need to Review
describe life at my college/university including the campus, things we need for school, etc. (pp. 76–77)	❏	❏
use the verb **estar** to express location and feelings/emotions (p. 78, 81)	❏	❏
say what I and others like and dislike (p. 82)	❏	❏
talk about sports and pastimes (p. 83)	❏	❏
list several sports and pastimes of the Hispanic world (p. 85)	❏	❏
practice listening for the gist (p. 87)	❏	❏
write a short personal description (p. 88)	❏	❏

SECTION GOALS FOR
Cultura

By the end of the *Cultura* section, students will be able to:

- scan the reading for important information about Mexico.
- compare the UNAM and Oaxaca with where they attend school.
- list several popular forms of *artesanía*.
- comprehend brief background information from the *almanaque*.

NATIONAL STANDARDS
Cultures, Comparisons

The information about Mexico in the cultural reading addresses the Cultures and Comparisons goals. Standard 2.2 is about understanding the relationship between the practices and perspectives of Hispanic cultures. Students learn that, in Mexico, unlike in the United States, there are fewer student residences on campus; therefore, many students live with their immediate family or with other family members. This is very different from American universities, where students who live on campus live in residence halls, town houses, or apartments. The reading also describes some of the common regional *artesanía* and the organic ingredients for chewing gum and some pharmaceuticals. The Mexican products differ from those produced in the United States because they have different natural resources. Students can make comparisons between university housing options and products in the United States and Mexico (Standard 4.2).

METHODOLOGY • Contrasting and Comparing

When possible, every effort will be made to have students make comparisons with the culture of their home/university community to what they are currently learning. Additionally, as appropriate, the students will be asked to compare what they are currently learning with previous chapters. Comparing cultures will be reinforced in *Capítulo 6* and *Capítulo 12* as well.

Araceli Gabriela
Campos Vega

México

Les presento mi país

Mi nombre es Araceli Campos y soy de Oaxaca, México. Soy una estudiante de la Universidad Nacional Autónoma de México (la UNAM) que está en la Ciudad de México. Vivo cerca de la universidad con la familia de mi tía porque normalmente hay pocas residencias estudiantiles en las universidades y muchos estudiantes viven con sus parientes (*relatives*). Con más de 270.000 estudiantes, la UNAM es la universidad más grande de México y de América Latina. ¿Cuántos estudiantes hay en tu universidad? En la UNAM, tenemos un equipo de fútbol, los «Pumas». El fútbol es muy popular en mi país, es el pasatiempo nacional. ¿Qué deporte es muy popular en tu país? Mi ciudad, Oaxaca, es un centro famoso de artesanía. En particular, hay hojalatería (*tin work*), cerámicas de barro negro (*black clay*), cestería (*basket making*), fabricación de textiles y de alebrijes (*painted wooden animals*) y mucho más. ¿Qué tipo de artesanía hay en tu región?

El tianguis de Tepotzlán, Morelia.

90

RECURSOS

| T2-9 | T2-9 | Cultural Background Notes |

ALMANAQUE

Nombre oficial:	Estados Unidos Mexicanos
Gobierno:	República federal
Población:	107.499.525 (est. 2006)
Idiomas:	español (oficial); maya, náhuatl
Moneda:	peso mexicano ($)

La biblioteca de la Universidad Nacional Autónoma de México. La fachada contiene un mosaico de la historia de México.

Frida Kahlo y Diego Rivera son pintores muy famosos: ella por sus autorretratos (*self-portraits*) psicológicos y él por sus pinturas y murales de temas históricos y sociales.

El fútbol es el pasatiempo nacional del país.

Oaxaca es un centro famoso de artesanía.

¿Sabías que...?

● El origen del chicle (*gum*) es el látex del chicozapote (*sapodilla tree* en inglés), un árbol tropical de la península de Yucatán. Los mayas, tribu antigua y muy importante del Yucatán, usaban (*used*) el látex como chicle.

● La planta, "cabeza de negro", del estado mexicano de Veracruz, forma la base del proceso para crear la cortisona y "la píldora", el contraceptivo oral.

PREGUNTAS

1. What is the most popular sport in Mexico?
2. What is a "tianguis"? What do we have in the United States that is similar?
3. What are the origins of cortisone and the birth control pill?
4. What are some of the handcrafted items from Mexico? What are similar handcrafted items made in your region?
5. What are some differences between the UNAM and your school?

En la Red
Amplía tus conocimientos sobre México en la página web de *¡Anda!*

91

Ambiciones siniestras

EPISODIO 2

lectura

2-52

2-42 Antes de leer. In this episode you will discover more information about three of the university students who are among the six protagonists of the story, specifically Alejandra, Manolo, and Cisco. You will learn their complete names, where they are from, and some of their interests.

1. Note that there are a few key words in the reading passage you may not know. They are written below with their English equivalents and are listed in order of appearance. They are also boldfaced in the body of the reading.

la seguridad (-dad = -ty)	*security*
las solicitudes	*applications*
mientras	*while*
los ensayos	*essays*
el oeste	*west*
el noreste	*northeast*

Based on this list of words, can you begin to guess what the context of the reading will be?

ESTRATEGIA Skimming

When you skim, or read quickly, you generally do so to capture the gist of the passage. Practice with skimming helps you learn to focus on main ideas in your reading.

2-43 A leer. To boost your comprehension, it is helpful to skim the passage for the first reading and then ask yourself what key information you have learned.

1. Skim the first two paragraphs of this episode, then answer the following questions.
   a. What is the person doing?
   b. Do you think what he is doing is part of his job?
   c. How many students has he located so far?
2. Now skim the remaining paragraphs and write down key points for each paragraph.
3. Then, reread the entire episode, this time more carefully, to add details to those main ideas. Do not forget to take advantage of cognates like **prestigiosa** and **paciencia** to boost your comprehension.

SECTION GOALS FOR
Lectura

By the end of the *Lectura* section, students will be able to:

- summarize information about each character.
- distinguish between when the narrator gives background information and when el Sr. Verdugo is speaking.
- read a text that includes cognates, new vocabulary, and unfamiliar words.
- organize the information they have read into a chart.

NATIONAL STANDARDS
Communication

The *Ambiciones siniestras* reading provides more in-depth information about the characters and their backgrounds. By reading information about the essays of the characters in Spanish, students understand written Spanish (Standard 1.2).

RECAP OF *AMBICIONES SINIESTRAS*
Episodio 1

Lectura: In the first episode of *Ambiciones siniestras*, there were three e-mail messages from some of the characters to various people. The first message was from Alejandra, and she wrote to her mother about a new friend, Manolo. In the e-mail, she described how handsome Manolo was and she asked about her other family members. In the second e-mail, Eduardo wrote to Cisco about a *macroeconomía* assignment he didn't understand. Eduardo needed help, and he wrote to Cisco since Cisco has a better grasp of the material. The last e-mail was forwarded from Marisol to her cousin, Ligia. Marisol received a personal ad from another student looking for a girlfriend, and she wanted to know if Ligia thought she should respond.
Video: In the video episode for *Capítulo 1*, the main characters (Marisol, Lupe, Alejandra, Manolo, Cisco, and Eduardo) of *Ambiciones siniestras* were introduced. The students attend three different universities in the Midwest, the Northeast, and the West. At the Northeast university, Cisco and Eduardo discussed the macroeconomics homework; at the Midwestern

92

Capítulo 2

university, Marisol introduced Phillip (not a recurring character) to Lupe; and at the Western university, Alejandra talked to Manolo.

Answers to 2-43

1.
a. Reading e-mails.
b. *Answers may vary.*
c. Three students.
2. and 3. *Answers may vary.*

Suggestion for reviewing *Episodio 1* In both the reading and the video, the main characters were introduced: Alejandra, Manolo, Cisco, Eduardo, Marisol, and Lupe.

Reading: 1. Which three characters wrote e-mails and to whom? (Alejandra to her mother, Eduardo to Cisco and Marisol to Ligia); 2. What were the e-mails about? (Alejandra wrote her mom to say hello; she asks about the family and tells her about her new friend, Manolo. Eduardo wrote about the tough time he is having in their macroeconomics class and to ask a question. Marisol sent Ligia an interesting personal ad she found.)

CD 1
Track 32

Las solicitudes

Un hombre joven está enfrente de° su computadora. Trabaja impacientemente y con rapidez. A su lado° tiene unos papeles con unos códigos misteriosos.

in front of
at his side

—A ver°. ¿Cómo paso por **la seguridad** de esta prestigiosa universidad? Ahhhh… sí. Paciencia. Ahora… para encontrar la lista de los estudiantes y sus **solicitudes**… Excelente. Es fácil dar con° jóvenes inteligentes, creativos e inocentes.—

Let's see

find

El hombre lee **los ensayos** de las solicitudes de varios estudiantes, dos de una universidad del oeste y uno de una universidad del noreste. **Mientras** lee, habla.

—De la universidad del **oeste**:

Fíjate

The dashes indicate dialogue or spoken words. In English we use quotation marks (" ").

Alejandra Sánchez Torres. Es de San Antonio, Texas; está lejos de su casa. Aquí habla mucho de su familia. Tiene muchos hermanos. Hmmm… le gusta pintar y escribir poesía. También le gusta viajar. ¡Perfecto! Y espera estudiar arte…

Manuel Rodríguez Ángulo. Manolo. Es de California, San Diego. Tiene cuatro hermanos… sus padres están divorciados. Le gustan todos los deportes, especialmente el fútbol americano. Es excelente estudiante también… desea especializarse en medicina.

De la universidad del **noreste**:

Francisco Quiroga Godoy, Cisco, es de familia hispana y vive en West Palm Beach. Cuando no estudia, trabaja en restaurantes, cafés y, ¡qué nombre°!, "El Golden Gal Day Spa". Con tantos° trabajos y tan° buenas notas debe ser un joven muy disciplinado. Especialidad: informática. Muy bien.—

what a name / so many
such

A este hombre tan sospechoso°… ¿por qué le interesan° estos estudiantes? ¿Qué quiere° de ellos?

suspicious / is he interested in
does he want

2-44 **Después de leer.** Answer the following questions.

1. How many applications does the man review in this episode? Who are the students about whom he reads?

2. Complete the following chart:

PERSONAJE	¿DE DÓNDE ES?	¿FAMILIA?	¿POSIBLE ESPECIALIDAD?	¿ACTIVIDADES?
Alejandra				
Manolo				
Cisco				

3. According to the information given, how might Manolo's family be different from those of the other two students? Do you notice any other major differences?

93

NATIONAL STANDARDS
Comparisons

Students are directed to skim the passage for the main idea. Standard 4.1 encourages students to understand the nature of language through comparisons between English and Spanish. This passage has new words, familiar words, and cognates. Students should read the notes in the passage to learn the unfamiliar words and see if they provide a clue about the reading. Early on, remind your students to skim when they read in Spanish and not to focus on every word that is unfamiliar, unless it interferes with comprehension of the sentence. Remember, their level of reception does not match their level of production.

METHODOLOGY • Checking Reading Comprehension

In the initial stages of foreign-language learning, it is suggested to check quickly for comprehension of reading passages by phrasing questions in English. Then students may answer in English to demonstrate comprehension. In the early stages of language acquisition, comprehension and verbal output are two very different skills. Students will comprehend before they can successfully produce the language.

Answers to 2-44

1. Three applications; Alejandra, Manolo, Francisco (Cisco)
2. Alejandra es de San Antonio, Texas; tiene muchos hermanos; su posible especialidad es el arte; sus actividades son pintar, escribir poesía y viajar.
   Manolo es de San Diego, California; tiene cuatro hermanos y sus padres son divorciados; su posible especialidad es la medicina; sus actividades son jugar a los deportes, especialmente el fútbol americano.
   Cisco es de West Palm Beach, Florida; posible especialidad es la informática; sus actividades son estudiar y trabajar.
3. Manolo's parents are divorced. Francisco has worked several jobs, including a day spa.

Suggestion (cont.)

Video: 1. Is Cisco and Eduardo's macroeconomic class large or small? (*small*) Do they sit together in class? (*yes*);
2. Lupe and Marisol are in psychology class. How large is it? (*around 30–40 students*) What is the professor like? (*He is young, disheveled, late, disorganized*);
3. With whom do the young women converse before class begins? (*Phillip*); What do they speak about? (*their families, and that the three of them speak Spanish*);

4. What is the class Manolo and Alejandra have together? (*Spanish literature*) Do they sit together in class? (*yes*)

SECTION GOALS FOR
Video

By the end of the video section, students will be able to:

- describe the characters in more detail.
- recap the events in chronological order.
- make predictions about the next episode.

Answers to 2-46

1. *Possible answers:* joven, alto, fuerte, impaciente, guapo, curioso.
2. An Internet café. No.
3. *Possible facts about Eduardo:* third-year student; major is Economics; speaks Spanish, English, and Portuguese; likes to play tennis and swim; volunteers to help poor children; spends time with his family.
Possible facts about Lupe: 25 years old; history and journalism major; spent 3 months in Brazil; speaks Spanish, English, German, and Portuguese; likes to write; family is important to her.
Possible facts about Marisol: born in New York; psychology major; junior; only child; likes to play golf and read detective novels; works as a volunteer in a hospital and in an elementary school.
4. He reads it and thinks about it.
5. He writes and sends an e-mail message.

video

2-53 to 2-57

2-45 **Antes del video.** In **Las solicitudes**, a suspicious man is reading information off the computer about three of our protagonists. In the second part of this episode you will watch him in video format as he continues to discover information about our characters. Before watching the episode, think about the possible answers to these questions:

1. Who is this person and why is he interested in Lupe, Cisco, Eduardo, Marisol, Manolo, and Alejandra?
2. What information could this man discover on the Internet about you?
3. What sites could provide him with information about you?
4. What do you have in common with the characters so far?

Otras actividades: trabajar como voluntario en una organización de ayuda a los niños.

Especialidad: periodismo e historia. Aficiones: jugar al básquetbol, nadar y correr.

¡Aquí comienza la aventura!

La aventura comienza

Episodio 2

Relax and watch the video, more than once if you choose; then complete the activity below.

2-46 **Después del video.** Answer the following questions.

1. What Spanish adjectives best describe the man at the computer?
2. Where might he be? Is he alone?
3. Which characters is he investigating now? List two facts he discovers about each one.
4. What does he do with the information he gets?
5. What is he doing as the episode ends?

94

Y por fin, ¿cómo andas?

Having completed this chapter, I now can...

	Feel Confident	Need to Review

Comunicación

- talk about my life as a university student (pp. 62, 76–77) ❑ ❑
- explain where the stress falls in written words and when to use written accents (p. 63) ❑ ❑
- describe my classroom (p. 66) ❑ ❑
- use regular **-ar, -er,** and **-ir** verbs in the present tense (p. 68) ❑ ❑
- formulate questions (p. 71) ❑ ❑
- use numbers 100–1,000 (p. 74) ❑ ❑
- use the verb **estar** (p. 78, 81) ❑ ❑
- tell what I and others like and do not like, using **gustar** (p. 82) ❑ ❑
- share information about my favorite and not-so-favorite pastimes and sports (p. 83) ❑ ❑
- listen for the gist, or main idea, in a passage (p. 87) ❑ ❑
- write a brief personal description for an application (p. 88) ❑ ❑

Cultura

- discuss diversity and stereotype issues (p. 65) ❑ ❑
- list some sports and pastimes of the Hispanic world (p. 85) ❑ ❑
- share three facts about Mexico that I find interesting (p. 90) ❑ ❑

Ambiciones siniestras

- skim the reading to get the main idea (p. 92) ❑ ❑
- name and briefly describe two of your favorite characters from the mystery story (p. 94) ❑ ❑

VOCABULARIO ACTIVO

CD 1
Tracks 33-42

Las materias y las especialidades — Subjects and majors

la administración de empresas	business
la arquitectura	architecture
el arte	art
la biología	biology
las ciencias (pl.)	science
el derecho	law
el idioma	language
los idiomas (pl.)	languages
la informática	computer science
la literatura	literature
las matemáticas (pl.)	mathematics
la medicina	medicine
la música	music
la pedagogía	education
el periodismo	journalism
la psicología	psychology

Los deportes y los pasatiempos — Sports and pastimes

bailar	to dance
caminar	to walk
escuchar música	to listen to music
hacer ejercicio	to exercise
ir de compras	to go shopping
jugar al básquetbol	to play basketball
jugar al béisbol	to play baseball
jugar al fútbol	to play soccer
jugar al fútbol americano	to play football
jugar al golf	to play golf
jugar al tenis	to play tennis
montar en bicicleta	to ride a bike
nadar	to swim
patinar	to skate
tocar un instrumento	to play an instrument
tomar el sol	sunbathe
ver la televisión	to watch TV

En la sala de clase — In the classroom

los apuntes (pl.)	notes
el bolígrafo	ballpoint pen
el borrador	eraser
el/la compañero/a de clase	classmate
la composición	composition
el cuaderno	notebook
el escritorio	desk
el/la estudiante	student
el examen	exam
el lápiz	pencil
el libro	book
el mapa	map
la mesa	table
la mochila	book bag; knapsack
el papel	paper
la pared	wall
la pizarra	chalkboard
el/la profesor/a	professor
la puerta	door
la sala de clase	classroom
la silla	chair
la tarea	homework
la tiza	chalk
la ventana	window

Emociones y estados — Emotions and states of being

aburrido/a	bored (with **estar**)
cansado/a	tired
contento/a	content; happy
enfermo/a	ill; sick
enojado/a	angry
feliz	happy
nervioso/a	upset; nervous
preocupado/a	worried
triste	sad

Los números 100–1.000 — *Numbers 100–1,000*

See page 74.

Las palabras interrogativas — *Interrogative words*

See page 71.

Los verbos — *Verbs*

abrir	*to open*
aprender	*to learn*
comer	*to eat*
comprar	*to buy*
comprender	*to understand*
contestar	*to answer*
correr	*to run*
creer	*to believe*
enseñar	*to teach; to show*
escribir	*to write*
esperar	*to wait for; to hope*
estar	*to be*
estudiar	*to study*
hablar	*to speak*
leer	*to read*
llegar	*to arrive*
necesitar	*to need*
preguntar	*to ask (a question)*
preparar	*to prepare; to get ready*
recibir	*to receive*
regresar	*to return*
terminar	*to finish; to end*
tomar	*to take; to drink*
trabajar	*to work*
usar	*to use*
vivir	*to live*

Los lugares — *Places*

el apartamento	*apartment*
la biblioteca	*library*
la cafetería	*cafeteria*
el centro estudiantil	*student center; student union*
el cuarto	*room*
el edificio	*building*
el estadio	*stadium*
el gimnasio	*gymnasium*
el laboratorio	*laboratory*
la librería	*bookstore*
la residencia estudiantil	*dormitory*
la tienda	*store*

La residencia — *The dorm*

la calculadora	*calculator*
el/la compañero/a de cuarto	*roommate*
la computadora	*computer*
el despertador	*alarm clock*
el dinero	*money*
el disco compacto (el CD)	*compact disk*
el DVD	*DVD*
el horario (de clases)	*schedule (of classes)*
el radio/la radio	*radio*
el reloj	*clock; watch*
el reproductor de CD/DVD	*CD/DVD player*
el televisor	*TV set*

Otras palabras útiles — *Other useful words*

a menudo	*often*
a veces	*sometimes; from time to time*
ayer	*yesterday*
cerca (de)	*close; near*
con	*with*
el curso	*course*
difícil	*difficult*
el equipo	*team*
fácil	*easy*
hasta	*until*
hay	*there is; there are*
hoy	*today*
lejos (de)	*far; far away*
mañana	*tomorrow*
más	*more*
menos	*less*
mucho	*a lot*
nunca	*never*
la pelota	*ball*
pero	*but*
poco	*a little; few*
el semestre	*semester*
también	*too; also*
y	*and*

97

3

Estamos en casa

From the most modern of skyscrapers, to Spanish colonial styles, to the variety of homes of indigenous populations, Hispanic architecture is as varied as the people who speak Spanish. **En los países hispanohablantes** (*Spanish-speaking countries*), **hay de todo.**

SECTION GOALS FOR
Chapter Opener

By the end of the *Chapter Opener* section, students will be able to:
- identify common elements of Spanish architecture.
- compare and contrast housing options in the Spanish-speaking world.
- identify how geographical and environmental variables affect construction.

OBJETIVOS

Comunicación
- To describe your house and household chores
- To discuss how you feel
- To give prices for some homes in Spain
- To listen for specific information
- To create an ad to sell a house

Cultura
- To describe general differences in housing in Spain
- To discuss the changing role of Hispanic women and their impact on society
- To list interesting facts about Spain

Ambiciones siniestras
- To scan a passage for specific information
- To read the enticing e-mail message that Alejandra and Manolo receive and share what you would do in a similar situation
- To discover who else receives the mysterious e-mail and their reactions to the message

CONTENIDOS

RECURSOS

IRM

Lesson Plan

Sevilla, España

PREGUNTAS

1 Why is Spanish architecture so prevalent throughout North, Central, and South America? Why can French influence be seen in Mexico?

2 How do geography and environment affect the design and construction of homes?

3 Is the style of your home found in any other region of the United States? Why or why not? Do you see any Spanish-inspired architecture in your region?

99

PLANNING AHEAD

For this chapter it is helpful if students bring in a die for actividad **3–8** and pictures of rooms from magazines for actividad **3–21**.

NOTE FOR *Chapter Opener*

In actividad **3–7,** as well as in other activities throughout the chapter, students will view additional photos that provide a variety of housing possibilities throughout the Spanish-speaking world.

Warm-up for *Chapter Opener* As in *Capítulo 1,* ask students to give their impressions of the photo and to describe different types of housing options available where they live. Also, have students read the chapter objectives silently. Spend no more than five to seven minutes on chapter openers.

Suggestion for *Chapter Opener* Take digital photos of the most recognizable buildings on campus or in your community. Ask students to identify the buildings, and, using drawings and cognates, ask them whether the buildings are *modernos, apartamentos, residencias, grandes,* and how many *pisos* they have. You could also take several pictures of housing options in the area and ask students to predict where you live and why.

Expansion for *Preguntas* Discuss the wide range of housing types that exists with students, from humble dwellings to mansions in the city, urban vs. rural housing, etc.

Answers to *Preguntas*

1. Spanish explorers carried that influence with them when they explored on both continents. The French also intervened in Mexico and the Emperor Maximilian ruled there from 1864 to 1867.
2. Dwellings are built to withstand the elements and out of materials that are readily available.
3. *Answers may vary.*

SECTION GOALS FOR

Comunicación

By the end of the *Comunicación* section, students will be able to:

- describe the interior rooms and exterior spaces of a house.
- compare the features of their house with the houses of others.
- explain how floors or stories of buildings are numbered in other countries.
- form the irregular verbs *dar, conocer, hacer, poner, salir, traer,* and *ver.*
- recognize patterns in the verbs with irregular *yo* forms.
- form the stem-changing verbs *decir, oír, poder, venir,* and *querer.*
- express preferences using *querer.*
- combine *poder* with other infinitives.
- report on the activities of classmates.
- talk about the housing options available to Spaniards.

NATIONAL STANDARDS

Communication

The activities in the *Comunicación* section address Standard 1.1. Students can partner with class-mates and engage in conversations about their houses. A simple sum-mary sheet containing the vocabu-lary related to a house, the number of rooms, and/or its square footage can provide the basis for giving and obtaining information and exchang-ing opinions. Students can draw a diagram or write an inventory of the things in their house and pre-sent a short narration to the class using the new vocabulary (Standard 1.3). The students at their seats can listen to the presenter and compare their sum-mary sheet with the information given by the speaker (Standard 1.2).

NOTE FOR *La casa*

Remind students that across the Spanish-speaking world there are many variations in vocabulary depending on where you are and with whom you are speaking. For example, the English word "bed-room" can mean *dormitorio, la alcoba, la habitación, la recámara,* etc.

Comunicación

- Describing my house

VOCABULARIO 1   La casa

3-1 to 3-6

4:00

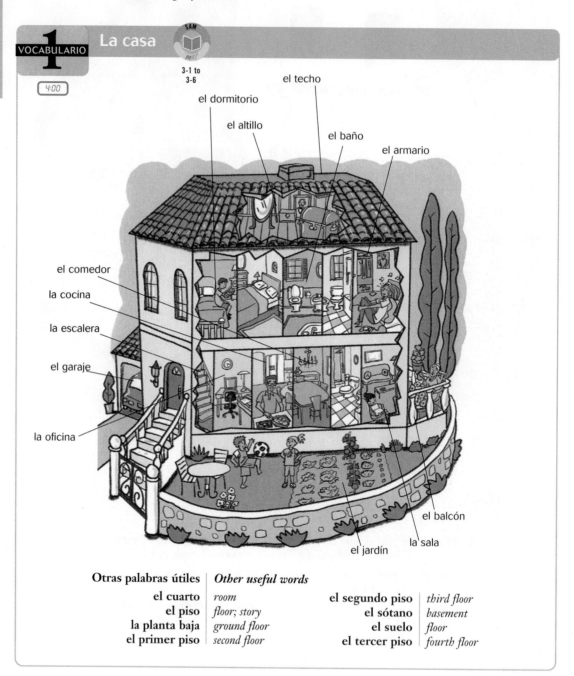

Otras palabras útiles	*Other useful words*		
el cuarto	*room*	**el segundo piso**	*third floor*
el piso	*floor; story*	**el sótano**	*basement*
la planta baja	*ground floor*	**el suelo**	*floor*
el primer piso	*second floor*	**el tercer piso**	*fourth floor*

METHODOLOGY • Teaching Vocabulary

With beginning language students, we believe in pre-senting vocabulary that is the most commonly used, and not giving many, if any, country/regional variations. Presenting several ways to say the same thing becomes too complicated for the novice learner. Having said that, as Spanish language instructors, we all know it is diffi-cult to determine exactly which words have the highest frequency of usage among Spanish-speakers in the world. In *¡Anda!* we have attempted to select what

appear to be the most commonly used words, but please feel free to use whatever words you may prefer. We encourage you to direct students to the *También se dice...* section in Appendix 3 for variations and additional vocabulary to enrich the basic *Vocabulario activo.*

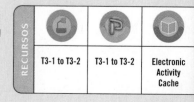

RECURSOS		
T3-1 to T3-2	T3-1 to T3-2	Electronic Activity Cache

PRONUNCIACIÓN `5:00`

CD 2
Track 1

3-7 to
3-9

The letters *h, j,* and *g*

1. The Spanish **h** is always silent and never pronounced.

   hombre   hola   hay   hora

2. The letter **j** is pronounced similar to the English *h* in *hot*.

   garaje   jardín   jueves   baja

3. The letter **g** is pronounced similar to the English *g* in *goal*, except when followed by *e* or *i*.

   garaje   globo   guitarra   gordo

   When **g** is followed by *e* or *i*, it is pronounced similar to the English *h* in *happy*.

   generalmente   gitano   agencia   agitado

3•1   **Las palabras**

Pronounce the following words, paying special attention to the letters **h, j,** and **g.**

1. hay
2. jardín
3. garaje
4. hospital
5. pongo
6. baja
7. generoso
8. ahora
9. guardar

> **Estrategia**
>
> Listen to the audio portion of your textbook prior to coming to class to practice the *h, j,* and *g* sounds.

3•2   **Las oraciones**

Pronounce the following sentences, paying special attention to the letters **h, j,** and **g.**

1. Hola, Javier. ¿Qué hay?
2. Gloria, tu guitarra está en el garaje.
3. Generalmente, me gustan los jueves en julio.

3•3   **Los dichos y refranes**

Now pronounce the following sayings and focus on the letters h, j, and g.

1. A la larga, lo más dulce amarga.
2. El hábito no hace el monje.

> **Estrategia**
>
> In *Capítulo 3* many of the directions for the activities are written in Spanish. New words that appear in the directions will be translated for you the first time they are used. Keep a list of those words to refer to; it helps you increase your vocabulary.

> Capítulo 2. El verbo *estar*, pág. 78.

3 4 ¿Dónde están?

`3:00`

Miren (*Look at*) el dibujo (*drawing*) de la casa en la página 100 y túrnense (*take turns*) para decir dónde están los siguientes (*following*) cuartos.

MODELO   E1:   el garaje

               E2:   *El garaje está en la planta baja.*

> **Fíjate**
>
> The first floor, or ground floor, is generally called *la planta baja; el primer piso* actually refers to the second floor. What is the third floor called?

	EN LA PLANTA BAJA	EN EL PRIMER PISO	EN EL SEGUNDO PISO
la sala	X		
el baño	X	X	
el dormitorio		X	
la cocina	X		
la oficina	X		
el altillo			X

3·5 Las partes de la casa

3:00

Dile (*Tell*) a tu compañero/a en qué parte de la casa haces (*you do*) las siguientes actividades.

MODELO estudiar
E1: *Yo estudio en la oficina. ¿Y tú?*
E2: *Yo estudio en mi dormitorio.*

1. hablar por teléfono
2. leer un libro
3. ver la televisión
4. organizar papeles
5. preparar enchiladas
6. tocar un instrumento
7. escuchar música
8. tomar el sol

3·6 ¿Y tu casa…?

5:00

Fíjate

In the directions, words like *miren, túrnense, comparen,* and *usen* are plural—they refer to both of you.

Túrnense para describir sus casas (o la de un miembro de su familia o amigo) y compararlas con la casa de la página 100. Usen el modelo para crear por lo menos (*at least*) **cinco** oraciones (*sentences*).

MODELO *En la casa del dibujo, la sala está en la planta baja y mi sala está en la planta baja también. En la casa del dibujo, el dormitorio está en el segundo piso, pero mi dormitorio está en la planta baja. No tenemos un altillo…*

NOTE FOR *La casa*

Remind students that when communicating with native speakers from different Spanish-speaking areas of the world, they can combine words that they may have learned already with new vocabulary to express their ideas. You can use the word *cuarto* to describe a room in general, and then tell what function the room has. For example, you can refer to a dining room as *un cuarto para comer.*

HERITAGE LANGUAGE LEARNERS

You might explain that for the true beginners in the class, you have been using more cognates, gestures, pictures, and speaking slightly slower than a native speaker would typically speak in order to facilitate their learning. You can tell the Heritage language learners that the pace of your speech and your word choice will change as the students acquire more Spanish.

HERITAGE LANGUAGE LEARNERS

Ask your Heritage language learners if they have any words related to the house that they use on a regular basis. Add those words to your vocabulary list so other students are familiar with them.

HERITAGE LANGUAGE LEARNERS

Your Heritage language learners may have a different concept of housing if they have spent time abroad with their families. Some families in Spain and Mexico, for example, are not considered wealthy by American standards, yet they have a summer chalet or a house in another part of the country where the family goes to spend time together. In many Spanish-speaking countries families have *empleadas domésticas* to help with the daily chores, but they are not the same type of personnel that we think of in the United States for those who are very wealthy (e.g. butlers, nannies, chauffeurs, cooks, gardeners, etc.).

METHODOLOGY • Writing

Research strongly supports our belief that class time should be spent engaging students almost exclusively in meaningful *oral* activities. Virtually all of the activities in *¡Anda!* are meant to be done orally in pairs or groups. This maximizes students' opportunities to speak and use Spanish in confidence-building *i+1* settings. Research confirms that strong oral skills translate into better writing skills. Therefore, students need a controlled environment to practice speaking so that outside of class, they will be more successful and confident writers.

3 7 Es una casa interesante...

Look at the photos and together, create a short description of one of the houses. Imagine the inside and the person(s) who may live there. Share your description with the class.

MODELO   *El apartamento está en Madrid en un edificio grande y tradicional. El apartamento es muy moderno. Tiene tres dormitorios, dos baños, una cocina pequeña, una sala grande y un balcón. Gastón y Patricia viven allí. No tienen hijos. Ellos trabajan en la ciudad.*

Vocabulario útil

antiguo/a	*old*	**humilde**	*humble*
la calle	*street*	**moderno/a**	*modern*
el campo	*country*	**nuevo/a**	*new*
la ciudad	*city*	**tradicional**	*traditional*
contemporáneo/a	*contemporary*	**viejo/a**	*old*

1.

2.

3.

4.

5.

6.

NOTE FOR 3–7

This activity exposes students to more variety on the subject of housing in the Spanish-speaking world. Further discussion may include housing in other parts of the Spanish-speaking world, the typical organization around the centralized urban state vs. provinces, economic disparity in Latin America, urban immigration and ghettos, etc.

Suggestion for 3–7 Remind students, or help them brainstorm, useful vocabulary they already know in addition to the *Vocabulario útil* listed, e.g., *alto, bajo, grande, pequeño, pobre, rico, bueno, malo, fuerte, débil, edificio,* etc.

Expansion for 3–7 Bring in a photo of a recognizable house or building, such as the White House, Trump Towers, or some other famous example of architecture in your area. Ask students to compare these buildings with the photos, or with the place in which they live.

Suggestion for *La casa* Encourage students to use this location strategy to learn the parts of a house: Imagine that you are in your house, or a house that is familiar to you, and you learn the vocabulary by arranging the list in the order that you see the rooms. You might enter through *la puerta*, then you see *la sala*, then *el comedor* and *la cocina*, and *el baño*. If you can, walk through the house and pronounce the vocabulary as you enter each room or hang a sign in each room with the corresponding vocabulary word. When it is time to take your test, close your eyes and remember the order in which you learned the rooms, just as they appear when you walk through them.

Additional activity for *La casa* Have your students create an architectural diagram or floor plan of the house or apartment where they grew up. Have them label the rooms in Spanish, using the correct definite articles. Along with labeling the rooms, they can write to whom the room belongs.

Additional activity for *La casa*. Give students the following list of "words" to unscramble.

MODELO   sipo
          piso

. louse   (suelo)
. reascale   (escalera)
. oñba   (baño)
. alas   (sala)
. naiciof   (oficina)
. mocored   (comedor)

Additional activity for *La casa* Play Twenty Questions with the parts of the house and the furniture. Hide a picture or a flashcard of the vocabulary word. Students can only ask questions that have yes or no answers. Model questions using the verb *hay,* such as *¿hay agua?, ¿hay mesas?, ¿hay una cama?,* etc.

NOTE FOR *Algunos verbos irregulares*

These common irregular verbs have been grouped by similarities—irregular *yo* forms, verbs with first-person "go" endings, and four stem-changing verbs. *Poder* and *querer* are included here because they are useful in practicing chapter vocabulary. They will also serve as a point of reference when stem-changing verbs are presented in *Capítulo 4*.

NOTE FOR *Algunos verbos irregulares*

The students who studied Spanish in high school might have learned about "shoe verbs" or "boot verbs." If you use the *vosotros/as* forms in your teaching, you might want to arrange the verb charts in two columns, with the singular forms on the left and the plural forms on the right. Then, you can draw a circle around the forms that change (excluding *nosotros/as* and *vosotros/as*) to form a boot or shoe. This helps students to remember which forms change and which do not.

If you are practicing with the *vosotros/as* forms in your class, point out that the verbs *dar* and *ver* have no accent in the *vosotros/as* forms.

NOTE FOR *Conocer*

We have chosen to introduce *conocer* in *Capítulo 3* as an irregular verb and to focus on the meaning "to be acquainted with." In *Capítulo 4 saber* is presented and contrasted with *conocer*.

METHODOLOGY • Teacher Talk

Although we simplify our spoken language in class in order to stay within the range of *i + 1*, we should strive to speak at a speed as close to natural as possible. Gradually increase speed as the semester progresses.

GRAMÁTICA 2 — Algunos verbos irregulares

3-10 to 3-15   13, 14

5:00

Estrategia

Memorizing information is easier to do when the information is arranged in chunks. You will notice that some of the *yo* forms end in *-go*, such as *salgo*, *traigo*, and *pongo*. Learning the information as a chunk of "go" verbs may make it easier to remember.

Look at the present tense forms of the verbs below. Notice that they all follow the same patterns that you learned in **Capítulo 2** to form the present tense of regular verbs, *except* in the **yo** form.

	dar (*to give*)	conocer (*to be acquainted with*)	hacer (*to do; to make*)	poner (*to put; to place*)
yo	doy	conozco	hago	pongo
tú	das	conoces	haces	pones
él, ella, Ud.	da	conoce	hace	pone
nosotros/as	damos	conocemos	hacemos	ponemos
vosotros/as	dais	conocéis	hacéis	ponéis
ellos/as, Uds.	dan	conocen	hacen	ponen

Estrategia

Organize the new verbs you are learning in your notebook. Note whether the verb is regular or irregular, what it means in English, if any of the forms have accents, and if any other verbs follow this pattern. You might want to highlight or color code the verbs that follow a pattern.

	salir (*to leave; to go out*)	traer (*to bring*)	ver (*to see*)
yo	salgo	traigo	veo
tú	sales	traes	ves
él, ella, Ud.	sale	trae	ve
nosotros/as	salimos	traemos	vemos
vosotros/as	salís	traéis	veis
ellos/as, Uds.	salen	traen	ven

Quiero comprar esta casa. ¿Qué dices?

Me gusta. ¡Yo digo que sí!

Capítulo 1. El verbo *tener*, pág. 35.

Two additional groups of very common irregular verbs follow. Note that **venir** is formed like **tener**.

	decir (*to say; to tell*)	**oír** (*to hear*)	**venir** (*to come*)
yo	digo	oigo	vengo
tú	dices	oyes	vienes
él, ella, Ud.	dice	oye	viene
nosotros/as	decimos	oímos	venimos
vosotros/as	decís	oís	venís
ellos/as, Uds.	dicen	oyen	vienen

	poder (*to be able to*)	**querer** (*to want; to love*)
yo	puedo	quiero
tú	puedes	quieres
él, ella, Ud.	puede	quiere
nosotros/as	podemos	queremos
vosotros/as	podéis	queréis
ellos/as, Uds.	pueden	quieren

5:00

3·8 La ruleta

How competitive are you? Listen as your instructor explains how to play this fast-paced game designed to practice the new verb forms. When you finish with this list, repeat the activity with different verbs and include **estar**, **ser**, and **tener**.

1. traer
2. hacer
3. oír
4. querer
5. conocer
6. dar
7. decir
8. venir
9. poder
10. poner
11. ver
12. salir

CAPÍTULO 3

INSTRUCTIONS FOR 3–8

Form groups of two to four students. Each group will need either a die or a small piece of paper on which numbers one through six have been written. Number 1 = *yo*; 2 = *tú*; 3 = *él, ella*; 4 = *Ud.*; 5 = *nosotros, nosotras*; 6 = *ellos, ellas*. The first person in the group rolls the die (or selects a numbered piece of paper) and gives the correct verb form, matching the number rolled. Other group members must verify the answer. After the correct verb form is given, the player passes the die to the next person. Players continue until the forms come quickly and automatically.

You may wish to keep 10 dice on hand to provide students for activities like **3–8**.

Suggestion for 3–8 Repeat the activity and include *tocar, mirar, trabajar, comprender*, etc.

Additional activity: *Jugar a la pelota* Use a softball or make one out of paper. Say an infinitive and a subject, then toss the ball to a student. The student must give the correct form of the verb. At this point, you can either remain in control of the ball by having the student toss it back to you so that you can continue as before, or students can take over the game. If students take control, then the one who catches the ball and gives the correct answer (sometimes with some coaching by the teacher or other students) then says another infinitive and subject and tosses the ball to a different student, who must give the correct verb form.

Be sure to say the infinitive and subject before tossing the ball so that all students formulate the answer instead of only the one who catches the ball.

NOTE FOR 3–8

Activities like *La ruleta* and *Jugar a la pelota* can be used regularly in class. The first time you give directions, a more detailed explanation may be required, but thereafter, setup for the activity is minimal.

METHODOLOGY • Direction Lines

Beginning in this chapter, direction lines will be in Spanish if they are *i+1*. The nomenclature *i+1* comes from research by Stephen Krashen known as the Input Hypothesis. (See Krashen, Stephen. *Principles and Practice in Second Language Acquisition*. New York: Pergamon Press, 1982, pp. 9–32). The Input Hypothesis states that learners can comprehend input (language) based on words they already know plus a few additional words they may not know but can intuit from context. A level higher than *i+1* is not comprehensible; it causes confusion and frustrates many learners, causing them to shut down to a point where they cannot comprehend anything. By the end of the first semester, virtually all direction lines will be in Spanish.

Suggestion for 3–10 *Paso 3* could also be used to follow up and summarize group work.

METHODOLOGY • Teaching Techniques

Most of the vocabulary and grammar activities are designed to be completed either in pairs or small groups. Krashen's Affective Filter Hypothesis states that students need a non-threatening environment, and having students work with each other provides just such an environment.

HERITAGE LANGUAGE LEARNERS

Remind students that *salir* is generally used with prepositions. A few common examples are:

salir de   to leave from
salir con to go out with
salir por to leave for an errand; to leave through (e.g., a window or door)
salir para to leave for (destination)

3·00

3·9 Combinaciones

Forma oraciones lógicas combinando los elementos de las dos columnas. Compara tus oraciones con las de tu compañero/a (*with those of your partner*).

1. ___f___ Hoy mis hermanos…
2. ___d___ Mis amigos y yo…
3. ___a___ Mi abuelo…
4. ___g___ Quiero…
5. ___h___ Mi perro (*dog*)…
6. ___b___ Mi profesor/a…
7. ___c___ Yo…
8. ___e___ Tú….

a. pone sus recuerdos (*mementos*) en el altillo.
b. conoce bien la arquitectura de España.
c. oigo música en la sala.
d. hacemos fiestas en el jardín.
e. ves la televisión en tu dormitorio.
f. no pueden salir de casa.
g. una casa con dos pisos, tres baños y un garaje.
h. siempre viene a la cocina para comer.

12·00

3·10 Otras combinaciones

Completa los siguientes pasos.

Paso 1 Escribe una oración con cada (*each*) verbo, combinando elementos de las tres columnas.

MODELO (A) nosotros, (B) hacer, (C) la tarea en la oficina
Nosotros hacemos la tarea en la oficina.

 Paso 2 En grupos de tres, lean las oraciones y corrijan (*correct*) los errores.

 Paso 3 Escriban juntos (*together*) **dos** oraciones nuevas y compártanlas (*share them*) con la clase.

COLUMNA A	COLUMNA B	COLUMNA C
Uds.	(no) hacer	estudiar ciencias
mamá y papá	(no) ver	programas interesantes en la
yo	(no) conocer	televisión los domingos
tú	(no) oír	de Madrid mañana
el profesor	(no) querer	la tarea en el dormitorio
nosotros/as	(no) salir	mis libros a clase
ellos/ellas	(no) traer	ruidos (*noises*) en el altillo
		por la noche
		bien el arte de España

3·11 Confesiones

Time for true confessions! Take turns asking each other how often you do the following things.

siempre (*always*)   a menudo (*often*)   a veces (*sometimes*)   nunca (*never*)

Capítulo 2. La formación de preguntas y las palabras interrogativas, pág. 71.

MODELO venir tarde (*late*) a la clase de español

> E1: *¿Vienes tarde a la clase de español?*
> E2: *Nunca vengo tarde a la clase de español. ¿Y tú?*
> E1: *Yo vengo tarde a veces.*

1. querer estudiar
2. oír lo que (*what*) dice tu profesor/a
3. poder contestar las preguntas de tu profesor/a de español
4. escuchar música en la clase de español
5. hacer preguntas tontas en clase
6. traer tus libros a la clase
7. salir temprano (*early*) de tus clases
8. querer comer en la sala para ver la televisión

3·12 Firma aquí

Complete the following steps.

Paso 1 Circulate around the room asking your classmates appropriate questions using the cues provided. Ask those who answer **sí** to sign in the chart.

Fíjate

Part of the enjoyment of learning another language is getting to know other people. Your instructor structures your class so that you have many opportunities to work with different classmates.

MODELO venir a clase todos los días

> E1: *Roberto, ¿vienes a clase todos los días?*
> E2: *No, no vengo a clase todos los días.*
> E1: *Amanda, ¿vienes a clase todos los días?*
> E3: *Sí, vengo a clase todos los días.*
> E1: *Muy bien. Firma aquí, por favor.* ___*Amanda*___

¿QUIÉN...?	
1. ver la televisión todas las noches	_____
2. hacer la tarea siempre	_____
3. salir con los amigos los jueves por la noche	_____
4. estar enfermo/a hoy	_____
5. conocer Madrid	_____
6. poder estudiar con música fuerte (*loud*)	_____
7. querer ser arquitecto	_____
8. tener una nota muy buena en la clase de español	_____

Paso 2 Report some of your information to the class.

MODELO *Joe ve la televisión todas las noches. Toni siempre hace la tarea. Chad está enfermo hoy.*

Suggestion for 3–11 Remind students that for activity **3–11**, they can confess what other people do. Sometimes shy students are more willing to participate if they can talk about other people, instead of themselves. They could say *yo no vengo tarde, pero mi hermana siempre viene tarde.* That way they also practice the other verb forms.

Suggestion for 3–12 As a follow-up, instead of just asking questions such as: *¿Quién ve la televisión todas las noches?* also ask *¿Quiénes ven la televisión todas las noches?* Or, after gathering some answers, check to make sure students are listening by asking questions like *¿Tom ve la televisión todas las noches?¿Shirley y Steve ven la televisión todas las noches?*

CAPÍTULO 3

8:00   **ii 3·13 Entrevista**

Complete the following steps.

Paso 1   Ask a classmate you do not know the following questions. Then change roles.

1. ¿Con quién(es) haces ejercicio? ¿Dónde?
2. ¿Cuándo ves la televisión? ¿Cuál es tu programa favorito?
3. ¿Con quiénes sales los fines de semana (*weekends*)? ¿Qué hacen Uds.?
4. ¿Qué días vienes a la clase de español? ¿A qué hora?
5. ¿Dónde pones tus libros? ¿Quién pone un examen en tu escritorio?
6. ¿Siempre dices la verdad?

Paso 2   Share a few of the things you have learned about your classmate with the class.

MODELO   *Mi compañero sale los fines de semana con sus amigos y no hace ejercicio.*

6:00   SAM   **¿Dónde viven los españoles?**

3-16

En Madrid, la capital de España, al igual que en Barcelona, una ciudad cosmopolita en el noreste del país, la vida es tan rápida y vibrante como en la ciudad de Nueva York y otras grandes ciudades. Muchas personas viven en pisos (apartamentos) en edificios grandes, mientras que muchas otras viven ahora en las afueras (*outskirts*) en complejos (grupos) de casas llamados «urbanizaciones», y van a la ciudad para trabajar. Para muchas personas, el costo de vivir en los centros urbanos resulta demasiado caro. Para otras, es preferible vivir donde la vida es un poco más tranquila y tener algo de naturaleza (*nature*) cerca de su vivienda.

Sin embargo (*Nevertheless*), en los pueblos pequeños y en el campo la vida es diferente. Generalmente, las casas son bajas y algunas (*some*) tienen corrales con animales. Muchas personas se dedican a la agricultura y la vida es más lenta.

Preguntas

1. ¿Dónde viven generalmente las personas que residen en Barcelona y en Madrid? ¿Qué es una urbanización? Viven en pisos/apartamentos. Una urbanización es un grupo de casas en las afueras de una ciudad.
2. ¿Dónde prefieres vivir tú, en el campo o en la ciudad? *Answers may vary.*

3 VOCABULARIO — Los muebles y otros objetos de la casa

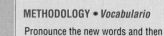

4:00

3-17 to
3-21

MUEBLES SÁNCHEZ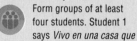

La sala y el comedor

el estante de libros
la lámpara
275€
el sillón
184€
899€
875€
1.200€ — el sofá
185€
400€
185€
148€
la alfombra

El baño

la ducha
222€
el lavabo
la bañera
387€
426€ 221€ 189€
el inodoro   el bidet

El dormitorio

el tocador
la almohada
450€
35€
36€
150€
42€
824€
las sábanas
la colcha   la manta   la cama

La cocina

el microondas   el refrigerador
295€
619€
875€
la estufa
479€
el lavaplatos

Otras palabras útiles	Other useful words		
amueblado/a	*furnished*	el mueble	*piece of furniture*
el armario	*armoire; closet; cabinet*	los muebles	*furniture*
la cosa	*thing*	el objeto	*object*
el cuadro	*picture; painting*	la planta	*plant*

METHODOLOGY • *Vocabulario*

Pronounce the new words and then have students repeat after you, both chorally and individually. You may also ask them to point to the part of the drawing in their books that represents each new word. Overhead transparencies and computer slides are another way to verify meaning and practice pronunciation, by pointing to different items and having students say the Spanish word that corresponds.

Suggestion for *Los muebles* Point out in the drawing of the faucets that "C" does not mean "cold" but rather "hot" (*caliente*) and "F" means "cold" (*fría*).

Additional activity for *Los muebles*
Form groups of at least four students. Student 1 says *Vivo en una casa que tiene...* and inserts something relevant. Student 2 says the phrase, inserting what his or her own house has, and then repeats what Student 1 has.

Modelo
E1 *Vivo en una casa que tiene un jardín grande.*
E2 *Vivo en una casa que tiene una estufa y un jardín grande.*
E3 *Vivo en una casa que tiene tres camas, una estufa y un jardín grande.*
Have students continue to see how many rooms or things in a house they can add.

Capítulo 1. El verbo *tener*, pág. 35.

NOTE FOR 3–14

Instruct students to organize their descriptions by rooms. They may also choose to describe their dorm rooms or apartments rather than their family homes.

[4:00]

3 · 14   En mi casa

Túrnense para describir qué muebles y objetos tienen en sus casas.

MODELO   E1: *Yo tengo una cama y dos sillas en mi dormitorio. ¿Qué tienes tú?*

E2: *Yo tengo una cama, un cuadro, una lámpara y un televisor. ¿Qué tienes en tu cocina?*

[4:00]

3 · 15   El dormitorio de Cecilia

Mira (*Look at*) la foto y con un/a compañero/a determina dónde está cada objeto.

Fíjate

The preposition *de* combines with the masculine definite article *el* to form the contraction *del*. The feminine article *la* does not contract. Note the following examples.

El tocador está a la derecha **de la** puerta.   *The dresser is to the right of the door.*

El tocador está a la derecha **del** armario.   *The dresser is to the right of the closet.*

MODELO   E1: ¿Dónde está el cuadro?

E2: *El cuadro está en la pared a la derecha de la cama, al lado de la lámpara.*

¿Dónde está(n)…?

1. la cama
2. el armario
3. las lámparas
4. los sillones
5. la puerta
6. el estante

Vocabulario útil

a la derecha (de)	*to the right (of)*
a la izquierda (de)	*to the left (of)*
al lado (de)	*beside*
encima (de)	*on top (of)*

Capítulo 2. El verbo
gustar, pág. 82.

8:00

3·16 ¿Quieres una casa estupenda?

You have received a grant to study abroad in Sevilla, Spain! Now you need a place to live. Look at the three apartment ads below and select one of them. Give your partner at least **three** reasons for your choice. Use expressions like **Me gusta(n)… o Tiene un/una…** Be creative!

MODELO   *Me gusta el edificio nuevo y tiene muebles. No me gustan…*

> Piso. Plaza de Cuba, Los Remedios. Edificio nuevo: dos dormitorios, baño, cocina, sala grande y balcón. Amueblado. 750€ al mes. Tel. 95 446 04 55.

> Piso. Colonia San Luis. Sala, cocina, dormitorio y baño. Sin muebles. 400€ al mes. Tel. 95 448 85 32.

> Alquilo piso de lujo en casa patio rehabilitada del siglo XVIII. Dos plantas, sala, cocina con zona de comedor, baño y dormitorio. Totalmente amueblado (junto a la Plaza Nueva, a dos minutos de la Catedral, Alcázar). Para más información por favor ponte en contacto con Teresa Rivas. Tel. 95 422 47 03.

¿Cómo andas?

Having completed the first **Comunicación,** I now can…

	Feel Confident	Need to Review
• describe my house and some of the items in it (p. 100)	❑	❑
• pronounce the letters **h, j,** and **g** properly in Spanish (p. 101)	❑	❑
• say and write the forms of the irregular **yo** verbs **dar, conocer, hacer, poner, salir, traer,** and **ver** and say what they mean (p. 104)	❑	❑
• create a simple sentence with each of the irregular **yo** verbs (p. 104)	❑	❑
• say and write the forms of the irregular verbs **decir, oír, venir, poder,** and **querer** (p. 105)	❑	❑
• create a simple sentence with the irregular verbs above (p. 105)	❑	❑
• describe some of the types of homes where Spaniards live (p. 108)	❑	❑

Expansion for 3–16 Ask students to write an ad to "sell" their own apartment or the apartment of a friend or family member.

CAPÍTULO 3

SECTION GOALS FOR
Comunicación

By the end of the *Comunicación* section, students will be able to:

- talk about household chores.
- discuss responsibilities and obligations using *tener + que + infinitive*.
- summarize daily activities related to running a household.
- compare their household chores with the chores of other students.
- talk about the role of women in the Spanish-speaking world.
- identify colors and use adjectives to modify nouns.
- inventory the contents of a house, including appliances and accessories.
- compare aspects of their house with the houses of classmates.
- experience Dalí's house by taking a virtual tour.
- use idiomatic expressions with *tener* to express feelings.
- write the numbers 1,000–100,000,000.
- review the numbers 0–999.
- report the price and features of a property for sale.
- analyze the population data of Spanish cities.
- budget euros and use the budget to furnish a house.
- recognize the meaning and uses of *hay*.
- listen for specific details about the rooms of a house.
- inventory the items in the classroom.

NATIONAL STANDARDS
Communication

Students can use household chores and everyday activities such as cleaning as a starting point for conversation. They engage in conversations comparing what types of chores they do, what responsibilities they have, how often they do specific chores, and their likes and dislikes (Standard 1.1). This topic lends itself well to exchanging opinions and providing and obtaining information, through interviews, signature activities, presentations or TPR modeling in front of the class, and role plays. One effective way of using role plays in this situation to elicit communication is to pair students and have one student be the parent and have the other student be the child. The division of household labor and the equities or inequities involved are familiar situations in most families.

Comunicación

- Talking about household chores   - Describing places and certain feelings

VOCABULARIO 4 — Los quehaceres de la casa

3-22 to 3-24

4:00

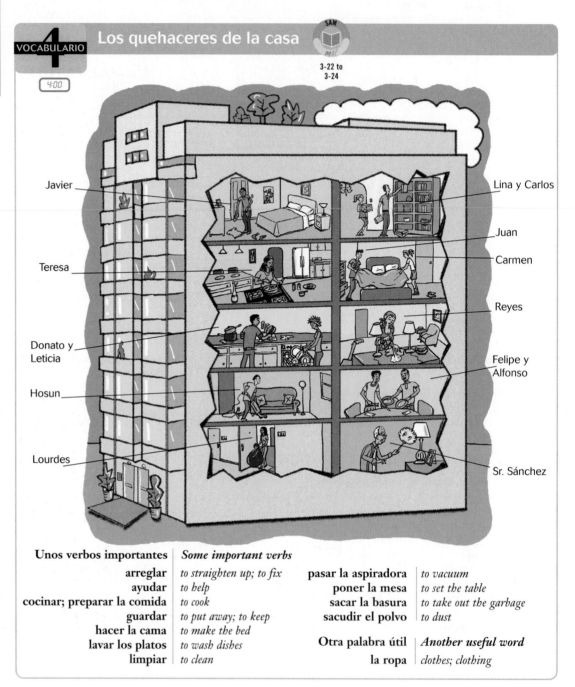

Unos verbos importantes	*Some important verbs*		
arreglar	*to straighten up; to fix*	**pasar la aspiradora**	*to vacuum*
ayudar	*to help*	**poner la mesa**	*to set the table*
cocinar; preparar la comida	*to cook*	**sacar la basura**	*to take out the garbage*
guardar	*to put away; to keep*	**sacudir el polvo**	*to dust*
hacer la cama	*to make the bed*		
lavar los platos	*to wash dishes*	**Otra palabra útil**	*Another useful word*
limpiar	*to clean*	**la ropa**	*clothes; clothing*

T3-5	T3-5	Electronic Activity Cache

RECURSOS

Answers to 3-17.
1. El Sr. Sánchez sacude el polvo.
2. Hosun pasa la aspiradora.
3. Javier arregla su dormitorio.
4. Reyes sacude el polvo y limpia la casa.
5. Donato y Leticia lavan los platos.
6. Lourdes saca la basura.
7. Lina y Carlos guardan los libros.
8. Teresa cocina/prepara la comida.
9. Felipe y Alfonso ponen la mesa.
10. Juan y Carmen hacen la cama.

3·17 ¡Mucho trabajo!

Mira el dibujo en la página 112 y con un/a compañero/a determina qué hacen las personas de la lista.

MODELO   E1:   Carmen
     E2:   *Carmen hace la cama.*

1. El Sr. Sánchez
2. Hosun
3. Javier
4. Reyes
5. Donato y Leticia
6. Lourdes
7. Lina y Carlos
8. Teresa
9. Felipe y Alfonso
10. Juan y Carmen

3·18 Responsabilidades

¿Cuáles son tus responsabilidades? ¿Cuánto tiempo dedicas a (*do you devote to*) estas tareas? ¿Cuándo? Completa el cuadro y comparte (*share*) oralmente tu información con un/a compañero/a.

Fíjate

The expression *tener que* + infinitive means "to have to do" something ¿*Qué tienes que hacer?* means "What do you have to do?" Later in this chapter you will learn more expressions with *tener*.

Vocabulario útil

desordenado/a	*messy*
limpio/a	*clean*
sucio/a	*dirty*
tener que + (*infinitive*)	*to have to (do something)*

MODELO   *Tengo que limpiar y arreglar mi dormitorio los lunes. Dedico dos horas porque está muy sucio.*

LUGAR	¿QUÉ TIENES QUE HACER?	¿CUÁNDO?	¿CUÁNTO TIEMPO DEDICAS?
1. mi dormitorio	limpiar y arreglar	el lunes	dos horas
2. el baño			
3. la cocina			
4. la sala			
5. el garaje			
6. el comedor			

Suggestion for 3–17 and 3–18 Pair students by the household chore they like the least, or by the appliance they could least/most live without.

NOTE FOR 3–18

Explain that days of the week are plural when talking in general, e.g., *los lunes* for "on Mondays" or *Limpio el apartamento los sábados.*

METHODOLOGY • *Tener + que + infinitive*

Tener + que + infinitive is introduced lexically in actividad **3–18** and then reinforced in *Capítulo 4.*

NATIONAL STANDARDS

Communication, Cultures, Comparisons.

The readings offer students two different examples of a modern Hispanic woman. The summary allows students to understand and interpret written Spanish (Standard 1.2) while explaining the social, cultural, and political implications of these women and their achievements. The first reading highlights how the practices of General Pinochet reflected the culture and political climate of the dictatorship. This, in turn, shaped the history of the country and later one of Pinochet's exiles became the first Chilean female president. This brief passage about Bachelet Jeria is an example of the practices and perspectives of Chile (Standard 2.1). In the United States, there has never been a female president or vice-president. Historically, Americans have elected a male, married president. Students can make comparisons between the political systems of the present and past in the United States and Chile (democracy and dictatorship). (Standard 4.2).

METHODOLOGY • Reading

You can introduce the reading in class and have students complete it at home, along with *Preguntas*. Then in class you can emphasize points and discuss the answers to *Preguntas*.

8:00　3-25 to 3-26

Las mujeres del mundo hispano

The roles of women in the Spanish-speaking world have changed dramatically in the past decades. Their quest for emancipation began somewhat later than in the United States. It has become more common for Hispanic women worldwide to work outside the home, own their own businesses, and have positions of responsibility, influence, and power. *El movimiento de las mujeres* is further along in the more industrialized Spanish-speaking countries.

These Hispanic women have achieved international recognition in different fields.

Verónica Michelle Bachelet Jeria (n. 1951), elegida presidenta de Chile en marzo de 2006.

Illy Nes (n. 1973), autora y periodista catalana.

Fue (*She was*) torturada y exiliada durante la dictadura del general Pinochet en Chile. Después de vivir en Australia y Alemania, vuelve a su país natal para trabajar como médica. Luego entra en el campo de la política. Habla español, francés, inglés y alemán. Es la primera mujer que sirve como presidenta en la historia del país.

Los temas de sus obras y de su trabajo como periodista y entrevistadora (*interviewer*) son el feminismo y la sexualidad. Ha recibido el premio (*She received the award*) Bigayles International dos veces: en 2000 por su novela *Morbo*, escrita a los quince años, y en 2004 por *Hijas de Adán: las mujeres también salen del armario*, una investigación de la homosexualidad dentro del mundo de las personas famosas.

Preguntas

1. ¿Por qué son importantes estas mujeres?　Verónica Michelle Bachelet Jeria es la primera mujer en servir como presidenta de Chile; Illy Nes ha recibido el premio Bigayles Internacional dos veces.
2. ¿Quiénes son otras mujeres hispanas famosas?　*Answers may vary but could include:* Nancy López, Arantxa Sánchez, Isabel Allende, Carolina Herrera, Antonia Novello, Ellen Ochoa, etc.

VOCABULARIO 5 — Los colores

3:00

3-27 to
3-29

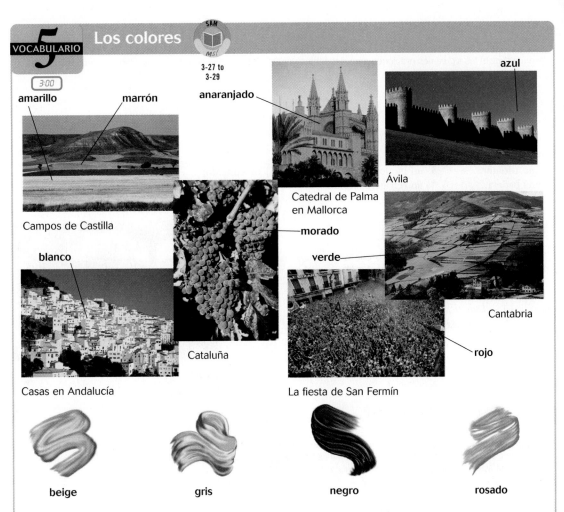

amarillo

marrón

Campos de Castilla

anaranjado

Catedral de Palma en Mallorca

azul

Ávila

blanco

morado

verde

Casas en Andalucía

Cataluña

La fiesta de San Fermín

Cantabria

rojo

beige

gris

negro

rosado

¿De qué color es...?   *What color is...?*

Colors are descriptive adjectives, and as such, they must agree with the noun they describe in number and gender.

- Adjectives ending in **-o** have four forms.

  rojo   roja   rojos   rojas

- Adjectives ending in a vowel other than **-o,** or in a consonant, have two forms.

  verde   verdes
  azul   azules

La casa es blanca y tiene un techo rojo.
Las casas son blancas y tienen techos rojos.
Tengo un armario marrón.
Tengo una alfombra marrón.
Tengo dos sillones marrones.

The house is white and has a red roof.
The houses are white and have red roofs.
I have a brown armoire.
I have a brown rug.
I have two brown armchairs.

How would you say "a black refrigerator," "a white sofa," "a green kitchen," and "some yellow chairs"?

Suggestion for *Los colores* Ask students to identify any additional colors they see in the photos.

NOTE FOR *Los colores*

Although "beige" is spelled the same in both English and Spanish, reinforce the proper Spanish pronunciation.

Expansion for *Los colores* For further practice with colors, use the photos *El dormitorio de Cecilia*, from activity **3-15**, and *La sala de Luis*, activity **3-20**. Ask specific questions like *¿Qué colores ves en la foto?, ¿De qué color es la alfombra?, ¿De qué color es la lámpara?*, or ask students to describe the two rooms orally and/or in writing.

Additional questions: *¿De qué color es tu dormitorio? ¿De qué color es tu silla favorita? ¿Qué color te gusta más? ¿Qué color no te gusta?*, etc.

Answer to question in *Los colores* presentation *Un refrigerador negro, un sofá blanco, una cocina verde, unas sillas amarillas.*

HERITAGE LANGUAGE LEARNERS

Remind students that so far they have been using colors as descriptive adjectives. They are also used as nouns when they do not describe an object, just as in English, e.g., the brown one (*el marrón*), the blue ones (*los azules*), etc.

Additional activity for *Los colores*

Túrnense para decir cuáles son sus colores favoritos y qué cosas de esos (*those*) colores hay en la sala de clase.

MODELO
E1   *Mis colores favoritos son el marrón, el azul y el verde. En la clase hay veinte escritorios marrones, un libro azul y una planta verde.*
E2   *Sí, y también hay una puerta marrón.*

RECURSOS

T3-6 to T3-7 | T3-6 to T3-7 | Electronic Activity Cache

CAPÍTULO 3

Suggestion for 3–21 This activity can be assigned as homework. Ask students to bring in photos from magazines, etc. Bring extra photos of your own in case some students forget theirs.

For additional practice, repeat the activity with other photos students bring in or have students pass their photos to someone else.

Suggestion for 3–22 Assign actividad **3–22** for homework. Students should bring answers to class to compare them with classmates' answers.

Additional activity for *Los colores*

 Assign students to work in groups of three. *Estudiante 1* selects a color and identifies something in the classroom with that color. *Estudiante 2* names something else that is the same color. *Estudiante 3* does the same. A student who cannot respond is "out." The last person left chooses the color for the next round.

MODELO
E1 *Veo una mochila roja.*
E2 *Veo un cuaderno rojo.*
E3 *Veo unos libros rojos.*
E1 *…*

3·19 La casa ideal [5:00]

Termina (*Finish*) las siguientes oraciones para describir tu casa ideal, incluyendo los colores. Comparte tus respuestas con un/a compañero/a.

MODELO E1: Quiero una casa con…   una cocina…
            E2: *Quiero una casa con una cocina amarilla.*

Quiero una casa con…

1. una alfombra…   3. un inodoro y un lavabo…   5. un comedor…   7. un techo
2. una bañera…   4. un refrigerador…   6. unos sillones…   8. ¿?

3·20 ¿Cómo son? [5:00]

Túrnense para comparar la sala de Luis con la tuya (*yours*) o la sala de un/a amigo/a. Usen los verbos **ser** y **tener**.

MODELO E1: *Luis tiene una sala grande pero yo tengo una sala pequeña.*
            E2: *La sala de Luis es grande y mi sala es grande también.*

La sala de Luis

3·21 Buena memoria [4:00]

Bring in colorful pictures of a house or rooms in a house. Select one picture and take a minute to study it carefully. Turn it over and relate to a partner as much detail as you can remember about the picture, especially pertaining to colors. Then listen to your partner talk about his or her picture. Who remembers more?

3·22 En la casa de Dalí [5:00]

Go to your *¡Anda!* web site to take a virtual tour of the home of the famous Spanish artist Salvador Dalí, el Castillo Gala Dalí in Púbol, Spain. While you are exploring his house, answer the following questions. Then compare your answers with those of a classmate.

El Castillo Gala Dalí

1. ¿Qué ves en el jardín?   Veo una piscina.
2. ¿Cuántas puertas tiene el salón de los escudos (*coats of arms*)? Tiene cinco puertas.
3. ¿Qué ves a la izquierda de la puerta cerrada en el salón de escudos?   Veo una silla.
4. ¿Qué muebles ves en el salón del piano? Veo tres sillones, un piano y dos puertas.
5. ¿Qué muebles ves en la biblioteca? ¿Cuántos cuadros ves? Veo un sofá grande y una mesa. Veo dos o tres cuadros.
6. ¿Cuáles son los colores principales que ves en la habitación de los invitados?   Los colores principales son rosado, blanco y amarillo.
7. ¿Ves algo (*something*) diferente o extraño en el comedor? No veo/no tiene sillas.
8. ¿De qué color son las paredes de la casa? Las paredes son blancas.

GRAMÁTICA 6 — Unas expresiones con *tener*

3-30 to
3-32

Susana

Rosario   Alicia

Beatriz   Julián

Pilar

Jorge   Ramón   Roberto

Carmen   David

The verb **tener,** besides meaning *to have,* is used in a variety of expressions.

tener… años	*to be… years old*	**tener miedo**	*to be afraid*
tener calor	*to be hot*	**tener prisa**	*to be in a hurry*
tener cuidado	*to be careful*	**tener razón**	*to be right*
tener éxito	*to be successful*	**tener sed**	*to be thirsty*
tener frío	*to be cold*	**tener sueño**	*to be sleepy*
tener ganas de + (*infinitive*)	*to feel like* + (*verb*)	**tener suerte**	*to be lucky*
tener hambre	*to be hungry*	**tener vergüenza**	*to be embarrassed*

—Mamá, **tengo hambre.** ¿Cuándo comemos?   *Mom, I'm hungry. When are we eating?*
—**Tienes suerte,** hijo. Salimos para   *You are lucky, son. We are leaving*
  el restaurante Tío Tapas en diez minutos.   *for Tío Tapas Restaurant in ten minutes.*

Fíjate

You have learned that some words in Spanish, like the color *amarillo,* have four forms (masculine singular, feminine singular, masculine plural, feminine plural). When you use the *tener* expressions like *tener frío* or *tener éxito,* you do not change the *o* of *frío* or *éxito* to make it feminine or plural.

Suggestion for *Unas expresiones con* tener Practice expressions with directed questions, such as *¿Qué no tienes ganas de hacer los lunes?,* *¿Cuándo tienes hambre?, ¿Cuándo tienes sueño?, ¿Cuántos años tienes?, ¿En qué meses tienes frío?, ¿En qué meses tienes calor?,* etc.

Suggestion for 3–23 and 3–24
Encourage students to take turns reading the sentences that they created aloud as they compare their answers.

NOTE FOR 3–24
Be sure that your students pay special attention to the *Modelos*. In this activity, students are doing more than matching; they are creating sentences.

Answers to 3-23.
Possible answers include:
Susana tiene 21 años.
Rosario tiene prisa.
Alicia tiene que estudiar.
Julián tiene suerte/éxito.
Beatriz tiene miedo.
Pilar tiene cuidado.
Jorge, Ramón y Roberto tienen frío.
Carmen tiene sed.
David tiene hambre.

`4:00`

3·23 ¿Qué pasa?

Mira los dibujos de la página 117 y, con un/a compañero/a, crea una oración para cada persona. Usa expresiones con **tener.**

MODELO   *Beatriz tiene miedo.*

`4:00`

3·24 ¿Qué haces cuando…?

¿Qué haces en casa en las siguientes situaciones? Contesta combinando los elementos de las dos columnas de la forma más lógica. Compara tus respuestas con las de un/a compañero/a.

MODELO   E1: tener ganas de descansar   ver la televisión
          E2: *Cuando tengo ganas de descansar, veo la televisión.*

Cuando…

1. __b__ tener hambre
2. __d__ tener suerte
3. __f__ tener miedo
4. __e__ tener prisa
5. __g__ tener frío
6. __a__ tener éxito
7. __c__ tener sed

a. estar muy feliz
b. preparar comida en la cocina
c. hacer una limonada
d. no tener que limpiar la casa
e. salir rápidamente en mi coche
f. llamar a la policía
g. tomar el sol en el jardín

`4:00`

3·25 ¿Qué tengo yo?

Expresa cómo te sientes (*you feel*) en las siguientes ocasiones usando (*using*) expresiones con **tener.** Compara tus respuestas con las de un/a compañero/a.

MODELO   E1: antes de comer
          E2: *Antes de comer tengo hambre.*

1. temprano en la mañana Temprano en la mañana tengo sueño.
2. los viernes por la tarde Los viernes por la tarde tengo ganas de salir.
3. después de correr mucho Después de correr mucho tengo sed.
4. en el verano En el verano tengo calor.
5. en el invierno En el invierno tengo frío.
6. cuando tienes tres minutos para llegar a clase Cuando tengo tres minutos para llegar a clase tengo prisa.
7. cuando sacas una "A" en un examen Cuando saco una "A" en un examen tengo suerte/éxito.
8. cuando lees un libro de Stephen King o ves una película (*movie*) de terror
   Cuando leo un libro de Stephen King o veo una película de terror tengo miedo.

3:00

3·26 Pobre Pablo

Poor Pablo, our new friend from Madrid, is having one of those days! Together retell his story using **tener** expressions.

MODELO

Pablo tiene prisa.

El despertador de Pablo no funciona (*does not work*). Tiene una clase a las 8:00 y es tarde. Sale de casa a las 8:10.

1. Es invierno y Pablo no tiene abrigo (*coat*).   Pablo tiene frío.

2. Pablo tiene un insuficiente (60% en EE.UU.) en un examen.   Pablo no tiene éxito./Pablo tiene que estudiar.

3. Pablo recibe una oferta (*offer*) de trabajo increíble.   Pablo tiene suerte.

4. Pablo ve que no tiene dinero para comer.   Pablo tiene vergüenza.

5. Pablo está en casa y quiere una botella de agua. En el refrigerador no hay ninguna (*none*).
Pablo tiene sed.

CULTURAL BACKGROUND FOR
Pobre Pablo

These vignettes are based on Pablo, a character from Madrid, Spain. Some students may need to have some information about the few cultural nuances that appear in the vignettes (e.g., grades). This can also lend itself to cultural comparison.

HERITAGE LANGUAGE LEARNERS

Have students create a complete narrative of Pablo's day, including as many details as possible.

`4:00`

3 • 27 Datos personales

Túrnense para hacerse esta entrevista (*interview*).

1. ¿Cuántos años tienes?
2. ¿Qué tienes que hacer hoy?
3. ¿Tienes ganas de hacer algo diferente? ¿Qué?
4. ¿En qué clase tienes sueño?
5. ¿En qué clase tienes mucha suerte?
6. ¿Siempre tienes razón?
7. ¿Cuándo tienes hambre?
8. ¿Cuándo tienes sueño?
9. Cuando tienes sed, ¿qué tomas?
10. ¿En qué tienes éxito?

VOCABULARIO 7

Los números 1.000– 100.000.000

SAM

3-33 to 3-37

`4:00`

1.000	mil	100.000	cien mil
1.001	mil uno	400.000	cuatrocientos mil
1.010	mil diez	1.000.000	un millón
2.000	dos mil	2.000.000	dos millones
30.000	treinta mil	100.000.000	cien millones

1. **Mil** is never used in the plural form when counting.

   mil   dos mil   tres mil

   > **Fíjate**
   > To express "a thousand," use *mil*, not *un mil*.

2. The plural of **millón** is **millones** and when followed by a noun, both take the preposition **de.**

   un millón de dólares   cinco millones de personas

   > **Fíjate**
   > Note that *millón* has an accent in the singular form but loses the accent in the plural, *millones*.

3. **Cien** is used before **mil** and **millones (de).**

   cien mil dólares   cien millones de dólares

4. Decimals are used instead of commas in some Hispanic countries to group three digits together, and commas are used to replace decimals.

   1.000.000 (un millón) $2.000,00 (dos mil dólares)

RECURSOS

Electronic Activity Cache

`4:00`

3·28 ¿Cuánto cuesta?

Look at the ads for houses in Spain. Take turns asking for the price and other details for each of the houses.

MODELO
E1: *¿Cuánto cuesta la casa en Cullera?*

E2: *Cuesta seiscientos veinte mil euros.*

E1: *¿Cuántos dormitorios tiene?*

E2: *Tiene cuatro dormitorios.*

Chalet en venta

6 dormitorios
3 baños
calefacción
aire acondicionado
piscina

Dos Hermanas,

Sevilla, España.

Precio: 1.262.125€

Tel. 95 467 51 83

Chalet independiente en venta

4 dormitorios, 3 baños, cocina amueblada, terrazas, piscina.

Cullera,   Precio: 620.000€
Valencia, España.   Tel. 96 264 79 51

Chalet independiente en venta

2 dormitorios, 1 baño, cocina amueblada, calefacción, terrazas, chimenea, jardín grande. Posibilidad de ampliación de dormitorios.

Fresno de la Vega,   Precio: 360.607€
León, España.   Tel. 98 721 52 60

Casa independiente en venta

Casa señorial de dos plantas. La construcción data de 1800. Muy buen estado de conservación.

5 dormitorios, 1 baño, chimenea, terrazas, jardín grande.

Toledo, España.
Precio: 420.000€
Tel. 92 592 72 23

NATIONAL STANDARDS
Communication, Connections

Actividad **3–28** asks students to engage in conversations about real estate advertisements. They look at the advertisement, and then they take turns providing and obtaining information about each property. The open-ended format of the activity also allows students to exchange opinions about the properties by using familiar expressions (*me gusta, es caro, es feo, es bonito,* etc.) (Standard 1.1).

This activity also reinforces their knowledge of other disciplines such as geography, math, international business, and political science. The prices listed are in euros, so students can convert the prices to American dollars and decide if the property is reasonably priced and how it compares to property values in their area. Students can use their knowledge of Spanish geography to make predictions about the climate, the location of the property relative to other Spanish cities, and how the location affects the value of the property. They can use their political science studies to examine what type of local government each city or community has, what types of property taxes a buyer might pay, and how owning real estate in a particular community impacts the local economy (Standard 3.1).

Suggestion for 3–28 For up-to-date exchange rates, please consult the web.

Suggestion for 3–28 Have students describe the houses, determine which one they would prefer to live in, imagine what they are like inside, etc.

Additional activity for *Los números 1.000 – 100.000.000* Students love to talk about the cost of their tuition each semester. Write the amounts of this year's tuition, room, board, and fees on the board or on a transparency and ask students to tell you the amounts in Spanish. For the upperclassmen, you might ask them to determine how much they have paid over the course of several years.

NOTE ON *LOS NÚMEROS 1.000 – 100.000.000*

Remind students that when writing numbers in Spanish, the decimal point is used where in English the comma is used.

NOTE FOR *Hay*

Hay was introduced lexically in *Capítulo 2*, actividad **2–7**, when students were asked to describe their classroom. The authors believe that structures should be introduced when needed. *Hay* is treated formally here.

4:00 **3·29** ¿Cuál es su población?

Lee las poblaciones de estas ciudades de España mientras (*while*) tu compañero/a te escucha y corrige. Después, cambien de papel (*change roles*).

1.	Madrid	5.423.384
2.	Barcelona	4.805.927
3.	Valencia	2.216.285
4.	Sevilla	1.728.603
5.	Granada	821.660

4:00 **3·30** ¿Qué compras?

Your rich Spanish uncle left you an inheritance with the stipulation that you use the money to furnish your house. Refer to the pictures on page 109 to spend 3,500 € on your house. Make a list of what you want to buy, assigning prices to those items without tags. Then share your list with your partner, who will keep track of your spending. Did you overspend?

MODELO   *Quiero comprar un televisor por (for) ochocientos noventa y nueve euros.*

> **Fíjate**
>
> The sentence in the model includes two verbs; the second verb is an infinitive (*-ar, -er, -ir*).
>
> Quiero comp**rar** un   *I want to buy a TV*
> televisor.   *set.*

  GRAMÁTICA **8** **Hay**   SAM   2:00   3-38 to 3-41

In **Capítulo 2**, you became familiar with **hay** when you described your classroom. To say *there is* or *there are* in Spanish you use **hay.** The irregular form **hay** comes from the verb **haber,** which you will learn more about in a later chapter.

Hay un baño en mi casa.   *There is one bathroom in my house.*
Hay cuatro dormitorios también.   *There are also four bedrooms.*
—¿**Hay** tres baños en tu casa?   *Are there three bathrooms in your house?*
—No, no **hay** tres baños.   *No, there aren't three bathrooms.*

¿Qué hay en ese cuarto?

RECURSOS   3-G8   Electronic Activity Cache

`3:00`

 **3•31** ¡Escucha bien!

Descríbele un cuarto de tu casa (real o imaginaria) a un/a compañero/a en **tres** oraciones. Él/Ella tiene que repetir las oraciones. Después, cambien de papel.

MODELO E1: *En mi dormitorio hay una cama, una lámpara y un tocador. También hay dos ventanas. No hay una alfombra.*

E2: *En tu dormitorio hay una cama, una lámpara y un tocador...*

`5:00`

 **3•32** ¿Qué hay en tu casa?

Descríbele tu casa a un compañero/a. Usen todas las palabras que puedan (*you can*) del vocabulario de *La casa*, p. 100, y *Los muebles y otros objetos de la casa*, p. 109.

MODELO E1: *En mi casa hay un garaje. ¿Hay un garaje en tu casa?*

E2: *No, en mi casa no hay un garaje.*

E2: *En mi baño hay una bañera y una ducha. ¿Qué hay en tu baño?*

E1: *Hay una ducha, un inodoro y un lavabo grande.*

`4:00`

 3•33 ¿Cuántos hay?

Túrnense para preguntar y contestar cuántos objetos y personas hay en su clase aproximadamente.

MODELO libros de español

E1: *¿Cuántos libros de español hay?*

E2: *Hay treinta libros de español.*

Capítulo Preliminar A. Los números 0–30, pág. 16; Capítulo 2. La formación de preguntas y las palabras interrogativas, pág. 71.

1. puertas
2. escritorios
3. mochilas azules
4. cuadernos negros
5. estudiantes contentos
6. estudiantes cansados
7. computadoras
8. estudiantes a quienes les gusta jugar al fútbol
9. estudiantes a quienes les gusta ir a fiestas
10. estudiantes a quienes les gusta estudiar

NOTE FOR 3–32

Time will vary for actividad **3–32**, depending on how thorough your students are. Encourage them to give complete descriptions. To discourage students from getting off-task and chatting, monitor them closely and end the activity when a third to a half of your students have finished.

SECTION GOALS FOR

Escucha

By the end of the *Escucha* section, students will be able to:

- practice pre-listening strategies.
- prepare questions they might ask a real estate agent.
- complete checklists of features of houses.
- listen for specific details.
- use the information from a listening passage to relay information to others.

NATIONAL STANDARDS

Communication

Once students are able to listen for cognates and the main idea, the next strategy they can apply is listening for specific information. The communicative mode is interpretive (Standard 1.2) as they understand and interpret spoken Spanish. The *Después de escuchar* activity allows students to practice role-playing, and the communication is interpersonal (Standard 1.1). If the students describe the house in front of an audience of listeners, they are also communicating in the presentational mode (Standard 1.3).

AUDIOSCRIPT FOR 3–35

AGENTE   Tengo la casa perfecta para usted y su familia. Es una casa bella de un solo piso. Tiene cuatro dormitorios —uno grande y los otros tres más pequeños— y tres baños. La cocina es enorme y muy moderna.

SR. JIMÉNEZ   ¿Y la sala? Siempre tenemos muchos amigos en casa.

AGENTE   La sala es grande y está al lado de la cocina. Hay mucho espacio para su familia y sus amigos.

SR. JIMÉNEZ   ¿Cuál es el precio de la casa?

AGENTE   Es muy razonable. Sólo 204.000 dólares.

ESCUCHA

3-42 to 3-43

ESTRATEGIA	Listening for specific information

To practice listening for specific information, first determine the context of the passage and then decide what information you need about that topic. For example, if you are listening to an ad about an apartment to rent, you may want to focus on size, location, and price. In *¡Anda!* the **Antes de escuchar** section will normally provide the context for each passage.

3•34   Antes de escuchar

A real estate agent is describing one of the homes she has listed to sell to the Jiménez family. Mr. Jiménez asks for a few details. Write a question Mr. Jiménez might ask the agent.

3•35   A escuchar

CW eBook

CD 2 Track 2

Listen to the passage and complete the following list based on the information the agent provides. Listen a second time to verify your answers.

1. Number of floors: ___1___
2. Number of bedrooms: ___4___
3. Number of bathrooms: ___3___
4. Size of kitchen: _large_
5. Size of living room: _large_
6. Price: $204.000

El Sr. Jiménez quiere comprar una casa.

3•36   Después de escuchar

In the role of Mr. Jiménez, describe the house to your partner using the information from **3-35**.

METHODOLOGY • Escucha

Students can complete this section at home or in class. Encourage them to practice and apply the listening strategy, rather than racing through the exercise. Follow up by checking answers.

ESCRIBE

3-44 to
3-45

3•37 **Antes de escribir**

You have accepted a new job and you must sell your house and move to a different town (real or imagined). Before creating the flyer to sell your house, make a list as detailed as possible of the features you want to include.

3•38 **Un anuncio** (*flyer*)

Organize your list and create your flyer, making it as informative and attractive as possible. The flyer should include the following information:

- Location (city, country, street, etc.)
- Type of house or building
- Number and types of rooms
- Appliances in the kitchen
- Pieces of furniture included
- Colors
- Price and contact information
- Special features

3•39 **Después de escribir**

Circulate among your classmates, sharing flyers, and determine which house you would most like to buy.

¿Cómo andas?

Having completed the second **Comunicación,** I now can…

	Feel Confident	Need to Review
● describe what I and others do around the house (p. 112)	❏	❏
● state at least one interesting fact about the famous Hispanic women presented in the chapter (p. 114)	❏	❏
● describe my ideal house using colors (p. 115)	❏	❏
● discuss certain feelings using **tener** expressions (p. 117)	❏	❏
● count, quote prices, and give population figures using numbers 1,000–100,000,000 (p. 120)	❏	❏
● describe places using **hay** (p. 122)	❏	❏
● practice listening for specific information (p. 124)	❏	❏
● create a flyer (p. 125)	❏	❏

SECTION GOALS FOR *Escribe*

By the end of the *Escribe* section, students will be able to:

- brainstorm and edit a list of the features of a property for sale.
- create a flyer for marketing the house.
- organize the contents of the flyer into appropriate categories.
- compare their flyer to those of their classmates.
- express their likes and dislikes about the flyers.
- choose the property whose flyer is most appealing.

NATIONAL STANDARDS
Communication, Connections

Creating a flyer as is done in activity **3–38** provides real-life experiences for students.

The listening and writing activities give students the opportunity to engage in conversations about renting, buying, or selling property. They must provide and obtain information about the house they wish to sell, or the property they want to buy. The listening activity (**3–35**) requires students to understand and interpret spoken Spanish. The flyer made in activity **3–38** uses written Spanish, but depending on how you implement the activity, the students could also present their flyers to the class; activity **3–39** combines written Spanish with the presentational mode of the classroom discussion about the flyers.

Students make connections between their real world experiences and what they are learning in school. The types of skills they practice while making flyers, taking inventories, listening for specific information, and preparing to relocate are practical skills they are learning in college. They use applications from the visual arts for the flyers, marketing for preparing their property, economics for calculating where they can afford to live, and life skills they will utilize upon their graduation. Students may also use these skills for making lodging arrangements while traveling or working abroad.

Suggestion for 3–39 You may want to use the flyers in a different way. For example, put students in groups of 4 or 5 and have them determine which house is the most interesting, will be the easiest to sell, etc.

Suggestion for 3–39 Bring in an episode of a show that features different homes. Play the video with no sound and ask them to make a list of the rooms and additional features of each house. Then ask them to report back to the class and share opinions about the value of the house, if they would want to live there, and if this type of house exists where they live.

Expansion of 3–39 Ask students to print a flyer of a house from a real estate web site such as http://www.realtor.com. Have them pretend they are the realtor and explain the features or selling points of the house to the class in Spanish. Have classmates guess the actual price of the home using the numbers they have just learned.

María Ángeles Solana Montoya

Espña

Les presento mi país

Mi nombre es María Ángeles Solana Montoya y soy de Madrid, la capital de España. Vivo con mis padres en un piso en el centro. ¿Dónde vives tú? ¿En una casa, en un apartamento o en una residencia estudiantil? Me gusta la vida en la capital porque hay mucha actividad. A veces, me gusta salir con mis amigos por la tarde para comer tapas y tomar algo. La Plaza Mayor es uno de los lugares más típicos para ir de tapas. ¿Cuál es tu lugar favorito para conversar y pasar tiempo con tus amigos? Frecuentemente, hablamos de los deportes, sobre todo el fútbol y los equipos españoles. ¡Cada uno tiene su favorito! ¿Cuál es tu deporte preferido? ¿Eres aficionado o jugador?

Don Quijote y Sancho Panza son personajes del autor Miguel de Cervantes Saavedra.
Picasso, Pablo (1881–1973), Don Quijote, 1955, Pen and Ink. Private Collection. Erich Lessing/Art Resource, NY. © 2004 Estate of Pablo Picasso/Artists Rights Society (ARS), NY.

El fútbol es el deporte más importante del país.

La Plaza Mayor de Madrid es un lugar agradable para comer tapas, tomar una bebida y conversar con amigos.

126

● ALMANAQUE ●

Nombre oficial:	Reino de España
Gobierno:	Monarquía parlamentaria
Población:	41.547.000 (est. 2006)
Idiomas oficiales:	español, catalán, gallego, eusquera (vasco)
Moneda:	euro (€)

La tortilla española es una tapa (un aperitivo) y un plato muy típico y popular.

Los *castells*—o castillos (*castles*) en español—son impresionantes construcciones humanas.

La Pedrera (la Casa Milà) en Barcelona es un ejemplo de la arquitectura creativa de Antonio Gaudí.

El patio de los leones de La Alhambra muestra la influencia árabe en Granada.

¿Sabías que...?

● La Organización Nacional de Ciegos Españoles, O.N.C.E., es una empresa que trabaja en beneficio de las personas ciegas (*blind*) y otros discapacitados.

● Los *castells* forman parte de una tradición empezada en Cataluña en el siglo (*century*) XVIII que consiste en competir por hacer la torre (*tower*) humana más alta. ¡Actualmente el récord es un castillo de nueve pisos!

PREGUNTAS

1. ¿Qué es una tapa?
2. ¿Qué evidencia hay de la presencia histórica de los árabes en España?
3. ¿Por qué son impresionantes los *castells*? Nombra una competencia famosa de tu país.
4. Describe la arquitectura de Antonio Gaudí. ¿Te gusta? ¿Por qué?
5. ¿Qué tienen en común México y España en cuanto a los deportes?

En la Red
Amplía tus conocimientos sobre España en la página web de *¡Anda!*

127

Suggestion for *Don Quijote y Sancho Panza* Ask students if they have heard of this novel, of the musical *"Man of La Mancha"* and of the ever-popular song "The Impossible Dream." The musical and song are takeoffs of the themes of the novel.

NOTE FOR
La tortilla española
You may wish to point out to your students the different types of *tortilla*, e.g., Spain's *tortilla* made with eggs and potatoes, and the corn or wheat *tortilla* of Latin America.

Suggestion for *La Alhambra* Ask students if they can identify any particular kind of architecture from their area. What influenced it? What makes it unique?

Suggestion for *Gaudí* Show students photos of *La Sagrada Familia* and ask them to compare this to churches in the United States. Do they like this structure by Gaudí? Why or why not? Students can learn more by visiting the *¡Anda!* web site.

Expansion for *O.N.C.E.* Sometimes students are bewildered as to how a blind person can differentiate between paper bills when selling lottery tickets and making change. Point out that in other countries such as Spain, the paper bills are different sizes, so that people can recognize the denomination by sight or by feeling the money.

Suggestion for *Los castells* Ask students if we have unusual contests involving physical activity in the United States (e.g., log rolling, ice sculpture, lumberjack sports). Ask why they think people participate in such activities. Ask if *they* would like to participate and, if so, in which activity?

Answers to *Preguntas*

1. Es un aperitivo.
2. La Alhambra en Granada es evidencia de la presencia histórica de los árabes.
3. Los *castells* son torres humanas. *Answers may vary.*
4. La arquitectura de Gaudí es muy creativa y moderna. *Answers may vary.*
5. El deporte más popular de México y de España es el fútbol.

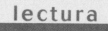

Ambiciones siniestras

EPISODIO 3

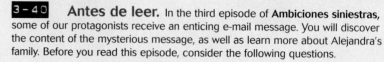

lectura

SAM
3-50

3-40 **Antes de leer.** In the third episode of **Ambiciones siniestras,** some of our protagonists receive an enticing e-mail message. You will discover the content of the mysterious message, as well as learn more about Alejandra's family. Before you read this episode, consider the following questions.

1. ¿Hablas sobre los miembros de tu familia con tus amigos? ¿Qué dices?
2. ¿Recibes mensajes curiosos que no vienen de amigos ni (*nor*) de personas de tu familia?
3. ¿Recibes mensajes sobre concursos (*contests*)?

ESTRATEGIA   Scanning

To enhance comprehension, you can scan or search a reading passage for specific information. When skimming, you read quickly to get the gist of the passage, the main	ideas. With scanning, you already know what you need to find out, so you concentrate on searching for that information.

3-41 **A leer.** Follow the steps below.

1. Scan the first two paragraphs of this episode, looking for the following specific information:
   a. the location of Alejandra and Manolo
   b. what they are doing there
   c. about whom Alejandra is talking
2. Now reread the second paragraph to determine why Alejandra is discussing this person. What is her concern?

Remember that successful reading in Spanish will require that you read the episodes more than once.

contest

CW
eBook
CD 2
Track 4

*message
to introduce him*

■ *El concurso°*

Manolo y Alejandra están en el cibercafé NetEscape. Hablan mientras se toman un café y leen sus correos electrónicos.

Alejandra le dice a Manolo que quiere mirar su e-mail para ver si tiene un mensaje° de su hermana Pili. Alejandra explica que Pili tiene un novio nuevo y que quiere presentárselo° a sus padres esta noche. Su hermana está muy nerviosa. El novio, Peter, tiene veintinueve años y la hermana tiene solamente diecinueve. ¡Con razón tiene miedo! Alejandra dice que sus padres son muy estrictos y creen que ella es demasiado joven para tener novio.

128

Alejandra lee varios mensajes y exclama:

—Manolo, ¡mira!

—¿Qué pasa? ¿Tienes un mensaje de tu hermana? —le pregunta Manolo.

—No, pero tienes que leer esto°. ¡Es increíble!   *this*

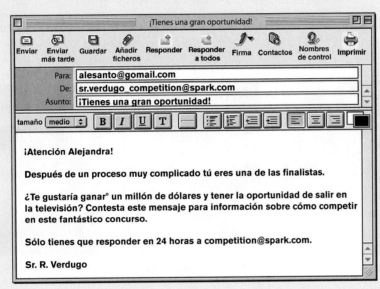

¡Tienes una gran oportunidad!

Para: alesanto@gomail.com
De: sr.verdugo_competition@spark.com
Asunto: ¡Tienes una gran oportunidad!

tamaño medio

¡Atención Alejandra!

Después de un proceso muy complicado tú eres una de las finalistas.

¿Te gustaría ganar° un millón de dólares y tener la oportunidad de salir en la televisión? Contesta este mensaje para información sobre cómo competir en este fantástico concurso.

Sólo tienes que responder en 24 horas a competition@spark.com.

Sr. R. Verdugo

Would you like to win?

Entonces Manolo decide ver si él tiene el mismo mensaje.

—¡Mira! —exclama Manolo. —¡Aquí está! ¡Qué bueno! Pero, seguramente el país entero° tiene el mismo mensaje. ¿Es legítimo? Alejandra, ¿respondemos?   *entire country*

—No sé. —le contesta Alejandra. —Mis padres siempre me dicen que debo° tener cuidado con las ofertas. ¿Pero qué nos puede pasar si sólo contestamos que deseamos más información?   *I must*

—Sí. —le responde Manolo. —¿Qué nos puede pasar?

3-42   **Después de leer.** Contesta las siguientes preguntas.

1. ¿Cómo se llama la hermana de Alejandra? ¿Cuál es su problema?

2. ¿Qué recibe Alejandra?

3. ¿Qué puede ganar?

4. Según (*According to*) Manolo, ¿quiénes reciben la oferta?

5. En tu opinión, ¿qué crees que hacen?

6. Hagan los papeles (*roles*) de unas personas que acaban (*have just*) de recibir el mensaje. ¿Cómo reaccionan? ¿Qué dicen? ¿Qué hacen?

129

Suggestion for reviewing *Episodio 2* Ask your students the following questions. Answers follow in italics.

1. ¿Quién es de San Antonio? (*Alejandra*) ¿San Diego? (*Manolo*) ¿West Palm Beach? (*Cisco*) ¿Nueva York? (*Marisol*)

2. ¿Quién estudia o desea estudiar psicología? (*Marisol*) ¿periodismo e historia? (*Lupe*) ¿economía? (*Eduardo*) ¿arte? (*Alejandra*) ¿medicina? (*Manolo*) ¿informática? (*Cisco*)

3. ¿A quién le gusta el fútbol americano? (*Manolo*) ¿pintar y escribir poesía? (*Alejandra*) ¿tener muchos trabajos diferentes? (*Cisco*) ¿jugar al tenis y nadar? (*Eduardo*) ¿escribir? (*Lupe*) ¿jugar al golf y leer novelas policíacas? (*Marisol*)

4. Por lo que sabemos hasta ahora, ¿quiénes tienen muchos hermanos? (*Alejandra y Manolo*) ¿Quién es hija única? (*Marisol*)

5. ¿Quiénes hacen trabajo voluntario? (*Marisol y Eduardo*)

6. ¿Qué tienen en común los estudiantes? (*todos tienen nombres hispanos*)

Answers to 3-42

1. Pili. Su novio, Peter, tiene 29 años.
2. Recibe un e-mail sobre un concurso.
3. Puede ganar un millón de dólares.
4. El país entero.
5. *Answers will vary.*
6. *Answers will vary.*

SECTION GOALS FOR
Video

By the end of the *Video* section, students will be able to:

- recognize the living space of Lupe.
- listen for specific pieces of information, such as the phrase *tal vez*.
- describe the homes and/or rooms of Eduardo and Cisco.
- narrate the characters' activities.
- summarize the messages the characters receive.
- arrange the events of the video in chronological order.

METHODOLOGY • Video

The video episode in each chapter, as well as the reading episode in the text, contextualizes new vocabulary and grammatical structures. This feature is a critical part of the *¡Anda!* program, as each episode (reading and video) ends in a mini-cliffhanger that is continued or resolved in the subsequent episode. If either the reading or the video is omitted, students will not be able to follow the story and a wonderful learning opportunity will be missed.

Suggestion for 3–44 You may want students to watch the video once for general comprehension, then a second time for specific information required to answer the questions.

Answers to 3-44

1. *Possible answers may include:* Es bonito y grande. Su dormitorio tiene una ventana. Etc.
2. Un e-mail sobre un concurso. También recibe el mismo e-mail.
3. En la biblioteca. Estudian matemáticas (*or whatever your students reply that would have mathematical problems*).
4. *Possible answers may include:* Es bastante grande con una cama grande, un armario, un sillón y una mesa para su computadora.
5. *Possible answers may include:* Es muy grande con una piscina grande. Es impresionante.
6. Eduardo y Cisco reciben el mismo e-mail que reciben Marisol, Lupe, Alejandra y Manolo.

video

3-51 to 3-54

3-43 **Antes del video.** Take a minute to think back to the first time you visited a friend in his or her dorm room, apartment, or house. Were you interested in seeing what the new living space was like? Did he/she take time to show you around and elaborate on some of the furnishings? In this video episode you will see Lupe's apartment as well as Eduardo's and Cisco's families' homes. They are also checking e-mail. Listen for the phrase **Seguro que es una broma.** (*It's got to be a joke.*) Who says it? Also listen for **Tal vez** (*perhaps*) **sea un mensaje en cadena. Cadena** means "chain." Can you guess what the sentence means?

¡Es una gran oportunidad! ¿No crees?

Tal vez sea un mensaje en cadena.

No lo puedo creer. ¡Qué piscina! ¡Es impresionante!

Episodio 3

¡Tienes una gran oportunidad!

Relax and watch the video, more than once if you choose. Then answer the questions that follow.

3-44 **Después del video.** Contesta las siguientes preguntas.

1. ¿Cómo es el apartamento de Lupe?
2. ¿Qué mensaje recibe Marisol? ¿y Guadalupe?
3. ¿Dónde están Cisco y Eduardo? ¿Qué estudian?
4. ¿Cómo es la nueva habitación de Eduardo?
5. ¿Cómo es la casa de los padres de Cisco?
6. ¿Qué ocurre al final del episodio?

130

RECURSOS

Video Script

Y por fin, ¿cómo andas?

Having completed this chapter, I now can...

	Feel Confident	Need to Review
Comunicación		
● describe my house and the things in it (p. 100, 109)	❑	❑
● use new verbs that have irregular **yo** forms and that are stem-changing (p. 104)	❑	❑
● talk about what I do or should do around my house (p. 112)	❑	❑
● use colors to describe things (p. 115)	❑	❑
● use idiomatic expressions with the verb **tener** to express physical and emotional states (p. 117)	❑	❑
● use numbers 1,000–100,000,000 (p. 120)	❑	❑
● say what things there are in a place, or how many there are, using **hay** (p. 122)	❑	❑
Cultura		
● describe some of the types and styles of homes in the Spanish-speaking world (p. 108)	❑	❑
● discuss the changing roles of Hispanic women, and share facts about at least one Hispanic woman who has made an impact on society (p. 114)	❑	❑
● list at least three facts about **España** (p. 126)	❑	❑
Ambiciones siniestras		
● scan for specific information when I read (p. 128)	❑	❑
● explain what is contained in the e-mail message the protagonists receive (p. 129–130)	❑	❑

VOCABULARIO ACTIVO

CW
eBook
CD 2
Tracks 5–16

La casa	The house
el altillo	attic
el balcón	balcony
el baño	bathroom
la cocina	kitchen
el comedor	dining room
el cuarto	room
el dormitorio	bedroom
la escalera	staircase
el garaje	garage
el jardín	garden
la oficina	office
el piso	floor; story
la planta baja	ground floor
el primer piso	second floor
la sala	living room
el segundo piso	third floor
el sótano	basement
el suelo	floor
el techo	roof
el tercer piso	fourth floor

Los verbos	Verbs
conocer	to be aquainted with
dar	to give
decir	to say; to tell
hacer	to do; to make
oír	to hear
poder	to be able to
poner	to put; to place
querer	to want; to love
salir	to leave; to go out
traer	to bring
venir	to come
ver	to see

Los muebles y otros objetos de la casa	Furniture and other objects in the house

La sala y el comedor	The living room and dining room
la alfombra	rug; carpet
el estante de libros	bookcase
la lámpara	lamp
el mueble	piece of furniture
los muebles	furniture
el sillón	armchair
el sofá	sofa

La cocina	The kitchen
la estufa	stove
el lavaplatos	dishwasher
el microondas	microwave
el refrigerador	refrigerator

El baño	The bathroom
la bañera	bathtub
el bidet	bidet
la ducha	shower
el inodoro	toilet
el lavabo	sink

El dormitorio	The bedroom
la almohada	pillow
el armario	armoire; closet; cabinet
la cama	bed
la colcha	bedspread; comforter
la manta	blanket
las sábanas	sheets
el tocador	dresser

132

Otras palabras útiles en la casa — Other useful words in the house

amueblado/a	*furnished*
la cosa	*thing*
el cuadro	*picture; painting*
el objeto	*object*
la planta	*plant*

Los quehaceres de la casa — Household chores

arreglar	*to straighten up; to fix*
ayudar	*to help*
cocinar, preparar la comida	*to cook*
guardar	*to put away; to keep*
hacer la cama	*to make the bed*
lavar los platos	*to wash dishes*
limpiar	*to clean*
pasar la aspiradora	*to vacuum*
poner la mesa	*to set the table*
sacar la basura	*to take out the garbage*
sacudir el polvo	*to dust*

Los colores — Colors

amarillo	*yellow*
anaranjado	*orange*
azul	*blue*
beige	*beige*
blanco	*white*
gris	*gray*
marrón	*brown*
morado	*purple*
negro	*black*
rojo	*red*
rosado	*pink*
verde	*green*

Expresiones con tener — Expressions with tener

tener … años	*to be… years old*
tener calor	*to be hot*
tener cuidado	*to be careful*
tener éxito	*to be successful*
tener frío	*to be cold*
tener ganas de + (*infinitive*)	*to feel like + (verb)*
tener hambre	*to be hungry*
tener miedo	*to be afraid*
tener prisa	*to be in a hurry*
tener razón	*to be right*
tener sed	*to be thirsty*
tener sueño	*to be sleepy*
tener suerte	*to be lucky*
tener vergüenza	*to be embarrassed*

Los números 1.000–100.000.000 — Numbers 1,000–100,000,000

See page 120

Otras palabras útiles — Other useful words

a la derecha (de)	*to the right (of)*
a la izquierda (de)	*to the left (of)*
al lado (de)	*beside*
antiguo/a	*old*
la calle	*street*
el campo	*country*
la ciudad	*city*
contemporáneo/a	*contemporary*
desordenado/a	*messy*
encima (de)	*on top (of)*
humilde	*humble*
limpio/a	*clean*
moderno/a	*modern*
nuevo/a	*new*
la ropa	*clothes; clothing*
siempre	*always*
sucio/a	*dirty*
tener que + (*infinitive*)	*to have to + (verb)*
tradicional	*traditional*
viejo/a	*old*

133

4

Nuestra comunidad

No importa si vivimos en el campo (*countryside*), en un pueblo, en una ciudad o en otro país (*country*), tenemos mucho en común. Todos comemos, trabajamos, compramos, pasamos tiempo con la familia y los amigos y ayudamos a los demás (*others*). Nuestra vida en comunidad es similar.

OBJETIVOS

Comunicación

- To relate information about your home and/or university town
- To talk about whom and what you know or are acquainted with in your area
- To share information about what will take place in the future
- To discuss some service opportunities in your community
- To paraphrase what you hear
- To write a postcard about your town or city

Cultura

- To compare your everyday, common tasks (such as shopping) with those of the Spanish-speaking world
- To list ways of serving your community
- To state three interesting facts about each of this chapter's feature countries: Honduras, Guatemala, and El Salvador

Ambiciones siniestras

- To practice the reading strategies of skimming and scanning
- To learn more about Lupe and Marisol, and which of the characters have not been truthful.

CONTENIDOS

RECURSOS

Lesson Plan

La plaza de Chichicastenango en Guatemala

PREGUNTAS

1 Generalmente, ¿qué haces durante un día normal?

2 ¿Conoces a personas de otros países o culturas? ¿Cuáles son sus actividades típicas?

3 ¿Qué tienes en común con las personas de otros países?

135

Suggestion for the *Chapter Opener*
Ask students to define *la comunidad*. Write their ideas on the board. Is it the people in the area? Is it the physical location? Is it the architecture and the landmarks? Is it the blending of cultures? Find out what they think the word *community* encompasses, and explain that this chapter includes all aspects of community. Ask students to think about what their school community is noted for.

Expansion for *Preguntas* What follows is another question you can ask your students regarding the chapter opener reading. Remember that they will understand the question in Spanish, but some of your beginning students may need to answer in English. That is pedagogically acceptable, since the goal is for them to demonstrate that they comprehend the question as well as the reading. Additionally, the following question will give you insight into which Spanish-speaking countries interest your students: ¿*Qué países quieres conocer?, ¿por qué?*

PLANNING AHEAD

You may want to assign *actividades* **4-6** and **4-17** as homework so that students come prepared to do the task in class. For *actividad* **4-35**, it is useful to have large sheets of newsprint paper and markers for your students, one sheet for every two students. Additionally, as a reminder, it is recommended that you assign the grammar explanations and the culture sections to be read before class. They are written in a clear language so that the students will be able to understand them. Then, you can maximize use of class time for students to ask for any possible clarification of the grammar, and to answer the comprehension and critical-thinking questions that accompany the culture readings.

METHODOLOGY • Checking for Reading Comprehension

The text and questions for this chapter opener are completely in Spanish. The reading is at an *i + 1* level for your students. Regarding checking for comprehension, you can use several techniques. If your students are true beginners, allow them to answer in English, since they will be learning new vocabulary in the chapter to help them answer the questions. Some of your beginning students will be able to answer the questions in Spanish, perhaps not as completely as they would like, but they will still be able to communicate. Your Heritage language learners will be able to answer the questions in a complete fashion in Spanish.

Comunicación

- Identifying places
- Discussing what and whom you know
- Stating what you have to do

VOCABULARIO 1 Los lugares

3:00

4-1 to 4-3

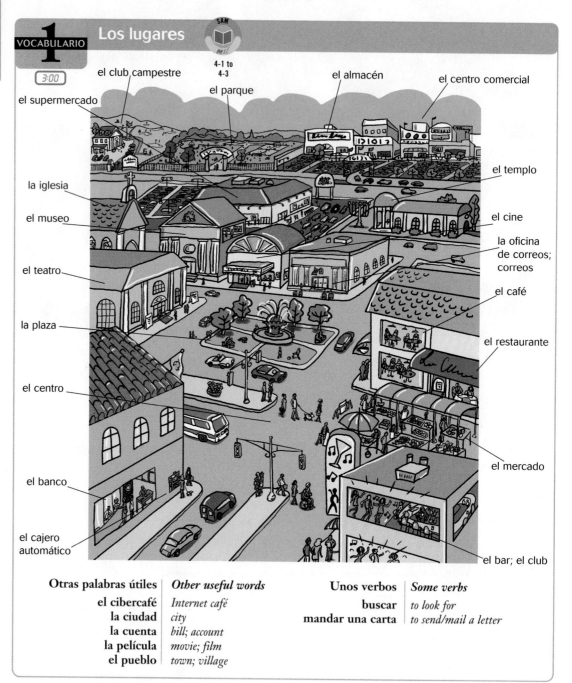

el club campestre
el parque
el almacén
el centro comercial
el supermercado
el templo
la iglesia
el cine
el museo
la oficina de correos; correos
el teatro
el café
la plaza
el restaurante
el centro
el mercado
el banco
el cajero automático
el bar; el club

Otras palabras útiles	*Other useful words*	Unos verbos	*Some verbs*
el cibercafé	*Internet café*	**buscar**	*to look for*
la ciudad	*city*	**mandar una carta**	*to send/mail a letter*
la cuenta	*bill; account*		
la película	*movie; film*		
el pueblo	*town; village*		

PRONUNCIACIÓN ⏱3:00

CD 2
Track 17

SAM

4-4 to 4-8

The letters *c* and *z*

1. Before the vowels **a**, **o**, and **u**, and when followed by a consonant, the Spanish **c** is pronounced like the *c* in the English word *car*.
2. Before the vowels **e** and **i**, the Spanish **c** is pronounced like the *s* in the English word *seal*.
3. The Spanish **z** is pronounced like the *s* in the English word *seal*.

4•1   Las palabras

Practice pronouncing the following words, focusing on the letters **c** and **z**.

1. almacén
2. banco
3. club
4. cuidado
5. cibercafé
6. cajero
7. lápiz
8. plaza

4•2   Las oraciones

Pronounce the following sentences, paying special attention to the letters **c** and **z**.

1. ¿Cuánto cuesta el lápiz?
2. Cecilia cocina con cuidado en la cocina.
3. Carlos tiene que buscar a sus amigos en la plaza.

4•3   Los trabalenguas

Pronounce the following tongue twister (*trabalenguas*), focusing on the letters **c** and **z**.

El cerdo del centro corre con cuidado hacia Zaragoza con una cerveza.

Capítulo 2. El verbo *estar*, pág. 78.

⏱2:00   **4•4**   ¿Dónde está?

Tu amigo está muy ocupado. Túrnate con un/a compañero/a para decir dónde está en este momento.

Capítulo 2. El verbo *estar*, pág. 78.

Fíjate

Notice that you use a form of *querer* + *infinitive* to express "to want to_____". For example:
Quiero mandar... = I want to send...
Queremos ver... = We want to see...

Answers to 4-4.
1. Está en el cine.
2. Está en el banco.
3. Está en un restaurante (mercado, supermercado, café).
4. Está en el museo.
5. Está en el parque.
6. Está en un bar (café, restaurante).
7. Está en el club campestre.
8. Está en la iglesia (el templo).

MODELO   E1:   Quiere mandar una carta.
            E2:   *Está en (la oficina de) correos.*

1. Quiere ver una película.
2. Necesita dinero para pagar una cuenta.
3. Quiere comer algo (*something*).
4. Quiere ver una exposición de arte.
5. Quiere caminar y hacer ejercicio.
6. Tiene sed y quiere tomar algo.
7. Quiere jugar al golf.
8. Tiene que ir a una boda (*wedding*).

SECTION GOALS FOR *Pronunciación*

By the end of the *Pronunciación* section, students will be able to:

- state the rules of pronunciation for the letter *c*.
- distinguish between the sounds the letters *c* and *z* make.

NOTE FOR *Pronunciación*

You may wish to tell your students that in Spain the pronunciation of the letter *c* (when followed by the letters *e* and *i*) and the letter *z* are pronounced like the *th* in the English word *think*.

NOTE FOR *Pronunciación*

The audio program for *¡Anda!* provides students with a wide array of native speakers from across the Spanish-speaking world. If your students will have multiple instructors throughout their language coursework, you can also explain that they will hear different accents depending on the instructor.

HERITAGE LANGUAGE LEARNERS

Remind Heritage language learners that Spanish pronunciation varies across countries. You may also share with them that their pronunciation might differ from yours, and that is fine.

Suggestion for 4-4 Remind students that the goal of the activity is to name the places in Spanish where the items are located. Specify that they use the vocabulary from the chapter, or they are likely to mention locations by their proper names (e.g., Bank of America instead of *el banco*).

CAPÍTULO 4

NOTE FOR 4-5

The new words *detrás* and *enfrente* are followed by the preposition *de* in parentheses. Use the preposition *de* after *detrás* and *enfrente* when you are talking about how one location is related to another: *La iglesia está enfrente de la plaza.*

Suggestion for 4-5 If your school is isolated and you don't have these places in the town where your school is located, you can either teach them the word *el único* (e.g., *el único banco es Sky Bank*), or use the city closest to your campus that most students would be familiar with to complete the activity.

NOTE FOR 4-5

Remind students that the feminine form is *la mejor* (or *las mejores*), as in the case of #7, *la tienda: La mejor tienda es Skippers.*

Expansion for 4-5 Have your students do a *El peor de los peores* version of this activity. This is a good activity for your pairs of students who finish the activity quickly.

Expansion for *Los lugares* As your students learn more prepositions of location, have them get a copy of your campus map to keep track of the new words. Have them label the building where they attend most of their classes and the building where they live, work, or park their car. Then have students write down how the buildings are related to one another in Spanish (behind, in front of, next to, etc.). This will help them remember the prepositions.

 4·5 El mejor de los mejores   `7:00`

¿Cuáles son, en tu opinión, los mejores lugares?

Estrategia

Remember that you learned vocabulary in *Capítulos 2* and *3*, such as *a la derecha, a la izquierda*, and *al lado de* that you can also practice with your new vocabulary.

Vocabulario útil

detrás (de)	*behind*
enfrente (de)	*in front (of)*
estar de acuerdo	*to agree*
el/la mejor	*the best*
el/la peor	*the worst*

Paso 1 Haz (*Make*) una lista de los mejores lugares de tu pueblo o ciudad según las siguientes categorías.

MODELO E1: restaurante

E2: *El mejor restaurante es* The Lantern.

1. almacén
2. banco
3. centro comercial
4. cine
5. café
6. teatro
7. tienda
8. restaurante
9. supermercado

Paso 2 Compara tu lista con la lista de los otros estudiantes de la clase. ¿Están de acuerdo?

MODELO E1: *En mi opinión, el mejor restaurante es* The Lantern. *¿Estás de acuerdo?*

E2: *No, no estoy de acuerdo. El mejor restaurante es* The Cricket.

Paso 3 Túrnense para explicar dónde están los mejores lugares.

MODELO E1: *Busco el mejor restaurante.*

E2: *El mejor restaurante es* The Lantern.

E1: *¿Dónde está?*

E2: *Está al lado del Banco Nacional.*

Fíjate

A reminder from *Capítulo 3*: The preposition *de* combines with the masculine singular definite article *el* to form the contraction *del*. The feminine article *la* does not contract.

CAPÍTULO 4

4·6 Chiquimula y mi ciudad... `9:00`

Chiquimula es un pueblo de 24.000 personas que está en el este de Guatemala.

Paso 1 Túrnense para describir el centro del pueblo. Mencionen dónde están los edificios principales.

MODELO *El Hotel Victoria está al lado del Restaurante el Dorado...*

Paso 2 Ahora dibuja (*draw*) un mapa del centro de tu pueblo o ciudad. El dibujo debe incluir los edificios principales. Después, túrnense para describirlo oralmente.

Paso 3 Túrnense para describir sus dibujos mientras tu compañero/a dibuja lo que dices.

Answers to Culture box: *Actividades cotidianas. Preguntas*
1. En las ciudades grandes hay centros comerciales. En los pueblos pequeños hay tiendas de todo tipo, la oficina de correos, bancos y restaurantes. También hay bullicio, especialmente durante los fines de semana. La gente va de compras, se encuentra para conversar y pasea por las calles y los parques.
   2. *Answers may vary.*

`2:00` 4-9 to 4-10

Actividades cotidianas: Las compras y el paseo

En los Estados Unidos, la gente hace gran parte de las compras en los centros comerciales. En los países hispanohablantes, también se hacen las compras en los centros comerciales, especialmente en las ciudades grandes. En Guatemala, Honduras y El Salvador algunos de los más conocidos son "Hiper Paiz", "Maxi Bodega" y "Despensa Familiar".

En los pueblos pequeños la gente va al centro de la ciudad. En el centro está el mercado y hay muchas tiendas además de la oficina de correos, el banco y los restaurantes. Se puede encontrar gente de todas las clases sociales y muchos vendedores ambulantes (*roving*).

Otro lugar importante en el centro de los pueblos es la plaza. Allí se encuentra la gente (*people meet*) para conversar, pasear, comprar o ir a la iglesia. Además, los lugareños (*locals*) pasean a diario por las calles principales y los parques del pueblo. En los pueblos hispanos siempre hay mucho bullicio (*hubbub*) y actividad, especialmente los fines de semana.

Preguntas

1. ¿Qué hay en las ciudades grandes? ¿Cómo son los pueblos pequeños? ¿Qué hace la gente todos los días?

> **Fíjate**
>
> Note that the word *gente*, unlike English, is singular: *La gente **va** al centro de la ciudad. Gente*, although made up of more than one person, is considered a collective noun like the singular nouns *la clase*, *el equipo*, or *la familia*.

2. ¿Dónde prefieres comprar, en las tiendas pequeñas o en los centros comerciales? ¿Por qué?

METHODOLOGY • Practicing Active Listening

It is important to provide students with active listening opportunities, hence the progression of actividad **4-6**.

Suggestion for 4-6 To save class time, ask your students to draw their maps for actividad **4-6** as homework.

NATIONAL STANDARDS

Cultures, Comparisons, Communities

The cultural reading, *Actividades cotidianas: Las compras y el paseo*, addresses the Goal Areas of Cultures, Comparisons, and Communities. In particular, Standards 2.1 and 2.2 refer to the practices, perspectives, and products of Hispanic cultures. By reading about shopping and daily activities, students learn about where shopping takes place, the types of products or services one can buy, and why for many Hispanic countries *la plaza* is the center of daily life. They also learn about how local businesses or shops are more common in Hispanic cultures than the giant malls and superstores typically found in the United States. Standard 4.2 is about developing insight into the nature of language and culture by making comparisons between Hispanic cultures and the students' cultures. The cultural reading also prepares them to participate in Hispanic communities in the United States and abroad by highlighting the differences in daily activities, illustrating how social the weekends are, and preparing them for shopping in cities.

GRAMÁTICA 2 — *Saber* y *conocer*

⏱ 3:00

4-11 to 4-13

¿Sabes dónde hay un cibercafé?

No, no conozco muy bien la ciudad.

In **Capítulo 3** you learned that **conocer** means *to know*. Another verb, **saber**, also expresses *to know*.

Fíjate

Note that *conocer* and *saber* both have irregular *yo* forms: *conozco* and *sé* respectively.

saber (*to know*)

Singular		Plural	
yo	**sé**	nosotros/as	**sabemos**
tú	**sabes**	vosotros/as	**sabéis**
él, ella, Ud.	**sabe**	ellos/as, Uds.	**saben**

The verbs are not interchangeable. Note when to use each.

    *Use **conocer** to express **being familiar or acquainted with people, places, and things.***

Ellos **conocen** los mejores restaurantes de la ciudad.   *They know the best restaurants in the city.*

Sí, **conozco** a tu hermano, pero no muy bien.   *Yes, I know your brother, but not very well.*

Note:

1. When expressing that *a person* is known, you must use **"a."** For example, *Conozco **a** tu hermano…*

2. When a is followed by **el, a + el = al.** For example, **Conozco *al* señor (a + el señor)**…

    *Use **saber** to express **knowing facts, pieces of information,** or **how to do something.***

¿Qué **sabes** sobre la música de Guatemala?   *What do you know about Guatemalan music?*

Yo **sé** tocar la guitarra.   *I know how to play the guitar.*

Fíjate

A form of *saber* + *infinitive* expresses knowing how to do something. For example:

Sé nadar. = I know how to swim.

Sabemos tocar la guitarra. = We know how to play the guitar.

4·7 ¿Sabes o conoces? ⏱ 2:00

Completa las siguientes preguntas usando **sabes** o **conoces**. Después, túrnate con un/a compañero/a para hacer y contestar las preguntas.

MODELO   E1:   *¿Conoces San Salvador?*

         E2:   *Sí, conozco San Salvador. / No, no conozco San Salvador.*

1. ¿ <u>Conoces</u> Tegucigalpa, Honduras?
2. ¿ <u>Conoces</u> al presidente de la universidad?
3. ¿ <u>Conoces</u> las películas de Alfred Hitchcock?
4. ¿ <u>Sabes</u> cuál es el mejor café de esta ciudad?

5. ¿ <u>Sabes</u> patinar?
6. ¿ <u>Sabes</u> usar una computadora?
7. ¿ <u>Conoces</u> el mejor restaurante mexicano?
8. ¿ <u>Sabes</u> hacer tortillas?

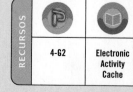

RECURSOS   4-G2   Electronic Activity Cache

4·8 ¿Qué sabemos de Honduras? `4:00`

Completen juntos el diálogo con la
forma correcta de **saber** o **conocer**.

Tegucigalpa, Honduras

PROF. DOMÍNGUEZ: ¿Qué (1) __saben__ ustedes sobre
Honduras?

DREW: Yo (2) __sé__ que la capital de
Honduras es Tegucigalpa.

DREW Y TANYA: Nosotros (3) __sabemos__ mucho sobre
el país.

PROF. DOMÍNGUEZ: ¿Y (4) __saben__ ustedes cómo se llaman las personas de Honduras?

TANYA: Sí, se llaman *hondureños*. (5) __Conocemos__ la cultura hondureña bastante bien. Nuestra
hermana, Gina, es una estudiante de intercambio allí este año y nos manda muchas
fotos y cartas. Ella (6) __conoce__ a mucha gente interesante, incluso al hijo del
Presidente.

PROF. DOMÍNGUEZ: ¡No me digan! ¿Estudia allí su hermana? ¿(7) __Saben__ ustedes que hay dos
universidades muy buenas en Tegucigalpa?

TANYA: Sí, el novio de Gina estudia allí pero no (8) __sé__ en qué universidad. Él es
salvadoreño y nuestros padres no lo (9) __conocen__ todavía. Gina dice que no quiere
volver a los Estados Unidos. Yo (10) __sé__ que mis padres van a estar muy
tristes si ella no vuelve.

PROF. DOMÍNGUEZ: Yo (11) __conozco__ a tu hermana y (12) __sé__ que es una mujer inteligente.
Va a pensarlo bien antes de tomar una decisión.

4·9 ¿Me puedes ayudar? `3:00`

Sofía acaba de llegar a San Salvador y se siente un poco perdida (*she
is feeling a little lost*). Túrnense para hacer y contestar sus preguntas
de manera creativa. Luego, creen (*create*) y contesten **dos** preguntas
más usando **saber** y **conocer**.

MODELO   SOFÍA: *¿Sabes dónde hay una iglesia?*

TÚ: *Sí, sé que hay una iglesia en la plaza.*

1. ¿Conoces un buen restaurante típico?
2. ¿Sabes dónde está el restaurante?
3. ¿Sabes cuáles son los platos típicos del restaurante?
4. ¿Conoces al cocinero (*chef*)?
5. ¿?
6. ¿?

METHODOLOGY • Chunking

A common pedagogical technique for breaking up complex tasks is to chunk information into manageable bits. We have done that with stem-changing verbs and the *¿Qué tienen que hacer? ¿Qué pasa?* presentation. These verbs are presented first as vocabulary, and then as stem-changing verbs. Practicing them as infinitives first helps students focus on and learn their meanings. The next step will be to introduce them as stem-changing verbs in the following grammar presentation on page 144.

NATIONAL STANDARDS

Communication

Notice that these stem-changing verbs are first practiced in their infinitive form. Then, in actividades **4-12** and **4-13**, students utilize the *tener que . . .* grammar point that they learned in the previous chapter. This is an excellent form of recycling, and it is a meaningful exercise for students, since they always have to do something!

    Standard 1.1 focuses on an interpersonal exchange for Communication. The stem-changing verbs such as *dormir, preferir, almorzar, entender, pensar,* etc. facilitate communication about things that students are familiar with. They can use the new verbs to exchange their opinions (*pensar*), express feelings and emotions (*preferir, pensar*), and provide and obtain information about each other (*almorzar, dormir, entender, recordar,* etc.) and how these verbs relate to their daily lives.

NOTE FOR

Vocabulario

Remind students that in *Capítulo 3* they learned some expressions with *tener*. They will recall that *tener + que + infinitive* means "to have to do something."

INSTRUCTIONS FOR 4-10

Although this activity may seem simple, it provides excellent practice with the new verbs. Provide these instructions to your students:

Make a tic-tac-toe grid on a sheet of paper. Write a different verb from the list of new verbs in each of the nine boxes. Do not show your grid to your partner. Take turns guessing

VOCABULARIO 3 — ¿Qué tienen que hacer? ¿Qué pasa?

4-14 to 4-16

almorzar · cerrar · comenzar · costar · dormir · encontrar · entender · mostrar · pedir · pensar · perder · preferir · recordar · repetir · seguir · servir · volver

2:00   **4·10   Tic-tac-toe**

Escucha mientras tu instructor/a explica el juego del *tic-tac-toe*.

MODELO   E1: *¿Tienes "volver"?*

              E2: *Sí, tengo "volver". / No, no tengo "volver".*

the words your partner has selected. Each time you guess correctly, your partner marks an X over the word.

2:00

4·11 ¿Y lo opuesto?

Decidan juntos qué verbo expresa lo opuesto (*opposite*) de las palabras o expresiones de la siguiente lista.

MODELO   E1:   no comer
E2:   *almorzar*

repetir	encontrar	volver	entender	pedir
perder	comenzar	querer	cerrar	almorzar

1. salir   volver
2. terminar   comenzar
3. abrir   cerrar
4. perder   encontrar
5. decir una vez   repetir
6. dar   pedir
7. encontrar   perder
8. no comprender   entender

4·12 Los quehaceres   2:00

Túrnense para expresar qué tienen que hacer ustedes generalmente.

MODELO   Tengo que comenzar…

E1:   *Tengo que comenzar la tarea para mi clase de español.*

E2:   *Tengo que comenzar la tarea para mi clase de inglés.*

1. Tengo que repetir…
2. Tengo que almorzar…
3. Tengo que recordar…
4. Tengo que dormir…

7:00

4·13 Entrevistas

Entrevista a tres compañeros para averiguar si (*to find out if*) hacen cosas similares. Después, comparte la información con la clase. ¿Qué tienen ustedes en común?

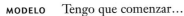

1. ¿Qué tienes que hacer para prepararte bien para las clases?
2. ¿Qué tienes que hacer durante la clase de español para sacar buenas notas?
3. Generalmente, ¿qué tienes que hacer cuando terminas con tus clases?

GRAMÁTICA 4 — Los verbos con cambio de raíz

¡Cierro la ventana, pido una pizza y empiezo a estudiar!

4-17 to 4-25

In **Capítulo 3,** you learned a variety of common verbs that are irregular. Two of those verbs were **querer** and **poder,** which are irregular due to some changes in their stems. Look at the following verb groups and answer the questions for each group.

Change e → ie

cerrar (*to close*)

Singular		Plural	
yo	cierro	nosotros/as	cerramos
tú	cierras	vosotros/as	cerráis
él, ella, Ud.	cierra	ellos/as, Uds.	cierran

1. Which verb forms look like the infinitive **cerrar**?
2. Which verb forms have a spelling change that differs from the infinitive **cerrar**?

Check your answers to the preceding questions in Appendix 1.

Other verbs like **cerrar** (e → ie) are:

comenzar	*to begin*	**mentir**	*to lie*	**preferir**	*to prefer*
empezar	*to begin*	**pensar**	*to think*	**recomendar**	*to recommend*
entender	*to understand*	**perder**	*to lose; to waste*		

Change e → i

pedir (*to ask for*)

Singular		Plural	
yo	pido	nosotros/as	pedimos
tú	pides	vosotros/as	pedís
él, ella, Ud.	pide	ellos/as, Uds.	piden

1. Which verb forms look like the infinitive **pedir**?
2. Which verb forms have a spelling change that differs from the infinitive **pedir**?

Check your answers to the preceding questions in Appendix 1.

Other verbs like **pedir** (e → i) are:

repetir	*to repeat*	**seguir***	*to follow; to continue (doing something)*	**servir**	*to serve*

*Note: The **yo** form of **seguir** is **sigo.**

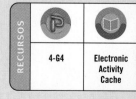

Change o → ue

encontrar (*to find*)

Singular		Plural	
yo	encuentro	nosotros/as	encontramos
tú	encuentras	vosotros/as	encontráis
él, ella, Ud.	encuentra	ellos/as, Uds.	encuentran

1. Which verb forms look like the infinitive **encontrar**?
2. Which verb forms have a spelling change that differs from the infinitive **encontrar**?

Check your answers to the preceding questions in Appendix 1.

Other verbs like **encontrar** (**o → ue**) are:

almorzar	*to have lunch*	**dormir**	*to sleep*	**mostrar**	*to show*	**volver**	*to return*
costar	*to cost*	**morir**	*to die*	**recordar**	*to remember*		

Change u → ue

jugar (*to play*)

Singular		Plural	
yo	juego	nosotros/as	jugamos
tú	juegas	vosotros/as	jugáis
él, ella, Ud.	juega	ellos/as, Uds.	juegan

1. Which verb forms look like the infinitive **jugar**?
2. Which verb forms have a spelling change that differs from the infinitive **jugar**?
3. Why does **jugar** not belong with the verbs like **encontrar**?

Check your answers to the preceding questions in Appendix 1.

To summarize…

1. What rule can you make regarding all four groups of stem-changing verbs and their forms?
2. With what group of stem-changing verbs would you put **querer**?
3. With what group of stem-changing verbs would you put the following verbs?

demostrar	*to demonstrate*	**encerrar**	*to enclose*
devolver	*to return (an object)*	**perseguir**	*to chase*

Check your answers to the preceding questions in Appendix 1.

5:00 **4•14** Categorías

Paso 1 With a partner, write the stem-changing verbs that were just presented on individual slips of paper. Next, make a chart with three categories: **e → ie, e → i, o → ue.**

Paso 2 Join another pair of students. When your instructor says **¡Empieza!**, place the verbs under the correct category (**e → ie, e → i,** or **o → ue**). Do several rounds of this activity, playing against different doubles partners.

METHODOLOGY • Reviewing and Recycling Grammatical Concepts

You may wish to have a warm-up each day at the beginning of class where you select a different stem-changing verb from each category and do a quick mechanical drill with the forms. You can also end a class with a quick mechanical drill if you have a few minutes to spare. These quick reviews should not last for more than a minute and a half.

Suggestion for *Los verbos con cambio de raíz* Drill the verb forms; say an infinitive and a pronoun in Spanish. The class should respond chorally with the correct form. Then drill by asking directed questions such as: ¿Juegas al tenis?, ¿Cuándo cierras las ventanas?, ¿Mientes a tu novio/a o tus amigos/as?, ¿A qué hora empiezan tus clases?, ¿Qué color prefieres, el azul o el rojo?, ¿A quién no entiendes?, etc.

Additional activity for *Los verbos con cambio de raíz*. ¿Conoces bien a tu compañero/a de clase? Túrnense para hacerse esta entrevista.

1. ¿Entiendes a tu profesor/a cuando habla español?
2. ¿A qué hora comienzas la tarea los lunes?
3. ¿Prefieres estudiar por la noche o por la mañana?
4. ¿Pierdes tus lápices o bolígrafos frecuentemente?
5. Generalmente, ¿con quién(es) almuerzas?
6. ¿Cuántas horas duermes cada noche?

4•15 Nuestras preferencias

`2:00`

Averigua cuáles son las preferencias de tu compañero/a. Comparte tus respuestas con la clase.

MODELO   el café o la Coca-Cola

E1: *¿Qué prefieres, el café o la Coca-Cola?*

E2: *Prefiero el café.*

¿Qué prefieres,...?

1. las matemáticas o las ciencias
2. la primavera o el otoño
3. el frío o el calor
4. el béisbol o el básquetbol
5. un sofá o un sillón
6. pasar la aspiradora o sacar la basura

4•16 ¿Quién hace qué?

`7:00`

Túrnense para decir qué personas que ustedes conocen hacen las siguientes cosas.

MODELO   E1: siempre perder la tarea

E2: *Mi hermano Tom siempre pierde la tarea.*

1. pensar ser profesor/a
2. almorzar en McDonald's a menudo
3. querer visitar Suramérica
4. siempre entender al/a la profesor/a de español
5. preferir dormir hasta el mediodía
6. volver tarde a casa a menudo
7. perder dinero
8. pensar que Santa Claus existe
9. nunca mentir
10. comenzar a hacer la tarea de noche

4•17 ¿Quién es?

`7:00`

Escribe las respuestas a las siguientes preguntas en forma de párrafos en una hoja de papel.

Primer párrafo

1. ¿Qué clases tienes este semestre?
2. ¿A qué hora empieza tu clase preferida? ¿Cuándo termina?
3. ¿Qué prefieres hacer si (*if*) tienes tiempo entre (*between*) tus clases?
4. ¿A qué hora vuelves a tu dormitorio/apartamento/casa?

Segundo párrafo

1. ¿Qué coche tienes (o quieres tener)? ¿Cuánto cuesta un coche nuevo?
2. ¿Cómo vienes a la universidad? (Por ejemplo, ¿vienes en coche?)
3. ¿Dónde prefieres vivir, en una residencia estudiantil, en un apartamento o en una casa?
4. ¿Dónde quieres vivir después de graduarte?

Tercer párrafo

1. ¿Qué deporte prefieres?
2. ¿Juegas a ese deporte? ¿Ves ese deporte en la televisión?
3. Normalmente, ¿cuándo y con quién(es) juegas?
4. ¿Qué otros deportes te gustan?

Capítulo Preliminar A. La hora, pág. 18; Capítulo 2. Las materias y las especialidades, pág. 62; Los deportes y los pasatiempos, pág. 83.

¿Cómo andas?

Having completed the first **Comunicación**, I now can…

	Feel Confident	Need to Review
• state where things are located around town and state what I could accomplish in each place (p. 136)	❑	❑
• pronounce the letters **c** and **z** correctly (p. 137)	❑	❑
• use **saber** and **conocer** appropriately (p. 140)	❑	❑
• list what I and others need to do using a form of **tener que…** (p. 142)	❑	❑
• use verbs that have stem changes correctly (p. 144)	❑	❑

Comunicación

- Describing what you will do
- Discussing volunteerism

SECTION GOALS FOR
Comunicación

By the end of the *Comunicación* section, students will be able to:

- form the verb *ir* correctly.
- combine what they have to do (*tener + que + infinitive*) with where they go (*ir*) to do it.
- construct sentences in the periphrastic future using *ir + a + infinitive*.
- discuss jobs and volunteer work.
- use negative and affirmative indefinite expressions.
- talk about their ideal professor.
- demonstrate their understanding of how *ser* and *estar* are used.

GRAMÁTICA 5

El verbo *ir*

SAM
M.S.L
4-26 to 4-28

1:00

Voy al almacén. ¿Adónde vas tú?

Another important verb in Spanish is **ir**. Note its irregular present tense forms below.

ir (*to go*)

Singular		Plural	
yo	**voy**	nosotros/as	**vamos**
tú	**vas**	vosotros/as	**vais**
él, ella, Ud.	**va**	ellos/as, Uds.	**van**

Voy al parque. ¿**Van** ustedes también?
No, no **vamos** ahora. Preferimos **ir** más tarde.

I'm going to the park. Are you all going too?
No, we're not going now. We prefer to go later.

METHODOLOGY • Presenting Information as Needed

We instructors love the Spanish language and are eager to share what we know with our students, yet sometimes we share more than students can grasp at a time. Too much information can confuse students and can also cause a raising of what Stephen Krashen calls the *affective filter*, where the students become hesitant to produce language for fear of making a mistake with the vast amount of information they have been given. Hence, we suggest simply presenting *¿Adónde?* in the context of use with *ir*. If you feel that your students will benefit from a more in-depth presentation (e.g., Heritage language learners), then please provide it.

Suggestion for *El verbo ir* After drilling *ir* forms mechanically by giving subjects and having students give the matching verb forms, practice with directed questions, such as *¿Adónde vas mañana? ¿Adónde vas de vacaciones? ¿Adónde van tus amigos este fin de semana?*

RECURSOS

4-G5 | Electronic Activity Cache

4·18　¿Adónde vas？　[2:00]

Túrnense para completar la conversación que tienen Memo y Esteban al salir de la clase de música. Usen las formas correctas del verbo **ir**.

MEMO:　　Hola, Esteban. ¿Adónde (1)＿＿vas＿＿ ahora?

ESTEBAN:　¿Qué hay? Pues, (2)＿＿voy＿＿ a la clase de física.

MEMO:　　Yo no. Mi compañero de cuarto y yo (3)＿＿vamos＿＿ al gimnasio. Tenemos un torneo (*tournament*) de tenis.

ESTEBAN:　Buena suerte. Oye, ¿tú (4)＿＿vas＿＿ a la fiesta de Isabel esta noche?

MEMO:　　No sé. ¿Quiénes (5)＿＿van＿＿? Creo que (yo) (6)＿＿voy＿＿ al cine para ver la película nueva de Steven Spielberg.

ESTEBAN:　¿Por qué no (7)＿＿vas＿＿ primero a la fiesta y después al cine?

MEMO:　　Buena idea. ¿(8)＿＿Vamos＿＿ (tú y yo) juntos?

ESTEBAN:　Muy bien. Mi amigo Roberto (9)＿＿va＿＿ también. Hablamos después del torneo.

MEMO:　　Bueno, hasta luego.

> **Fíjate**
> In *Capítulo 2* you learned two words for the question word "Where?" Use ¿*Adónde?* with *ir*.

> **Fíjate**
> Remember that *a + el = al*.

4·19　Los "¿por qué?"　[2:00]

Esperanza tiene una sobrina que está en la etapa de los "¿por qué?", tiene muchas preguntas. Túrnense para darle las respuestas de Esperanza a Rosita.

MODELO　ROSITA:　　　¿Por qué va mi papá al gimnasio?
　　　　　ESPERANZA:　*Tu papá va al gimnasio porque quiere hacer ejercicio.*

1. ¿Por qué va mi mamá al mercado?
2. ¿Por qué va mi hermana a la oficina de correos?
3. ¿Por qué van mis hermanos al parque?
4. ¿Por qué vas a la universidad?
5. ¿Por qué no vamos al cine ahora?

Capítulo Preliminar A.
La hora, pág. 18.

4·20 ¿Adónde van?

Miren los horarios de las siguientes personas. Túrnense para decir adónde van, a qué hora y qué hacen en cada (*each*) lugar.

MODELO *A las diez mis padres van a la librería para buscar y comprar unos libros. Luego…*

Mis padres

16 de marzo
10:00AM buscar y comprar unos libros
2:00PM comer
6:00PM ver un programa de televisión
10:00PM dormir

Mi hermano

16 de marzo
9:00AM matemáticas
10:00AM estudiar
4:00PM leer correo electrónico
8:00PM ver *Romeo y Julieta* con Beatriz

Yo

16 de marzo
8:00AM comprar comida
10:00AM mandar una carta
12:00PM ver la exposición de Picasso con mi clase de arte
2:00PM jugar al fútbol
8:00PM ir al cine a ver la película *Drácula* con amigos

GRAMÁTICA 6   *Ir + a + infinitivo*

SAM

4-29 to 4-31

¿Vamos a almorzar pronto? ¡Tengo hambre!

Sí. Voy a pedir comida salvadoreña.

Study the following sentences and then answer the questions that follow.

Voy a mandar esta carta. ¿Quieres ir conmigo?	*I'm going to mail this letter. Do you want to come with me?*
Sí. Luego, **¿vas a almorzar?**	*Yes. Then, are you going to have lunch?*
Sí, **vamos a comer** comida guatemalteca en el restaurante Tikal.	*Yes, we are going to eat Guatemalan food at Tikal Restaurant.*
¡Perfecto! Ya sé que **voy a pedir** unas empanadas.	*Perfect! I already know that I am going to order some empanadas.*
Muy bien. Pero, primero, tengo que ir al banco. **¡Vamos a necesitar** dinero!	*OK. But first I have to go to the bank. We are going to need money!*

1. When do the actions in the previous sentences take place: in the *past*, *present*, or *future*?
2. What is the first bold type verb you see in each sentence?
3. In what form is the second bolded verb?
4. What word comes between the two verbs? Does this word have an equivalent in English?
5. What is your rule, then, for expressing future actions or statements?

Check your answers to the preceding questions in Appendix 1.

NATIONAL STANDARDS
Communication

Speaking in the future tense is one of the main time frames. When an individual can sustain communication in the present, future, and past tenses, they are emerging into the ACTFL Advanced Level of oral proficiency.

   The new verb *ir* and the *ir + a + infinitive* construction allow students a greater range of communication, because they can talk about where they are going and what they are doing in the immediate future. Learning the new construction provides more opportunities for communication in the interpersonal mode (Standard 1.1), as they engage in conversations about their plans and provide and obtain information. The *ir + a + infinitive* construction works well with Standard 1.3, because students are able to present about their future plans to an audience of listeners or readers. With the appropriate vocabulary, they can communicate their weekend plans, what they want to do after they graduate, how they will spend the next five years, and the characteristics of their ideal mate. You could also ask them to predict what their hometown city or university town will be like in ten years.

Suggestion for *ir + a + infinitivo*
After the initial presentation, the following directed questions can be used to practice *ir + a + infinitive*. They can also be used as warm-up questions to begin a class: *¿Cuándo vas a almorzar?, ¿Cuándo vas a trabajar?, ¿Cuándo vas a hacer tu tarea?, ¿Adónde vas a estudiar?, ¿Qué vas a estudiar?, ¿Cuándo vas a limpiar tu casa?, ¿Cuándo vas a lavar los platos?, ¿Adónde vas a ir este verano?*

HERITAGE LANGUAGE LEARNERS

If your Heritage language learners have a good understanding of the future expression *ir + a + infinitive*, they could use the future tense for actividades **4-21** through **4-23** to talk about their future plans.

2:00
4·21 ¿Y en el futuro?

Túrnense para contestar las siguientes preguntas sobre el futuro.

1. ¿Vas a dedicar más tiempo a tus estudios?
2. ¿Vas a vivir en una casa grande?
3. ¿Tu familia va a visitar Honduras?
4. ¿Los doctores van a encontrar la cura para el cáncer?
5. ¿Vamos a poder acabar con (*end*) el terrorismo?

4·22 Mi agenda 2:00

¿Qué planes tienes para la semana que viene? Termina las frases sin (*without*) repetir los quehaceres.

Capítulo Preliminar A. Los días de la semana, los meses y las estaciones, pág. 20.

MODELO

E1: El lunes...

E2: *El lunes voy a lavar mi coche.*

1. El lunes...
2. El martes...
3. El miércoles...
4. El jueves...
5. El viernes...
6. El sábado...
7. El domingo...
8. El fin de semana...

3:00 **4·23 Qué será, será...**

¿Qué tiene el futuro para ti, tus amigos y tu familia? Escribe **cinco** predicciones de lo que va a ocurrir en el futuro.

MODELO

Mi primo va a ir a la Universidad Autónoma el año que viene. Mis padres van a limpiar el armario y el altillo. Yo voy a estudiar en Suramérica....

VOCABULARIO 7 — Trabajos y servicios voluntarios

3:00

SAM
4-32 to
4-34

el campamento de niños

el/la consejero/a

la residencia de ancianos

las personas mayores, los mayores

la campaña política

apoyar a un/a candidato/a

la canoa

la artesanía

hacer una caminata

la hoguera

repartir comidas

organizar

la tienda de campaña

circular una petición

llevar a alguien al médico

ir de excursión

CORREO

Guchigami

VOTEN

Unos verbos	*Some verbs*	Otras palabras útiles	*Some useful words*
deber	*ought to; should*	el deber	*obligation; duty*
trabajar como voluntario/a	*to volunteer*	el voluntariado	*volunteerism*

NATIONAL STANDARDS
Communication, Connections, Communities

This vocabulary connects with other disciplines, such as health care professions. It also provides students with ideas of where they can use Spanish in their community. Some of your institutions require or encourage community service projects, and this vocabulary connects directly with many university offerings or initiatives. This vocabulary also ties in well with the chapter title *Nuestra comunidad*.

The vocabulary in the section, *Trabajos y servicios voluntarios*, provides a glimpse into the many types of volunteer work and paid work available to students. Ask the career center of your school what types of volunteer jobs are available and bring that vocabulary to class. Standards 1.1 and 1.3 apply to volunteer work because students can communicate interpersonally about the types of work they would like to do and they can present about the types of work. To integrate Standard 1.3, ask students to research a particular volunteer position (or internship) available in their community and make a presentation to the class about their job. You could also invite a local organization in need of Spanish-speaking volunteers to present to students. Standard 3.1 states that students reinforce and further their knowledge of other disciplines through Spanish. Have the students research an internship or volunteer position that ties in with their major so that they make connections and they are able to work in the community, applying their major and the skills they have acquired in Spanish (Standard 5.1).

NOTE FOR 4-24

Give students the definitions on slips of paper and have them act out the definitions. You could also use the board for help on some of the items, or simply play charades.

2:00

4·24 Definiciones

Túrnense para leer las siguientes definiciones y decir cuál de las palabras o expresiones de la lista de **Trabajos y servicios voluntarios** corresponde a cada una.

MODELO   E1:   personas que tienen muchos años

E2:   *las personas mayores*

1. un bote (*boat*) para una o dos personas   la canoa
2. dar un documento a personas para obtener firmas (*signatures*)   circular una petición
3. una estructura portátil (no permanente) que se usa para dormir fuera de casa   la tienda de campaña
4. acompañar a una persona a una cita (*appointment*) con el médico   llevar a alguien al médico
5. una persona que trabaja con los niños en un campamento   el/la consejero/a
6. servir a las personas sin recibir dinero a cambio (*in exchange*)   el voluntariado
7. un tipo de arte que puedes crear con materiales diversos   la artesanía
8. un lugar donde van los niños, generalmente en el verano, para hacer muchas actividades diferentes   el campamento de niños
9. trabajar para un candidato político   apoyar a un/a candidato/a
10. un lugar donde viven las personas mayores   la residencia de ancianos

4:00

4·25 En tu opinión...

Termina las siguientes frases sobre el voluntariado. Después, comparte tus respuestas con un/a compañero/a.

MODELO   *Yo soy una consejera perfecta porque me gustan los niños. También escucho muy bien....*

1. Yo (no) soy un/a consejero/a perfecto/a porque…
2. Dos trabajos voluntarios que me gustan son…
3. Hay muchas residencias de ancianos en los Estados Unidos porque…
4. Yo apoyo al candidato _____ porque…
5. Cuando repartes comidas, puedes…

4·26 Elaborando el tema [4:00]

En grupos de tres o cuatro, discutan las siguientes preguntas.

1. ¿Cuáles son las actividades más interesantes en los campamentos de niños?
2. ¿Cuáles son las oportunidades de voluntariado que existen en tu universidad?
3. ¿Cuáles son los trabajos voluntarios que se asocian más con apoyar a un candidato?
4. ¿Crees que servir a la comunidad es un deber?

[2:00]

4-35 to
4-37

La conciencia social

Tanto en los Estados Unidos como en los países hispanohablantes, la gente se interesa cada día más en servir a la comunidad. Su conciencia social se puede manifestar tanto *(as much as)* en un trabajo remunerado *(job with a salary)* como en trabajos voluntarios, por ejemplo ser entrenadores de deportes, llevar a los ancianos a pasear por los centros comerciales, trabajar para los congresistas, etc. En los Estados Unidos muchos trabajos voluntarios tienen que ver con *(are related to)* las personas mayores o con los jóvenes.

En los países hispanohablantes, el voluntariado todavía no existe de la misma forma que conocemos en los Estados Unidos. Sin embargo *(Nevertheless)*, cuando la gente necesita ayuda, por ejemplo después de un desastre natural, los hispanos están allí para servir a su comunidad.

Preguntas

1. ¿Qué trabajos voluntarios hay en tu comunidad?
2. ¿Cómo sirves a tu comunidad?

NATIONAL STANDARDS
Communication, Connections, Communities

The cultural note provides a starting point for discussing how students can help others in the community. Students can engage in conversations about how they contribute to the community and if they feel they are doing enough to participate in their community (Standard 1.1). They can also brainstorm with other students to use what they are learning in their programs of study and apply their content knowledge to improving the community (3.1). Lastly, depending upon the size of the Hispanic population in your area, students could think of a way to improve the community now, during their experience as a college student (Standard 5.1) or by using *ir + a + infinitive* to talk about how they might combine their Spanish skills and their major to improve the community after they graduate (Standard 5.2).

METHODOLOGY • Maximizing Class Time

None of us ever has enough class time to do what we feel is important and necessary. The authors of *¡Anda!* are committed to helping students spend as much of the class period as possible speaking Spanish. Hence, as was suggested from the beginning, we highly recommend that all of the culture readings are assigned to be read before class, especially as they become longer in length.

NOTE FOR

La conciencia social

The concept of volunteerism is expanding throughout the Spanish-speaking world, but still does not exist to the degree that it exists in the United States. In the United States, many schools and communities have highly developed programs for volunteering. In some schools, it is a requirement to volunteer a certain number of hours each year.

NOTE FOR *Las expresiones afirmativas y negativas*

You may begin this presentation by asking students what they do on a regular basis and changing their affirmative responses to negative ones, stating that you do the opposite. E.g., *Yo voy al gimnasio.* ➔ *¡Jamás voy al gimnasio!*

GRAMÁTICA 8   ## Las expresiones afirmativas y negativas

4-38 to 4-39   9, 38, 40

3:00

> Siempre me gusta hacer artesanía con los niños, ¡pero jamás voy a ir en una canoa con ellos!

In the previous chapters you have seen and used a number of the affirmative and negative expressions listed below. Study the list and learn the ones that are new to you.

Expresiones afirmativas		Expresiones negativas	
a veces	*sometimes*	**jamás**	*never; not ever* (emphatic)
algo	*something; anything*	**nada**	*nothing*
alguien	*someone*	**nadie**	*no one; nobody*
algún	*some; any*	**ningún**	*none*
alguno/a/os/as	*some; any*	**ninguno/a/os/as**	*none*
siempre	*always*	**nunca**	*never*
o… o	*either… or*	**ni… ni**	*neither… nor*

Look at the sentences below, paying special attention to the position of the negative words, and answer the questions that follow.

—¿Quién llama?   *Who is calling?*

—**Nadie** llama. (**No** llama **nadie**.)   *No one is calling.*

—¿Vas al gimnasio todos los días?   *Do you go to the gym every day?*

—No, **nunca** voy. (No, **no** voy **nunca**.)   *No, I never go.*

> **Fíjate**
>
> Unlike English, Spanish can have two or more negatives in the same sentence. A double negative is actually quite common. For example, *No tengo nada que hacer* is *I don't have anything to do.*

1. When you use a negative word (**nadie, nunca,** etc.) in a sentence, does it come before or after the verb?

2. When you use the word **no** and then a negative word in the same sentence, does **no** come before or after the verb? Where does the negative word come in these sentences?

3. Does the meaning change depending on where you put the negative word? (e.g., **Nadie llama** *versus* **No llama nadie**).

Check your answers to the preceding questions in Appendix 1.

Algún **and** *ningún*

1. Forms of **algún** and **ningún** need to agree in gender and number with the noun they modify.

2. Use **algún** and **ningún** when they are followed by *masculine, singular nouns*.

3. When no noun follows, use **alguno** or **ninguno** when referring to masculine, singular nouns, and **alguna** or **ninguna** when referring to feminine singular nouns.

RECURSOS   4-G8   Electronic Activity Cache

Study the following sentences.

María:	¿Tienes **alguna** clase fácil este semestre?
Juan:	No, no tengo **ninguna**. ¡Y **ningún** profesor es simpático!
María:	Vaya, ¿y puedes hacer **algún** cambio?
Juan:	No, no puedo hacer **ninguno**. (No, no puedo tomar **ningún** otro curso.)

4·27 ¿Con qué frecuencia? ⏱ 7:00

Indica con una **X** con qué frecuencia tus compañeros/as de clase hacen las siguientes actividades. Escribe el nombre de tu compañero/a debajo de la **X** y comparte los resultados con la clase.

MODELO   ir de excursión con niños
A veces Josefina va de excursión con niños.

	SIEMPRE	A VECES	NUNCA
1. ir de excursión con niños		*Josefina*	
2. trabajar en una campaña política			
3. hacer una hoguera			
4. circular una petición			
5. firmar una petición			
6. repartir comidas a los mayores			
7. visitar una residencia de ancianos			
8. trabajar en un campamento para niños			
9. trabajar como voluntario en un hospital o una clínica			
10. dormir en una tienda de campaña			

4·28 El/La profesor/a ideal ⏱ 2:00

Túrnense para decir si las siguientes características son ciertas (*true*) o no en un/a profesor/a ideal.

MODELO   E1: a veces duerme en su trabajo
E2: *No. Un profesor ideal nunca duerme en su trabajo.*
E1: jamás va a clase sin sus apuntes
E2: *Sí, un profesor ideal jamás va a clase sin sus apuntes.*

Un/a profesor/a ideal…

1. siempre está contento/a en su trabajo.
2. a veces llega a clase cinco minutos tarde.
3. prepara algo interesante para cada clase.
4. piensa que sabe más que nadie.
5. falta (*misses*) a unas clases.
6. nunca pone a los estudiantes en grupos.
7. jamás asigna tarea para la clase.
8. siempre prefiere leer sus apuntes.
9. no pierde nada (la tarea, los exámenes, etc.)
10. no habla con nadie después de la clase.

4·29 ¿Sí o no? `3:00`

Túrnense para contestar las siguientes preguntas.

MODELO   E1: *¿Siempre almuerzas a las cuatro de la tarde?*

E2: *No, nunca almuerzo a las cuatro de la tarde. / No, no almuerzo nunca/jamás a las cuatro de la tarde.*

1. ¿Pierdes algo cuando vas de vacaciones?
2. ¿Siempre encuentras las cosas que pierdes?
3. ¿A veces duermes más de diez horas?
4. ¿Haces algo para ayudar a los pobres?

5. ¿Siempre almuerzas en restaurantes caros (*expensive*)?
6. ¿Conoces a alguien de Guatemala?
7. ¿Siempre piensas en el amor?
8. ¿Hay algo más importante que el dinero?

`2:00` ## 4·30 No tienes razón

Tu amigo/a es muy idealista. Túrnense para decirle (*tell him/her*) que debe ser más realista, usando expresiones negativas.

MODELO

Tengo que encontrar el curso perfecto.

No hay ningún curso perfecto.

1. Tengo que buscar una profesión sin estrés.
2. Quiero el coche perfecto, un Lexus.
3. Voy a tener hijos perfectos.
4. Pienso que no voy a estudiar esta semana que viene.
5. Voy a encontrar unos muebles muy baratos y elegantes.

GRAMÁTICA 9   Un repaso de *ser* y *estar*

SAM

4-40 to 4-43

`5:00`

Son las ocho. ¿Dónde está Beto?

You have learned two Spanish verbs that mean **to be** in English. These verbs, **estar** and **ser,** are contrasted below.

*Estar is used:

- **To describe physical or personality characteristics that can change, or to indicate a change in condition**

María **está** enferma hoy.	*María is sick today.*
Jorge y Julia **están** tristes.	*Jorge and Julia are sad.*
La cocina **está** sucia.	*The kitchen is dirty.*

- **To describe the location of people or places**

El museo **está** en la calle Quiroga.	*The museum is on Quiroga Street.*
Estamos en el centro comercial.	*We're at the mall. Where are*
¿Dónde **estás** tú?	*you?*

***Ser** is used:

- **To describe physical or personality characteristics that remain relatively constant**

Gregorio **es** inteligente.	*Gregorio is intelligent.*
Yanina **es** guapa.	*Yanina is pretty.*
Su tienda de campaña **es** amarilla.	*Their tent is yellow.*
Las casas **son** grandes.	*The houses are large.*

- **To explain what or who someone or something is**

El Dr. Suárez **es** profesor de literatura.	*Dr. Suárez is a literature professor.*
Marisol **es** mi hermana.	*Marisol is my sister.*

- **To tell time, or to tell when or where an event takes place**

¿Qué hora **es**?	*What time is it?*
Son las ocho.	*It's eight o'clock.*
Mi clase de español **es** a las ocho y **es** en Peabody Hall.	*My Spanish class is at eight o'clock and is in Peabody Hall.*

- **To tell where someone is from and to express nationality**

Somos de Honduras.	*We are from Honduras.*
Somos hondureños.	*We are Honduran.*
Ellos **son** de Guatemala.	*They are from Guatemala.*
Son guatemaltecos.	*They are Guatemalan.*

Compare the following sentences and answer the questions below.

    Su hermano **es** simpático.
    Su hermano **está** enfermo.

> **Estrategia**
>
> Review the forms of *ser* (p. 13) and *estar* (p. 78).

1. Why do you use a form of **ser** in the first sentence?
2. Why do you use a form of **estar** in the second sentence?

Check your answers to the preceding questions in Appendix 1.

You will learn several more uses for **estar** and **ser** by the end of *¡Anda!*

Additional activity for *Ser y estar* **Quiero conocerte mejor.** Túrnense para hacer y contestar las siguientes preguntas.

1. ¿De dónde eres?
2. ¿Cómo eres?
3. ¿Cómo estás hoy?
4. ¿A qué hora son tus clases?
5. ¿Cómo es tu casa?
6. ¿Dónde está tu casa?
7. ¿De qué color es tu casa?
8. ¿Dónde está tu dormitorio?
9. ¿Cómo es tu dormitorio?
10. ¿Cuál es tu color favorito?
11. Descríbele la persona más importante para ti.
12. ¿Dónde está él/ella ahora (*now*)?

You may wish to tell your students to interpret *casa* in this activity as either *casa, apartamento,* or *residencia estudiantil.*

4·31 ¿Quién es Margarita?   3·00

Margarita es una estudiante de la Universidad Francisco Marroquín en la ciudad de Guatemala. Completen juntos el párrafo siguiente con las formas correctas de **ser** o **estar** para conocerla (*to know her*) mejor.

(1) _____Son_____ las siete y media de la mañana. Margarita (2) _____está_____ cansada pero tiene que tener prisa porque su clase de física (3) _____es_____ a las ocho. ¿Me dices que no la conoces? Pues, Margarita (4) _____es_____ la hermana de mi amigo Roberto. (5) _____Es_____ una mujer alta, inteligente y muy simpática. Le gusta estudiar. (6) _____Es_____ de la ciudad de Antigua y sus padres viven allí (*there*) todavía (*still*). Ellos (7) _____están_____ muy contentos porque ella tiene muy buenas notas en todos sus cursos.

Bueno, casi (8) _____son_____ las ocho. ¿Dónde (9) _____está_____ Margarita ahora? Pues, como siempre, llega a tiempo a su clase; (10) _____es_____ muy puntual y no le gusta llegar tarde.

Answers to 4-32.
2. physical condition
3. when an event takes place
4. who someone is
5. physical characteristics
6. tell where someone is from
7. condition
8. telling time
9. location of people
10. personality characteristic

3·00   ## 4·32 Así es

Expliquen por qué usaron (*you used*) **ser** o **estar** en la actividad **4-31**.

1. (*Son*) telling time   telling time

4·33 Nuestro conocimiento   1·00

¿Qué sabes de Guatemala, Honduras y El Salvador? Túrnense para hacerse y contestar las siguientes preguntas.

1. ¿Dónde están estos países, en Norteamérica, Centroamérica o Suramérica?
2. ¿Cuál está más cerca de México? ¿Cuál está más cerca de Panamá?
3. ¿Son países grandes o pequeños?
4. ¿Cuáles son sus capitales?

Answers to 4-33.
1. Están en Centroamérica.
2. Guatemala está más cerca de México. Honduras está más cerca de Panamá.
3. Son países pequeños.
4. La capital de Guatemala es Guatemala. La capital de Honduras es Tegucigalpa. La capital de El Salvador es San Salvador.

4·34 ¡A jugar!   5·00

Vamos a practicar **ser** y **estar.**

Paso 1   Draw two columns on a piece of paper. Label one column **ser** and the other **estar.** Your instructor will give you three minutes to write as many sentences with **ser** and **estar** as you can.

Paso 2   After you have finished writing, form groups of four to check your sentences and uses of the verbs. How many correct sentences do you have?

4·35 Somos iguales   ⏱ 10:00

Paso 1 Draw **three** circles, as per the model below, and ask each other questions to find out what things you have in common and what sets you apart. In the center circle write sentences using **ser** and **estar** about things you have in common, and in the side circles write sentences about things that set you apart.

MODELO

E1: *¿Cuál es tu color favorito?*

E2: *Mi color favorito es el negro.*

E1: *Mi color favorito es el negro también.*

(E1/E2 WRITE: *Nuestro color favorito es el negro.*)

E2: *Hoy estoy nerviosa. ¿Cómo estás tú?*

E1: *Yo estoy cansado.*

(E2 WRITES: *Hoy estoy nerviosa.*;
E1 WRITES: *Hoy estoy cansado.*)

Hoy estoy nerviosa.   Nuestro color favorito es negro.   Hoy estoy cansado.

Paso 2 Share your drawings with the class. What are some of the things that all of your classmates have in common?

ESCUCHA

4-44

ESTRATEGIA   **Paraphrasing what you hear**

When you know the context and listen carefully, you can repeat or paraphrase what you hear. Start by saying one or two words about what you hear, working up to complete sentences.

Marisol y Lupe conversan sobre el trabajo voluntario.

4·36   Antes de escuchar

Do you volunteer? What service opportunities exist in your city/town? You are going to hear a conversation between Marisol and Lupe, where Marisol shares her experiences with volunteering. Think of three Spanish words dealing with volunteering that you might hear.

Answers to 4-37. *Answers may include:*
Marisol hace trabajo voluntario. En la escuela ayuda a los niños con la tarea. Quiere trabajar en el hospital y visitar a los pacientes y llevarles las comidas. Mañana va a ir con Lupe al hospital.

4·37   A escuchar

CD 2
Track 18

After listening to Marisol and Lupe's conversation for the first time, jot down three main points, words, or topics. After listening to their conversation a second time, paraphrase their conversation with at least **three** complete sentences. You may use the following questions to guide your listening.

1. ¿Quién hace trabajo voluntario?

2. ¿Qué trabajo hace ella en la escuela? ¿Qué más quiere hacer?

3. ¿Adónde va a ir mañana? ¿Con quién?

4·38   Después de escuchar

Form *three* sentences about your volunteering experiences, or what you can do in your community, and tell them to your classmate. Your classmate will paraphrase what you have said.

ATIONAL STANDARDS

ommunication

he listening strategy for *Capítulo 4* is paraphrasing hat you hear. This section represents Standard 1.2 s students listen, understand, and interpret what ey have heard. Students also use Standard 1.1, e interpersonal mode, when they pair off and scuss volunteerism. The practice in a small group nds itself well to reinforcing the new strategy of araphrasing.

Suggestion for 4-35 For actividad **4-35**, pair students by their favorite colors. Also, for this activity, you can use notebook paper, but it is more enjoyable for the students if you use approximately three feet of newsprint and markers. They can then hold up their work at the end of the activity and report to the rest of the class. If you are interested in acquiring a roll of newsprint, your local newspaper is usually happy either to donate or sell "end rolls" to educators at a very nominal price. The end rolls are wonderful for all sorts of classroom activities.

SECTION GOALS FOR
Escucha

By the end of the *Escucha* section, students will be able to:

• paraphrase what they hear in short sentences.

• practice brainstorming in pre-listening activities for words they might hear.

• narrate how they volunteer and repeat what their classmates say about volunteering.

AUDIOSCRIPT FOR 4-37

LUPE:	Marisol, ¿es verdad que tú haces trabajo voluntario?
MARISOL:	Sí, para mí el voluntariado es muy importante.
LUPE:	¿Qué tipo de trabajo haces?
MARISOL:	Pues, me gusta trabajar con los niños. Generalmente voy a la escuela y les ayudo con la tarea.
LUPE:	¿Qué más?
MARISOL:	Quiero trabajar en el hospital. Quiero visitar a los pacientes y llevarles las comidas.
LUPE:	¿Vas a hacer trabajo voluntario ahora que estás en la universidad?
MARISOL:	Pienso que sí. Mañana voy a ir al hospital. Quiero saber si hay oportunidades. ¿Quieres venir?
LUPE:	¡Sí! Quiero ir también.

SECTION GOALS FOR

Escribe

By the end of the *Escribe* section, students will be able to:

- organize their writing by first making a list of things they will write about.
- write a minimum of five complete sentences.
- describe their town using the postcard format.
- read the postcards their classmates have written.

NATIONAL STANDARDS

Communication, Comparisons

Actividades **4-39** and **4-40** afford students a real-life situation where they can describe their town, perhaps compare it to either a country they have already learned about, or the feature countries, as well as use the present and future tenses.

The activities in the *Escribe* section focus on Standards 1.3 and 4.1. Standard 1.3 is the presentational mode of communication. Students write and illustrate postcards to an audience of readers (their classmates and teacher) or present the postcards to an audience of listeners by talking about their postcards in Spanish. Standards 1.1 and 1.2 could also be incorporated if you ask students to compare the postcards with each other (Standard 1.1- interpersonal), or if you have a pen pal from a Hispanic country whose postcards were written in Spanish, you could make copies for the students to read (Standard 1.2). The Comparisons Standard 4.1 is addressed by comparing how to write a postcard in English and Spanish. You could address Standard 4.2 by bringing in photocopies of blank postcards you have collected from different Hispanic countries and encouraging students to write about the kinds of activities they see on the postcard.

Suggestion for *Escribe* The activities in the *Escribe* section lend themselves well to homework. You could provide students with index cards of whatever size postcard you want, and bring in a completed postcard or a postcard from your travels, so they are clear about your expectations. You might have a gallery of completed postcards that you display.

ESCRIBE

4-45 to
4-46

4•39   Antes de escribir

Escribe una lista de los lugares importantes o interesantes de tu pueblo o ciudad. Luego escribe por qué son importantes o interesantes. Usa el vocabulario de este capítulo y de **También se dice...** Appendix 3.

4•40   Una tarjeta postal

Organiza tus ideas usando las siguientes preguntas como guía. Escribe por lo menos **cinco** oraciones completas. Si necesitas ayuda, puedes usar el modelo.

1. ¿Qué lugares hay en tu pueblo o ciudad?
2. ¿Por qué son importantes o interesantes?
3. Normalmente, ¿qué haces allí?
4. ¿Adónde vas los fines de semana?
5. ¿Qué te gusta de tu pueblo?

Querido/a_____:

Tienes que conocer mi pueblo, Roxborough.
Hay _____. Me gusta(n) _____. Es
interesante porque _____. Los fines de semana
_____. etc. . . .

Con cariño,
__(Tu nombre)__

4•41   Después de escribir

Tu profesor/a va a recoger las tarjetas y "mandárselas" (*mail them*) a otros miembros de la clase para leerlas.

¿Cómo andas?

Having completed the second **Comunicación,** I now can...

	Feel Confident	Need to Review
express where I and others wish to go using the correct forms of **ir** (p. 147)	❏	❏
talk about the future using **ir** + **a** + *infinitive* (p. 149)	❏	❏
give examples of volunteer and service opportunities (p. 151)	❏	❏
express concepts both affirmatively and negatively (p. 154)	❏	❏
use **ser** and **estar** in the correct contexts (p. 156)	❏	❏
paraphrase what I hear (p. 159)	❏	❏
write a postcard (p. 160)	❏	❏

Alfonso Guillermo Rivera Zúñiga

Honduras

`15:00`

CW
eBook

CD 2
Track 19

SAM

4-47 to
4-49

DVD/VHS

Vistas
culturales

Les presento mi país

Mi nombre es Alfonso Guillermo y soy de San Pedro Sula, Honduras. Mi país tiene un pasado cultural muy rico, ya que los mayas viven aquí desde la época precolombina. Las ruinas más importantes que tenemos están en Copán. **¿Hay ruinas importantes en tu pueblo?** Mi país es muy hermoso (*beautiful*) porque los bosques (*forests*) ocupan más del cincuenta por ciento del país, pero están en peligro (*danger*). **¿Te gustan los bosques? ¿Vives cerca de alguno?**

La Escalinata de Copán

La tala de bosques

• ALMANAQUE •

Nombre oficial:	República de Honduras
Gobierno:	República democrática constitucional
Población:	7.326.496 (2006)
Idiomas:	español (oficial); miskito, garífuna, otros dialectos amerindios
Moneda:	Lempira (L)

¿Sabías que…?

● El nombre original de esta región es *Higüeras,* que es el nombre de una planta nativa. Al llegar a la costa norteña, Cristóbal Colón renombra la región *Honduras* a causa de la profundidad del agua en la bahía.

PREGUNTAS

1. ¿Qué significa *Honduras*? ¿De dónde viene el nombre?

2. ¿Quiénes construyeron las ruinas de Copán?

3. ¿Qué semejanzas hay entre Honduras y México?

 En la Red
Amplía tus conocimientos sobre Honduras en la página web de *¡Anda!*

161

SECTION GOALS FOR
Cultura

By the end of the *Cultura* section, students will be able to:

• identify the ruins of Copán in Honduras.

• describe how Honduras was named.

• identify the Mayan ruins and pyramids of Tikal, Guatemala.

• discuss the volcanoes located in Guatemala.

• compare the indigenous populations and languages of Honduras, Guatemala, and El Salvador.

• discuss the sports, pastimes, and activities of Salvadorans.

• highlight the similarities and differences between Honduras, Guatemala, and El Salvador.

NATIONAL STANDARDS
Cultures, Comparisons

This three-page culture spread introduces students to basic information about Honduras, Guatemala, and El Salvador. Encourage students to compare and contrast these three Central American countries to each other as well as to the other feature countries up to this point.

The *Les presento mi país* section compares the cultural information of Honduras, Guatemala, and El Salvador. Goal Two, Cultures, states that students gain knowledge and understanding of the cultures of the world. These readings encompass the practices, perspectives, and products of Hispanic cultures (Standards 2.1, 2.2). They present information about the indigenous people, the local economy, the tourism sector, pastimes, geography, and flora and fauna. Students are able to compare (Standard 4.2) the cultures of Honduras, Guatemala, and El Salvador with their own culture.

Answers to *Honduras:* Preguntas

1. Profunda. De Cristóbal Colón, por la profundidad del agua en la bahía.

2. Los mayas en la época precolombina

3. Ruinas, la presencia maya (You may want to discuss comparisons beyond the scope of the reading to geography, history, food, etc.)

RECURSOS

T4-6	T4-6	Cultural Background Notes

Expansion for *La tala de bosques* Ask students if there is a problem with illegal logging elsewhere in the world, including the United States. Discuss the problems of deforestation, including concepts such as erosion and loss of habitat for endangered and protected species.

Expansion for *¿Sabías qué. . .?* Ask students about names of places in the United States and their meaning. If your students are not native to the United States, ask about their home country.

NOTE FOR
Tajumulco

Tajumulco is the highest volcano in Central America and the highest elevation in Guatemala. It is 4,220 meters high, which is 13,845 feet. It is a peak in the Sierra Madre de Chiapas mountain range, which extends from southern Mexico into Guatemala. It is possible to climb this volcano.

Suggestion for *Tajumulco* Ask students if they have climbed a mountain or volcano. What was the experience like?

Answers to *Guatemala:* **Preguntas**
1. Hay muchas montañas y volcanes
2. Español y 23 idiomas amerindios reconocidos oficialmente. En total, 24 oficialmente.
3. México y Honduras

Itzel Fabiola Guerra Cruz

CD 2
Track 20

DVD/VHS

Vistas
culturales

Guatemala

Les presento mi país

Mi nombre es Itzel Fabiola Guerra Cruz y soy de Quezaltenango, Guatemala. Soy maya y mi nombre, Itzel, significa "ella del arco iris (*rainbow*)". Muchas mujeres mayas llevan ropa tradicional de colores brillantes y diseños (*designs*) simbólicos. Mi país es montañoso (*mountainous*) con muchos volcanes, algunos de ellos muy activos. También hay ruinas mayas muy antiguas, como las de Tikal y algunas de nuestras pirámides son las más altas de las Américas. ¿En qué otros lugares encuentras pirámides?

Tajumulco es el volcán más alto de Centroamérica y la montaña más alta de Guatemala.

Un templo muy alto de Tikal es El Gran Jaguar.

MÉXICO

Tikal

Lago Petén Itzá

Flores

BELICE

Puerto Barrios

GUATEMALA

Quetzaltenango

Lago de Izabal

SIERRA MADRE

Tajumulco

Guatemala

HONDURAS

Mazatenango

Pacaya

Lago de Atitlán

Antigua Guatemala

EL SALVADOR

● ALMANAQUE ●

Nombre oficial:	República de Guatemala
Gobierno:	República democrática constitucional
Población:	12.293.545 (2006)
Idiomas:	español (oficial); idiomas amerindios (23 reconocidos oficialmente)
Moneda:	Quetzal (Q)

¿Sabías que…?

● Los mayas tienen un calendario civil, *El Haab*. Consiste en 18 "meses" de 20 días cada uno. Los últimos cinco días del año, conocidos como *el Wayeb*, se consideran de muy mala suerte.

PREGUNTAS

1. Nombra dos cosas que sabes de la geografía guatemalteca.
2. ¿Cuántos idiomas se hablan en Guatemala?
3. ¿Qué otros países tienen herencia maya?

En la Red
Amplía tus conocimientos sobre Guatemala en la página web de *¡Anda!*

RECURSOS

C	P	IRM
T4-7	T4-7	Cultural Background Notes

Alba Violeta Orellana Barrillas

CW
eBook

CD 2
Track 21

DVD/VHS

Vistas culturales

Les presento mi país

Mi nombre es Alba Violeta Orellana Barrillas. Soy de un pueblo pequeño cerca de la playa El Sunzal, en la costa del Pacífico, donde mucha gente practica los deportes acuáticos. ¿Te gustan los deportes acuáticos? El Salvador es el único país de Centroamérica que no tiene costa caribeña. En mi casa viven tres generaciones de mi familia y nos gusta mucho la comida salvadoreña, como las pupusas. ¿Cuál es tu comida favorita?

El Salvador

La playa El Sunzal es un lugar excelente para el surfing, el snorkeling y el buceo.

Las pupusas son la comida nacional de El Salvador.

NOTE FOR

El Sunzal

The beach at El Sunzal is touted as one of the ten best places in the world for surfing. It is also ideal for other aquatic sports, such as snorkeling and scuba diving.

Suggestion for *El Sunzal* Ask students: How are El Salvador and the United States similar? How are they different? What do you have in common with people your age in El Salvador, Guatemala, and Honduras?

NOTE FOR

Las pupusas

Pupusas are the national food of El Salvador. They are thick corn tortillas stuffed with various fillings, such as refried beans, cheese, pork rinds (*chicharrones*), and *loroco* (the flower from a shrub that grows in Central America). Restaurants that specialize in these are called *pupuserías*.

Suggestion for *Las pupusas* Ask students: Do we have restaurants that specialize in certain foods?

Answers to *El Salvador*: Preguntas

1. Los mayas lo usaron como dinero.
2. Los deportes acuáticos
3. *Possible answers:* Es el único país de Centroamérica que no tiene costa caribeña; es un país pequeño, etc.

● ALMANAQUE ●

Nombre oficial:	República de El Salvador
Gobierno:	República democrática constitucional
Población:	6.822.378 (2006)
Idiomas:	español (oficial)
Moneda:	Dólar estadounidense

¿Sabías que...?

● Durante la antigüedad, los mayas usaron (*used*) los granos de cacao como dinero.

● Algunos salvadoreños, sobre todo los que viven en las partes rurales del país, van a los curanderos (*folk healers*) para buscar ayuda médica.

PREGUNTAS

1. ¿Qué importancia tiene el cacao en la historia maya?
2. ¿Qué deportes practican en El Salvador?
3. ¿Qué cosas de El Salvador son únicas o diferentes a las de otros países hispanos?

En la Red
Amplía tus conocimientos sobre El Salvador en la página web de *¡Anda!*

163

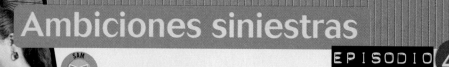

Ambiciones siniestras

lectura

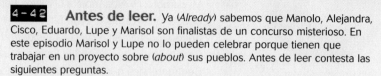

4-54

4-42 **Antes de leer.** Ya (*Already*) sabemos que Manolo, Alejandra, Cisco, Eduardo, Lupe y Marisol son finalistas de un concurso misterioso. En este episodio Marisol y Lupe no lo pueden celebrar porque tienen que trabajar en un proyecto sobre (*about*) sus pueblos. Antes de leer contesta las siguientes preguntas.

1. ¿Cómo es tu pueblo? ¿Es un buen lugar donde vivir? ¿Por qué?
2. ¿De dónde son tus mejores amigos? ¿Sabes mucho sobre sus familias y sus pueblos?

ESTRATEGIA **Skimming and Scanning (II)**

Continue to practice focusing on main ideas and important information. Remember, when you *skim* a passage you read quickly to get the gist of the passage. When

you *scan* a passage you already know what you need to find out, so you concentrate on searching for that particular information.

4-43 **A leer.** Complete the following steps.

1. *Skim* the first paragraph, looking for the answers to the following questions.
   a. About whom is this paragraph?
   b. Which statement best describes where they are?
      They are in sociology class.
      They are at a party.
      They are in an apartment.
2. Now *scan* the second paragraph, looking for the following information:
   a. Where is Lupe's parents' home—in the country or in the middle of town?
   b. Is her parents' home large or small?
   c. What city is next to Lupe's hometown?

This gives you a good start to discovering what happens next in **Ambiciones siniestras**.

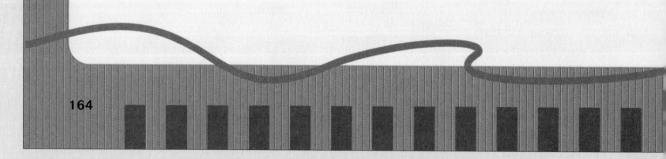

CD 2
Track 22

Las cosas no son siempre lo que parecen°

seem

Alejandra, Manolo, Cisco, Eduardo, Marisol y Lupe —están emocionados al saber que son finalistas del concurso. Muchos van a celebrarlo, pero Marisol y Lupe no pueden. Están ahora en el apartamento de Lupe. Tienen que terminar un proyecto sobre sus pueblos para la clase de sociología.

Las fotos que tiene Lupe de la casa de sus padres y de su pueblo en general representan un lugar muy tranquilo en el campo°, con una casa pequeña y un jardín muy grande. Sin embargo°, Lupe nunca quiere hablar de su familia ni de su pueblo. Sólo dice que es de un pueblo de las afueras° de Akron, Ohio.

countryside
Nonetheless
outskirts

En cambio, a Marisol le encanta hablar de su familia y de su pueblo que está muy cerca de la ciudad de Nueva York. Marisol viene de una familia muy grande. Es hija única pero tiene muchos tíos y primos. Todos viven cerca de Nueva York.

Marisol está muy orgullosa° de su pueblo. Siempre le dice a Lupe que tiene de todo cerca de su casa. Por ejemplo, dice que hay un cine donde ponen quince películas diferentes a la vez. Ella vive en un apartamento y enfrente hay un supermercado pequeño, una librería y un restaurante que siempre recibe la distinción de ser el mejor restaurante chino del pueblo. Según ella, ¡no comprende cómo alguien puede vivir en otro lugar!

proud

Mientras Marisol trabaja de manera muy seria, escucha a Lupe reírse° y hacer comentarios casi inaudibles. De pronto Lupe le dice a Marisol que tiene que salir un momento para hacer una llamada por teléfono. Marisol, muy curiosa, decide mirar lo que Lupe escribe. Se acerca a su computadora y lee allí algo muy extraño° —Lupe no escribe sobre su pueblo en Ohio. ¡Escribe sobre Los Ángeles!

laugh

strange

4-44 Después de leer. Contesta las siguientes preguntas.

1. ¿Qué tipo de proyecto hacen Lupe y Marisol?
2. ¿Qué no quiere hacer Lupe?
3. ¿Cómo es la familia de Marisol?
4. ¿Dónde vive Marisol? ¿Cómo es su pueblo?
5. ¿Qué escribe Lupe en su computadora?

NATIONAL STANDARDS
Comparisons

You may wish to ask students how well they skim and scan in their first language. For those who say they skim and scan well in their first language, you may wish to follow up and have those students describe the techniques they use to the class.

Standard 4.1 promotes making comparisons between Spanish and English. You can encourage students to use reading strategies (like skimming and scanning) from their first language and apply them to learning Spanish. Brainstorm the vocabulary in Spanish (such as question words) that they will need to answer when they skim the passage. Highlight the words that they will be looking for in Spanish as they scan for specific information. When they are finished, ask them if the strategies they use for reading in Spanish are different from those strategies they use when reading in English.

Answers to 4-44

1. Es un proyecto acerca de sus pueblos para la clase de sociología.
2. No quiere hablar de su familia.
3. Es una familia grande con muchos tíos y primos. Es hija única.
4. Vive en un pueblo cerca de Nueva York. Tiene de todo cerca de su casa.
5. Escribe sobre Los Ángeles, no sobre su pueblo en Ohio.

165

video

4-55 to
4-56

4-45 **Antes del video.** Do you volunteer your time with a group or organization? In the video episode of **Ambiciones siniestras** you will learn about Cisco's and Eduardo's volunteerism experiences (or the lack thereof!). Also listen for "**¡No toques** (*touch*) **mis cosas nunca más! ¿Me oyes?**" Why do you think the character says this? And finally, you will discover that either Cisco or Eduardo is not being totally honest! Who do you think it is? Why?

Trabajo como voluntario en una organización que ayuda a los niños.

¡No toques mis cosas nunca más! ¿Me oyes?

Cisco piensa que lo sabe todo…

Episodio 4

¿Quiénes son en realidad?

Relax and watch the video, more than once if you choose. Then complete the questions that follow.

4-46 **Después del video.** Contesta las siguientes preguntas.

1. ¿Adónde van Cisco y Eduardo?
2. ¿Qué hacen allí?
3. ¿Quién trabaja como voluntario? ¿A quiénes ayuda?
4. ¿Por qué está enojado Cisco?
5. ¿Qué hace Eduardo al final?

Y por fin, ¿cómo andas?

Having completed this chapter, I now can…

	Feel Confident	Need to Review
Comunicación		
share information about places in my home and/or university town (p. 136)	❑	❑
correctly pronounce **c** and **z** (p. 137)	❑	❑
use **saber** and **conocer** correctly (p. 140)	❑	❑
relate what I need to do (p. 142)	❑	❑
use stem-changing verbs appropriately (p. 144)	❑	❑
state where I and others are going with the verb **ir** (p. 147)	❑	❑
talk about things that will happen using the construction **ir** + **a** + *infinitive* (p. 149)	❑	❑
describe different types of community service (p. 151)	❑	❑
use affirmative and negative expressions (p. 154)	❑	❑
use **ser** and **estar** correctly (p. 156)	❑	❑
paraphrase what I hear (p. 159)	❑	❑
write a postcard about my hometown (p. 160)	❑	❑
Cultura		
compare and contrast shopping and going out and about town in the United States with the Spanish-speaking world (p. 139)	❑	❑
share ways that individuals demonstrate social consciousness (p. 153)	❑	❑
state three facts about Honduras, Guatemala, and El Salvador (pp. 161–163)	❑	❑
Ambiciones siniestras		
skim and scan for meaning (p. 164)	❑	❑
state who are the finalists in the Internet contest of **Ambiciones siniestras** and which characters may not be telling the truth (p. 166)	❑	❑

VOCABULARIO ACTIVO

CD 2
Tracks 23-30

Los lugares	Places
el almacén	department store
el banco	bank
el bar; el club	bar; club
el café	cafe
el cajero automático	ATM machine
el centro	downtown
el centro comercial	mall; business/shopping district
el cibercafé	Internet café
el cine	movie theater
el club campestre	country club
la iglesia	church
el mercado	market
el museo	museum
la oficina de correos; correos	post office
el parque	park
la plaza	town square
el restaurante	restaurant
el supermercado	supermarket
el teatro	theater
el templo	temple

Unos verbos	Some verbs
buscar	to look for
estar de acuerdo	to agree
mandar una carta	to send/mail a letter

Otras palabras útiles	Other useful words
detrás (de)	behind
enfrente (de)	in front (of)
el/la mejor	the best
el/la peor	the worst
la ciudad	city
la cuenta	bill; account
la película	movie; film
el pueblo	town; village

Trabajos y servicios voluntarios	Volunteerism opportunities
apoyar a un/a candidato/a	to support a candidate
la artesanía	arts and crafts
el campamento de niños	summer camp
la campaña política	political campaign
la canoa	canoe
circular una petición	to circulate a petition
el/la consejero/a	counselor
deber	ought to; should
hacer una caminata	to take a walk
la hoguera	campfire
ir de excursión	to take a short trip
llevar a alguien al médico	to take someone to the doctor
trabajar como voluntario/a	to volunteer
organizar	to organize
las personas mayores, los mayores	elderly people
repartir comidas	to hand out/deliver food
la residencia de ancianos	nursing home/assisted living facility
la tienda de campaña	tent
trabajar como voluntario/a	to volunteer

¿Qué tienen que hacer?	What do they have to do?
(Verbos con cambio de raíz)	*(Stem-changing verbs)*
almorzar (ue)	*to have lunch*
cerrar (ie)	*to close*
comenzar (ie)	*to begin*
costar (ue)	*to cost*
demostrar (ue)	*to demonstrate*
devolver (ue)	*to return (an object)*
dormir (ue)	*to sleep*
empezar (ie)	*to begin*
encerrar (ie)	*to enclose*
encontrar (ue)	*to find*
entender (ie)	*to understand*
jugar (ue)	*to play*
mentir (ie)	*to lie*
morir (ue)	*to die*
mostrar (ue)	*to show*
pedir (i)	*to ask for*
pensar (ie)	*to think*
perder (ie)	*to lose; to waste*
perseguir (i)	*to chase*
preferir (ie)	*to prefer*
recomendar (ie)	*to recommend*
recordar (ue)	*to remember*
repetir (i)	*to repeat*
seguir (i)	*to follow; to continue (doing something)*
servir (i)	*to serve*
volver (ue)	*to return*

Otros verbos	Other verbs
ir	*to go*
saber	*to know*

Otras palabras útiles	Other useful words
el deber	*obligation; duty*
el voluntariado	*volunteerism*

Expresiones afirmativas y negativas	Affirmative and negative expressions
a veces	*sometimes*
algo	*something; anything*
alguien	*someone*
algún	*some; any*
alguno/a/os/as	*some; any*
jamás	*never; not ever (emphatic)*
nada	*nothing*
nadie	*no one; nobody*
ni…ni	*neither…nor*
ningún	*none*
ninguno/a/os/as	*none*
nunca	*never*
o…o	*either…or*
siempre	*always*

169

5

¡A divertirse!
La música y el cine

En el mundo hispanohablante la gente trabaja pero también sabe divertirse (*enjoy themselves*). La música, el baile y el cine son formas de expresión y de distracción comunes. Estos pasatiempos, además de otros como los deportes o leer un buen libro, nos hacen la vida muy agradable. Sobre todo (*Above all*), es importante buscar maneras de relajarse y aliviar el estrés.

SECTION GOALS FOR
Chapter Opener

By the end of the Chapter Opener section, students will be able to:
- name some forms of diversion in Hispanic countries.
- think about ways to alleviate stress.
- reflect on the concept of *trabajar para vivir* or *vivir para trabajar*.

OBJETIVOS

Comunicación
- To discuss different types of music, including your personal preferences
- To point out specific persons, places, things, and ideas
- To state how or in what manner something is done
- To express what is happening at the moment
- To share information about your favorite movies and television programs
- To rank people, places, and things
- To state what needs to be accomplished
- To listen with the goal of anticipating content
- To write a movie review

Cultura
- To talk about Hispanic music in the United States
- To begin exploring information regarding famous actors from the Spanish-speaking world
- To create a list of at least three interesting facts about this chapter's featured countries: Nicaragua, Costa Rica, and Panama

Ambiciones siniestras
- To learn to anticipate content
- To discover what Cisco does in his search for Eduardo
- To learn about the videoconference the characters have and find out who is the second student to disappear

CONTENIDOS

RECURSOS

Lesson Plan

Un concierto de
Marc Anthony

PREGUNTAS

1 ¿Qué haces cuando no estudias?

2 ¿Qué hacen los miembros de tu familia para relajarse y aliviar el estrés?

3 Hay una expresión en español que dice: "Algunas personas viven para trabajar y otras trabajan para vivir". ¿Cuál es tu filosofía de la vida?

171

NOTE FOR
Chapter Opener

Note that the introduction talks about other pastimes such as sports, reading, and ways to alleviate stress, but the main focus of the chapter is music and cinema. You might also want to expand on the importance of theater in Hispanic cultures, such as *El teatro campesino*, whose roots were in the United Farm Workers Union in California. It was started by Luis Valdez and featured Chicano themes. Other classic plays such as *La Celestina* or *La casa de Bernarda Alba* are offered throughout the United States by traveling theater groups. Browse the Internet for Spanish theater groups that might be coming to a city near you.

Suggestions for *Chapter Opener*
Bring in a photo of your favorite Hispanic recording artist or group (or an American artist who sings in Spanish) and ask students to identify who they think the artist is. Play a track from your favorite CD or download the song and play a clip of the song. Ask your students to identify characteristics about the song and the artist from the clip. What genre of music do they think it is? Is this artist's music representative of his/her country? What is the tempo? What kinds of instruments do they hear?

PLANNING AHEAD

You will want to play music in class for the students to listen to, or ask students to bring in music they want to share. It is helpful to have access to a compact disc player or computer for music files, and blank CDs for students to bring in their music to share. You may also wish to plan on playing music daily in the background while students are working in their groups. Students find this technique adds to the immersion-style atmosphere.

METHODOLOGY • Making Topics Relevant for Students

The text and questions for this chapter opener are completely in Spanish, just as in *Capítulo 4*. Notice that the questions begin with your learners and their preferences, something that we have learned from educational philosopher John Dewey. Try having your students turn to a partner and answer the questions in pairs. Then have them share the answers their partners gave. This has them practice listening and paraphrasing.

PLANNING AHEAD

Remember that all grammar explanations and culture presentations should be assigned to be read before class. Class time should be spent answering clarification questions for the grammar presentations, or answering the comprehension/critical thinking questions that follow the culture presentations. *Actividades* **5-7** and **5-12** are activities that can be assigned to be written at home and then shared in class.

SECTION GOALS FOR
Comunicación

By the end of the *Comunicación* section, students will be able to:

- talk about the world of music, including genres and characteristics of each genre.
- pronounce strong vowels (*a, e, o*), weak vowels (*i, u*), and diphthongs.
- link words and pronounce identical vowels and consonants.
- discuss musical preferences.
- form demonstrative adjectives and demonstrative pronouns.
- review the agreement rules of nouns and adjectives.
- form adverbs from adjectives.
- produce the forms of the present progressive using regular and irregular gerunds.

NATIONAL STANDARDS
Communication, Cultures, Comparisons

If you have a collection of different types of music from the Spanish-speaking world, this chapter is an excellent opportunity for you to expose your students to a wide variety. Encourage them to compare and contrast the music within *el mundo hispanohablante* as well as with music from the English-speaking world.

The activities related to music provide you with multiple ways to address the Standards. In particular, you can address the Communication Goal (Standards 1.1, 1.2, and 1.3) by incorporating music into the class. Play your favorite Hispanic artist's music and have your students share their opinions and preferences about the artist and the music (Standard 1.1) in pairs or small groups. Give students a copy of the lyrics in Spanish, and ask them to interpret what the song is about. The combination of hearing the words and following along with the written lyrics facilitates interpretation (Standard 1.2). Ask students to present part of the song (reading aloud or singing in front of the class) or a different song of their choosing (Standard 1.3). They can bring in the Spanish lyrics for others to read along (Standard 1.2) as they present (Standard 1.3). Goal Two, Cultures, is also easily addressed through music. Highlight the different types of music in Spanish-speaking countries, how different

cultures incorporate music into daily life, and the types of commercially produced music with which students might be familiar. Encourage students to make comparisons (Standard 4.2) between what role music has in the United States and Hispanic countries, and the different types of music available. When you analyze the lyrics, you can explain the literal meaning versus the figurative meaning, or how it translates versus what it means. That allows students to make comparisons between Spanish and English (Standard 4.1).

Comunicación

- Sharing thoughts about music
- Pointing out people and things
- State how or in what manner something is done
- Expressing what is happening at the moment

VOCABULARIO 1 — El mundo de la música

5-1 to 5-7

3:00

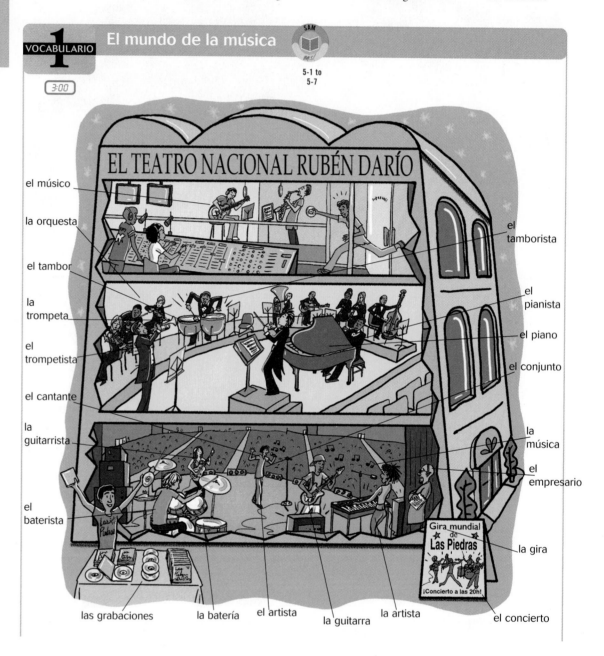

el músico
la orquesta
el tambor
la trompeta
el trompetista
el cantante
la guitarrista
el baterista
las grabaciones
la batería
el artista
la guitarra
la artista
el tamborista
el pianista
el piano
el conjunto
la música
el empresario
la gira
el concierto

EL TEATRO NACIONAL RUBÉN DARÍO

Gira mundial de **Las Piedras**

¡Concierto a las 20h!

RECURSOS | T5-1 to T5-2 | T5-1 to T5-2 | Electronic Activity Cache

Unos géneros musicales	*Some musical genres*
el jazz	*jazz*
la música clásica	*classical music*
la música popular	*pop music*
la ópera	*opera*
el rock	*rock*
la salsa	*salsa*

Unas características	*Some characteristics*
apasionado/a	*passionate*
fino/a	*fine; delicate*
lento/a	*slow*
suave	*smooth*

Unos verbos	*Some verbs*
dar un concierto	*to give/perform a concert*
ensayar	*to practice/rehearse*
grabar	*to record*
hacer una gira	*to tour*
sacar un CD	*to release a CD*
tocar	*to play (a musical instrument)*

Otras palabras útiles	*Other useful words*
el/la aficionado/a	*fan*
la fama	*fame*
el género	*genre*
la habilidad	*ability; skill*
la letra	*lyrics*
el ritmo	*rhythm*
el sabor	*flavor*
la voz	*voice*

  5·1 Dibujemos

7:00

Escuchen mientras su instructor/a les da (*gives you*) las instrucciones de esta actividad.

 5·2 Listas

3:00

Túrnate con un/a compañero/a para decir y escribir todas las palabras nuevas que recuerden (*you both remember*) de las tres categorías en el modelo. ¿Cuántas palabras son?

MODELO

TIPOS DE MÚSICA	INSTRUMENTOS	OTRAS PALABRAS
el jazz	*la trompeta*	*el conjunto*

METHODOLOGY • Comprehensible Input

Notice that virtually all of the direction lines in this chapter are in Spanish. For all students, this provides reading practice. You may choose to model some of the activities such as actividad **5-2** to make sure that students understand what they are supposed to do with their partner.

METHODOLOGY • Visual Organizers

For actividad **5-2**, you may wish to put up the transparency of the new vocabulary that does not have the words written on it. Students can then use the transparency as a visual organizer to assist them in remembering the vocabulary they have just learned.

NOTE FOR
El mundo de la música,
Unos géneros musicales

You will notice that the genres listed here are mostly cognates. Students should be able to discuss the instruments and artists most commonly associated with each genre. *Salsa* is the genre that may require the most explanation. You can discuss the roots of *salsa* in the United States during the 1960s and 1970s, stemming from Puerto Rican immigration and Cuban influences. *Salsa* is quite popular in Latin America and is sometimes referred to as *música tropical* or Latin jazz.

Suggestion for *El mundo de la música* Have students brainstorm five artists/musical groups from each decade and decide what musical genres dominated each decade. Depending on the age and composition of your class, you might start in the 1970s or later. Come prepared with a list of your most influential artists and see if they match those of your students.

NOTE FOR 5-1

Actividad **5-1** continues with the mechanical practice for your students to learn the new vocabulary. This activity can be used in other chapters as well, to either present or review vocabulary. It is also a good activity for pairs who finish early. Please give the following extended directions to your students, if you are familiar with the game *Pictionary*, it is very similar. It is like charades, but they have to draw pictures rather than act it out. **INSTRUCTIONS:** Divide your class into groups of four. Each group of four will work as two teams of two students. "Captains" from each team select the same word that they are going to draw. Their teammate needs to try to guess what the word is in Spanish as they draw. The round is over when one of the teams guesses the word. The roles are then switched, and the two team members who did the guessing now select the same word that each will draw for his/her partner. We suggest doing this activity for at least 4 rounds. It is a motivating way to practice vocabulary.

CD 2
Track 31

SAM

5-8 to
5-13

PRONUNCIACIÓN ⏱3:00

Diphthongs and linking

In Spanish, **a**, **e**, and **o** are what are known as *strong vowels*. The **i** and **u** are known as *weak vowels*. A **diphthong** is the combination of a strong and a weak vowel, or two weak vowels. Diphthongs are pronounced as a single syllable.

concierto   empresaria   grabaciones   pianista

When pronouncing words in Spanish, *linking* occurs. Linking is what makes spoken Spanish appear to flow and be seamless. What follows is a summary of how words are linked.

1. A **consonant** at the *end* of one word is linked to a **vowel** at the *beginning* of the next word.

   el artista   un aficionado   ellos ensayan

2. A **vowel** at the *end* of one word is linked to a **vowel** at the *beginning* of the next word.

   su (h)abilidad   tu orquesta   nuestra ópera   ella ensaya

3. **Identical consonants** (or consonant sounds) at the *end* of one word and at the *beginning* of the next word are linked.

   sus sabores   con negro   sabor rítmico   voz suave

4. **Identical vowels** (or vowel sounds) at the *end* of one word and the *beginning* of the next word.

   la artista   música apasionada   la (h)abilidad   la alfombra

> **Fíjate**
>
> Remember that the letter **h** in Spanish is silent and not pronounced.

5•3 Las palabras

Practice pronouncing the following words, focusing on the diphthongs and linking.

1. concierto
2. empresaria
3. grabaciones
4. pianista
5. el artista
6. un aficionado
7. ellos ensayan
8. tu orquesta
9. su (h)abilidad
10. nuestra ópera
11. ella ensaya
12. sus sabores
13. con negro
14. sabor rítmico
15. voz suave
16. la artista
17. música apasionada
18. la (h)abilidad

5•4 Las oraciones

Pronounce the following sentences, paying special attention to the diphthongs and linking.

1. La orquesta ensaya todos los días.
2. Toca con una habilidad impresionante.

5•5 Los dichos y refranes

Pronounce the following saying, focusing on diphthongs and linking.

Aquellos que tienen amigos son ricos.

5·6 A conocerte mejor `7:00`

Hazle las siguientes preguntas a un/a compañero/a. Toma apuntes y luego comparte las respuestas con otros dos compañeros.

1. ¿Con qué frecuencia vas a conciertos?
2. ¿Qué género de música prefieres?
3. ¿Cuál es tu grupo favorito?
4. ¿Cuál es tu cantante favorito/a? ¿Cómo es su voz?
5. ¿Qué instrumento te gusta?
6. ¿Cuál es tu canción favorita?
7. ¿Sabes tocar un instrumento? ¿Cuál?
8. ¿Sabes cantar bien? ¿Te gusta cantar? ¿Cuándo y dónde cantas?
9. ¿En qué tienes mucha habilidad o talento?
10. ¿Conoces algún conjunto o cantante hispano? ¿Cuál?

Estrategia

When reporting your information, make complete sentences, and remember to use the *él* or *ella* form of the verb. Also, simply refer to your notes; do not read from them. This technique will help you to speak more fluidly and will help you speak in paragraphs, an important skill to perfect when learning a language.

`7:00` ## 5·7 Los famosos

Capítulo 2. La formación de preguntas y las palabras interrogativas, pág. 71.

Completa los siguientes pasos.

Paso 1 Como reportero/a de la revista *Rolling Stone* tienes la oportunidad de entrevistar a los hermanos Mejía, dos músicos populares de Nicaragua. Escribe por lo menos **cinco** preguntas que vas a hacerles.

Fíjate

Remember that if you are interviewing people whom you don't know, use the *usted/ustedes* form.

Ramón (Perrozompopo) Mejía

Luis Enrique Mejía

 Paso 2 Ve a la página web de *¡Anda!* para ver si puedes descubrir las respuestas a tus preguntas y para escuchar la música de Luis y Ramón Mejía. Después, comparte tus resultados y tu opinión con la clase; díles (*tell them*) qué canción te gusta más y por qué.

NOTE FOR 5-6

Remind students that in actividad **5-6** they are asked to share their answers with two other classmates. If they work in groups of three, they could change the questions to the *ustedes* form.

CULTURAL BACKGROUND FOR 5-7

The Mejía brothers are currently the most popular Nicaraguan artists; Ramón for his combination of rock, rap, and flamenco, and Luis for his popularity with salsa music. Ramón was politically active during the 2006 elections and wrote and performed a highly popular song, *Rompe el silencio,* that encouraged young Nicaraguans to get out and vote.

Suggestion for 5-7 We suggest assigning the writing of the questions outside of class. Encourage your students to go to the Internet to hear a bit of these brothers' music.

HERITAGE LANGUAGE LEARNERS

Ask your Heritage language learners what types of Spanish language music they enjoy. If the artists are not commonly known, ask them to bring in a sample of their music to share with the class.

METHODOLOGY • Having Students Create Questions

Research has confirmed what instructors have observed time and again: One of the most difficult skills for language learners is to create questions. Our classes tend to focus on questions we ask our students, but rarely are they asked to create their own questions. Actividad **5-7** is excellent practice for your students.

METHODOLOGY • Peer Editing

You may wish to check your students' questions for actividad **5-7** either with peer editing in pairs, or on the board. If you use the board, have each student write a question and let the class help edit them.

NATIONAL STANDARDS
Communities

One way of having some of your students use their Spanish in the community is to plan a talent show focusing on Hispanic music.

CAPÍTULO 5

NOTE FOR
Los pronombres demostrativos

The Real Academia Española has determined that it is permissible to omit the written accent from demonstrative pronouns if the meaning is clear from the context. You can choose to share this if you have a class of Heritage language learners; you may choose not to include this with true beginners, since it may be too much additional information and would be difficult for them to process.

Suggestion for *Los adjetivos demostrativos* Use the demonstrative adjectives with classroom objects to indicate the distance from the speaker, using *this*, *that*, and *that one over there*: *Este lápiz es rojo, ese lápiz es azul y aquel lápiz es amarillo*. You can also use demonstrative adjectives as a way to review possession and possessive adjectives. Borrow various items from your students while the class is watching. Then ask *¿De quién es esta mochila?* and have them answer by using *ser + de* or an appropriate possessive adjective.

METHODOLOGY • Streamlining the Syllabus

Based on research, as well as consultation with hundreds of instructors, the decision was made that *¡Anda!* will teach a more streamlined syllabus so that students may learn well (acquire) what is being presented. This is a departure from how it has been done in the past: to introduce everything and have students leave the course with little or nothing that they can do with the language. You have noticed that, when presenting grammar, we have not presented all of the exceptions to the rules or nuances of the language that can be presented at a later time so that students will comprehend the differences. Having said that, if you have Heritage language learners or false beginners, feel free to present them. As always, we as instructors must ultimately decide what is best for our students.

GRAMÁTICA 2   Los adjetivos demostrativos

5-14 to 5-16   4, 21

3:00

> Esta mujer toca muy bien. Ese hombre toca bien y aquel hombre toca muy mal.

When you want to point out a specific person, place, thing, or idea, you use a *demonstrative adjective*. In Spanish, they are:

DEMONSTRATIVE ADJECTIVES	MEANING	REFERRING TO...
este, esta, estos, estas	*this, these*	something nearby
ese, esa, esos, esas	*that, those over there*	something farther away
aquel, aquella, aquellos, aquellas	*that, those (way) over there*	something even farther away in distance and/or time... perhaps not even visible

Since forms of **este, ese,** and **aquel** are adjectives, they must agree in gender and number with the nouns they modify. Note the following examples.

Este conjunto es fantástico.	*This group is fantastic.*
Esta cantante es fenomenal.	*This singer is phenomenal.*
Estos conjuntos son fantásticos.	*These groups are fantastic.*
Estas cantantes son fenomenales.	*These singers are phenomenal.*
Ese conjunto es fantástico.	*That group is fantastic.*
Esa cantante es fenomenal.	*That singer is phenomenal.*
Esos conjuntos son fantásticos.	*Those groups are fantastic.*
Esas cantantes son fenomenales.	*Those singers are phenomenal.*
Aquel conjunto es fantástico.	*That group (over there) is fantastic.*
Aquella cantante es fenomenal.	*That singer (over there) is phenomenal.*
Aquellos conjuntos son fantásticos.	*Those groups (over there) are fantastic.*
Aquellas cantantes son fenomenales.	*Those singers (over there) are phenomenal.*

> **In summary:**
>
> 1. When do you use **este, ese,** and **aquel**?
> 2. When do you use **esta, esa,** and **aquella**?
> 3. When do you use **estos, esos,** and **aquellos**?
> 4. When do you use **estas, esas,** and **aquellas**?
>
> Check your answers to the preceding questions in Appendix 1.

Suggestion for *Los adjetivos demostrativos* You may wish to use the following saying for students who need extra help with demonstratives. "*This* and *these* both have *t*'s in Spanish; *that* and *those* do not in Spanish; (e.g., *Este, esta,* and *estos, estas* mean *this* and *these* and have *t*'s. *Ese, esa, esos,* and *esas* mean *that* and *those* and do not have *t*'s.)

RECURSOS

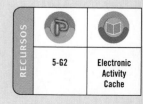

5-G2   Electronic Activity Cache

`1:00` ii **5·8** Amiga, tienes razón

Tu amigo/a te da su opinión y tú respondes con una opinión similar. Cambia la forma de **este/a** a (*to*) **ese/a** y añade (*add*) la palabra **"también"**.

> MODELO   TU AMIGO/A: Esta música es muy suave.
>
> TÚ: *Sí, y esa música es suave también.*

1. Este grupo es fenomenal.
2. Estos cantantes son muy jóvenes.
3. Esta gira empieza en enero.

4. Este CD sale ahora.
5. Estas canciones son muy apasionadas.
6. Estos pianistas tocan muy bien.

`2:00` ii **5·9** En el centro estudiantil

Completen el diálogo de Lola y Tina con la forma correcta de **este, ese** y **aquel**.

LOLA: Tina, mira (1) ____este____ (*this*) grupo de estudiantes que acaba de entrar.

TINA: Sí, creo que conozco a (2) ____este____ (*this*) hombre alto. Es guitarrista del trío de jazz *Ritmos*.

LOLA: Tienes razón. Y (3) ____esta____ (*this*) mujer rubia es pianista en la orquesta de la universidad.

TINA: ¿Quiénes son (4) ____esas____ (*those*) dos mujeres morenas?

LOLA: Están en nuestra clase de química. ¿No las conoces? Y (5) ____aquellos____ (*those over there*) dos hombres de las camisas rojas ¡son muy guapos!

`2:00` ii **5·10** ¿Qué opinas?

Miren el dibujo y expresen su opinión sobre las casas. Usen las formas apropiadas de **este, ese** y **aquel**.

 Capítulo 2. El verbo *gustar*, pág. 82; Capítulo 4. Los verbos con cambios de raíz, pág. 144.

> MODELO   *Me gusta esta casa blanca pero prefiero esa casa beige. Pienso que aquella casa roja es fea. También creo que este jardín de la casa blanca es bonito.*

METHODOLOGY • Instructional Delivery

There are many ways to make instructional delivery more efficient. One way is pairing your students for the day, you put the activities on the board that you want them to do. You suggest the amount of time they may want to spend. Some partners will spend/need more time than others. Give directions in advance for any activities that may need extra explaining. Otherwise, students should be permitted to negotiate meaning together. Finally, always have one or more activities for groups that finish early. That might be reviewing the vocabulary from previous chapters, or you may want to list activities from previous chapters that they should go back and redo.

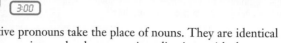

GRAMÁTICA 3 · Los pronombres demostrativos

`3:00`

Demonstrative pronouns take the place of nouns. They are identical in form and meaning to the demonstrative adjectives, with the exception of the **accent mark**.

¡Éste es muy bueno! Ése no me gusta, pero ¡aquél es fenomenal!

Masculino	Femenino	*Meaning*
éste	ésta	*this one*
éstos	éstas	*these*
ése	ésa	*that one*
ésos	ésas	*those*
aquél	aquélla	*that one (way over there/not visible)*
aquéllos	aquéllas	*those (way over there/not visible)*

A demonstrative pronoun must agree in gender and number with the noun it replaces. Observe how demonstrative adjectives and demonstrative pronouns are used in the following sentences.

Yo quiero comprar **este CD** pero mi hermana quiere comprar **ése.**

I want to buy this CD but my sister wants to buy that one.

—¿Te gusta **esa guitarra**?

Do you like that guitar?

—No, a mí me gusta **ésta.**

No, I like this one.

Estos instrumentos son interesantes, pero prefiero tocar **ésos.**

These instruments are interesting, but I prefer to play those.

En **esta** calle hay varios cines. ¿Quieres ir a **aquél**?

There are several movie theaters on this street. Do you want to go to that one over there?

`2:00` 👥 **5·11 Comparando cosas**

Tu compañero/a te propone (*proposes*) una cosa pero tú siempre prefieres otra (*another one*). Responde a sus comentarios usando la forma correcta de **éste, ése** o **aquél.**

MODELO E1: ¿Quieres ir a este concierto?

E2: *No, quiero ir a ése/aquél.*

1. ¿Quieres escuchar estos músicos?
2. ¿Vamos a ir a ese teatro?
3. ¿Entiendes la letra de esta canción?
4. ¿Tus amigos tocan en aquel conjunto?
5. ¿Vas a comprar aquellas camisetas (*T-shirts*)?
6. ¿Piensas arreglar este cuarto para (*for*) la fiesta?

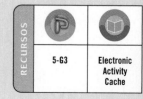

RECURSOS

5-G3 | Electronic Activity Cache

3:00

5 • 12 ¡Vamos a un concierto!

¡Qué suerte! Tienes dos entradas gratis (*free tickets*) para ir a un concierto.

Paso 1   Ve a la página web de *¡Anda!* para escuchar la música de El Gran Combo, Marc Anthony, Juan Luis Guerra y Los Tigres del Norte.

Paso 2   Tú compañero/a y tú tienen que decidir a qué concierto quieren ir. Túrnense para describir a quién prefieren escuchar y por qué. Usen **éste**, **ése** y **aquél** en sus descripciones.

MODELO   *Prefiero ir al concierto de Marc Anthony. ¡Él canta muy bien! Pero es difícil decidir porque los músicos de Los Tigres del Norte son muy buenos también. Éstos saben tocar y cantar muy bien. Y aquéllos…*

El Gran Combo   Marc Anthony   Juan Luis Guerra   Los Tigres del Norte

SAM

3:00   5-19 to 5-21

La música latina en los Estados Unidos

Néstor Torres

La música latina abarca (*encompasses*) muchos géneros, estilos e intérpretes (músicos, cantantes). Entre los géneros más populares en los Estados Unidos se encuentran la salsa, el merengue, el Tex-Mex o norteño y otros. Algunos intérpretes de estos tipos de música son El Gran Combo, Marc Anthony, Juan Luis Guerra y Los Tigres del Norte.

El rock y el jazz son influencias que están presentes en la música latina en los Estados Unidos, aunque ésta ha evolucionado (*has evolved*) y producido nuevos géneros como el merenhouse, el rock latino, el rap en español, el jazz latino, el reggaetón y otros.

La influencia de los países hispanohablantes del Caribe —Cuba, Puerto Rico y la República Dominicana— y su herencia africana forma parte de los ritmos, las melodías y la instrumentación de la música y los bailes latinos. También les dan vida (*they give life*) a géneros como la plena, la cumbia y la bachata.

Entre los artistas populares de hoy en día se encuentra Néstor Torres, flautista de música de jazz latino. Torres ganó un premio Grammy latino por su interpretación de "This Side of Paradise".

Preguntas

1. ¿Cuáles son cuatro de los géneros de la música latina? ¿Cuáles conoces tú?
   La salsa, el merengue, el Tex-Mex, el merenhouse, el rock latino, el rap, el reggaetón, etc.
2. ¿Quiénes son los artistas latinos más conocidos en este momento?
   Answers may vary.

CAPÍTULO 5

Suggestion for *La música latina en los Estados Unidos* Remember to assign these readings in advance of class so that class time is spent discussing the answers to the questions.

NATIONAL STANDARDS
Communication, Cultures, Connections, Comparisons

Determine if you have any music majors or devotees among your students who may wish to do additional reports for class. You may wish to bring samples of the music of some of the genres listed as well as from several of the artists.

This reading discusses various artists, genres, and influences in Latin music. Standard 1.2 requires communication through understanding and interpreting written Spanish, like the Spanish used in a cultural reading. The Cultures Goal is for students to gain knowledge and understanding of the cultures of the world through the practices, perspectives, and products of Hispanic cultures. The history of Latin music, the famous Latin artists, and the evolution of genres all contribute to Standards 2.1 and 2.2. Students can make connections (Standard 3.2) about how music has evolved in the United States and how religious festivals, indigenous populations, African influences, and political leaders have shaped Latin music. They can make comparisons (Standard 4.2) between the genres, how artists are rewarded for their music (Grammy awards), and the way music has changed over the past decades or eras.

NOTE FOR
Los adverbios

Although a complete grammatical explanation of adverbs would include the fact that they can also modify verbs, whole phrases, clauses, or sentences, we have chosen to simplify the presentation. Also note that we have chosen to use the word *describe* rather than the word *modify* in the presentation. Although both words are grammatically acceptable, *describe* is a bit more casual and user-friendly.

GRAMÁTICA **4** Los adverbios

5-22 to 5-24   45

`3:00`

Many Spanish adverbs end in **-mente,** which is equivalent to the English *-ly*. They describe the verb and usually answer the question *how*. These Spanish adverbs are formed as follows:

1. Add **-mente** to the *feminine singular* form of an *adjective*.

Este baterista toca horriblemente.

Adjetivos		**Adverbios**
Masculino	**Femenino**	
rápido →	*rápida* + -mente →	**rápidamente**
lento →	*lenta* + -mente →	**lentamente**
tranquilo →	*tranquila* + -mente →	**tranquilamente**

2. If an *adjective* ends in a *consonant* or in **-e**, simply add **-mente.**

Adjetivos		**Adverbios**
Masculino	**Femenino**	
fácil →	*fácil* + -mente →	**fácilmente**
suave →	*suave* + -mente →	**suavemente**

*Note that if an adjective has a written accent, it is retained when **-mente** is added.

`1:00` **5·13** Lógicamente

Capítulo 1. Los adjetivos descriptivos, pág. 44.

Estrategia

Remember to first determine the *feminine singular* form of the adjective and then add *-mente.*

Túrnense para transformar en adverbios los siguientes adjetivos.

MODELO   E1: normal
              E2: *normalmente*

1. interesante   interesantemente
2. perezosos   perezosamente
3. feliz   felizmente
4. nervioso   nerviosamente
5. fuertes   fuertemente
6. claro   claramente

7. seguro   seguramente
8. apasionadas   apasionadamente
9. difícil   difícilmente
10. débil   débilmente
11. rápida   rápidamente
12. pacientes   pacientemente

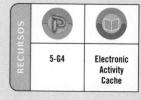

RECURSOS   5-G4   Electronic Activity Cache

2:00

5·14 Para conocerte

Túrnense para
hacerse y
contestar las
siguientes
preguntas. Pueden
usar los adjetivos
de la lista.

alegre	constante	paciente	difícil	divino
fácil	horrible	perfecto	rápido	tranquilo

MODELO   E1:   ¿Cómo bailas? (divino)

E2:   *Bailo divinamente.*

1. ¿Cómo cantas?
2. ¿Cómo duermes?
3. ¿Cómo hablas español?
4. ¿Cómo juegas al béisbol?
5. ¿Cómo tocas el piano?
6. ¿Cómo cocinas?
7. ¿Cómo lavas los platos?
8. ¿Cómo manejas (*drive*)?

Capítulo 2. Presente
indicativo de verbos
regulares, pág. 68;
Capítulo 4. Los
verbos con cambio
de raíz, pág. 144.

2:00

5·15 Di la verdad

Hazle (*Ask*) a tu
compañero/a las
siguientes
preguntas.
Después, cambien
de papel.

MODELO   E1:   ¿Qué haces diariamente (todos los días)?

E2:   *Limpio mi dormitorio, voy a clase, estudio, como,
hago ejercicio y duermo.*

1. ¿Qué haces perfectamente?
2. ¿Qué haces horriblemente?
3. ¿Qué haces fácilmente?
4. ¿Qué debes hacer rápidamente?
5. ¿Qué debes hacer lentamente?

Estrategia

Answer in complete
sentences when
working with your
partner. Even though
it may seem
mechanical at times,
it leads to increased
comfort speaking
Spanish.

Expansion for 5-14 Ask students
who finish early to repeat the activity, answering how they think you
do those things. When they have
finished, tell them if you agree with
their assessment by saying *estoy de
acuerdo* or *no estoy de acuerdo*, and
correct the items they have
assessed incorrectly.

METHODOLOGY • Recycling

Please note that for students to
complete these activities, they are
required to review verbs and vocabulary not only from this chapter, but
from previous chapters as well.
Adverbs are a simple enough concept, so we're having the students
practice them while also reviewing
concepts that require more practice,
such as regular and irregular
present tense verbs.

GRAMÁTICA 5 — El presente progresivo

¿Qué estamos haciendo aquí afuera?

Estoy esperando al trompetista de la orquesta. Están grabando un CD.

3:00

So far you have been learning and using the present tense to communicate ideas. If you want to emphasize that an action is occurring at the moment and is in progress, you can use the *present progressive* tense.

The English present progressive is made up of a form of the verb *to be* + *present participle* (*-ing*). Look at the following sentences and formulate a rule for creating the present progressive in Spanish. Use the questions below to guide you.

—¿Qué *estás* **haciendo**?   *What are you doing?*
—*Estoy* **estudiando.**   *I'm studying.*

—¿*Está* **escuchando** música tu hermano?   *Is your brother listening to music?*
—No, *está* **tocando** la guitarra.   *No, he is playing the guitar.*

—¿*Están* ustedes **viendo** la televisión?   *Are you watching television?*
—No, les *estamos* **escribiendo** una carta a   *No, we are writing a letter to our*
nuestros padres.   *parents.*

> **Fíjate**
>
> The present progressive is *not* used to express the future.
>
> Present progressive: *Están ensayando.* They are rehearsing (right now).
>
> Future: *Van a ensayar.* They are going to rehearse (in the future).

1. What is the infinitive of the first verb in each sentence that is in *italics*?
2. What are the infinitives of **haciendo, estudiando, escuchando, tocando, viendo, and escribiendo**?
3. How do you form the verb forms in **boldface**?
4. In this new tense, the *present progressive*, do any words come between the two parts of the verb?
5. Therefore, your formula for forming the *present progressive* is:
   a form of the verb _____ + a verb ending in _____ or _____

Check your answers to the preceding questions in Appendix 1.

*The following are some verbs that are irregular in this tense. Please note them below.

creer	creyendo	pedir	pidiendo	seguir	siguiendo
leer	leyendo	preferir	prefiriendo	servir	sirviendo
ir	yendo	perseguir	persiguiendo		
		repetir	repitiendo	dormir	durmiendo
decir	diciendo			morir	muriendo
mentir	mintiendo				

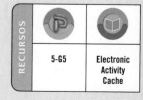

5•16 Progresando

Escuchen mientras su instructor/a les da (*gives you*) las instrucciones de esta actividad. ¡Diviértanse! (*Enjoy!*)

MODELO
E1: *hablar, yo*
E2: *estoy hablando*
E2: *comer, nosotros*
E3: *estamos comiendo*

5•17 ¿Tienes telepatía?

Es sábado. Túrnense para decir qué está haciendo su profesor/a en varios momentos del día.

MODELO
E1: Le gusta tomar café por la mañana. Son las siete y media.
E2: *Está tomando café en su terraza.*

1. Le gusta hacer ejercicio para comenzar su día.
2. Le gusta la música latina y está en una tienda.
3. Su coche está muy sucio y esta noche lleva a unos amigos a una gran fiesta.
4. Está trabajando en la computadora y resulta que tiene muchos mensajes de sus estudiantes.
5. Quiere comer algo ligero (*light*) antes de ir a la fiesta.
6. Está con sus amigos en la fiesta y los músicos están tocando.

5•18 ¿Qué está ocurriendo?

Túrnense para decir qué están haciendo estas personas.

MODELO
E1: Felipe
E2: *Felipe está preparando su comida y está comiendo también.*

Felipe   Manuel   Sofía

Raúl y Mari Carmen   José   Mercedes y Guillermo

1. Manuel   Manuel está lavando los platos.
2. Sofía   Sofía está sacando la basura.
3. Raúl y Mari Carmen   Raúl y Mari Carmen están tocando música. Raúl está tocando el piano y Mari Carmen la flauta.
4. José   José está viendo la televisión.
5. Mercedes y Guillermo   Mercedes y Guillermo están escuchando música.

NOTE AND INSTRUCTIONS FOR 5-16

¡Anda! believes in offering highly creative activities while at the same time keeping the direction lines at an *i + 1* level. There are activities, such as this one, where it is more efficient for you to give the directions in English, unless you have a large number of Heritage language learners or false beginners, in which case you may choose to give the following directions in Spanish.

INSTRUCTIONS: Work in groups of at least four students. One student makes a ball out of a piece of paper, says an infinitive and a subject (noun or pronoun), then tosses the ball to someone in the group. The person who catches the ball must give the correct form of the verb in the present progressive. If correct, he or she receives a point. The activity continues until you, the teacher, call "time."

Follow-up to 5-17 If a student is absent, you can ask the class to predict what that student might be doing during the time when the other students are in class. If no one is absent, you might ask them what they think the university administrators are currently doing, or what the students in the other Spanish classes are doing.

NOTE FOR 5-19

Rather than having your students create a dialogue, you may choose to have them write song lyrics.

`8:00` **5·19** ¡Qué creativo!

Creen juntos un diálogo de por lo menos **seis** oraciones usando los siguientes verbos. Usen el presente progresivo un mínimo de **tres** veces (*times*).

| decir | dormir | repetir | creer | morir |
| mentir | leer | ir | seguir | servir |

¿Cómo andas?

Having completed the first **Comunicación**, I now can…

	Feel Confident	Need to Review
● talk about the kinds of music that my friends and I like and dislike (p. 172)	❏	❏
● pronounce diphthongs correctly and use "linking" when speaking (p. 174)	❏	❏
● use demonstrative adjectives and pronouns (**este, ese,** and **aquel; éste, éste,** and **aquél**) in sentences (pp. 176, 178)	❏	❏
● state three facts about Latin music (p. 179)	❏	❏
● explain how something is done using adverbs (**-mente**) (p. 180)	❏	❏
● state what is happening right now using the present progressive (form of **estar + -ando, -iendo**) (p. 182)	❏	❏

Comunicación

- Sharing information and opinions about movies and actors
- Ranking items
- Stating what needs to be accomplished

VOCABULARIO 6
3:00

El mundo del cine

5-28 to 5-30

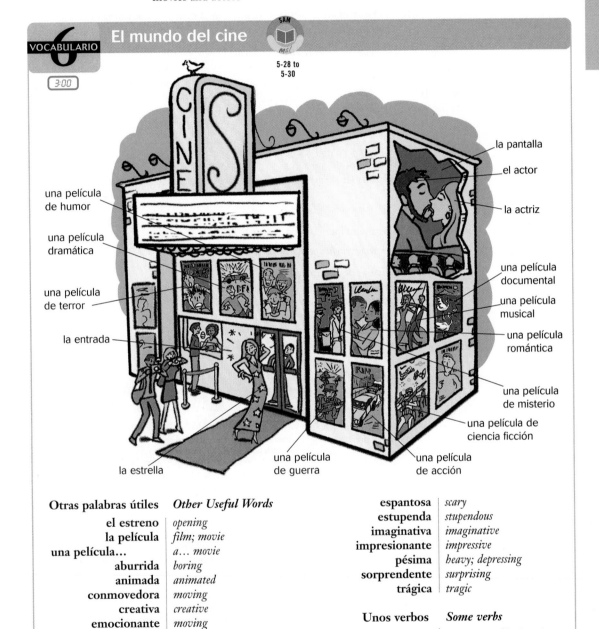

- la pantalla
- el actor
- la actriz
- una película de humor
- una película dramática
- una película de terror
- la entrada
- una película documental
- una película musical
- una película romántica
- una película de misterio
- una película de ciencia ficción
- una película de acción
- una película de guerra
- la estrella

Otras palabras útiles	Other Useful Words
el estreno	opening
la película	film; movie
una película...	a... movie
aburrida	boring
animada	animated
conmovedora	moving
creativa	creative
emocionante	moving
entretenida	entertaining
épica	epic

espantosa	scary
estupenda	stupendous
imaginativa	imaginative
impresionante	impressive
pésima	heavy; depressing
sorprendente	surprising
trágica	tragic

Unos verbos	Some verbs
estrenar una película	to release a film/movie
presentar una película	to show a film/movie

SECTION GOALS FOR
Comunicación

By the end of the *Comunicación* section, students will be able to:

- discuss their favorite films and current releases.
- categorize films by genre.
- identify the Hispanic influence and presence in North American movies.
- rank items using ordinal numbers.
- construct sentences using the expression *hay* + *que* + *infinitive*.
- identify direct objects and use direct object pronouns.

NATIONAL STANDARDS
Communication

This vocabulary is optimal because so many of the words are cognates in English. Also, students enjoy talking about what interests them, and most students enjoy some genre of film. This vocabulary motivates students to share orally, which will then lead to meaningful communication in writing with the guidance that *¡Anda!* provides.

The activities in the *Comunicación* section provide opportunities for communication in the interpersonal and presentational modes. Students are encouraged to share their opinions and observations with others about their favorite movies and actors (Standard 1.1). Actividades **5-21** and **5-22** can be adapted to address Standard 1.3 by having students present a poster for their favorite movie and try to persuade others to see it. They can vote for the movie they would most like to see, and then write a review of that movie in Spanish, practicing the new chapter vocabulary. If you have a particular movie that you like, you can write a description of the movie in Spanish, and students can practice listening as you present your movie. They could also practice reading if you make a pamphlet or jacket cover that summarizes what you said about the movie (Standard 1.2).

RECURSOS
T5-3 to T5-4	T5-3 to T5-4	Electronic Activity Cache

Answers to 5-20.
Possible answers include:
1. dramática / épica / conmovedora
2. musical / entretenida
3. dramática / trágica / romántica
4. animada / creativa / imaginativa / de humor
5. de acción / de ciencia ficción
6. dramática / épica
7. de guerra / impresionante / trágica
8. de acción / entretenida
9. de terror / espantosa

[3:00]

5•20 ¿Cuál es el género?

Clasifiquen las siguientes películas según su género y usen el mayor (*the largest*) número de palabras posibles para describirlas.

MODELO   E1:   Jaws (*Tiburón*)

E2:   *Tiburón es una película dramática, de acción. Es emocionante, entretenida, impresionante y trágica.*

1. Gone With the Wind (*Lo que el viento se llevó*)
2. Chicago
3. Titanic
4. Shrek II
5. Spiderman II (*El hombre araña II*)
6. Ben-Hur
7. Saving Private Ryan
8. Rush Hour (*Hora punta*)
9. The Exorcist (*El exorcista*)
10. ¿?

[3:00]

5•21 En mi opinión

Túrnense para completar las siguientes oraciones sobre las películas. ¿Están ustedes de acuerdo?

Capítulo Preliminar A.
El verbo *ser*, pág. 13.

MODELO   E1:   La mejor película de terror…

E2:   *La mejor película de terror es* Saw.

1. Las mejores películas de humor…
2. Una película épica pésima…
3. Mis actores favoritos de las películas de acción…
4. La película de misterio que más me gusta…
5. Unas películas animadas creativas…
6. La película más conmovedora…

[5:00]

5•22 Mis preferencias

Lee las reseñas (*reviews*) siguientes de unas películas. Después, túrnate con un/a compañero/a para describir la película que prefieren ver y por qué.

MODELO   *Prefiero ver _____. Es una película _____ y_____. Me gusta _____. También es _____ …*

En el cine

Cartas desde Iwo Jima (2006, EE.UU.)
Género: Película de guerra
Director: Clint Eastwood
Interpretación: Ken Watanabe, Kazunari Ninomiya…

Un tributo al rostro de la derrota en la célebre y decisiva batalla de Iwo Jima.

Dreamgirls (2006, EE.UU.)
Género: Película musical
Director: Bill Condon
Interpretación: Beyoncé Knowles, Jamie Foxx, Eddie Murphy…

Un festín bailable para los amantes del Motown y el Rhythm & Blues.

Invencible (2006, EE.UU)
Género: Película dramática
Director: Ericsson Core
Interpretación: Mark Wahlberg, Greg Kinnear…

La historia real de un ciudadano que se convirtió por sorpresa en estrella de la NFL.

5·23 En nuestra opinión...

Paso 1 Habla de algunas películas que conoces con un/a compañero/a, usando las preguntas siguientes como guía (*guide*).

1. ¿Cuáles son las películas que más te gustan? ¿Por qué?
2. ¿Quiénes son tus actores o actrices favoritos?
3. ¿Qué películas que van a estrenar pronto quieres ver?

Paso 2 Ahora hablen sobre unos programas de televisión.

5-31 to
5-32

La influencia hispana en el cine norteamericano

Antonio Banderas

La influencia hispana en el cine norteamericano empieza a tener importancia en los años cincuenta. Actores como Gilbert Roland, Anthony Quinn y Ricardo Montalbán se destacan (*stand out*) en películas de habla inglesa. Les siguen más tarde estrellas del cine y de la televisión como Raquel Welch y Rita Moreno y continúan hasta el presente con Antonio Banderas, Jimmy Smits, John Leguizamo, Edward James Olmos, Jennifer López, Andy García, Salma Hayek, Cameron Díaz, Freddie Prinze, Jr. y Penélope Cruz, entre muchos otros. Su presencia en la industria representa el cambio en la demografía de los Estados Unidos.

Preguntas

1. De los actores mencionados, ¿a cuáles conoces? ¿Qué sabes de ellos?

2. ¿Quiénes son los actores hispanos más populares en este momento?

Salma Hayek

Cameron Díaz

Jennifer López

NATIONAL STANDARDS
Communication, Cultures, Connections, Comparisons

When discussing the National Standards, it is always interesting to note how the 5C's overlap. If you have a film festival at your school, you may wish to request either vintage movies or current films with Hispanic actors.

This reading highlights the four goal areas of Communication, Cultures, Connections, and Comparisons. Students are able to communicate about this reading in one of three ways. First, you can ask them to work in pairs or small groups and have them research one of the profiled actors. You can bring the information to class, they can bring the information to class, or you can take them to the language lab for research. The discussions that they have about the actors satisfy Standard 1.1. The reading they are doing in Spanish contributes to Standard 1.2. If you have them present the information they have read as a group or turn in a report of the information, it addresses Standard 1.3. If you have time to show a film, or film clip, from one of these actors, you can also use that as a starting point for discussion, assignments, and presentations. Students see the products and perspectives (Standard 2.2) through the contributions that Hispanics have made to the film industry. They can connect the new information to what they might have known about the actor(s) or topics discussed in the movie (Standard 3.2) and think about it in the context of learning Spanish. (The films by Spanish director Pedro Almodóvar are especially useful for Standard 3.2). Students can make comparisons between Spanish and English (subtitled movies work well to show the difference between translation and interpretation) and the cultural differences they see in the films (Standards 4.1 and 4.2).

Expansion for 5-24 through 5-26
Other practice for the ordinal numbers could include having students complete the following lists, e.g., *El primer día de la semana es lunes, el segundo día es martes,* etc., *El primer mes es enero, el segundo mes es. . .* , etc. You can start them with an example, and they can continue the list.

GRAMÁTICA 7 — Los números ordinales

[2:00]

5-33 to 5-35 · 42

¿Te gusta la primera sinfonía de Beethoven?

Sí, pero prefiero la novena.

The first ten ordinal numbers in Spanish are listed below. They are the most commonly used.

primer, primero/a	*first*	**sexto/a**	*sixth*
segundo/a	*second*	**séptimo/a**	*seventh*
tercer, tercero/a	*third*	**octavo/a**	*eighth*
cuarto/a	*fourth*	**noveno/a**	*ninth*
quinto/a	*fifth*	**décimo/a**	*tenth*

1. Ordinal numbers are adjectives and agree in number and gender with the nouns they modify.

el **cuarto** año   *the fourth year*
la **octava** sinfonía   *the eighth symphony*

2. Before a masculine, singular noun, **primero** and **tercero** are shortened to **primer** and **tercer.**

el **primer** concierto   *the first concert*
el **tercer** curso de español   *the third Spanish course*

3. As seen in the examples above, ordinal numbers usually *precede* the noun.

5·24 Orden de preferencia [4:00]

Asigna un orden de preferencia a las actividades de la lista: desde la más importante (primero) hasta la menos importante (octavo). Después, comparte tu lista con un/a compañero/a usando oraciones completas.

MODELO   *Primero, me gusta ver una película con mi actor favorito, Tom Hanks. Segundo, quiero visitar a mis hermanos. Tercero, prefiero…*

1. ir a un concierto de tu conjunto favorito
2. visitar a tus amigos
3. ver una película con tu actor/actriz favorito/a
4. leer una novela buena
5. ir a un partido de fútbol americano
6. estudiar para un examen
7. visitar Costa Rica
8. conocer al presidente de los Estados Unidos

Answers to 5-25.
1. *Answers may vary.*
2. *Answers may vary.*
3. El tercer mes del año es marzo y el sexto es junio.
4. El séptimo día de la semana es el domingo (en los países hispanohablantes).
5. El primer presidente de los Estados Unidos es George Washington.
6. *Answers may vary.*

5·25 Preguntas de trivia [2:00]

Túrnense para hacerse y contestar las siguientes preguntas.

1. ¿En qué piso está esta sala de clase?
2. ¿A qué hora es tu primera clase los lunes? ¿y la segunda?
3. ¿Cuál es el tercer mes del año? ¿y el sexto?
4. ¿Cuál es el séptimo día de la semana?
5. ¿Cómo se llama el primer presidente de los Estados Unidos?
6. ¿Cómo se llama la cuarta persona de la tercera fila (*row*) en la clase de español?

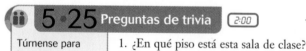

Capítulo Preliminar A. Los días, los meses y las estaciones, pág. 20.

Estrategia

Remember that when asked a question with *tu/tus*, you need to answer *mi/mis.*

RECURSOS · 5-G7 · Electronic Activity Cache

5·26 La lista de los mejores

¿Cuáles son las mejores películas para los estudiantes de tu clase?

Paso 1 Entrevista a cinco estudiantes y pregúntales cuáles son sus tres películas favoritas. Usa las palabras **primera, segunda** y **tercera**.

Paso 2 Con el/la profesor/a, haz una lista de las **diez** películas más populares de la clase.

Paso 3 Organiza por orden de preferencia la lista de las películas más populares de la clase. Escribe el número ordinal apropiado para cada película.

PELÍCULAS FAVORITAS	ESTUDIANTE 1	ESTUDIANTE 2	ESTUDIANTE 3	ESTUDIANTE 4	ESTUDIANTE 5
Primera					
Segunda					
Tercera					

 GRAMÁTICA

Hay que + infinitivo

5-36 to 5-37

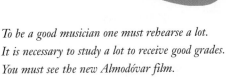

Hay que trabajar. ¡No hay que ser perezoso!

So far when you have wanted to talk about what someone should do, needs to do, or has to do, you have used the expressions **debe, necesita,** or **tiene que.** The expression **hay que** + *infinitive* is another way to communicate responsibility, obligation, or the importance of something. **Hay que** + *infinitive* means:

It is necessary to…

You must…

One must/should…

Para ser un músico bueno **hay que** ensayar mucho.   *To be a good musician one must rehearse a lot.*

Hay que estudiar mucho para sacar buenas notas.   *It is necessary to study a lot to receive good grades.*

Hay que ver la nueva película de Almodóvar.   *You must see the new Almodóvar film.*

5·27 Para generalizar

Túrnense para sustituir **tener que** por **hay que.** Sigan el modelo.

MODELO   E1:   Tenemos que consultar al profesor para confirmar la información.

          E2:   *Hay que consultar al profesor para confirmar la información.*

1. Ustedes tienen que leer más si quieren sacar buenas notas en el examen.
2. Marisol, tú tienes que ser más paciente si quieres tener muchos amigos.
3. Mamá, tienes que comprar un carro nuevo. Tu carro es muy viejo.
4. Jorge y Catrina, ustedes tienen que preparar el almuerzo para sus padres.
5. Rafael, tienes que visitar a tu hermana porque está enferma.
6. Sara, tú tienes que terminar el proyecto antes del primero de diciembre.

METHODOLOGY • Chunking

You will note that *¡Anda!* presented *tener* + *que* + *infinitive* separately from *hay que* + *infinitive*. Once again, the purpose is to chunk information so that the students focus on smaller bits, giving them one way to express an idea and then providing them with another way to vary their repertoire.

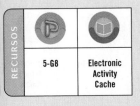

RECURSOS

5-G8	Electronic Activity Cache

[3:00] 🗣🗣 **5·28** ¿Obligaciones?

¿Qué hay que hacer para llegar a tener las siguientes características? Túrnense para completar las frases dando por lo menos **dos** ideas.

MODELO E1: Para ser un pintor excelente...

E2: *hay que pintar mucho y hay que ser muy creativo.*

Para ser...

1. un músico impresionante...
2. un político honesto...
3. un cantante estupendo...

4. un director de cine sorprendente...
5. una actriz conmovedora...
6. una novelista entretenida...

[4:00] 👥👥 **5·29** y todos necesitamos...

¿Qué debemos hacer para tener un futuro mejor? Compartan sus ideas y comuniquen sus resultados a la clase usando **tres** oraciones completas.

MODELO E1: Hay que...

E2: *Hay que respetar las otras culturas.*

Vocabulario útil	
el idioma/la lengua	*language*
la paz	*peace*
respetar	*to respect*

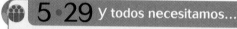

GRAMÁTICA ⑨ Los pronombres de complemento directo y la "a" personal

SAM 5-38 to 5-40   Guide **G** 6, 19, 20

[3:00]

¿Mi trompeta y mi guitarra? Sí, las tengo.

Direct objects receive the action of the verb and answer the questions *What?* or *Whom?* Note these examples.

A: I need to do *what?*

B: You need to pay *the bills* by Monday.

A: Yes, I do need to pay *them.*

A: I have to call *whom?*

B: You have to call *David.*

A: Yes, I do have to call *him.*

Note the following examples of *direct objects* in Spanish.

María toca **dos instrumentos** muy bien.	*María plays two instruments very well.*
Sacamos **un CD** el primero de septiembre.	*We are releasing a CD the first of September.*
¿Tienes **las entradas**?	*Do you have the tickets?*
No conozco a **Antonio Banderas.**	*I do not know Antonio Banderas.*
Siempre veo a **Shakira** en la televisión.	*I always watch Shakira on TV.*

Note: In *Capítulo 4*, you learned that to express knowing a person, you put "**a**" after the verb (*conocer* + *a* + person). Now that you have learned about direct objects, a more global way of stating the rule is: when direct objects refer to *people*, you must use the personal "**a.**" Review the following examples.

People	Things
¡Veo **a** *Cameron Díaz*!	¡Veo *el coche* de Cameron Díaz!
Hay que ver **a** *mis padres*.	Hay que ver *la película*.
¿**A** qué *actores* conoces?	¿Qué *ciudades* conoces?

As in English, we can replace direct objects nouns with *direct object pronouns*. Note the following examples.

María **los** toca muy bien.	*María plays them very well.*
Lo sacamos el primero de septiembre.	*We are releasing it the first of September.*
¿**Las** tienes?	*Do you have them?*
No **lo** conozco.	*I do not know him.*
Siempre **la** veo en la televisión.	*I always see her on TV.*

In Spanish, direct object pronouns *agree in gender and number with the nouns they replace*. The chart below lists the direct object pronouns.

Singular		Plural	
me	*me*	nos	*us*
te	*you*	os	*you all*
lo, la	*him, her, it, you*	los, las	*them, you all*

Placement of direct object pronouns

Direct object pronouns are:

1. Placed before the verb.
2. Attached to *infinitives* or to the *present participle* (**-ando, -iendo**).

¿Tienes los discos compactos?	→	Sí, **los** tengo.
Tengo que traer los instrumentos.	→	**Los** tengo que traer. / Tengo que traer**los.**
Tiene que llevar su guitarra.	→	**La** tiene que llevar. / Tiene que llevar**la.**

—¿Por qué estás preparando la comida para tu madre?

—**La** estoy preparando porque mi madre está enferma. /

Estoy preparándo**la** porque mi madre está enferma.

METHODOLOGY • *Personal a*

You may choose to present exceptions to the rule given to students regarding the personal *a*, e.g., *Tengo un hermano,* or talk about variations in the Spanish-speaking world. Your own personal philosophy, and your knowledge of your students and their abilities, will be your guide when making these types of decisions.

NOTE FOR

os

You may wish to remind your students about *vosotros*. Also, remember that the forms are presented as a point of information in the charts, but they are not practiced in the activities.

NOTE FOR

Placement of Direct Object Pronouns

¡Anda! will present more information regarding accent marks in relation to direct and indirect objects in *Capítulo 10*, when commands are introduced.

5·30 ¿Estás listo? `2:00`

Capítulo 2. Presente indicativo de verbos regulares, pág. 68.

¿Estás preparado/a para el concierto de Perrozompopo? Túrnate con un/a compañero/a para revisar la lista, esta vez usando **lo, la, los** o **las**.

> **MODELO** E1: confirmar *la hora* del concierto
> E2: *La confirmo hoy.*

1. comprar *las entradas*   Las compro.
2. invitar *a mis amigos*   Los invito.
3. leer *el artículo* de *The New York Times* sobre Perrozompopo   Lo leo.
4. compartir (*share*) *el artículo y los CD de Perrozompopo* con mis amigos   Los comparto.
5. preparar *comida* para un pícnic   La preparo.
6. traer *la cámara*   La traigo.

5·31 ¿Hay deberes? `2:00`

El concierto de Perrozompopo fue increíble, pero hay que volver al mundo real. Siempre hay trabajo, sobre todo en la casa. Túrnate con un/a compañero/a para hacer y contestar las siguientes preguntas.

> **MODELO** E1: ¿Lavas los pisos?
> E2: *Sí, los lavo. / No, no/nunca los lavo.*
> *All can be either* sí *or* no.

Capítulo 3. Los quehaceres de la casa, pág. 112.

1. ¿Limpias la cocina?   ... la limpio
2. ¿Arreglas tu cuarto?   ... lo arreglo
3. ¿Lavas los platos?   ... los lavo
4. ¿Guardas tus cosas?   ... las guardo
5. ¿Sacudes los muebles?   ... los sacudo
6. ¿Haces las camas?   ... las hago
7. ¿Preparas la comida?   ... la preparo
8. ¿Pones la mesa?   ... la pongo
9. ¿Nos ayudas a arreglar el jardín?   ... los ayudo
10. ¿Me invitas a un concierto?   ... te invito

5·32 Una hora antes `3:00`

Carlos Santana, como muchos músicos, es una persona muy organizada. Antes de cada concierto repasa con su ayudante (*assistant*) personal los preparativos. Aquí tienes las preguntas del ayudante. Contesta como si fueras (*as if you were*) Santana, usando **lo, la, los** o **las**.

> **MODELO** E1: ¿Tienes tu anillo (*ring*) de la buena suerte?
> E2: *Sí, lo tengo.*

1. Juan está enfermo. ¿Conoces al trompetista que toca esta noche con el conjunto?   Sí, lo conozco.
2. ¿Traes tu guitarra nueva?   Sí, la traigo.
3. ¿Los cantantes saben la letra de la canción nueva?   Sí, la saben.
4. ¿Traemos todos los trajes (*suits, outfits*)?   Sí, los traemos.
5. ¿Quieres unas botellas de agua (*water*)?   Sí, las quiero.
6. ¿Oyes al público? ¡Está listo para el concierto!   Sí, lo oigo.
7. ¿Me van a necesitar después del concierto?   Sí, te vamos a necesitar.
8. ¿El empresario te va a anunciar?   Sí, me va a anunciar. *or* Sí, va a anunciarme.

Carlos Santana

5·33 Mis preferencias

Túrnense para hacerse y contestar las siguientes preguntas usando el pronombre de complemento directo correcto.

MODELO E1: ¿Lees los poemas de Rubén Darío? ¿Por qué?

E2: *No, no los leo. No los leo porque no los conozco.*

1. ¿Escuchas música clásica? ¿Por qué?
2. ¿Tu amigo y tú tienen ganas de ver una película de acción de Antonio Banderas? ¿Por qué?
3. ¿Sus amigos limpian sus casas todos los días? ¿Por qué?
4. ¿Escuchas música jazz en tu iPod? ¿Por qué?
5. ¿Tocas un instrumento? ¿Por qué?

ESCUCHA

5-41 to 5-43

ESTRATEGIA Anticipating content

Use all clues available to you to anticipate what you are about to hear. That includes photos, captions, and body language if you are looking at the individual(s) speaking. If there are written synopses, they are important to read in advance. Finally, if you are doing a listening activity such as these, look ahead at the comprehension questions to give you an idea of the topic and important points.

5·34 Antes de escuchar

Mira la foto y contesta las siguientes preguntas.
1. ¿Quiénes están en la foto?
2. ¿De qué hablan Eduardo y Cisco?

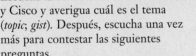

Eduardo y Cisco

5·35 A escuchar

CD 2 Track 32

Escucha la conversación entre Eduardo y Cisco y averigua cuál es el tema (*topic*; *gist*). Después, escucha una vez más para contestar las siguientes preguntas.
1. ¿Quién va al concierto de Audioslave? Eduardo
2. ¿Qué música prefiere Cisco? el jazz
3. Deciden no estudiar. ¿Adónde van a ir? Van al Club Ritmo.

5·36 Después de escuchar

Describe una canción que te guste en **tres** oraciones y dibuja un cuadro (*picture*) que la represente. Preséntaselo a un/a compañero/a.

SECTION GOALS FOR *Escucha*

By the end of the *Escucha* section, students will be able to:
- practice anticipating content.
- summarize the main idea of the conversation.

NATIONAL STANDARDS
Communication

Capítulo 5 introduces a new listening strategy: anticipating content. Communication Standard 1.2 emphasizes understanding and interpretation of spoken Spanish. After listening, students discuss in small groups what they have heard. They can then create mini-dialogues as if they were the teacher, in which they describe one of their favorite films. Conversations take place in pairs, allowing students to practice interpersonal communication, Standard 1.1.

AUDIOSCRIPT FOR 5-35

EDUARDO: Oye, ¿vas al concierto de Audioslave el viernes?

CISCO: No, tengo que trabajar. ¿Tú vas a ir?

EDUARDO: Sí. Me gusta mucho el baterista del grupo. El último CD es fenomenal, ¿sabes?

CISCO: Sí, y dicen que sacan un CD nuevo el mes que viene.

EDUARDO: ¿Te gusta el rock?

CISCO: Sí, pero prefiero el jazz.

EDUARDO: ¿Tienes un grupo favorito de jazz?

CISCO: Pues. . . el Grupo Pat Metheny. Wynton Marsalis, Nestor Torres, Norah Jones—son todos increíbles. ¿Cuál es tu grupo favorito de rock?

EDUARDO: Hmmm. Hay muchos muy buenos. . . U2, Coldplay, Molotov. . .

CISCO: Mira, vamos al Club Ritmo ahora. Siempre ponen una música muy buena.

EDUARDO: ¿Sí? Pues vamos. ¡Esta noche no estudiamos!

ESCRIBE

5·44

5·37 Antes de escribir

Piensa en una película que te guste mucho. Anota algunas ideas sobre los aspectos que te gustan más de esa película.

• ¿Qué tipo de película es?
• ¿Para qué grupo(s) es apropiada?
• ¿Cuál es el tema?
• ¿Tiene una lección para el público?

5·38 Una reseña

Organiza tus ideas y escribe una reseña (*review*), como una de las de la actividad **5-22**, de **cuatro** a **seis** oraciones. Puedes usar las siguientes preguntas para organizar tu reseña.

1. ¿Cómo se llama la película?
2. ¿De qué género es?
3. ¿Cómo la describes?
4. ¿A quiénes les va a gustar? ¿Por qué?
5. ¿La recomiendas? ¿Por qué?

5·39 Después de escribir

Tu profesor/a va a leer las reseñas. La clase tiene que adivinar cuáles son las películas.

¿Cómo andas?

Having completed the second **Comunicación**, I now can…

	Feel Confident	Need to Review
talk about my favorite movies (p. 185)	❑	❑
name at least three famous Hispanic actors (p. 187)	❑	❑
rank things using ordinal numbers (p. 188)	❑	❑
express things that need to be done by using **hay que…** (p. 189)	❑	❑
replace direct objects with the direct object pronouns (**me, te, lo, la, nos, los, las**) in sentences (p. 190)	❑	❑
explain the use of the personal "**a**" (p. 191)	❑	❑
listen with the goal of anticipating content (p. 193)	❑	❑
write a movie review (p. 194)	❑	❑

Mauricio Morales Prado

Nicaragua

15:00

CW
eBook

CD 2
Track 33

SAM
MSI
5-45

DVD/VHS
MSI

Vistas
culturales

Les presento mi país

Mi nombre es Mauricio Morales Prado y soy de Managua, Nicaragua. Mi país es conocido como la tierra de volcanes y lagos (*lakes*). Hay dos lagos principales y muchos volcanes. Siete están activos todavía. **¡Localiza estos lugares en el mapa!** Bluefields es la ciudad principal en la costa caribeña; allí se celebra la fiesta del Palo de Mayo. **¿Qué fiestas celebras en tu ciudad?** Mi familia y yo somos muy aficionados al béisbol. Vamos frecuentemente a los partidos en el Estadio Nacional en Managua.

El béisbol es muy popular en Nicaragua.

HONDURAS
Río Coco
Puerto Cabezas
Cayos Miskitos
NICARAGUA
Mar Caribe
Matagalpa
San Cristóbal
Momotombo
León
Managua
Masaya
Bluefields
Islas del Maíz
Granada
Lago de Nicaragua
OCÉANO PACÍFICO
Río San Juan
COSTA RICA

La fiesta del Palo de Mayo en Bluefields

• ALMANAQUE •

Nombre oficial:	República de Nicaragua
Gobierno:	República
Población:	5.570.129 (2006)
Idiomas:	español (oficial); miskito, otros idiomas indígenas
Moneda:	Córdoba (C$)

¿Sabías que...?

● El Lago de Nicaragua es el único lago de agua dulce (*fresh water*) del mundo donde se encuentran tiburones (*sharks*) y atunes.

● El 23 de diciembre de 1972, un terremoto (*earthquake*) desastroso de 6,5 en la escala Richter destruyó (*destroyed*) la ciudad de Managua.

PREGUNTAS

1. ¿Por qué se llama Nicaragua la tierra de lagos y volcanes?

2. ¿Qué tiene el Lago de Nicaragua de especial?

3. ¿Qué deporte es muy popular en Nicaragua? ¿En qué otros países hispanohablantes es popular?

En la Red
Amplía tus conocimientos sobre Nicaragua en la página web de *¡Anda!*

195

SECTION GOALS FOR
Cultura

By the end of the *Cultura* section, students will be able to:

• locate Nicaragua's lakes and volcanoes on a map.
• discuss Nicaraguan pastimes.
• explain what *ticos* are.
• identify the national symbol of Costa Rica.
• list main exports and industries of Costa Rica.
• summarize the significance of the Panama Canal.
• compare and contrast Nicaragua, Costa Rica, and Panama.

NATIONAL STANDARDS
Cultures, Comparisons

The cultural information about Nicaragua, Costa Rica, and Panama highlights Standards 2.1 and 2.2. Students read about each country, what makes that country unique, and some of the daily activities and products the country is known for. The cultural information presented in each chapter allows students to make comparisons among the Hispanic countries and their own countries (Standard 4.2), as well as comparisons between the Hispanic countries presented here and in earlier chapters. They learn how geography, climate, exports, and natural resources contribute to the differences among the Hispanic countries, and how those countries differ from the United States or their country of origin.

NOTE FOR
Bluefields

Inhabitants of Bluefields are largely descended from English colonizers and black immigrants from Caribbean islands. The language of Bluefields is English and/or English Creole, and reggae music is often heard there. It was part of a British protectorate for decades, and many British customs remain. One of these is the celebration of May Day, the beginning of spring. The MayPole dance and festivities in Bluefields take place during the entire month of May. There are dance contests, beauty pageants, parades, sporting events, and food fairs in which a mixture of the local cultures is evident.

NOTE FOR
El béisbol

Baseball is very important in Nicaragua. On any given Sunday, you can find a baseball game going on in places everywhere, from small villages to large cities. There are several professional baseball teams in Nicaragua, and Managua has a large baseball stadium that holds 40,000 fans. It was built in 1948 and survived the devastating earthquake of 1972. Baseball is the sport most played in this stadium. Denis Martínez, "el presidente," is perhaps the most famous player.

NOTE FOR
Ecoturismo

Ecotourism is big business in Costa Rica. Because the geography, flora, and fauna are so varied, there is something for everyone: such as beautiful beaches, rain and cloud forests, volcanoes, two- and three-toed sloths, howler monkeys, butterflies, tapirs, green turtles and their nesting sites. In recent years, sailing through the trees on zip lines or walking through tree canopies over hanging bridges have been two popular diversions offered to tourists. You and your students can look for additional information on the web by using the key words: *Costa Rica* and *ecotourism*.

NOTE FOR
La carreta

The oxcart has played a big role in Costa Rica's economic history and traditions. Originally the oxcart was the only method for transporting coffee beans to coastal commerce centers. Because coffee was the economic livelihood of many farmers, the carts were extremely important. Eventually, the owners began to paint them to indicate their region, their town, and their own distinct personalities. These painted carts are rarely seen now, but they remain a cultural symbol and are a source of pride for many Costa Ricans, reflecting their history and industriousness. They were declared a national symbol on March 22, 1988.

Alejandra Cecilia Montero Valverde

CD 2
Track 34

Vistas culturales

Les presento mi país

Mi nombre es Alejandra Cecilia Montero Valverde y soy *tica*. *Ticos* es el apodo que tenemos todos los costarricenses. Soy de Sarchí, un pueblo famoso por su artesanía, sobre todo por la carreta, que es un símbolo nacional. **¿Cuáles son algunos símbolos de tu país y qué representan?** Si piensas visitar Costa Rica, te recomiendo una visita a los parques nacionales. Son bonitos y tienen flora y fauna únicas en el mundo. **¿Cuál es tu animal favorito?** ¡Costa Rica es pura vida!

Costa Rica

Una carreta pintada de Sarchí

El ecoturismo es muy importante para la economía de Costa Rica.

El café, un producto principal de exportación.

● ALMANAQUE ●

Nombre oficial: República de Costa Rica

Gobierno: República democrática

Población: 4.075.261 (2006)

Idiomas: español (oficial); inglés

Moneda: Colón (₡)

¿Sabías que...?

● El ejército (*army*) se abolió en Costa Rica en 1948. Los recursos monetarios desde aquel entonces apoyan (*support*) el sistema educativo. A causa de su dedicación a la paz (*peace*), la llaman "La Suiza de Centroamérica".

PREGUNTAS

1. ¿Qué artesanía es un símbolo nacional costarricense?
2. ¿Cuál es uno de los productos de exportación importantes de Costa Rica? ¿Qué otros países exportan productos similares?
3. ¿Qué otra industria es importante para la economía de Costa Rica?

En la Red
Amplía tus conocimientos sobre Costa Rica en la página web de *¡Anda!*

RECURSOS | T5-6 | T5-6 | Cultural Background Notes

Aída Elena Flores Solís

Panamá

CW
eBook

CD 2
Track 35

DVD/VHS

Vistas
culturales

Les presento mi país

Mi nombre es Aída Elena Flores Solís y soy de la ciudad de Panamá, la capital. Mi país es famoso por el canal. **¿Qué sabes tú de la historia del canal?** La economía de Panamá se basa principalmente en el sector de los servicios, la banca, el comercio y el turismo. Los turistas van al canal y también a las Islas San Blas. Allí pueden apreciar la artesanía de las mujeres indígenas. Los Kunas son un grupo de indígenas que viven en este lugar y las mujeres hacen *molas* como parte de su ropa tradicional.

Una mujer Kuna haciendo una mola, artesanía tradicional

El Canal de Panamá

Mar Caribe

COSTA RICA
Bocas del Toro
Golfo de los Mosquitos
Canal de Panamá
Islas San Blas
Colón
Balboa
Panamá
Golfo de Panamá
La Palma
Barú
PANAMÁ
David
Santiago
Archipiélago de las Perlas
Isla de Coiba
COLOMBIA
OCÉANO PACÍFICO

● ALMANAQUE ●

Nombre oficial:	República de Panamá
Gobierno:	Democracia constitucional
Población:	3.191.319 (2006)
Idiomas:	español (oficial); chibcha, inglés
Moneda:	Balboa (B/)

¿Sabías que...?

● Richard Halliburton nadó el canal en 1928 y la tarifa fue (*was*) 36 centavos. Hoy la tarifa promedio (*average*) por cruzar el canal es $40.00 U.S.

● Hay un palíndromo famoso en inglés asociado con el canal: *A man, a plan, a canal: ¡Panamá!*

PREGUNTAS

1. ¿Por qué es importante el canal?
2. Compara Panamá con Costa Rica y Nicaragua. ¿En qué son similares? ¿En qué son diferentes?
3. Compara Panamá, Costa Rica y Nicaragua con México. ¿En qué son similares? ¿En qué son diferentes?

En la Red
Amplía tus conocimientos sobre Panamá en la página web de *¡Anda!*

197

NOTE FOR
El Canal de Panamá

The Panama Canal reverted to Panamanian ownership and directorship on December 31, 1999. The canal greatly decreases the travel time from Atlantic Ocean destinations to Pacific Ocean ones; the trip is also much safer than going around the tip of South America. Five years after the takeover by Panama, the canal is profitable and the accident rate has been reduced.

Suggestion for *El Canal de Panamá*
We believe in the need to use English at some points so that the students will have the richest experience possible. These brief questions bring forward the National Foreign Language Standards of Cultures, Comparisons, and Connections since through culture, they have students use knowledge from political science/history and make comparisons culturally. Ask students: Why is this canal so strategically important? Ask if anyone has ever been through the canal or through a system of locks (from lake to lake). Why is the Panama Canal economically important?

NOTE FOR
Los kunas

The Kuna Indians live in the Islas San Blas and in the province of Darién. The Kuna society is a matriarchal one; when a couple marries, the man moves to the woman's household. Kuna women are known for their colorful traditional dress that includes the *mola*, insets on both the front and back of a blouse with an intricate pattern and/or design. This is made by interleaving several layers of different colored cloth and cutting out shapes accordingly. This handicraft is highly prized and is a symbol of this indigenous culture.

RECURSOS

T5-7	T5-7	Cultural Background Notes
IRM		

NOTE FOR
Palíndromo

A palindrome is a "word, phrase, verse, or sentence which reads the same backward or forward." (*American Heritage Dictionary*, 1982.) A very famous one that appears in *The American Heritage Dictionary* is "A man, a plan, a canal, Panama!" Another palindrome in Spanish is *OSO*.

Suggestion for *Las molas* A brief English discussion of *molas* might include the following questions: What is traditional clothing like in indigenous groups in the United States? (*Possible answer: Some indigenous groups have animal skins or woven fabrics. The skins are natural tones, and the woven fabrics can be bright or more subdued, depending on the vegetation available for dying.*) How does it compare with the *molas*? (*Possible answer: They can be as colorful, depending on the dying materials available in nature. They reflect the culture with either geometric shapes or those of flora or fauna.*)

Ambiciones siniestras

EPISODIO 5

lectura

5-40 **Antes de leer.** En el **Episodio 4,** Marisol tiene sus dudas sobre Lupe. Cree que Lupe miente (*lies*) sobre su pueblo y posiblemente sobre otras cosas. En el **Episodio 4** del video, Cisco está enojado con Eduardo porque toca sus cosas. Luego, Eduardo se va misteriosamente. Teniendo esto en cuenta, contesta las siguientes preguntas.

• ¿Qué piensas? ¿De dónde es Lupe, de Akron, de Los Ángeles o de otro lugar?
• ¿Adónde va Eduardo?

ESTRATEGIA	Anticipating content

You can often anticipate the content of a reading passage by paying attention to the title, to any available illustrations, and by quickly reading through the comprehension questions that may follow the passage.

5-41 **A leer.** Complete the following activities.

1. Take a look at the title of the episode, **La búsqueda de Eduardo,** and answer these questions.
   • What verb does **búsqueda** look like?
   • Who would be looking for Eduardo?
   • What might Cisco do to look for him?
2. Now read the **Después de leer** questions. What do you glean from the questions? Employ this new reading strategy along with the others you have been learning (identifying cognates, skimming, and scanning), and enjoy the episode!

CW
eBook
CD 2
Track 36

La búsqueda de Eduardo

Cuando Cisco regresa a la sala, Eduardo no está. Pasa dos días haciendo llamadas y preguntándoles a otros amigos si saben algo de él. Nada. Nadie sabe nada. Cisco ya no° sabe qué hacer. ¿Debe llamar a la policía? ¿Debe avisar a los padres de Eduardo?

no longer

Por fin va a la computadora de Eduardo para ver si hay alguna pista°. Como Cisco es muy hábil con las computadoras, puede entrar en el correo electrónico de Eduardo. ¡Allí ve unos mensajes que le dan miedo!

clue

Lo piensa bien y finalmente decide mandarle un e-mail a su primo Manolo. Cisco admira y respeta mucho a su primo porque tiene mucha experiencia en la vida. Piensa que Manolo es muy responsable y casi siempre tiene respuestas para todo. Va a la computadora y empieza a escribir:

METHODOLOGY • Checking for Comprehension in English

When encouraging students to hypothesize regarding what will happen, it is acceptable to encourage them to brainstorm in English.

Answers to 5-42

1. Llama a sus amigos, lo busca y le escribe a su primo Manolo.
2. A Manolo, porque es muy inteligente y sabe qué hacer.
3. Va a un concierto. Es muy divertido y conoce a una chica bonita.
4. De Eduardo.
5. Alejandra, Marisol, Lupe y Manolo.

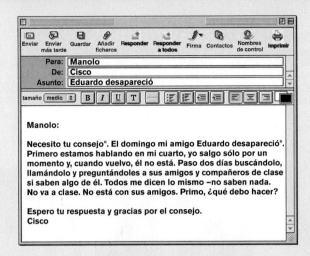

Manolo:

Necesito tu consejo°. El domingo mi amigo Eduardo desapareció°. Primero estamos hablando en mi cuarto, yo salgo sólo por un momento y, cuando vuelvo, él no está. Paso dos días buscándolo, llamándolo y preguntándoles a sus amigos y compañeros de clase si saben algo de él. Todos me dicen lo mismo −no saben nada. No va a clase. No está con sus amigos. Primo, ¿qué debo hacer?

Espero tu respuesta y gracias por el consejo.
Cisco

advice
disappeared

—Bueno, —piensa Cisco— necesito algo para distraerme°. Creo que voy al concierto.

entertain myself/get my mind off the situation

Su universidad siempre tiene buenos programas de música. Esta noche toca un grupo de fama internacional. Sus grabaciones son fenomenales y el cantante principal también tiene mucha habilidad como guitarrista. Cisco tiene todos sus CD.

—Sé quien va a estar sentada a mi lado—, piensa, —aquella chica guapísima de mi clase de economía compró su entrada al mismo tiempo que yo. ¡Ay! Las cosas se ven mucho mejor ahora.

Después de regresar del concierto, Cisco está de muy buen humor. Es muy tarde pero no quiere dormir. Quiere pensar en el concierto y en la chica. Decide ir a ver si tiene un mensaje de ella o de su primo. Al abrir su correo electrónico encuentra un mensaje de Eduardo con la fecha del mismo día de la «discusión»: ¡hace dos días!

¡Es increíble! Y algo igualmente increíble es que los destinatarios del mensaje sean Cisco y cuatro personas más: Alejandra Sánchez, María Soledad Valenzuela, Guadalupe Iriarte y Manolo Rodríguez. ¿Manolo? Su primo Manolo se llama *Rodríguez* también. ¿Puede ser el mismo?

5-42 **Después de leer.** Contesta las siguientes preguntas.

1. ¿Qué hace Cisco para buscar a Eduardo?
2. ¿A quién le escribe Cisco para pedirle consejo? ¿Por qué?
3. ¿Qué hace Cisco para distraerse? Describe el evento.
4. ¿De quién tiene Cisco un mensaje en su correo electrónico?
5. ¿Quiénes reciben el mismo mensaje?

199

SECTION GOALS FOR
Video

By the end of the *Video* section, students will be able to:

- discuss possible theories regarding Eduardo's whereabouts.
- report the events of the videoconference.
- predict what secrets Lupe might be hiding.

Answers to 5-44

1. Cisco, porque quiere hablar de Eduardo y del correo electrónico.
2. De la música.
3. En la biblioteca.
4. Comparten información personal como sus especialidades, etc.
5. A Lupe. Piensa que la conoce de una clase de sociología el año pasado.
6. Alejandra desaparece al final.

video

5-48 to
5-50

5-43 **Antes del video.** ¿Qué podemos hacer cuando alguien desaparece? En tu opinión, ¿por qué Cisco no llama a la policía? En la segunda parte del episodio, vas a ver una videoconferencia entre todos los estudiantes menos Eduardo. ¿Qué piensas que van a decir? También, Alejandra va a decir, "Creo que te conozco". ¿A quién crees que le dice Alejandra esa oración?

¿Te gusta la música latina?

Creo que te conozco.

Debemos informar a la policía.

Episodio 5

Se conocen

Relájate y disfruta el video.

5-44 **Después del video.** Contesta las siguientes preguntas.

1. ¿Quién organiza la videoconferencia y por qué?
2. ¿De qué hablan Marisol y Lupe antes de la videoconferencia?
3. ¿Dónde están Alejandra y Manolo antes de la videoconferencia?
4. ¿Qué información comparten los estudiantes durante la videoconferencia?
5. Alejandra piensa que reconoce a alguien. ¿A quién? ¿Por qué?
6. ¿Quién desaparece al final de la videoconferencia?

RECURSOS

Video
Script

Y por fin, ¿cómo andas?

Having completed this chapter, I now can…

	Feel Confident	Need to Review
Comunicación		
● share my likes and dislikes with regard to music (p. 172)	❏	❏
● pronounce diphthongs correctly and use "linking" when speaking (p. 174)	❏	❏
● point out specific persons, places, things, and ideas using demonstrative adjectives and pronouns (**este, ese, aquel** and **éste, ése, aquél**) (pp. 176, 178)	❏	❏
● state how or in what manner something is done using adverbs (**-mente**) (p. 180)	❏	❏
● state what is going on right now using the present progressive (form of **estar + -ando, -iendo**) (p. 182)	❏	❏
● discuss information regarding movies and television shows (p. 185)	❏	❏
● rank people, places, and things (p. 188)	❏	❏
● express the importance or necessity of doing something with **hay que** (p. 189)	❏	❏
● use direct object pronouns in complete sentences (p. 190)	❏	❏
● know when to use the personal "**a**" correctly when speaking and writing (p. 191)	❏	❏
● anticipate content when listening to someone (p. 193)	❏	❏
● write a brief movie review (p. 194)	❏	❏
Cultura		
● state two interesting things about Hispanic music and musicians (p. 179)	❏	❏
● share the names of two Hispanic actors that have influenced film and television (p. 187)	❏	❏
● give at least two interesting facts about each country: Nicaragua, Costa Rica, and Panama (pp. 195–197)	❏	❏
Ambiciones siniestras		
● anticipate content by looking for visual cues and other clues (p. 198)	❏	❏
● explain two things that Cisco does when he realizes Eduardo is missing (p. 198)	❏	❏
● share what happens when the contestants, minus Eduardo, have a videoconference (p. 200)	❏	❏

VOCABULARIO ACTIVO

CD 2
Tracks 37-46

El mundo de la música	The world of music
el/la artista	artist
la batería	drums
el/la baterista	drummer
el/la cantante	singer
el concierto	concert
el conjunto	group; band
el/la empresario/a	agent; manager
la gira	tour
las grabaciones	recordings
la guitarra	guitar
el/la guitarrista	guitarist
el/la músico/a	musician
la música	music
la orquesta	orchestra
el/la pianista	pianist
el piano	piano
el tambor	drum
el/la tamborista	drummer
la trompeta	trumpet
el/la trompetista	trumpet player

Unos géneros musicales	Some musical genres
el jazz	jazz
la música clásica	classical
la música popular	pop music
la ópera	opera
el rock	rock
la salsa	salsa

Unas características	Some characteristics
apasionado/a	passionate
cuidadoso/a	careful
fino/a	fine; delicate
lento/a	slow
suave	smooth

Unos verbos	Some verbs
dar un concierto	to give/perform a concert
ensayar	to practice/rehearse
grabar	record
hacer una gira	to tour
sacar un CD	to release a CD
tocar	to play (a musical instrument)

Otras palabras útiles	Some useful words
el/la aficionado/a	fan
la fama	fame
el género	genre
la habilidad	ability; skill
la letra	lyrics
el ritmo	rhythm
el sabor	flavor
la voz	voice

El mundo del cine — *The world of cinema*

el actor	*actor*
la actriz	*actress*
la entrada	*ticket*
la estrella	*star*
la pantalla	*screen*
una película...	*a... film; movie*
de acción	*action*
de ciencia ficción	*science fiction*
documental	*documentary*
dramática	*drama*
de guerra	*war*
de humor	*funny; comedy*
de misterio	*mystery*
musical	*musical*
romántica	*romantic*
de terror	*horror*

Otras palabras útiles — *Other useful words*

el estreno	*opening*
la película	*movie*
una película...	*a... movie*
aburrida	*boring*
animada	*animated*
conmovedora	*moving*
creativa	*creative*
emocionante	*moving*
entretenida	*entertaining*
épica	*epic*
espantosa	*scary*
estupenda	*stupendous*
imaginativa	*imaginative*
impresionante	*impressive*
pésima	*heavy; depressing*
sorprendente	*surprising*
trágica	*tragic*

Los números ordinales — *Ordinal numbers*

primer, primero/a	*first*
segundo/a	*second*
tercer, tercero/a	*third*
cuarto/a	*fourth*
quinto/a	*fifth*
sexto/a	*sixth*
séptimo/a	*seventh*
octavo/a	*eighth*
noveno/a	*ninth*
décimo/a	*tenth*

Unos verbos — *Some verbs*

estrenar una película	*to release a film/movie*
presentar una película	*to show a film/movie*

Vocabulario útil — *Useful vocabulary*

el idioma/la lengua	*language*
la paz	*peace*
respetar	*to respect*

203

6

¡Sí, lo sé!

Comunicación

- To describe your family and other families (Communication)
- To talk about your school and relate information about your university campus (Communication)
- To share information about homes that you and your friends like and dislike (Communication)
- To talk about what will take place in the future (Communication)
- To share what you and others like to do and what you need to do (Communication)
- To describe service opportunities in your community (Communication, Connections, Communities)
- To discuss music and movies (Communication, Connections, Comparisons)

Cultura

- To share information about Mexico, Spain, Honduras, Guatemala, El Salvador, Nicaragua, Costa Rica, and Panama, as well as about Hispanics in the United States (Communication, Cultures, Comparisons)
- To compare and contrast the countries you learned about in *Capítulos 1–5* (Cultures, Comparisons)

OBJETIVOS

Comunicación

- To describe your family and families
- To talk about your school and relate information about your university campus
- To share information about homes that you and your friends like and dislike
- To talk about what will take place in the future
- To share what you and others like to do and what you need to do
- To describe service opportunities in your community
- To discuss music and movies

Cultura

- To share information about Mexico, Spain, Honduras, Guatemala, El Salvador, Nicaragua, Costa Rica, and Panama, as well as about Hispanics in the United States
- To compare and contrast the countries you learned about in **Capítulos 1–5**

This chapter is a recycling chapter, designed for you to see just how much Spanish you have learned thus far. The *major points* of **Capítulos 1–5** are included in this chapter, providing you with the opportunity to "put it all together." You will be pleased to realize how much you are able to communicate in Spanish.

Since this is a recycling chapter, no new vocabulary is presented. The intention is that you review the vocabulary of **Capítulos 1–5** thoroughly, focusing on the words that you personally have difficulty remembering.

METHODOLOGY • Philosophy on Recycling

This chapter is unique in *¡Anda!* because it presents an opportunity for instructors and students to have yet another assessment regarding language acquired. In this chapter, *¡Anda!* has synthesized the main points of the first five chapters in a recycled format for students to practice the new skills they are learning. You will note that all of these activities have the students *put it all together;* in other words, *all of the activities in Capítulo 6 are communicative.* There are no discrete point, mechanical activities. Instead, we direct the students to make use of the activities in *MySpanishLab™* or to repeat the activities in their *Student Activities Manual* or in the textbook itself for mechanical practice.

Prior to beginning the activities in this chapter, if your students choose (or you strongly encourage them) to gain more mechanical practice, repeating the activities they

have already done both in the *¡Anda!* textbook and in their *Student Activities Manual™* is an excellent start for their review. Redoing activities already done is an important review tool that is based on learning theory. This works for the following reasons: First, they are already familiar with the context of the activity, know what they got correct and missed the first time, and hence they are able

to observe if they have improved. They also are repeating the activities on a different level. Since they have already completed the activity, these repetitions go to a meta-analysis level, where they need to analyze why they continue to miss certain items. The same learning theory concept is similar in music, where we practice the same scales and arpeggios over and over.

Finally, if you have advanced or Heritage language learners, you may wish to skip this chapter or assign it as extra practice that the students can do by themselves.

IRM

RECURSOS

Lesson Plan

METHODOLOGY • Organizing a Review for Students

Researchers and reviewers of *¡Anda!* agree. After giving the students strategies on how to conduct an overall review, this chapter is organized by beginning with communicative and engaging activities that focus on grammar and vocabulary from *Capítulo 1*. The review continues to move through the chapters, ending with *Capítulo 5*. This is followed by a more comprehensive review, truly *putting it all together*, combining all of the chapters. Finally, there is a review of countries presented in *Capítulos 1–5*.

METHODOLOGY • Recycling vs. Reviewing

In *¡Anda!*, *recycling* up to this point has meant taking previously learned material and recombining it with new material. This concept is supported by Gagné's learning concept of spiraling information. In *Capítulo 6*, we are not presenting any new material, but rather recombining what your students have already learned and expanding the level. This also constitutes *recycling*. The concept of *review* is revisiting a topic, much like one does before an exam. *Review* is best illustrated in *Capítulo 4* (*Un repaso de ser y estar*) as well as this chapter. No new information is introduced in a *review*, nor is there any true spiraling. Instead, a *review* affords students the opportunity to practice in a systematic fashion.

Everyone learns at a different pace. You and your classmates will vary in terms of how much of the material presented thus far you have mastered and what you still need to practice.

Remember, language learning is a process. Like any skill, learning Spanish requires practice, review, and then more practice!

205

6-1 to
6-29

Organizing Your Review

There are processes used by successful language learners for reviewing a world language. The following tips can help you organize your review. There is no one correct way, but these are some suggestions that will best utilize your time and energy.

❶ REVIEWING STRATEGIES

1. Make a list of the *major* topics you have studied and need to review, dividing them into three categories: *vocabulary, grammar,* and *culture*. These are the topics where you need to focus the majority of your time and energy.

   Note: The two-page chapter openers can help you determine the *major* topics.

2. Allocate a minimum of an hour each day over a period of time to review. Budget the majority of your time for the major topics. After beginning with the most important grammar and vocabulary topics, review the secondary/supporting grammar topics and the culture. Cramming the night before a test is *not* an effective way to review and retain information.

3. Many educational researchers suggest that you start your review with the most recent chapter, or in this case, **Capítulo 5.** The most recent chapter is the freshest in your mind, so you tend to remember the concepts better, and you will experience quick success in your review.

4. Spend the most amount of time on concepts where you determine *you* need to improve. Revisit the self-assessment tools **y por fin, ¿cómo andas?** in each chapter to see how you rated yourself. Those tools are designed to help you become good at self-assessing what you need to work on the most.

❷ REVIEWING GRAMMAR

1. When reviewing grammar, begin with the *major* points, that is, begin with the *present tense* of regular, irregular, and stem-changing verbs. After feeling confident with using the major grammar points correctly, proceed to the additional grammar points and review them.

2. Good ways to review include redoing activities in your textbook, redoing activities in your **Student Activities Manual**, and (re)doing activities on your *¡Anda!* web site.

❸ REVIEWING VOCABULARY

1. When studying vocabulary, it is usually most helpful to look at the English word, and then say or write the word in Spanish. Make a special list of words that are difficult for you to remember, writing them in a small notebook. Pull out the notebook every time you have a few minutes (in between classes, waiting in line at the grocery store, etc.) to review the words. The **Vocabulario activo** pages at the end of each chapter will help you organize the most important words of each chapter.

2. Saying vocabulary (which includes verbs) out loud helps you retain the words better.

④ OVERALL REVIEW TECHNIQUE

1. Get together with someone with whom you can practice speaking Spanish. If you need something to spark the conversation, take the composite art pictures from *¡Anda!* and say as many things as you can about each picture. Have a friendly challenge to see who can make more complete sentences or create the longest story about the pictures. This will help you build your confidence and practice stringing sentences together to speak in paragraphs.

2. Yes, it is important for you to know "mechanical" pieces of information such as

verb endings, or how to take a sentence and replace the direct object with a pronoun. *But*, it is *much more important* that you are able to take those mechanical pieces of information and put them all together, creating meaningful and creative samples of your speaking and writing on the themes of the first five chapters.

3. You are well on the road to success if you can demonstrate that you can speak and write in paragraphs, using a wide variety of verbs and vocabulary words correctly. Keep up the good work!

> **Estrategia**
>
> Before beginning each activity, make sure that you have reviewed the identified recycled concepts carefully so that you are able to move through the activities seamlessly as you put it all together! *¡Sí, lo sabes!*

> **Estrategia**
>
> Being a good listener is an important life skill. Repeating what your classmate said gives you practice in demonstrating how well you listen.

Comunicación

Capítulos Preliminar A, 1 y 2

> **Estrategia**
>
> With situations like those in actividad **6-1**, it is not essential that *all* details be remembered. Nor is it essential in this type of scenario to repeat *verbatim* what someone has said; it is totally acceptable to express the same idea in different words. When necessary ask him/her to repeat or clarify information.

6 1 Nuestras familias

Completen los siguientes pasos en grupos de cuatro.

Paso 1 Con un/a compañero/a, túrnense para describir a varios miembros de sus familias usando por lo menos **diez** oraciones con un mínimo de **cinco** verbos diferentes. Incluyan *(Include):* aspectos de personalidad, descripción física, qué hacen en su tiempo libre, cuántos años tienen, etc.

MODELO E1: *Mi familia no es muy grande. Mi madre es simpática, inteligente y trabajadora. Tiene cuarenta y cinco años…*

Paso 2 Ahora describe a la familia de tu compañero/a a otro miembro del grupo usando por lo menos **cinco** oraciones. Si no recuerdas bien los detalles o si necesitas clarificación, pregúntale *(ask him/her)*.

MODELO E2: *La familia de Adriana es pequeña. Su madre es simpática y trabajadora… Adriana, perdón, pero ¿cuántos años tiene tu madre? …*

RECURSOS

Electronic Activity Cache

METHODOLOGY • Making Learning Meaningful for Students

The three photos that accompany activity **6-1** are intended to act as advance organizer photos. Advance organizers are meant in this case to help students envision their own families. If you teach in a community that is in some way not represented by one of these three images, you may want to bring in a photo that depicts your community, or you may wish to have students bring in their own photos.

METHODOLOGY • Using This Chapter

Although most of the activities in this chapter utilize the pair icon, you will note that most can be done at home. You can choose whether you want these activities to be oral, written, or a combination of oral and written. You can also choose whether you want the activities to be prepared outside of class or done in class. The decisions are yours to personalize the chapter in a manner that best suits your and your students' needs.

PLANNING AHEAD

Activity **6-1** is enhanced if students bring in photos of their families to act as advanced organizers. You will note, though, that we have included a variety of family photos as visual organizers that you can suggest they use. You can also suggest that students bring in photos from magazines as their "imaginary" families. We are very sensitive to the fact that the term "family" is highly diverse in the 21st century.

Suggestion for *Planning Ahead*

Students who live on campus do not always have access to personal family photos or to magazines without going home for the weekend. You might want to have pictures of families available for those students who are not able to bring in photos.

6 2 ¿Cómo eres?

Conoces un poco a los estudiantes que estudiamos en *Les presento mi país* en los Capítulos **1–5**. ¿Qué más quieres saber de ellos? Escribe por lo menos **diez** preguntas que quieres hacerles. Sé *(Be)* creativo/a.

MODELO
1. *¿Dónde estudias?*
2. *¿Te gusta leer libros de deportes?*
3. *¿Qué comes?*
4. …

> **Estrategia**
>
> Although these activities are focusing on *Capítulos Preliminar A, 1,* and *2,* feel free to use additional vocabulary from later chapters to create your questions. For example, in actividad **6-2**, you may want to use vocabulary from *Capítulo 5.*

> **Estrategia**
>
> Pay attention to the particular grammar point you are practicing. If you are supposed to write sentences using *tener,* underline each form of *tener* that you use, and then check to make sure it agrees with the subject. Using strategies such as underlining can help you focus on important points.

Alberto Martínez Vergara

Araceli Gabriela Campos Vega

María Ángeles Solana Montoya

Alfonso Guillermo Rivera Zúñiga

Itzel Fabiola Guerra Cruz

Alba Violeta Orellana Barrillas

Mauricio Morales Prado

Alejandra Cecilia Montero Valverde

Aída Elena Flores Solís

6 3 Una gira

Trabajas en tu universidad como guía para los nuevos estudiantes. Crea una gira para ellos. Incluye por lo menos **cinco** lugares y **dos** deportes.

MODELO *Esta universidad tiene diez mil estudiantes. Ésta es la biblioteca. Los estudiantes estudian aquí y usan las computadoras. Allí está el gimnasio donde juegan al básquetbol. Tenemos las especialidades de matemáticas, español, …*

Vocabulario útil

aquí	*here*
allí	*there / over there*
allá	*over there (and potentially not visible)*

6 4 Mi casa favorita

Mira los dibujos y descríbele tu casa favorita a un/a compañero/a. Dile *(Tell)* por qué te gusta la casa y explícale por qué no te gustan las otras *(the other)* casas.

Capítulo 3

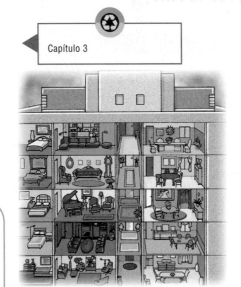

Estrategia

As you study vocabulary or grammar, it might be helpful to organize the information into a word web. Start with the concept you want to practice, such as *la casa*, write the word in the center of the page, and draw a circle around it. Then, as you brainstorm how your other vocabulary fits into *la casa*, you can create circles that branch off from your main idea, for example, *la cocina, la sala, el dormitorio*, etc. and list the furniture that belongs in each room.

6 5 Mi horario personal

Escribe tu horario *(schedule)* para una semana académica. Incluye por lo menos **siete** actividades usando **siete** verbos diferentes. Después comparte tu horario con un/a compañero/a.

Estrategia

When reviewing vocabulary, one strategy is to fold your paper lengthwise and have one column dedicated to the words in English and another column in Spanish. That way, you can fold the page over and look at the words, testing yourself to see if you really know the vocabulary.

METHODOLOGY • Learning Theory

Learning research has taught us that when reviewing/studying lists of vocabulary, it is most efficient for the brain to begin with the native language and then move to the target language word. When a beginning Spanish language student is searching for a word in the target language, that individual defaults to the most common language — their native language. If your students are not strong speakers of English, adjust this study tip to meet their needs.

Expansion for 6-4 After completing the activity, take a student poll to determine which house is the most popular. If there is a clear favorite, encourage discussion regarding their reasons for choosing it.

Expansion for 6-5 Compare student schedules to determine who begins the day earliest, who ends the day latest, who has the most entries, which days seems to be the busiest for the majority, etc.

RECURSOS

T6-1 to T6-3   T6-1 to T6-3

6 6 Quiero saber...

Completa los siguientes pasos para entrevistar a un/a compañero/a.

Paso 1 Escribe tus preguntas usando los siguientes verbos.

hacer	oír	querer	salir	venir
poder	poner	saber	traer	conocer

MODELO   E1:   *¿Qué traes a tus clases todos los días?*

Paso 2 Entrevista a tu compañero/a.

MODELO   E1:   *¿Qué traes a tus clases todos los días?*

E2:   *Traigo mi mochila a mis clases todos los días. …*

Paso 3 Comparte la información con tus compañeros de clase.

MODELO   *Mi compañero Jake trae su mochila a sus clases. También,…*

6 7 ¿Qué tienen?

Túrnense para describir a las personas de los dibujos usando expresiones con **tener**.

MODELO   *Jorge recibe una buena nota en su examen. Tiene éxito en su clase de periodismo.*

Julia   Susana   Mirta   Beatriz   Jorge

Guadalupe   Guillermo   Miguel   Beto   Adriana   David

RECURSOS   T6-4   T6-4

6 8 Lo conocemos y lo sabemos

Juntos hagan un diagrama de Venn sobre lo que conocen y saben, y sobre lo que no conocen o no saben. Escriban por lo menos **diez** oraciones.

Capítulo 4

MODELO

Janet
1. Mi familia y yo sabemos hablar español.
2. Mi amiga Julia y sus hermanos saben tocar el piano.

Nosotras
1. Sabemos patinar.
2. No sabemos hablar chino.
3. Conocemos a la profesora.

Audrey
1. Mi amiga Sally y su familia conocen al presidente de la universidad.

6 9 Un cuento divertido

Escriban en grupos un cuento creativo usando los siguientes verbos. Empiecen con la oración en el modelo. ¡Sean creativos!

almorzar (nosotros)	devolver (él)	mostrar (ella)	servir (ellos)
cerrar (ellas)	dormir (ellos)	pedir (tú)	volver (yo)
costar (los libros)	encontrar (nosotros)	seguir (yo)	comenzar (él)

MODELO

¡Qué día tan horrible! Primero pierdo la tarea para la clase de _____.

Vocabulario útil

entonces	*then*
después	*afterward*
finalmente	*finally*
luego	*then*
sin embargo	*nevertheless*

NOTE FOR 6-9

This activity forces practice with stem-changing verbs and with a variety of subject nouns and pronouns. With advanced students, you can make it less structured and either have them use the word bank in the textbook in the order it is given, or not. Again, the objective for this writing activity is to practice stem-changing verbs and to create a fun context. If not guided, most beginning students will look for an easier way to complete the assignment, for example, having all of their sentences begin with *yo*. Hence the structure we suggest. Encourage students to include other verbs and/or details in their sentences. For example, Student 1 might write: *Pienso, "¿Qué hago? Mi profesor pide la tarea todos los días." Finalmente, vuelvo a mi casa para buscarla.*

NOTE FOR 6-11

For additional practice with *ser* versus *estar*, direct your students to redo activities in their *Student Activities Manual* and *MySpanishLab™*, as well as to repeat the activities in their *¡Anda!* textbook.

6·10 Mi comunidad ideal

Eres un/a arquitecto/a urbano/a y planeas tu ciudad ideal.

Paso 1 Dibuja el plano de tu ciudad con los lugares más necesarios (apartamentos, bancos, parques, etc.).

Paso 2 Descríbele tu ciudad a un/a compañero/a. Usa por lo menos **diez** oraciones con una variedad de verbos y vocabulario.

MODELO   *Mi ciudad ideal se llama Ciudad Feliz. Hay una plaza en el centro. Tiene…*

6·11 Querida familia:…

Trabajas como consejero/a en un campamento de niños. Un día ayudas a los niños a escribirles una carta a sus padres y piensas que es una buena idea escribirle a tu familia también. En tu carta, incluye oraciones que incorporen todos los usos que puedas (*all of the uses that you can*) de **ser** y **estar**.

MODELO

> Querido José:
>
> Estoy muy, muy cansada hoy. Tengo ganas de dormir pero ¡solamente son las 9! . . .

RECURSOS   T6-5   T6-5

6·12 Mi tiempo libre

¡Tus compañeros y tú van a tener diez gloriosos días de vacaciones después de los exámenes! ¿Qué van a hacer? Túrnense **cinco** veces para decir oraciones usando **el futuro**. Después de decir tu oración, repite todo lo que dijeron (*you both said*) antes (*before*). Usen también diferentes pronombres (**yo, tú, ellos, nosotros,** etc.).

MODELO   E1: *Voy a dormir diez horas cada día.*

E2: *Mis amigos van a ir a Cancún y tú vas a dormir diez horas cada día.*

E1: *Mi familia y yo vamos a nadar, tus amigos van a ir a Cancún, y voy a dormir diez horas cada día.*

E2: *…*

Capítulo 5

6·13 ¡El concierto del siglo!

Quieres ir al concierto de tu conjunto (*group*) o cantante favorito, pero tu compañero/a no quiere ir. Creen un diálogo sobre su situación y preséntenlo a la clase. Su diálogo debe incluir por lo menos **doce** oraciones. Usen: formas de **este, ese, aquel;** unos adverbios (**-mente**); **hay que…;** pronombres de objeto directo (**me, te, lo, la, nos, los, las**).

MODELO   E1: *David, quiero ir al concierto de Marc Anthony. Es este sábado a las ocho. Las entradas no cuestan mucho. Te invito.*

E2: *No gracias, Mariela. No quiero ir. Realmente, no puedo ir. Tengo mucha tarea.*

E1: *Pero David,…*

6·14 ¡Bienvenido, estrella!

¡Tienes el trabajo ideal! Puedes entrevistar (*interview*) a tu actor o actriz favorito/a del cine. Escribe **diez** preguntas que vas a hacerle. Después, con un/a compañero/a de clase, hagan los papeles de (*play the roles of*) estrella y entrevistador/a para la clase.

NOTE FOR 6-12

Many of us may have played a game as youngsters where we began by saying, "*I'm going on a trip and I'm taking X.*" Then the person sitting next to us says "*I'm going on a trip and I'm taking Y and X.*" That is the design and goal of activity **6-12.** Based on educational research, repetition is an excellent way to learn. This is the same technique that is used in children's books like *The Cat in the Hat*, where the narrative has predictable repetition. This technique works with adult learners too. Although this activity can be done in larger groups, we recommend doing it in pairs, so each student will have more opportunities to speak and hence be less likely to become distracted and go off task.

Follow-up to 6-12 You can modify the activity by telling your students that you need a vacation after grading all of their exams. You can create a scenario explaining where you are going and with whom. They can take notes and then either say or write sentences using the future and the present, e.g., *Mi profesor/a va a viajar a España, pero yo tengo que trabajar. Mi profesor/a y su familia van a nadar en la playa, pero yo necesito limpiar mi casa.*

Expansion for 6-12 Another approach would be to have students make their own list of ten things they and their family and friends are going to do. Then students can switch papers and say what their classmate and his/her friends are going to do. This would force them to change the forms of the verb *ir*. For example, if one student writes, "*Yo voy a nadar en la piscina,*" the classmate would have to say, "*Él/Ella va a nadar en la piscina.*"

Suggestion for 6-14 You can set this up like an *Oprah, David Letterman,* or *Cristina* show, where you have students come to the front of the room and pretend they are on a talk show.

NOTE FOR 6-15

You may choose to have students create a dialogue between the lottery winner and the interviewer to perform in class.

NOTE FOR 6-16

Before starting this activity, encourage students to make a list of the household chores and work-related tasks for which they might need help. This is also a great opportunity to encourage creativity and humor.

Un poco de todo

6·15   ¡Ganaste la lotería!

Ganaste (*You won*) un millón de dólares en la lotería y te invitan a un programa de televisión para explicar qué vas a hacer con el dinero. Dile al/a la entrevistador/a (tu compañero/a) qué vas a hacer con el dinero en por lo menos **diez** oraciones. Después cambien de papel (*Take turns playing each role*).

6·16   Busco ayuda...

Con el dinero que ganaste en la lotería, decides buscar un ayudante personal (*personal assistant*) para ayudar con los quehaceres de la casa y con algunos asuntos (*matters*) de tu trabajo. Entrevista a un/a compañero/a que hace el papel de ayudante. Después cambien de papel.

MODELO
- E1: *Debe mandar mis cartas y escribir unos e-mails.*
- E2: *Bueno, pero no limpio las ventanas.*
- E1: *¿Cómo? ¿No las limpia? ¿Pasa la aspiradora?*
- E2: *…*

6·17   Mi horario para la semana

Crea un horario para una semana durante el verano. Usa por lo menos **diez** verbos diferentes para explicar lo que tienes que hacer. Comparte tu horario con un/a compañero/a.

junio						
L	**M**	**M**	**J**	**V**	**S**	**D**
	1	2	3	4	5	6
7	8	9	10	11	12	13
14	15	16	17	18	19	20
21	22	23	24	25	26	27
28	29	30				

julio						
L	**M**	**M**	**J**	**V**	**S**	**D**
			1	2	3	4
5	6	7	8	9	10	11
12	13	14	15	16	17	18
19	20	21	22	23	24	25
26	27	28	29	30	31	

agosto						
L	**M**	**M**	**J**	**V**	**S**	**D**
						1
2	3	4	5	6	7	8
9	10	11	12	13	14	15
16	17	18	19	20	21	22
23	24	25	26	27	28	29
30	31					

RECURSOS

T6-6	T6-6

CAPÍTULO 6

6 · 18 Mis planes para el verano

Escribe un e-mail a tus primos de **ocho** a **diez** oraciones sobre lo que vas a hacer este verano: **cuándo, dónde** y **con quién.**

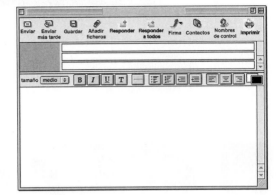

6 · 19 Para la comunidad

Escribe un poema en verso libre o una canción sobre el voluntariado y sus beneficios para los que dan y para los que reciben ayuda.

6 · 20 Mi comunidad

Túrnense para describir detalladamente su comunidad. Incluyan en su descripción oral detalles de su pueblo o ciudad (edificios, lugares para diversión, etc.), su casa y también las oportunidades que existen para hacer servicio voluntario.

METHODOLOGY • Peer Editing

Activities **6-18, 6-19, 6-20,** and **6-21** provide starting points for simple narrations about familiar topics. You might assign these exercises for homework so that each student has something written for class. Instead of correcting the writing assignments yourself, have your students peer edit. Peer editing affords students the opportunity to read carefully in order to help their classmates.

Suggestion for 6-19 For actividad **6-19,** you may want to provide students with a free verse poem in English to activate schemata.

NOTE FOR 6-21

Students can begin the activity by brainstorming, jotting down the basic plot so far. They can then refer to this list to keep them on track as they add details in their oral narrations.

Episodio 6

6 21 El juego de la narración

Túrnense para crear una narración oral sobre **Ambiciones siniestras.** ¡Incluyan muchos detalles!

MODELO E1: Ambiciones siniestras *es un misterio muy imaginativo.*

E2: *Hay seis estudiantes que se llaman...*

E1: *...*

Cisco   Eduardo   Manolo   Alejandra   Lupe   Marisol

Estrategia

The ability to retell information is an important language-learning strategy. Practice summarizing or retelling in your own words in Spanish the events from *Ambiciones siniestras*, chapter by chapter. Set a goal for yourself of saying or writing at least five important events in each episode that move the story along. Another technique is to recap as if you were retelling the story to another student who was absent.

6 22 ¿Me quiere?

Cisco, de **Ambiciones siniestras,** le escribe un correo electrónico a la chica que conoció *(he met)* en el concierto. En el e-mail habla de sus planes para el fin de semana y la invita a acompañarlo *(accompany him)*. Escríbele ese mensaje para Cisco en **diez** oraciones.

MODELO

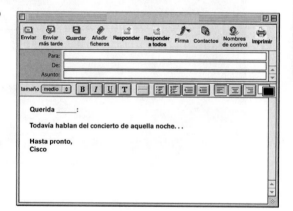

Querida _____:

Todavía hablan del concierto de aquella noche...

Hasta pronto,
Cisco

RECURSOS

IRM

Video Script

6 23 Su versión

En la actividad **6-21**, narraron (*you narrated*) una versión del cuento **Ambiciones siniestras.** Ahora es su turno como escritores. Sean muy creativos y creen su propia (*own*) versión creativa. Su instructor les va a explicar cómo hacerlo. Empiecen con la oración del modelo. ¡Diviértanse!

MODELO   *Hay seis estudiantes de tres universidades.*

6 24 Tu propia película

Eres cinematógrafo y puedes crear tu propia versión de **Ambiciones siniestras.** Primero, pon las fotos en el orden correcto y luego escribe el diálogo para la película. Luego, puedes filmar tu versión.

NOTE FOR 6-23

This activity makes use of what we call *accordion stories*. They are a wonderful way to stimulate writing and creativity with language. You need a group of at least three students, but we recommend no more than four for this assignment. Any more than four, and you will have students off task while waiting for their classmates to finish. You proceed as follows:

1. Student 1 takes the *Modelo* sentence and writes it at the top of the paper. Then he/she writes a sentence that moves the story along. Student 1 then folds the paper over the original sentence and all that shows is Student 1's sentence. Student 1 passes the paper to Student 2. Student 2 reads what Student 1 has written and then adds the next sentence to the story. Student 2 then folds the paper over Student 1's sentence and passes the paper to Student 3. All Student 3 can see/read is the sentence written by Student 2. And so the process continues. You can control the number of times that the students pass the paper to each other. We suggest for this activity that each student write at least 7 sentences. For a group of 3, you will have a "story" of 21 sentences. The more sentences they write, the more involved, and usually more enjoyable, the story becomes. The students should write their sentences for up to 10 minutes. Once the 10 minutes are up, you or a member of each group can read their story aloud to the class. When the paper is unfolded, it looks like an accordion or fan.

2. Encourage students to include a wide variety of verbs and/or details in their sentences.

NOTE FOR 6-25

Jeopardy! is a highly popular, long-running television quiz show in the United States. The premise of the game is that the contestant sees the answer and must formulate the appropriate question. The "answers" are grouped by categories and each "answer" has a dollar value. Easier answers have lower dollar values. In almost every community across the United States, it is on every night of the week for 30 minutes. This game show phenomenon has been wildly successful in Spanish classrooms for decades as a review tool. It provides students with a motivating way to review categories, helps them to organize material thematically, and forces them to create questions—a skill that the research says students seldom perform since they are usually answering our questions!

6 25 ¡A jugar!

En grupos de tres o cuatro, preparen las respuestas para las siguientes categorías de **¿Lo sabes?**, un juego como *Jeopardy!*, y después las preguntas correspondientes. Pueden usar valores de dólares, pesos, euros, etc. ¡Buena suerte!

CATEGORÍAS

VOCABULARIO
la vida estudiantil
las materias y las especialidades
los deportes y los pasatiempos
la casa y los muebles
los quehaceres de la casa
el cine
la música
el voluntariado

VERBOS
verbos regulares
verbos irregulares
saber y **conocer**
ser y **estar**
ir, ir + a + infinitivo
estar + -ando, -iendo

CULTURA
los Estados Unidos
México
España
Honduras
Guatemala
El Salvador
Nicaragua
Costa Rica
Panamá

Estrategia

You have read numerous cultural notes throughout the first five chapters. To help you organize the material, make a chart of the most important information, or dedicate a separate page in your notebook for each country, recording the unique cultural items of that particular country.

MODELOS

CATEGORÍA: LA VIDA ESTUDIANTIL
Respuesta: en la residencia estudiantil
Pregunta: *¿Dónde viven los estudiantes?*

CATEGORÍA: LOS DEPORTES Y LOS PASATIEMPOS
Respuesta: Sammy Sosa
Pregunta: *¿Quién juega al béisbol muy bien?*

NOTE FOR 6-25

The images in this activity are as follows:

¿Lo sabes?

México: (top) Mexico D.F.; (bottom) La biblioteca de la Universidad Nacional Autónoma de México.

España: (top) Madrid; (bottom) La Pedrera (la Casa Milá) en Barcelona.

Honduras: (top) Tegucigalpa; (bottom) La Escalinata de Copán.

Guatemala: (top) Ciudad de Guatemala; (bottom) Tikal.

¿Lo sabes? Doble

El Salvador: (top) San Salvador; (bottom) La playa El Sunzal.

Nicaragua: (top) Managua; (bottom) El béisbol.

Costa Rica: (top) San José; (bottom) El café, producto principal de exportación.

Panamá: (top) Ciudad de Panamá; (bottom) El Canal de Panamá.

Expansion for 6-27 You may choose to use actividad **6-27** as the first step, or as an organizer to be used for completing actividades **6-28** and **6-29.**

6 · 26 Los hispanos en los Estados Unidos

Escribe **cinco** influencias hispanas en los Estados Unidos.

MODELO 1. *St. Augustine fue fundada por los españoles.*

6 · 27 Aspectos interesantes

Escribe por lo menos **tres** cosas interesantes sobre cada uno de los siguientes países.

MÉXICO	ESPAÑA	HONDURAS	GUATEMALA

EL SALVADOR	NICARAGUA	COSTA RICA	PANAMÁ

PLANNING AHEAD FOR 6-28

You may want to encourage students to bring in travel brochures or copies of web pages from the countries mentioned in *Capítulos 1–5* to help them plan their writing.

NOTE FOR 6-29

Although this activity is similar in nature to **6-28,** you can take one of several approaches: (1) encourage your students to select a different country from the one they did in **6-28;** (2) differentiate instruction; that is, for students who are weaker, have them use **6-28** as a basis to expand for **6-29;** (3) for students who are stronger, suggest for **6-28** that they choose a country that is not necessarily their favorite but which is most suited for their clients.

6 28 Un agente de viajes

Durante el verano tienes la oportunidad de trabajar en una agencia de viajes (*travel agency*). Tienes unos clientes que quieren visitar un país hispanohablante. Escoge uno de los países que estudiamos y recomienda el país en por lo menos **seis** oraciones.

6 29 Mi país favorito

Describe tu país favorito entre los que hemos estudiado (*we have studied*). En por lo menos **ocho** oraciones explica por qué te gusta y lo que encuentras interesante e impresionante de ese país.

6 30 Compáralos

Escoge dos países que estudiamos y escribe las diferencias y semejanzas *(similarities)* entre los dos.

MODELO   *México es un país grande en Norteamérica y Nicaragua es pequeño y está en Centroamérica.*

Y por fin, ¿cómo andas?

Having completed this chapter, I now can...

	Feel Confident	Need to Review
Comunicación		
● describe my family and other families	❏	❏
● talk about my school and relate information about my university campus	❏	❏
● state which homes I like and dislike	❏	❏
● tell what I and others need to do (**tener + que / hay que**)	❏	❏
● share information about what will take place in the future	❏	❏
● discuss some service opportunities in my community	❏	❏
Cultura		
● share information about Mexico, Spain, Honduras, Guatemala, El Salvador, Nicaragua, Costa Rica, and Panama, as well as Hispanics in the United States	❏	❏
● compare and contrast the countries I learned about in **Capítulos 1–5**	❏	❏

NATIONAL STANDARDS

Comunicación

- To greet, take leave of, and introduce others (Communication)
- To describe yourself and others (Communication)
- To talk about your school and your life as a student (Communication)
- To share information about the sports and pastimes you and your friends like and dislike (Communication)
- To describe your home and household chores (Communication)
- To relate information about your home and/or university town (Communication)
- To tell what you and others need to do (Communication)
- To share information about what will take place in the future (Communication)
- To discuss some service opportunities in your community (Communication, Connections, Communities)
- To discuss different types of music, movies, and television programs, including your personal preferences (Communication, Cultures, Comparisons)

Ambiciones siniestras

- To describe what has happened thus far to the protagonists: Alejandra, Manolo, Cisco, Eduardo, Marisol, and Lupe (Communication)
- To hypothesize about what you think will happen next (Communication)

SECTION GOALS FOR

Chapter Opener

By the end of the Chapter Opener section, students will be able to:

- familiarize themselves with the text
- summarize the main points of *Capítulo Preliminar A* to *Capítulo 6*
- locate vocabulary and grammar presentations from the first half of the text
- review the *Ambiciones siniestras* storyline

Introducciones y repasos

OBJETIVOS

Comunicación

- To greet, take leave of, and introduce others
- To describe yourself and others
- To talk about your school and your life as a student
- To share information about the sports and pastimes you and your friends like and dislike
- To describe your home and household chores
- To relate information about your home and/or university town
- To tell what you and others need to do
- To share information about what will take place in the future
- To discuss some service opportunities in your community
- To discuss different types of music, movies, and television programs, including your personal preferences

Ambiciones siniestras

- To describe what has happened thus far to the protagonists: Alejandra, Manolo, Cisco, Eduardo, Marisol, and Lupe
- To hypothesize about what you think will happen next

This chapter is a review of vocabulary and grammatical concepts that you are already familiar with in Spanish. Some of you are continuing with *¡Anda!* while others may be coming from a different program. As you begin the second half of *¡Anda!,* it is important for all students to feel confident about what they already know about the Spanish language as they continue to acquire knowledge and proficiency. This chapter will help you determine what you already know, and also help you focus on what you personally need to improve upon.

If you are new to *¡Anda!,* you will want to review not only the grammar concepts already introduced, but also familiarize yourself with the active vocabulary used in the textbook. *¡Anda!* recycles vocabulary and grammar concepts frequently to help you learn better, and this chapter will help you with what we consider to be the basics of the preceding chapters.

For all students, this chapter also reviews what has occurred to date in the thrilling episodic adventure, **Ambiciones siniestras.** Students who haven't seen the first episodes will have an

METHODOLOGY • Creating a Cohesive Group

This preliminary chapter is meant to assist you with the beginning of the semester. Many of you teaching this course will have a wide array of students with different backgrounds in Spanish. It is necessary to start with a review, based on the *¡Anda!* chapters, that will familiarize the students with the vocabulary and grammar concepts to help them be successful as they continue on with their study of Spanish chapters.

METHODOLOGY • Reviewing at the Beginning of the Term

Learning theory informs our practice of beginning with a review before presenting new material. We recommend that this review be conducted as follows:

1. First day of class: take care of administrative details (e.g., course enrollments, going over the syllabus, which includes your expectations, etc.), followed by organizing basic speaking activities, such as having students turn to greet each other, etc.

2. Have students review *Capítulo Preliminar A* and *Capítulo 1* of *¡Anda!* for homework. This makes students accountable for their review. Then, the students will be able to do the pair activities in this chapter the next day in class.

3. We suggest spending no more than 5 days on review at the beginning of the semester. The grammar concepts and vocabulary will be recycled throughout *Capítulos 7–11.*

opportunity to do so. The episodes in the text and the video build upon each other, just like a **telenovela,** and starting in **Capítulo 7,** will continue from where the episode in **Capítulo 5** left off. **Capítulo 6** is a recycling chapter and no new episodes for **Ambiciones siniestras** were introduced.

Before you begin this chapter, you may wish to review the study and learning strategies on page 206 in **Capítulo 6.** These strategies are applicable to your other subjects as well. So on your mark, get set, let's review!

223

THE NATIONAL STANDARDS

¡Anda! is committed to and based on the National Foreign Language Standards. These National Standards, known as *the 5C's,* are: Communication, Cultures, Connections, Comparisons, and Communities. The beginning of each chapter will highlight how each of the 5C's will be addressed in that chapter.

Each of the five goal areas has corresponding standards. When possible, the goal areas have been expanded to include each standard that the activities address. In *¡Anda!,* you will find ways to incorporate the standards into your teaching, and sometimes we will present alternative directions or assignments in order to meet more than one standard. If you are new to *¡Anda!* or you are unfamiliar with the 5C's, please consult the explanations provided in *Capítulo Preliminar A* or in the Preface.

METHODOLOGY • Reviewing (*Capítulo Preliminar B*) vs. Recycling (*Capítulo 6*)

There were different goals and objectives used for creating *Capítulo 6* and this current chapter, *Capítulo Preliminar B.* The goal of *Capítulo 6* was to *recycle* material and to "put it all together," acting as culminating activities after a semester of study. Your students have been together for an extended period of time working with you and each other. They are familiar with you, your expectations, and those of *¡Anda!* With *Capítulo Preliminar B,* there is the *potential* for a very different scenario. Some of you will not have taught the first semester, some of your students may have had a different instructor in the first semester, some of your students may be coming directly from high school or from another institution of higher education, and still other students may have taken time off from studying Spanish and are re-entering the course of study. Hence the intention of *Capítulo Preliminar B* is to methodically *review* and guide all students to begin at a similar point. You will notice that *Capítulo Preliminar B* moves more by small chunks of material than *Capítulo 6* does. *Capítulo Preliminar B* assumes that students need more step-by-step guidance and remediation so they can all arrive at a common starting point.

Having provided this rationale, it is up to you how (and if!) you will use this chapter. *¡Anda!* was created to afford you, the instructor, the maximum flexibility in your planning. What follows are several options:

1. You may choose to use *Capítulo 6* at the end of first semester to recycle, and *Capítulo Preliminar B* at the beginning of second semester as a review.
2. You may choose to use Option #1, modifying it by picking and choosing the activities in *Capítulo Preliminar B* that best suit your needs.
3. You may choose not to use *Capítulo 6* at the end of the first semester, but to begin this semester with it, and skip *Capítulo Preliminar B.*
4. You may choose to move directly to *Capítulo 7.*

The bottom line is that you know your students and your curriculum better than anyone else. Choose the option that works best for you and your circumstances.

Comunicación

● Capítulo Preliminar A ●

1. Para empezar. This chapter provided an introduction to Spanish via the following topics: greetings and farewells; classroom expressions; the alphabet; cognates; subject pronouns and the verb **ser**; adjectives of nationality; numbers 1–30; telling time; days and months; the weather; and the verb **gustar.** If you need to review any of these topics before proceeding, consult pages 4–25.

● Capítulo 1 ●

2. La familia. Review the **La familia** vocabulary on page 32 and then do the following activities.

> **Estrategia**
>
> In **B-1,** you are directed to write at least five sentences. See how many more than five you can write in the time allotted.

🕖 7:00

B·1 Mi familia

Túrnense para describir a sus familias o a una de las familias de las fotos. Digan por lo menos **cinco** oraciones.

MODELO *George es mi tío. Mis primos son Stacy y Scott. …*

RECURSOS

Electronic Activity Cache

3. El verbo *tener*.   Review the verb **tener** on page 35. What are all of the present tense forms of **tener**?

B-3

 7:00 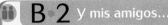 **B·2** Y mis amigos...

Túrnense para hablar de sus familias y de la familia de uno de sus amigos usando el verbo **tener**. Digan por lo menos **ocho** oraciones.

MODELO   *Tengo un hermano. Mi amigo, Joe, tiene dos hermanos. Mis amigas, Jennifer y Marty, no tienen abuelos. ...*

4. El singular y el plural.   Review how to make singular nouns plural on page 37 and explain the rules to your partner. Then complete the following activity.

B-4

Fíjate

The rules for accents are listed in *Capítulo 2*, p. 63. Some words keep their accent marks in the plural while other words lose theirs in the plural.

7:00   **B·3** Te toca a ti

Digan el plural de estas palabras.

MODELO   E1: primo
         E2: *primos*

1. madre madres   3. taxi taxis   5. abuela abuelas
2. francés franceses   4. nieto nietos   6. joven jóvenes

5. El masculino y el femenino.   Review the differences between masculine and feminine nouns on page 38. State the rules to a partner, and then do the following activity.

B-5

7:00   **B·4** ¿Recuerdas?

Digan si las siguientes palabras son masculinas o femeninas. **¡OJO!** Hay unas excepciones.

Fíjate

Some words that end in a consonant, like *profesor,* also have a feminine form, *profesora.* Pay attention to the form when making the noun plural, as in the case of *profesores* or *profesoras.*

MODELO   E1: tía
         E2: *femenina*

1. padrastros m   3. foto f   5. hermano m   7. tía f
2. televisión f   4. universidad f   6. mano f   8. hijo m

NOTE ON *Actividades*

¡Anda! provides many activities for diverse groups of learners and learning styles. As the instructor, you should decide which activities to use based on how well they meet the needs of your students. Depending on how often your class meets, you might decide to use class time exclusively for speaking and to assign the writing activities for homework. Select and use the activities that are relevant to your learning goals. We have color-coded the activity direction lines for easy usage. The orange ones are vocabulary-focused, while the green ones are grammar-focused.

METHODOLOGY • Helping Your Students with their Study Habits

References will be made to the page numbers in the first half of the book that your students can consult if they need more guidance. Students who need additional mechanical practice in addition to what is in this chapter will find *MySpanishLab*™ to be an excellent resource.

EXPANSION FOR METHODOLOGY • Helping Your Students with their Study Habits

You can flag certain pages from *Capítulo Preliminar A* through *Capítulo 5* in your book and model the study skill of using sticky notes to flag important pages. If you used *¡Anda!* for the first half, you have a good idea of what vocabulary or grammar your students will need to review. This technique works well because it is a non-permanent way to efficiently organize the text.

Follow-up to *El singular y el plural*
Your students should be able to form the plurals, but they will need a review of the rules for accents. In number 2, *francés,* and in number 6, *joven,* they will need a reminder about why *francés* drops the accent in the plural and why *joven* adds the accent in the plural.

METHODOLOGY • Pair Work

¡Anda! is based on the research that states that students learn best from other students. Stephen Krashen would explain it as *lowering the affective filter.* Still other researchers would call this a *constructivist approach* to teaching and learning. Hence, most of the activities are suggested to be pair activities. This is predicated on students changing partners daily (or nearly daily). Once again, we encourage you to determine what works best for you. You may decide that you would like to assign some of the activities as homework to be turned in for a grade. Still other activities you may decide to skip altogether. The goals of *¡Anda!* are to maximize student talk time in class and to make your job as instructor as streamlined as possible, providing you with all the tools to make the best instructional delivery decisions.

CAPÍTULO PRELIMINAR B

6. **Los artículos definidos e indefinidos.** How do you say *the* and *some* in Spanish? For a reminder, see page 39. Then do the following activity.

B-6

B·5 Vamos a practicar   1:00

Túrnense para añadir el equivalente de *"the"* y *"a"* o *"some"* a estas palabras.

MODELO   E1: tías
         E2: *las tías/unas tías*

1. padrastro el/un   3. madre la/una   5. hijos los/unos   7. nieto el/un
2. hermanas las/unas 4. tío el/un   6. primas las/unas   8. padres los/unos

7. **Los adjetivos posesivos y descriptivos.** How do you say *my, your, his, her, our,* and *their?* If you need help, see page 42. Also consult pages 44–45 to review words you may use to describe yourself and others. Then do the following activity.

B-7 to B-8

B·6 Nuestras familias   7:00

Túrnense para hablar de y describir a su familia o a las familias de sus amigos. Digan por lo menos **ocho** oraciones.

Fíjate
When you see the 👥 by the activity number, you work with a partner. Words in the direction lines like *miren, túrnense, comparen,* and *usen* are plural—they refer to both of you.

MODELO   *Mis padres son trabajadores. La mamá de mi amigo John es trabajadora. Nuestros primos son simpáticos. ...*

● **Capítulo 2** ●

8. **Las materias y las especialidades.** Review the **Las materias y las especialidades** vocabulary on page 62 of **Capítulo 2.** Then practice the vocabulary words with the following activity.

B-9 to B-10

B·7 ¿Cuál es más fácil?   5:00

Expresa tu opinión sobre las materias y las especialidades. Comparte tus respuestas con un/a compañero/a. Puedes consultar **También se dice...** en el Apéndice 3.

Estrategia
For actividad **B-7** about *Las materias y las especialidades,* change partners and find someone whose major is different than yours. See if you have the same opinions.

MODELO   *Las especialidades más difíciles son las matemáticas y los negocios. Las especialidades más fáciles son...*

Vocabulario útil
difícil   *difficult*
fácil   *easy*
aburrido/a   *boring*

LAS ESPECIALIDADES...				
MÁS DIFÍCILES	MÁS FÁCILES	MÁS CREATIVAS	MÁS INTERESANTES	MÁS ABURRIDAS
1.	1.	1.	1.	1.
2.	2.	2.	2.	2.

9. **La sala de clase.** Review the **La sala de clase** vocabulary on page 66 and then do the following activity.

B-11

B·8 ¿Qué tienen tus compañeros/as?

Escoge (*Choose*) a unos/as de tus compañeros/as y completa el cuadro siguiente.

5:00

MODELO ESTUDIANTE 1: *Sarah*

1. *Sarah tiene dos cuadernos, un libro, un bolígrafo y dos lápices.*
2. *¡Sarah no tiene la tarea!*
3. ...

Estrategia

For actividad **B-8**, you and your partner may wish to ask other classmates questions such as: *¿Qué tienes en tu mochila? ¿Qué tienes en tu escritorio?*

ESTUDIANTE 1 _Sarah_	ESTUDIANTES 2 Y 3 _____	TÚ Y YO _____
(no) tiene	(no) tienen	(no) tenemos
1. _tiene dos cuadernos_	1.	1.
2. _tiene un libro_	2.	2.
3. _tiene un bolígrafo_	3.	3.
4. _tiene dos lápices_	4.	4.
5. _no tiene la tarea_	5.	5.

10. **Presente indicativo de verbos regulares.** How do you form the *present tense* of *regular* **-ar, -er, -ir** *verbs*? If you need help, consult pages 68–69. Finally, before you complete the following activities, review the common verbs that are presented on the same page.

B-12 to B-13

B·9 ¿A quién o quiénes conoces que...? 5:00

Túrnense para preguntarse y contestar para qué personas que ustedes conocen son ciertas (*true*) o falsas las siguientes afirmaciones.

Estrategia

You will notice that nearly all activities in *¡Anda!* are pair activities. You will be encouraged or required to change partners frequently, perhaps even daily. The purpose is for you to be able to practice Spanish with a wide array of speakers. Working with different classmates will help you to improve your spoken Spanish more quickly.

MODELO hablar poco

E1: *¿Quién habla poco?*

E2: *Mi hermano, Tom, habla poco.*

E2: *¿Quiénes hablan poco?*

E1: *Mis padres hablan poco. / Mis hermanos y yo hablamos poco.*

1. hablar demasiado
2. correr mucho
3. vivir lejos
4. escribir muchos e-mails
5. usar los apuntes de sus amigos
6. estudiar mucho
7. necesitar estudiar más
8. tomar un examen hoy
9. enseñar español

NOTE ON B-8

Actividad **B-8** is a good way for students to learn the names of their classmates and to build trust within a classroom community. When students know the names of their classmates and can talk to them on a familiar basis, they are more likely to take risks with their language learning and enjoy practicing Spanish with new people. As students report back to the class and repeat information, you can learn the names of your new students.

METHODOLOGY • Working in Pairs

If you are an instructor using *¡Anda!* for the first time, you will note that we recommend that virtually all our activities be done with students working with a partner. The research is conclusive that students learn best from other students, and that working with partners in a student-centered class gives them more opportunities to become proficient in Spanish than if they were in a teacher-centered class.

Expansion for B-9 You can have students ask each other: *¿Tú hablas mucho? ¿Tú corres mucho? ¿Tú vives lejos?* The students will jot down their answers and then you can ask the class: *¿Quién en la clase habla mucho? ¿Quién corre mucho? ¿Quién vive lejos?*

RECURSOS | TB-1 | TB-1

Additional Activity for *Presente indicativo de verbos regulares*

Hay que practicar. On ten small pieces of paper, write the nouns and pronouns that follow. Then on six different slips of paper, write the six infinitives listed below. Take turns selecting a noun and a verb, and give the correct forms. After practicing the verbs listed below, select your own group of regular **-ar, -er,** and **-ir** verbs to practice. While doing this activity, focus not only on the forms of the verbs, but also on their meanings.

LOS NOMBRES Y PRONOMBRES:

tú	usted	yo
nosotros	ustedes	ellas
Marco	Juan y Eva	Mariela

LOS VERBOS:

estudiar	correr	escribir
hablar	comer	vivir

MODELO

E1: *yo / estudiar*

E2: *estudio*

Additional activity for *Presente indicativo de verbos regulares*

A conocerte mejor. Sit in a circle. Your instructor will give you directions on how to proceed. Enjoy! This activity is outstanding for students to get to know each other and to practice stringing small sentences together.

Directions:

1. If you have 25 students or fewer, have students sit in one large circle.
2. You can orchestrate the seating (unbeknownst to the students) so that your weakest students are sitting toward the beginning of the activity. Therefore, you can either quickly tell students where to sit in the circle, or you can insert yourself in the circle, close to the weakest student.
3. Model the activity demonstrating that Student 1 says his/her name and one brief sentence about himself/herself. Student 2 says his/her name and one brief sentence about himself/herself, and then says who Student 1 is and his/her brief sentence. Your model should use only the verbs they have had up to this point.
4. Proceed around the circle until each student has had a turn with you at the end delivering the final entry.
5. Students should not write any notes about what their classmates are saying. Rather, students are to help each other, so if someone forgets, students can coach/help/tell each other.
6. You can control the sentences, e.g., two students have already said "Tengo un hermano." You then can intervene by saying, *Ya no queremos más oraciones con "tengo hermanos". Usen otros verbos.*
7. Encourage applause by all classmates after approximately Student #10.
8. After the first few students, your entire class will understand that this is a very supportive activity. As the class leader, you should ensure that students feel good after having said the sentences. Students truly enjoy getting to know all of the names of their classmates.

Note for Additional activity A conocerte mejor. Additional comments to accompany this additional activity:

⏱ 7:00   **B·10** **Dime quién, dónde y cuándo**

Miren el dibujo y creen juntos una historia.

MODELO
E1: *Josefina le escribe una carta a su novio.*
E2: *Ella escribe cartas todos los días.*
E1: *En otro apartamento Raúl y Mariela...*

Estrategia

¡Anda! encourages you to be creative when practicing and using Spanish. One way is to create mini-stories about photos or drawings that you see. Being creative includes giving individuals in drawings names and characteristics.

Costa del Sol

11. La formación de preguntas y las palabras interrogativas. How do you form questions in Spanish? What are the question words in Spanish? To review this topic, consult pages 71–72 and then do the following activity.

B-14 to B-15

Fíjate

Remember that all question words have accents. Also remember that when writing a question, there are two question marks, one at the beginning and one at the end of the question.

⏱ 2:00 **B·11** **Preguntas y más preguntas**

Túrnense para formar una pregunta con cada oración.

MODELO
E1: *Estudio **matemáticas.***
E2: *¿Qué estudias?*

1. Pilar estudia **en la biblioteca.** ¿Dónde estudia Pilar?
2. **Guillermo y yo** estudiamos. ¿Quiénes estudian?
3. Comen **entre las 7:00 y las 8:00 de la noche.** ¿Cuándo comen?
4. Aprendemos español **fácilmente.** ¿Cómo aprenden español?
5. Leo **tres libros.** ¿Cuántos libros lees?
6. Estudiamos español **porque nos gusta el profesor.**
¿Por qué estudian español?

---

1. This is an excellent practice of the first person singular and third person singular forms of all of the verbs they know.
2. Because the students are not writing the information, it is an excellent listening activity. At the same time they aare also learning about acceptable in-class behavior, where they support each other while learning Spanish.
3. This activity inherently encourages students to pay attention to each other, since with each student's turn, an individual hears about himself/herself and is interested in assisting if a classmate has a mental block.

Suggestion for Additional activity A conocerte mejor. Point out the *También se dice. . .* section in Appendix 3 to your students and encourage them to use the section if they want to express words ideas that are not in the *Vocabulario Activo* lists at the end of each chapter.

12. Los números 1–1.000. Review the numbers 1–1,000, consulting pages 16, 48, and 74 if you need help. Then do the following activity.

B-16

2:00

B·12 ¡Dilo!

Túrnense para decir los precios de los artículos en el catálogo.

MODELO E1: (325 €) *El precio es trescientos veinticinco euros.*
E2: (999 €) *El precio es…*

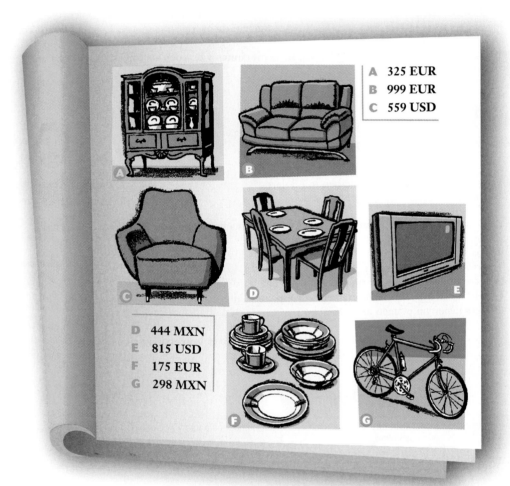

A 325 EUR
B 999 EUR
C 559 USD

D 444 MXN
E 815 USD
F 175 EUR
G 298 MXN

METHODOLOGY • Repeating Activities as a Learning Tool

You will notice that *¡Anda!* encourages students to repeat activities they may have already done in the text and *Student Activities Manual.* This study technique is based on thousands of research studies dealing with general learning theory for all subject areas which show that we learn by gaining confidence with what we already know and by analyzing our errors. By reviewing previously completed activities, your students are already familiar with the contexts, and they are able to observe and note their improvements. They are also better able to ask questions regarding what they still do not understand. This same learning theory applies to all other skills, such as music, where we practice the same scales and arpeggios over and over in order to become more proficient.

Finally, you will note in this chapter that some of the activities are similar in nature to those in *Capítulos Preliminar A–Capítulo 5.* That is intentional, since students respond well to similar contexts. We want our students to succeed and to feel successful. It is important to begin a semester with students gaining confidence. It sets the tone for a positive learning experience for all.

METHODOLOGY • Teaching Culture

You will notice that the cultural concepts from the first five chapters are not formally reviewed. The reason is that this review is meant to consist of the basic grammar and vocabulary so that the students will quickly feel success and begin the new material presented in *Capítulo 7.*

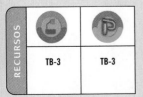
CAPÍTULO PRELIMINAR B

13. El verbo *estar.* What are the present tense forms of **estar**? When do you use **estar**? Check pages 78–79 if you need help before doing the following activity.

B-17

B·13 ¿Cómo se dice? `3:00`

Túrnense para hacerse preguntas y responder usando **estar.**

MODELO el mapa/libro

E1: *¿Dónde está el mapa?*

E2: *El mapa está en el libro.*

> **Fíjate**
>
> Remember that four forms of *estar* have accents in the present tense: *estás, está, estáis,* and *están.*

1. mis amigos y yo/la clase de ciencias
2. tú/el apartamento
3. los escritorios/la sala de clase
4. el papel/la silla
5. los apuntes/el cuaderno
6. Jorge y tú/la puerta
7. los libros/la mochila
8. José/bien
9. Lupe y Mariela/contenta

14. Emociones y estados. Review the **Emociones y estados** vocabulary on page 81 and then do the following activity.

B-18

B·14 ¿Qué pasa? `2:00`

Digan qué adjetivo describe las siguientes situaciones.

MODELO E1: Jorge y María reciben mil dólares.

E2: *Están contentos.*

1. Esperas y esperas pero tu amigo no llega (¡y no te llama por teléfono!). Estoy enojado/a / preocupado/a.
2. Corres quince millas (*miles*). Estoy cansado/a.
3. Tus padres están en el hospital. Estoy nervioso/a / triste / preocupado/a.
4. Tu novio/a está en Panamá y ¡no regresa! Estoy triste / enojado/a.
5. El profesor de literatura lee sin parar durante una hora y quince minutos. Estoy aburrido/a.
6. Ustedes sacan una "A" en sus exámenes de español e informática. Estamos contentos / felices.
7. Ustedes tienen un examen muy difícil hoy. Estamos nerviosos/as / preocupados/as / tristes.

> **Fíjate**
>
> In **B-14** you see *sus exámenes de español e informática.* The word **y** changes to **e** when the **i** sound appears immediately after the **y,** as in the case of the word *informática.*

15. En la universidad. Review the **En la universidad** vocabulary on page 76 and do the following activity.

B-19

`2:00` ## B·15 ¡Lo sé!

Digan qué lugar asocian con las siguientes palabras y acciones. Después formen una oración completa.

MODELO estudiar

E1: *Voy a la biblioteca para estudiar.*

E2: *Estudio en mi apartamento.*

1. fútbol
2. comprar libros
3. hamburguesas, pizza, café, etc.
4. básquetbol
5. experimentos científicos
6. leer libros, estudiar, escribir composiciones, etc.

16. El verbo *gustar*. How do you say *to like* in Spanish? Review page 82 and then do the following activity.

B-20 to
B-21

Estrategia

With actividad **B-16**, ask each other: *¿Qué materias te gustan? ¿Qué escritores te gustan? ¿Qué películas te gustan?*

`10:00` **B·16** Opiniones

Compara tu opinión con la de otros/as dos compañeros/as e informa después a la clase.

MODELO   E1:   *Las materias que más me gustan son las ciencias y las matemáticas. La escritora que más me gusta es J.K. Rowling…*

E2:   *Las materias que más le gustan a David son las ciencias y las matemáticas. La escritora que más le gusta es J.K. Rowling…*

LAS MATERIAS…	LOS/AS ESCRITORES/AS…	LAS PELÍCULAS (*MOVIES*)…
que más me gustan son:	que más me gustan son:	que más me gustan son:
1.	1.	1.
que menos me gustan son:	que menos me gustan son:	que menos me gustan son:
1.	1.	1.

17. Los deportes y los pasatiempos. Review the **Los deportes y los pasatiempos** vocabulary on pages 83–84 and then do the following activity.

B-22 to
B-23

`5:00` **B·17** Tus preferencias

Selecciona los **tres** deportes o pasatiempos **que más te gustan** y luego los tres **que menos te gustan.** Después de completar el cuadro, comparte la información con un/a compañero/a, según el modelo.

MODELO   *Los deportes o pasatiempos que más me gustan son patinar, bailar y leer. Los deportes o pasatiempos que menos me gustan son el fútbol, el fútbol americano y nadar.*

LOS DEPORTES Y PASATIEMPOS QUE MÁS ME GUSTAN	LOS DEPORTES Y PASATIEMPOS QUE MENOS ME GUSTAN
1.	1.
2.	2.
3.	3.

METHODOLOGY • Differentiating Instruction

We are well aware that different students have different abilities and needs. For your Heritage language learners and students who are more advanced or creative with the language, you may wish to direct them to the *También se dice. . .* section in Appendix 3. There, they will find additional vocabulary that they can incorporate into their repertoire.

CAPÍTULO PRELIMINAR B

METHODOLOGY • Use of English

The majority of the reviewers/instructors involved in developing *¡Anda!* preferred the use of both English and Spanish in this chapter to help ease all of your students into the course. You will notice that all references to grammar review are in English. This is because all grammar is presented throughout *¡Anda!* in English. The philosophy is that students will be more successful by quickly understanding concise explanations in English rather than laboring to decode Spanish explanations. Also, you will note that in this chapter, students are asked to review the grammar themselves and, in most cases, to state the rule(s). This is based on the learning theory concept that learners demonstrate comprehension when they can state or explain the rules. Directions to the activities are in Spanish when they are at what Krashen calls *the comprehensible input level of i + 1.*

● **Capítulo 3** ●

18. La casa.   Review the vocabulary about **La casa** on page 100 and do the following activities.

B-24 to
B-25

2:00   **B·18** Las actividades

Túrnense para decir en qué parte o partes de la casa hacen estas actividades.

MODELO   E1:   estudiar

E2:   *Estudio en la oficina y también en el dormitorio y en la cocina.*

1. escuchar música y ver la televisión
2. organizar papeles
3. echar una siesta (*take a nap*)
4. preparar tacos
5. tocar el piano
6. hablar por teléfono
7. tomar el sol
8. trabajar en la computadora

4:00   **B·19** ¿Y tu casa...?

Descríbele tu casa o apartamento a un/a compañero/a. O si quieres, puedes describir tu casa ideal. Usa por lo menos **ocho** oraciones.

MODELO   *Mi casa tiene dos pisos. Mi dormitorio está en la planta baja. No tenemos un altillo. Mi dormitorio está al lado del baño. La cocina es pequeña. ...*

RECURSOS | TB-4 | TB-4

19. Algunos verbos irregulares. Review the irregular verbs on pages 104–105 and then practice them with the following activities.

B-26 to B-27

5:00

B•20 Otras combinaciones

Túrnense para formar oraciones completas combinando elementos de las tres columnas. Formen una oración distinta con cada verbo de la columna B.

MODELO   *Nosotros hacemos la tarea todos los días.*

COLUMNA A	COLUMNA B	COLUMNA C
Uds.	(no) hacer	estudiar ciencias
el profesor	(no) oír	a clase tarde
él, ella, Ud.	(no) querer	la tarea todos los días
nosotros/as	(no) salir	mis libros a clase
ellos/ellas	(no) traer	temprano de la universidad
yo	(no) venir	los viernes
tú		con mis abuelos los domingos
mamá y papá		ruidos (*noises*) por la noche

7:00

B•21 Entrevista

Túrnense para hacerse la siguiente entrevista.

1. ¿Practicas algún deporte?
2. ¿Haces ejercicio todos los días?
3. ¿Qué te dice tu mamá siempre? (Mi mamá me dice…)
4. ¿Siempre traes todo lo que necesitas a tus clases?
5. ¿Sales los fines de semana? ¿Con quién o quiénes sales?
6. ¿Qué quieres ser (o hacer) en el futuro?
7. ¿Conoces a una persona famosa?
8. ¿Qué pones en tu mochila los lunes? ¿Los martes?
9. ¿Vienes a la clase de español todos los días?
10. ¿A qué hora sales para la clase?

Estrategia

Getting to know your classmates helps you build confidence. It is much easier to interact with someone you know.

Additional activity for *Algunos verbos irregulares*

La conjugación. Practice the following verbs until you can correctly determine each form quickly. Also pay attention to their meanings.

conocer	oír	traer
dar	poder	venir
decir	querer	ver
hacer	salir	

NOTE FOR B-20

This activity can be expanded into a listening activity. Student 1 reads his/her sentences to a partner without showing his/her paper. Student 2 listens carefully and connects the words from each of the three columns on his/her sheet using a different color pen or pencil.

  Student 2 shows Student 1 what he/she has connected to check listening comprehension. They then change roles.

Additional activity for *Algunos verbos irregulares*

Confesiones. Túrnense para hacerse y contestar preguntas usando **siempre** (*always*), **a menudo** (*often*), **a veces** (*sometimes*) o **nunca** (*never*). Si necesitan repasar cómo formar preguntas, consulten el **Capítulo 2,** página 71.

MODELO
venir tarde a la clase de español
E1: *¿Vienes tarde a la clase de español?*
E2: *Nunca vengo tarde a la clase de español.*
E1: *Yo siempre vengo tarde a la clase de español.*

1. oír lo que (*what*) dice tu profesor/a
2. darles tus apuntes a tus amigos
3. querer estudiar
4. hacer preguntas tontas en la clase
5. querer comer en la sala para ver la televisión
6. salir temprano de tus clases
7. poder contestar las preguntas de tu profesor/a de español
8. traer tus libros a las clases

METHODOLOGY • Lesson Planning

Due to time constraints that all instructors have, we suggest that you decide if you wish to formally review the cultural topics of this and previous chapters. In *Capítulo 3,* for example, one of the topics dealt with housing in the Spanish-speaking world. If you have the time in your schedule, you may wish to go to page 108 in *Capítulo 3* and select some of the questions on those topics to ask your students.

20. Hay. What does **hay** mean? Review page 122 if you need help. Then do the following activity.

B-28

3:00

B·22 ¿Qué hay en tu casa?

Descríbele tu casa a un/a compañero/a y averigua (*find out*) cómo es la suya (*his/hers*) usando **hay.**

MODELO   E1: *En mi casa hay un garaje. ¿Hay un garaje en tu casa?*

Fíjate

Remember that you can form questions by adding question marks to the statement or inverting the order of the subject and the verb.

E2: *Sí, en mi casa hay un garaje. / No, en mi casa no hay un garaje.*

E1: *Mi casa tiene dos pisos. ¿Cuántos pisos hay en tu casa?*

21. Los muebles y otros objetos de la casa. Review the **Los muebles y otros objetos de la casa** vocabulary on page 109. Then do the following activity.

B-29 to B-30

5:00

B·23 En mi casa

¿Qué muebles y objetos tienes en casa? Descríbele los siguientes cuartos a un/a compañero/a y averigua qué tiene él/ella.

sala	comedor	cocina	baño	dormitorio	garaje

MODELO   E1: *Yo tengo una cama y dos sillas en mi dormitorio. ¿Qué tienes tú?*

E2: *Yo tengo un cuadro, una lámpara y un televisor.*

NOTE FOR B-24
This activity can also be used as an interview. Each student completes the chart, answers his/her partner's questions, and then switches roles with his/her partner.

Expansion for B-24 As a follow-up to this activity, choose a student to report on his/her partner's responses. Tell everyone to listen carefully, and when he/she is finished, ask questions to verify comprehension. This encourages students to be active listeners and holds them accountable for what others say.

22. Los quehaceres de la casa y los colores. Review the vocabulary dealing with **Los quehaceres de la casa** and **Los colores** on pages 112 and 115. Then, do the following activities.

B-31 to B-33

3:00

B·24 Responsabilidades

¿Cuáles son tus responsabilidades? Túrnense para contestar las siguientes preguntas y explicar cuándo hacen estas tareas y cuánto tiempo dedican a hacerlas.

MODELO E1: mi dormitorio

E2: *Tengo que limpiar y arreglar mi dormitorio el lunes. Necesito dos horas porque está muy sucio.*

Estrategia

Group the rooms of the house with the verbs associated with each room. For example, match *comer* and *el comedor, bañarse* and *el baño, dormir* and *el dormitorio, cocinar* and *la cocina.*

1. mi dormitorio
2. el baño
3. la cocina
4. la sala
5. el garaje
6. el comedor

¿QUÉ TIENES QUE HACER?	¿CUÁNDO?	¿CUÁNTO TIEMPO?
limpiar y arreglar mi dormitorio	el lunes	dos horas

3:00 **B·25** La casa ideal

¿Cómo es tu casa ideal? ¿Y los colores? Descríbele tu casa ideal a un/a compañero/a usando las palabras siguientes en por lo menos **ocho** oraciones.

MODELO   *Quiero una casa con una cocina amarilla. ...*

 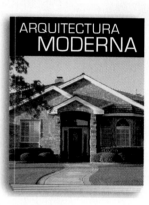 

 23. Unas expresiones con *tener*.   Review the **tener** expressions on page 117 and then do the following activities.

B-34

2:00 **B·26** ¿Qué tengo yo?

Túrnense para expresar cómo se sienten (*you feel*) en estas situaciones. Usen las expresiones con **tener.**

MODELO   E1:   antes de comer

E2:   *Antes de comer tengo hambre.*

1. los lunes
2. los viernes
3. tarde en la noche
4. temprano en la mañana
5. antes de tener un examen
6. cuando ves una película de terror
7. en el verano
8. en el invierno
9. durante (*during*) la semana de los exámenes finales
10. cuando sacas una "A" en un examen

B·27 Datos personales   3:00

Túrnense para hacerse esta entrevista.

1. ¿Cuántos años tienes?
2. ¿Cuándo tienes hambre?
3. ¿Qué tienes que hacer hoy?
4. ¿Qué tienes ganas de hacer?
5. ¿En qué clase tienes sueño?
6. ¿En qué clase tienes mucha suerte?
7. ¿Siempre tienes razón?
8. ¿Cuándo tienes sueño?
9. Cuando tienes sed, ¿qué tomas?

24. Los números 1.000–100.000.000. Review the numbers on page 120 and then do the following activity.

B-35

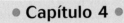

B·28 ¿Cuál es su población?

Túrnense para leer las poblaciones de las siguientes capitales del mundo hispano en voz alta.

1. Buenos Aires, Argentina	12.000.000
2. La Paz, Bolivia	713.400
3. Bogotá, Colombia	1.945.488
4. La Habana, Cuba	2.241.000
5. San José, Costa Rica	315.909
6. México, D.F., México	18.731.000

Answers to B-28.

1. doce millones
2. setecientos trece mil, cuatrocientos
3. un millón, novecientos cuarenta y cinco mil, cuatrocientos ochenta y ocho
4. dos millones, doscientos cuarenta y un mil
5. trescientos quince mil, novecientos nueve
6. dieciocho millones, ciento treinta y un mil

● Capítulo 4 ●

25. Los lugares. Review the **Los lugares** vocabulary on page 136 and then do the following activity.

B-36

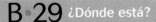

B·29 ¿Dónde está?

Tus amigos y tú están muy ocupados. Túrnate con un/a compañero/a para decir dónde están.

MODELO E1: Uno de mis amigos quiere mandar una carta.

E2: *Está en la oficina de correos.*

1. Marta quiere leer y necesita comprar un libro.
2. Dos de mis amigos necesitan dinero.
3. Julio tiene hambre y quiere comer algo (*something*).
4. Queremos ver una exposición de arte.
5. Ustedes quieren ver una película.
6. Jorge tiene sed y quiere tomar algo.
7. Vamos a jugar al golf.
8. Tienen que ir a una boda (*wedding*).

Answers to B-29.

1. Está en la librería.
2. Están en el banco.
3. Está en el restaurante / el café / el bar.
4. Estamos en el museo.
5. Están en el cine.
6. Está en el bar / el café / el restaurante.
7. Estamos en el campo de golf.
8. Están en la iglesia / el templo.

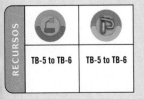

TB-5 to TB-6	TB-5 to TB-6

RECURSOS

Additional activity for *Saber y conocer*

Decisiones. Escojan la palabra correcta para completar las oraciones.

1. *Conocemos/Sabemos* que el cibercafé es nuevo.
2. Sus amigos *conocen/saben* tocar el piano.
3. Los turistas *conocen/saben* el Teatro Colón.
4. *Conozco/Sé* al presidente de la organización.
5. ¿*Conoces/Sabes* si en la biblioteca hay libros en español?

Answers:
1. Sabemos
2. saben
3. conocen
4. Conozco
5. Sabes

Additional activity for *La "a" personal*

¿Sí o no? Decide si la **"a"** personal es necesaria o no en las oraciones siguientes. Comparte tus respuestas con un/a compañero/a.

MODELO:
¿Escribes ___X___ la carta?

1. ¿Quieres _____ un café?
2. Mi madre siempre dice: Trae _____ tu hermano a casa después de la escuela.
3. ¿Siempre escuchas _____ tu mamá cuando te habla?
4. Conozco _____ una chica que se llama Alejandra.
5. ¿Siempre traes _____ tus libros?

Answers: 1. X, 2. a, 3. a, 4. a, 5. X

Additional activity for *La "a" personal*

Preguntas. Formen preguntas con las palabras de la lista y luego contéstenlas. ¿Hay que usar la **a** personal?

MODELO:
él / esperar / padres

E1: ¿Espera a sus padres?
E2: Sí, espera a sus padres. No, no espera a sus padres.

1. nosotros / necesitar / mochila / nueva
2. yo / no / ver / David
3. ¿tú / conocer / hermanas / de Pepe?
4. yo / no escribir / cartas
5. el profesor / enseñar / dos clases
6. mamá / ayudar / presidente de los Estados Unidos

B-37 to B-38

26. *Saber y conocer* **and the personal** *a.*   Make a list of when you use **saber** and when you use **conocer.** You can review the uses on page 140. Then do the following activity.

2:00   **B·30** ¿Lo sabes o lo conoces?

Completa las siguientes preguntas usando **sabes** o **conoces**. Después, túrnate con un/a compañero/a para hacerse y contestar las siguientes preguntas.

MODELO   E1:   ¿Conoces Buenos Aires?
         E2:   Sí, conozco Buenos Aires. / No, no conozco Buenos Aires.

1. ¿__Conoces / Conozco__ un buen lugar para comprar una televisión?
2. ¿__Sabes / Sé__ preparar tortillas?
3. ¿__Sabes / Sé__ cuál es el mejor café de esta ciudad?
4. ¿__Conoces / Conozco__ San Juan, Puerto Rico?
5. ¿__Sabes / Sé__ jugar al ráquetbol?
6. ¿__Sabes / Sé__ dónde están tus amigos ahora?
7. ¿__Sabes / Sé__ usar una computadora?
8. ¿__Conoces / Conozco__ al presidente de los Estados Unidos?
9. ¿__Conoces / Conozco__ el mejor restaurante chino de nuestra ciudad?
10. ¿__Conoces / Conozco__ las películas de Will Smith?

Fíjate

For more information about the personal **a**, consult *Capítulo 5*, page 191.

B-39 to B-40

27. ¿Qué tienen que hacer?   What does **tener que + infinitivo** mean? Review page 142 if you have any questions before doing this activity.

5:00   **B·31** Entrevistas

¿Hacen tus compañeros/as cosas similares?

Paso 1 Usando las siguientes preguntas, entrevista a tres compañeros/as.

1. ¿Cuáles son las cosas que haces para prepararte (*prepare yourself*) bien para tus clases?
2. Generalmente, ¿qué tienes que hacer después de terminar con tus clases?

Paso 2 Comparte la información con otros compañeros/as de la clase. ¿Qué tienen ustedes en común?

MODELO   *Para prepararse bien para las clases Jack y Sally tienen que estudiar cinco horas cada día. Sally tiene que ir a la biblioteca. Jack tiene que organizar sus apuntes. Después de terminar nuestras clases, nosotros tenemos que limpiar nuestros apartamentos. …*

B-41 to B-42

28. Los verbos con cambio de raíz.   Review the stem-changing verbs on page 144 and then practice with the following activities.

`2:00` **B·32** ¿Quién es?

Digan a cuales personas conocen que hacen las siguientes actividades.

MODELO   siempre perder la tarea

     E1:   *Mi novia Adriana siempre pierde la tarea.*

     E2:   *Mis primos siempre pierden la tarea.*

1. almorzar en Burger King a menudo
2. siempre entender al/a la profesor/a de español
3. jugar al fútbol muy bien
4. preferir dormir hasta el mediodía
5. volver a casa tarde a menudo
6. nunca tener dinero y siempre tener que pedirlo
7. nunca encontrar sus cosas
8. querer visitar Centroamérica
9. pensar que Santa Claus existe
10. nunca mentir

`7:00` **B·33** Un poco de mi vida

Listen as your partner answers the following questions. Then repeat the information back to your partner. How good a listener are you? How much did you remember?

Estrategia

Being an "active listener" is an important skill in any language. *Active listening* means that you have heard and understood what someone is saying. Being able to repeat what someone says helps you practice and perfect the skill of active listening.

1. ¿Qué clases tienes este semestre?
2. ¿A qué hora empieza tu clase preferida?
3. ¿Qué prefieres hacer si tienes tiempo entre (*between*) las clases?
4. ¿A qué hora vuelves a tu residencia/apartamento/casa?
5. ¿Qué coche tienes (o quieres tener)?
6. ¿Cuánto cuesta el coche nuevo?
7. ¿Cómo vienes a la universidad? (Por ejemplo, ¿vienes en coche?)
8. ¿Dónde prefieres vivir, en una residencia estudiantil, en un apartamento o en una casa?
9. ¿Dónde quieres vivir después de graduarte?
10. ¿Qué deporte prefieres?

Suggestion for B-33. Tell students that for actividad **B-33**, they should have their partners answer questions 1–5. Then repeat back to him/her what they heard. Then it's their turn to do questions 1–5, and their partners will repeat what is said. Have them continue with the rest of the activity in this manner.

Additional Activity for *Los verbos con cambio de raíz*

¿Conoces bien a tu compañero/a de clase? Túrnense para hacerse esta entrevista.
1. ¿Con quién(es) almuerzas generalmente?
2. ¿Prefieres estudiar por la noche o por la mañana?
3. ¿Cuántas horas duermes cada noche?
4. ¿A qué hora comienzas la tarea los lunes?
5. ¿Pierdes tus lápices o bolígrafos frecuentemente?
6. ¿Entiendes a tu profesor/a cuando habla español?

Expansion for *Additional activity for* **Los verbos con cambio de raíz:**
¿Conoces bien a tu compañero/a de clase?
Have the students add original questions at the end.

Expansion for B-35 Turn this activity into an add-on game in which students sit in a circle, state their names, and tell one thing they are going to do this week. Each student repeats what everyone has said up to that point before adding his/her information.

E1: *Soy Sally y voy a estudiar mucho.*

E2: *Ella es Sally y va a estudiar mucho. Soy Rick y voy a jugar al fútbol.*

E3: *Ella es Sally y va a estudiar mucho. Él es Rick y va a jugar al fútbol. Soy Tina y voy al cine.*

…

29. El verbo *ir* e *ir* + a + infinitivo. What are the present tense forms of **ir**? How do you express the future with **ir**? Consult pages 147 and 149 if you need to do so and then do the following activities.

SAM
B-43 to
B-45

B·34 ¡Vámonos! [2:00]

Completa las oraciones según el modelo. Túrnate después con un/a compañero/a para decir adónde van sus parientes y sus amigos en las siguientes situaciones.

Estrategia

When you write sentences that require more than one verb, as in **B-34**, make sure that your verbs match your subject throughout the sentence.

MODELO   E1:   Cuando tengo que estudiar…

        E2:   *Cuando tengo que estudiar voy a la biblioteca.*

1. Cuando quiere comer, mi compañero de cuarto…
2. Cuando queremos hacer ejercicio, nosotros…
3. Cuando tienes ganas de bailar, tú…
4. Para almorzar muy bien, mis amigos…
5. En la primavera me gusta…
6. Cuando mi hermana quiere comprar música, ella…
7. Para ver una película, tú…
8. Cuando llueve, yo…
9. Cuando hace frío, mis padres…
10. En el verano prefiero…

[2:00] B·35 Nuestra agenda

¿Qué van a hacer la semana que viene? Termina las siguientes oraciones con planes diferentes. Compara tus respuestas con las de un/a compañero/a.

lunes _____	
martes _____	
miércoles _____	
jueves _____	
viernes _____	
sábado _____	
domingo _____	

MODELO   E1:   El lunes, yo…

        E2:   *El lunes voy a lavar mi coche.*

1. El lunes, yo…
2. El martes, la profesora…
3. El miércoles, mis amigos…
4. El jueves, tú y yo…
5. El viernes, mis primos…
6. El sábado, tú…
7. El domingo, mi madre…

NOTE FOR B-37

In an effort to become better acquainted with your students, and them with each other, ask them who has participated in volunteer activities, what they did, where, and when.

2:00

B·36 Qué será, será...

¿Qué tiene el futuro para ti, tus amigos y tu familia? Hagan **cinco** predicciones de lo que va a ocurrir en el futuro y compartan sus respuestas.

MODELO *Mi primo va a ir a la Universidad Autónoma el año que viene. Nosotros vamos a estudiar mucho para sacar buenas notas. Mis padres van a trabajar en Baltimore. ...*

SAM
MSL
B-46

30. Trabajos y servicios voluntarios. Review the vocabulary **Trabajos y servicios voluntarios** on page 151 and then do the following activity.

2:00

B·37 Definiciones

Túrnense para leer las siguientes definiciones y decir a qué palabra o expresión corresponde cada una.

MODELO E1: personas que tienen muchos años

E2: *Las personas que tienen muchos años son los mayores.*

1. servir a las personas sin (*without*) recibir dinero a cambio (*in exchange*)   el voluntariado
2. un lugar donde viven las personas mayores   la residencia de ancianos
3. acompañar a una persona a una cita (*appointment*) con el médico   llevar a alguien al médico
4. dar un documento a las personas para obtener firmas   circular una petición
5. trabajar para un candidato político sin recibir dinero a cambio (*in exchange*)   apoyar a un/a candidato/a
6. una persona que trabaja con los niños en un campamento   el/la consejero/a
7. un bote (*boat*) para una o dos personas   la canoa
8. un tipo de arte que puedes crear de muchos materiales   la artesanía
9. una estructura portátil (no permanente) que se usa para dormir fuera de casa   la tienda de campaña
10. un lugar adonde van los niños, generalmente en el verano, para hacer muchas actividades diferentes   el campamento de niños

CAPÍTULO PRELIMINAR B

Additional Activity for *Las expresiones afirmativas y negativas*

¿Sí o no? Túrnense para contestar las siguientes preguntas.

MODELO
E1: ¿*Siempre almuerzas al mediodía?*
E2: *No, nunca almuerzo al mediodía. / No, no almuerzo nunca/jamás al mediodía.*

1. ¿Siempre almuerzas en restaurantes caros (*expensive*)?
2. ¿Hay algo más importante que el dinero?
3. ¿Haces algo para ayudar a los pobres?
4. ¿Pierdes algo cuando vas de vacaciones?
5. ¿Siempre piensas en el amor?
6. ¿A veces duermes más de diez horas en una noche?
7. ¿Conoces a alguien de Bolivia?
8. ¿Siempre encuentras las cosas que pierdes?

31. Las expresiones afirmativas y negativas. Review the affirmative and negative expressions on page 154 and then do the following activity.
B-47 to B-48

B·38 El/La profesor/a ideal [2:00]

Túrnense para decir si las siguientes características son ciertas o falsas en un profesor ideal.

MODELO Un/a profesor/a ideal… siempre da buenas notas.
E1: *A veces un profesor ideal da buenas notas.*
E2: *No, el profesor ideal no siempre da buenas notas. A veces tiene que dar malas notas.*

Un/a profesor/a ideal…

1. nunca falta (*misses*) a una clase.
2. prepara algo interesante para cada clase.
3. siempre prefiere leer sus apuntes.
4. piensa que sabe más que nadie.
5. a veces organiza a sus estudiantes en grupos para discutir (*discuss*) ideas.
6. a veces llega a clase cinco minutos tarde.
7. jamás manda (da) tarea para la clase.
8. no pierde nada—por ejemplo la tarea, los exámenes, los trabajos escritos (*papers*), etc.
9. no habla con nadie después de la clase.
10. siempre está contento/a con su trabajo.

Answers to B-39.
1. están
2. estoy
3. está
4. están
5. está
6. está
7. estoy
8. está
9. Son
10. estoy
11. son
12. son
13. están
14. es

32. Un repaso de *ser* y *estar*. When do you use **ser** and **estar**? Write the reasons on a sheet of paper, and then check your list against the one on pages 156–157. Next, do the following activities.
B-49

[5:00] **B·39** ¿Qué tal?

Adriana le escribe un e-mail a su familia. Llenen los espacios en blanco con la forma correcta de **ser** o **estar** para conocerla (*to know her*) mejor.

Para: **Mamá**
De: **Adriana**
Asunto: **Saludos**

Querida familia:
¿Cómo (1) _____ todos? Yo (2) _____ muy bien, pero muy ocupada. La casa (3) _____ muy sucia y los niños (4) _____ enfermos. Raúl (5) _____ en Boston con su trabajo nuevo. Su oficina nueva (6) _____ en el centro. Yo (7) _____ muy orgullosa (*proud*) de él, pero ¿dónde (8) _____ cuando lo necesito? (9) _____ las dos de la tarde y (10) _____ cansada.

La próxima semana, los primos de Raúl van a venir a nuestra casa. Ellos (11) _____ de Los Ángeles. No los conozco pero Raúl me dice que (12) _____ simpáticos. Ahora ellos (13) _____ en Nueva York.

Bueno, ya (14) _____ tarde y me tengo que ir. Cuídense mucho (*Take care of yourselves*).
Besos,
Adriana

Suggestion for B-42 Ask students to use the Internet to research popular Hispanic groups, singers, and/or musicians. They should choose one to report on in class, providng a photo and basic information.

B·40 Así es

Ahora expliquen por qué usaron (*you used*) **ser** o **estar** en la actividad **B-39**.

MODELO *están, physical condition*

1. están, physical condition	6. está, location	11. son, tell where someone is from
2. estoy, physical condition	7. estoy, mental condition	12. son, personality characteristics
3. está, physical condition	8. está, location	13. están, location
4. están, physical condition	9. Son, tell time	14. es, telling time
5. está, location	10. estoy, physical condition	

B·41 A conocernos mejor

Túrnense para hacerse y contestar las siguientes preguntas.

1. ¿De dónde eres?
2. ¿A qué hora son tus clases?
3. ¿Cómo es tu casa?
4. ¿Dónde está tu casa?
5. ¿Cómo es tu dormitorio?
6. ¿Dónde está tu dormitorio?

7. ¿De qué color es tu casa?
8. ¿Cuál es tu color favorito?
9. ¿Cómo es tu novio/a (esposo/a, amigo/a)?
10. ¿Dónde está él/ella ahora (*now*)?
11. ¿Cómo eres?
12. ¿Cómo estás hoy?

● Capítulo 5 ●

33. El mundo de la música.   Review the **El mundo de la música** vocabulary on page 172 and then do the following activities.

B-50 to B-51

B·42 ¿Qué quiere decir?

Lee las siguientes descripciones. Después, túrnate con un/a compañero/a para decir a qué palabra o expresión se refieren.

MODELO   E1: dar conciertos en muchos lugares

E2: *Dar conciertos en muchos lugares es "hacer una gira".*

1. ser muy popular y conocido entre muchas personas la fama
2. las palabras que cantas en una canción la letra
3. la música de Mozart y Beethoven, por ejemplo la música clásica
4. una persona que canta un/a cantante
5. lo que usas para cantar y hablar la voz
6. un instrumento de percusión el tambor / la batería
7. sinónimo de grupo el conjunto
8. hacer sonido bonito con un instrumento tocar
9. cuando haces algo muy bien, dicen que tienes mucha _____
   habilidad

Suggestion for B-43 The Internet is an excellent resource for music, lyrics, and music videos that you may want to share with your students. For suggested links, visit the *¡Anda!* web site.

3:00 | ii | **B·43** La música

Túrnense para hacerse esta entrevista.

1. ¿Cuál es tu grupo favorito?
2. ¿Cuál es tu cantante favorito?
3. ¿Cuál es tu instrumento favorito?
4. ¿Cuál es tu tipo de música favorito?
5. ¿Cuál es tu canción favorita?
6. ¿Sabes tocar un instrumento? ¿Cuál?
7. ¿Te gusta cantar? ¿Cuándo y dónde cantas?
8. ¿En qué tienes mucha habilidad o talento?

B-52

34. Los adjetivos y pronombres demostrativos. How do you say *this*, *that*, *these*, and *those* in Spanish? Review the demonstrative adjectives and pronouns on pages 176 and 178 and then do the following activities.

3:00 | ii | **B·44** Comparando cosas

Tu mejor amigo/a te propone una cosa pero tú siempre prefieres otra. Túrnense para responder a sus comentarios usando una forma de **éste**, **ése** o **aquél**.

MODELO   TU MEJOR AMIGO/A: ¿Quieres ir a este cine?

             TÚ: *No, no quiero ir a éste. Quiero ir a aquél.*

1. ¿Vamos a ir a ese teatro?
2. ¿Tus hermanos tocan en aquel grupo?
3. ¿Quieres escuchar este CD?
3. ¿Piensan ustedes arreglar este cuarto para (*for*) la fiesta?
5. ¿Vas a comprar aquellas entradas?
6. ¿Entiendes la letra de esta canción?

2:00 | ii | **B·45** En la universidad

Túrnense para hablar de lo que les gusta o no les gusta usando formas de **este**, **ese** y **aquel**. Hagan por lo menos **cinco** oraciones positivas y **cinco** oraciones negativas.

MODELO   *Me gusta esta clase. Nuestro profesor de español es interesante, pero aquel profesor de sociología es un poco aburrido. Este libro es bueno pero ese libro de matemáticas es difícil. …*

35. Los adverbios. In Spanish, how do most adverbs end? How are they formed? Check page 180 to verify your answers. Then do the following activity.

B-53

2:00 **B·46** ¿Qué ocurre en el concierto?

Vas a un concierto de varios conjuntos en el estadio de tu universidad. Para saber qué pasa, completa estas oraciones con los adverbios apropiados. Comparte tus respuestas con un/a compañero/a.

MODELO E1: Vamos al concierto (rápido, cuidadoso).

E2: *Vamos al concierto rápidamente.*

1. La gente espera a los conjuntos (paciente, lento). pacientemente
2. El primer conjunto toca (triste, feliz). felizmente
3. Un grupo llega tarde y entra al estadio (seguro, nervioso). nerviosamente
4. Los otros músicos escuchan (cansado, atento). atentamente
5. De repente (*Suddenly*), empieza a llover (rápido, fuerte). rápidamente o fuertemente
6. Terminan el concierto (inmediato, final). inmediatamente o finalmente

 36. El presente progresivo. How do you form the present progressive in Spanish (*I am _____ing, We are _____ing*, etc.)? Check your answer on page 182 and then do the following activity.

B-54

2:00 **B·47** ¿Qué están haciendo?

Túrnense para decir qué están haciendo las siguientes personas.

MODELO E1: Son las siete y media de la mañana y mi papá está en su terraza.

E2: *Está tomando café.*

1. A mi hermano le gusta hacer ejercicio para comenzar su día.
2. A mi prima le gusta la música hispana y está en una tienda.
3. Esta noche mis abuelos llevan a unos amigos a una gran fiesta y su coche está muy sucio.
4. Nuestro/a profesor/a está en la computadora y resulta que tiene muchos mensajes de sus estudiantes.
5. Nuestros amigos quieren comer algo ligero (*light*) antes de ir a la fiesta.
6. Estamos con nuestros amigos en la fiesta y un grupo está tocando.

Suggestion for B-47 Before beginning the activity, take a few minutes to play an abbreviated version of charades. Give a few students a slip of paper on which you have written an action verb from *Capítulos 1–5*. Each student must act out his/her verb while the others guess. Students should use the present progressive tense.

Expansion for B-48 You may wish to ask your students questions based on this activity or have your students create their own questions, e.g., ¿Cuál es la mejor película de humor?

37. El mundo del cine. Review the **El mundo del cine** vocabulary on page 185 and practice it with the following activity.

B-55

B·48 En mi opinión

Termina las oraciones sobre las películas que tú has visto (*have seen*). Pueden ser películas viejas o nuevas, buenas o malas. Comparte tus respuestas con un/a compañero/a.

MODELO　　E1:　La mejor película de terror…

　　　　　E2:　*La mejor película de terror es* Ring 2.

1. La mejor película de humor…
2. Una película épica pésima…
3. La película de misterio que más me gusta…
4. Mi actor/actriz favorito/a de las películas de acción…
5. La película animada más creativa…
6. La película más conmovedora…

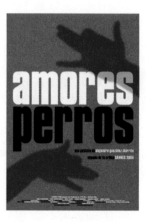

38. Los números ordinales. How do you say *first*, *second*, *third*, etc. in Spanish? Check your answers on page 188 and then do the following activity.

B-56

B·49 Orden de preferencia

Asigna un orden de preferencia a las actividades de la lista: de la más importante (primero) a la menos importante (octavo). Luego compara tu lista con la de un/a compañero/a usando oraciones completas.

MODELO　　*Primero, me gusta ver una película de mi actor favorito Johnny Depp. Segundo, me gusta visitar a mis parientes…*

1. ir a un concierto de un grupo fabuloso 　　　＿＿＿＿＿＿＿＿
2. visitar a tus parientes 　　　＿＿＿＿＿＿＿＿
3. ver una película de tu actor/actriz favorito/a 　　　＿＿＿＿＿＿＿＿
4. leer una novela buena 　　　＿＿＿＿＿＿＿＿
5. ir a un partido de fútbol americano 　　　＿＿＿＿＿＿＿＿
6. estudiar para un examen 　　　＿＿＿＿＿＿＿＿
7. viajar a Venezuela 　　　＿＿＿＿＿＿＿＿
8. conocer al presidente de los Estados Unidos 　　　＿＿＿＿＿＿＿＿

39. *Hay que* + infinitivo. What does **hay que** + **infinitivo** mean? Check your answer on page 189 and then do the following activity.

B-57

2:00

B·50 ¿Obligaciones?

Digan qué hay que hacer o cómo hay que ser para tener las siguientes profesiones.

MODELO   un pintor

E1:   *Hay que pintar mucho.*

E2:   *Hay que ser muy creativo.*

1. novelista   3. músico/a   5. director/a de cine
2. cantante   4. actriz   6. político/a

40. Los pronombres de complemento directo. What is a *direct object*? What is a *direct object pronoun*? What are the direct object pronouns in Spanish? Where do you place direct object pronouns? Review pages 190–191 and then practice with the following activities.

B-58

2:00

B·51 ¿Estás listo/a?

¡Qué suerte! Vas al concierto del año en el anfiteatro Pine Park. Revisa la lista de preparativos con un/a compañero/a usando **lo, la, los** o **las.**

MODELO   E1:   ¿Tienes que comprar *las entradas* del concierto?

E2:   *Sí, las tengo que comprar hoy. / Tengo que comprarlas hoy.*

1. ¿Vamos a preparar *una comida* (meal)?
2. ¿Vamos a invitar *a nuestros amigos*?
3. ¿Escuchan ellos *los CD del grupo*?
4. ¿Tengo que leer *la reseña* (review)?
5. ¿Vas a llevar *la cámara*?

Answers to B-51.
1. Sí, vamos a hacerla. / Sí, la vamos a hacer.
2. Sí, los vamos a invitar. / Sí, vamos a invitarlos.
3. Sí, los escuchan.
4. Sí, tienes que leerla. / Sí, la tienes que leer.
5. Sí, la voy a llevar. / Sí, voy a llevarla.

NOTE FOR B-51

Prior to beginning this activity, ask students to create sentence pairs using the present progressive tense with direct objects and direct object pronouns. The first sentence should contain a direct object noun while the second sentence replaces that noun with a direct object pronoun:
Mi padre está lavando el carro. Mi padre está lavándolo. /Mi padre lo está lavando.

`3:00` **B·52** ¿Hay deberes?

Siempre hay cosas que hacer. Usen **lo, la, los** o **las** para hablar de sus deberes.

MODELO ¿lavar los pisos todos los días?

E1: *Sí, tengo que lavarlos todos los días. /*
Sí, los tengo que lavar todos los días.

E2: *No, nunca los lavo. / No, los lavo los fines de semana.*

1. ¿sacudir los muebles?
2. ¿poner la mesa por la tarde?
3. ¿limpiar la cocina los sábados?
4. ¿preparar la comida todos los días?

5. ¿lavar los platos cada (*each*) día?
6. ¿hacer las camas por la mañana?
7. ¿guardar tus cosas?
8. ¿arreglar tu cuarto?

Episodio 6

B-59

41. Ambiciones siniestras. Read and then view the synopsis of the first five text and video episodes of **Ambiciones siniestras.** Then do the following activities.

`10:00` **B·53** ¿Qué pasó?

Escribe un resumen de lo que ha pasado (*has happened*) en **Ambiciones siniestras.** Puedes describir a cada personaje o puedes escribir una síntesis de cada capítulo.

`7:00` **B·54** ¿Qué va a ocurrir?

Escribe un párrafo sobre lo que tú piensas que va a ocurrir en los próximos episodios de **Ambiciones siniestras.**

The *¿Cómo andas?* and *Y por fin, ¿cómo andas?* sections are designed to help you assess your understanding of specific concepts. In *Capítulo Preliminar B,* there is one opportunity for you to reflect on how well you understand the concepts. Beginning with *Capítulo 7* there will be three opportunities for you to stop and reflect on what you have learned. These checks help you become accountable for your own learning, and help you determine what you need to review. Also use the checklist as a way to communicate with your instructor about any concepts you still need to review. Additionally, you might also use your checklist as a way to study with a peer group or peer tutor. If you need to review a particular concept, more practice is available on your *¡Anda!* web site. There you will find quizzes online.

Y por fin, ¿cómo andas?

Having completed this chapter, I now can…

	Feel Confident	Need to Review
Comunicación		
● greet and take leave of others	❑	❑
● describe myself, my family, and my life as a student	❑	❑
● describe my house and jobs around the house	❑	❑
● talk about places in my community as well as community service opportunities	❑	❑
● relate my preferences for music and cinema	❑	❑
Ambiciones siniestras		
● narrate what has happened thus far to the protagonists in **Ambiciones siniestras** and hypothesize about what will happen in future episodes	❑	❑

NOTE FOR

Y por fin, ¿cómo andas?

Each chapter will normally have three *self-checks:* two entitled, *¿Cómo andas?* and the third, entitled, *Y por fin, ¿cómo andas?* Each time the students complete a self-check, they are responsible for more information and they are able to more accurately assess their progress. Since *Capítulo Preliminar B* is meant to be a quick introduction to Spanish, there is only one self-check for the students. Encourage them to use these self-checks, since they help your students become accountable for their own learning and promote self-actualization.

Suggestion for *Y por fin, ¿cómo andas?* If you have time constraints, we recommend that these self-assessments be completed by the students outside of class. You may want to spot-check some students and ask how they are doing (e.g., "How many of you feel confident with greeting, saying goodbye, and introducing someone?"). For those students who do not raise their hands, remind them that they need to consult the pages listed to review the material. If you have time to do them in class, one approach is to have students write short answers to the topics, then check in their textbook to verify their answers. Based on this verification, they can rate themselves on the concept and hand in their ratings to you at the end of class.

7

¡A comer!

Comer bien es un gran placer (*pleasure*). Dentro del mundo hispanohablante hay una tremenda variedad de comidas (*foods*) y la comida tiene una función social muy importante.

OBJETIVOS	CONTENIDOS	
Comunicación		
• To discuss your food preferences and compare them with those from the Spanish-speaking world	1 Food	252
	2 Review of the direct object	257
• To talk and write about things you did and events that occurred in the past	3 The preterit tense	258
	4 Food preparation	263
• To order some of your favorite foods in a restaurant	5 Irregular verbs in the preterit tense	266
	6 In the restaurant	271
• To combine listening strategies to maximize comprehension	Pronunciación: The letters **r** and **rr**	253
• To describe, in writing, a special day from your past	Escucha:	274
	Estrategia: Combining strategies	
	Escribe: Relating a memory	275
Cultura		
• To talk about eating habits and foods from different parts of the Hispanic world	Meals in the Spanish-speaking world	256
	Food in the Spanish-speaking world	265
• To share important facts about this chapter's featured countries: Chile and Paraguay	*Chile* and *Paraguay*	276–277
Ambiciones siniestras		
• To predict what will happen in a reading	Episodio 7	
• To discover the voice-mail message that frightens Cisco	Lectura: *El rompecabezas*	278
	Estrategia: Predicting	
• To determine who has received the riddle and what they have figured out so far	Video: *¡Qué rico está el pisco!*	280

RECURSOS

Lesson Plan

METHODOLOGY • ¡Anda!

If you are new to using the ¡Anda! program, please refer to the preface where we describe our philosophy of language education. These teacher notes will assist you as you progress through the rest of the program to help your students acquire Spanish and become effective communicators in the language. Also, a reminder that the questions that follow the brief reading on this page are meant to start with what the students already know (activating their prior knowledge), and help to entice them to learn more about the topic.

Warm-up for *Chapter Opener* The students should already be familiar with the word *comer*, from the title *¡A comer!* so ask them to think about the types of foods and Hispanic dishes they have already learned about in previous chapters.

METHODOLOGY • Making Topics Relevant for Students

The text and questions for this chapter opener are completely in Spanish, just as in *Capítulos 4* and *5*. Notice that the questions begin with your learners and their preferences, a technique we have learned from educational philosopher John Dewey. Try having your students turn to their partners and answer the questions in pairs. Then have them share the answers their partners gave. This has them practice listening and also paraphrasing.

Expansion for *Preguntas* Ask students if they are aware of dishes with the same names that are prepared differently. You may want to tell them about the difference between *la tortilla mexicana* (of corn or flour) and *la tortilla española* (potato omelette).

You may also want to ask your students the following questions:
1. *En tu experiencia, ¿a qué tipo de comida se refiere la expresión "Spanish food"?*
2. *¿Hay restaurantes hispanos en nuestra ciudad?, ¿qué platos tienen?*

¡Buen provecho!

PREGUNTAS

1 ¿Cuáles son tus platos *(dishes)* favoritos?

2 ¿Hay alguna comida típica de la región donde vives tú? ¿Cuáles son algunas comidas típicas de los Estados Unidos?

3 ¿Qué platos de otras culturas te gustan?

251

NOTE FOR *Chapter Opener*

If your campus has a diverse student population and the students are familiar with different types of ethnic foods, you will want to anticipate the kinds of cuisine they might mention so you can tell them how to say those foods in Spanish.

HERITAGE LANGUAGE LEARNERS

Ask your Heritage language learners if there is a specific *comida casera* they enjoy and what ingredients they use to make the dish. If the vocabulary differs from that of the *Vocabulario activo*, ask them to explain how the dish is made and whether the products are available in American grocery stores.

Comunicación

• Talking about food   • Discussing past actions

VOCABULARIO 1   La comida

7-1 to 7-6

5:00

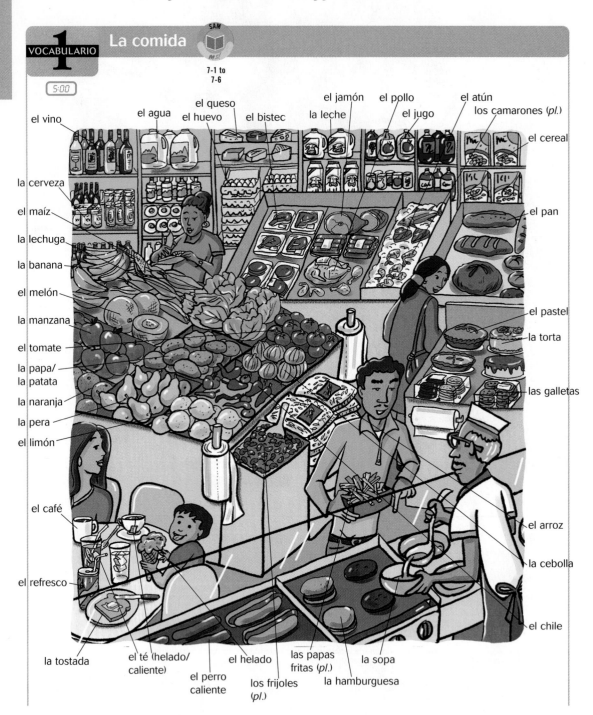

el vino
el agua
el queso
el huevo
el bistec
la leche
el jamón
el pollo
el atún
los camarones *(pl.)*
el jugo
el cereal
la cerveza
el maíz
la lechuga
la banana
el melón
la manzana
el tomate
la papa/ la patata
la naranja
la pera
el limón
el pan
el pastel
la torta
las galletas
el arroz
la cebolla
el chile
el café
el refresco
la tostada
el té (helado/ caliente)
el helado
el perro caliente
las papas fritas *(pl.)*
los frijoles *(pl.)*
la sopa
la hamburguesa

RECURSOS		
T7-1 to T7-2	T7-1 to T7-2	Electronic Activity Cache

las aves	*poultry*
las bebidas	*beverages*
la carne	*meat*
la comida	*food; meal*
los dulces	*sweets*
la ensalada	*salad*
la fruta	*fruit*
el hielo	*ice*
los mariscos	*seafood*
el pescado	*fish*
el postre	*dessert*
la verdura	*vegetable*

Otras palabras útiles	*Other useful words*
el desayuno	*breakfast*
el almuerzo	*lunch*
la merienda	*snack*
la cena	*dinner*

Unos verbos	*Some verbs*
almorzar (ue)	*to have lunch*
beber	*to drink*
cenar	*to have dinner*
desayunar	*to have breakfast*
merendar (ie)	*to have a snack*

CW
eBook

CD 3
Track 1

SAM

7-7 to
7-10

PRONUNCIACIÓN 5:00

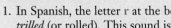

The letters *r* and *rr*

1. In Spanish, the letter **r** at the beginning of a word, and the **rr** between vowels are *trilled* (or rolled). This sound is the equivalent to the trill in English when imitating a motor sound (*brrrrrr*).

   refresco   **R**odríguez   arroz   perro caliente

2. All other **r** positions are pronounced with a *flap* of the tongue. The sound is similar to the English pronunciation of the *tt* in *Betty* or the *dd* in *ladder*.

   camarones   naranja   pera   torta

7•1 Las palabras

Pronounce the following words, paying special attention to the letters **r** and **rr**.

1. cerveza
2. merienda
3. frijoles
4. Ramón
5. rápidamente
6. refresco
7. guitarra
8. ritmo

7•2 Las oraciones

Pronounce the following sentences, paying special attention to the letters **r** and **rr**.

1. Rafael corre rápidamente.
2. Quiero arroz, camarones, un refresco y, de postre, una torta.
3. Me gustan las películas de guerra, humor, misterio y terror.

7•3 Dichos y trabalenguas

Now pronounce the following tongue twister and saying, focusing on the letters **r** and **rr**.

1. Erre con erre cigarro, erre con erre barril, rápido corre el ferrocarril.
2. Cuando una puerta se cierra dos mil se abren.

SECTION GOALS FOR
Pronunciación

By the end of the *Pronunciación* section, students will be able to:
• distinguish between the sounds for *r* and *rr*.
• spell words correctly by hearing the *r* sound or *rr* sound.

METHODOLOGY • Making Students Accountable for Their Own Learning

By creating a student-centered class, you reinforce the fact that your students are ultimately accountable for their own learning.

METHODOLOGY • Organizing the Student-Centered Classroom

When we say that *¡Anda!* supports and helps create a student-centered classroom, we mean that the presentations and activities afford students the maximum amount of time to practice Spanish in a classroom-controlled setting. By having your students work with partners, it provides them with an increased amount of time to speak Spanish. What follows are some ideas to help you maximize the effectiveness of your student-centered class.

1. Change partners daily. This gives all students the opportunity to work with everyone in the class on multiple occasions. Some days you can place two strong students together; other days you can pair a strong and weak student. Still other days you may choose to pair students with similar hobbies or interests. You can also pair students randomly or in fun ways, such as according to their birth dates or their favorite color.

2. You may wish to assign a variety of pair activities on the board at the beginning of the class so that students may work with their partner in 15–20 minute intervals. This might mean assigning up to 10 activities that the groups can work on at their own pace.

3. During pair work, students need to know that they are accountable for staying on task and for performing up to your expectations. Therefore, after 15–20 minute intervals, you may choose to have several groups report on some of their responses.

. You may be familiar with the term *classroom management (discipline) by proximity*. You will have pairs of students that will find it difficult to stay on task. As you circulate around the room while the students are working together, make a point of positioning yourself frequently in close proximity to the pairs that need more monitoring.

. Giving a significant grade in class participation helps to keep students on task. When students understand that you expect them to speak in Spanish, to take turns, and to work well with others, AND that you will be grading them on their classroom behavior, it helps them understand the importance of their work in the classroom.

6. Not all groups will finish all items of all activities during a class period. That is fine, since students have been moving at the pace necessary for them to learn. During a subsequent class period when students are working with new partners, you can have a list of review pair activities that students can work on if they finish early. These would be the communicative activities at the end of each *chunk*. Even though your students are repeating an activity that they may have already done, the fact that they are working with a new partner and a new context will help to retain their interest.

CAPÍTULO 7

METHODOLOGY • Working in Pairs

As a reminder, it is ideal to change partners daily. In this way, students have the opportunity to work with all students, and you build community within your classroom. At the very least, partners should be changed weekly.

Expansion for 7-4 Actividad 7-4 can also be done as a race, with the teacher choosing the letter as teams of students supply the words.

Suggestion for 7-5 Bring in a mystery food that you enjoy or a food that you know your students enjoy from the vending machine, kiosk, or cafeteria. Find out how many calories are in the food and ask them to guess the nutritional information. Reveal the nutritional information in Spanish and see how the answers differ.

METHODOLOGY • Environmental Print

Environmental print in *¡Anda!* consists of words such as *proteína* and *carbohidratos*, which are cognates but not active vocabulary.

Expansion for 7-5 Ask the following questions: *¿A quién le gustan las hamburguesas con queso? ¿A quién no le gusta la carne? ¿Qué frutas prefieren?*

Expansion for 7-5 Ask students to create their own descriptions for different foods. This will allow them further practice with descriptive words.

4:00

7·4 Concurso

Escoge **cinco** letras diferentes. Bajo cada letra escribe todas las palabras del vocabulario de **La comida** que recuerdes. Después, compara tu lista con la de un/a compañero/a.

MODELO   **a**   **d**   **p**

arroz   *desayuno*   *papas fritas*

agua   *dulce*

Fíjate

Although *agua* and *ave* are feminine nouns, the masculine singular article *el* is used with them, as a way to separate and differentiate the similar stressed vowel sounds in each word (*la* and *a*). *Las* is used with the plurals of these words (*las aguas, las aves*). All adjectives describing these words are feminine.

4:00

7·5 ¡Ay, las calorías!

Túrnense para decir a qué comida corresponden las siguientes descripciones. Usen el cuadro de los valores nutritivos.

CUADRO DE LOS VALORES NUTRITIVOS

Comida	Calorías	Proteína	Grasa	Carbohidratos	Vitaminas
bistec	455	27	36	0	A, B
hamburguesa con queso	950	50	60	54	B
jugo de naranja	100	1	0	16	A, B, C
naranja	50	1	0	16	A, B, C
pan	150	6	2	38	B
papa	100	3	0	23	B, C
perro caliente	200	5	14	1	B, C
salmón	200	24	10	0	A, B
torta	455	4	13	76	A, B, C
lechuga	10	1	0	2	A, B, C

Capítulo Preliminar A. Los números 0–30, pág. 16; Capítulo 1. Los números 31–100, pág. 48; Capítulo 2. Los números 100–1.000, pág. 74.

Estrategia

¡Anda! has provided you with recycling references to help guide your continuous review of previously learned material. Make sure to consult the indicated pages if you need to refresh your memory about numbers.

MODELO   E1:   *Esta comida tiene mucha agua, es verde y tiene diez calorías.*

           E2:   *Es la lechuga.*

Esta comida tiene…

1. 60 gramos (*grams*) de grasa, 50 gramos de proteína y 950 calorías.   la hamburguesa con queso
2. muchas proteínas, es un pescado y tiene 200 calorías.   el salmón
3. vitamina C y 100 calorías. Es una verdura.   la papa
4. muchos carbohidratos y 150 calorías.   el pan
5. 27 gramos de proteína, es una carne y tiene 455 calorías.   el bistec
6. es una fruta y tiene 50 calorías.   la naranja
7. es una bebida y tiene 16 carbohidratos.   el jugo de naranja
8. las vitaminas B y C, sólo un carbohidrato y 14 gramos de grasa.   el perro caliente

7·6 La dieta de Nico

Paso 1 Nico es un estudiante universitario de Santiago de Chile. Mira lo que (*what*) come normalmente, a qué hora y compara la dieta de Nico con la tuya.

MODELO *Yo nunca tomo té para el desayuno. Generalmente desayuno más temprano que Nico.*

Vocabulario útil

| más temprano que | *earlier than* |
| más tarde que | *later than* |

Mi pirámide
PASOS HACIA UNA SALUD MEJOR

AGUA
DIARIAMENTE

Haga ejercicio casi todos los días 30 minutos

Recomendación diaria para cada grupo de alimentos.

ACEITE GRASAS AZÚCAR OCASIONALMENTE

GRANOS	VERDURAS	FRUTAS	PRODUCTOS LÁCTEOS	CARNES Y FRIJOLES
7 onzas	3 tazas	2 tazas	3 tazas	6 onzas
Consuma la mitad en granos integrales Trate de consumir por lo menos **3 onzas y media** de granos integrales cada día	**Varíe las verduras** Intente alcanzar estas cantidades cada semana: **Verduras verdes -** 3 tazas **Verduras con almidón -** 6 tazas **Otras verduras -** 7 tazas	**Enfóquese en las frutas** Coma frutas variadas No tome mucha cantidad de jugo de frutas	**Coma alimentos ricos en calcio** Al escoger leche, yogur o queso, opte por productos bajos en contenido graso	**Escoja proteínas bajas en grasas** Escoja carnes y aves de bajo contenido graso o magras Varíe su rutina de proteínas; coma más pescado, frijoles, guisantes, nueces y semillas

Encuentre un equilibrio entre la alimentación y la actividad física

Manténgase físicamente activo por lo menos durante 30 minutos la mayoría de los días de la semana

Conozca los límites de las grasas, los azúcares y el sodio

Su dosis de aceites es **6 cucharaditas por día**

Limite las grasas sólidas y azúcares - **a 290 calorías por día**

Fíjate

The word *galleta* means both *cookie* and *cracker*.

LA DIETA DE NICO

	DESAYUNO	ALMUERZO	MERIENDA	CENA
	8:30	**12:00**	**5:30**	**8:00**
DÍA 1:	*té con galletas*	*ensalada, arroz con pollo, uvas*	*manzana*	*atún con una ensalada de lechuga con tomate y fruta*
DÍA 2:	*té y pan con mantequilla*	*sopa, tortilla de papas, flan*	*galletas*	*pan con mermelada*

TU DIETA

	DESAYUNO	ALMUERZO	MERIENDA	CENA
DÍA 1:				
DÍA 2:				

Paso 2 Comparte tus conclusiones con un/a compañero/a.

Paso 3 Miren la pirámide de alimentación para determinar si todos los grupos están representados en sus dietas.

NATIONAL STANDARDS
Communication

Actividad **7-6** is an excellent opportunity for students to communicate meaningful preferences. Also, if you are beginning a new semester and have new students, the next activity is a good way to help them get acquainted and build classroom community.

The interpersonal communicative activities like actividad **7-6,** where students are working together to piece together information, promote Standard 1.1. They are engaging in conversations, providing and obtaining information, and exchanging their opinions about their eating habits and foods they like or dislike. If you asked students to write down their daily eating schedule and menu and to present it to the class you can satisfy Standard 1.3 as well.

Expansion for 7-6 You may wish to have each student interview another student so that when reporting, he/she will say, *Él/Ella...*

7·7 ¿Cuáles son tus preferencias?

Capítulo 2. El verbo *gustar.* pág. 82.

¿Qué comidas te gustan?

Paso 1   Completa el cuadro según tus preferencias.

Estrategia

You may want to talk about foods that are not included here. Refer to the *También se dice...* section in Appendix 3 for additional vocabulary.

1. Las carnes, las aves, el pescado y los mariscos que...	
a. más me gustan son...	b. menos me gustan son...
1.	1.
2.	2.

2. Las frutas y verduras que...	
a. más me gustan son...	b. menos me gustan son...
1.	1.
2.	2.

Paso 2   Ahora, compara tus preferencias con las de los compañeros de la clase: ¿cuáles son las comidas favoritas? ¿Qué comidas les gustan menos?

7·8 ¿Qué comes tú?

Entrevista a un/a compañero/a usando las siguientes preguntas.

1. ¿Comes bien o mal? Explica.
2. ¿Qué tipo de comida prefieres?
3. ¿Qué te gusta merendar?
4. ¿Qué comidas tienen vitaminas A y C?
5. ¿Qué comidas tienen mucha proteína?

7-11 to 7-12

Las comidas en el mundo hispano

La palabra "comida" significa varias cosas en español: *food, meal* y *lunch (the main meal of the day)*. Las comidas en los países hispanoamericanos son similares a las comidas norteamericanas pero también existen algunas diferencias. Por ejemplo, el desayuno en el mundo hispano normalmente consiste en café y pan o panes dulces. Generalmente es una comida ligera (*light*).

El almuerzo es normalmente la comida más grande y más fuerte del día. En lugares con una cultura más tradicional, el almuerzo puede empezar a eso de (*around*) las dos de la tarde. Los niños regresan de la escuela y el papá (y la mamá si trabaja fuera [*outside*] de la casa) comen juntos en casa. Entonces, hay tiempo para descansar (*to rest*) antes de volver al trabajo y a la escuela. En los países y las zonas con más industria y comercio puede haber un horario de almuerzo similar al horario de los Estados Unidos.

La cena generalmente es una comida más ligera. La gente en los países hispanohablantes cena más tarde que la mayoría de los norteamericanos. ¡Algunos no cenan hasta las diez o las once de la noche!

Preguntas

1. ¿Cómo es un desayuno típico en el mundo hispano? ¿un almuerzo? ¿una cena?
   Un desayuno típico es ligero, como café con pan o pan dulce. Un almuerzo típico es una comida grande. Una cena típica es una comida ligera.
2. ¿Cuál es el horario de las comidas en los países hispanos?
   Generalmente, el desayuno es por la mañana, el almuerzo empieza a las dos y la cena es tarde.

GRAMÁTICA 2 — Repaso del complemento directo

`3:00`

7-13 to 19, 20
7-16

¿Postre? Tenemos...

¡Los quiero todos!

In **Capítulo 5** you learned to use direct object pronouns in Spanish. Return to pages 190–191 for a quick review, then answer the following questions:

1. What are direct objects? What are direct object pronouns?
2. What are the pronouns (forms)? With what must they agree?
3. Where are direct object pronouns placed in a sentence?

Check your answers to the preceding questions in Appendix 1.

NOTE FOR

Repaso del complemento directo

Direct object pronouns are reviewed here and recycled throughout the chapter in anticipation of the presentation of indirect object pronouns in *Capítulo 8*.

`3:00`

7·9 Las dietas

¿Piensas mucho en lo que *(what)* comes?

Paso 1 Subraya *(Underline)* los complementos directos en las siguientes preguntas. Compara tus respuestas con las de un/a compañero/a.

MODELO ¿Conoces <u>la dieta Weight Watchers</u>?

Paso 2 Ahora contesten juntos las siguientes preguntas, usando los pronombres de complemento directo en sus respuestas.

MODELO E1: ¿Conoces la dieta Weight Watchers?

E2: *Sí, la conozco. / No, no la conozco.*

1. ¿Sigues la dieta South Beach?
2. ¿Prefieres los postres de chocolate?
3. ¿Sabes preparar bien el arroz?
4. ¿Comes muchas frutas diferentes?
5. ¿Preparas los huevos con queso?
6. ¿Lavas la lechuga bien antes de comerla?

`3:00`

7·10 Las buenas decisiones

Dile a tu compañero/a cómo te gusta tomar las siguientes comidas y bebidas y con qué frecuencia las tomas.

| nunca | algunas veces | generalmente | constantemente | siempre |

MODELO E1: la torta

E2: *La como con helado. La como algunas veces. / No la como nunca.*

1. el cereal
2. las tostadas
3. los tomates
4. las galletas
5. la cebolla
6. el café

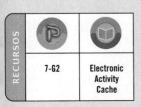

GRAMÁTICA 3 — El pretérito

7-17 to 7-23   35

`5:00`

¿Dónde compraste el helado?

Lo compré en Big Scoop.

Up to this point, you have been expressing ideas or actions that take place in the present and future. To talk about something you did or something that occurred in the past, you can use the **pretérito** (*preterit*). Below are the endings for regular verbs in the **pretérito.**

Los verbos regulares

Note the endings for regular verbs in the **pretérito** below and answer the questions that follow.

	-ar: comprar	**-er: comer**	**-ir: vivir**
yo	compré	comí	viví
tú	compraste	comiste	viviste
él, ella, Ud.	compró	comió	vivió
nosotros/as	compramos	comimos	vivimos
vosotros/as	comprasteis	comisteis	vivisteis
ellos/as, Uds.	compraron	comieron	vivieron

1. What do you notice about the endings for **-er** and **-ir** verbs?
2. Where are accent marks needed?

Check your answers to the preceding questions in Appendix 1.

> **Estrategia**
>
> Remember that there are two types of grammar presentations in *¡Anda!*:
>
> 1. You are given the grammar rule.
> 2. You are given guiding questions to help *you* construct the grammar rule, and state the rule in your own words.

—¿Dónde está el vino que **compré** ayer?

—Mis primos se lo **bebieron** anoche.

—¿Ah, sí? ¿**Comieron** Uds. en casa?

—No, **comimos** en un restaurante chino. ¡**Terminaron** el vino antes de salir a cenar!

Where is the wine that I bought yesterday?

My cousins drank it last night.

Really? Did you all eat at home?

No, we ate at a Chinese restaurant. They finished the wine before we went out to dinner!

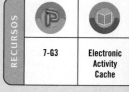

RECURSOS   7-G3   Electronic Activity Cache

Los verbos que terminan en *-car, -zar* y *-gar* **y el verbo** *leer*

Hoy corrí cinco millas, jugué al tenis, toqué el piano por dos horas, leí una novela, empecé la tarea para la clase de español. . .

Several verbs have small spelling changes in the preterit. Look at the charts below.

METHODOLOGY • The Preterit

The authors have chosen to present both regular and irregular preterits in the same chapter to allow for greater focus on form and practice. You will note that this is the primary grammatical focus for *Capítulo 7*. In *Capítulos 8–11*, the preterit will be continually recycled (along with the present tense) for additional practice and reinforcement.

> **Fíjate**
>
> The *-ar* and *-er* stem-changing verbs in the present tense do not have stem changes in the preterit. There may be spelling changes, however, as with *empezar* and *jugar*.

tocar (c → qu)	
yo	to**qu**é
tú	tocaste
él, ella, Ud.	tocó
nosotros/as	tocamos
vosotros/as	tocasteis
ellos/as, Uds.	tocaron

* (**sacar** and **buscar** have the same spelling change)

empezar (z → c)	
yo	empe**c**é
tú	empezaste
él, ella, Ud.	empezó
nosotros/as	empezamos
vosotros/as	empezasteis
ellos/as, Uds.	empezaron

* (**comenzar** and **organizar** have the same spelling change)

jugar (g → gu)	
yo	ju**gu**é
tú	jugaste
él, ella, Ud.	jugó
nosotros/as	jugamos
vosotros/as	jugasteis
ellos/as, Uds.	jugaron

* (**llegar** has the same spelling change)

leer (i → y)	
yo	leí
tú	leíste
él, ella, Ud.	le**y**ó
nosotros/as	leímos
vosotros/as	leísteis
ellos/as, Uds.	le**y**eron

* (**creer** and **oír** have the same spelling change)

—**Toqué** la trompeta por seis horas ayer porque tengo un concierto esta noche.

—¿A qué hora **empezaste**?

—**Empecé** a las nueve.

—¿**Jugaron** tus hermanos al béisbol hoy?

—No, **leyeron** una novela para la clase de inglés.

I played the trumpet for six hours yesterday because I have a concert tonight.

At what time did you begin?

I began at nine.

Did your brothers play baseball today?

No, they read a novel for English class.

Some things to remember:

1. With verbs that end in **-car,** the **c** changes to **qu** in the **yo** form to preserve the sound of the hard **c** of the infinitive.

2. With verbs that end in **-zar,** the **z** changes to **c** before **e.**

3. With verbs that end in **-gar,** the **g** changes to **gu** to preserve the sound of the hard **g** (**g** before **e** or **i** sounds like the **j** sound in Spanish).

4. For **leer, creer,** and **oír,** change the **i** to **y** in the third-person singular and plural.

NATIONAL STANDARDS
Communication

Actividades **7-12** through **7-15** lead students through a series of practice exercises that have them work with the endings of preterit verbs as well as review the direct object pronouns. Students are asked to give their opinions on a favorite topic, and these activities are highly motivating for them.

The pair activities such as **7-13** and **7-16** require interpersonal communication (Standard 1.1) as students ask and answer questions using the past tense. For actividad **7-13**, you could assign roles of chef and sous-chef and have them role play the activity. These role-plays support Standard 1.3, the presentational mode. Actividad **7-16** can be turned into a writing activity if, once the answers from the chart are compiled, you assign an expansion paragraph to each student who answered a topic affirmatively. If students answered that they ate in a restaurant last Saturday, for example, you could ask them for more details in the preterit, such as what they ordered, if they spoke with the waiter, if they left a tip, how the food tasted, etc.

NOTE FOR
Actividades 7-12* through *7-15

Actividades **7-12** through **7-15** provide a variety of interesting scenarios to practice the preterit. The activities are mechanical and meaningful in nature and move toward becoming communicative.

Additional Activity for *El pretérito* With *¡Anda!* we recommend finding ways of making mechanical practice enjoyable. One such way is with activities like the following, which can be used when introducing any new tense. Here are the directions to give your students:

INSTRUCTIONS FOR STUDENTS: Make a grid, like one for tic-tac-toe. With a partner, select one *-ar* verb. Write a different preterit form of the verb in each blank space on your grid. Each of you should write each preterit form with a different pronoun. Do not show your partner what you have written. Take turns randomly selecting pronouns and say the corresponding verb forms. When you say a form of the verb that your partner has, your partner marks an X over the word. The first person to get three X's either vertically, horizontally, or diagonally wins the round. After doing an *-ar* verb, repeat with *-er* and *-ir* verbs.

MODELO

tú comiste	*ellas comieron*
yo comí	*ellos comieron*
ella comió	*vosotros comisteis*
nosotros comimos	*él comió*
Uds. comieron	

3:00

7-11 De la teoría a la práctica

Write six different infinitives on six small pieces of paper. Next, on six different small pieces of paper, write six different subject pronouns. Take turns selecting a paper from each pile and give the correct **pretérito** form of the verb. After several rounds, write six different verbs.

4:00

7-12 Creaciones

Paso 1 Combinen elementos de las tres columnas para escribir **ocho** oraciones que describan lo que hicieron estas personas.

MODELO Yolanda comprar un coche nuevo.
Yolanda compró un coche nuevo.

Yolanda	beber	el piano durante la cena
Ud.	limpiar	cuatro botellas de agua
los estudiantes	preparar	un coche nuevo
yo	buscar	dos hamburguesas con queso
mi mejor amigo y yo	leer	la cocina después del almuerzo
tú	tocar	una cena deliciosa
mis primos	comprar	el restaurante La Frontera
el/la profesor/a	comer	sobre el gran cocinero Emeril Lagasse

Paso 2 Túrnense para preguntarse cuándo occurrió cada actividad mencionada en **Paso 1.**

E1: *¿Cuándo compró Yolanda un coche nuevo?*
E2: *Compró un coche nuevo el año pasado./Lo compró el año pasado.*

Vocabulario útil

anoche	*last night*
anteayer	*the day before yesterday*
ayer	*yesterday*
el año pasado	*last year*
el fin de semana pasado	*last weekend*
el martes/viernes/domingo, etc. pasado	*last Tuesday/Friday/Sunday, etc.*
la semana pasada	*last week*

Fíjate

In the list of *Vocabulario útil*, note that for the words "last weekend" (*el fin de semana pasado*), the adjective *pasado* agrees with the masculine noun *el fin* and not *semana*. In contrast, for "last week" (*la semana pasada*), the word "last" agrees with the feminine noun *semana*.

NOTE FOR 7-12

This activity provides an opportunity to practice listening. In pairs, have students take turns reading their sentences aloud. As one reads, the other traces a light line connecting the appropriate items from each column. You may also want students to write some of their sentences on the board for follow-up.

Expansion for 7-13 Have students write a brief paragraph about the preparations surrounding a meal they prepared for a friend or for a party they gave or attended.

[3:00]

7·13 Cocinero/a

Tu compañero/a y tú van a preparar un almuerzo especial para sus amigos. Para saber si todo está listo, túrnense para contestar las siguientes preguntas usando el pretérito y un pronombre de complemento directo (**lo, la, los, las**).

MODELO   E1: ¿Compraste la carne?

E2: *Sí, la compré.*

1. ¿Compraste los refrescos?   Sí, los compré. / No, no los compré.
2. ¿Buscaste las recetas (*recipes*) de tu abuela?   Sí, las busqué. / No, no las busqué.
3. ¿Cocinaste tus platos (*dishes*) favoritos?   Sí, los cociné. / No, no los cociné.
4. ¿Encontraste fruta muy fresca para la ensalada?   Sí, la encontré. / No, no la encontré.
5. ¿Preparaste una mesa bonita?   Sí, la preparé. / No, no la preparé.
6. ¿Limpiaste el comedor?   Sí, lo limpié. / No, no lo limpié.
7. ¿Mandaste las invitaciones?   Sí, las mandé. / No, no las mandé.

[4:00]

7·14 Los quehaceres de Inés

Capítulo 3. Los quehaceres de la casa, pág. 112.

Paso 1   Escribe una oración para cada quehacer que terminó Inés. Después, compara tus oraciones con las de un/a compañero/a.

MODELO   E1: el suelo

E2: *Inés barrió el suelo.*

1. la ropa   3. el baño   5. la basura
2. la aspiradora 4. los muebles   6. el armario

Paso 2   Túrnense para decir qué hizo Inés en el centro después de terminar sus quehaceres. Sigan el modelo.

MODELO   E1: el correo

E2: *Compró sellos.*

1. la librería   3. el banco   5. la biblioteca   7. el supermercado
2. el cine   4. el cibercafé 6. el café   8. la tienda

7·15 ¿Y cuándo…?   [4:00]

Entrevista a un/a compañero/a para saber cuándo ocurrieron las siguientes cosas.

MODELO   ¿Cuándo… (tú) comprar esta lechuga?

E1: *¿Cuándo compraste esta lechuga?*

E2: *La compré el sábado pasado.*

¿Cuándo…?

empezaste/empecé

1. (tú) tocar un instrumento   tocaste/toqué
2. (tus amigos) visitar a sus padres   visitaron/visitaron
3. (tú) comprar un CD nuevo   compraste/compré
4. (tus amigos y tú) comer en un restaurante muy bueno
   comieron/comimos
5. (tú) empezar tus estudios universitarios
6. (tu profesor/a) leer una novela de Dan Brown
   leyó/leyó
7. (tus amigos y tú) bailar   bailaron/bailamos
8. (Uds.) invitar a un amigo a ir a una fiesta
   invitaron/invitamos

Expansion for 7-16 Have each student write a sentence about something they have done recently. Collect the slips of paper and read them to the class, having students guess who wrote each one.

7·16 ¿Te puedo hacer una pregunta? 5:00

Entrevista a cinco estudiantes diferentes y anota sus respuestas (**sí** o **no**). Después, compara tus respuestas con las de los otros estudiantes de la clase. ¿Cuáles son las tendencias?

MODELO   arreglar el cuarto hoy

TÚ: *¿Arreglaste tu cuarto hoy?*
E1: *Sí, lo arreglé.*
E2: *No, no lo arreglé.*
E3: *Sí, arreglé mi cuarto.*
E4: *No, no arreglé mi cuarto.*
E5: *No, yo no lo arreglé, pero mi compañero lo arregló.*

	E1	E2	E3	E4	E5
1. arreglar el cuarto hoy arreglaste/arreglé					
2. comer en un restaurante el sábado pasado comiste/comí					
3. estudiar anoche estudiaste/estudié					
4. lavar los platos ayer lavaste/lavé					
5. hablar por teléfono con los padres anteayer hablaste/hablé					
6. jugar al golf el verano pasado jugaste/jugué					
7. escribir un ensayo para la clase de inglés la semana pasada escribiste/escribí					
8. terminar la tarea para la clase de español anoche terminaste/terminé					

¿Cómo andas?

Having completed the first **Comunicación**, I now can…

	Feel Confident	Need to Review
● talk about food that I like and dislike (p. 252)	❏	❏
● pronounce the letters **r** and **rr** properly in Spanish (p. 253)	❏	❏
● talk about past actions using direct object pronouns (p. 257)	❏	❏
● correctly use verbs that are regular in the preterit (p. 258)	❏	❏
● talk about past actions and events (p. 258)	❏	❏
● use verbs that end in **-car, -zar,** and **-gar** and the verb **leer** in the preterit correctly (p. 259)	❏	❏

Comunicación

- Describing food preparation and restaurant activity
- Describing past actions

VOCABULARIO 4

La preparación de las comidas

7-24 to
7-26

3:00

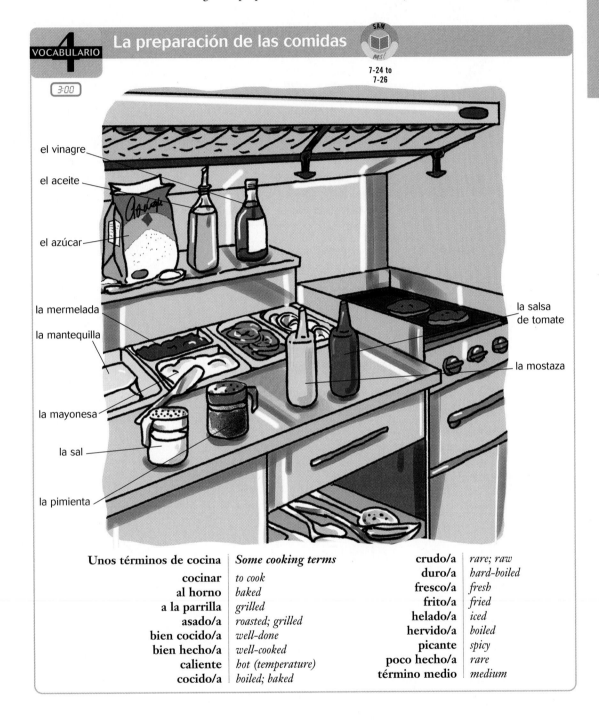

el vinagre
el aceite
el azúcar
la mermelada
la mantequilla
la mayonesa
la sal
la pimienta
la salsa de tomate
la mostaza

Unos términos de cocina	*Some cooking terms*
cocinar	*to cook*
al horno	*baked*
a la parrilla	*grilled*
asado/a	*roasted; grilled*
bien cocido/a	*well-done*
bien hecho/a	*well-cooked*
caliente	*hot (temperature)*
cocido/a	*boiled; baked*

crudo/a	*rare; raw*
duro/a	*hard-boiled*
fresco/a	*fresh*
frito/a	*fried*
helado/a	*iced*
hervido/a	*boiled*
picante	*spicy*
poco hecho/a	*rare*
término medio	*medium*

CAPÍTULO 7

Suggestion for 7-18 Encourage your
students to answer the questions
with direct object pronouns.

Additional Activity for
La preparación de las comidas
Have students pair each new
vocabulary word or phrase with an
appropriate word or phrase from
pages 252–253. E.g. *cocinar las
verduras,* etc.

7·17 La asociación `2:00`

Digan una palabra o
expresión que asocian
con cada condimento,
especia o término de la
siguiente lista.

MODELO E1: picante

E2: *salsa*

1. frito/a
2. la salsa de tomate
3. crudo/a
4. la mayonesa
5. el azúcar
6. a la parrilla
7. fresco/a
8. al horno
9. la mostaza
10. la mantequilla

7·18 ¿Cómo lo prefieres? `5:00`

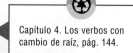

Capítulo 4. Los verbos con
cambio de raíz, pág. 144.

Entrevista a un/a compañero/a para conocer sus preferencias. Después cambien de papel.

MODELO E1: ¿Cómo quieres tu hamburguesa?

E2: *La quiero término medio.*

1. ¿Cómo quieres tu bistec?
2. ¿Con qué condimento(s) lo quieres?
3. ¿Cómo quieres tu ensalada?
4. ¿Cómo prefieres el pescado?
5. ¿Cómo quieres tu refresco, con o sin hielo?
6. ¿Cómo te gustan los huevos?
7. ¿Cómo prefieres la pizza?
8. ¿Cómo te gusta el té, helado o caliente?
9. ¿Cómo pides la sopa, con mucha o poca sal?
10. ¿Cómo tomas el café?

5:00 7-27 to 7-28

La comida hispana

La parrillada

La comida hispana es muy variada. En España se comen muchos pescados y mariscos, pero cada región tiene sus platos típicos. Por ejemplo, en Asturias tienen la fabada (*bean stew*), en Valencia la paella y en Andalucía el gazpacho. La parte central de España es conocida por su carne asada.

La comida mexicana se define por sus técnicas y por los ingredientes propios del país. Las diferentes formas de preparar el maíz y los chiles son exclusivas a la cocina mexicana; también se destacan (*they distinguish themselves*) en la manera de cocinar verduras, carnes, mariscos, huevos, salsas, sopas y aves. Desde Baja California hasta la península de Yucatán, se encuentran platos típicos mexicanos de cada región.

Las islas del Caribe tienen en común la herencia de las culturas española, indígena y africana combinadas con la cultura nativa. Las comidas de estos países llevan una gran variedad de condimentos (*seasonings*) como la bija (*annatto*) o el achiote, el orégano, la cebolla, el ajo, el cilantro y muchos más. El arroz es indispensable en la dieta caribeña, también los plátanos, los mariscos y los frijoles (o habichuelas). El arroz es muy importante también en la dieta centroamericana, igual que el maíz, los frijoles, las tortillas, las enchiladas, las verduras, el pollo, los tamales y las frutas.

En los países de Suramérica comen mucho arroz, frijoles, pollo, carne, frutas y mariscos. En Paraguay y Uruguay se comen muchas sopas, verduras, pan de maíz con queso y carne de cerdo (*pork*). En Chile, igual que en Argentina, las parrilladas (*mixed grills*) son muy populares. Las empanadas o empanadillas (un *turnover* de carne de res, legumbres, queso, mariscos o pollo) son famosas en toda la América Latina, desde Cuba hasta Argentina.

Preguntas

1. ¿Cuáles de los platos típicos (o ingredientes) mencionados te gustan?   *Answers may vary.*

2. ¿Cómo se compara la comida del Caribe con la comida de otras partes del mundo hispanohablante?

2. *Possible answer.* La comida del Caribe tiene/lleva muchos condimentos y el arroz, el plátano, los mariscos y los frijoles son importantes. El arroz y los frijoles también son importantes en los países centroamericanos y en México. La comida de Suramérica tiene mucha carne.

NATIONAL STANDARDS
Cultures, Comparisons

The reading, *La comida hispana*, provides cultural information about various Spanish-speaking regions throughout the world. Students learn about the main dishes, the ingredients, and the seasonings commonly used in Hispanic cooking. This information explains how the geographic location affects the diet and food choices, determining which ingredients and products are readily available. Students see how geography and climate affect the practices, the products, and the perspectives of Hispanic cultures (Standards 2.1, 2.2). There is great variety in the Hispanic diet, and the reading offers a brief outline of how food differs across the regions of Spain, Mexico, the Caribbean, and South America. Students can compare how *la cominda hispana* differs from their own diet, and they can also compare how it varies across Spanish-speaking countries. (Standard 4.2).

Expansion for *La comida hispana*
Additional questions include:

1. *¿Dónde preparan muchos platos con arroz?*
2. *¿Cuál es una de las especialidades de España? ¿Cuáles son algunos de los ingredientes de los platos típicos de México?*
3. *¿Por qué crees que comen tanta (so much) carne de res en Uruguay y Argentina?*
4. *¿Cuáles son algunos platos típicos de la región donde vives?, ¿y de tu familia?*

GRAMÁTICA 5

Unos verbos irregulares en el préterito

7-29 to
7-33

8:00

In the first **Comunicación** you learned about verbs that are regular in the **pretérito** and others that have spelling changes. The following verbs are *irregular* in the **pretérito;** they follow a pattern of their own. Study the verb charts to determine the similarities and differences among the forms.

	andar *(to walk)*	estar	tener
yo	anduve	estuve	tuve
tú	anduviste	estuviste	tuviste
él, ella, Ud.	anduvo	estuvo	tuvo
nosotros/as	anduvimos	estuvimos	tuvimos
vosotros/as	anduvisteis	estuvisteis	tuvisteis
ellos/as, Uds.	anduvieron	estuvieron	tuvieron

Ayer anduvimos diez millas.

El verano pasado **anduvimos** mucho por la playa.   *Last summer we walked along the beach a lot.*
¿En qué bar **estuvieron** Uds.?   *In which bar were you all?*
Juan **tuvo** muy buena suerte. ¡Ganó la lotería!   *Juan was really lucky. He won the lottery!*

	conducir *(to drive)*	traer	decir
yo	conduje	traje	dije
tú	condujiste	trajiste	dijiste
él, ella, Ud.	condujo	trajo	dijo
nosotros/as	condujimos	trajimos	dijimos
vosotros/as	condujisteis	trajisteis	dijisteis
ellos/as, Uds.	condujeron	trajeron	dijeron

> **Fíjate**
> Note that the third-person plural ending of *conducir, decir,* and *traer* is *-eron.*

Conduje el coche nuevo de mi padre anoche.   *I drove my father's new car last night.*
Rubén **trajo** a su madre a la fiesta.   *Rubén brought his mother to the party.*
¿**Dijeron** la verdad sobre el accidente?   *Did they tell the truth about the accident?*

	ir	ser
yo	fui	fui
tú	fuiste	fuiste
él, ella, Ud.	fue	fue
nosotros/as	fuimos	fuimos
vosotros/as	fuisteis	fuisteis
ellos/as, Uds.	fueron	fueron

> **Fíjate**
> Note that *ser* and *ir* have the same forms in the preterit. You must rely on the context of the sentence or conversation to determine the meaning.

Ayer cené con Ana.   *I had dinner with Ana yesterday.*
La cena **fue** deliciosa.   *The dinner was delicious.*
Fuimos al mercado para comprar mariscos.   *We went to the market to buy seafood.*
La gente del mercado **fue** muy amable.   *The people at the market were very kind.*

RECURSOS

P	📖
7-G5	Electronic Activity Cache

	dar	ver	venir
yo	di	vi	vine
tú	diste	viste	viniste
él, ella, Ud.	dio	vio	vino
nosotros/as	dimos	vimos	vinimos
vosotros/as	disteis	visteis	vinisteis
ellos/as, Uds.	dieron	vieron	vinieron

	hacer	querer
yo	hice	quise
tú	hiciste	quisiste
él, ella, Ud.	hizo	quiso
nosotros/as	hicimos	quisimos
vosotros/as	hicisteis	quisisteis
ellos/as, Uds.	hicieron	quisieron

	poder	poner	saber
yo	pude	puse	supe
tú	pudiste	pusiste	supiste
él, ella, Ud.	pudo	puso	supo
nosotros/as	pudimos	pusimos	supimos
vosotros/as	pudisteis	pusisteis	supisteis
ellos/as, Uds.	pudieron	pusieron	supieron

—**Vimos** a mucha gente en tu fiesta.   *We saw a lot of people at your party.*
—Sí, ¡y todos me **dieron** un regalo!   *Yes, and everyone gave me a gift!*
—¿**Vinieron** tus tíos también?   *Did your aunt and uncle come as well?*
—No, no **pudieron** venir por sus trabajos.   *They couldn't come because of their jobs.*
—¡Que lástima! ¿Qué **hiciste** después de la fiesta?   *What a shame! What did you do after the party?*

Verbos con cambio de raíz

¿Cuántas horas durmió anoche?

Por lo menos doce.

The next group of verbs also follows its own pattern. In these stem-changing verbs, the first letters next to the infinitives, listed in parentheses, represent the present tense spelling changes; the last letter indicates the spelling change in the **él** and **ellos** forms of the **pretérito**.

> **Fíjate**
>
> The -*ir* stem-changing verbs are irregular in the third person singular and plural forms only.

	dormir (o → ue → u)	pedir (e → i → i)	preferir (e → ie → i)
yo	dormí	pedí	preferí
tú	dormiste	pediste	preferiste
él, ella, Ud.	durmió	pidió	prefirió
nosotros/as	dormimos	pedimos	preferimos
vosotros/as	dormisteis	pedisteis	preferisteis
ellos/as, Uds.	durmieron	pidieron	prefirieron

¿Qué comida **pidieron** Sara y Manolo?   *What food did Sara and Manolo order?*
Mis abuelos **prefirieron** la carne de res.   *My grandparents preferred the beef.*
Después de comer, los niños se **durmieron**.   *After eating, the children fell asleep.*

Suggestion for *Unos verbos irregulares en el pretérito* If you think now is an appropriate time, point out to your students that the verbs *querer* and *saber* change meaning in the preterit. For example, in the preterit, *querer* usually means "tried to," *no querer* means "refused," and *saber* means "found out."

CAPÍTULO 7

Expansion for 7-20 Have students prepare a dialogue to perform based on the market scene in actividad 7-20.

4:00

7·19 Más práctica

Repite el juego de verbos de la actividad **7-11**, esta vez usando los nuevos verbos irregulares.

7·20 El mercado 8:00

El año pasado, Amanda fue estudiante de intercambio y vivió con una familia en Asunción. Completa el siguiente párrafo sobre su primera visita al mercado y después compártelo con un/a compañero/a.

andar	traer	decidir	ir
pedir	poder	poner	tener

Ayer mis nuevas "hermanas", Patricia y Gloria, y yo (1) _____fuimos_____ al mercado por primera vez. Como perdimos el autobús, (2) _____tuvimos_____ que ir caminando. (3) ¡Nosotras _____anduvimos_____ por más de media hora! Por fin llegamos y (4) _____decidimos_____ tomar un café antes de entrar en el mercado. Yo pedí un café doble con leche y ellas (5) _____pidieron_____ café con leche y tostada. Cuando el señor nos (6) _____trajo_____ los cafés, Patricia (7) _____puso_____ seis cucharadas (*spoonfuls*) de azúcar en el suyo (*hers*). (Yo) No lo (8) _____pude_____ creer, ¡demasiado dulce para mí!

comprar	decir	estar	poner
ser	tomar	ver	volver

Al entrar en el mercado, yo (9) _____vi_____ un montón de verduras y frutas de muchos colores brillantes. (10) _____Fue_____ impresionante. Después yo les (11) _____tomé_____ varias fotos a las chicas. Primero compramos una lechuga, dos cebollas, ajo, medio kilo de zanahorias y un pimiento verde. Hablamos unos cinco minutos con la vendedora sobre su sobrina. Ella (12) _____estuvo_____ seis meses en los Estados Unidos como estudiante de intercambio. Después miramos las frutas y por fin escogimos dos melones y medio kilo de peras. Las chicas (13) _____pusieron_____ las verduras en el bolso grande y la fruta en el bolso más pequeño. Entonces pasamos a la parte del pescado donde nosotras (14) _____compramos_____ atún. La señora lo envolvió (*wrapped*) en papel antes de ponerlo en una bolsa de plástico. Hicimos las compras en menos de media hora. A las nueve y cuarto les (15) _____dijimos_____ adiós a todos y (16) _____volvimos_____ a casa …esta vez en autobús.

Fíjate

Amanda refers to a *medio kilo de zanahorias*. Remember that in most parts of the world the metric system is the preferred system of measurement.

NOTE FOR 7-22
Actividad **7-22** is based on the game "Twenty Questions." The goal of the game is to arrive at the answer by asking only *yes* or *no* questions and getting the answer before your 20 questions run out. Remind students that they need to phrase questions that can be answered just by *sí* or *no*, and they will want to keep track of their questions so they do not repeat. It might be a good idea to have them write out their questions as homework, in case they need all of the questions to find out what their classmate did last summer.

Estrategia

Remember that *una vez* means *once* and *veces* means *times*: *Yo fui al restaurante una vez pero tú fuiste tres veces.* = *I went to the restaurant once but you went three times.*

[8:00] **7·21 ¿Hay rutina en tu semana?**

¿Cuántas veces hiciste estas cosas la semana pasada?

Paso 1 Escribe las respuestas a las siguientes preguntas, según el modelo.

MODELO E1: La semana pasada, ¿cuántas veces viste una película en la televisión?

E2: *Vi una película en la televisión una vez (dos veces, tres veces, etc.).*

La semana pasada, ¿cuántas veces…?
Verb forms:
1. hiciste tu tarea Hice
2. diste la respuesta correcta en clase Di
3. no viniste a la clase de español No vine
4. condujiste a la universidad Conduje
5. dormiste ocho horas Dormí
6. anduviste por el centro Anduve
7. fuiste al cine Fui
8. jugaste a un deporte Jugué
9. viste un partido en la televisión Vi
10. comiste comida rápida Comí

Paso 2 Pídele a tu compañero/a que advine (*guess*) cuántas veces hiciste las actividades anteriores. Sigue el modelo.

MODELOS E1: *La semana pasada, ¿cuántas veces piensas que (yo) hice la tarea?*

E2: *Pienso que la hiciste una vez.*

E1: *Sí, tienes razón. ¡La hice una vez!*

(o)

E1: *¿Cuántas veces piensas que fui al cine?*

E2: *Pienso que no fuiste.*

E1: *No, no tienes razón. Fui una vez.*

[5:00] **7·22 ¿Adónde fui?**

Hazle a tu compañero/a las siguientes preguntas para averiguar adónde fue de vacaciones. Después, cambien de papel. (**¡OJO!** *Before asking the last question, try to guess where he or she went.*)

MODELO E1: ¿Fuiste en verano?

E2: *No, fui en otoño. / Sí, fui en verano.*

Verb forms:
1. ¿Fuiste a la playa? Fui
2. ¿Visitaste un museo? Visité
3. ¿Viste un partido de béisbol? Vi
4. ¿Montaste en bicicleta? Monté
5. ¿Qué compraste? Compré
6. ¿Comiste mariscos? Comí
7. ¿Tomaste el sol? Tomé
8. ¿Jugaste al golf? Jugué
9. ¿Nadaste? Nadé
10. ¿Dormiste en un hotel? Dormí
11. ¿Jugaste al tenis? Jugué
12. ¿Fuiste a un parque? Fui
13. ¿Qué más hiciste? Answers may vary.
14. ¿Adónde fuiste? Fui

7•23 Chismes (*Gossip*)

Imagina que eres el/la editor/a de la columna de chismes de un periódico. Escribe en el cuadro tus respuestas a las siguientes preguntas. Después, entrevista a tres compañeros/as y anota sus respuestas. ¿Están de acuerdo?

1. ¿Qué película tuvo mucho éxito el año pasado?
2. ¿Qué actor salió en una película que **no** tuvo éxito?
3. ¿Qué miembro del gobierno (*member of the government*) dijo algo tonto?
4. ¿Quién hizo un CD recientemente?
5. ¿Cuál de tus amigos estuvo en la playa recientemente?
6. ¿Quién vino tarde a la clase una vez?
7. ¿Quién no trajo sus libros a clase?
8. ¿Quién les dio un examen muy difícil la semana pasada?

	YO	ESTUDIANTE 1	ESTUDIANTE 2	ESTUDIANTE 3
1.				
2.				
3.				

 ## 7•24 ¿Qué dijo?

Form groups of at least six students and sit in a circle. **Estudiante 1** starts by saying his/her name and something that he/she did yesterday, last week, or last year. **Estudiante 2** gives his/her name, says something he/she did, and then tells what the preceding person (**Estudiante 1**) did. **Estudiante 3** tells his/her name, says what he/she did, and then tells what **Estudiante 2** and **Estudiante 1** did (in that order). Follow the model.

MODELO   E1:   *Soy Fran y ayer fui a la playa.*

E2:   *Soy Tom y ayer jugué al tenis. Fran fue a la playa.*

E3:   *Soy Chris y ayer tuve que llamar a mis padres. Tom jugó al tenis y Fran fue a la playa.*

VOCABULARIO 6

En el restaurante

7-34 to
7-37

4:00

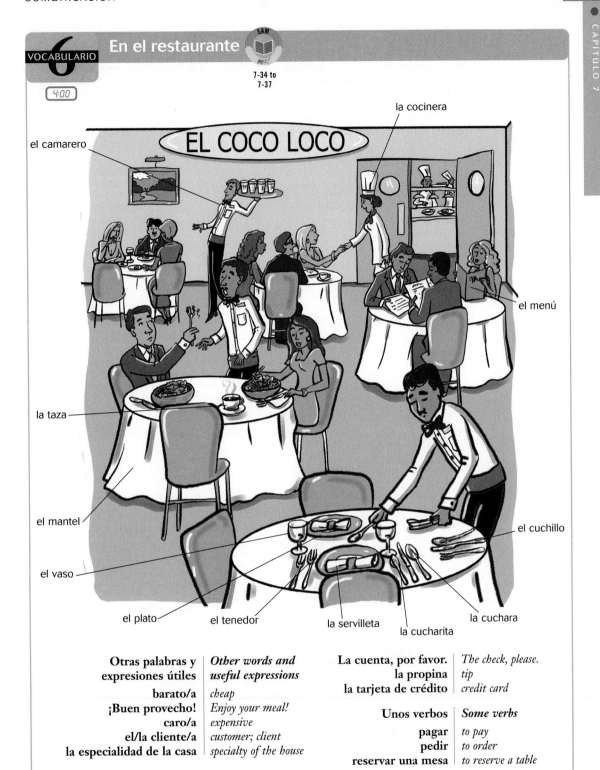

EL COCO LOCO

el camarero

la cocinera

el menú

la taza

el mantel

el vaso

el plato — el tenedor — la servilleta — la cucharita — la cuchara — el cuchillo

Otras palabras y expresiones útiles	Other words and useful expressions
barato/a	cheap
¡Buen provecho!	Enjoy your meal!
caro/a	expensive
el/la cliente/a	customer; client
la especialidad de la casa	specialty of the house

La cuenta, por favor.	The check, please.
la propina	tip
la tarjeta de crédito	credit card

Unos verbos	Some verbs
pagar	to pay
pedir	to order
reservar una mesa	to reserve a table

Suggestion for *En el restaurante*
You might want to add the word *cash* to your payment options. You can say *dinero en efectivo* for those students who pay for their meals in cash. You might also add the word *un descuento* for the university establishments that offer a discount to students with photo identification.

NOTE FOR 7-25

This activity can also be done as a class. Have one student be the scribe for each list, with classmates supplying the items.

`4:00` **7·25** La organización es clave

Juntos escriban las siguientes categorías en una hoja de papel: **cosas en la mesa, pedir y pagar, personas en el restaurante**. Después, organicen el vocabulario de **En el restaurante** bajo esas categorías.

MODELO	COSAS EN LA MESA	PEDIR Y PAGAR	PERSONAS EN EL RESTAURANTE
	el cuchillo	la propina	el camarero

`2:00` **7·26** ¿Cómo se dice?

Túrnense para decir qué palabra o frase corresponde a las siguientes descripciones.

MODELO   E1:   el "Gran Especial"
          E2:   la especialidad de la casa

1. persona que sirve la comida   el/la camarero/a
2. dinero que das por buen servicio   la propina
3. lista de comidas y bebidas   el menú
4. necesario para limpiar las manos   la servilleta
5. persona que prepara la comida en un restaurante   el/la cocinero/a
6. necesario para comer *Frosted Flakes*   una cuchara/cucharita, la leche
7. necesario para beber café   una taza
8. persona que come en el restaurante   el/la cliente

> **Estrategia**
>
> As you acquire more Spanish in each chapter, try to write definitions in Spanish of your new vocabulary words like in the model. Learning new vocabulary will become easier the more you practice. Also, it will help you use your new vocabulary in sentences.

`5:00` **7·27** Una mesa bien puesta

Dibuja la mesa de tu familia o de la familia de un/a buen/a amigo/a para una cena especial con todo bien puesto (*well set*). Ahora, sin mostrar tu dibujo, descríbeselo a un/a compañero/a mientras él/ella lo dibuja. ¿Lo dibujó bien? Luego cambien de papeles.

Vocabulario útil

al lado (de)	*beside; next to*
a la izquierda (de)	*to the left (of)*
a la derecha (de)	*to the right (of)*
cerca (de)	*near*
debajo (de)	*under; underneath*
encima (de)	*on top of; above*

`3:00` **7·28** ¿Qué pasó?

Miren el dibujo en la página 271 y digan por lo menos **cinco** oraciones acerca de lo que pasó anoche en el restaurante El Coco Loco.

7·29 ¿Me puede servir…?

Vas con dos amigos/as al restaurante más popular de Asunción para cenar.

Paso 1 Miren el menú y determinen qué van a pedir sabiendo que tienen 60.000 guaraníes para pagar.

EL RESTAURANTE BUEN PROVECHO

SÁNDWICHES CALIENTES

Sándwich de queso	36.000
Sándwich de pollo, jamón y queso	48.000
Sándwich de jamón	38.000

SÁNDWICHES FRÍOS

Sándwich de pollo, tomate y lechuga	43.000
Sándwich de ensalada de pollo	45.000
Sándwich de jamón y queso	46.000

HELADOS Y POSTRES

Tres Marías	14.500
Helado de chocolate	12.000
Helado especial	12.000
Flan de la casa	14.500

BEBIDAS Y REFRESCOS

Café	5.500
Vaso de leche	6.600
Chocolate en taza	7.200
Té caliente	5.500
Té frío	5.500
Refrescos fríos	7.000
Cervezas	12.500
Copa de vino	14.000

SOPAS Y CREMAS

Sopa de cebolla gratinada	15.500 PYG
Sopa de pescado	32.000
Sopa de pollo y verduras	27.000
Consomé de pollo	17.000

ENSALADAS

Mixta de verduras	19.500
Ensalada de jamón, pollo o atún	45.000
Ensalada de frutas	35.000

Paso 2 Ahora, utilizando esa información, realicen *(act out)* una escena en un restaurante para la clase. Una persona debe ser el/la camarero/a y las otras dos personas deben ser los clientes.

Capítulo 2. Presente indicativo de verbos regulares, pág. 68.

7·30 De compras en el mercado

Algunos estudiantes van a hacer el papel de vendedores y otros de clientes. Tu profesor/a te va a dar una lista de los productos que tienes para vender o de los que necesitas comprar. Los vendedores deben ganar cincuenta mil guaraníes y los clientes sólo pueden gastar cincuenta mil guaraníes. Va a haber competencia entre los vendedores y sí, ¡puedes regatear *(bargain; negotiate the price)*!

NATIONAL STANDARDS
Communication, Cultures, Communities

Ordering from the menu in actividad **7-29** gives your learners the opportunity to use language in a real context and to experience the Spanish language from a part of the Spanish-speaking world that is apart from the usual. If your community has restaurants with cuisine from the Spanish-speaking world, encourage your students to use their Spanish when ordering from the menu.

NOTE AND INSTRUCTIONS FOR 7-30

This activity takes a bit of planning, but is well worth the effort. Half the class will be vendors, while the other half will be shoppers. There should be 2 meat and poultry vendors, 2 fruit and vegetable vendors, 2 bakery vendors, and 2 vendors of housewares. You may add other vendors, depending on the size of your class. The pairs of vendors sell the same type of goods but with some different varieties and/or slightly different prices. The shoppers should be given a context; for example, they may be shopping for a party or a holiday meal.

Ideally, the shops can be positioned in front of chalkboards so that the vendors can draw signs and advertisements. You can also provide them with pictures of products that are typical for their shops. The shopping lists should have drawings to represent what should be purchased, with the amount written to the side. Shoppers may add to the list, or simply create their own based on the type of meal or party they choose to prepare. Encourage bargaining.

With regard to recycling prior concepts that the students have already learned, they should review and practice daily greetings, numbers, and interrogatives, as well as food vocabulary.

Sample of partial list for shopper:

14 eggs	1 tablecloth
3 chickens	12 forks
2 hams	6 spoons
kilo potatoes	6 knives
lettuce	paper napkins
3 tomatoes	bread for 12 people
kilo grapes	pastries for 12 people

(cont. of Note and Instructions for 7–30)

Sample of partial list for vendors (in kilos except where indicated):

Eggs	$,50 each
Chicken	$ 2,00
Ham	$12,00
Steak	$6,50
Lettuce	$,40
Tomatoes	$,30
Grapes	$,40
Bread	$,20 "loaf"

Attempt to make the prices as realistic as possible. Also, to keep with the country/regional theme of this chapter, you may want the prices to reflect the Chilean peso or the Paraguayan guaraní. Consult your *¡Anda!* web site for current conversion rates.

Expansion for 7-30 This activity can also center on a restaurant experience with some students acting as patrons and others as owners or servers. The patrons could have a certain amount to spend and the owners or servers must try to convince the patrons to order specific items (or to mount the largest bill possible). Students could create sample menus for homework or work together in groups in class.

ESCUCHA

7-38 to
7-39

ESTRATEGIA **Combining strategies**

To begin the new term it is useful to review and combine all the listening strategies you have practiced thus far. Remember to use all clues available to you to anticipate what you are about to hear, including photos, captions, and pre-listening synopses or questions. If you are performing a listening activity like the one to follow, also look ahead at the comprehension questions. Once you have an idea of the context, consider what you already know about it. Taking time to think about and practice these specific strategies will enhance your ability to listen effectively.

7·31

Antes de escuchar

Contesta las siguientes preguntas.

1. Mira la foto. ¿Dónde está la mujer? ¿Qué hace?
2. ¿Haces las compras (*Do you shop*) en un mercado como éste, donde hay muchos vendedores en un solo lugar, o en un supermercado?
3. ¿Qué tipo de vocabulario necesitas saber para poder hacer las compras en un mercado?

La madre de Alejandra

7·32

CD 3
Track 2

A escuchar

Escucha la conversación entre la madre de Alejandra y un vendedor para averiguar el propósito (*purpose*) de la conversación. Después, escucha una vez más para contestar las siguientes preguntas.

1. ¿Qué compra? Pon una tacha (✓) delante de los ingredientes o condimentos que ella compra.

✓ mantequilla	____ vinagre
____ azúcar	✓ huevos
✓ queso	____ pan
____ mayonesa	✓ leche

2. Determina si las siguientes oraciones son verdaderas (**V**) o falsas (**F**).
   a. La madre necesita ingredientes para preparar un plato nuevo. V
   b. El Sr. Gómez tiene todo lo que la madre necesita comprar. F

7·33

Después de escuchar

Realiza (*Act out*) con un/a compañero/a la escena entre la madre y el Sr. Gómez.

MADRE: Bueno, entonces sólo quiero seis. ¿Mañana va a tener los blancos?

VENDEDOR: Sí, por supuesto. Aquí tiene los huevos. Y el queso, ¿cuánto necesita? *(pause as if reaching for the cheese and indicating an amount)* ¿Así está bien?

MADRE: Sí. Sólo quiero un poco. Lo necesito para un plato nuevo que quiero preparar de verduras al horno con una salsa de queso.

VENDEDOR: Excelente.

MADRE: ¿Cuánto es?

VENDEDOR: A ver —la leche, dos setenta y cinco; la mantequilla, uno cincuenta; seis huevos, 70 centavos; y el queso, uno noventa y cinco . . . *(pause)* son seis dólares noventa centavos.

MADRE: Aquí lo tiene. Ahora necesito comprar las verduras.

VENDEDOR: Muy bien. Gracias, señora. ¡Qué le vaya bien!

MADRE: Adiós. Hasta mañana.

ESCRIBE

7-40 to
7-41

7·34 Antes de escribir

Piensa en el mejor día festivo que pasaste de niño. Haz una lista de los siguientes detalles:

- las personas con quienes celebraste o las que fueron a la fiesta
- lo que comieron y bebieron
- las cosas que hicieron
- los regalos que dieron y recibieron

7·35 Un recuerdo (*memory*)

Ahora, usando los detalles de la lista, escribe un párrafo bien desarrollado (*well developed*) sobre ese día, con introducción y conclusión.

7·36 Después de escribir

En grupos de cuatro o cinco estudiantes, lean los párrafos de la actividad **7-35**. Ofrezcan (*Offer*) ideas a sus compañeros para mejorar su trabajo. Después, escriban la versión final para entregársela (*turn it in*) a su profesor/a.

¿Cómo andas?

Having completed the second **Comunicación,** I now can...

	Feel Confident	Need to Review
● discuss foods that I like and dislike and say how I like them prepared (p. 263)	❏	❏
● describe actions in the past using a variety of regular and irregular verbs (p. 266)	❏	❏
● describe how to set a table (p. 271)	❏	❏
● order food in a restaurant (p. 271)	❏	❏
● buy food in a market (p. 273)	❏	❏
● combine listening strategies (p. 274)	❏	❏
● write about a special day from my past (p. 275)	❏	❏

SECTION GOALS FOR
Escribe

By the end of the *Escribe* section, students will be able to:

- brainstorm ideas about a major childhood holiday they celebrated.
- organize and write a well-developed paragraph.
- practice reading aloud what they have written.
- revise the paragraph based on the feedback of others.
- edit the writing of others.
- finish a final draft of the paragraph.

NATIONAL STANDARDS
Communication

The *Escribe* section focuses on all three Communication Standards. First, students plan a list of details pertaining to their best childhood holiday. They write a detailed paragraph about that special day for peer review. Then, in groups of 4–5 students, they receive feedback about their writing. This requires that all students read at least 4 paragraphs that their classmates have written. Students follow Standard 1.1 when they engage in conversations and provide feedback about the writing process to their classmates. They use Standard 1.2 when they read the paragraphs written by other students, and students might also read the paragraphs aloud to their small groups. Reading aloud requires that the other group members listen to spoken Spanish. Lastly, students prepare to present their paragraphs in written form to the teacher. The teacher might display the paragraphs for an audience of readers (Standard 1.3).

TPR activity for 7-34 Give students simple sentences in the preterit tense that they can act out. Pretend you are remembering a birthday party from your childhood and retell the story about your presents, the cake, the decorations, etc.

Gino Breschi Arteaga

CW
eBook

CD 3
Track 3

SAM
MSL
7-42

DVD/VHS
MSL
Vistas culturales

10:00

Chile

Les presento mi país

Mi nombre es Gino Breschi Arteaga y soy de Viña del Mar, Chile. Viña del Mar es una ciudad turística en la costa y tiene una playa hermosa. El país es muy largo y estrecho, con un promedio (*average*) de 180 kilómetros de ancho (*wide*) y aproximadamente 4.300 kilómetros de largo. Al oeste, tenemos el océano Pacífico y al este, la cordillera majestuosa de los Andes. **¿Prefieres vivir cerca del océano o de las montañas?** Al norte, está el desierto de Atacama, el más árido del mundo. Al sur, hay una serie de glaciares en parques nacionales. Soy soltero (*bachelor*) así que todavía vivo con mis padres, como la mayoría de los chilenos antes de casarse (*to marry*). Así puedo comer el pastel de choclo que mi madre me hace con frecuencia. ¡Qué rico!

El glaciar San Rafael, Patagonia

El pastel de choclo es un plato favorito de los chilenos.

La playa en Viña del Mar

OCÉANO PACÍFICO

Arica
Iquique
San Pedro
Antofagasta
La Serena
Viña del Mar
Valparaíso
Santiago
Concepción
Río Bío Bío
Puerto Montt
Isla de Chiloé
Archipiélago de Los Hornos

BOLIVIA
BRAZIL
PARAGUAY
Lascar
ARGENTINA
URUGUAY

CORDILLERA DE LOS ANDES

Estrecho de Magallanes
Isla Grande de Tierra del Fuego
Punta Arenas
Cabo de los Hornos

Isla de Pascua

● ALMANAQUE ●

Nombre oficial:	República de Chile
Gobierno:	República
Población:	16.134.219 (2006)
Idiomas:	español
Moneda:	Peso chileno ($)

¿Sabías que...?

- Además del (*In addition to*) desayuno, el almuerzo y la cena, los chilenos toman una merienda llamada "las onces", que comen entre las 4:00 y las 7:00 de la tarde.

- El baile nacional de Chile es la cueca. Este baile se inspira en el rito de cortejo (*courting*) del gallo (*rooster*) y la gallina (*hen*).

PREGUNTAS

1. ¿Qué extremos geográficos y climatológicos se mencionan? ¿Hay algo parecido en los Estados Unidos?

2. Generalmente, ¿cuándo salen de casa los jóvenes chilenos para vivir por su cuenta (*on their own*)? ¿Cuál es la costumbre en los Estados Unidos?

3. Describe el baile nacional. En tu opinión, ¿cuál debe ser el baile nacional de los Estados Unidos? ¿Por qué?

> **En la Red**
> Amplía tus conocimientos sobre Chile en la página web de *¡Anda!*

RECURSOS

C	P	IRM
T7-6	T7-6	Cultural Background Notes

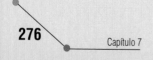

CW
eBook

CD 3
Track 4

DVD/VHS

Vistas
culturales

Mirta Beatriz Chávez
Villalba

Paraguay

Les presento mi país

Mi nombre es Mirta Beatriz Chávez Villalba y vivo en Asunción, Paraguay. Como un gran porcentaje de los paraguayos, soy bilingüe: hablo español y guaraní. **¿En qué otros países hay una población bilingüe?** El guaraní es el idioma hablado por los indígenas originales del país: los guaraníes. Hoy día, el noventa por ciento de los paraguayos somos **mestizos,** una mezcla (*mixture*) de los indígenas y los conquistadores españoles. Los indígenas cultivaron la mandioca (*yucca*), la batata (*yam*), el maíz y la yerba mate entre otras cosechas (*crops*). Estas comidas se usan hoy día en nuestros platos y bebidas principales. Durante el día, se ve a los paraguayos tomando su **tereré,** una infusión fría de yerba mate. **¿Qué refresco te gusta tomar?**

El tereré, una infusión fría de yerba mate, es la bebida preferida en Paraguay.

El ñandú es una especie de ave nativa y amenazada (*endangered*) de El Chaco.

La Represa Hidroeléctrica de Itaipú, en la frontera entre Paraguay y Brasil.

BOLIVIA

GRAN CHACO

Fuerte Olimpo

BRAZIL

Río Paraguay

PARAGUAY

Concepción

San Pedro

Río Paraná

Asunción

Ciudad del Este

ARGENTINA

● ALMANAQUE ●

Nombre oficial:	República del Paraguay
Gobierno:	República constitucional
Población:	6.506.464 (2006)
Idiomas:	español (oficial); guaraní (oficial)
Moneda:	Guaraní (G)

¿Sabías que...?

● Muchos paraguayos son aficionados a los remedios caseros (*homemade remedies*).

● El Chaco cubre el 60% de la superficie de Paraguay pero contiene solamente un 2% de la población del país.

PREGUNTAS

1. ¿Qué comidas se comen en Paraguay?

2. ¿Por qué un gran porcentaje de los paraguayos son bilingües?

3. ¿En qué aspectos son Chile y Paraguay diferentes y similares? ¿Cómo se comparan con los otros países que hemos estudiado?

En la Red
Amplía tus conocimientos sobre Paraguay en la página web de *¡Anda!*

277

NOTE FOR *El Chaco*

El Chaco, or *El Gran Chaco,* is a vast area of empty plains and forests. (The name *Chaco* supposedly comes from the Quechuan word for *great hunting ground*). It contains several of Paraguay's national parks and biological reserves. It is a prime area for ecotourism due to the variety of flora and fauna located there, e.g., the jaguar, the tapir, the elusive guanaco, the maned wolf, and the giant armadillo. It is also home to many aviary species, including the flamingo and the ostrich-like rhea or *ñandú,* which is endangered.

NOTE FOR *La Represa Hidroeléctrica de Itaipú*

The Itaipú Hydroelectric Dam is a joint venture of enormous proportions between Brazil and Paraguay. Construction began in 1975 and was completed in 1991. Harnessing the hydroelectric potential of the Paraná River, this dam and power plant provide more than 80% of the electrical power consumption of Paraguay and more than 25% of that of Brazil. It has become a huge tourist attraction.

NOTE FOR *Tereré*

Tereré is the cold infusion form of yerba mate, the grass-like tea that is the preferred drink in Paraguay, Uruguay, and Argentina. When it is hot, it is called *yerba mate*; as a cold drink, it is called *tereré.*

NOTE FOR *Remedios Caseros*

Beliefs in herbal and folk remedies abound in Paraguay. Sometimes they are combined with modern medical practices, depending on the person with an ailment, his/her background, and his/her geographic location— rural populations being more prone to these practices. Nevertheless, in the marketplaces in Asunción, a modern capital city, medicine women set up their stalls and do brisk business.

Expansion for *Preguntas* Additional questions include:

1. *¿Qué significa ser bilingüe?*

2. *¿Qué idiomas hablan los paraguayos? ¿Qué idiomas hablan los canadienses?, ¿los puertorriqueños?*

3. *¿Dónde vive la mayoría de los paraguayos?, ¿por qué piensas que es así?*

4. *¿Cómo se compara la comida paraguaya con la comida de otros países hispanos?*

Web activity for *¿Sabías que...?*
Have your students do the following research on the Internet.

1. *¿Qué piensas de los remedios caseros? ¿Prefieres las curas alternativas o ir al médico?, ¿por qué? Busca en la Red más información sobre los remedios caseros y la clasificación de alimentos en la medicina herbal. (Palabras clave: la medicina herbal o alternativa, los remedios caseros)*

2. *La represa de Itaipú es un proyecto de construcción enorme. ¿Hay algún proyecto de este tipo en los EE.UU.? ¿Por qué se llevaron a cabo estos proyectos? ¿Cuáles son los beneficios y las desventajas para los países? (Palabras clave: represas estadounidenses, proyectos hidroeléctricos, energía eléctrica)*

RECURSOS

T7-7	T7-7	Cultural Background Notes

Ambiciones siniestras

lectura

SECTION GOALS FOR

Lectura

By the end of the *Lectura* section, students will be able to:

- implement the new reading strategy of prediction.
- integrate previously learned reading strategies with predicting new content.
- recognize the new verb forms written in the preterit tense.
- make predictions about what will happen to the characters.

NATIONAL STANDARDS

Communication

Episode 7 of *Ambiciones siniestras* introduces the strategy of predicting. The students are exposed to more complex grammatical structures in the reading, and they are encouraged to activate their prior knowledge and link what they anticipate will happen with what they already know. The reading aligns with Standard 1.2, as students are reading authentic text in Spanish and interpreting what they believe has happened and what will happen. The video portion of *Ambiciones siniestras* also aligns with Standard 1.2, as students are listening to authentic Spanish and viewing the events. Both the reading and the video require that students interpret Spanish, and the video requires students to interpret the actions and gestures of the characters when there is no dialogue.

RECAP OF *AMBICIONES SINIESTRAS*

Episodio 5

Lectura: In *Capítulo 5, La búsqueda de Eduardo*, Cisco snooped into Eduardo's e-mail account to see if he could find any information about Eduardo's whereabouts. Cisco also consulted his cousin Manolo for advice about what to do about Eduardo's disappearance. While he waited for a response from his cousin, Cisco attended a concert at the university and saw a girl from his economics class who interested him. He returned home, checked his e-mail, and discovered a message

---

7-37 **Antes de leer.** En el **Episodio 5**, Eduardo desaparece. Cisco no sabe qué hacer y le pide consejo a su primo, Manolo. Después, todos los estudiantes menos Eduardo y Alejandra tienen una videoconferencia. Antes de continuar con el siguiente episodio contesta estas preguntas.

1. Mira el título. ¿Cuál es un ejemplo de un rompecabezas? ¿Qué experiencia tienes con los rompecabezas?
2. ¿Quién está en la foto? ¿Qué hace?

ESTRATEGIA   Predicting

To predict what a reading passage is about, first anticipate the content by considering the title, visual cues (illustrations, photos), and comprehension questions. Once you have a general idea of what the passage is about, connect any personal knowledge or experience you have with it. Then, quickly skim the reading for the main idea(s). At that point you can predict what will happen in the reading.

7-38 **A leer.** Completa los siguientes pasos.

1. Lee superficialmente (*skim*) el episodio para averiguar cuáles son los personajes y dónde están.
2. Escribe **dos** predicciones de lo que crees que va a ocurrir en el episodio.
3. Lee el episodio y determina si las predicciones que hiciste son correctas.

CD 3
Track 5

El rompecabezas°   *riddle*

Cisco está muy preocupado por Alejandra. Por eso después de la videoconferencia llamó a Manolo y le preguntó por ella. Manolo le dijo que Alejandra no respondió al último correo electrónico. Tampoco° estuvo en la   *Nor* clase de literatura. Manolo le dijo a Cisco que la esperó por media hora después de la clase y no vino. No sabe nada de ella.

Ellos dos están muy preocupados acerca de lo que está pasando. ¿Por qué fueron escogidos°? ¿Qué pasó con Eduardo? ¿Dónde está Eduardo? ¿Y   *selected* dónde está Alejandra?

---

from Eduardo to the other contestants dated three days earlier. He recognized the name Manolo Rodríguez and wondered if Eduardo had written to his cousin.

Video: In *Episodio 5, Se conocen*, the characters finally met each other via a video conference organized by Cisco. Cisco read Eduardo's e-mail confronting el Sr. Verdugo about a fake contest, and found the names of the other finalists. Manolo revealed to Alejandra that Cisco was his cousin.

When the finalists met online, they discovered that Eduardo was missing. Lupe seemed aloof, as if she had something to hide, and at the end of the video Alejandra's picture faded. We learned that Alejandra might have been taken by force by a mysterious stranger.

Con los nervios y la preocupación, Cisco tenía mucha hambre así que decidió ir a su restaurante favorito, Mamá Mía. Ahí siempre puede comer algo y pensar en todo lo que está pasando. Pidió lo que su madre llama *comfort food*: pollo frito, papas, maíz y frijoles. Durante la comida, conversó con sus amigos que trabajan allí. Cuando pagó, le sonó el teléfono celular. Cisco contestó y oyó una voz de hombre: —*Cisco Quiroga. Tiene cuatro pistas° para resolver este rompecabezas o Eduardo va a morir. Aquí están:*

clues

Conocido por su longitud

Por la razón o la fuerza

Qué rico está el pisco

Para quien baile la cueca

Recuerde, tiene dos días para resolver el rompecabezas o Eduardo va a morir. No vaya a la policía.—

CLIC…

Cisco se quedó sin palabras, le temblaron las manos. Tomó el teléfono y llamó a Manolo. La línea estaba ocupada. —Vamos Manolo, cuelga° el teléfono, —pensó Cisco— necesito hablar contigo.— Por fin, después de llamar varias veces, Manolo contestó con voz de pánico.

(colgar) hang up

—¿Quién es? —contestó Manolo.

—Soy yo, Cisco —respondió Cisco. —Mira…
(Manolo interrumpe)

—Cisco, recibí una llamada antes de la tuya°…

yours

—¿De un hombre con una voz muy rara? —le preguntó Cisco.

—Así que te llamó a ti también —respondió Manolo. —Cisco, tenemos que llamar a los demás. Yo llamo a Lupe y a Alejandra y tú llamas a Marisol, ¿está bien?

—De acuerdo. Muy bien. —dijo Cisco.

Manolo llamó a Alejandra pero no consiguió hablar con ella. La voz del contestador automático era la de un hombre… «*Lo sentimos, no estamos en casa en estos momentos. Pueden dejar un mensaje.*» Intentó llamar de nuevo. Otra vez el contestador. ¿Dónde está Alejandra? Cree que conoce la voz del hombre del contestador.

De repente°, Manolo, pensando en voz alta y horrorizado, gritó: —¡Por favor no… No puede ser…!—

Suddenly

7-39 **Después de leer.** Contesta las siguientes preguntas.

1. ¿Qué dijo Manolo de Alejandra?
2. ¿Dónde estaba *(was)* Cisco cuando recibió la llamada misteriosa?
3. ¿Qué acababa *(had just done)* de hacer cuando recibió la llamada?
4. ¿De qué se trató la llamada?
5. ¿Por qué estaba *(was)* Cisco asustado *(frightened)*?
6. ¿Qué hizo Cisco después de colgar el teléfono?
7. ¿Qué ocurrió cuando Manolo llamó a Alejandra?

279

video

7-48 to 7-50

7-40 **Antes del video.** ¿Dónde puede estar Alejandra? ¿De quién es la voz en su contestador automático? ¿Quién más recibió el rompecabezas? En la segunda parte del episodio, vas a ver a Lupe trabajando en su computadora. ¿Qué piensas que está haciendo? También Manolo, Cisco, Marisol y Lupe van a tener otra videoconferencia. ¿De qué necesitan hablar ahora?

¿Qué lees?

Esto es muy peligroso.

¡No tengo nada que ver con la desaparición de Eduardo!

¡Qué rico está el pisco!

Episodio 7

Relájate y disfruta el video.

7-41 **Después del video.** Contesta las siguientes preguntas.

1. ¿Dónde estaba Lupe? ¿Qué hizo?

2. ¿Dónde estaba Cisco? ¿Qué hizo?

3. ¿Cuál es la mentira (*lie*) de Lupe?

4. ¿Qué **no** les va a mencionar Cisco a los otros?

5. ¿De qué le "acusó" Manolo a Lupe?

6. ¿Por qué le respondió Cisco a Manolo de una manera defensiva?

7. ¿Qué descubrió Cisco al final del episodio?

280

RECURSOS   **Video Script**

Y por fin, ¿cómo andas?

Having completed this chapter, I now can...

	Feel Confident	Need to Review
Comunicación		
● discuss my food preferences (p. 252)	❏	❏
● pronounce **r** and **rr** correctly, distinguishing between the two (p. 253)	❏	❏
● talk and write about things I did and events that occurred in the past (p. 258)	❏	❏
● explain how I like my food prepared (p. 263)	❏	❏
● order food in a restaurant (p. 271)	❏	❏
● buy food in a market or supermarket (p. 273)	❏	❏
● combine strategies to better understand when listening (p. 274)	❏	❏
● write about a childhood memory (p. 275)	❏	❏
Cultura		
● discuss meals of the Spanish-speaking world and when they are eaten (p. 256)	❏	❏
● give examples of the variety of foods in the Spanish-speaking world (p. 265)	❏	❏
● give at least two interesting facts about Chile and Paraguay (pp. 276–277)	❏	❏
Ambiciones siniestras		
● predict what will happen in a reading (p. 278)	❏	❏
● share the content of the latest message the students have received (p. 280)	❏	❏

VOCABULARIO ACTIVO

CD 3
Tracks 6-19

Las carnes y las aves *Meat and poultry*

las aves	*poultry*
el bistec	*steak*
la carne	*meat*
la hamburguesa	*hamburger*
el jamón	*ham*
el perro caliente	*hot dog*
el pollo	*chicken*

El pescado y los mariscos *Fish and seafood*

el atún	*tuna*
los camarones (*pl.*)	*shrimp*
el pescado	*fish*

Las frutas *Fruit*

la banana/el plátano	*banana*
el limón	*lemon*
la manzana	*apple*
el melón	*melon*
la naranja	*orange*
la pera	*pear*
el tomate	*tomato*

Las verduras *Vegetables*

la cebolla	*onion*
el chile	*chili pepper*
la ensalada	*salad*
los frijoles (*pl.*)	*beans*
la lechuga	*lettuce*
el maíz	*corn*
la papa /la patata	*potato*
las papas fritas (*pl.*)	*french fries; potato chips*
la verdura	*vegetable*

Los postres *Desserts*

los dulces	*candy; sweets*
las galletas	*cookies; crackers*
el helado	*ice cream*
el pastel	*pastry; pie*
el postre	*dessert*
la torta	*cake*

Las bebidas *Beverages*

el agua (con hielo)	*water (with ice)*
el café	*coffee*
la cerveza	*beer*
el jugo	*juice*
la leche	*milk*
el refresco	*soft drink*
el té (helado/caliente)	*tea (iced/hot)*
el vino	*wine*

Más comidas *More foods*

el arroz	*rice*
el cereal	*cereal*
el huevo	*egg*
el pan	*bread*
el queso	*cheese*
la sopa	*soup*
la tostada	*toast*

Las comidas *Meals*

el almuerzo	*lunch*
la cena	*dinner*
la comida	*food; meal*
el desayuno	*breakfast*
la merienda	*snack*

Verbos · *Verbs*

almorzar (ue)	*to have lunch*
andar	*to walk*
beber	*to drink*
cocinar	*to cook*
conducir	*to drive*
cenar	*to have dinner*
desayunar	*to have breakfast*
merendar	*to have a snack*

Los condimentos y las especias · *Condiments and spices*

el aceite	*oil*
el azúcar	*sugar*
la mantequilla	*butter*
la mayonesa	*mayonnaise*
la mermelada	*jam; marmalade*
la mostaza	*mustard*
la pimienta	*pepper*
la sal	*salt*
la salsa de tomate	*ketchup*
el vinagre	*vinegar*

Unos términos de cocina · *Cooking terms*

a la parrilla	*grilled*
al horna	*baked*
asado/a	*roasted; grilled*
bien cocido/a	*well done*
bien hecho/a	*well cooked*
caliente	*hot (temperature)*
cocido/a	*boiled; baked*
crudo/a	*rare; raw*
duro/a	*hard-boiled*
fresco/a	*fresh*
frito/a	*fried*
helado/a	*iced*
hervido/a	*boiled*
picante	*spicy*
poco hecho/a	*rare*
término medio	*medium*

En el restaurante · *In the restaurant*

el/la camarero/a	*waiter/waitress*
el/la cliente/a	*customer; client*
el/la cocinero/a	*cook*
la cuchara	*soup spoon; tablespoon*
la cucharita	*teaspoon*
el cuchillo	*knife*
la especialidad de la casa	*specialty of the house*
el mantel	*tablecloth*
el menú	*menu*
el plato	*plate; dish*
la propina	*tip*
la servilleta	*napkin*
la tarjeta de crédito	*credit card*
la taza	*cup*
el tenedor	*fork*
el vaso	*glass*

Verbos · *Verbs*

pagar	*to pay*
pedir	*to order*
reservar una mesa	*to reserve a table*

Otras palabras útiles · *Other useful words*

anoche	*last night*
anteayer	*the day before yesterday*
el año pasado	*last year*
ayer	*yesterday*
barato/a	*cheap*
¡Buen provecho!	*Enjoy your meal!*
caro/a	*expensive*
cerca (de)	*near*
debajo (de)	*under; underneath*
encima (de)	*on top (of); above*
el fin de semana pasado	*last weekend*
el… (jueves) pasado	*last… (Thursday)*
La cuenta, por favor.	*The check, please.*
la semana pasada	*last week*
más tarde que	*later than*
más temprano que	*earlier than*

283

¿Qué te pones?

En los países hispanohablantes la gente lleva (*wears*) ropa (*clothing*) muy similar a la que llevan por todo el mundo pero también se usa ropa más tradicional. Por ejemplo, en México se encuentran sarapes, ponchos y huaraches y en Colombia usan rebozos (*ponchos*) y alpargatas (*espadrilles*).

NATIONAL STANDARDS

Comunicación

- To describe what you and others are wearing as well as your clothing preferences (Communication, Cultures, Comparisons)
- To talk about to whom and for whom things are done (Communication)
- To discuss what delights, fascinates, bothers, matters, and is needed by you and others (Communication)
- To describe your typical day and compare it to that of a classmate (Communication, Comparisons)
- To describe situations in the past and share how things used to be (Communication)
- To guess the meaning of unfamiliar words, when listening, from the context (Communication, Connections)
- To write an e-mail about your childhood (Communication, Cultures, Comparisons, Connections, Communities)

Cultura

- To talk about a Spanish clothing company (Communication, Cultures, Connections, Comparisons)
- To discuss shopping in the Spanish-speaking world (Communication, Cultures, Connections, Comparisons)
- To share important facts about this chapter's featured countries: Argentina and Uruguay (Cultures, Comparisons)

Ambiciones siniestras

- To guess the meaning of unfamiliar words in a reading passage (Connections, Communication)
- To explain the significance of the latest e-mail from el Sr. Verdugo (Communication)
- To reveal some secrets regarding Lupe (Communication)

SECTION GOALS FOR
Chapter Opener

By the end of the Chapter Opener section, students will be able to:

- identify in what country the people wear certain items of clothing.
- make comparisons between American and Hispanic fashions.

OBJETIVOS

Comunicación

- To describe what you and others are wearing as well as your clothing preferences
- To talk about to whom and for whom things are done
- To discuss what delights, fascinates, bothers, matters, and is needed by you and others
- To describe your typical day and compare it to that of a classmate
- To describe situations in the past and share how things used to be
- To guess the meaning of unfamiliar words, when listening, from the context
- To write an e-mail about your childhood

Cultura

- To talk about a Spanish clothing company
- To discuss shopping in the Spanish-speaking world
- To share important facts about this chapter's featured countries: Argentina and Uruguay

Ambiciones siniestras

- To guess the meaning of unfamiliar words in a reading passage
- To explain the significance of the latest e-mail from el Sr. Verdugo
- To reveal some secrets regarding Lupe

NATIONAL STANDARDS
Communities

If you have a large Hispanic community in your area, you might ask students to volunteer their time at a local church, women's shelter, or other social service agency that collects clothing. There are several organizations throughout the United States, such as Dress for Success, Goodwill, and the Salvation Army, that accept clothing donations for resale. Some churches and welfare agencies collect new and gently used items of clothing for redistribution. If you have a children's hospital, cancer treatment facility, or hospice in the area, you might consider asking students to collect clothing that can be turned into quilt squares. Then students can cut the squares for hand or machine piecing. Donate the quilts to children, homeless, senior citizens, or relatives of hospice patients.

RECURSOS

Lesson Plan

NATIONAL STANDARDS
Cultures

It is important to reinforce the idea that students around the Spanish-speaking world share the same clothing "uniform" of jeans/slacks and T-shirts/shirts. Too often American students have the stereotypical notion that indigenous clothing is the only way of dressing. Nevertheless, it is important to share photos of indigenous peoples from the Spanish-speaking world so that your students will have a clearer picture of the diversity of *los hispanohablantes*. Actividad **8-5** involves students describing the dress of indigenous people from different parts of Latin America, as depicted in the photos on p. 288.

NOTE FOR

Chapter Opener

You may wish to ask your students to give their impressions regarding the photo for this chapter opener. Also, have the students read the objectives for the chapter silently. We suggest you spend no more than 5 to 7 minutes on chapter openers.

PLANNING AHEAD

Inform students that they will need to bring in photos of fashion models from magazines, catalogs, or the Internet for actividad **8-6.** You will want to have extras on hand for the students who have trouble gathering the materials or forget to bring them to class.

METHODOLOGY • Contrasting and Comparing

Whenever possible, every effort will be made to have students make comparisons between the culture of their home/university community and what they are currently learning. Additionally, as appropriate, the students will be asked to compare what they are currently learning with what they learned in previous chapters.

*Óscar de la Renta:
diseñador dominicano*

PREGUNTAS

1 ¿Qué tipo de ropa te gusta? ¿Prefieres la ropa formal o la ropa informal?

2 ¿Te interesa la moda *(fashion)*? ¿Te interesan distintos tipos de ropa? Explica.

3 ¿Qué semejanzas hay entre la ropa de la gente joven y la gente mayor en los Estados Unidos? ¿Qué diferencias hay?

285

METHODOLOGY • Making Topics Relevant for Students

The opening questions for each chapter begin with your learners and their preferences, something that we have learned from educational philosopher John Dewey. Try having your students turn to a partner and answer the questions in pairs. Then have them share the answers their partners gave. This has them practice listening and paraphrasing.

METHODOLOGY • Meaningful Learning

One purpose of the discussion questions is to begin with a topic with which your students are familiar so they can see how the major theme of the chapter relates to their lives. This facilitates learning by encouraging active mental participation in relating new material to existing knowledge, the basic tenet of Ausubel's "meaningful learning." (Ausubel, D. *Educational Psychology: A cognitive view.* New York: Holt, Rinehart & Winston 1968)

CAPÍTULO 8

Comunicación

- Discussing clothing
- Talking about to whom and for whom something is done
- Expressing likes and dislikes

VOCABULARIO 1 La ropa

8-1 to 8-8

7:00

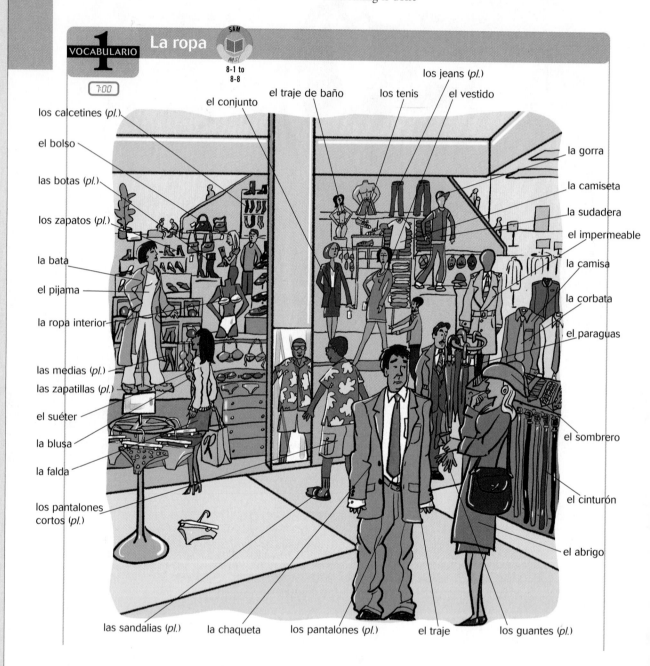

los calcetines (*pl.*)
el bolso
las botas (*pl.*)
los zapatos (*pl.*)
la bata
el pijama
la ropa interior
las medias (*pl.*)
las zapatillas (*pl.*)
el suéter
la blusa
la falda
los pantalones cortos (*pl.*)
las sandalias (*pl.*)
la chaqueta
los pantalones (*pl.*)
el traje
los guantes (*pl.*)
el conjunto
el traje de baño
los tenis
los jeans (*pl.*)
el vestido
la gorra
la camiseta
la sudadera
el impermeable
la camisa
la corbata
el paraguas
el sombrero
el cinturón
el abrigo

RECURSOS		
T8-1 to T8-3	T8-1 to T8-3	Electronic Activity Cache

Las telas y los materiales	*Fabrics and materials*	elegante	*elegant*
el algodón	cotton	estampado/a	print; with a design or pattern
el cuero	leather	estrecho/a	narrow; tight
la lana	wool	formal	formal
el poliéster	polyester	informal	casual
la seda	silk	largo/a	long
una tela/falda/pantalón etc. …		liso/a	solid-colored
de cuadros	checked	oscuro/a	dark
de lunares	polka-dotted		
de rayas	striped	**Unos verbos**	*Some verbs*
		llevar	to wear; to take; to carry
Unos adjetivos	*Some adjectives*	llevar puesto	to wear; to have on
ancho/a	wide	quedar bien/mal	to fit well/poorly
atrevido/a	daring		
claro/a	light (colored)	**Otras palabras útiles**	*Other useful words*
cómodo/a	comfortable	la moda	fashion; style
corto/a	short	el modelo	male model
		la modelo	female model

Fíjate

In your vocabulary list you see the letters (*pl.*) beside words such as *las medias* or *los jeans* to indicate that they are plural in Spanish. You will also notice (*pl.*) beside *los calcetines*. Each sock is a *calcetín*.

CW eBook
CD 3
Track 20

SAM
8-9 to
8-11

PRONUNCIACIÓN 5:00

The letters ll and ñ

1. The **ll** is pronounced by most Spanish speakers like the *y* in the English word *yellow*.

   zapatilla   llevar   cuchillo   servilleta

2. The **ñ** is pronounced like the *ny* in the English word *canyon*.

   año   mañana   campaña   bañera

8·1   **Las palabras**

Pronounce the following words, paying special attention to the letters **ll** and **ñ**.

1. llamo
2. llegamos
3. millón
4. ella
5. señores
6. niños
7. enseñamos
8. pequeñas
9. años

8·2   **Las oraciones**

Pronounce the following sentences, paying special attention to the letters **ll** and **ñ**.

1. ¿Llevas las zapatillas amarillas?
2. Enseño a niños pequeños.

8·3   **Los dichos y refranes**

Now pronounce the following sayings and focus on the letters **ll** and **ñ**.

1. El que busca, halla.
2. Donde hay gana hay maña.

[4:00]

8·4 ¡Señoras y señores!

Dibujen un diagrama de Venn según el modelo. En el círculo izquierdo, hagan una lista de la ropa que generalmente llevan las mujeres. En el círculo derecho, hagan una lista de la ropa que generalmente llevan los hombres. En el centro donde se juntan los círculos (*where circles overlap*), hagan una lista de la ropa que los hombres y las mujeres llevan. ¿Que lista es más larga?

Fíjate

You have noticed that *¡Anda!* makes extensive use of pair and group work in the classroom to provide you with many opportunities during the class period to practice Spanish. When working in pairs or groups, it's imperative that you make every effort to speak only Spanish.

MODELO

la ropa de mujeres   la ropa que sirve para hombres y mujeres   la ropa de hombres

[3:00]

8·5 ¿Cómo se visten?

Túrnense para describir qué ropa llevan las personas en las fotos.

MODELO: *Los hombres llevan pantalones blancos.*

Estrategia

Remember that adjectives describe nouns and agree in number (singular/plural) and gender (masculine/feminine) with the nouns they are describing.

[4:00]

8·6 ¿Qué está de moda?

Trae a la clase tres o cuatro fotos de modelos (pueden ser de una revista (*magazine*), un catálogo o del Internet). Túrnate con un/a compañero/a para describir en por lo menos **tres** frases lo que los modelos llevan puesto. Digan qué ropa les gusta más y qué ropa les gusta menos. ¿Están de acuerdo?

NUESTRA MODA
¡Prepárate para la primavera!
Una entrevista con la gran diseñadora Carolina Herrera

LOS HOMBRES
¡El mundo deportivo!

Answers to 8-7.
Sample answers include:
1. un abrigo, unos guantes, un suéter, pantalones largos, pantalones vaqueros, camisas/blusas, zapatos
2. un traje de baño, pantalones cortos, zapatos de tenis, sandalias, pantalones largos, camisetas, camisas/blusas
3. pantalones largos y cortos, unas camisas/blusas, una chaqueta, camisetas
4. un traje de baño, pantalones cortos, zapatos de tenis, sandalias, pantalones largos, camisetas, camisas/blusas
5. pantalones largos y cortos, unas camisas/blusas, una chaqueta, camisetas
6. un abrigo, unos guantes, un suéter, pantalones largos, pantalones vaqueros, camisas/blusas, zapatos

[5:00]

8·7 Señora, ¿qué debo llevar?

Trabajas para una agencia de viajes y, para ayudar a tus clientes, tienes que preparar una lista de la ropa que deben llevar a cada destino (*destination*). Compara tu lista con la de un/a compañero/a.

Capítulo Preliminar A. Los días, los meses y las estaciones, pág. 20.

1. Argentina en julio
2. Costa Rica en junio
3. México en septiembre
4. Cuba en diciembre
5. Uruguay en marzo
6. España en febrero

8·8 El juego del viaje (*travel*)   5:00

¿Te gusta viajar? Formen un círculo de cinco estudiantes o más. Primero, decidan dónde quieren ir de viaje. Después, túrnense para decir sus nombres y un artículo de ropa que quieren llevar. Cada estudiante tiene que repetir lo que dijeron los estudiantes anteriores. **¡OJO!** Si no recuerdan (*If you don't remember*), tienen que preguntar: **¿Qué dijiste, por favor?** o **¿Puedes repetir, por favor?**

MODELO   Vamos a Cancún.

E1:   *Soy Beverly y voy a llevar un traje de baño.*

E2:   *Soy Tim y voy a llevar una camiseta blanca.*
       Beverly va a llevar un traje de baño.

E3:   *Soy Kelly y voy a llevar una chaqueta.*
       Tim va a llevar una camiseta blanca.
       Beverly va a llevar un traje de baño.

E4:   …

Estrategia

It is important to be supportive of your fellow classmates during these activities, which includes making suggestions and helpful comments and corrections. Because you will be learning from each other, it is good to know the following expressions to help you interact with each other:

(No) Estoy de acuerdo.	I agree./I don't agree.
Yo pienso que es…	I think it's…
¿No debería ser…?	Shouldn't it be…?

Capítulo 4. Ir + a + infinitivo, pág. 149;
Capítulo 5. Los pronombres de complemento directo, pág. 190;
Capítulo 7. El pretérito, pág. 258.

6:00   ## 8·9 ¿Tienes un presupuesto (*budget*)?

Completa el siguiente cuadro con las prendas que acabas de comprar (*have just bought*) y con las que necesitas comprar. Después, comparte tus respuestas con un/a compañero/a.

Fíjate

The expression *acabar de + infinitive* means *to have just done something*. Use this expression in the present tense when you want to refer to the very recent past. As in the *modelo*, this expression is useful for establishing a context for the use of the preterit.

MODELO   *Acabo de comprar una blusa. La compré en J.C. Penney la semana pasada.*
       Pagué quince dólares. Necesito comprar una falda.

ACABO DE COMPRAR…	LO(S)/LA(S) COMPRÉ…	PAGUÉ…	VOY A/NECESITO COMPRAR…
1. *una blusa*	*en J.C. Penney*	*$15*	*una falda*
2.			
3.			

Additional activity for *La ropa*

Mi definición de "atractivo". Escoge un/a modelo que te parezca atractivo/a en una revista o catálogo. Tu compañero/a te va a hacer por lo menos tres preguntas sobre cinco páginas para tratar de localizar al/a la modelo en la revista. Túrnense.

MODELO

¿Lleva pantalones o falda? ¿Lleva una corbata?

4:00 **8·10 ¿Quién puede ser?**

Escoge a una persona de tu clase y piensa en la ropa que lleva incluyendo el estilo (*style*), el color y la tela. Describe **cuatro** de sus prendas a tu compañero/a, quien tiene que adivinar a quién describes. Túrnense para describir a **tres** compañeros de clase.

MODELO E1: *Esta persona lleva unos pantalones largos de rayas blancas, una camiseta oscura, una chaqueta informal y unos zapatos de tenis blancos.*

E2: *Es Mayra.*

3:00 8-12 to 8-13

Zara: la moda internacional

En España, uno de los negocios más florecientes (*flourishing*) es la empresa de ropa Zara. El fundador, Amancio Ortega Gaona, empezó el negocio (*business*) en La Coruña, en el norte de España, con unas 5.000 pesetas ($83.00 US). Ahora el Sr. Ortega es uno de los hombres más ricos de este país.

> **Fíjate**
>
> In 2002, Spain converted to the *euro*. Previously, its currency was the *peseta*.

Una de las razones del gran éxito del negocio es que continuamente ofrece lo que la gente quiere. Su filosofía es vender ropa "barata y de buena calidad". Tiene unos doscientos diseñadores (*designers*) que son los responsables de crear la moda Zara. Las diferentes líneas creadas por los diseñadores proporcionan un *look* completo para hombres y mujeres.

La mayoría de la ropa se hace en una fábrica (*factory*) muy moderna en La Coruña. Desde el momento que surge la idea hasta que la prenda llega a la tienda, sólo pasan unas tres semanas. Dos o tres veces por semana llegan productos nuevos a las tiendas y así se renueva más del cuarenta por ciento del inventario.

Ahora se puede comprar la moda Zara en más de 626 tiendas en 46 países, por catálogo y por el Internet. Para conocer la moda internacional del momento, hay que conocer Zara.

Preguntas

1. ¿Quién empezó el negocio Zara y dónde? ¿Cuánto le costó?
   Amancio Ortega Gaona empezó Zara. Le costó 5.000 pesetas ($83.00 US).
2. ¿Por qué tiene tanto éxito el negocio? Zara tiene tanto éxito porque vende ropa barata y de buena calidad.

Suggestion for *Los pronombres de complemento indirecto* You may want to remind students or make the connection between *me* and *te* in *me gusta/te gusta (Capítulo 2)* and this new grammar presentation.

METHODOLOGY • Presenting Grammar Inductively

You will recall that we suggested having students read the grammar presentations before coming to class. They have been written clearly and simply so that all students can understand them. With the inductive presentations, we have provided a series of questions that the students should answer at home that help guide them to state their rules. In class, we suggest checking for comprehension by quickly reviewing all of the questions.

2 GRAMÁTICA Los pronombres de complemento indirecto

8-14 to
8-16

33, 34

5:00

The indirect object indicates *to whom* or *for whom* an action is done. Note these examples:

A: My mom bought this dress *for whom?*

B: She bought this dress *for you.*

A: Yes, she bought *me* this dress.

Review the chart of the indirect object pronouns and their English equivalents:

¿Éste es el vestido que mi madre me compró?

Los pronombres de complemento indirecto	
me	*to/for me*
te	*to/for you*
le	*to/for him, her, you* (Ud.)
nos	*to/for us*
os	*to/for you all* (vosotros)
les	*to/for them, you all* (Uds.)

Now study the sentences in the following box and answer the questions that follow.

Mi madre	**me**	compra mucha ropa.
Mi madre	**te**	compra mucha ropa.
Mi madre	**le**	compra mucha ropa a mi hermano.
Mi madre	**nos**	compra mucha ropa.
Mi madre	**os**	compra mucha ropa.
Mi madre	**les**	compra mucha ropa a mis hermanos.

In each of the above sentences:

1. Who is *buying* the clothing?

2. Who is *receiving* the clothing?

Check your answers to the preceding questions in Appendix 1.

Now, look at the following examples. Can you identify the direct objects along with the indirect object pronouns?

¿Me traes la falda de rayas?   *Will you bring me the striped skirt?*

Su novio le regaló la chaqueta de cuero.   *Her boyfriend gave her the leather jacket.*

Mi hermana me compró la blusa de seda.   *My sister bought me the silk blouse.*

Nuestra compañera de cuarto nos lavó la ropa. *Our roommate washed our clothes for us.*

RECURSOS

8-G2	Electronic Activity Cache

Some things to remember:

1. Like direct object pronouns, indirect object pronouns *precede* the verb and can also be *attached to infinitives and present participles* (**-ando, -iendo**).

¿**Me** quieres dar el dinero?
¿Quieres dar**me** el dinero?
} *Do you want to give me the money?*

¿**Me** vas a dar el dinero?
¿Vas a dar**me** el dinero?
} *Are you going to give me the money?*

¿**Me** estás dando el dinero?
¿Estás dándo**me** el dinero?
} *Are you giving me the money?*

Manolo **te** puede comprar la gorra en la tienda.
Manolo puede comprar**te** la gorra en la tienda.
} *Manolo can buy you the hat at the store.*

Su hermano **le** va a regalar una camiseta.
Su hermano va a regalar**le** una camiseta.
} *Her brother is going to give her a T-shirt.*

2. To clarify or emphasize the indirect object, a prepositional phrase (**a** + *prepositional pronoun*) can be added, as in the following sentences. Clarification of **le** and **les** is especially important since they can refer to different people (*him, her, you, them, you all*).

Le presto el abrigo **a él** pero no **le** presto nada **a ella.**
I'm loaning him my coat but I'm not loaning her anything. (clarification)

¿**Me** preguntas **a mí**?
Are you asking me? (emphasis)

3. As you have seen, indirect object pronouns are used without the indirect object noun when the person to/for whom the action is being done is known.

 8·11 Amigos perfectos

Cuando sus mejores amigos celebran sus cumpleaños, tu pareja y tú siempre organizan las fiestas. Juntos escriban frases sobre las cosas que hacen, usando **me, te, nos, le** y **les.**

MODELO E1: yo/preparar/las fiestas de cumpleaños/para mis amigos

E2: *Yo preparo las fiestas de cumpleaños <u>para mis amigos</u>. / <u>Les</u> preparo las fiestas.*

1. yo/preparar/una fiesta de sorpresa/para él o ella
2. yo/mandar/invitaciones/a todos nuestros amigos
3. mis otros amigos y yo/comprar/unos regalos cómicos/para él o ella
4. yo/hacer/una torta/para mi amigo
5. nosotros/dar/unas flores bonitas/a nuestra amiga
6. nosotros/cantar/a nuestro amigo/una canción especial

Expansion for 8-12 Play the role of the counselor and have students respond with the appropriate verb and indirect object pronoun changes. You can also offer the following similar activity:

¡Qué consejos! Los consejeros normalmente les dan mucha información a los estudiantes nuevos durante la orientación. De los siguientes comentarios posibles, ¿cuáles son probables y cuáles son improbables?

MODELO

Les digo que tenemos una universidad muy buena.

E1 *Nos dice que tenemos una universidad muy buena. Es probable.*

1. Les pido información sobre sus familias.
2. Les pregunto cuáles son sus especialidades.
3. Les doy las reglas (*rules*) de la universidad.
4. Les prometo mi ayuda.
5. Les recomiendo la cafetería.
6. También les recomiendo el restaurante El Pollo Loco.
7. Les explico que no deben (*should not, must not*) estudiar mucho.
8. Les recomiendo clases fáciles.
9. Les digo que pueden salir hasta muy tarde todas las noches.
10. Les digo que no tienen que regresar a la residencia hasta las dos de la mañana.
11. Finalmente, les recomiendo que tomen una clase de español.

NOTE FOR 8-14

You may wish to prepare a list of possible "presents" for the students to choose from if time is a factor.

NOTE ON *Gustar*

We have chosen to utilize natural English and to present the verb *gustar* as "to like." You may differ and choose to present *gustar* as "to be pleasing."

8·12 ¿Qué me recomienda? `5:00`

Una persona hace el papel de consejero/a y la otra de estudiante de primer año (*freshman*). Deben hacer y contestar las siguientes preguntas según el modelo. Al terminar, cambien de papel.

MODELO E1: ¿Me recomienda la clase de Conversación 101?

E2: *No, no le recomiendo esa clase. Le recomiendo la clase de civilización española.*

1. ¿Me está pidiendo Ud. información sobre mi familia?
2. ¿Me recomienda Ud. algunas clases fáciles?
3. ¿Me ayuda Ud. con mis estudios?
4. ¿Me recomienda Ud. jugar algún deporte?
5. ¿Me recomienda Ud. hablar con mis profesores fuera de clase?
6. ¿Me recomienda Ud. la cafetería?

Capítulo 3. Los quehaceres de la casa, pág. 112; Capítulo 7. El pretérito, pág. 258.

8·13 ¡Qué suerte! `5:00`

Haz una lista de por lo menos **cuatro** cosas que tú hiciste por tu compañero/a de cuarto o tu familia la semana pasada. Después, haz otra lista de tres o cuatro cosas que esa persona hizo por ti. Compara tu lista con la de un/a compañero/a.

MODELO E1: *A mi compañero de cuarto le arreglé la sala y le contesté el teléfono.*

E2: *Mi compañera de cuarto me lavó la ropa. Me preparó la comida…*

8·14 Los regalos `5:00`

Capítulo 7. El pretérito, pág. 258.

¿Te regalaron muchas cosas este año? ¿Regalaste muchas cosas tú? Escribe una lista de **cuatro** regalos que te dieron y de **cuatro** cosas que tú les regalaste. Después comparte tu lista con un/a compañero/a según el modelo. ¡Hay que ser creativos!

MODELO E1: *Le di una corbata a mi padre.*

E2: *¿Ah sí? ¿De qué color? ¿Le gustó a tu padre?*

E1: *Sí, le gustó mucho la corbata azul. Y mis padres me regalaron una bicicleta.*

E2: *¡Qué suerte! ¿Te gusta andar en bicicleta?*

Fíjate

As in English, there are word "families." *El regalo* (noun) means "gift" and *regalar* (verb) means "to give a gift."

GRAMÁTICA 3 — *Gustar* y **verbos como** *gustar*

`3:00`

¡Me encanta el vestido!

8-17 to 8-20   11, 12, 15, 19

As you already know, the verb **gustar** is used to express likes and dislikes. **Gustar** functions differently from other verbs you have studied so far.

• The person, thing, or idea that is liked is the *subject* (S) of the sentence.

• The person who likes the other person, thing, or idea is the *indirect object* (IO).

Consider the chart below:

(A mí) **me** gusta el traje.	*I like the suit.*	(A nosotros/as) **nos** gusta el traje.	*We like the suit.*
(A ti) **te** gusta el traje.	*You like the suit.*	(A vosotros/as) **os** gusta el traje.	*You (all) like the suit.*
(A él) **le** gusta el traje.	*He likes the suit.*	(A ellos/as) **les** gusta el traje.	*They like the suit.*
(A ella) **le** gusta el traje.	*She likes the suit.*	(A Uds.) **les** gusta el traje.	*You (all) like the suit.*
(A Ud.) **le** gusta el traje.	*You like the suit.*		

Note the following:

1. The construction **a** + *pronoun* (**a mí, a ti, a él,** etc.) or **a** + *noun* is optional most of the time. It is used for clarification or emphasis. Clarification of **le gusta** and **les gusta** is especially important since the indirect object pronouns **le** and **les** can refer to different people (*him, her, you, them, you all*).

A él le gusta llevar ropa cómoda. (clarification)	*He likes to wear comfortable clothes.*
A Ana le gusta llevar ropa cómoda. (clarification)	*Ana likes to wear comfortable clothes.*
Me gustan esos pantalones de lunares.	*I like those pants with the polka dots.*
A mí me gustan más ésos de rayas (emphasis).	*I like those striped ones even more.*

2. Use the plural form **gustan** when what is liked (the subject of the sentence) is plural.

Me gusta **el traje.** → Me gusta**n** **los trajes.**
I like the suit.   *I like the suits.*

3. To express the idea that one likes *to do* something, **gustar** is followed by an infinitive. In that case you always use the singular **gusta,** even when you use more than one infinitive in the sentence:

Me gusta ir de compras por la mañana.	*I like to go shopping in the morning.*
A Pepe **le gusta leer** revistas de moda y **llevar** ropa atrevida.	*Pepe likes to read fashion magazines and wear daring clothing.*
Nos gusta hacer ejercicio y **andar** antes de ir a clase.	*We like to exercise and walk before going to class.*

The verbs listed below function like **gustar:**

encantar	*to love; delight*	**importar**	*to matter; to be important*
fascinar	*to fascinate*	**molestar**	*to bother*
hacer falta	*to need; to be lacking*		

Me encanta ir de compras.	*I love to go shopping. (Shopping delights me.)*
A Doug y a David **les fascina** la tienda de ropa Rugby.	*The Rugby clothing store fascinates (is fascinating to) Doug and David.*
¿**Te hace falta** dinero para comprar el vestido?	*Do you need (are you lacking) money to buy the dress?*
A Juan **le importa** el precio de la ropa, no la moda.	*The price of the clothing, not the style, matters (is important) to Juan.*
Nos molestan las personas que llevan sandalias en invierno.	*People who wear sandals in the winter bother us.*

Additional activity for *Gustar y verbos como gustar*

Ideas incompletas
Completa las siguientes oraciones. Después, compártelas con un/a compañero/a.
1. En invierno me encanta(n) . . .
2. A mis profesores les molesta(n) . . .
3. A mi mejor amigo/a no le importa(n) . . .
4. A los estudiantes de español les fascina(n) . . .
5. A mis compañeros de clase y a mí nos hace(n) falta . . .

CULTURAL BACKGROUND
FOR 8-16

Some of the people mentioned in
actividad **8-16** might not be familiar
to you or your students.
Salvador Dalí: Spanish surrealist
painter.
Diego Rivera: Mexican muralist (his
wife was Frida Kahlo, a famous
Mexican painter).
Gloria Estefan: Cuban singer (for-
merly of the Miami Sound Machine)
came to the United States in 1959
and has been making music in
Miami for decades.
Carlos Santana: Mexican musician,
but has spent the majority of his life
in the United States making Grammy
Award-winning music with his band
Santana.
Pablo Neruda: Chilean author, won a
Nobel Prize in Literature for his
poetry.
Isabel Allende: contemporary
Chilean author who incorporates
magical realism in some of her
work.
Antonio Banderas: Spanish actor.
Salma Hayek: Mexican actress.

Sugggestion for 8-16 Actividad
8-16 encourages students to give
their opinions about the famous
people listed. In addition to practicing with *gustar* and similar verbs,
you can use this activity to reinforce
their mastery of *saber* and *conocer*
with direct object pronouns. For
each question, think of a follow-up
question to practice with direct
object pronouns and *saber* or
conocer. ¿Sabes quién es Óscar de
la Renta? ¿Conoces las novelas
de Isabel Allende? ¿Conoces las
pinturas de Salvador Dalí? ¿Sabes
cómo se llama el grupo musical de
Gloria Estefan? ¿Sabes quién es la
esposa de Antonio Banderas?
¿Conoces las pinturas de la esposa
de Diego Rivera? ¿Conoces el país
de origen de Salma Hayek?, etc.

Capítulo 5. El mundo de la música, pág. 172.

8·15 Hablando de la música... 5:00

A Jaime y a Celia les gusta mucho la música. Completa las oraciones para descubrir sus preferencias. Después, comparte tu párrafo con un/a compañero/a.

MODELO A nosotros *nos fascina* (fascinar) la música rap.

A nosotros (1) __nos encanta__ (encantar) la música rock. A mí (2) __me gustan__ (gustar) los grupos como Aerosmith y Tool. Mi cantante favorito es Dave Matthews y (3) __me gusta__ (gustar) su grupo también. A Celia (4) __le fascina__ (fascinar) el grupo No Doubt. Celia tiene casi todos los CD pero (5) __le hace falta__ (hacer falta) uno que se llama *Running*. A nuestros compañeros (6) __les molesta__ (molestar) tener que escuchar nuestra música favorita. Ellos prefieren la música jazz. A Celia y a mí no (7) __nos importa__ (importar) su opinión, ¡somos amigos pero no nos tienen que gustar las mismas cosas siempre!

5:00 ## 8·16 ¿Qué opinas?

Da tu opinión sobre estas personas famosas poniendo una equis (**X**) en la columna apropiada. Después, comparte tu opinión con un/a compañero/a.

MODELO E1: *¿Te fascinan los diseños de Óscar de la Renta y Narciso Rodríguez?*
E2: *Sí, me fascinan. / No, no me importan mucho. / No sé, no los conozco.*

Salvador Dalí

Gloria Estefan

Antonio Banderas

Isabel Allende

Diego Rivera

Carlos Santana

Salma Hayek

Pablo Neruda

	ME FASCINA(N)	ME ENCANTA(N)	NO ME IMPORTA(N) MUCHO	NO LO(S)/LA(S) CONOZCO
1. las pinturas de Salvador Dalí				
2. las canciones de Gloria Estefan				
3. las películas de Antonio Banderas				
4. las novelas de Isabel Allende				
5. los murales de Diego Rivera				
6. la música de Carlos Santana				
7. las películas de Salma Hayek				
8. los poemas de Pablo Neruda				

8·17   En mi opinión...

¿Qué te gusta y no te gusta de tu universidad?

Paso 1   Completa el siguiente cuadro según tu opinión.

ME MOLESTA(N)...	ME ENCANTA(N)...	NOS HACE(N) FALTA...
1.	1.	1.
2.	2.	2.
3.	3.	3.

Paso 2   Ahora, circula por la clase para pedirles a tres compañeros su opinión.

MODELO   E1 (TÚ):   *¿Qué te molesta?*

                E2:   *Me molesta la comida de la cafetería.*

A ____ LE MOLESTA(N)...	A ____ LE ENCANTA(N)...	NOS HACE(N) FALTA...
1.	1.	1.
2.	2.	2.
3.	3.	3.

METHODOLOGY • Practice in the Classroom

Up to this point, we have spent a good deal of time addressing the benefits of pair and group work. Practice is the way that students gain confidence as well as improve their speaking skills. Another piece of research states that if "students can say it, they can write it." This research comes from the literature of English as a Second Language (ESL), as well as literacy literature. It states that an individual usually cannot write at a higher level than he/she can speak. Yes, there are some exceptions to this rule, but for the most part this is true. Think about your students in the past. The best writers tend to have the best verbal skills. This does not mean that their spelling will be perfect, but they should be able to express themselves. Hence, we encourage you to give your students as many opportunities as possible to use Spanish in the classroom.

Follow-up to 8-16 Once students have paired up and shared their opinions about the famous people, have them report what they have learned about their partner's opinions to the class. Do they share the same opinions? Is there a person that the entire class likes?

Additional activity for *Gustar y verbos como gustar*

 Preferencias ¿Qué opinas? Responde a estas situaciones usando **encantar, fascinar, importar** y **molestar.** Comparte tus respuestas con un/a compañero/a.

MODELO
E1: *comprar ropa en Target*
E2: *Me encanta comprar ropa en Target. Me queda muy bien. / No me gusta comprar ropa en Target. Me queda grande.*

1. llevar ropa estrecha
2. combinar ropa de rayas con ropa de lunares
3. llevar sandalias en el invierno
4. comprar ropa de seda
5. tener que ponerme (*put on*) ropa formal
6. correr con zapatos elegantes
7. ponerme un traje de baño
8. llevar pantalones sin cinturón

GRAMÁTICA **Los pronombres de complemento directo e indirecto usados juntos**

SAM 8-21 to 8-25   Guide **G** 20, 34

`3:00`

> ¡Me encanta la blusa verde de seda!

> ¿Sí, amor? Pues, entramos. Te la compro ahora mismo.

You have worked with two types of object pronouns, direct and indirect. Now note how they are used together in the same sentence.

La profesora **nos** está devolviendo **los exámenes**.	→ La profesora **nos los** está devolviendo.
The professor is giving us back the exams.	*The professor is giving them back to us.*
¡Ella no **nos** regala **las notas**!	→ ¡Ella no **nos las** regala!
She does not give away grades!	*She does not give them to us!*
Tatiana **me** pide **dinero** ahora.	→ Tatiana **me lo** pide ahora.
Tatiana is asking me for money now.	*Tatiana is asking me for it now.*
Mi novio **me** trae **la comida**.	→ Mi novio **me la** trae.
My boyfriend brings me food.	*My boyfriend brings it to me.*

1. You know that direct and indirect objects come after the verb. Where do you find the direct and indirect object pronouns?
2. Reading from left to right, which pronoun comes first (direct or indirect)? Which pronoun comes second?

Check your answers for the preceding questions in Appendix 1.

¡OJO! A change occurs when you use **le** or **les** along with a direct object pronoun that begins with **l**: (**lo, la, los, las**): **le** or **les** changes to **se**.

   le → se

Tatiana **le** pide un favor a él.	→	Tatiana **se lo** pide a él.
Memo **le** lleva comida a su novia.	→	Memo **se la** lleva a su novia.
La profesora no **le** regala la nota al estudiante.	→	La profesora no **se la** regala al estudiante.

   les → se

La profesora **les** devuelve los exámenes a ellos.	→	La profesora **se los** devuelve a ellos.
Ella **les** da buenas notas a todos los estudiantes.	→	Ella **se las** da a todos los estudiantes.
Yo no **le** pido un favor al profesor.	→	Yo no **se lo** pido al profesor.

RECURSOS   8-G4   Electronic Activity Cache

Direct and indirect object pronouns may also be attached to infinitives and present participles. Note that when attached, an accent is placed over the final vowel of the infinitive and the next-to-last vowel of the participle.

¿Aquel abrigo? Mi madre **me lo** va a comprar.

¿Aquel abrigo? Mi madre va a comprár**melo.**

    } *That coat over there? My mother is going to buy it for me.*

Me lo está comprando ahora.

Está comprándo**melo** ahora.

    } *She is buying it for me now.*

Capítulo 7. El pretérito, pág. 258; Unos verbos irregulares en el pretérito, pág. 266.

`3:00` **8·18** Combinaciones

Escribe oraciones completas sobre Pablo y su hermano Antonio usando los pronombres de complemento directo e indirecto. Comparte tus frases con un/a compañero/a.

MODELO   Mi hermano Antonio/prestar/(a mí)/sus libros favoritos/ayer

E1: *Mi hermano Antonio **me** prestó **sus libros favoritos** ayer.*

E2: *Mi hermano Antonio **me los** prestó ayer.*

1. Yo/dar/(a Antonio)/unos CD/la semana pasada
2. Mis padres/regalar/(a Antonio)/un coche nuevo/el año pasado
3. Yo/lavar/la ropa/(a Antonio)/anteayer
4. Antonio/cantar/una canción/(a mí)/anoche
5. Antonio y yo/decir/la verdad sobre el accidente/(a nuestros padres)/ayer

Answers to 8-19.
1. ¿Me prestas los zapatos negros?
Sí, te los presto. / No, no te los presto.
2. ¿Me prestas la corbata de rayas azules?
Sí, te la presto. / No, no te la presto.
3. ¿Me prestas una camiseta blanca y una camisa azul de manga larga?
Sí, te las presto. / No, no te las presto.
4. ¿Me prestas el cinturón de cuero negro?
Sí, te lo presto. / No, no te lo presto.
5. Me prestas tu coche nuevo?
Sí, te lo presto. / No, te lo presto.

`4:00` **8·19** Antonio, ¿me prestas...?

Ahora Pablo va a una fiesta y quiere usar la ropa de su hermano Antonio. Túrnense para hacer los papeles de Pablo y Antonio usando los pronombres de complemento directo e indirecto.

MODELO   prestar/un abrigo

E1: (Pablo):   *¿Me prestas el abrigo?*

E2: (Antonio):   *Sí, te lo presto. / No, no te lo presto.*

1. prestar/los zapatos negros
2. prestar/la corbata de rayas azules
3. prestar/una camiseta blanca y una camisa azul de manga larga (*long sleeved*)
4. prestar/el cinturón de cuero negro
5. prestar/tu coche nuevo

Expansion for 8-20 Have students personalize this activity by substituting the proper nouns with their own choices and/or changing the persons to whom the recommendations are given.

Expansion for 8-21 After completing this activity, have students role-play the situations between the assistant and his/her boss.

[4:00]

8·20 Mis recomendaciones

¿Qué recomiendas? Lee la lista y pon una equis (**X**) en la columna apropiada. Después, comparte tus opiniones con un/a compañero/a según el modelo.

MODELO los libros de Tom Clancy (a tus primas)

E1: *¿Les recomiendas los libros de Tom Clancy a tus primas?*

E2: *No, no se los recomiendo.*

	SÍ	NO
1. las novelas de Stephen King (a tus tíos)		
2. la música de Eminem (a tu compañero/a de cuarto)		
3. el restaurante Taco Bell (a nosotros)		
4. el hotel Hilton (a tu amiga que no tiene mucho dinero)		
5. la película *Drácula* (a tus primos de cinco años)		
6. Disney World (a tu hermano)		
7. el Museo de Arte Moderno (a tu profesor/a)		
8. la clase de español (a tu mejor amigo/a)		

8·21 ¿En qué puedo servirle? [4:00]

Acabas de empezar un trabajo en prácticas (*internship*). En vez de (*Instead of*) tareas productivas asociadas con la profesión, te dan el trabajo de ayudante de una de las vice presidentas. Túrnense para contestar sus preguntas.

MODELO E1: *¿Me puede comprar un periódico?*

E2: *Sí, se lo puedo comprar. / Sí, puedo comprárselo.*

1. ¿Me puede traer un café?
2. ¿Me puede comprar los boletos (*tickets*) para un viaje a Nueva York?
3. ¿Me puede arreglar los apuntes y los papeles para la reunión de esta tarde?
4. ¿Me puede buscar un artículo en el periódico?
5. ¿Me puede reservar una mesa en un restaurante elegante para esta noche?
6. ¿Me puede comprar unas rosas para la recepcionista? Es su cumpleaños hoy.

Estrategia

Remember that when addressing an employer, you would use *Usted*, not *tú*. Also, be sure to practice both ways of structuring the sentence with two object pronouns, as in the *modelo*.

¿Cómo andas?

Having completed the first **Comunicación,** I now can...

	Feel Confident	Need to Review
● describe clothing (p. 286)	❏	❏
● pronounce the letters **ll** and **ñ** properly in Spanish (p. 287)	❏	❏
● talk about a Spanish clothing company (p. 291)	❏	❏
● talk about to whom and for whom things are done (p. 292)	❏	❏
● talk about clothing I like and dislike (p. 294)	❏	❏
● share what delights, fascinates, bothers, and matters to me and others, as well as what I and others need using the verbs **encantar, fascinar, hacer falta, importar,** and **molestar** (p. 295)	❏	❏
● use **me, te, le, nos, les** (indirect object pronouns) correctly in sentences as well as in combination with **me, te, lo, la, nos, los, las** (direct object pronouns) in the same sentence (p. 298)	❏	❏

Comunicación

- Discussing daily routines
- Describing situations in the past

GRAMÁTICA 5 Las construcciones reflexivas

8-26 to 8-31   25, 26

Study the captions for the drawings below.

5:00

In each drawing:

- Who is performing/doing the action?
- Who or what is receiving the action?

When the subject both performs and receives the action of the verb, a reflexive verb and pronoun are used.

- Which of the drawings and captions demonstrate reflexive verbs?

Look at the chart that follows; the reflexive pronouns are highlighted.

La fiesta **los** despierta.

Alberto **la** acuesta.

Beatriz **lo** lava.

Raúl y Gloria **se** despiertan.

Alberto **se** acuesta.

Beatriz **se** lava la cara.

Reflexive pronouns			
Siempre	**me**	divierto	en las fiestas.
Siempre	**te**	diviertes	en las fiestas.
Siempre	**se**	divierte	en las fiestas.
Siempre	**nos**	divertimos	en las fiestas.
Siempre	**os**	divertís	en las fiestas.
Siempre	**se**	divierten	en las fiestas.

Reflexive pronouns follow the same rules for position as other object pronouns. Reflexive pronouns:

1. precede a conjugated verb.
2. can be attached to *infinitives* and *present participles* (**-ando, -iendo**).

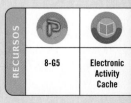

RECURSOS

8-G5   Electronic Activity Cache

Te vas a dormir.
Vas a dormir**te**.
} *You are falling asleep.*

¿**Se** van a dormir esta noche?
¿Van a dormir**se** esta noche?
} *Are they going to fall asleep tonight?*

¿**Se** están durmiendo?
¿Están durmiéndo**se**?
} *Are you all falling asleep?*

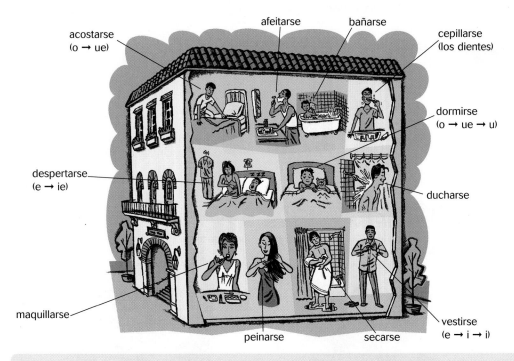

afeitarse   bañarse

acostarse
(o → ue)

cepillarse
(los dientes)

dormirse
(o → ue → u)

despertarse
(e → ie)

ducharse

maquillarse

vestirse
(e → i → i)

peinarse   secarse

Unos verbos reflexivos

acordarse de (o → ue)	*to remember*	**ponerse (la ropa)**	*to put on (one's clothes)*
arreglarse	*to get ready*	**ponerse (nervioso/a)**	*to get (nervous)*
callarse	*to get/keep quiet*	**quedarse**	*to stay; to remain*
divertirse (e → ie → i)	*to enjoy oneself; to have fun*	**quitarse (la ropa)**	*to take off (one's clothes)*
irse	*to go away; to leave*	**reunirse**	*to get together; to meet*
lavarse	*to wash oneself*	**secarse**	*to dry off*
levantarse	*to get up; to stand up*	**sentarse (e → ie)**	*to sit down*
llamarse	*to be called*	**sentirse (e → ie → i)**	*to feel*

Note: To identify all of the previous verbs as *reflexive*, the infinitive ends in **-se.**

Estrategia

When a new infinitive is presented, if it is a stem-changing verb, the irregularities will be given in parentheses. For example, if you see *divertirse* (*e → ie → i*) you know that this infinitive is an *-ir* stem-changing verb, that the first "e" in the infinitive changes to "ie" in the present indicative, and that the "e" changes to "i" in the 3rd person singular and plural of the preterit.

Fíjate

Some verbs change their meaning slightly between non-reflexive and reflexive verbs, for example: *dormir* (to sleep) and *dormirse* (to fall asleep); *ir* (to go) and *irse* (to leave).

METHODOLOGY • Reviewing and Recycling Grammatical Concepts

You may wish to have a warm-up each day at the beginning of class where you select different verbs and vocabulary words from this and previous chapters. For example, you can do a quick mechanical drill with the forms of different tenses, such as the *pretérito* from *Capítulo 7.* You can also end a class with a quick mechanical drill. These quick reviews should last no more than 2 minutes.

Additional activity for *Las construcciones reflexivas*

 El juego de la pelota. En grupos de cuatro a seis estudiantes, van a tirar (*throw*) una pelota de papel. Turnándose, una persona del grupo nombra uno de los verbos reflexivos y un sujeto, y tira la pelota a un/a compañero/a. Si el/la compañero/a dice la forma correcta, gana un punto y tiene que continuar el juego. Cuando terminen, jueguen otra vez con los verbos en el pretérito.

MODELO

E1: ducharse . . . yo (tira la pelota)
E2: *me ducho*
E2: vestirse . . . mi madre (tira la pelota)
E3: *mi madre se viste*
E3: acordarse . . . tú (tira la pelota)
E4: *te acuerdas*

NOTE FOR 8-23

INSTRUCTIONS: Draw a 9 square tic-tac-toe board and write a different reflexive verb in each of the nine squares. With a partner, and without showing your squares, play tic-tac-toe. For example, your partner says one of the verbs. If the verb is in your square, mark an X on the verb; if not, you don't have to do anything. Now you have to say one of your verbs, and you take turns until one of you has 3 Xs in a row going horizontally, vertically, or diagonally.

METHODOLOGY • Pair Work

You will want to identify daily who is Student "A" and who is Student "B," and then ask Student "A" to do the even-numbered items while Student "B" does the odd items. It is important for you to overtly tell students to take turns when working in pairs. If not, one student may tend to monopolize the pair work.

TPR Activity for 8-24 Use actividad **8-24** as a model to narrate a typical day using reflexive verbs. You can talk about your day or what we do, as in *primero nos despertamos y nos levantamos*, and have students act out the actions along with you. If you add extra information that is not in the book, make sure you write down those verbs so they can see them as they act out the day.

8·22 El juego de la asociación `3:00`

Juntos decidan qué verbos reflexivos asocian con las siguientes palabras y expresiones.

1. no decir nada   *callarse*
2. una silla   *sentarse*
3. recordar algo   *acordarse*

4. tener sueño   *dormirse*
5. no recordar algo   *olvidarse de*
6. triste o alegre, por ejemplo   *ponerse*

7. un sombrero   *ponerse*
8. estar sucio   *lavarse/ducharse/bañarse*
9. no ir a ningún lugar   *quedarse*

8·23 ¡Batalla! `5:00`

Van a jugar con un/a compañero/a a *tic-tac-toe*. Escuchen mientras el/la profesor/a les explica el juego.

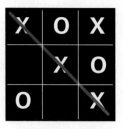

`3:00`

Capítulo 7. El pretérito, pág. 258. Unos verbos irregulares en el pretérito, pág. 266.

8·24 Un día en la vida

Ordena las actividades diarias de María y Tomás de forma cronológica. Después, compara tu lista con la de un/a compañero/a.

El día de María

1. Antes de irse a la universidad, se acordó de la tarea que no hizo para su clase de historia.
2. Se duchó.
3. Se maquilló.
4. Llegó a la clase de historia y se quitó el abrigo.
5. Se vistió.
6. Se secó.
7. Se levantó.

El día de Tomás

1. Se acostó tarde.
2. Se levantó rápidamente a las ocho.
3. Se despertó tarde.
4. No se durmió inmediatamente.
5. Se divirtió con sus amigos.
6. Después de las clases se fue con los amigos para pasar el fin de semana en la playa.
7. Se fue para la clase de química.

[4:00] **8·25** Un día normal

Capítulo Preliminar A. La hora, pág. 18.

Escribe por lo menos **cinco** actividades que haces normalmente y a qué hora las haces. Usa verbos reflexivos. Después, comparte tu lista con un/a compañero/a.

8·26 A conocerte más aún [4:00]

Túrnense para hacerse esta entrevista y conocer mejor sus hábitos.

MODELO
E1: *¿Qué te pones para ir al cine?*
E2: *Me pongo pantalones vaqueros con una camiseta. ¿Y tú? ¿Qué te pones?*
E1: *Generalmente me pongo pantalones con una blusa o un suéter.*
E2: *¿Qué...?*

1. ¿Qué te pones cuando sales con esa "persona especial"?
2. Cuando estás durmiéndote, ¿te acuerdas de las cosas que no hiciste durante el día?
3. ¿Cómo te diviertes?
4. Si tienes tiempo, ¿con quién(es) te reúnes?
5. ¿Cuándo te pones nervioso/a?
6. ¿Cuándo te sientes feliz?

[5:00] **8·27** Mímica

Hagan mímica (*charades*) en grupos de cuatro. Túrnense para escoger un verbo reflexivo para representar al grupo. El grupo tiene que adivinar qué verbo es. Sigan jugando hasta que cada estudiante represente **cuatro** verbos diferentes.

8·28 ¿Conoces bien a tus compañeros? [7:00]

Trabaja en grupos de cuatro para hacer esta actividad.

Paso 1 Un/a compañero/a debe salir de la sala de clase por un momento. Los otros estudiantes escriben **cinco** preguntas sobre la vida diaria del/de la compañero/a, usando los verbos reflexivos.

MODELO *¿A qué hora te despiertas?*
¿Te duchas todos los días?

Paso 2 Antes de entrar el/la compañero/a, el grupo de estudiantes debe adivinar cuáles van a ser las respuestas a esas preguntas.

MODELO *Me despierto a las siete.*
Sí, me ducho todos los días.

Paso 3 Entra el/la compañero/a y los otros le hacen las preguntas.

Paso 4 Comparen las respuestas del grupo con las del/de la compañero/a. ¿Tenían razón? Pueden repetir la actividad con los otros miembros del grupo.

NOTE FOR 8-25
You can make actividad **8-25** a writing exercise:
MODELO *Me despierto a las ocho y me levanto inmediatamente. Después . . .*

Expansion for 8-25 You may wish to ask your students about their daily routine this morning and last night: e.g., *¿Qué hiciste esta mañana? ¿Qué hiciste anoche?*

Follow-up to 8-26 You can ask questions so that your students use the third person: e.g., *¿Qué se pone _____ cuando sale con esa "persona especial"? ¿Qué se ponen _____ y _____ cuando salen. . .? ¿Cuándo se sienten _____ y _____ felices?*, etc.

SAM

8-32 to
8-33

4:00

Los centros comerciales en Latinoamérica

Ir de compras en Latinoamérica se asocia muchas veces con los mercados al aire libre donde se vende la artesanía y la comida típica de la región. Es cierto que estos lugares existen y son muy populares, sobre todo con los turistas. Pero en las últimas décadas ha surgido (*has emerged*) la cultura del centro comercial y los grandes almacenes en las sociedades latinoamericanas.

Los grandes centros comerciales, como los Unicentros en El Salvador y los centros Sambil en Venezuela, las tiendas de Falabella en Chile, Argentina y Perú, y los almacenes Liverpool en México son buenos ejemplos de mercados modernos que atraen a la población latina de varias clases económicas. Estas tiendas son modernas y ofrecen de todo a los clientes que buscan una gran variedad de productos como, por ejemplo, ropa, artículos y aparatos domésticos y muebles.

La gente va a los centros comerciales para pasear, mirar y entretenerse (*to entertain oneself*). En muchos hay hipermercados donde se puede comprar comida y artículos diversos para el hogar. Los centros comerciales son lugares para citas, para pasar el tiempo, para ir al cine, para reunirse con amigos, para observar a la gente, para ojear las vitrinas (*window shop*) y para enterarse de las últimas tendencias de la moda. Verdaderamente, estos centros han cambiado (*have changed*) mucho el estilo de vida de la gente hoy en día.

Preguntas

1. Antes de leer "Los centros comerciales en Latinoamérica", ¿qué entendías tú (*did you understand*) por "mercado latinoamericano"? ¿Qué imagen tenías (*did you used to have*)?   *Answers may vary.*

2. ¿Qué hace la gente en los centros comerciales latinoamericanos? ¿Cómo se comparan estas actividades con las de los centros comerciales estadounidenses?   *La gente pasea, mira y se entretiene. También van al cine, a citas, etc. Son muy similares a las de los centros comerciales estadounidenses.*

GRAMÁTICA **6**

El imperfecto

SAM

Guide **G**

8-34 to
8-38

36, 41

5:00

In **Capítulo 7** you learned how to express certain ideas and notions that happened in the past with the preterit. Spanish has another past tense, **el imperfecto,** that *expresses habitual or ongoing past actions, provides descriptions, or describes conditions.*

	-ar: hablar	-er: comer	-ir: vivir
yo	hablaba	comía	vivía
tú	hablabas	comías	vivías
él, ella, Ud.	hablaba	comía	vivía
nosotros/as	hablábamos	comíamos	vivíamos
vosotros/as	hablabais	comíais	vivíais
ellos/as, Uds.	hablaban	comían	vivían

Cuando Pepe vivía en la playa, nadaba en el mar todas las mañanas.

Estrategia

Focus on the forms and when to use the *imperfecto*. Note that the *-er* and *-ir* forms are exactly the same, and that they have accents in every form. Also note that in the *-ar* verbs the *nosotros/nosotras* form has an accent.

RECURSOS

8-G6 | Electronic Activity Cache

There are only *three irregular verbs* in the imperfect: **ir, ser,** and **ver.**

	ir	ser	ver
yo	iba	era	veía
tú	ibas	eras	veías
él, ella, Ud.	iba	era	veía
nosotros/as	íbamos	éramos	veíamos
vosotros/as	ibais	erais	veíais
ellos/as, Uds.	iban	eran	veían

The imperfect is used to:

1. provide background information, set the stage, or express a condition that existed

Llovía mucho.   *It was raining a lot.*

Era una noche oscura y nublada.   *It was a dark and cloudy night.*

Estábamos en el segundo año de la universidad.   *We were in our second year of college.*

Adriana **estaba** enferma y no **quería** levantarse. *Adriana was ill and didn't want to get up/get out of bed.*

> **Fíjate**
>
> Repeated actions are usually expressed in English with *used to...* or *would...*

2. describe habitual or often repeated actions

Íbamos al cine todos los viernes. Nos   *We went (used to go) to the movies every Friday.*
divertíamos mucho.   *We had a lot of fun.*

Cuando **era** pequeño, Lebron **jugaba** al   *When he was little Lebron played (used to play)*
básquetbol por lo menos dos horas al día.   *basketball for at least two hours a day.*

Mis padres siempre **se levantaban** a las seis   *My parents always got up (used to get up) at 6:00 A.M.*
de la mañana.

Some words or expressions for describing habitual and repeated actions are:

a menudo	*often*	**muchas veces**	*many times*
casi siempre	*almost always*	**mucho**	*a lot*
frecuentemente	*frequently*	**normalmente**	*normally*
generalmente	*generally*	**siempre**	*always*
mientras	*while*	**todos los días**	*every day*

3. express *was* or *were* + *-ing*

¿Dormías?   *Were you sleeping?*

Me duchaba cuando Juan llamó.   *I was showering when Juan called.*

Alberto **leía** mientras Alicia **escuchaba** música. *Alberto was reading while Alicia was listening to music.*

4. tell time in the past

Era la una y yo todavía **estudiaba.**   *It was 1:00 and I was still studying.*

Eran las siete y media y los niños **se dormían.** *It was 7:30 and the children were falling asleep.*

Suggestion for *El imperfecto* Drill
el imperfecto by giving infinitives
and subject pronouns and having
the class respond chorally with the
correct form.

Suggestion for *El imperfecto* Drill
with directed questions such as:
*¿Dónde vivías?, ¿Quién era tu mejor
amigo/a?, ¿Cómo era?, ¿Cómo se
llamaba tu mejor amigo/a de la
escuela primaria?, ¿Qué te ponías
cuando tenías cinco años?, Cuando
tenías cinco años, ¿con quién
jugabas?, ¿Qué no te gustaba
comer que ahora te gusta?*

Additional Activity for *El imperfecto*

¿Cierto o falso? Lee las
frases siguientes y decide si
son ciertas o falsas en tu
caso. Después, túrnate con un/a
compañero/a para hacer preguntas y
contestar según el modelo.

MODELO
E1: *Antes de venir a la universidad,
    ¿vivías en un apartamento?*
E2: *No, no vivía en un aparta-
    mento. Vivía con mis padres en
    una casa.*

Antes de venir a la universidad...
 1. vivir en un apartamento
 2. tener un animal
 3. ver mucho la televisión
 4. gustarte comer verduras
 5. ser un/a buen/a estudiante
 6. tener muchos amigos
 7. estudiar todo el tiempo
 8. tener mucho dinero para gastar
 9. llevar pantalones cortos
10. tocar un instrumento
11. sacar la basura
12. manejar mucho

CAPÍTULO 8

`3:00`

8·29 La práctica

Repitan el juego de la actividad **7-11** en la página 260, esta vez para practicar el imperfecto.

8·30 Cuando era joven   `5:00`

Completa el párrafo sobre Eva Perón para saber cómo pudo ser su vida cuando era joven. Después, compara tus respuestas con las de un/a compañero/a.

ayudar	encantar	gustar	poder	querer
preferir	sentirse	ser	tener	trabajar

María Eva Duarte, como primero se llamaba, nació en una provincia de Buenos Aires en 1919. Cuando
(1) _____ tenía _____ seis o siete años su padre murió. Eva y sus cuatro hermanos
(2) _____ se sentían _____ muy tristes y para ellos la vida (3) _____ era _____ muy difícil porque les faltaban
dinero y comida. La madre (4) _____ trabajaba _____ como costurera (*seamstress*) y los niños le
(5) _____ ayudaban _____ en la casa. Imaginamos que a Eva le (6) _____ encantaba _____ el verano cuando
(7) _____ podía _____ estar en casa con sus hermanos. No le (8) _____ gustaban _____ las muñecas y
(9) _____ prefería _____ inventar juegos o imaginar situaciones diferentes. Parece que desde el principio (*from the start*) Eva (10) _____ quería _____ ser actriz.

`5:00`

8·31 En el colegio...

¿Qué hacías cuando estabas en el colegio? ¿Con qué frecuencia? Escribe una equis (**X**) en la columna apropiada. Luego, compara tus respuestas con las de un/a compañero/a.

Fíjate

In actividad **8-31**, you see the word *el colegio*. Remember that *colegio* is a false cognate in Spanish; it can mean *school* or *high school*.

MODELO   E1: *¿Escuchabas música de Frank Sinatra?*

E2: *No, nunca escuchaba música de Frank Sinatra. /*
Sí, a veces escuchaba música de Frank Sinatra.

	TODOS LOS DÍAS	MUCHAS VECES	A VECES	NUNCA
1. escuchar música de Frank Sinatra				
2. nadar en la playa				
3. leer obras de Shakespeare				
4. bañarse				
5. acostarse temprano				
6. dormirse en las clases				
7. ponerse nervioso/a antes de un examen				
8. reunirse con los amigos				
9. vestirse como querías				
10. querer ir a la escuela				
11. levantarse muy tarde				
12. no hacer nada por la noche				

[4:00] **8·32** Mi primera casa

Capítulo 3. La casa, pág. 100.

¿Cómo era tu primera casa o la casa de tu amigo/a? Descríbesela a un/a compañero/a dándole por lo menos **cinco** detalles. Después, cambien de papel.

MODELO   *Mi primera casa estaba en una ciudad pequeña. Tenía dos dormitorios. La cocina era amarilla. El comedor y la sala eran pequeños. Tenía solamente (only) un baño.*

[4:00] **8·33** Cómo ha cambiado la vida

Miren el dibujo y escriban **siete** oraciones que contesten la pregunta "¿cómo era la vida en los años setenta?". Usen verbos como **tener, estar, ser, haber, ayudar, limpiar** y **jugar.** Sean creativos.

 8·34 Preguntas personales   [8:00]

Cuando tenían dieciséis años, ¿qué hacían tus compañeros/as de clase? Circula por la clase para preguntárselo.

MODELO   E1:   ¿Jugabas al fútbol con los amigos?

           E2:   *Sí, jugaba todos los días después de salir del colegio.*

           E3:   *Sí, jugaba con el equipo del colegio.*

           E4:   *No, nunca jugaba al fútbol. No me gustaba.*

	ESTUDIANTE 1:	ESTUDIANTE 2:	ESTUDIANTE 3:
1. ¿Te quedabas en casa los fines de semana?			
2. ¿Qué hacías los fines de semana?			
3. ¿Manejabas?			
4. ¿Tenías coche?			
5. ¿Trabajabas?			
6. ¿Qué hacías cuando hacía mal tiempo?			
7. ¿Qué hacías cuando hacía buen tiempo?			
8. ¿Qué hacías cuando tenías dinero?			
9. ¿Qué hacías cuando no tenías dinero?			
10. ¿Qué hacías para divertirte?			

METHODOLOGY • Students Learning from Students

The authors of *¡Anda!* firmly believe in the importance of students learning from students. In this way, they construct knowledge, build confidence, and become highly motivated. They truly learn best from each other. Hence, *¡Anda!* makes frequent use of activities in which students must either work with a partner or circulate around the classroom to interact with their classmates. You will find that students love these activities and truly use their Spanish. It is important that you set these activities up with several strong expectations.

1. They must speak solely in Spanish.
2. When they have a survey to conduct, they must speak to at least six different students.
3. They must ask the question, and not just point to the paper.

Another technique to always keep in mind is to end an activity when students are still enjoying it. Never wait until *all* groups have completed the activity; the others will become bored and go off task. A technique that works well is to have additional activities from the text listed on the board for groups who finish first.

ESCUCHA

8-39 to
8-42

ESTRATEGIA   Guessing meaning from context

You do not need to know every word to understand a listening passage or to get the gist of a conversation. | Think about the overall message, then use the surrounding words or sentences to guess at meaning.

8·35

Antes de escuchar

Beatriz, la prima de Marisol, es estudiante de intercambio en Buenos Aires. Va de compras con su "hermana" argentina, Luz. Están en la tienda Zara, comprando ropa.

1. ¿Cómo es la tienda Zara? *Zara es una tienda española. Vende ropa de buena calidad pero no es muy cara.*
2. ¿Piensas que ir de compras en Zara en Buenos Aires es igual que ir de compras en Zara en Nueva York (o en cualquier otra ciudad)? *Answers may vary.*

8·36

CD 3
Track 21

A escuchar

Completa las siguientes actividades.

1. Escucha la conversación entre Beatriz y Luz y después selecciona la opción que mejor conteste la pregunta. ¿De qué se trata (*What is the gist of*) la conversación? *b*

   _____ a. A Beatriz no le gustan las blusas de la tienda y tampoco la tienda. Jamás va de compras allí.

   _____ b. A Beatriz le encanta el dependiente. Vive cerca de Luz.

   _____ c. A Luz le gustan los perros negros. Alguien tiene un perro que se llama Toro o posiblemente Goro.

2. Escucha una vez más y termina las siguientes frases.

   a. Marisol y Beatriz visitaron una de las tiendas Zara… (dónde y cuándo)
   b. Marisol y Beatriz no compraron nada porque…
   c. Luz no quiere comprar la blusa de seda o la falda de lana porque…
   d. Beatriz reconoce (*recognizes*) al dependiente porque…

3. ¿Qué significa "dependiente"? *Significa "salesperson".*

Beatriz y Luz van de compras.

8·37

Después de escuchar

En grupos de tres, realicen (*act out*) la escena entre Beatriz, Luz y el dependiente.

ESCRIBE

SAM 8-43 to 8-44

8•38 Antes de escribir

Haz una lista de las **ocho** cosas que más te gustaba hacer cuando eras niño/a.

8•39 Cuando era niño/a

Organiza tus ideas y escribe un e-mail a tu hermano/a (o a tu mejor amigo/a), recordando las cosas que hacías en tu niñez.

8•40 Después de escribir

Tu profesor/a va a leer los e-mails a la clase para ver si ustedes pueden adivinar quiénes los escribieron.

¿Cómo andas?

Having completed the second **Comunicación,** I now can...

	Feel Confident	Need to Review
• describe my daily routine (p. 302)	❑	❑
• talk about shopping in a department store in a Spanish-speaking country (p. 306)	❑	❑
• use regular and irregular verbs in the imperfect tense correctly (p. 306)	❑	❑
• talk about how things were in the past and what I used to do (p. 307)	❑	❑
• glean meaning from context when listening (p. 310)	❑	❑
• write an e-mail about my childhood (p. 311)	❑	❑

SECTION GOALS FOR *Escribe*

By the end of the *Escribe* section, students will be able to:

- pre-write by brainstorming childhood activities.
- organize their pre-writing.
- write an e-mail about childhood memories.
- listen to what other people wrote and guess who wrote each narration.

NATIONAL STANDARDS *Communication*

The *Escribe* section focuses on communication in the presentational mode (Standard 1.3) when students listen to the instructor read aloud the writing samples from various students. The activity can be modified to include interpretation of written Spanish (Standard 1.2): e.g., you could write a brief narration of your childhood for your students to read. By working in groups and discussing their writing before handing it in, students practice interpersonal communication (Standard 1.1). The writing exercise reinforces the sound writing practices they have learned when writing in English: pre-writing, organizing, and brainstorming. (Standard 4.1).

Alternate Activities for *Escribe* The writing exercise in the *Escribe* section can be expanded to include other topics. One such topic could be that of one's first best friend. You can assign this writing exercise for homework and collect the assignment. Sometimes assignments that require students to reveal personal information are better suited for homework than for sharing with the class. Another topic that would work well would be their first pet.

CULTURA

By the end of the *Cultura* section, students will be able to:

- explain the ethnic roots represented in Argentina.
- describe the geographical diversity of Argentina.
- discuss the climate and culture of Uruguay.
- compare Argentina and Uruguay to the previously featured countries.

NATIONAL STANDARDS
Cultures, Comparisons

In *Les presento mi país*, the readings highlight the unique features of Argentina and Uruguay. Students learn about the culture of these two countries (Standard 2.1), and with the information presented they can make comparisons about how these countries differ from the United States (Standard 4.2). One comparison they learn is that many Italians immigrated to Argentina and therefore many Argentines have Italian surnames; also, Italian cuisine has been incorporated into the Argentine diet. In Uruguay there is a temperate climate, which differs from the extreme temperature variations in regions across the United States.

NOTE FOR
Les presento mi país

People from the city of Buenos Aires are called *porteños*. They are said to have their own mannerisms and idiomatic expressions as well as accent. The pronunciation of *y* and *ll* are closer to the *sh* sound in English than in Spanish elsewhere.

NOTE FOR
Les presento mi país

Argentines use "che" to call attention to people, to begin sentences, as a nickname, and as a sentence interjection. It is an all-purpose word. In some indigenous languages, it means "man" or "people." It was, of course, the nickname of Ernesto Guevara, the revolutionary from Rosario, Argentina.

Marina Claudia
Luschini Ojeda

Argentina

 CW eBook
CD 3 Track 22
SAM 8-45 to 8-46
DVD/VHS Vistas culturales

10:00

Les presento mi país

Mi nombre es Marina Claudia Luschini Ojeda y vivo en la capital de Argentina, Buenos Aires. Soy porteña (*una persona de Buenos Aires*) y de herencia italiana, como puedes ver por mi apellido. Muchos argentinos tienen apellidos italianos a causa de la gran inmigración europea a fines del siglo diecinueve. ¿De qué herencia sos vos, che? Mi país es grande y la geografía es muy variada: desde la montaña más alta del hemisferio occidental, el Cerro Aconcagua, hasta la ciudad más sureña (*del sur*) del mundo, Ushuaia. También tenemos lugares naturales como los glaciares, las pampas, la región de Patagonia, las cataratas del Iguazú y unas playas hermosas, como la del Mar del Plata. ¿Qué regiones y riquezas naturales hay en tu país?

Las Cataratas del Iguazú en la frontera con Brasil y Paraguay

El tango en San Telmo, un antiguo barrio en la capital.

Las Galerías Pacífico en la calle Florida

OCÉANO PACÍFICO
PARAGUAY BRAZIL
Salta Formosa
San Miguel de Tucumán
Córdoba URUGUAY
Cerro Aconcagua Mendoza Rosario
Buenos Aires La Plata
PAMPAS Río de la Plata
Mar del Plata
Bahía Blanca
PATAGONIA
OCÉANO ATLÁNTICO

● ALMANAQUE ●

Nombre oficial:	República de Argentina
Gobierno:	República
Población:	39.921.833 (2006)
Idioma:	español
Moneda:	Peso argentino ($)

¿Sabías que...?

● El **lunfardo** es un dialecto o jerga que tuvo su origen en los barrios de Buenos Aires a finales del siglo XIX. Es la lengua del tango y también de la jerga de las prisiones a principios del siglo XX. Se forman palabras diciendo las sílabas al revés (*reversing the syllables*): "tango" en lunfardo es *gotan*.

PREGUNTAS

1. ¿Cuáles son tres de las distintas regiones geográficas del país? Cuando es verano en Argentina, ¿en qué estación estamos aquí? ¿Por qué?

2. ¿Dónde puedes ir de compras en Buenos Aires?

3. ¿Qué tienen en común Argentina y Chile?

 En la Red
Amplía tus conocimientos sobre Argentina en la página web de *¡Anda!*

NOTE FOR
Les presento mi país

While *voseo*, the use of the pronoun *vos* for second person singular, is widespread throughout many parts of Latin America, it is very widespread in Argentina. Though it is not taught in Spanish textbooks in the United States, millions of people in the Southern Cone and elsewhere use this linguistic form on a daily basis.

Expansion for *Preguntas* Additional questions include: ¿Cómo se usa la palabra "che" en Argentina?, ¿Por qué se dice que Buenos Aires es una ciudad cosmopolita?, ¿Qué es el lunfardo?

RECURSOS		
T8-4	T8-4	Cultural Background Notes

Francisco Tomás
Bacigalupe Bustamante

Uruguay

El chivito es un plato
típico uruguayo.

La Rambla de
Montevideo

Les presento mi país

Mi nombre es Francisco Tomás Bacigalupe Bustamante, aunque de pequeño me llamaban Paquito. Soy de Montevideo, la capital de Uruguay. Mi país es pequeño pero tranquilo y bonito, y la mayoría de la población, el ochenta por ciento, vive en los centros urbanos. El clima es templado (no hace mucho calor ni mucho frío) y perfecto para nuestras playas increíbles. Cuando era niño las playas eran nuestro destino favorito para ir de vacaciones. ¿Dónde ibas tú de vacaciones? Tenemos mucho en común con nuestros vecinos los argentinos: el tango, la yerba mate, los gauchos y una dieta que contiene mucha carne. También comemos mucha pizza y pasta, debido a nuestra herencia italiana. ¿Qué comida de otros países te gusta comer?

Punta del Este es un balneario (*resort*) muy turístico.

ALMANAQUE

Nombre oficial:	República Oriental del Uruguay
Gobierno:	República democrática
Población:	3.431.932 (2006)
Idiomas:	español (oficial); portuñol/brazilero
Moneda:	Peso uruguayo ($U)

¿Sabías que...?

- Debido al índice de alfabetización (*literacy*), el clima agradable y templado, la belleza del paisaje y la hospitalidad de la gente, Uruguay se le conoce como "la Suiza de América".

PREGUNTAS

1. ¿Dónde vive la mayoría de los uruguayos?
2. Muchos uruguayos son de herencia italiana. ¿En qué se ve esta herencia?
3. ¿Qué tiene en común Uruguay con su país vecino Argentina?

En la Red
Amplía tus conocimientos sobre Uruguay en la página web de *¡Anda!*

313

NOTE FOR *La Rambla*
La Rambla of Montevideo is an avenue that stretches for miles and miles along the northern coast of the Río de la Plata and reflects the diversity of Uruguay. From the bustling background of high-rise buildings to the tranquility of sandy beaches to the activity of marinas and fishing boats, this walkway provides a backdrop for Uruguayans to stroll along through life. You can find people walking, talking, eating in restaurants, engaging in all manner of water sports, and simply sunbathing.

Suggestion for *La Rambla* Ask students where else there are walkways like this near or on beaches in the United States (Atlantic City, etc.).

NOTE FOR *Punta del Este*
Punta del Este is one of the most popular resorts in all of South America. It is a mecca for glamorous tourists who enjoy golfing, casinos, beautiful beaches, and other resort pastimes.

Suggestion for *Punta del Este* Ask students: What are some famous resorts in the United States?, Are some more exclusive than others?, Why do they think that happens?

Suggestion for *El chivito* Ask students: What is our most common fast food? (hamburgers), Do we have food in common with other cultures, or is it exclusively "United Statesian"?

Expansion for *Preguntas*
1. ¿Qué importancia tiene la Rambla en Montevideo?
2. ¿Qué plato de "comida rápida" es típico en Uruguay? ¿Cómo se compara este plato con la "comida rápida" estadounidense? ¿Y con los otros países que hemos estudiado?

NOTE FOR *El chivito*
El chivito is a steak sandwich that contains cheese, ham, bacon, tomatoes, eggs, lettuce, and mayonnaise. It is the Uruguayan version of "fast food", and is quite popular. Another typical dish is *asado*, which we read about in the section on Argentina. Italian food is also popular, due to the large number of people of Italian descent in the country.

RECURSOS | T8-5 | T8-5 | Cultural Background Notes

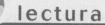

Ambiciones siniestras

lectura

SAM
M.S.I
8-50 to
8-51

EPISODIO 8

SECTION GOALS FOR
Lectura

By the end of the *Lectura* section, students will be able to:

- utilize the new reading strategy of guessing from the context.
- apply the new strategy in combination with the previous strategies.
- narrate the main events of the reading.

RECAP OF *AMBICIONES SINIESTRAS*
Episodio 7

Lectura: In *Capítulo 7, El rompecabezas,* Cisco called Manolo to check on Alejandra and learned that no one had heard from her. Cisco went to his favorite restaurant to do some thinking and received a phone call from a man who said he would have two days to solve a riddle or Eduardo would die. Upon further investigation, Cisco learned from Manolo that he too had received the mysterious phone call. When Manolo called Alejandra, he heard a man's voice on her answering machine.
Video: In *Episodio 7, ¡Qué rico está el pisco!,* Cisco organized a video-conference about Eduardo's and Alejandra's disappearances. Both Cisco and Lupe acted very mysteriously when asked about the disappearances. It appeared that Lupe was hiding her true identity, and that Cisco knew more about the disappearances than he was letting on. At the end of the episode, Cisco suspected that the answer to the riddle was Chile, and he wondered if el Sr. Verdugo could be holding Eduardo in Chile.

NATIONAL STANDARDS
Communication

The *lectura* provides authentic text in Spanish that students have to read and interpret for understanding (Standard 1.2). The video provides listening practice as students interpret what is happening and why, and how these actions might affect future actions (Standard 1.2).

8-41   Antes de leer. En el **Episodio 7**, los protagonistas seguían preocupados por Eduardo y tampoco sabían dónde estaba Alejandra. Cuando Manolo intentó llamarla, salió la voz de un hombre en su contestador automático. Tuvieron otra videoconferencia para hablar de Eduardo, Alejandra y el rompecabezas que recibieron. Para prepararte bien para el **Episodio 8**, contesta las siguientes preguntas basadas en el **Episodio 7**.

1. ¿Cómo se sentía Marisol? ¿Manolo? Explica.
2. ¿Por qué era importante resolver el rompecabezas?
3. ¿Cuáles eran las dudas que tenían?

ESTRATEGIA   Guessing meaning from context

Before consulting a dictionary, always try to guess the meaning of an unfamiliar word from the context of the reading. In other words, looking closely at the surrounding words and sentences can help you determine the meaning. Even if you cannot come up with an exact translation, you can get the general idea of what the word means.

Estrategia

The new strategy *guessing meaning from context* is especially useful to beginning language students. It is much easier to focus on what you can understand and make logical guesses about the new information instead of trying to focus on what you cannot understand and attempting to look up every word. Only look up a word if it interferes with your ability to comprehend the sentence, question, or the main idea.

8-42   A leer. Completa las siguientes actividades.

1. Al empezar el episodio, sabemos que Marisol estaba "preocupada" y "no tenía ganas" de hacer nada ni de comer nada (primer párrafo). En el segundo párrafo, cuando ella fue a su computadora *"Tenía varios mensajes, pero inmediatamente vio uno del hombre del concurso. Empezó a temblar sin saber por qué."*

   ¿Qué significa la palabra "temblar"? ¿Cómo podía sentirse Marisol al recibir otro mensaje del hombre del concurso? ¿feliz? ¿contenta? ¿asustada? Si leemos el mensaje podemos imaginar la reacción de ella. Creemos que Marisol se puso nerviosa al leerlo, entonces "temblar" es más una reacción de miedo que de felicidad, ¿no? En realidad, "temblar" significa *"to tremble."*

2. Lee superficialmente el episodio y subraya (*underline*) las palabras que no conoces. Intenta adivinar el significado de cada una, según el contexto. (Sigue el proceso indicado en el apartado 1.) Después, compara tus palabras subrayadas y sus posibles significados con las de tu compañero/a.

3. Lee el episodio una vez más, revisando los posibles significados cuando sea necesario (*as needed*). Al terminar, comparte tus resultados con el/la profesor/a.

The new strategy, guessing meaning from the context, prepares students to become more efficient readers as they scan for the main ideas and supporting ideas for enhanced understanding. If students work together to discuss the comprehension questions, they engage in conversations and provide and obtain information (Standard 1.1).

Answers to 8-41

1. Marisol y Manolo estaban preocupados porque Eduardo desapareció y no sabían dónde estaba Alejandra.
2. Tenían que resolver el rompecabezas para salvar la vida de Eduardo.
3. Manolo pensaba que Cisco sabía algo de Eduardo, y Marisol no sabía si Lupe le estaba diciendo la verdad.

CD 3
Track 24

¿Quién fue?

Eran las ocho y Marisol estaba en la cama, preocupada y confusa. No quería levantarse. No tenía ganas de arreglarse… no podía comer porque no tenía hambre ni para sus dulces favoritos.

Sonó el teléfono pero Marisol decidió no contestarlo. Prefería escuchar un mensaje que hablar con alguien en estos momentos. Nada: nadie dejó un mensaje. Decidió levantarse e ir a la computadora para leer su correo electrónico. Tenía varios mensajes, pero inmediatamente vio uno del hombre del concurso. Empezó a temblar sin saber por qué. Por fin lo abrió y leyó:

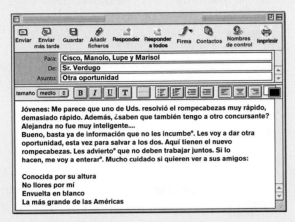

Para:	Cisco, Manolo, Lupe y Marisol
De:	Sr. Verdugo
Asunto:	Otra oportunidad

Jóvenes: Me parece que uno de Uds. resolvió el rompecabezas muy rápido, demasiado rápido. Además, ¿saben que también tengo a otro concursante? Alejandra no fue muy inteligente…. Bueno, basta ya de información que no les incumbe°. Les voy a dar otra oportunidad, esta vez para salvar a los dos. Aquí tienen el nuevo rompecabezas. Les advierto° que no deben trabajar juntos. Si lo hacen, me voy a enterar°. Mucho cuidado si quieren ver a sus amigos:

Conocida por su altura
No llores por mí
Envuelta en blanco
La más grande de las Américas

you do not need to know

warn

find out

Marisol no podía creerlo. ¡Qué pesadilla°! ¿Quién resolvió el primer rompecabezas? Ella no tuvo nada que ver con eso°. ¿Y qué pasó con Lupe en estos últimos días? Estaba portándose° muy rara y misteriosamente. Dijo que las cosas no eran importantes, pero sí, lo son. Parecía que escondía° algo. ¡Podía ser que este último mensaje fuera° de ella! En ese momento sonó el teléfono.

nightmare
She had nothing to do with that /
behaving /
was hiding /
was

—Marisol, soy Manolo. Encontré tu número en el Internet.

—Manolo, gracias por llamar —respondió Marisol —Tengo que hablar contigo. Tengo mucho miedo. ¿Recibiste el nuevo rompecabezas? ¿Fuiste tú quien solucionó el primer rompecabezas? —le preguntó.

—Sí, —explicó Manolo, —recibí el nuevo pero no, no fui yo quien solucionó el primero —explicó Manolo.

—¿Sabes qué? —empezó a decir Marisol. —Creo que es Lupe quien nos manda los e-mails. Creo que ella es el «Sr. Verdugo», —le dijo muy convencida.

—¿Sí? —respondió Manolo —y yo creía que era Cisco. Él tiene mucho talento con las computadoras. Me da mucho miedo. Creo que Cisco sí sabe lo que pasa con Eduardo y no nos dice nada. Temo que él sea el culpable°.

I'm afraid he may be the guilty one

METHODOLOGY • Reading

¡Anda! supports both top-down and bottom-up approaches to reading. In the top-down, or reader-driven, approach, the pre-existing knowledge the reader brings to the text is critical to comprehension. The *Antes de leer* section supports this approach. The text-driven, or bottom-up, approach relies on the decoding of words, phrases, and sentences.

NATIONAL STANDARDS

Communication, Comparisons

Note that the readings are kept at a level of comprehensible input that entices the students to read. Also, follow-up questions encourage students to think beyond the content of the story and make informed guesses about what they would do in the same circumstance.

315

—No sé—le refutó Marisol—. No lo sé. Hay cosas muy misteriosas con Lupe también. Siempre está en el Internet y cuando me acerco° a ella, cierra su computadora y me dice que no está haciendo nada. ¿Qué hacemos? —le preguntó. *approach*

Manolo se quedó pensando.

—Tal vez debemos llamar a la policía—contestó Manolo—, pero ¿qué decimos? No sabemos nada en concreto ni de Eduardo ni de Alejandra. Vamos a pensarlo bien. ¿Y si es una broma° de mal gusto? Te llamo pronto. *joke*

—Bueno. —respondió Marisol angustiada—. Adiós.

Marisol, temblando de nuevo, volvió a sus mensajes. Miró la lista y vio una dirección que no reconoció: muchasuerte@comando.com. Abrió el mensaje y gritó°. *screamed*

8-43 Después de leer

1. ¿Qué hora era? ¿Qué hacía Marisol al empezar el episodio?
2. ¿Cuál era el nuevo rompecabezas?
3. ¿Qué amenaza (*threat*) había al final de su mensaje?
4. ¿Quién llamó por teléfono?
5. ¿Cuáles eran las dudas de Manolo? ¿y de Marisol?

8-52 to
8-53

video

8-44 Antes del video. ¿Quién resolvió el primer rompecabezas? ¿Por qué gritó Alejandra? En la segunda parte del episodio vas a saber quién resolvió el rompecabezas, pero al mismo tiempo vas a tener más dudas sobre algunos de los protagonistas. También, Manolo va a hablar de algo peligroso (*dangerous*). Y finalmente, ¿quién tiene una pistola?

Eso es todo lo que necesito.

Cisco, te lo digo en serio, esto puede ser muy peligroso.

Oye, Manolo. Perdón pero tengo que irme.

Episodio 8

«El misterio crece»

Relájate y disfruta el video.

8-45 **Después del video.** Contesta las siguientes preguntas.

1. ¿Qué hacía Lupe mientras hablaba con Manolo?
2. ¿Quién resolvió el primer rompecabezas? ¿Cuál era la respuesta?
3. Según Lupe, ¿quién debía saber algo sobre Eduardo?
4. ¿Qué ocurrió justo antes de colgar los teléfonos?
5. ¿Por qué se puso nervioso Manolo al final del episodio?
6. ¿A quién vimos al final del episodio?

Y por fin, ¿cómo andas?

Having completed this chapter, I now can…

	Feel Confident	Need to Review
Comunicación		
• describe clothing (p. 286)	❏	❏
• pronounce **ll** and **ñ** correctly (p. 287)	❏	❏
• talk about to whom and for whom things are done (p. 292)	❏	❏
• discuss likes and dislikes, what is and is not important, what is bothersome, and what is lacking or needed (p. 294)	❏	❏
• describe my daily routine (p. 302)	❏	❏
• talk and write about the past, describing situations and telling how things used to be (p. 306)	❏	❏
• guess the meaning of unfamiliar words using contextual clues when listening (p. 310)	❏	❏
• write an e-mail about my childhood (p. 311)	❏	❏
Cultura		
• talk about a Spanish clothing company (p. 291)	❏	❏
• talk about shopping in a department store in a Spanish-speaking country (p. 306)	❏	❏
• share at least two interesting facts about each country: Argentina and Uruguay (pp. 312–313)	❏	❏
Ambiciones siniestras		
• guess the meaning of unfamiliar words from context in a reading passage (p. 314)	❏	❏
• tell who solved the first riddle (p. 316)	❏	❏
• list doubts that Marisol and Manolo have about Lupe and Cisco (p. 316)	❏	❏

317

VOCABULARIO ACTIVO

CW
eBook
CD 3
Tracks 25-31

La ropa / Clothing

el abrigo	overcoat
la bata	robe
la blusa	blouse
el bolso	purse
las botas (pl.)	boots
los calcetines (pl.)	socks
la camisa	shirt
la camiseta	T-shirt
la chaqueta	jacket
el cinturón	belt
el conjunto	outfit
la corbata	tie
la falda	skirt
la gorra	cap
los guantes	gloves
el impermeable	raincoat
los jeans (pl.)	jeans
las medias (pl.)	stockings; hose
los pantalones (pl.)	pants
los pantalones cortos (pl.)	shorts
el paraguas	umbrella
el pijama	pajamas
la ropa interior	underwear
las sandalias (pl.)	sandals
el sombrero	hat
la sudadera	sweatshirt
el suéter	sweater
los tenis (pl.)	tennis shoes
el traje	suit
el traje de baño	swimsuit; bathing suit
el vestido	dress
las zapatillas (pl.)	slippers
los zapatos (pl.)	shoes

Las telas y los materiales / Fabrics and materials

el algodón	cotton
el cuero	leather
la lana	wool
el poliéster	polyester
la seda	silk
la tela	fabric

Unos adjetivos / Some adjectives

ancho/a	wide
atrevido/a	daring
claro/a	light (colored)
cómodo/a	comfortable
corto/a	short
de cuadros	checked
de lunares	polka-dotted
de rayas	striped
elegante	elegant
estampado/a	print; with a design or pattern
estrecho/a	narrow; tight
formal	formal
informal	casual
largo/a	long
liso/a	solid-colored
oscuro/a	dark

318

Unos verbos	Some verbs
llevar	to wear; to take; to carry
llevar puesto	to wear; to have on
quedar bien/mal	to fit well/poorly

Otras palabras útiles	Other useful words
la moda	fashion; style
el/la modelo	model

Unos verbos como *gustar*	Verbs similar to *gustar*
encantar	to love; delight
fascinar	to fascinate
hacer falta	to need; to be lacking
importar	to matter; to be important
molestar	to bother

Unos verbos reflexivos	Some reflexive verbs
acordarse de (o → ue)	to remember
acostarse (o → ue)	to go to bed
afeitarse	to shave
arreglarse	to get ready
bañarse	to bathe
callarse	to get/keep quiet
cepillarse (el pelo, los dientes)	to brush (one's hair, teeth)
despertarse (e → ie)	to wake up; to awaken
divertirse (e → ie → i)	to enjoy oneself; to have fun
dormirse (o → ue → u)	to fall asleep
ducharse	to shower
irse	to go away; to leave
lavarse	to wash oneself
levantarse	to get up; to stand up
llamarse	to be called
maquillarse	to put on make up
peinarse	to comb one's hair
ponerse (la ropa)	to put on (one's clothes)
ponerse (nervioso/a)	to get (nervous)
quedarse	to stay; to remain
quitarse (la ropa)	to take off (one's clothes)
reunirse	to get together; to meet
secarse	to dry off
sentarse (e → ie)	to sit down
sentirse (e → ie → i)	to feel
vestirse (e → i → i)	to get dressed

319

9

Estamos en forma

Todos queremos tener una buena calidad de vida y prolongarla lo más posible. No podemos cambiar nuestra herencia genética transmitida de padres a hijos, pero sí tenemos control sobre decisiones que pueden afectar nuestro estilo de vida: el ejercicio, la dieta, la prevención de accidentes y el uso de sustancias adictivas como el tabaco.

NATIONAL STANDARDS

Comunicación

- To describe parts of the human body (Communication)
- To avoid repetition of previously mentioned people and things (Communication)
- To describe what one does to himself/herself (Communication)
- To explain what ails you and suggest treatments for certain ailments (Communication, Comparisons, Connections)
- To make exclamatory or emphatic statements (Communication)
- To narrate in the past (Communication, Communities)
- To ask yourself questions when listening to a passage to help organize and summarize what you heard (Communication, Connections)
- To write a summary using the past tenses (Communication, Comparisons)

Cultura

- To discuss the importance of water in maintaining good health (Communication, Connections)
- To talk about pharmacies in Latin America and how they differ from those in the United States (Communication, Comparisons, Connections)
- To talk about this chapter's featured countries: Peru, Bolivia, and Ecuador (Communication, Cultures, Connections, Comparisons)

Ambiciones siniestras

- To create check questions to facilitate comprehension when reading (Communication, Connections)
- To discuss the contents of the new e-mail message (Communication)
- To talk about the progress the characters are making in deciphering the new riddle (Communication)

SECTION GOALS FOR

Chapter Opener

By the end of the Chapter Opener section, students will be able to:

- list environmental and personal factors that contribute to longevity.
- compare healthy lifestyle choices with unhealthy choices.
- narrate how their choices contribute to or detract from living healthily.

OBJETIVOS / CONTENIDOS

Comunicación

OBJETIVOS	CONTENIDOS	
• To describe parts of the human body	The human body	322
• To avoid repetition of previously mentioned people and things	Review of direct and indirect object pronouns and reflexive pronouns	325
• To describe what one does to himself/herself	Some illnesses and medical treatments	328
• To explain what ails you and suggest treatments for certain ailments	The exclamations ¡qué! and ¡cuánto!	332
• To make exclamatory or emphatic statements	The preterit and imperfect	334
• To narrate in the past	Expressions with hacer (*hace* + time, etc.)	341
• To talk about how long something has been going on and how long ago something occurred	Pronunciación: The letters d and t	323
• To ask yourself questions when listening to a passage to help organize and summarize what you heard	Escucha:	343
• To write a summary using the past tenses	Estrategia: Asking yourself questions	
	Escribe: Writing a summary using the past tenses	344

Cultura

OBJETIVOS	CONTENIDOS	
• To discuss the importance of water in maintaining good health	Water and good health	331
• To talk about pharmacies in Latin America and how they differ from those in the United States	Pharmacies in the Spanish-speaking world	340
• To talk about this chapter's featured countries: Peru, Bolivia, and Ecuador	*Perú, Bolivia,* and *Ecuador*	345–347

Ambiciones siniestras

OBJETIVOS	CONTENIDOS	
• To create check questions to facilitate comprehension when reading	Episodio 9	
• To discuss the contents of the new e-mail message	Lectura: *¡Qué mentira!*	348
• To talk about the progress the characters are making in deciphering the new riddle	Estrategia: Asking yourself questions	
	Video: *No llores por mí*	350

RECURSOS

Lesson Plan

¡A ponerse en forma!

PREGUNTAS

1 ¿Vives una vida sana (*healthy*)? ¿Qué haces (o no haces) para tener
una vida más sana?

2 ¿Qué tipo de ejercicio te gusta hacer?

3 ¿Crees que es más fácil vivir una vida sana a ciertas edades?
¿Por qué?

321

NATIONAL STANDARDS
Communities

This chapter is about health and
wellness. If you have a health/well-
ness major at your school (especially nutrition/dietetics or exercise
science) you could ask a faculty
member to provide materials that
your students could translate and
use to make presentations to the
Hispanic community about topics
such as the food pyramid, diet,
exercise, and preventive medical
care. They could get healthy recipes
and translate those into Spanish for
the Spanish-speaking community as
well. You could also ask local health
clinics or doctors' offices if they
have simple materials or signs they
would like to post in Spanish, such
as to whom to make checks, the
rules of the office regarding the use
of cell phones, or fees for certain
services like flu shots or copies of
forms. If you have a sizable Hispanic
community, you could ask the
hospital for upcoming wellness
programs and have students make
flyers in Spanish, posting the
details of the events. As always,
use good judgment when thinking
of service projects, remember the
skill level of your students, and
consider how they could serve the
community.

METHODOLOGY • Teacher Talk

In the classroom, although we simplify our language when we speak,
attempting to stay within the range
of *i + 1*, we should strive to deliver
our speech at a speed that is as
close to natural as possible. As the
semester progresses, that speed
gradually increases.

SECTION GOALS FOR
Comunicación

By the end of the *Comunicación* section, students will be able to:

- identify body parts and things associated with the human body.
- pronounce the letters *d* and *t* correctly.
- match body parts with clothing items worn on the body.
- review formation and placement of direct and indirect object pronouns and reflexive pronouns.
- describe ailments and medical treatments for ailments.
- tell where to go to treat certain symptoms and explain what symptoms they have.
- read about the importance of water to health.
- use *qué* and *cuánto* for exclamations.

NATIONAL STANDARDS
Communication

Talking about how one feels appeals to the basic sense that we all have; we love to talk about ourselves! Your students will enjoy the associated activities that help them acquire the vocabulary. The vocabulary associated with *el cuerpo humano* and *unas enfermedades y tratamientos médicos* is rich with communicative possibilities because the topic is universal. Most of the activities are for pairs and small groups, thus students are engaging in interpersonal communication (Standard 1.1). If you have students play doctor and patient, pretending to have ailments, or are acting out ailments you suggest, you satisfy Standard 1.3, the presentational mode. You could bring in the Spanish dosage instructions from packages of over-the-counter medications for students to read and discuss, and that would meet Standard 1.2, the interpretive mode. You could also read the instructions to them and use that as a listening activity.

Comunicación

- Describing the human body
- Avoiding repetition of previously mentioned people and things
- Describing what one does to oneself
- Making exclamations

VOCABULARIO 1

El cuerpo humano

`4:00`

9-1 to 9-6

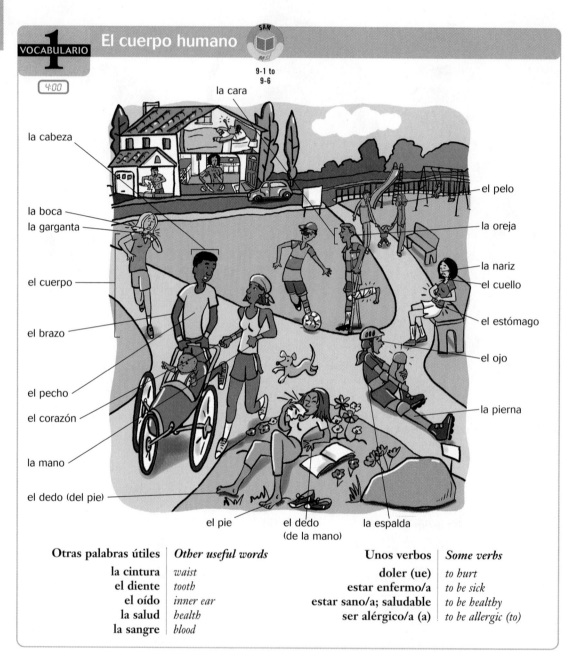

Otras palabras útiles	***Other useful words***
la cintura	*waist*
el diente	*tooth*
el oído	*inner ear*
la salud	*health*
la sangre	*blood*

Unos verbos	***Some verbs***
doler (ue)	*to hurt*
estar enfermo/a	*to be sick*
estar sano/a; saludable	*to be healthy*
ser alérgico/a (a)	*to be allergic (to)*

Additional activity for *El cuerpo humano*

 Categorías Juntos escriban todas las palabras de la lista que corresponden a las diferentes partes del cuerpo.

MODELO   E1: la cabeza
E2: *la cara, el pelo*, etc.

1. la cabeza
2. de la cintura para arriba (*from the waist up*)
3. de la cintura para abajo
4. el interior del cuerpo

RECURSOS | T9-1 to T9-2 | T9-1 to T9-2 | Electronic Activity Cache

CW eBook
CD 4
Track 1

SAM

9-7 to
9-10

PRONUNCIACIÓN 5:00

The letters *d* and *t*

1. The Spanish **d** is pronounced with a hard sound when it appears at the beginning of a sentence or phrase, or after the letters **n** or **l**. The sound is similar to the *d* in the English word *dog*.

doctor   Daniel   espalda   dónde

2. In all other cases, the Spanish **d** is pronounced like the *th* in the English words *they* or *father*.

oído   quedarse   antiácido   algodón

3. When pronouncing the Spanish **t**, the tongue touches the back of the upper teeth. It sounds like the *t* in the English word *star*.

diente   garganta   estómago   quitarse

9•1 Las palabras

Pronounce the following words, paying special attention to the letters **d** and **t**.

1. dedo
2. doctora
3. despertarse
4. David
5. vestido
6. diente
7. frecuentemente
8. todos
9. tenedor

9•2 Las oraciones

Pronounce the following sentences, paying special attention to the letters **d** and **t**.

1. A David le duelen los dientes y la garganta.
2. Estas sandalias y esa sudadera son cómodas. ¿Te gustan?
3. Deseo algo dulce como un helado u otro postre.

9•3 Los dichos y refranes

Now pronounce the following sayings and focus on the letters **d** and **t**.

1. Aunque la mona se vista de seda, mona se queda.
2. Del dicho al hecho hay mucho trecho.

2:00   **9•4** ¿Cómo nos vestimos?

Capítulo 8. La ropa, pág. 286.

Túrnense para decir qué partes del cuerpo asocian con la siguiente lista de ropa.

MODELO E1: los zapatos
          E2: *los pies*

1. las botas   los pies
2. los guantes   las manos
3. los pantalones   las piernas
4. la gorra   la cabeza
5. la corbata   el cuello
6. la camiseta   el pecho/la espalda
7. los calcetines   los pies
8. la chaqueta   el pecho/la espalda/los brazos

SECTION GOALS FOR
Pronunciación

By the end of the *Pronunciación* section, students will be able to:

- pronounce the letters *d* and *t* correctly.
- practice pronunciation skills using *dichos* and *refranes*.

METHODOLOGY • Group Work

What follows are some suggestions for pairing students using the body parts:

1. You will need one small piece of paper for each student. Write a different body part on half of the slips. On the other half of the slips, write a related body part or other word. For example, you might write *las manos* on one slip, and *los dedos* on another; *el ojo* on one, and *ver* on yet another. Put your slips of paper in a hat, box, or bag, and let each student draw a paper. Then tell them to get up and find the person who has the body part/word most closely "related" to their own. This is a critical thinking activity.
2. Again, you will need one slip of paper for each student in your class. Write the first part of the word on one slip, and finish the word on a second slip. For example, one slip might have *ca...* and its mate would have *...ra*. Another pair could be *estó...* and its partner would be *...mago*.
3. A third way is to write a body part on one slip and draw it on another (or cut the pictures out of a magazine). For example, on one slip of paper you write *la nariz* and on its match you draw (or cut out) a nose.

You will want to collect these slips of paper at the end of the activity so that you can reuse them in the future. A good way to organize them is to put them in sandwich bags and mark on the bags what vocabulary topic they are and which chapter they correspond to in *¡Anda!*

Additional activity for *El cuerpo humano*

¿Cómo se escribe? Escribe la primera y la última letra de una de las palabras nuevas. Un/a compañero/a tiene que terminarla. Túrnense para practicar la ortografía de por lo menos ocho palabras.

MODELO E1: e _ _ _ _ _ a
          E2: e s p a l d a

INSTRUCTIONS FOR 9-6

This activity has two parts. Draw a monster on the board, a transparency, etc. and have students work in pairs with one student facing the drawing and the other with his/her back to the drawing. The student facing the drawing describes what he/she sees (the instructor's drawing) and the other student draws it. When finished, the student compares the drawing he/she created with the original and then the students switch places and repeat the activity.

Suggestion for 9-6 Make your "monster" as unusual as you like, since the more you deviate from a real person, the more closely the student who is drawing must listen to his/her partner. Perhaps the monster you draw has one eye, three noses, two mouths, one tooth, one big ear, one small ear, three legs, and five hearts. If you have an odd number of students, one pair has to draw while the third student gives directions. Also, you may ask the extra student to draw the second monster after you have modeled the procedure. You may wish to teach additional words like *cuadrado, círculo, línea, triángulo*, etc. Finally, encourage the student giving the directions *not* to use his/her hands since this is a listening activity and he/she needs to work toward making himself/herself understood. By the way, this is a very popular activity with students and instructors alike. The students feel a real sense of accomplishment when they are able to carry on extended descriptions.

NOTE FOR 9-6

The objective of this activity is for students to listen to each other and to instantly demonstrate comprehension via the drawing. If the student who has his/her back to the *monstruo* does not understand, he/she must ask questions for clarification. Although couched in an enjoyable context where students are practicing their new vocabulary, the objective is much more important. Your students are communicating on an interpersonal level in an attempt to be mutually understood.

9·5 Una obra de arte [4:00]

Capítulo 3. *Hay*, pág. 122.

Miren el cuadro y descríbenlo usando las siguientes preguntas como guía.

1. ¿Cuántas personas hay en la pintura?   dos
2. ¿Cuántas caras hay?   cuatro
3. ¿Cuántas manos pueden ver?   seis
4. ¿Cuántos ojos pueden ver?   cinco
5. ¿Cuántas narices hay?   cuatro
6. ¿Qué otras cosas ven en la pintura?   pelo, cabezas, etc.
7. Estas personas son…   madre e hijo
8. La pintura representa…   *Answers may vary.*

Fíjate

Note that *la mano* is irregular; it ends in *o* but the word is feminine.

Estrategia

Being an "active listener" is an important skill in any language; it means that you have heard and understood what someone is saying. Being able to demonstrate that you have understood correctly, as in reproducing this drawing of the monster, helps you practice and perfect the skill of active listening.

9·6 ¿Es un monstruo o una obra de arte? [6:00]

Su instructor va a dibujar un monstruo. En parejas, un estudiante va a describir lo que ve y el otro estudiante va a dibujar lo que su compañero le describe. Al terminar, cambien de papel.

El monstruo tiene…

a la derecha	a la izquierda	encima de	debajo de

Additional activity for *El cuerpo humano* The following activity requires markers (or crayons) and end roll or butcher-type paper. If your institution does not have any paper readily available, you can acquire end rolls from your local newspaper. Newspapers usually donate end rolls to educators.

Vamos a dibujar Su profesor/a les va a dar un papel largo y unos marcadores (*markers*). Una persona del grupo va a acostarse (*lie down*) encima del papel. Otra persona va a calcar (*trace*) alrededor del/de la compañero/a. Después de calcarlo/a, cada persona en el grupo tiene que marcar (*label*) por lo menos (*at least*) tres partes del cuerpo.

GRAMÁTICA 2 — Un resumen de los pronombres de complemento directo, indirecto y reflexivos

9-11 to 9-15 · 20, 26, 34

4:00

¡Mamá! ¡La muñeca! ¡Me la robó!

Let's review the forms, functions, and positioning of the *direct* and *indirect object pronouns*, as well as the *reflexive pronouns*:

LOS PRONOMBRES DE COMPLEMENTO **DIRECTO**	LOS PRONOMBRES DE COMPLEMENTO **INDIRECTO**	LOS PRONOMBRES **REFLEXIVOS**
Direct object pronouns tell *what* or *who* receives the action of the verb. They replace direct object nouns and are used to avoid repetition.	Indirect object pronouns tell *to whom* or *for whom* something is done or given.	Reflexive pronouns indicate that the *subject* of a sentence or clause *receives the action of the verb.*

me	*me*		**me**	*to/for me*		**me**	*myself*	
te	*you*		**te**	*to/for you*		**te**	*yourself*	
lo, la	*him/her/you/it*		**le (se)**	*to/for him/her/you*		**se**	*himself/herself/yourself*	
nos	*us*		**nos**	*to/for us*		**nos**	*ourselves*	
os	*you (all)*		**os**	*to/for you (all)*		**os**	*yourselves*	
los, las	*them/you*		**les (se)**	*to/for them/you*		**se**	*themselves/yourselves*	

Compré el coche ayer. **Lo** compré por diez mil euros. Quiero regalárse**lo** a mi hijo.

I bought the car yesterday.
I bought it for ten thousand euros.
I want to give it to my son.

Le compré el coche ayer. **Le** voy a regalar el coche para su cumpleaños.

I bought him the car yesterday.
I am going to give him the car for his birthday.

Me cepillo los dientes tres veces al día.

I brush my teeth three times a day.

Remember the following guidelines on position and sequence:

Position

- Object pronouns and reflexive pronouns come **before** the verb.

Mi asistente **le** mandó la carta.
Después **se** sintió aliviado.

My assistant sent him the letter.
Then he felt relieved.

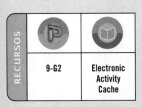
METHODOLOGY • Recycling and Spiraling

We firmly believe in recycling and spiraling. *Recycling* concepts means bringing them back for additional practice, usually including new vocabulary or additional grammar concepts. *Spiraling* means taking an already introduced concept (or vocabulary) and taking it to new and higher levels. It can mean the incorporation of higher order/critical thinking skills. In *Capítulo 9*, we recycle/spiral the direct, indirect, and reflexive pronouns, a grammar concept that is always important to practice because the placement of the pronouns differs from English.

NOTE FOR

Un resumen de los pronombres de complemento directo, indirecto y reflexivos

This grammar presentation provides an opportunity to review not only the object pronouns and reflexive pronouns, but also verb phrases: *ir + a + infinitive* and the present progressive tense.

- Object pronouns and reflexive pronouns can also be placed before or be attached to the end of:

   a. **infinitives**

El señor Rodríguez **me** va a contestar rápidamente. ⎫
El señor Rodríguez va a contestar**me** rápidamente. ⎭ *Mr. Rodríguez will respond to me quickly.*

Después **se** va a reunir con los gerentes. ⎫
Después va a reunir**se** con los gerentes. ⎭ *Then he will meet with the managers.*

   b. **present participles (-ando, -endo and -iendo)**

La está leyendo ahora. ⎫
Está leyéndo**la** ahora. ⎭ *He is reading it now.*

Se está poniendo nervioso. ⎫
Está poniéndo**se** nervioso. ⎭ *He is getting nervous.*

Sequence

- When a direct (DO) and indirect object (IO) pronoun are used together, ***the indirect object precedes the direct object.***

- If both the direct and the indirect object pronoun begin with the letter "*l*" the indirect object pronoun changes from **le** or **les** to **se,** as in the example below.

Quiero mandar la carta al director ahora.   *I want to send the letter to the director now.*

↓	↓		↓	↓
DO	IO		DO	IO
la	le (se)			
IO	DO			
se	la			

Se la quiero mandar ahora mismo. ⎫
Quiero mandár**se**la ahora mismo. ⎭ *I want to send it to him right now.*

9•7 Un animal muy extraño   `3:00`

Juntos respondan a las oraciones exclamativas con el pronombre de complemento directo apropiado y un adjetivo.

MODELO   E1: ¡Mira la nariz!

E2: *Sí, la tiene muy grande (pequeña/fea/bonita…).*

Fíjate

In Spanish, an animal's legs are referred to as *patas. Pierna(s)* is only used for people.

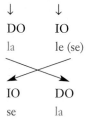

1. ¡Mira la boca!
2. ¡Mira las orejas!
3. ¡Mira los dientes!
4. ¡Mira las patas!

5. ¡Mira la cabeza!
6. ¡Mira el estómago!
7. ¡Mira la cara!
8. ¡Mira el cuello!

Capítulo 8. *Gustar* y verbos como *gustar*, pág. 294.

`3:00`

9·8 Las preferencias

Escribe oraciones completas usando siempre los pronombres de complemento indirecto. Después compara tus oraciones con las de un/a compañero/a.

MODELO   A Betty / gustar despertarse temprano
A Betty le gusta despertarse temprano.

1. A mis padres / importar el dinero   A mis padres les importa el dinero.
2. A mí / molestar las personas irresponsables   (A mí) Me molestan las personas irresponsables.
3. A Manolo / encantar las novelas de Rushdie   A Manolo le encantan las novelas de Rushdie.
4. A nosotros / hacer falta estudiar mucho más   (A nosotros) Nos hace falta estudiar mucho más.
5. A nuestro/a profesor/a / fascinar el cine japonés   (A nuestro profesor) Le fascina el cine japonés.

`7:00`

9·9 En el restaurante

¿Qué les ocurrió ayer a Paco y a Pati en el Restaurante Boca Grande?

Paso 1   Completa las oraciones con los pronombres de complemento directo, indirecto o reflexivo apropiados. Después, compara tus respuestas con las de un/a compañero/a.

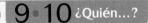

Paco y Pati se conocieron en el gimnasio. Decidieron cenar juntos y llegaron al restaurante con mucha hambre. (1) __Se R__ sentaron en una mesa grande al lado de las ventanas. Primero pidieron el menú. El camarero (2) __se IO__ (3) __lo DO__ trajo en seguida (inmediatamente). Después, (4) __les IO__ recomendó unos platos muy ricos. Paco pidió un bistec para él y a Pati (5) __le IO__ pidió pollo asado con ajo. ¡Pati no (6) __lo DO__ podía creer! ¡Paco ni (7) __le IO__ preguntó qué quería! Ella (8) __se R__ sentía muy incómoda—ningún hombre, excepto su padre, (9) __la DO__ había tratado (*had treated*) así antes. Pati (10) __se R__ calló mientras Paco hablaba de su día, su trabajo y su familia. Cuando por fin el camarero (11) __les IO__ sirvió la comida, Pati miró su plato y (12) __se R__ levantó gritando. ¡Su plato era del «Menú para niños»!

Paso 2   Digan qué tipo de pronombre es cada uno que usaron.

Answers to 9-10.
1. Patricia te los va a traer./ Patricia va a traértelos.
2. Paco te la está comprando. / Paco está comprándotela.
3. Guadalupe y Lina te lo van a limpiar. / Guadalupe y Lina van a limpiártelo.
4. Tu madre te la está lavando. / Tu madre está lavándotela.
5. Tina y Luisa te la están preparando. / Tina y Luisa están preparándotela.
6. Nadie te la va a hacer. / Nadie va a hacértela.

`4:00`

9·10 ¿Quién...?

Jacobo está enfermo y no puede levantarse de la cama. Es un poco exigente (*demanding*) y quiere saber quiénes lo van a atender (*wait on him*). Contesta sus preguntas y después comparte tus respuestas con un/a compañero/a.

MODELO   ¿Quién va a traerme la tarea? (hermano)
Tu hermano te la va a traer. / Tu hermano va a traértela.

1. ¿Quién va a traerme los libros que pedí? (Patricia)
2. ¿Quién está comprándome la medicina que necesito? (Paco)
3. ¿Quién me va a limpiar el cuarto? (Guadalupe y Lina)
4. ¿Quién me está lavando la ropa? (tu madre)
5. ¿Quién está preparándome la comida? (Tina y Luisa)
6. ¿Quién me va a hacer la tarea? (nadie)

NATIONAL STANDARDS

Communication, Comparisons, Connections

The vocabulary about illness, injury, and explaining symptoms to medical personnel encompasses many of the National Standards. Any of the pair or small group activities that require students to engage in conversations, provide and obtain information, express their feelings and emotions, and exchange opinions address Standard 1.1. The idea of using verbs reflexively and non-reflexively or the concept of using articles with body parts instead of using possessive adjectives helps students see the differences between Spanish and English. They make comparisons (Standard 4.1) between how they express pain or discomfort in Spanish and in English. They are able to connect their prior knowledge of science/health with the new vocabulary in Spanish.

VOCABULARIO 3 — Unas enfermedades y tratamientos médicos

9-16 to 9-21

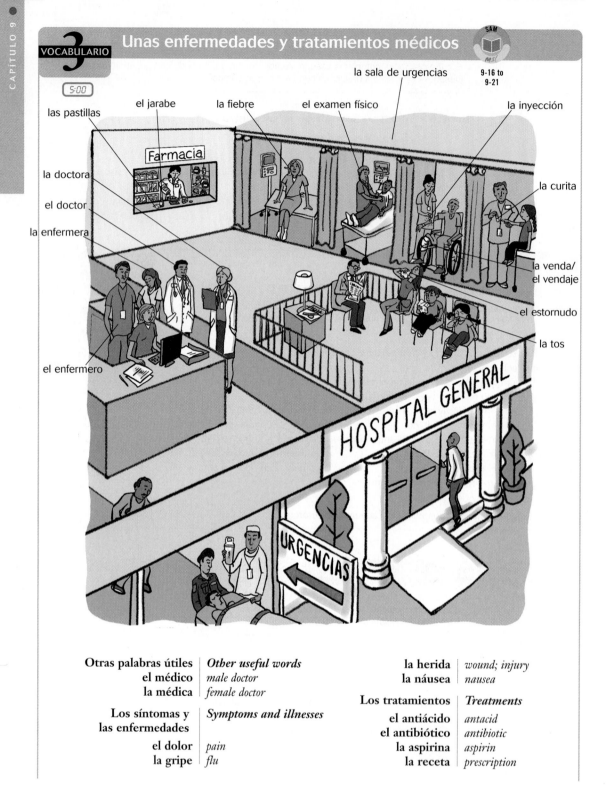

Otras palabras útiles	*Other useful words*
el médico	*male doctor*
la médica	*female doctor*

Los síntomas y las enfermedades	*Symptoms and illnesses*
el dolor	*pain*
la gripe	*flu*

la herida	*wound; injury*
la náusea	*nausea*

Los tratamientos	*Treatments*
el antiácido	*antacid*
el antibiótico	*antibiotic*
la aspirina	*aspirin*
la receta	*prescription*

RECURSOS			
	T9-3 to T9-4	T9-3 to T9-4	Electronic Activity Cache

Unos verbos	Some verbs
acabar de + infinitivo	to have just finished + (something)
cortar(se)	to cut (oneself)
curar(se)	to cure; to be cured
enfermar(se)	to get sick
estornudar	to sneeze
evitar	to avoid
guardar cama	to stay in bed
lastimar(se)	to get hurt
mejorar(se)	to improve; to get better
ocurrir	to occur
quemar(se)	to burn; to get burned
romper(se)	to break

tener...	
alergia (a)	to be allergic (to)
(un) catarro, resfriado	to have a cold
(la/una) gripe	to have the flu
una infección	to have an infection
tos	to have a cough
un virus	to have a virus
tener dolor de...	
cabeza	to have a headache
espalda	to have a backache
estómago	to have a stomachache
garganta	to have a sore throat
toser	to cough
tratar de	to try to
vendar(se)	to bandage (oneself); to dress (a wound)

Fíjate

A verb with **se** in parentheses indicates that it can be also used as a reflexive verb.

quemar(se): Ayer me quemé. (reflexive)   *Yesterday I burned myself.*
Ayer quemé los papeles viejos.   *Yesterday I burned the old papers.*

5:00

9·11 Unos tratamientos

¿Adónde tienes que ir para poder curarte o buscar tratamiento para las siguientes condiciones? Pon una equis (**X**) en la columna apropiada. Después, túrnate con un/a compañero/a para decir adónde van.

MODELO   un brazo roto (*broken*)

E1:   *Si tengo un brazo roto, voy a la sala de urgencias.*

CONDICIÓN	A LA CAMA	A LA FARMACIA	AL CONSULTORIO DEL MÉDICO	AL HOSPITAL	A LA SALA DE URGENCIAS
1. tos					
2. náusea					
3. (la) gripe					
4. (un) dolor de garganta					
5. una infección de la sangre					
6. una herida en la pierna					
7. (un) catarro					
8. fiebre					

Fíjate

Body parts are usually referred to with an article, not a possessive adjective.

Me duele   **My** hand
la mano.   hurts.

TPR activity for *Unas enfermedades y tratamientos médicos* Have students act out certain symptoms as you say them. E.g., *Cuando tengo la gripe, me duele mucho el estómago. Tengo náusea y me entran ganas de vomitar. A veces estornudo y tengo que guardar cama.*

HERITAGE LANGUAGE LEARNERS

If you have Heritage language learners, they can role play doctors, and your other students can be patients with various ailments. Either give the "patients" slips of paper with symptoms, or have them create their own that they present to the doctor. The "doctor" then prescribes a course of treatment.

CAPÍTULO 9

NOTE FOR 9-12

Soroche, or altitude sickness, can strike anyone, regardless of whether he/she is in good or poor health. People in really good physical shape can fall victim to *soroche*, and feeble folks can be immune. The best remedy is to move slowly, avoid alcohol, meat, and tobacco the first few days, and acclimatize. Symptoms can also be lessened by drinking a tea made from the local coca leaves, a local herbal remedy.

Additional activity for *Unas enfermedades y tratamientos médicos*

No sirve ¿Qué palabra o expresión no pertenece (*doesn't belong*) a cada uno de los siguientes grupos de palabras? Túrnense para leer la lista y contestar.

MODELO

E1: el estómago, la cara, el ojo, la nariz

E2: *el estómago*

1. el hospital, el doctor, el enfermero, el oído
2. toser, estornudar, la receta, tener catarro
3. el jarabe, la farmacia, las pastillas, quemarse
4. lastimarse, la sala de urgencias, la tos, romperse la pierna
5. la venda, la herida, cortarse, el resfriado

Answers: 1. el oído, 2. la receta, 3. quemarse, 4. la tos, 5. el resfriado

---

9·12 El soroche 5:00

El verano pasado Nina fue a Bolivia como voluntaria para ayudar a construir una escuela en el altiplano (*high plateau*).

Paso 1 Juntos terminen la conversación entre Nina y su padre con las palabras de la lista.

corazón	enfermedad	evitar	me duele
mejorar	náusea	pastillas	estómago

NINA: Hola, Papá.

PAPÁ: ¡Ay, Nina! ¿Cómo estás, hija? ¿Llegaste bien?

NINA: Sí. Ayer llegamos bien pero hoy me siento enferma. (1) __Me duele__ la cabeza. No me duele mucho el (2) __estómago__ pero tengo (3) __náusea__ cuando pienso en la comida—me entran ganas (*I get the urge*) de vomitar.

PAPÁ: Pobrecita. ¿Qué te pasa? ¿Comiste ayer?

NINA: Sí, un poco. Pero desde que (*since*) llegamos no tengo mucha hambre.

PAPÁ: ¿Tienes otros síntomas?

NINA: Sí. El (4) __corazón__ me late (*is beating*) rápidamente y no puedo respirar (*breathe*) muy bien. ¿Crees que tengo alguna (5) __enfermedad__?

PAPÁ: Nina, me parece que tienes soroche.

NINA: ¿Soroche? ¿Qué es eso?

PAPÁ: Es el mal de altura (*altitude sickness*). Debes empezar a sentirte mejor (*better*) en un par de días. Mientras tanto, necesitas intentar relajarte, tomar mucha agua y (6) __evitar__ el alcohol y el tabaco. También puedes tomar unas (7) __pastillas__ de ibuprofén y beber un té medicinal hecho de (*made from*) hojas de coca (*coca leaves*).

NINA: Gracias, Papá. Ya que entiendo qué me ocurre, creo que me voy a (8) __mejorar__ pronto.

Paso 2 Ahora, contesten las siguientes preguntas.

1. ¿Qué es el soroche? Es la enfermedad de la altura.
2. ¿Cuáles son los síntomas? Con el soroche puedes tener dolor de cabeza, náusea, no tener hambre, el corazón late rápidamente y no puedes respirar bien.
3. ¿Qué tratamiento le recomienda su papá? Le recomienda tomar ibuprofén, descansar/relajarse, beber mucha agua, evitar el alcohol y el tabaco y tomar un té de hojas de coca.

9·13 Para evitar lo inevitable

¿Cómo tratan de evitar tus compañeros las siguientes enfermedades y condiciones? Circula por la clase para hacerles estas preguntas. Necesitas **tres** respuestas para cada pregunta.

MODELO TÚ: ¿Cómo tratas de evitar el dolor de garganta?

E1: *Bebo mucho jugo de naranja.*

E2: *Llevo una bufanda* (scarf) *en el cuello.*

E3: *Tomo mucha vitamina C.*

1. ¿Cómo tratas de evitar el dolor de cabeza?	4. ¿Cómo evitas enfermarte?
E1: _____	E1: _____
E2: _____	E2: _____
E3: _____	E3: _____
2. ¿Cómo tratas de evitar el dolor de estómago?	5. ¿Cómo evitas cortarte?
E1: _____	E1: _____
E2: _____	E2: _____
E3: _____	E3: _____
3. ¿Cómo tratas de evitar el dolor de espalda?	6. ¿Cómo tratas de evitar la depresión?
E1: _____	E1: _____
E2: _____	E2: _____
E3: _____	E3: _____

El agua y la buena salud

¿Sabías que tres cuartas partes de tu peso corporal son de agua? Tu vida empezó en un mar de líquido amniótico y ahora, como adulto, alrededor del ochenta y cinco por ciento de la sangre, el setenta por ciento de los músculos y el veintidós por ciento de tu cerebro consiste en agua.

Para mantener la buena salud se debe beber por lo menos dos litros (seis a ocho vasos) de agua al día. El cuerpo elimina de unos quinientos a setecientos centímetros cúbicos diarios de agua al sudar (sweat) y es muy importante reponer esa cantidad y más.

Los alimentos son una fuente importante de agua para el cuerpo, sobre todo las frutas y las verduras. También cuentan otras bebidas además del agua, pero hay que considerar que algunas tienen el efecto contrario. El café y las bebidas alcohólicas deshidratan. Para compensar esta deshidratación hay que beber agua. Por ejemplo, por cada vaso de cerveza se debe tomar otro vaso de agua.

Answers to *Preguntas.* 1. El cuerpo contiene mucha agua, pero cada día elimina de 500 a 700 centímetros cúbicos al sudar.

Preguntas
2. Todos los órganos del cuerpo funcionan mejor; beber agua es bueno para la piel y el pelo; beber agua ayuda a eliminar toxinas del cuerpo.

1. ¿Por qué es importante beber tanta (so much) agua? ¿Cuántos vasos de agua bebes al día?

2. ¿Qué otros beneficios tiene beber suficiente agua al día?

METHODOLOGY • Reading

Always activate students' schemata, tap into their pre-existing knowledge, prior to assigning a reading. For example, prepare students for this reading by asking them what they usually drink, how much water they drink per day, and in what ways they think water is important to our health. You may also want to pick out a few key words from the reading and ask students what they mean.

NATIONAL STANDARDS
Communication, Cultures, Connections

The cultural reading about *el aguá y la buena salud* encompasses Communication and Connections. Students read and interpret the text (Standard 1.2). Students have prior knowledge about the benefits of water from their science and health courses, so they are able to connect what they read in Spanish to what they learned in those disciplines (Standard 3.1).

HERITAGE LANGUAGE LEARNERS

You may wish to assign Heritage language learners or advanced learners the project of researching water issues in Latin America.

HERITAGE LANGUAGE LEARNERS

Your Heritage language learners or advanced students may enjoy www.buenasalud.com. It has a wealth of information that students can take advantage of for writing reports or sending e-mails to other students, to name just a few activities.

Juntos respondan a estas situaciones. Pueden utilizar estas expresiones o responder con sus propias.

| ¡Qué (mala) suerte! | ¡Qué cruel! | ¡Qué dolor! ¡Cuánto tiempo! |
| ¡Qué horrible! | ¡Qué romántico! | ¡Qué triste! ¡Qué interesante! |

1. Mis padres celebran este mes su aniversario de boda—¡25 años ya!
2. Félix, no te quiero desilusionar después de tantos meses juntos, pero quiero salir con otros hombres.
3. Silvia es la mujer más increíble del mundo. Quiero ser más que su novio. Quiero pasar mi vida a su lado.
4. Nadie quiere salir conmigo (*with me*). Nadie me mira. Me gusta ir al cine, comer en buenos restaurantes, ir a partidos de básquetbol, bailar—pero no me gusta hacer estas cosas solo (*alone*).
5. Soy muy joven para tener novia. Me divertí contigo (*with you*) anoche en la fiesta pero me divierto con muchas mujeres....
6. Adriano es el hombre perfecto para mí. Es muy respetuoso, considerado y me trata bien siempre.

GRAMÁTICA 4 — ¡Qué! y ¡cuánto!

9-24 to 9-26

So far you have used **qué** and **cuánto** as interrogative words, but these words can also be used in exclamatory sentences.

—Felipe, **¡qué** anillo! — *Felipe, what a ring!*
—María, **¡cuánto** te quiero! — *María, I love you so much!*
—Mi cabeza, **¡qué** dolor! — *My head—what pain!*
—**Cuánto** lo siento. — *I'm so sorry. (How sorry I am.)*
—**¡Qué** susto! ¡Se cortó el dedo! — *What a scare! He cut his finger!*
—Se ve muy mal. **¡Qué** feo! — *It looks really bad. How awful! (It looks awful/ugly.)*
—**¡Qué** doctor! Le salvó la vida. — *What a doctor! He saved his life.*
—**Cuánto** se lo agradezco. — *I'm so thankful. (How grateful I am.)*

*Note that in the examples above, **cuánto** accompanies *verbs* and is masculine and singular. When **cuánto** accompanies *nouns* it must agree with them in gender and number:

—**¡Cuántas** recetas y todavía estoy tosiendo! — *So many prescriptions and I am still coughing!*
—Sí, y **¡cuántos** estudiantes con la misma cosa! — *Yes, and so many students with the same thing.*

9•14 ¿Cómo respondes?   3:00

Elige la respuesta apropiada para cada comentario. Después, comparte tus respuestas con un/a compañero/a.

1. __d__ ¡Ay, el estómago!
2. __c__ Su novia se graduó con honores.
3. __h__ Pepe me compró veinticuatro rosas rojas.
4. __e__ Esta comida es deliciosa.
5. __f__ Este doctor es el novio de aquella enfermera.
6. __g/b__ Mi madre preparó tapas para cincuenta personas.
7. __a__ Tiene la cara de un monstruo.
8. __b__ Tengo que leer dos libros para mi clase de historia y preparar un informe.

a. ¡Qué feo!
b. ¡Cuánto trabajo!
c. ¡Qué inteligente!
d. ¡Cuánto me duele!
e. ¡Cuánto me gusta!
f. ¡Qué interesante!
g. ¡Cuánta comida!
h. ¡Qué romántico!

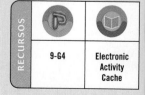

9-G4   Electronic Activity Cache

Follow-up to 9-15 Bring in photos (try Google Images for faster browsing) of ailments, broken bones, and diseases, and ask students how they would respond in Spanish. Give them some additional choices such as: *¡Qué susto!, ¡Qué horror!, ¡Cuánto me duele!,* etc.

3:00 ii **9·15** ¿Qué tiene?

¿Cómo responden Uds. a las siguientes situaciones?

MODELO   E1:   Tito está muy mal porque tiene un dolor terrible de estómago.

E2:   *¡Cuánto le duele!*

E1:   Yo no puedo hablar porque estoy tosiendo mucho.

E2:   *¡Qué tos tengo!*

Answers to 9-15.
1. ¡Qué catarro/resfriado tengo!
2. ¡Qué mala suerte tiene!
3. ¡Cuánto me duele el estómago!
4. ¡Qué caro! ¡Cuánto dinero le va a costar!
5. ¡Qué enferma estás!

1. No puedo respirar, me duele la garganta, estornudo todo el tiempo y no tengo hambre.
2. A mi hermano siempre le ocurre algo malo: un accidente, se rompe algo…
3. ¡Ay! Necesito un antiácido ahora mismo, por favor.
4. Mi abuelo acaba de salir del hospital después de pasar mucho tiempo allí. No tiene seguro médico (*insurance*).
5. Tú tienes mucha fiebre y te duele el cuerpo.

¿Cómo andas?

Having completed the first **Comunicación**, I now can…

	Feel Confident	Need to Review
describe the human body (p. 322)	❑	❑
pronounce the letters **d** and **t** correctly (p. 323)	❑	❑
identify and use direct object, indirect object, and reflexive pronouns with more confidence (p. 325)	❑	❑
explain what ails me and understand others when they say where "it" hurts (p. 328)	❑	❑
suggest treatments for various ailments (p. 328)	❑	❑
explain the importance of water in maintaining good health (p. 331)	❑	❑
use the exclamations **¡qué!** and **¡cuánto!** (p. 332)	❑	❑

Comunicación

- Talking about the past
- Narrating in the past
- Explaining how long something has been going on
- Telling how long ago something happened

GRAMÁTICA 5 El pretérito y el imperfecto

9-27 to 9-34   35, 36, 41

5:00

In **Capítulos 7** and **8** you learned about two aspects of the past tense in Spanish, **el pretérito** and **el imperfecto,** which are not interchangeable. Their uses are contrasted below.

Fuimos a Cuzco y subimos a Machu Picchu. Hacía buen tiempo.

THE **PRETERIT** IS USED:	THE **IMPERFECT** IS USED:
1. To relate an event or occurrence that refers to *one specific time in the past* • **Fuimos** a Cuzco el año pasado. *We went to Cuzco last year.* • **Comimos** en el restaurante El Sol y **nos gustó** mucho. *We ate at El Sol restaurant and liked it a lot.*	**1.** To express *habitual* or often *repeated actions* • **Íbamos** a Cuzco todos los veranos. *We used to go to Cuzco every summer.* • **Comíamos** en el restaurante El Sol todos los lunes. *We used to eat at El Sol Restaurant every Monday.*
2. To relate an act *begun or completed in the past* • **Empezó** a llover. *It started to rain.* • **Comenzaron** los juegos. *The games began.* • La gira **terminó.** *The tour ended.*	**2.** To express *was/were + -ing* • **Llovía** sin parar. *It rained without stopping.* • **Comenzaban** los juegos cuando llegamos. *The games were beginning when we arrived.* • La gira **transcurría** sin ningún problema. *The tour continued without any problems.*
3. To relate a *sequence of events*, each completed and moving the narrative along toward its conclusion • **Llegamos** en avión, **recogimos** las maletas y **fuimos** al hotel. *We arrived by plane, picked up our luggage, and went to the hotel.* • Al día siguiente **decidimos** ir a Machu Picchu. *The next day we decided to go to Machu Picchu.* • **Vimos** muchos ejemplos de la magnífica arquitectura incaica. Después **anduvimos** un poco por el camino de los incas. **Nos divertimos** mucho. *We saw many examples of the magnificent Incan architecture. Afterward we walked a bit on the Incan road. We had a great time.*	**3.** To provide *background* information, set the stage, or express a pre-existing condition • **Era** un día oscuro. **Llovía** de vez en cuando. *It was a dark day and it rained once in a while.* • Los turistas **llevaban** pantalones cortos y lentes de sol. *The tourists were wearing shorts and sunglasses.* • El camino **era** estrecho y **había** muchos turistas. *The path was narrow and there were many tourists.*

4. To relate an action that took place within a specified or *specific amount* (segment) *of time.*

Caminé (por) dos horas.
I walked for two hours.

Hablamos (por) cinco minutos.
We talked for five minutes.

Contemplaron el templo un rato.
They contemplated the temple for a while.

Viví en Ecuador (por) seis años.
I lived in Ecuador for six years.

4. To *tell time* in the past

Era la una.
It was 1:00.

Eran las tres y media.
It was 3:30.

Era muy tarde.
It was very late.

Era la medianoche.
It was midnight.

> **Fíjate**
> The use of *por* is optional in these cases.

WORDS AND EXPRESSIONS THAT COMMONLY SIGNAL:

PRETERIT	IMPERFECT
anoche	a menudo
anteayer	cada semana/mes/año
ayer	con frecuencia
de repente (*suddenly*)	de vez en cuando (*once in a while*)
el fin de semana pasado	mientras
el mes pasado	muchas veces
el lunes pasado/el martes pasado, etc.	frecuentemente
esta mañana	todos los lunes/martes, etc.
una vez, dos veces, etc.	todas las semanas
siempre (when an end point is obvious)	todos los días/meses/años
	siempre (when an event is repeated with no particular end point)

Please note: The **pretérito** and the **imperfecto** can be used in the same sentence.

Miraban la tele cuando **sonó** el teléfono.

They were watching TV when the phone rang.

In the preceding sentence, an action was going on **(miraban)** when it was interrupted by another action **(sonó el teléfono).**

Suggestion for *El pretérito y el imperfecto* Begin each class with directed questions using both the *pretérito* and the *imperfecto*. Some sample questions might be: *¿A qué hora te acostaste anoche?, ¿A qué hora te acostabas el verano pasado?, ¿Qué te pusiste ayer?, ¿Qué te ponías cuando tenías cinco años?,* etc.

Suggestion for *El pretérito y el imperfecto* To assist in remembering the *pretérito* and *imperfecto* and the rules for each, have students recall a humorous story from their childhood. Have students write the story in English and decide which verbs in their story would be *preterit* and which would be *imperfect*. They can use the examples from their humorous story to help them remember which to use and why.

Additional activity for *El pretérito y el imperfecto* What follows is an additional activity that can help to ease students into using the preterit and the imperfect correctly. It is intentionally in English so that students are able to connect how the preterit and imperfect relate to expressing the past in English.

Una mañana muy extraña Lee el siguiente texto sobre una experiencia muy extraña. Señala si el verbo debe estar en pretérito (P) o imperfecto (I) y explica por qué.

MODELO
1. was (P/I) #4 (*To relate an action that took place within a specified or specific amount [segment] of time—"yesterday morning."*)

Yesterday morning (1) was (P/I) strange. When I (2) woke up (P/I), I (3) was feeling (P/I) a little sick. My head (4) was hurting (P/I) and my back (5) ached (P/I) as well. The weather (6) was (P/I) damp and cold so I (7) was (P/I) not anxious to get out of bed. Suddenly I (8) heard (P/I) a crash. I (9) glanced (P/I) at the clock and (10) saw (P/I) that it (11) was (P/I) already 8:45. My

roommate always leaves by 8:00 so I (12) believed (P/I) that I (13) was (P/I) alone. I (14) jumped (P/I) out of bed and (15) ran (P/I) to the window. I (16) didn't see (P/I) anything unusual. I (17) was thinking (P/I) I (18) should look (P/I) around outside when I (19) heard (P/I) an eerie sound, like a cross between a whimper and a howl.

By that time my head (20) was throbbing (P/I) along with my back, but I (21) could not pay attention (P/I) to the pain. I (22) struggled (P/I) to overcome it so I (23) could focus (P/I) on the situation at hand. Without grabbing a coat, I (24) ran out the door. I (25) did not realize (P/I) that the wooden steps (26) were (P/I) icy and I immediately (27) slipped (P/I) and (28) fell (P/I). I (29) banged (P/I) both my back and my head on the hard, wooden steps. I (30) screamed (P/I) loudly but (31) did not feel (P/I) the fall because to my right there (32) was (P/I) a big black bear digging in our garbage can. He (33) was staring (P/I) at me, apparently (34) feeling

(P/I) just as startled as I (35) was (P/I). At exactly the same moment we (36) began (P/I) to back away from each other—me up the steps and the bear away from the garbage can. As I (37) was reaching (P/I) up to open the screen door, the bear (38) turned (P/I) and (39) ran (P/I).

Once I (40) calmed (P/I) down I (41) realized (P/I) that I (42) was no longer feeling (P/I) pain. The fear and the hard fall had cured me!

9·16 Una (muy) breve historia de los incas 6:00

¿Qué sabes sobre los incas? Lee el siguiente fragmento y completa las actividades que siguen con un/a compañero/a.

Machu Picchu, la ciudad perdida de los incas.

El imperio de los incas.

El imperio de los incas <u>fue</u> uno de los imperios más importantes de las civilizaciones precolombinas. <u>Se encontraba</u> (*It was located*) en lo que es hoy Perú, Bolivia, el norte de Chile y parte de Ecuador. El imperio <u>se dividía</u> en tres partes iguales: una tercera parte <u>pertenecía</u> (*pertained to*) a los indígenas y <u>pasaba</u> de padre a hijo; otra tercera parte <u>era</u> del Inca, o sea, del Gobierno; la otra tercera parte <u>pertenecía</u> a la Iglesia.

Los incas <u>adoraban</u> al hijo del Sol. Según la leyenda (*legend*), el hijo <u>cayó</u> (*fell*) en algún lugar cerca del lago Titicaca. Con él <u>llegó</u> su hermana y según la leyenda, ellos <u>eran</u> los padres de todos los incas. Esta civilización <u>practicaba</u> sacrificios de animales y algunas veces sacrificios humanos. También le <u>ofrecían</u> objetos preciosos y joyas (*jewels*) al sol. El último cacique (o jefe político) famoso de los incas <u>fue</u> Atahualpa.

1. Subrayen los verbos.
2. Digan cuáles son pretéritos y cuáles son imperfectos.
3. Expliquen por qué usaron cada uno de estos tiempos verbales.

CULTURAL BACKGROUND FOR 9-16

The lost city of Machu Picchu (8,000 feet, 2,438 meters) was rediscovered in 1911 by Hiram Bingham, an archaeologist from Yale University. It had been hidden for centuries in the mountains of the Andes northwest of Cuzco. Its amazing construction and architecture demonstrate the achievements of the Incan civilization. The stones of the buildings there are cut precisely to fit together tightly; not even a knife blade can be inserted between them. There is no mortar holding the stones in place. As the Incas did not use the wheel, it is a mystery how they could construct such massive buildings so high up in the mountains. The Urubamba River snakes along 2,000 feet (610 meters) below. Cuzco is at 11,000 feet (3,353 meters), much higher than Machu Picchu.

NOTE ON 9-16

In some texts you will see definite articles before the names of countries, as in *el Perú* or *el Ecuador*. We have not included the articles here in *Una (muy) breve historia de los incas*, but you have the option to use them.

Expansion for 9-16 You may want to ask students these comprehension questions:

1. ¿Dónde se encontraba el imperio de los incas?
2. ¿Cómo se dividía el imperio?
3. ¿En qué consiste la leyenda del hijo del sol?
4. ¿Qué practicaban los incas?

9·17 Un cuento de hadas `4:00`

En grupos de tres o cuatro personas, pongan las siguientes oraciones en orden cronológico para terminar el cuento de Ricitos de Oro (*Goldilocks*). Después, analicen los usos del pretérito y el imperfecto dentro del cuento como lo hicieron en la actividad **9-16**.

Había una vez una niña muy curiosa. Un día, mientras caminaba por el bosque, encontró una casa muy bonita. En la casa vivían tres osos. Mientras los osos no estaban, …

__9__ Los osos la asustaron *(scared her)*.

__3__ Entró en el dormitorio de los osos.

__7__ Mientras ella dormía entraron los osos.

__10__ La niña se levantó y salió corriendo de la casa.

__2__ Tenía sueño.

__4__ Buscó una cama.

__1__ La niña entró en la casa.

__5__ Vio que una cama era muy grande, otra era muy pequeña y la otra tenía el tamaño perfecto.

__8__ Encontraron a la niña dormida en la cama.

__6__ Se acostó.

9·18 En el consultorio `6:00`

Capítulo 8. Las construcciones reflexivas, pág. 302.

Completa el siguiente pasaje con la forma correcta del pretérito o el imperfecto de cada verbo. Después, comparte las respuestas con un/a compañero/a y explícale por qué usaste el pretérito o el imperfecto.

Ayer en el consultorio del Dr. Fuentes (1. haber) ___había___ mucha actividad. Muchos pacientes (2. esperar) ___esperaban___ al médico y yo no (3. encontrar) ___encontraba___ dónde sentarme. Dos horas (4. pasar) ___pasaron___ lentamente. (5. Ser) ___Eran___ las once cuando por fin la recepcionista me (6. llamar) ___llamó___ y la enfermera (7. salir) ___salió___ para buscarme. Juntas (8. entrar) ___entramos___ al cuarto donde (9. estar) ___estaba___ el médico. El Dr. Fuentes (10. levantarse) ___se levantó___ y me (11. mirar) ___miró___ con mucha curiosidad. (12. Empezar) ___Empezó___ a examinarme y a hacerme preguntas.

Yo (13. ponerse) ___me puse___ nerviosa y (14. callarse) ___me callé___. Sólo (15. esperar) ___esperaba___ un examen anual típico pero las preguntas (16. ser) ___eran___ demasiadas específicas. Por ejemplo, me (17. preguntar) ___preguntó___ si (18. sentirse) ___me sentía___ mareada *(faint)* por la mañana y si (19. comer) ___comía___ bien cuando (20. tener) ___tenía___ hambre.

Por fin (21. darse cuenta [*to realize*]: yo) ___me di cuenta___ de lo que (22. ocurrir) ___ocurría___. ¡El Dr. Fuentes (23. pensar) ___pensaba___ que yo (24. estar) ___estaba___ embarazada *(pregnant)*! Por lo visto la enfermera (25. equivocarse [*to be mistaken*]) ___se equivocó___ y ¡le (26. dar) ___dio___ al médico la información de otra paciente!

`4:00` 9·19 En el pasado

Termina las siguientes oraciones. Después, compártelas con un/a compañero/a.

MODELO Cuando era niño/a…

E1: *Cuando era niño me gustaba subirme a los árboles.*

1. Cuando era niño/a…
2. Cuando tenía entre catorce y dieciséis años, frecuentemente…
3. Una vez el verano pasado…
4. Ayer tenía ganas de _____ pero…
5. Anoche…
6. Cuando vivía con mis padres, todas las semanas…

5:00 **9·20** Nuestro cuento

En grupos de tres, van a contar una historia (en el pasado) basada en los dibujos. Al terminar van a compartir su historia con los otros miembros de la clase.

Estrategia

In this variation of "Cinderella," remember to use the *imperfect* for *description* and *background* information. Use the *preterit* for *sequences of actions*.

La Cenicienta

9·21 Y en el hospital 〔8:00〕

Imagina que trabajas como enfermero/a en la sala de urgencias de un hospital. Un día entra un joven de unos veinte años con unos síntomas raros.

Paso 1 Llena el siguiente formulario médico para el joven enfermo como si fueras un/a enfermero/a.

FORMULARIO MÉDICO

Por favor complete este formulario con la mayor precisión posible. Toda la infomación en este formulario es confidencial y será utilizada en caso de emergencia. Por favor escriba legiblemente.

HISTORIA MÉDICA

Nombre _____
Dirección _____
Ciudad y estado _____
Código postal _____
Número de teléfono _____
Edad _____
Fecha de nacimiento _____
Sexo _____ Peso _____ Altura _____
Grupo sanguíneo _____

1. ¿Está bajo tratamiento por alguna enfermedad? Explique._____
_____

2. ¿Toma algún tipo de medicamento? _____
_____

3. ¿Tiene algún tipo de alergia?_____
_____

4. ¿Ha tenido cirugía alguna vez?_____
_____

CONDICIONES MÉDICAS

Por favor marque cualquier enfermedad que haya tenido en el pasado y la fecha en que comenzó.

_____artritis	_____asma	_____dolor de espalda
_____mareos	_____tos crónica	_____dolor de pecho
_____diabetes	_____epilepsia	_____fracturas
_____dolor de cabeza	_____hernia	_____presión alta

¿Ha tenido otra condición que no hemos mencionado?_____
_____

Paso 2 Crea seis preguntas para determinar cuál es su problema, según el modelo.

MODELO E1: ¿Dar / todos sus datos / en recepción?

E2: *¿Dio todos sus datos en recepción?*

1. ¿Cuándo / llegar / la sala de urgencias? ¿Cuándo llegó Ud. a la sala de urgencias?
2. ¿Cuándo / le empezar / a doler? ¿Cuándo le empezó a doler?
3. ¿Qué / hacer / cuando / le empezar / a doler? ¿Qué hacía cuando le empezó a doler?
4. ¿Quién / estar / con Ud.? ¿Quién estaba con Ud.?
5. ¿Cómo / sentirse / cuando / acostarse / anoche? ¿Cómo se sentía Ud. cuando se acostó anoche?
6. ¿Qué / hacer / para causar el dolor? ¿Qué hizo Ud. para causar el dolor?

Paso 3 Crea un diálogo con un/a compañero/a entre el joven y el/la enfermero/a usando las preguntas que escribiste.

Additional activity for *El pretérito y el imperfecto*
Los días del verano. ¿Qué hiciste el verano pasado? Usando por lo menos cinco oraciones, descríbele a un/a compañero/a un día normal, y después, en otras cinco oraciones, un día que fue diferente.

Additional activity for *El pretérito y el imperfecto*
Entrevista a un/a compañero/a sobre un accidente que sufrió. Debe incluir la siguiente información:

- que hacía cuando ocurrió
- cuando ocurrió
- dónde ocurrió
- cómo ocurrió el accidente
- quién le ayudó
- qué pasó después

Additional activity for *El pretérito y el imperfecto*
This grammar topic is the perfect opportunity for a round robin story. Divide students into 5 or 6 groups. Write the first sentence or two of a possible story on the board (e.g., *Era una noche oscura. Roberto estaba solo en su casa...; Había una vez una niña muy, muy mala...*). Tell the groups to continue the story. Give them five or six minutes to write collectively. Then, have each group pass their story to the group to their left (or right). The groups now read what the previous group has written and continue that story for another five or six minutes. This continues until all groups have contributed to each story. At that time, the stories go back to their original group to be finished. You may want to devote an entire class to this activity or divide it over two class periods.

NOTE FOR

Las farmacias en el mundo hispanohablante

You may want to share the following information with students regarding health systems in Spanish-speaking countries.

    En el mundo hispano hay una variedad de sistemas de salud:

- nacionales de salud pública con cobertura (*coverage*) para todos
- privados para la gente con mayores recursos (*greater financial resources*)
- mixtos (público y privado) con todo rango (*level*) de servicios según el nivel económico del paciente
- de cobertura (*coverage*) para los trabajadores que contribuyen al seguro social (pero también hay opciones para las personas que no tienen recursos propios)

NATIONAL STANDARDS

Communication, Comparisons, Connections

The cultural reading, *Las farmacias en el mundo hispanohablante*, provides the context for Communication, Comparisons, and Connections. Students are reading an authentic text that requires them to understand and interpret written Spanish (Standard 1.2), but if you read it aloud to them for listening comprehension, you could satisfy written and spoken Spanish. When students discuss the differences between Latin American pharmacies and American pharmacies, they engage in conversations in the interpersonal mode (Standard 1.1) and compare the cultural differences between pharmacies (Standard 4.2). Students use their background information about what role pharmacies have in the United States and they connect this knowledge to their understanding of how pharmacies in Latin America operate (Standard 3.2).

9·22 La última vez que me enfermé `5:00`

Túrnense para describir la última vez que se enfermaron. Incluyan esta información.

- ¿Cuándo fue?
- ¿Cómo te sentías?
- ¿Cuáles fueron los síntomas?
- Si fuiste al médico, ¿qué te hizo? ¿Qué te dijo?
- ¿Te recetó (*recetar = to prescribe*) algo? ¿Cuánto pagaste por la visita? Si no fuiste al médico, ¿qué hiciste para curarte?
- ¿Cuánto tiempo duró (*durar = to last*) la enfermedad?

> **Fíjate**
>
> Use the term *médico* when referring to the profession of a doctor. Use *doctor* for the title of the person.
>
> El <u>Doctor</u> Ramírez es un <u>médico</u> excelente.

> **Fíjate**
>
> When the preterit and imperfect are used together in narratives in which events are retold, you will notice that the *imperfect* provides the background information such as the time, weather, and location. The *preterit* relates the specific events that occurred.

9·23 ¿Y ayer? `5:00`

Descríbele a un/a compañero/a tu día de ayer en por lo menos **cinco** oraciones.

MODELO   *Ayer hacía mal tiempo cuando me desperté. No quería levantarme, pero por fin salí de la cama. Fui a mi clase de español. El profesor nos dio mucha tarea. Luego fui a la biblioteca. Estudiaba cuando llegó mi mejor amigo Jeff.*

9·24 Luces, cámara, acción `5:00`

Capítulo 5. El mundo del cine, pág. 185.

¿Te gustan las películas? ¿Vas al cine a menudo? Cuéntale (*Narrate*) a un/a compañero/a una película que hayas visto (*you have seen*) últimamente. Usa por lo menos **siete** oraciones. ¡Recuerda! Generalmente el imperfecto se usa para la descripción y el pretérito para la acción.

`3:00`   SAM 9-35

Las farmacias en el mundo hispanohablante

En Latinoamérica, las farmacias son, por la mayor parte, dispensarios de medicina únicamente. El farmacéutico (*pharmacist*) muchas veces ofrece consejos sobre los medicamentos (medicinas). Es fácil conseguir muchos tipos de medicina sin receta en las farmacias. Por ejemplo, puedes ir a la farmacia, describir los síntomas (como tos y fiebre) y pedir que te den unos antibióticos. Todo ello sin consultar al médico. Muchos países tienen *farmacias de turno* o *de guardia* que atienden al público las veinticuatro horas al día.

En algunos países (como Argentina, Chile y Perú) hay un nuevo tipo de farmacia al estilo estadounidense, que vende de todo. Estas farmacias pertenecen a grandes cadenas (Farmacity en Argentina, FASA en Chile, Inka Farma en Perú) que atraen a los consumidores con una gran variedad de productos, aparte de los medicamentos.

Preguntas

1. Es una farmacia que está abierta 24 horas al día/nunca cierra. Algunas farmacias en los Estados Unidos son farmacias de turno o de guardia (como Walgreens).
2. En las farmacias hispanas tradicionales puedes pedir consejo a los farmacéuticos y conseguir medicina sin receta (como los antibióticos), pero sólo venden medicina, no la gran variedad de productos que compramos en las farmacias de EE.UU.

1. ¿Qué es una *farmacia de turno* o *farmacia de guardia*? ¿Existe este sistema en los Estados Unidos?

2. ¿Qué diferencias hay entre las farmacias hispanas tradicionales y las de los Estados Unidos?

GRAMÁTICA 6 — Expresiones con *hacer*

9-36 to 9-39

`4:00`

The verb **hacer** means *to do* or *to make*. You have also used **hacer** in idiomatic expressions dealing with weather. There are some additional special constructions with **hacer** that deal with time. **Hace** is used:

> Hace seis meses que no te veo.

1. to discuss an action that began in the past but is still going on in the present.

> **hace** + *period of time* + **que** + *verb in the present tense*

Hace cuatro meses **que** estudio español.	*I've been studying Spanish for four months.*
Hace dos años **que** vivo aquí.	*I've been living here for two years.*

2. to ask how long something has been going on.

> **cuánto (tiempo)** + **hace** + **que** + *verb in present tense*

¿Cuántos meses **hace que** estudias español?	*How many months have you been studying Spanish?*
¿Cuánto tiempo **hace que** estudias español?	*How long have you been studying Spanish?*
¿Cuántas semanas **hace que** vives aquí?	*How many weeks have you been living here?*

3. in the preterit to tell how long ago something happened.

> **hace** + *period of time* + **que** + *verb in the preterit*

Hace cuatro meses **que** empecé a estudiar español.	*I began to study Spanish four months ago.*
Hace dos años **que** me mudé aquí.	*I moved here two years ago.*

or

> *verb in the preterit* + **hace** + *period of time*

Empecé a estudiar español **hace** cuatro meses.	*I began to study Spanish four months ago.*
Me mudé aquí **hace** dos años.	*I moved here two years ago.*

*Note that in this construction **hace** can either precede or follow the rest of the sentence. When it follows, **que** is not used.

4. to ask how long ago something happened.

> **cuánto (tiempo)** + **hace** + **que** + *verb in preterit*

¿Cuánto tiempo **hace que** empezaste a estudiar español?	*How long ago did you begin to study Spanish?*
¿Cuánto tiempo **hace que** te enfermaste?	*How long ago did you get sick?*

RECURSOS

| 9-G6 | Electronic Activity Cache |

NOTE FOR *Expresiones con hacer*

Discuss the difference in meaning in the sentences between having the verbs in the present tense vs. the preterit with students.

Haciendo oraciones

Paso 1 Escribe seis oraciones diferentes utilizando palabras de cada columna, más otras palabras necesarias. Comparte las oraciones con un/a compañero/a.

MODELO
Hace una hora que estudio francés.

Hace	una hora	que estudiar...
	un día	escuchar la música de...
	una semana	ir a un museo de...
	un mes	comprar...
	un año	visitar a...
	mucho tiempo	viajar a...

Paso 2 Juntos pongan los verbos en las oraciones en el pretérito. ¿Cómo cambia el significado de las frases?

MODELO
Hace una hora que estudio francés.
Hace una hora que estudié francés.

NOTE FOR 9-26

Encourage students to move around the room, asking as many different classmates as possible. You may want to make this a competition—the student who gets the most signatures in the amount of time you set, wins.

9·25 ¿Qué pasa? `3:00`

Juntos completen el diálogo entre Julián, Pati y su mamá con las palabras apropiadas.

> Julián, ¡ese sofá es horrible!

MAMÁ: Julián (1) ¿ __Cuánto__ tiempo hace (2) __que__ vives en esta casa?

JULIÁN: Bueno, creo que (3) __hace__ unos dos años que vivo aquí.

MAMÁ: Y (4) ¿ __cuánto__ __tiempo__ __hace__ que tienes ese sofá? Está muy sucio.

JULIÁN: No sé, mamá. Fue un regalo de un amigo. Lo tenía en su apartamento.

MAMÁ: Creo que (5) __hace__ por lo menos diez años (6) __que__ tiene esas manchas (*stains*) negras. ¡Es horrible!

JULIÁN: Mamá, (7) __hace__ media hora (8) __que__ criticas mi casa y…

PATI: ¡Mamá! (9) ¡ __Hace__ cinco minutos (10) __que__ te estoy llamando! ¡Tráeme agua!

> **Fíjate**
>
> Note that *cuánto* agrees with the amount of time: cuánto tiempo cuántas semanas/horas; cuántos años/días

9·26 Firma aquí `8:00`

Circula por la clase hasta encontrar a un estudiante que pueda contestar afirmativamente tu pregunta.

MODELO empezar a estudiar español hace menos de (*less than*) un año

E1: *¿Empezaste a estudiar español hace menos de un año?*

E2: *No, empecé a estudiar español hace dos años.*

E1: (a otro estudiante)*¿Empezaste a estudiar español hace menos de un año?*

E3: *Sí, empecé a estudiar español hace seis meses.*

E1: *Muy bien. Firma (Sign) aquí por favor.*

Janet _____

1. empezar a estudiar español hace menos de un año	_____
2. graduarse de la escuela secundaria (*high school*) hace dos años	_____
3. conocer a su mejor amigo/a hace muchos años	_____
4. ver una película de terror hace dos o tres semanas	_____
5. ir a un concierto hace uno o dos meses	_____
6. tomar café hace una hora	_____
7. comer en un restaurante elegante hace unos (*some*) días	_____
8. hacer ejercicio hace unas horas	_____
9. hablar con alguien de su familia hace una semana	_____
10. enfermarse hace una semana	_____

`5:00` 9·27 Conversando

Habla con varios compañeros de clase utilizando las siguientes preguntas para guiar la conversación.

1. ¿Cuánto tiempo hace que vives en este estado (*state*)? ¿Dónde vivías antes?
2. ¿Cuánto tiempo hace que estudias en esta universidad? ¿En qué año te gradúas?
3. ¿Cuánto tiempo hace que conoces a tu mejor amigo/a? ¿Dónde lo/la conociste?
4. ¿Cuánto tiempo hace que viste a tus padres? ¿Volviste a casa o te visitaron?
5. ¿Cuánto tiempo hace que fuiste al médico? ¿Qué te recomendó?

SECTION GOALS FOR *Escucha*

By the end of the *Escucha* section, students will be able to:

- incorporate previously presented listening strategies with new strategies.
- apply the new strategy of asking themselves questions for comprehension checks.
- practice pre-listening skills to organize the information they are about to hear.
- act out the scene they have just heard.

NATIONAL STANDARD

Communication, Connections

The new strategy of listening and asking themselves questions reinforces the ability to be a good listener. All interpersonal communication with pairs or groups requires the ability to listen well and follow a conversation (Communication Standard 1.1). Standard 1.2 focuses on interpreting and understanding spoken Spanish on a variety of topics. Standard 1.3 also focuses on presenting information

to an audience of listeners, and, as other people present to the class, students have to apply their strategies as they listen and check their comprehension. The ability to be a good listener is interdisciplinary, as many classes are lecture-based. Students transfer their strategies for listening in Spanish to other courses and can apply the new strategy of asking themselves questions to check their comprehension (Standard 3.1).

ESCUCHA

9-40 to
9-42

ESTRATEGIA   Asking yourself questions

A useful tool for boosting comprehension is asking yourself check questions to help you organize information and summarize what you have heard. | To practice this strategy be sure to complete the **Antes de escuchar** section.

9•28   ### Antes de escuchar

Marisol no se siente bien y llama a su madre para pedirle consejo. Cuando tú no te sientes bien, ¿qué haces generalmente: llamas al médico, hablas con un/a amigo/a, llamas a tu madre u otro pariente o te cuidas solo/a (*take care of yourself*)?

Marisol llama a su madre.

9•29   ### A escuchar

CD 4
Track 2

Completen las siguientes actividades.

1. La conversación entre Marisol y su madre se divide en tres partes. Escucha la primera parte y después escoge la pregunta que mejor resuma (*summarizes*) lo que escuchaste. Repite el proceso con cada parte.

   PRIMERA PARTE   b
   a. ¿Por qué llama Marisol a su madre?
   b. ¿Cuáles son los síntomas de Marisol?
   c. ¿Qué hizo Marisol cuando se levantó?

   SEGUNDA PARTE   c
   a. ¿Con quiénes salió Marisol anoche?
   b. ¿A Marisol le gustan las galletas?
   c. ¿Qué comió Marisol anoche?

   TERCERA PARTE   c
   a. ¿Debe ir a clase?
   b. ¿Debe comer mucho hoy?
   c. ¿Qué puede hacer Marisol para sentirse mejor?

2. Escucha una vez más para averiguar si escogiste las preguntas apropiadas. Compáralas con las de un/a compañero/a. Expliquen por qué son las mejores preguntas.

3. Ahora escucha la conversación por última vez para contestar las siguientes preguntas.
   a. ¿Por qué llama Marisol a su madre?   Llama a su madre porque no se siente bien y no sabe qué hacer.
   b. ¿Cuáles son sus síntomas?   Le duele mucho la cabeza y el estómago. No tiene ganas de comer.
   c. ¿Qué comió Marisol anoche?   Comió dos hamburguesas con queso y papas fritas, helado y galletas.
   d. ¿Cuál es el consejo de su mamá?   Le dice que no debe comer mucho pero debe beber mucha agua y té. Si come, debe comer cosas ligeras como sopa, arroz y fruta.

9•30   ### Después de escuchar

Realicen la escena entre Marisol y su madre.

(cont.)

TERCERA PARTE
MARISOL: ¿Qué puedo hacer? Tengo clase en dos horas.
MAMÁ: Primero debes tomar un té caliente, como un té de manzanilla. Si no te hace sentir mejor, puedes tomar un Alka Seltzer.
MARISOL: Gracias, mamá. Voy a mirar a ver si tengo Alka Seltzer aquí. Estoy segura de que tengo té.

MAMÁ: Muy bien, hija. Y Marisol...
MARISOL: ¿Sí?
MAMÁ: No debes comer mucho hoy. Tienes que beber mucha agua, y té también, si quieres. Además, debes comer cosas ligeras como sopa, arroz y fruta.
MARISOL: ¡Gracias, mamá! Adiós. ¡Te quiero!
MAMÁ: Bueno, cuídate. Adiós, hija. ¡Un beso!

NOTE FOR
Escucha

For the *Escucha* section, you will need to pause the CD after each part (*primera, segunda, tercera*) so that students can choose the question that best summarizes what they heard. Tell your students that they will be listening in small chunks and that you will stop the audio after each part to check their comprehension. If your students do the *Escucha* section at home, please ask them to pause the CD.

AUDIOSCRIPT FOR 9-29

PRIMERA PARTE
MARISOL: Hola, mamá. ¿Cómo estás?
MAMÁ: Bien, hija. ¿Cómo estás tú hoy?
MARISOL: Bueno, por eso te llamo. No me siento muy bien.
MAMÁ: ¿Ah sí? ¿Qué te pasa? ¿Estás enferma?
MARISOL: Sí, anoche no dormí bien y cuando me desperté esta mañana, me dolían mucho la cabeza y el estómago.
MAMÁ: Pues... ¿comiste algo cuando te levantaste?
MARISOL: No, mamá. No tengo ganas de comer nada.
MAMÁ: ¿Tomaste una aspirina o un Tylenol?
MARISOL: No. Todavía no.
(15 second pause)

SEGUNDA PARTE
MAMÁ: Vamos a ver... ¿qué comiste anoche?
MARISOL: Salí con unos amigos. Primero cenamos en el restaurante Hamburger Shack. Comí dos hamburguesas con queso y unas papas fritas. Después caminamos al centro y compramos helado. A las diez fuimos al apartamento de Tina y comimos chocolate con galletas.
MAMÁ: Marisol, ¿cuántas galletas comiste?
MARISOL: No sé... quizás seis o siete. Tú sabes que me encantan las galletas.
MAMÁ: Sí, hija. Pero eso es mucha comida en muy poco tiempo. Por eso te sientes mal.

(15 second pause)

SECTION GOALS FOR
Escribe

By the end of the *Escribe* section, students will be able to:

• review the events from *Episodio 8* and write a synopsis in Spanish.
• embellish the events they brainstormed to include a more detailed description of the events.
• compare their summaries with their classmates' summaries.
• write the story in the past tense, practicing the uses of the preterit and imperfect.
• edit the events based on feedback from their classmates or their instructor.

NATIONAL STANDARDS
Communication, Comparisons

Students write their summary of the *Episodio 8* events in the past tense. When they share their narrations with the class, it becomes the presentational mode of communication (Standard 1.3). You could turn the activity into a jigsaw; you tell them what happened in English (10 sentences), one student writes the even events and the other student writes the odd events. They then meet in pairs or small groups to discuss the story (Standard 1.1). They use their past tense narrations to compare which form (preterit or imperfect) is more appropriate, based on how they would say the sentence in English. They process and compare their understanding of the past tense with their understanding of the English past tense (Standard 4.1).

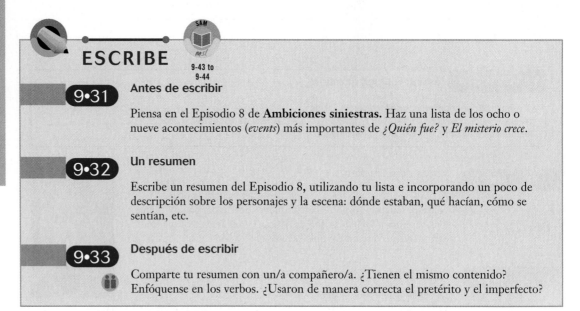

ESCRIBE

9-43 to
9-44

9•31 Antes de escribir

Piensa en el Episodio 8 de **Ambiciones siniestras.** Haz una lista de los ocho o nueve acontecimientos (*events*) más importantes de *¿Quién fue?* y *El misterio crece.*

9•32 Un resumen

Escribe un resumen del Episodio 8, utilizando tu lista e incorporando un poco de descripción sobre los personajes y la escena: dónde estaban, qué hacían, cómo se sentían, etc.

9•33 Después de escribir

Comparte tu resumen con un/a compañero/a. ¿Tienen el mismo contenido? Enfóquense en los verbos. ¿Usaron de manera correcta el pretérito y el imperfecto?

¿Cómo andas?

Having completed the second **Comunicación**, I now can…

	Feel Confident	Need to Review
• talk about how things used to be and narrate events in the past (p. 334)	❏	❏
• talk about how long something has been going on (p. 335)	❏	❏
• talk about pharmacies in Latin America and how they differ from those in the United States (p. 340)	❏	❏
• talk about how long ago something occurred (p. 341)	❏	❏
• ask myself questions when listening to a passage to help organize and summarize what I hear (p. 343)	❏	❏
• write a summary of a story using the preterit and imperfect (p. 344)	❏	❏

15:00

CW
eBook

CD 4
Track 3

SAM

9-45

DVD/VHS

Vistas
culturales

Milagros Alejandra
Romero Zárate

Perú

Les presento mi país

Mi nombre es Milagros Alejandra Romero Zárate y soy de Arequipa, Perú. Soy estudiante de arqueología en la Universidad Nacional Mayor de San Marcos en Lima. Mientras estudio, vivo con unos parientes en Miraflores, un barrio de la capital. Quiero ser arqueóloga porque me fascina la historia del país; hay muchas ruinas de la civilización incaica en Perú. **¿Qué sabes de la historia de tu país y sus pueblos antiguos?** Perú es un país de extremos geográficos: tenemos la costa, al nivel del mar, los Andes, montañas impresionantes, cañones profundos, la selva y los principios del río Amazonas. ¡Puedes mantenerte en forma caminando por estas regiones!

Miraflores, en las afueras
de Lima, Perú

Las líneas de Nazca

OCÉANO
PACÍFICO

● ALMANAQUE ●

Nombre oficial:	República del Perú
Gobierno:	República constitucional
Población:	28.302.603 (2006)
Idiomas:	español (oficial); quechua (oficial); idiomas indígenas
Moneda:	Nuevo sol (S/)

¿Sabías que...?

● Las líneas de Nazca, que se encuentran en un desierto del sur del país, son un enigma. Consisten en una serie de dibujos de diferentes animales, plantas y flores, y figuras geométricas que se reconocen solamente desde el aire.

● Hay casi 3,5 millones de llamas en los Andes.

PREGUNTAS

1. ¿Por qué Milagros quiere ser arqueóloga?

2. ¿Por qué se dice que Perú es un país de geografía muy variada?

3. ¿Qué otros países comparten algunas de las características geográficas de Perú?

En la Red
Amplía tus conocimientos sobre Perú en la página web de *¡Anda!*

345

NOTE FOR *Las líneas de Nazca*

Las líneas de Nazca are still a mystery today. There are hundreds of different figures, plus additional cross-hatching lines, spread out over an area of 400 square miles. Some of the figures are distinctive (e.g., a monkey, a hummingbird, a spider, flowers), and others are difficult to decipher even now. Several theories exist as to the origin and meaning of the lines.

Suggestion for *Les presento mi país* Ask students: What is the oldest university in the United States? When was it founded, why, and by whom? How old is your university?

SECTION GOALS FOR
Cultura

By the end of the *Cultura* section, students will be able to:

- discuss the geography of Peru.
- highlight geographical and historical sites in Peru.
- contrast Peru with Bolivia.
- identify the indigenous people of Bolivia.
- describe the indigenous ruins in Bolivia.
- explain how Bolivia differs from other South American countries.
- describe the geographical variation in Ecuador.
- explain the role of the shaman.
- make comparisons between Peru, Bolivia, and Ecuador.

NATIONAL STANDARDS

Communication, Cultures, Connections, Comparisons

The readings from *Les presento mi país* relate to Communication, Cultures, Connections, and Comparisons. The readings encompass interpretive communication because students are reading written Spanish and they have to interpret and understand the information (Standard 1.2). If you also read the cultural notes aloud, they would be interpreting and understanding spoken Spanish (Standard 1.2). Your students are engaging in interpersonal communication when discussing the readings in small groups and answering the questions that follow (Standard 1.1). The readings about Peru, Bolivia, and Ecuador explain how the cultures differ between the three countries, and students can relate to how the cultural differences shape the practices, perspectives, and products of the countries (Standards 2.1, 2.2). These cultural differences provide the basis for making comparisons between these cultures and the cultures of the United States (Standard 4.2). Students can also make connections between their studies in history, geography, and science to the new information about Peru, Bolivia, and Ecuador.

NOTE FOR

Les presento mi país

The University of San Marcos was founded May on 12, 1551, by an order of Dominican friars; it is the oldest university in Latin America.

Bolivia

Raúl Eduardo Loza Arce

CW eBook

CD 4 Track 4

DVD/VHS MSL

Vistas culturales

Les presento mi país

Mi nombre es Raúl Eduardo Loza Arce y soy de La Paz, la capital administrativa de Bolivia. Hay otra capital, Sucre, que es la sede (*headquarters*) constitucional; allí se mantiene el Tribunal Supremo del país. La Paz es la capital más alta del mundo, a unos 3.650 m.s.n.m. en los Andes. **¿A qué altura está tu ciudad?** La gente indígena constituye más del cincuenta por ciento de la población del país, y muchos viven en el altiplano, un área cerca del lago Titicaca, que es el lago navegable más alto del mundo. En el altiplano se encuentran las ruinas de una civilización antigua preincaica, anterior a los aymara, que pueblan la región hoy en día.

> **Fíjate**
> The abbreviation *m.s.n.m.* means *metros sobre nivel del mar*, or meters above sea level.

Una mujer aymara con ropa tradicional

En las islas flotantes del lago Titicaca viven algunos indígenas.

● ALMANAQUE ●

Nombre oficial:	República de Bolivia
Gobierno:	República
Población:	8.989.046 (2006)
Idiomas:	español (oficial); quechua (oficial); aymara (oficial)
Moneda:	Boliviano (Bs)

¿Sabías que...?

● La papa, nativa de Suramérica, es un alimento básico en Bolivia. Se cultivan más de doscientos tipos de papa en el país.

● Aunque no tiene salida al mar, Bolivia tiene una fuerza marina: la Armada Boliviana.

PREGUNTAS

1. ¿Por qué crees que Bolivia tiene tres idiomas oficiales?

2. ¿Qué distinción tiene La Paz como capital?

3. ¿Qué riesgo para la salud (*health risk*) comparten Bolivia y Perú?

> **En la Red**
> Amplía tus conocimientos sobre Bolivia en la página web de *¡Anda!*

María Yolanda
Palacios Mena

Ecuador

CW
eBook

CD 4
Track 5

DVD/VHS

Vistas
culturales

Les presento mi país

Mi nombre es María Yolanda Palacios Mena y soy de Santo Domingo de los Colorados. Ecuador tiene tres diferentes tipos de geografía: la costa, la sierra y el oriente o la selva. La población, principalmente mestiza e indígena, se concentra en la sierra y la costa. **¿Dónde vive la mayoría de la población en tu país?** Uno de los grupos indígenas de Ecuador son los tsáchilas, también llamados "los colorados", debido a la costumbre de los hombres de pintarse (*dye*) el pelo de color rojo. Los chamanes (*shamans*) de esta tribu tienen gran conocimiento de las plantas medicinales y, por lo tanto, tienen mucho poder en la comunidad.

Un sombrero Panamá

Un tsáchila de Santo
Domingo de los Colorados

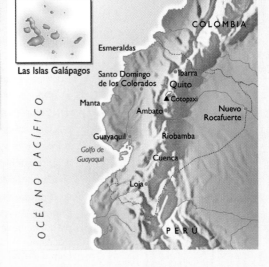

Las Islas Galápagos

COLOMBIA
Esmeraldas
Santo Domingo
de los Colorados · Ibarra
· Quito
Manta ▲ Cotopaxi
Ambato Nuevo
Rocafuerte
Guayaquil Riobamba
Golfo de
Guayaquil Cuenca
Loja
PERÚ

OCÉANO PACÍFICO

● ALMANAQUE ●

Nombre oficial:	República del Ecuador
Gobierno:	República
Población:	13.547.510 (2006)
Idiomas:	español (oficial); quechua y otros idiomas indígenas
Moneda:	El dólar estadounidense ($)

¿Sabías que...?

● El famoso sombrero panamá es en realidad de Ecuador.

● El volcán Cotopaxi se considera el volcán activo más alto del mundo.

PREGUNTAS

1. ¿Cuál es una costumbre de los tsáchilas?
2. ¿Qué tiene Ecuador en común geográficamente con Perú y Bolivia?
3. ¿En qué otros países se encuentra un gran porcentaje de mestizos e indígenas?

En la Red
Amplía tus conocimientos sobre Ecuador en la página web de *¡Anda!*

347

RECURSOS

T9-7 | T9-7 | Cultural Background Notes

NOTE FOR
Los Tsáchilas

The Tsáchilas or *Colorados* are a distinctive indigenous group in the province of Pichincha, some 40 miles west of Quito. Although many of their traditions are being lost due to the encroachment of modernization and the lure of the "big cities" for the younger members of the community, this group maintains some easily recognizable traits. The men wear a rectangular piece of cloth, navy blue and white striped, which resembles a skirt. They shave their heads up to the crown, maintaining the hair on top rather long. This is then coated with a mixture of a vaseline-like substance tinted with the *achiote* seed, which makes it bright orange-red. The women weave a cloth of many colors for their skirts and wear necklaces of glass beads. Both sexes paint their bodies with black lines. The shamans of the Tsáchilas are well-known for their knowledge and use of medicinal plants.

Suggestion for *Los Tsáchilas* Ask students: Why is it hard to maintain tribal or community customs in the present day? What do you think of shamans? Can they cure people? Why do you think they can or can't?

Suggestion for *El sombrero panamá* Ask students: Can you think of other products or practices that have geographic misnomers, e.g., have names that do not truly reflect their origins (e.g., the Russian flu, which didn't begin in Russia, but was first documented there)?

NOTE FOR
El sombrero panamá

Despite the name, Panama hats (*el sombrero panamá*) are made only in Ecuador. They are woven by hand from the toquilla plant. Monticristi and Jipijapa are two places where the hats are made. The true Panama hat is woven so tightly that it passes the water test: Turn the hat upside down and pour water into it. The best hats yield not a drop of water leaking out!

Ambiciones siniestras

lectura

9-48

SECTION GOALS FOR
Lectura

By the end of the *Lectura* section, students will be able to:

- use the new strategy, asking themselves questions as they read the passage.
- incorporate familiar reading strategies with the new reading strategy.
- recall the events from *Episodio 8* and make predictions about what will happen in *Episodio 9*.
- summarize the main events from the story.

Expansion for *Antes de leer* This is a good time to have students re-tell *Ambiciones siniestras* from the first lesson (reading and video) through *Capítulo 8* in the format of a story, using the preterit and imperfect. They could work in pairs.

RECAP OF *AMBICIONES SINIESTRAS*
Episodio 8

Lectura: In *Ambiciones siniestras*, *Capítulo 8*, Marisol read her e-mail and discovered that someone had solved the puzzle, and she received a new puzzle to solve. As she read her e-mail, the phone rang and it was Manolo. Marisol confessed that she thought Lupe was el Sr. Verdugo, and Manolo told her that he thought Cisco was el Sr. Verdugo. They decided not to call the police and hung up. Marisol saw a new e-mail message from an unfamiliar sender, read the message, and screamed.

Video: Marisol received a threatening message over e-mail. Manolo called Lupe and she revealed that she solved the puzzle. She had photos of Alejandra and Eduardo from wherever they were being held, but the other characters do not know that she has the information. Toward the end of their conversation it appeared as if someone had been listening to their entire conversation. Lupe realized something important, packed a suitcase, and added a gun to her suitcase. Manolo called Cisco to tell him that Lupe solved the puzzle and their call was dropped. We saw Cisco find a paper he was looking for, change his clothes, and then he finished getting dressed and walked out.

9-34 Antes de leer. En el **Episodio 8** Marisol y Manolo hablan de las dudas que tienen sobre Lupe y Cisco. Teniendo esto en cuenta, contesta las siguientes preguntas.

- ¿Es posible que Lupe sea (*is*) el Sr. Verdugo?
- ¿Por qué actúa Cisco de manera tan misteriosa?
- Si resuelven el nuevo rompecabezas, ¿van a poder salvar (*save*) a Alejandra y a Eduardo?

ESTRATEGIA **Asking yourself questions**

Just as with listening, it is helpful to learn to ask yourself check questions as you read, which help you summarize and organize information.

9-35 A leer. Completa las siguientes actividades.

1. Lee el primer párrafo y elige la pregunta que mejor lo resuma (*summarizes it*).
   a. ¿Dónde están los protagonistas?
   b. ¿Cómo están Eduardo y Alejandra?
   c. ¿Qué saben Manolo, Cisco, Marisol y Lupe de Eduardo y Alejandra?
2. Ahora lee el segundo párrafo y elige la pregunta que mejor lo resuma.
   a. ¿Por qué tienen miedo Manolo, Cisco, Marisol y Lupe?
   b. ¿Por qué Manolo, Cisco, Marisol y Lupe participaron en el concurso?
   c. ¿Por qué se desaparecieron Eduardo y Alejandra?
3. Continúa leyendo el episodio pero ahora, en vez de elegir la mejor pregunta, tú vas a escribir una pregunta para cada sección indicada (secciones de 3 a 9). Al terminar, compara tus preguntas con las de tus compañeros.

CD 4
Track 6

¡Qué mentira!

[1] En distintas partes del país hay cuatro estudiantes universitarios muy preocupados. Todavía no saben ni dónde ni cómo están Eduardo y Alejandra. Sólo saben que desaparecieron y que un tal Verdugo tiene algo que ver con todo eso°.

°has something to do with it

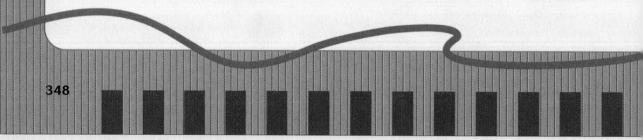

Answers to 9-35

1. c
2. a
3. *Possible answers include:*
   ¿Cómo está Manolo hoy?
   ¿Por qué Cisco llama a Manolo?
   ¿Por qué Marisol llama a Manolo?
   ¿Tienen tiempo para descifrar el rompecabezas?
   ¿Qué oportunidad les da el Sr. Verdugo?
   ¿Cómo les amenaza?
   ¿Qué hace Manolo después de leer el mensaje?

[2] El concurso —¡Qué mentira°!— ¿Cómo pudieron creerlo? Este   *lie*
tipo de cosas tan increíbles generalmente terminan siendo
falsas. Para Manolo, Cisco, Marisol y Lupe es mucho más serio.
Hay dos desaparecidos° ya y los otros con el miedo de no saber   *missing*
si les va a pasar lo mismo a ellos. El Sr. Verdugo les dijo que no
hablaran° con nadie —especialmente con la policía— o les haría   *not to talk*
daño a todos°. Así que todos los días se levantan y se acuestan   *would hurt*
con miedo.   *all of them*

[3] Hoy Manolo se despertó asustado° y se levantó   *scared*
inmediatamente. Durmió mal anoche y ahora le duele todo el
cuerpo. Decidió tomar tres aspirinas y volvió a acostarse. Pocos
minutos después, sonó el teléfono celular. Era Cisco.

[4] —¿Manolo? ¿Estás levantado?

—Sí —respondió Manolo— hace media hora. ¿Qué pasa?

—Acabamos de recibir otro mensaje. Este hombre está loco
—explicó Cisco.

—Voy a leer el mensaje y te llamo más tarde —le dijo Manolo.

[5] Colgaron°. Otra llamada. Esta vez fue Marisol.   *They hung up*

—¿Manolo? Tienes que leer el último mensaje. No sé qué
hacer…

—Mira Marisol, voy a leerlo ahora mismo. Ya me llamó Cisco
hace unos minutos. Llama tú a Lupe y dentro de diez minutos te
llamo. ¿Está bien? ¿Estás en tu teléfono celular?

—Sí. Bueno, te espero.

[6] Manolo encendió° la computadora y leyó: *turned on*

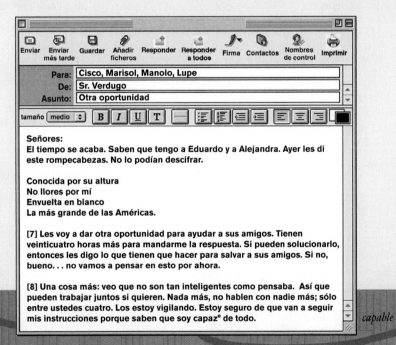

Para: Cisco, Marisol, Manolo, Lupe
De: Sr. Verdugo
Asunto: Otra oportunidad

Señores:
El tiempo se acaba. Saben que tengo a Eduardo y a Alejandra. Ayer les di
este rompecabezas. No lo podían descifrar.

Conocida por su altura
No llores por mí
Envuelta en blanco
La más grande de las Américas.

[7] **Les voy a dar otra oportunidad para ayudar a sus amigos. Tienen**
veinticuatro horas más para mandarme la respuesta. Si pueden solucionarlo,
entonces les digo lo que tienen que hacer para salvar a sus amigos. Si no,
bueno. . . no vamos a pensar en esto por ahora.

[8] **Una cosa más: veo que no son tan inteligentes como pensaba. Así que**
pueden trabajar juntos si quieren. Nada más, no hablen con nadie más; sólo
entre ustedes cuatro. Los estoy vigilando. Estoy seguro de que van a seguir
mis instrucciones porque saben que soy capaz° de todo.   *capable*

349

NATIONAL STANDARDS
Communication, Comparisons

Note that the readings are kept at a
level of comprehensible input that
entices the students to read. Also,
the follow-up questions encourage
your students to think beyond the
content of the story and make
informed guesses about what they
would do in the same circumstances.
The *Ambiciones siniestras* reading
for *Capítulo* 9 focuses on asking
questions while reading. If students
work together and discuss the questions as they read, they are communicating interpersonally (Standard
1.1). The students can also make
comparisons between the past tense
in English and the preterit and imperfect in Spanish (Standard 4.1) as
they read the story and decide why
parts of the story required the preterit or the imperfect.

NATIONAL STANDARDS
Communication, Connections

The reading and writing activities
from *Ambiciones siniestras* are
designed to practice the new strategy of asking yourself questions.
Students read the passage or
engage in pre-writing activities that
facilitate their communication in
Spanish (Standard 1.2), and if they
communicate with others in the
interpersonal mode, they also apply
Standard 1.1. They can use this new
strategy and apply it to other
subjects as they read for comprehension (Standard 3.1) while they
strengthen their reading skills and
increase their comprehension in
other disciplines.

Suggestion for *Lectura* You may
want to explain that *Verdugo* means
tormenter.

[9] Con un gran suspiro, Manolo buscó su teléfono y empezó a marcar°… De pronto dejó de marcar, se quedó mirando el teléfono un momento y lo tiró° con fuerza contra la pared…

dial

threw it

9-36 **Después de leer.** Contesta las siguientes preguntas.

1. ¿Por qué se levantan y se acuestan con miedo nuestros protagonistas?
2. ¿Cómo se sentía Manolo cuando se levantó?
3. ¿Quiénes llamaron a Manolo? ¿Por qué?
4. Además de un rompecabezas, ¿qué información nueva contiene el mensaje?
5. En tu opinión, ¿qué fue lo más aterrador (*frightening*) de todo lo que dijo el mensaje?

9-49 to
9-50

video

9-37 **Antes del video.** ¿Por qué crees que Manolo tiró el teléfono contra la pared? ¿Los protagonistas van a poder descifrar ese nuevo rompecabezas? ¿Van a trabajar juntos esta vez? ¿Van a poder salvar a Eduardo y a Alejandra?

Sin embargo, creo que ya tenemos una pista (*clue*).

Todo este lío (*mess*) con los rompecabezas me tiene bastante nerviosa.

Tengo que confesar algo.

Episodio 9

«No llores por mí»

Relájate y disfruta el video.

9-38 **Después del video.** Contesta las siguientes preguntas.

1. ¿Dónde estaban Marisol y Lupe?
2. ¿Qué hacían ellas?
3. ¿Qué información tenía Marisol que creía que podía ayudar con la primera pista?
4. ¿Cómo respondió Lupe a su idea?
5. ¿Por qué decidieron ellas llamar a Cisco y a Manolo?
6. ¿Qué dijo Cisco sobre la segunda pista, "No llores por mí"?
7. ¿Qué propuso Manolo sobre las dos últimas pistas?
8. ¿Cuántas horas tenían para terminar de descifrar el rompecabezas?
9. ¿Cómo terminó el episodio?

350

Y por fin, ¿cómo andas?

Having completed this chapter, I now can…

	Feel Confident	Need to Review
Comunicación		
● describe the human body (p. 322)	❏	❏
● pronounce **d** and **t** correctly (p. 323)	❏	❏
● identify and use the direct and indirect object pronouns and reflexive pronouns with more confidence (p. 325)	❏	❏
● talk about what ails me and understand when others tell me where "it" hurts (p. 328)	❏	❏
● discuss certain ailments and treatments (p. 328)	❏	❏
● make exclamatory and emphatic statements using **¡qué!** and **¡cuánto!** (p. 332)	❏	❏
● explain when to use the preterit and the imperfect (p. 334)	❏	❏
● narrate in the past (p. 334)	❏	❏
● talk about how long something has been going on and how long ago something occurred (pp. 335, 341)	❏	❏
● organize and summarize a listening passage by asking myself check questions (p. 343)	❏	❏
● write a summary of a story using past tenses (p. 344)	❏	❏
Cultura		
● discuss the importance of water in maintaining good health (p. 331)	❏	❏
● talk about pharmacies in the Spanish-speaking world (p. 340)	❏	❏
● share at least two interesting facts about each country: Peru, Bolivia, and Ecuador (pp. 345–347)	❏	❏
Ambiciones siniestras		
● create check questions to facilitate comprehension when reading (p. 348)	❏	❏
● discuss the contents of the new e-mail message (p. 349)	❏	❏
● talk about the progress the characters are making in deciphering the new riddle (p. 350)	❏	❏

VOCABULARIO ACTIVO

CD 4
Tracks 7-11

El cuerpo humano	*The human body*
la boca	*mouth*
el brazo	*arm*
la cabeza	*head*
la cara	*face*
la cintura	*waist*
el corazón	*heart*
el cuello	*neck*
el cuerpo	*body*
el dedo (de la mano)	*finger*
el dedo (del pie)	*toe*
el diente	*tooth*
la espalda	*back*
el estómago	*stomach*
la garganta	*throat*
la mano	*hand*
la nariz	*nose*
el oído	*inner ear*
el ojo	*eye*
la oreja	*ear*
el pecho	*chest*
el pelo	*hair*
el pie	*foot*
la pierna	*leg*

Unos verbos	*Some verbs*
doler (ue)	*to hurt*
estar enfermo/a	*to be sick*
estar sano/a; saludable	*to be healthy*
ser alérgico/a (a)	*to be allergic (to)*

Otras palabras útiles	*Other useful words*
la salud	*health*
la sangre	*blood*

Unas enfermedades y tratamientos médicos	*Illnesses and medical treatments*
el antiácido	*antacid*
el antibiótico	*antibiotic*
la aspirina	*aspirin*
el catarro/el resfriado	*cold*
la curita	*adhesive bandage*
el/la doctor/a	*doctor*
el dolor	*pain*
el/la enfermero/a	*nurse*
el estornudo	*sneeze*
el examen físico	*physical exam*
la farmacia	*pharmacy*
la fiebre	*fever*
la gripe	*flu*
la herida	*wound; injury*
el hospital	*hospital*
la inyección	*shot*
el jarabe	*cough syrup*
el/la médico/a	*doctor*
la náusea	*nausea*
las pastillas	*pills*
la receta	*prescription*
la sala de urgencias	*emergency room*
la tos	*cough*
la venda/el vendaje	*bandage*

Unos verbos	Some verbs
acabar de + infinitivo	to have just finished + (something)
cortar(se)	to cut (oneself)
curar(se)	to cure; to be cured
enfermar(se)	to get sick
estornudar	to sneeze
evitar	to avoid
guardar cama	to stay in bed
lastimar(se)	to get hurt
mejorar(se)	to improve; to get better
ocurrir	to occur
quemar(se)	to burn; to get burned
romper(se)	to break
tener...	
alergia (a)	to be allergic (to)
(un) catarro, resfriado	to have a cold
(la/una) gripe	to have the flu
una infección	to have an infection
tos	to have a cough
un virus	to have a virus
tener dolor de...	to have a...
cabeza	headache
espalda	backache
estómago	stomachache
garganta	sore throat
toser	to cough
tratar de	to try to
vendar(se)	to bandage(oneself); to dress (a wound)

353

¡Viajemos!

¿Vas a viajar al extranjero (*abroad*)? Debes averiguar (*find out*) todo lo que puedas acerca del sitio que piensas visitar, pensar en tus gastos (*expenses*) y hacer un presupuesto (*budget*) y poner tu información personal afuera de cada maleta (*suitcase*). Y ahora… ¡viajemos!

NATIONAL STANDARDS

Comunicación

- To discuss travel and different modes of transportation (Communication, Comparisons)
- To list the various parts of a car in Spanish (Communication, Cultures, Connections)
- To influence others by using commands (Communication)
- To discuss what belongs to you and others (Communication)
- To compare people, places, and things (Communication, Comparisons)
- To focus on linguistic cues when listening to a passage to enhance comprehension (Communication, Connections)
- To write and present a report about an interesting tourist spot in Colombia or Venezuela (Communication, Cultures, Connections)

Cultura

- To list some public transportation options and discuss procedures for getting a driver's license in Hispanic countries (Communication, Cultures, Connections, Comparisons)
- To discuss travel/tourism opportunities in Venezuela (Communication, Cultures)
- To share important facts about this chapter's featured countries: Colombia and Venezuela (Communication, Cultures, Comparisons)

Ambiciones siniestras

- To determine when it is appropriate to skip unfamiliar words and still comprehend when reading a passage (Communication, Comparisons)
- To discover the truth about what Cisco knows (Communication)
- To confirm that Lupe is not what she appears to be (Communication)

OBJETIVOS

Comunicación

- To discuss travel and different modes of transportation
- To list the various parts of a car in Spanish
- To influence others by using commands
- To discuss what belongs to you and others
- To compare people, places, and things
- To focus on linguistic cues when listening to a passage to enhance comprehension
- To write and present a report about an interesting tourist spot in Colombia or Venezuela

Cultura

- To list some public transportation options and discuss procedures for getting a driver's license in Hispanic countries
- To discuss travel/tourism opportunities in Venezuela
- To share important facts about this chapter's featured countries: Colombia and Venezuela

Ambiciones siniestras

- To determine when it is appropriate to skip unfamiliar words and still comprehend when reading a passage
- To discover the truth about what Cisco knows
- To confirm that Lupe is not what she appears to be

CONTENIDOS

SECTION GOALS FOR

Chapter Opener

By the end of the Chapter Opener section, students will be able to:

- list preparations of smart travelers.
- make suggestions for planning a trip.

NATIONAL STANDARDS

Communities

There are several service learning options available for integrating travel, transportation, and the use of Spanish. If you have a large Hispanic population, you could plan a travel fair, where students have a table or booth for each Spanish-speaking country. You could invite community members from those countries to represent their country of origin with realia, photos, souvenirs, artifacts, or food. This could be done during the day, during your class time, at night, or on a weekend. Students could research the country of their Hispanic partner and act as the travel agent for the public, offering advice for what to see, excursions to take, and general travel tips. If you do not have a large Hispanic population, you could ask the students to do research as if they were travel agents and offer a "get to know my country" event where community members could find out what each Spanish-speaking country has to offer tourists. Students could research the current cost of travel, immunizations, and documentation required, and the best places to see; they could also plan a virtual trip using the Internet.

RECURSOS

IRM

Lesson Plan

Expansion for *Preguntas* Ask your students the following questions: *¿Tuviste problemas alguna vez en un viaje?, explica. ¿Qué puedes hacer para evitar este problema en futuros viajes?*

METHODOLOGY • Student Motivation

Motivation plays a large role in learning another language. All of the activities in *¡Anda!* focus on having students interact with each other in a non-threatening and highly engaging way. You should notice your students becoming more and more comfortable and confident as they learn Spanish. This chapter continues our goal of providing students with fun, enjoyable opportunities to practice Spanish with their classmates.

¡Buen viaje!

PREGUNTAS

1 Cuando viajas, ¿adónde vas generalmente?

2 Antes de viajar, ¿qué haces normalmente?

3 ¿Qué precauciones tomas?

355

SECTION GOALS FOR
Comunicación

By the end of the *Comunicación* section, students will be able to:

- identify the parts of a car and their functions.
- discuss different modes of transportation.
- pronounce the letters *b* and *v* correctly.
- give affirmative and negative *tú* commands.
- give affirmative and negative *Ud.* and *Uds.* commands.
- contrast public transportation options in the United States and abroad, and report about learning how to drive in Colombia.

NATIONAL STANDARDS
Communication

The vocabulary and activities in this section are highly motivational since a number of the transportation words are cognates. Also, it is very easy for students to access and use this vocabulary in real-life situations using the Internet, since there is an abundance of travel web sites for each country.

Depending on where one lives, there are multiple modes of transportation available. In the large cities, people walk or use public transportation such as trains or buses, whereas in small cities and suburbs many people drive cars. In *Capítulo 10,* students learn about different modes of transportation and how in many Hispanic countries there is a greater reliance on public transportation than on cars. They are able to make comparisons (Standard 4.2) about how transportation options differ among countries.

The vocabulary in *Capítulo 10* is focused on transportation, the parts of a car, and verbs associated with driving and maintaining vehicles. Students communicate in the interpersonal mode when they identify the parts of a car and discuss proper car maintenance (Standard 1.1). They can use this information, coupled with commands, to express themselves to others (rental car agents, mechanics, police, cab drivers, chauffeurs, bus drivers, etc.) about their transportation needs when traveling abroad (Standard 2.2). Students are able to connect what they already know about transportation and car parts with the new information they have learned in Spanish (Standard 3.1).

Comunicación

- Discussing different modes of transportation
- Naming the parts of a car
- Telling people what to do and what not to do

VOCABULARIO 1 — Los medios de transporte

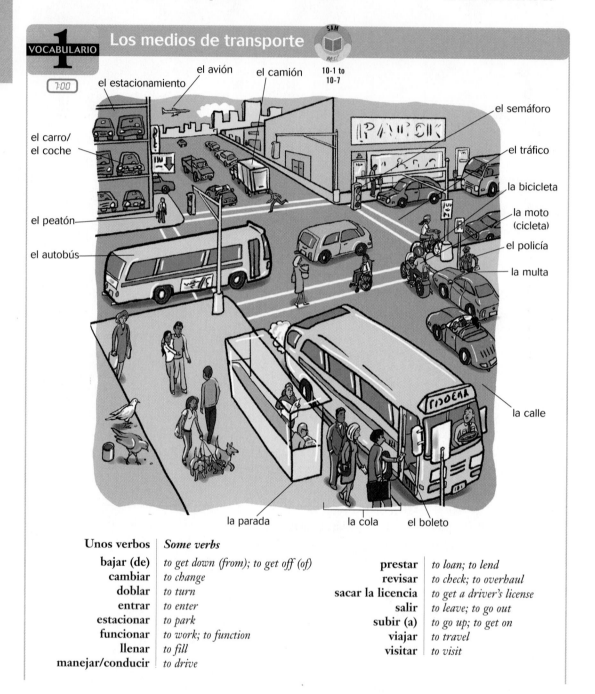

el avión · el camión · el estacionamiento · el carro/el coche · el peatón · el autobús · el semáforo · el tráfico · la bicicleta · la moto (cicleta) · el policía · la multa · la calle · la parada · la cola · el boleto

Unos verbos	Some verbs		
bajar (de)	*to get down (from); to get off (of)*	**prestar**	*to loan; to lend*
cambiar	*to change*	**revisar**	*to check; to overhaul*
doblar	*to turn*	**sacar la licencia**	*to get a driver's license*
entrar	*to enter*	**salir**	*to leave; to go out*
estacionar	*to park*	**subir (a)**	*to go up; to get on*
funcionar	*to work; to function*	**viajar**	*to travel*
llenar	*to fill*	**visitar**	*to visit*
manejar/conducir	*to drive*		

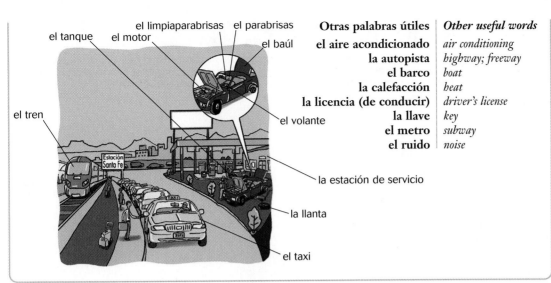

el tanque
el limpiaparabrisas   el parabrisas
el motor
el baúl
el tren
el volante
la estación de servicio
la llanta
el taxi

Otras palabras útiles	Other useful words
el aire acondicionado	*air conditioning*
la autopista	*highway; freeway*
el barco	*boat*
la calefacción	*heat*
la licencia (de conducir)	*driver's license*
la llave	*key*
el metro	*subway*
el ruido	*noise*

NOTE FOR *Los medios de transporte*

If you wish, point out other ways of saying some of the following vocabulary. For example: *el autobús/camión (Mex.)/guagua (Caribe); el coche/el carro/el auto; el boleto/el billete*. If you choose to expand their knowledge by explaining that different countries have different ways of saying things, we recommend that you explain to beginning students that they will still be understood using the basic vocabulary we are presenting in *¡Anda!* Otherwise, they will become frustrated, thinking that native speakers in country X will not understand them. As always, remind them of the *También se dice...* section in Appendix 3.

SECTION GOALS FOR
Pronunciación

By the end of the *Pronunciación* section, students will be able to:

• pronounce the letters *b* and *v* correctly.
• state the rules that state when the *v* is pronounced like *b*.
• pronounce some popular *dichos y refranes* with *v* and *b* sounds in them.

CW
eBook
CD 4
Track 12

SAM
10-8 to
10-11

PRONUNCIACIÓN 5·00

The letters *b* and *v*

1. In Spanish, the letters **b** and **v** are pronounced alike. When each letter comes at the beginning of a word or phrase, or after the letters **m** or **n**, they are both pronounced like the **b** in the English word *bat*.

   vaso   **b**oleto   tam**b**ién   in**v**ierno

2. In all other instances, the Spanish **b** and **v** have an identical, soft pronunciation. There is no equivalent in English. The lips come together but do not close so some air may pass between the lips.

   para**b**risas   re**v**isar   a**v**ión   auto**b**ús

10·1 Las palabras

Pronounce the following words, paying special attention to the letters **b** and **v**.

1. **b**arco
2. **b**oleto
3. **b**aúl
4. cam**b**iar
5. **v**iajar
6. ser**v**icio
7. limpiapara**b**risas
8. do**b**lar
9. **v**olar

10·2 Las oraciones

Pronounce the following sentences, paying special attention to the letters **b** and **v**.

1. **B**eto y **V**erónica **v**iajaron a **B**arcelona en a**v**ión para **v**isitar a sus a**b**uelos.
2. Esperá**b**amos el auto**b**ús cuando hu**b**o un accidente de **b**icicletas.
3. El **b**oleto para **v**iajar en **b**arco costa**b**a menos que el **b**oleto para **v**olar.

10·3 Los dichos y refranes

Now pronounce the following sayings and focus on the letters **b** and **v**.

1. No hay mal que por bien no venga.
2. Vale más tarde que nunca.

METHODOLOGY • Timing Activities

You will see that in some cases suggested times for activities may be slightly longer than in past chapters. As students are able to manipulate and create more with the language, more time may be allotted for activities in which students are encouraged to elaborate on responses or engage in more extended conversation. Whenever possible, extend your follow-up to engage students further by posing related questions and holding them accountable for what classmates are saying. E.g., *¿Cambió Carla el aceite de su coche?*

Additional activity for *Los medios de transporte*

No pertenece ¿Qué palabra no pertenece a cada uno de los siguientes grupos? Túrnense para leer la lista y contestar.

1. el parabrisas, el tráfico, el limpiaparabrisas, el baúl
2. el carro, el semáforo, la moto, el metro
3. revisar, estacionar, manejar, caminar
4. el tanque, el motor, la rueda, la multa
5. el taxi, el coche, el avión, el camión

Answers: 1. el tráfico, 2. el semáforo, 3. caminar, 4. la multa, 5. el avión

---

Answers to 10-4.
avión: el motor, el parabrisas, el limpiaparabrisas, el aire acondicionado, la calefacción, la llanta, la rueda, el tanque
autobús: el aire acondicionado, el baúl, la calefacción, el parabrisas, el limpiaparabrisas, la llanta, la llave, el motor, la rueda, el tanque
moto: la llanta, el motor, la rueda, el tanque, la llave
tren: el aire acondicionado, la calefacción, el motor, el tanque, el parabrisas, el limpiaparabrisas
center circle: el motor, el tanque

[5:00] 📖 👥 **10·4 ¿Qué tienen en común?**

Escriban características específicas de cada medio de transporte en cada uno de los círculos pequeños. En el círculo grande del centro, escriban lo que todos estos medios de transporte tienen en común. Después comparen su diagrama con otros compañeros.

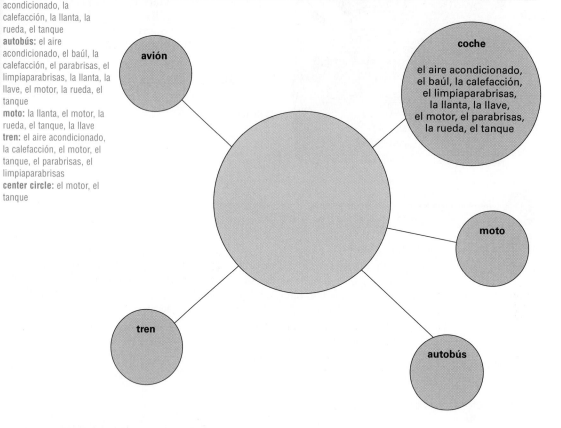

👥 **10·5 ¿Es verdad?** [4:00]

Decide si estas frases son ciertas o falsas. Si son falsas, corrígelas *(correct them)*. Compara tus respuestas con las de un/a compañero/a.

MODELO   Un carro tiene seis llantas.
Un carro tiene cuatro llantas.

> **Estrategia**
>
> When correcting true/false statements, instead of simply adding a negative word, correct the word that is false to make the statement true.

1. Hay semáforos en las autopistas.   F   en las calles
2. Para llegar a la universidad yo puedo tomar el autobús o ir a pie.   C/F
3. Ir en avión es más rápido que ir en tren.   C
4. Un coche no puede funcionar sin limpiaparabrisas.   F   un motor, gasolina, etc.
5. Hay que cambiar el aceite de un coche cada 100.000 millas.   F   de cada 3.000 a 5.000
6. Puedes llenar el tanque con gasolina en la estación de servicio.   C
7. Usamos la calefacción en el verano.   F   Usamos la calefacción en el invierno *or* Usamos el aire acondicionado en el verano.
8. Si manejamos muy rápido el policía nos puede dar una llave.   F   una multa

---

Additional activity for *Los medios de transporte*

👥 **¿Cómo vas?** Completa los siguientes pasos.

Paso 1 Pon una equis (X) en la columna apropiada. Después, pregúntale a un/a compañero/a qué medios de transporte usa él/ella.

MODELO
E1: *¿Qué medio de transporte usas a menudo?*
E2: *Uso el autobús a menudo. ¿Y tú?*
E1: *Uso el carro.*
E2: *¿Qué medio de transporte usas a veces?*
E1: *Uso la bicicleta a veces. ¿Y tú?*

¿QUÉ USAS . . .?	A MENUDO	A VECES	NUNCA
bicicleta			
autobús			
avión			
carro			
tren			

Paso 2 Túrnense para hacer las siguientes preguntas.

¿Qué medio de transporte usas . . .
1. más?
2. menos?
3. para ir a la universidad?
4. para ir al centro comercial?
5. para ir a visitar a tus amigos?
6. para ir a la casa de tus padres o unos parientes?
7. para ir a Los Ángeles?
8. para ir a Caracas, Venezuela?
9. para ir a Europa?

6:00 **10·6** Cinco preguntas

En grupos de tres o cuatro estudiantes, escriban **cinco** preguntas interesantes relacionadas con el vocabulario nuevo. Después, para cada pregunta, deben escoger a una persona de otro grupo para contestarla.

MODELO

GRUPO 1:	¿Cambiaste el aceite del coche la semana pasada?
GRUPO 2 (PHILIP):	No, no cambié el aceite la semana pasada pero tengo que cambiarlo pronto.
GRUPO 1:	¿Viajaste a México el verano pasado?
GRUPO 2 (GENA):	Sí, fui a Cancún con mi familia.

8:00   **10·7** Firma aquí

Estrategia

When performing a signature search (or *Firma aquí*) activity, remember to circulate around the classroom, speaking to many different classmates. You should try to have a different student's signature for each item.

Circula por la clase hasta encontrar a un estudiante que pueda contestar afirmativamente a tu pregunta. **¡OJO!** Debes usar **el pretérito** en muchas de las preguntas.

MODELO manejar un camión

E1: ¿Manejas un camión?
E2: Sí, manejo un camión.
E1: Pues, firma aquí.
      Rosario

manejar un camión	ir a una gasolinera esta mañana	saber manejar un barco
tener más de tres llaves contigo	llegar a la universidad por autopista	tener un coche sin calefacción
perder sus llaves alguna vez	viajar a algún lugar exótico durante las últimas vacaciones	recibir una multa el año pasado
tener un accidente en la autopista en los últimos dos años	llevar su coche al mecánico el mes pasado	viajar en tren el año pasado

GRAMÁTICA **2** ## Los mandatos informales

10-12 to 10-16

`6:00`

When you need to give instructions, advise, or ask people to do something, you use commands. If you are addressing a friend or someone you normally address as **tú,** you use informal commands. You have been responding to **tú** commands since the beginning of *¡Anda!*: **escucha, escribe, abre tu libro en la página…,** etc.

¡A la derecha, Pepe! Dobla a la derecha, no a la izquierda…

1. The affirmative *tú* command form is the same as the *él, ella,* **Ud.** form of the present tense of the verb:

Infinitive		Present tense	Affirmative *tú* command
llen**ar**	él, ella, Ud.	llen**a**	llen**a**
le**er**	él, ella, Ud.	le**e**	le**e**
ped**ir**	él, ella, Ud.	pid**e**	pid**e**

Llen**a** el tanque.	*Fill the tank.*
Dobl**a** a la derecha.	*Turn to the right.*
Conduc**e** con cuidado.	*Drive carefully.*
Pid**e** permiso.	*Ask permission.*

There are eight common verbs that have irregular affirmative *tú* commands:

decir	**di**	ir	**ve**	salir	**sal**	tener	**ten**
hacer	**haz**	poner	**pon**	ser	**sé**	venir	**ven**

Sé respetuoso con los peatones.	*Be respectful of pedestrians.*
Ten cuidado al conducir.	*Be careful when driving.*
Ven al aeropuerto con tu pasaporte.	*Come to the airport with your passport.*
Pon las llaves en la mesa.	*Put the keys on the table.*

2. **To form the negative *tú* commands:**
   1. Take the **yo** form of the present tense of the verb.
   2. Drop the **-o** ending.
   3. Add *-es* for **-ar** verbs, and add *-as* for **-er** and **-ir** verbs.

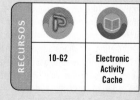

Infinitive	Present tense		Negative *tú* command
llenar	yo llen**ø**	+ es	no llen**es**
leer	yo le**ø**	+ as	no le**as**
ped**ir**	yo pid**ø**	+ as	no pid**as**

No llen**es** el tanque.   *Don't fill the tank.*

No dobl**es** a la derecha.   *Don't turn to the right.*

No conduzc**as** muy rápido.   *Don't drive very fast.*

No pid**as** permiso.   *Don't ask permission.*

Verbs ending in **-car**, **-gar**, and **-zar** have a spelling change in the negative **tú** command. These spelling changes are needed to preserve the sound of the infinitive ending.

Infinitive	Present tense		Negative *tú* command
sa**car**	yo sa**c**o	c → qu	no sa**qu**es
lle**gar**	yo lle**g**o	g → gu	no lle**gu**es
empe**zar**	yo empie**z**o	z → c	no empie**c**es

3. Object and reflexive pronouns are used with *tú* commands in the following ways.

    a. They are *attached* to the end of *affirmative* commands. When the command is made up of more than two syllables after the pronoun(s) is/are attached, a written accent mark is placed over the stressed vowel.

Se pinchó una llanta. **¡Cámbiamela!**   *I got a flat tire. Change it for me!*

Tu bicicleta no funciona. **Revísala.**   *Your bike does not work. Check it.*

Me gusta tu coche. **Préstamelo.**   *I like your car. Loan it to me.*

Llegamos tarde. **¡Estaciónate,** por favor!   *We are late. Park, please!*

    b. They are placed *before negative* **tú** commands.

No se nos pinchó una llanta.   *We don't have a flat tire.*

¡No **me la** cambies!   *Don't change it for me!*

Tu bicicleta funciona.   *Your bicycle works.*

No **la** vendas.   *Don't sell it.*

No me gusta ese coche.   *I don't like that car.*

No **me lo** compres.   *Don't buy it for me.*

Llegamos tarde.   *We are late.*

No **te** estaciones aquí, por favor.   *Do not park here, please.*

Additional activity for *Los mandatos informales*
Por favor… ¿Qué les pides a tus amigos? Con un/a compañero/a, da los mandatos siguientes.

MODELO
E1: llamarme mañana
E2: *Llámame mañana, por favor.*

1. venir a verme
2. tener paciencia conmigo
3. decirme la verdad siempre
4. divertirse
5. no salir con personas antipáticas
6. acordarse de la fiesta
7. no ser tonto/a
8. no vestirse de manera atrevida

Answers: 1. ven, 2. ten, 3. dime, 4. diviértete, 5. no salgas, 6. acuérdate, 7. no seas, 8. no te vistas

 10·8 ¿Qué diría el profesor? `3:00`

Túrnense para decir cuál de los dos mandatos diría (*would say*) un/a profesor/a de una escuela de conducir.

MODELO   a. Toma apuntes mientras hablo.

b. No tomes apuntes mientras hablo.

E1: *Toma apuntes mientras hablo.*

1. (a.) Estudia las reglas.
   b. No estudies las reglas.
2. a. Ven tarde a la clase.
   (b.) No vengas tarde a la clase.
3. (a.) Lee el manual con cuidado.
   b. No leas el manual con cuidado.
4. (a.) Practica fuera de la clase.
   b. No practiques fuera de la clase.
5. a. Ponte nervioso/a.
   (b.) No te pongas nervioso/a.
6. (a.) Conduce con cuidado.
   b. No conduzcas con cuidado.
7. a. Sal de la clase antes de tiempo.
   (b.) No salgas de la clase antes de tiempo.
8. (a.) Trae tu manual a clase.
   b. No traigas tu manual a clase.

Capítulo 5. Los pronombres de complemento directo, pág. 190.

Estrategia

For activities like **10-9** you can take turns by having one student do the even-numbered items while the other does the odd-numbered ones. Or, one can give the affirmative commands while the other gives the negatives, then switch roles.

 10·9 Hazlo, por favor `3:00`

Túrnense para expresar mandatos afirmativos y negativos usando los pronombres de complemento directo.

MODELO   esperar el autobús

E1: *¡Espéralo!*

E2: *¡No lo esperes!*

1. tomar el autobús
2. prestarme las llaves
3. conducir el carro

4. usar la calefacción
5. hacer un ruido
6. limpiar el parabrisas

7. subir la ventana
8. estacionar el coche en el garaje
9. buscar un estacionamiento

Answers to 10-9.
1. ¡Tómalo! ¡No lo tomes!
2. ¡Préstamelas! ¡No me las prestes!
3. ¡Condúcelo! ¡No lo conduzcas!
4. ¡Úsala! ¡No la uses!
5. ¡Hazlo! ¡No lo hagas!
6. ¡Límpialo! ¡No lo limpies!
7. ¡Súbela! ¡No la subas!
8. ¡Estaciónalo en el garaje! ¡No lo estaciones en el garaje!
9. ¡Búscalo! ¡No lo busques!

[4:00] **10·10** ¡Ayúdame!

¡Tu compañero/a de apartamento te vuelve loco/a!

Paso 1   Usa los verbos siguientes para decirle lo que debe y no debe hacer y compara tus respuestas con las de un/a compañero/a.

MODELO   no poner tus libros en mi cama

No pongas tus libros en mi cama.

1. no dormirse en el sofá   No te duermas en el sofá.
2. sacar la basura   Saca la basura.
3. no comer en la sala   No comas en la sala.
4. no beber de mi vaso   No bebas de mi vaso.
5. decirme la verdad siempre   Dime la verdad siempre.
6. no vestirse en la cocina   No te vistas en la cocina.
7. tener más paciencia con mi gato (*cat*)   Ten más paciencia con mi gato.
8. no invitar siempre a tus amigos después de las once de la noche
   No invites siempre a tus amigos después de las once de la noche.

Paso 2   Para cada mandato negativo que dieron juntos, den otra alternativa. *Answers may vary.*

MODELO   E1:   *No pongas tus libros en mi cama.*

          E2:   *Ponlos en la mesa.*

[5:00] **10·11** ¡Una fiesta!

Uds. organizan una fiesta para sus amigos. Tienen mucho que hacer: limpiar el apartamento, organizar la música, comprar y preparar la comida, vestirse, etc. Un amigo se ofrece a ayudarles. Hagan una lista de las cosas que él puede hacer.

MODELO   *1. Organiza los CD.*

GRAMÁTICA 3 — Los mandatos formales

10-17 to 10-20

When you need to influence others by making a request, giving advice, or giving orders to people you normally treat as **Ud.** or **Uds.**, you are going to use a different set of commands: **Ud.** and **Uds.** commands. The forms of these commands are similar to the negative **tú** command forms.

1. To form the *Ud.* and *Uds.* commands:
   1. Take the **yo** form of the present tense of the verb.
   2. Drop the **-o** ending.
   3. Add **-e(n)** for **-ar** verbs, and add **-a(n)** for **-er** and **-ir** verbs.

Infinitive	Present tense		Ud. commands	Uds. commands
limpi**ar**	yo limpi**ø**	+ e(n)	(no) limpi**e**	(no) limpi**en**
le**er**	yo le**ø**	+ a(n)	(no) le**a**	(no) le**an**
ped**ir**	yo pid**ø**	+ a(n)	(no) pid**a**	(no) pid**an**

Llene el tanque. **Llénelo.** — *Fill up the tank. Fill it.*
No limpie el parabrisas. **No lo limpie.** — *Don't clean the windshield. Don't clean it.*
Conduzca el camión para su tío. **Condúzcalo.** — *Drive the truck for your uncle. Drive it.*
No ponga esa gasolina cara en el coche. — *Don't put that expensive gasoline in the car.*
No la ponga en el coche. — *Don't put it in the car.*
Traiga su licencia. **Tráigala.** — *Bring your license. Bring it.*
No busquen sus llaves. **No las busquen.** — *Don't look for your keys. Don't look for them.*

1. Where do the object pronouns appear in affirmative commands? In negative commands? In what order?
2. Why are there written accents on some of the commands and not on others?

Check your answers to the preceding questions in Appendix 1.

2. Verbs ending in *-car, -gar,* and *-zar* have a spelling change in the *Ud.* and *Uds.* commands. These spelling changes are needed to preserve the sound of the infinitive ending.

Infinitive	Present tense		Ud. /Uds. commands
sac**ar**	yo sac**o**	c → qu	sa**que**(n)
lleg**ar**	yo lleg**o**	g → gu	lle**gue**(n)
empez**ar**	yo empiez**o**	z → c	empie**ce**(n)

3. These verbs also have irregular forms for the *Ud./Uds.* commands:

dar	**dé(n)**	ir	**vaya(n)**	ser	**sea(n)**
estar	**esté(n)**	saber	**sepa(n)**		

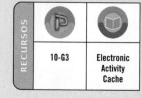

4. Finally, compare the forms of the *tú* and *Ud./Uds.* commands:

	Tú commands		*Ud./Uds.* commands	
	affirmative	**negative**	**affirmative**	**negative**
hablar	habla	no hables	hable(n)	no hable(n)
comer	come	no comas	coma(n)	no coma(n)
pedir	pide	no pidas	pida(n)	no pida(n)

10·12 Consejos `4:00`

> Capítulo 8. Las construcciones reflexivas, pág. 302.

Dos estudiantes de intercambio (*exchange students*) van a llegar a tu universidad y necesitan tu ayuda con lo que deben y no deben hacer antes de llegar a los Estados Unidos. Comparte la lista con un/a compañero/a.

MODELO   E1: acostarse temprano la noche antes de viajar
           E2: *Acuéstense temprano la noche antes de viajar.*
              Levántense temprano el día del viaje.

1. levantarse temprano el día del viaje   Preparen el equipaje el
2. preparar el equipaje (*luggage*) el día anterior   día anterior.
3. ponerse ropa cómoda   Pónganse ropa cómoda.
4. no ponerse nervioso/a   No se pongan nerviosos.
5. evitar el alcohol   Eviten el alcohol.
6. tener su pasaporte a mano (*on hand*)   Tengan su pasaporte a mano.
7. sentarse en el asiento correcto   Siéntense en el asiento correcto.
8. dormirse durante el vuelo   Duérmanse durante el vuelo.

10·13 La multa `7:00`

Termina el diálogo entre Mayra y el policía. Después realicen la escena con un/a compañero/a.

> Capítulo 9. Un resumen de los pronombres de complemento directo, indirecto y reflexivos, pág. 325.

MAYRA: Buenas noches. ¿Iba muy rápido, señor policía?

POLICÍA: Sí, señorita. (1) ____Muéstreme____ (mostrarme) su licencia, por favor.

MAYRA: Aquí la tiene (*here you go*), señor. Sé que la foto es muy mala.

POLICÍA: No (2) ____se preocupe____ (preocuparse). Ahora, (3) ____cuénteme____ (contarme), señorita. ¿A qué velocidad (*speed*) iba?

MAYRA: Pues… la verdad es que no estoy segura. (4) ____Dígamelo____ (decírmelo) usted.

POLICÍA: Iba a ochenta kilómetros por hora y el límite aquí es sesenta y cinco.

MAYRA: ¡Ay! ¡Mi padre me va a matar! Por favor, no (5) ____me dé____ (darme) una multa. Lo siento. Le aseguro que voy a manejar mucho más lento ahora.

POLICÍA: No es mi decisión. Es la ley (*law*).

MAYRA: Entonces, por lo menos no (6) ____escriba____ (escribir) ochenta kilómetros por hora en la multa. (7) ____Ponga____ (poner) setenta, por favor.

POLICÍA: No puedo hacer eso. Bueno, (8) ____tómela____ (tomarla).

MAYRA: (*silencio*)

POLICÍA: Y no (9) ____maneje____ (manejar) tan rápidamente en el futuro. (10) ____Tenga____ (tener) más cuidado.

Warm-up for *Los mandatos formales* Drill command forms by saying an infinitive and asking for a choral class response for the command. Start with just the command form, then add more information. For example: *hablar (más despacio), regresar (temprano), levantarse (por favor), comprar (estos zapatos), comer (verduras), beber (leche), traer (tu traje de baño), ponerse (guantes), divertirse (esta noche).*

Additional Activity for *Los mandatos formales*

¿Cómo contestaría tu profe de español? Túrnense para hacer los papeles de profesor (**P**) y estudiante (**E**).

MODELO
E: ¿Debemos hacer la tarea para mañana?
P: *Sí, hagan la tarea para mañana. /*
    Sí, háganla para mañana.

1. ¿Debemos traer el cuaderno a la clase?
2. ¿Podemos llegar cinco minutos tarde?
3. ¿Hay que hablar en español todo el tiempo?
4. ¿Tenemos que tomar un examen pasado mañana?
5. ¿Podemos usar nuestros apuntes durante el examen?
6. ¿Está bien si no venimos a clase mañana?
7. ¿Podemos desayunar en la sala de clase?
8. ¿Buscamos la lectura en el Internet?
9. ¿Empezamos la tarea en clase?
10. ¿Podemos salir temprano?

CAPÍTULO 10

NOTE FOR 10-14

In addition to the *Transmilenio* bus system, Bogotá has more than 20,000 buses and microbuses that transport around 7 million passengers daily. For more information on *Transmilenio*, visit www.transmilenio.gov.co/transmilenio/.

Expansion for 10-14 Ask students if these regulations are any different from the ones that apply to public transportation where they live.

NATIONAL STANDARDS

Communication, Culture, Connections, Comparisons

In the reading *¿Cómo nos movemos?*, students learn about public transportation in Hispanic countries and driving in Colombia. The *Preguntas* that follow are for interpersonal communication (Standard 1.1), and the reading itself provides authentic written Spanish for understanding and interpretation (Standard 1.2). The reading is about how transportation differs from that of the United States, so students read about the culture (Standard 2.1) and note the differences. These differences allow them to make comparisons between driving in the United States and driving in Colombia (Standard 4.2). Lastly, students make the comparisons based on what they have connected from other disciplines about learning how to drive and how transportation affects society (Standard 3.2).

Expansion for *Preguntas* Ask students the following question: *¿Por qué no es tan importante tener que conducir si vives en una ciudad?*

10·14 El transporte rápido [5:00]

El Transmilenio es un sistema de transporte masivo de pasajeros (*passengers*) en autobús que permite llegar rápidamente a cualquier (*any*) lugar de la ciudad de Bogotá. Lee las siguientes reglas del Transmilenio y completa la lista con mandatos formales. Luego, compártela con un/a compañero/a.

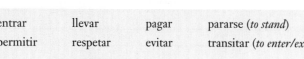

| entrar | llevar | pagar | pararse (*to stand*) |
| permitir | respetar | evitar | transitar (*to enter/exit*) |

MODELO   Siempre *evite* correr.

- Instrucciones para el uso adecuado (*suitable*) del sistema:

1. Cuando espere al autobús, __párese__ detrás de la línea amarilla de seguridad.
2. Antes de entrar, __permita__ que salgan los pasajeros.
3. __Pague__ con su tarjeta al entrar.
4. Al usar las rampas, túneles o plataformas, __transite__ por la derecha.
5. No __lleve__ paquetes (*packages*) grandes ni mascotas (*pets*).
6. No __entre__ en el autobús bebiendo o fumando ni en estado de embriaguez (*intoxication*).
7. __Respete__ las sillas azules que son para personas con discapacidad, mujeres embarazadas, niños de brazos y adultos mayores.

[4:00]   **¿Cómo nos movemos?**

10-21

El saber conducir o manejar un auto no suele ser tan importante en los países hispanohablantes como en los Estados Unidos. Por lo general, la gente camina más y usa el transporte público, ya sea el autobús, el metro o el taxi. Las personas que sí quieren conducir, generalmente tienen que tomar un curso en una escuela privada de conducir.

En Colombia, por ejemplo, para obtener (*get*) una licencia de conducir es necesario:

- tener 16 años.
- saber leer y escribir.
- aprobar un examen teórico o presentar un certificado de aptitud en conducción (*driving*) emitido por una escuela aprobada (*approved*) por el Ministerio de Educación Nacional en coordinación con el Ministerio de Transporte.
- presentar un certificado de aptitud física y mental expedido por (*completed by*) un médico.

Una de las escuelas de conducir más conocidas en Colombia es ConducirColombia. Los cursos y los precios varían según la experiencia previa del estudiante. Hay cursos básicos de diez clases por unos ciento cincuenta y nueve dólares hasta cursos avanzados de catorce clases por unos doscientos dólares.

Preguntas

1. ¿Sabes conducir? ¿Cuándo aprendiste? ¿Quién te enseñó? ¿Cuándo sacaste la licencia de conducir?
   Answers may vary.
2. Según esta lectura, ¿crees que es generalmente más fácil o más difícil obtener una licencia en Colombia que en los Estados Unidos? Explica.   Puede ser más difícil obtener una licencia de conducir en Colombia porque es necesario presentar un certificado de aptitud física y mental.

4:00

Answers to 10-15.
1. Lléneme el tanque, por favor. / Llénemelo.
2. Límpieme el parabrisas, por favor. / Límpiemelo, por favor.
3. Arrégleme el limpiaparabrisas, por favor. / Arréglemelo, por favor.
4. Revíseme el motor, por favor. / Revísemelo, por favor.
5. Póngame aire en las llantas, por favor. / Póngamelo, por favor.
6. Cámbieme el aceite, por favor. / Cámbiemelo, por favor.

10·15 La estación de servicio

Acabas de llegar a una gasolinera. Dile a la persona responsable lo que necesitas.

MODELO   No puedo abrir el baúl.
           Ábrame el baúl, por favor. /
           Ábramelo, por favor.

1. Necesito gasolina.
2. El parabrisas está sucio.
3. El limpiaparabrisas no funciona.
4. El motor tiene un ruido extraño.
5. Las llantas necesitan aire.
6. El aceite está sucio.

Capítulo 8. Los pronombres de complemento indirecto, pág. 292; Los pronombres de complemento directo e indirecto usados juntos, pág. 298.

5:00

10·16 ¡A su servicio!

Capítulo 3. La casa, pág. 100; Los muebles y otros objetos de la casa, pág. 109; Los quehaceres de la casa, pág. 112.

Uds. son compañeros/as de apartamento y acaban de ganar el concurso ¡A su servicio! Reciben como premio la ayuda de Jaime, un mayordomo (*butler*) por una semana. Díganle **ocho** cosas que quieren que haga (*you want him to do*) para ayudarles hoy con los quehaceres. Después, díganle **tres** cosas que no debe hacer.

MODELO   *Jaime, saque la basura, por favor.*

Additional activity for *Los mandatos formales* **Los compañeros de cuarto del infierno** Este año tus compañeros de cuarto/apartamento (¡o unos miembros de tu familia!) son horribles. Haz una lista de cinco cosas que deben (o no deben) hacer. Después, comparte tu lista con un/a compañero/a. (Verbos posibles: *cerrar, dejar, limpiar, sacar, sacudir, pasar la aspiradora, lavar*)

MODELO
Cierren la puerta del refrigerador.
No dejen la ropa sucia en el suelo.

¿Cómo andas?

Having completed the first **Comunicación**, I now can...

	Feel Confident	Need to Review
• discuss different modes of transportation (p. 356)	❑	❑
• name the various parts of a car (p. 357)	❑	❑
• pronounce **b** and **v** properly in Spanish (p. 357)	❑	❑
• influence others by using commands (pp. 360, 364)	❑	❑
• list some public transportation options and discuss procedures for getting a driver's license in Hispanic countries (p. 366)	❑	❑

Comunicación

- Discussing travel
- Describing a past trip
- Discussing to whom things belong
- Comparing people, places, and things

VOCABULARIO 4 El viaje

10-22 to 10-27

5:00

la playa   las montañas

Agencia de Viajes Mundotur

MÉXICO   PERÚ

el lago

el parque de atracciones

la agente de viajes

el agente de viajes

el pasaporte

el boleto de ida y vuelta

el aeropuerto

la estación de autobús

el cuarto individual

arreglar/hacer la maleta

la maleta

el barco

el cuarto doble

el botones

Otras palabras útiles	*Other useful words*
la agencia de viajes	*travel agency*
la estación de tren	*train station*
el extranjero	*abroad*
la recepción	*front desk*
la reserva	*reservation*
el sello	*postage stamp*
la tarjeta postal	*postcard*
las vacaciones	*vacation*
los viajeros	*travelers*
el vuelo	*flight*

Unos verbos útiles	*Some useful verbs*
caminar, ir a pie	*to walk; to go on foot*
dejar	*to leave*
ir de vacaciones	*to go on vacation*
ir de viaje	*to go on a trip*
irse del hotel	*to leave the hotel; to check out*
registrarse (en el hotel)	*to check in*
volar (o → ue)	*to fly; to fly away*

RECURSOS

T10-6	T10-6	Electronic Activity Cache

Additional activity for *El viaje*

¿Adónde van? Ustedes trabajan en una agencia de viajes y un/a cliente quiere ir de viaje a La Isla de Margarita en Venezuela. Tiene un presupuesto de 2.000 dólares.

Paso 1 Escriban una conversación entre el/la agente de viajes y el/la cliente. Incluyan:

1. como mínimo dos preguntas sobre las preferencias del cliente.
2. los planes —el destino, cómo va a viajar, cuánto cuesta el boleto, qué puede hacer y ver allí y qué ropa necesita para hacer la maleta.

Paso 2 Realicen la escena para la clase.

While the students are writing, circulate often among them to offer suggestions and make corrections. That way, when they present their skits there won't be as many errors. You may also have them turn the skits in, correct them, and give them back the following class for students to act out. How you handle *Paso 2* will determine the amount of time you need to set aside for the activity.

Expansion for 10-17 For additional practice, create teams of 3 or 4 students and challenge them to write a logical sentence with as many new vocabulary words as possible in 3 minutes.

Expansion for 10-18 Have students create their own grid relating to their university, city, or area.

10·17 Categorías

Tienes tres minutos para escribir todas las palabras que pertenecen (*pertain*) a las siguientes categorías. No debes repetir palabras. Después, compara tus listas con las de un/a compañero/a. Date un punto por cada palabra que tienes que tu compañero/a no tiene.

EL AEROPUERTO	EL HOTEL	LAS VACACIONES

10·18 ¿Quiénes lo hacen?

Circula por la clase hasta encontrar a un/a estudiante que pueda contestar afirmativamente a tu pregunta. **¡OJO!** Debes usar el pretérito en **dos** de las preguntas.

MODELO ¿Quién…?

siempre dejar una buena propina cuando va a un restaurante

TIFFANY: *¿Siempre dejas una buena propina cuando vas a un restaurante?*

ROB: *Sí, siempre dejo una buena propina.*

TIFFANY: *Pues, firma aquí.*

Rob

¿QUIÉN…?		
siempre dejar una buena propina cuando va a un restaurante	nunca ir a un parque de atracciones	viajar al extranjero
ir a la playa el verano pasado	nunca volar en avión	coleccionar tarjetas postales
quedarse en un hotel elegante una vez	vivir en las montañas	tener más de tres maletas

10·19 Antes de ir

Tu amigo tiene que ir a Venezuela para una reunión (*meeting*) de negocios. Dale **cinco** consejos sobre lo que debe o no debe hacer para prepararse para el viaje y compara tu lista con la de tu compañero.

MODELO 1. *Busca tu pasaporte.*

10·20 Las mejores vacaciones

Capítulo 7. El pretérito, pág. 258; Unos verbos irregulares en el pretérito, pág. 266.

Piensa en tus mejores vacaciones al contestar las siguientes preguntas. Después, circula por la clase para entrevistar a tus compañeros/as.

1. ¿Adónde fuiste?
2. ¿Cómo viajaste?
3. ¿Dónde te quedaste?
4. ¿Cuánto tiempo estuviste allí?
5. ¿Qué hiciste durante aquellas vacaciones especiales?
6. ¿A quién le mandaste una tarjeta postal? ¿una tarjeta electrónica?

Venezuela, país de aventuras

Venezuela, país de aventuras

¿Es Ud. aventurero/a? En Venezuela tenemos muchas oportunidades para conocer nuestro país a base de la aventura. Le proponemos (propose) una excursión de dos días en el Canaima. El primer día le ofrecemos un paseo en barco por la Laguna Ucaima y una visita al Salto Ucaima. La excursión del segundo día le permite conocer el Salto Ángel, donde podemos nadar al pie de la cascada (waterfall).

Si le gusta hacer trekking, puede disfrutar de una excursión a los tepuyes (una palabra indígena que significa "montaña"). Se puede subir el Pico Humboldt; a unos 4.942 m.s.n.m. es el segundo pico del país. Una excursión de este tipo está dentro de los considerados "deportes extremos" que se pueden practicar.

Si quiere combinar la aventura con una estancia en un hotel de lujo (luxury), debe considerar La Isla de Margarita. Está situada al norte de Caracas a sólo treinta y cinco minutos en avión o a un par de horas en ferry. Allí puede disfrutar de todos los deportes de agua, pescar, jugar al golf y explorar las numerosas y variadas playas. Por la noche hay restaurantes, clubes de baile, bares y casinos. Para informarse mejor, póngase en contacto hoy con su agencia de viajes preferida.

Preguntas En el Canaima puedes ver al Salto Ucaima y al Salto Ángel. En los tepuyes puedes subir el Pico Humboldt. En la Isla de Margarita puedes disfrutar de todos los deportes de agua, pescar, jugar al golf y explorar las playas.

1. ¿Qué puedes hacer durante la excursión en el Canaima? ¿en la excursión a los tepuyes? ¿en la Isla de Margarita?

2. De las "aventuras" que ofrece Venezuela, ¿cuál prefieres? ¿Por qué? *Answers may vary.*

3. ¿Eres aventurero/a? ¿Cuál es la aventura más atrevida que has tenido (you have had)? *Answers may vary.*

CAPÍTULO 10

GRAMÁTICA 5 — Otras formas del posesivo

SAM 10-28 to 10-29

Guide G 17, 61

5:00

¿Dónde están tus llaves? Tengo las mías aquí.

Pues, las llaves mías deben estar en el carro.

In **Capítulo 1** you learned how to say *my, your, his, ours*, etc. (**mi/s, tu/s, su/s, nuestro/a/os/as, vuestro/a/os/as, su/s**). In Spanish you can also show possession with the long (or stressed) forms, the equivalent of the English *of mine, of yours, of his, of hers, of ours*, and *of theirs*.

| Singular | | Plural | | |
Masculine	Feminine	Masculine	Feminine	
mío	mía	míos	mías	*mine*
tuyo	tuya	tuyos	tuyas	*yours* (fam.)
suyo	suya	suyos	suyas	*his, hers, yours, theirs* (form.)
nuestro	nuestra	nuestros	nuestras	*ours*
vuestro	vuestra	vuestros	vuestras	*yours* (fam.)

Study the following examples.

Mi coche funciona bien.	**El coche mío** funciona bien.	**El mío** funciona bien.
Nuestros boletos cuestan mucho.	**Los boletos nuestros** cuestan mucho.	**Los nuestros** cuestan mucho.
¿Dónde están **tus** llaves?	¿Dónde están **las llaves tuyas**?	¿Dónde están **las tuyas**?
Su multa es de $100.	**La multa suya** es de $100.	**La suya** es de $100.

Compare the possessives in the above sentences.

1. What is the position of each possessive in the left-hand column? the middle column?
2. How do the possessive adjectives and pronouns agree?
3. What do the sentences mean in the column on the right? What have you removed from the previous sentence?

Check your answers to the preceding questions in Appendix 1.

*Note that the third person forms (**suyo/a/os/as**) can have more than one meaning. To avoid confusion, you can use:

article + noun + de *+ subject pronoun:*

el coche suyo

- el coche de él/ella
- el coche de Ud.
- el coche de ellos/ellas
- el coche de Uds.

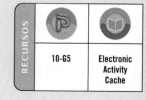

⏲ 3:00 👥 **10·21** Entre hermanos

Cambia todos los posesivos a la forma nueva (larga) en la conversación entre Marco y Mari.
Después compara los cambios con los de un/a compañero/a.

MODELO   El problema que tienes con tu coche es serio.

El problema que tienes con el coche tuyo es serio.

MARCO: Mari, parece que tu llanta pierde aire.

MARI: Ah ¿sí? Tampoco funciona bien mi coche.

MARCO: Pues, mi mecánico es muy bueno.

MARI: Gracias, pero pienso llevar el coche a nuestro mecánico. Hace
         muchos años que Tom y yo lo conocemos.

MARCO: ¿Él tiene su negocio en la calle Bolívar?

MARI: Sí, y trabaja con uno de sus hermanos.

MARCO: ¿Puedes usar uno de sus coches mientras arregla el tuyo?

MARI: Sí, pero prefiero sacar tu BMW del garaje. Nunca lo manejas.

MARCO: Escucha, hermana. Ese BMW es un tesoro (*treasure*) y nadie lo
         maneja.

Answers to 10-22.
1. No, son de Tina.
   Los pantalones (cortos
   azules) son suyos.
2. No, es de Susana.
   La camisa (de rayas) es
   suya.
3. Sí, son los míos.
   Los calcetines
   (estampados) son míos.
4. No, es de Felipe.
   La chaqueta (negra) es
   suya.
5. Sí, es mío. El suéter (de
   algodón) es mío.
6. No, son de Tina. Las
   camisetas (blancas) son
   suyas.

⏲ 4:00 👥 **10·22** ¡Problemas!

♻ Capítulo 8. La
ropa, pág. 286.

Están de viaje con algunos de sus mejores amigos. El hotel
les lavó la ropa pero ahora Uds. no saben de quiénes son
las prendas. Túrnense para hacer y contestar las preguntas
de Ana, quien está intentando organizar la ropa.

MODELO   E1 (ANA):   Los calcetines rojos, ¿son los
                      tuyos? (de Felipe)

          E2:   *No, son de Felipe.*
                     Los calcetines son suyos.

1. Los pantalones cortos azules, ¿son los tuyos? (de Tina)
2. La camisa de rayas, ¿es la mía? (de Susana)
3. Los calcetines estampados, ¿son los tuyos? (mío)
4. La chaqueta negra, ¿es la tuya? (de Felipe)
5. El suéter de algodón, ¿es el tuyo? (mío)
6. Las camisetas blancas, ¿son las tuyas? (de Tina)

⏲ 4:00 👥 **10·23** Personalmente...

Termina las siguientes
oraciones sobre tu
mejor amigo/a y tú y
después compártelas
con un/a
compañero/a.

1. El mejor amigo mío...
2. La casa suya...
3. La especialidad mía...
4. La materia favorita suya...
5. El restaurante favorito nuestro...
6. A los otros amigos nuestros les encanta(n)...

NATIONAL STANDARDS
Communication

The activities that accompany the
presentation of possessive pronouns help students master speech
typical of native speakers. They have
already learned the possessive
adjectives and how to use *de* for
possession, and now they have
learned another way to express possession. The activities recycle the
possessive adjectives in combination with the new material, and
students are able to communicate
in the interpersonal mode
(Standard 1.1) about what they and
others possess.

Expansion for 10-21 Ask students
to create a list of their 5 favorite
possessions. Then have them circulate around the room and offer those
possessions to other students.

E.g. Mi iPod negro.→¿Quieres el
iPod negro mío?
No, no quiero el iPod tuyo. / Sí,
quiero el iPod tuyo.

NATIONAL STANDARDS
Communication, Comparisons

In *Capítulo 10*, students learn how to compare things that are similar and dissimilar. They also learn how to form comparatives and superlatives. This new information allows for greater depth of conversation with others when they express their feelings and emotions and exchange opinions. They can discuss familiar topics in Spanish with classmates (Standard 1.1), and, if they travel abroad, they can form useful questions, such as where the cheapest place to stay is, or what restaurant has the best food. If they are deciding between two things featured in their guide books, they can ask which one is better. The new grammar allows them to compare how to phrase comparisons in English and Spanish (Standard 4.1).

Suggestion for *El comparativo y el superlativo* Use your students and objects in the classroom to demonstrate forming comparisons and superlatives. Have two students stand up. Offer a couple of comparisons as a model (e.g., *Mary es más baja que Gena. El pelo de Gena es tan rubio como el pelo de Mary*). Then have students create as many comparisons of equality and inequality as possible on their own. Together, create superlative statements about the students and the classroom. Another great topic for comparison is your institution with a rival institution.

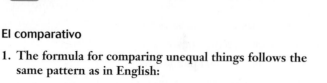

GRAMÁTICA 6
El comparativo y el superlativo

10-30 to   28, 29, 30
10-35

6:00

El comparativo

No tengo tantas maletas como tú.

1. The formula for comparing unequal things follows the same pattern as in English:

> **más** + *adjective/adverb/noun* + **que**
>
> **menos** + *adjective/adverb/noun* + **que**

El Hotel Hilton es **más** caro **que** el Motel 6.	*The Hilton is **more** expensive **than** Motel 6.*
El Motel 6 hace reservas **más** rápidamente **que** el Hotel Hilton.	*Motel 6 makes reservations **faster than** the Hilton.*
En esta ciudad hay **menos** hoteles **que** moteles.	*In this city there are **fewer** hotels **than** motels.*

- When comparing numbers, **de** is used instead of **que**:

El Hilton de Bogotá tiene **más de** doscientas habitaciones.	*The Bogotá Hilton has **more than** two hundred rooms.*

2. The formula for comparing two or more *equal* things also follows the same pattern as in English:

> **tan** + *adjective/adverb* + **como**   *as... as*
>
> **tanto(a/os/as)** + *noun* + **como**   *as much/many... as*

La agencia de viajes Mundotur es **tan** conocida **como** Meliá.	*The Mundotur travel agency is **as** well known **as** Meliá.*
Estos vuelos son **tan** caros **como** ésos.	*These flights are **as** expensive **as** those.*
Mi coche va **tan** rápido **como** un Ferrari.	*My car is **as** fast **as** a Ferrari.*
No tengo **tantas** maletas **como** tú.	*I don't have **as many** suitcases **as** you (do).*
No hay **tanto** tráfico **como** ayer.	*There isn't **as much** traffic **as** yesterday.*

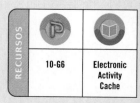

NOTE FOR
El comparativo y el superlativo

Diminutives and augmentatives are presented in *¡Anda! Curso intermedio.*

Suggestion for *El superlativo* As a class, create as many superlatives as possible in 2 to 3 minutes about your Spanish class and/or your institution.

El superlativo

1. **To compare three or more people or things, use the superlative. The formula for expressing the superlative is:**

> **el, la, los, las** *(noun)* + **más/menos** + *adjective* (+ **de**)

La agencia de viajes Viking es **la** agencia **más** popular **de** nuestro pueblo.

The Viking Travel Agency is the most popular (travel) agency in our town.

—¿Es el aeropuerto Hartsfield de Atlanta **el** aeropuerto **más** concurrido **de** los Estados Unidos?

Is Atlanta's Hartsfield Airport the busiest airport in the United States?

—Sí, ¡y el aeropuerto de mi ciudad es **el menos** concurrido!

Yes, and my city's airport is the least busy!

2. **The adjectives** *bueno/a, malo/a, grande,* **and** *pequeño/a* **are irregular in the comparative and the superlative.**

	Comparative			Superlative	
bueno/a	*good*	**mejor**	*better*	**el/la mejor**	*the best*
malo/a	*bad*	**peor**	*worse*	**el/la peor**	*the worst*
grande	*big*	**mayor**	*bigger*	**el/la mayor**	*the biggest*
pequeño/a	*small*	**menor**	*smaller*	**el/la menor**	*the smallest*

Comparative:

Mi clase de español es **mejor que** mis otras clases.

My Spanish class is better than my other classes.

Superlative:

Mi clase de español es **la mejor de** mis clases.

My Spanish class is the best (one) of my classes.

CAPÍTULO 10

10·24 ¿Cierto o falso? ⟨4:00⟩

¿Qué sabes de la geografía? Indica si las siguientes oraciones son ciertas o falsas; si son falsas, corrígelas. Comparte tus oraciones con las de un/a compañero/a siguiendo el modelo.

MODELO   México es más grande que Uruguay.

E1:   *¿Es México más grande que Uruguay?*

E2:   *Sí. México es mucho más grande que Uruguay. ¿Es Chile tan grande como Argentina?*

E1:   *No. Chile es más pequeño que Argentina, pero creo que es tan grande como Venezuela.*

1. México es más pequeño que Colombia.   F   México es más grande que Colombia.
2. Colombia es tan grande como Venezuela.   C
3. Panamá es más grande que Venezuela.   F   Panamá es más pequeño que Venezuela.
4. De estos países, Panamá es el más pequeño.   C
5. Bogotá se encuentra a mayor altura sobre el nivel del mar (es más alta) que Lima.   C
6. Colombia es más grande que los Estados Unidos.   F   Colombia es más pequeño que los EE.UU.
7. Caracas es tan grande como México, D.F.   F   Caracas no es tan grande como México, D.F.
8. La Paz es la capital situada a la mayor altitud (es la más alta).   C

⟨4:00⟩ ## 10·25 ¡Así son!

Capítulo 1. Los adjetivos descriptivos, pág. 44.

Haz una lista de **cuatro** o **cinco** adjetivos descriptivos. Después, en grupos de cinco o seis, discutan "quién es la persona más _____".

MODELO   de la clase (alta)

E1:   *¿Quién es la persona más alta de la clase?*

E2:   *La persona más alta de la clase es Catalina.*

1. de la televisión
2. del cine
3. del mundo de los deportes
4. de la música
5. de la universidad
6. de la política

10·26 ¿El mejor o el peor?

Circula por la clase para averiguar qué opinan los estudiantes sobre "los mejores" y "los peores". Necesita al menos **dos** opiniones para cada categoría.

Estrategia

You can also use the following expressions to express your opinions:

Pienso que…, Creo que…, Estoy de acuerdo, No estoy de acuerdo, and *En mi opinión…*

MODELO   E1:   *¿Cuál es el mejor supermercado?*

E2:   *En mi opinión, Whole Foods es el mejor supermercado. Y tú, ¿qué piensas?*

E1:   *Creo que el mejor supermercado es Kroger.*

	ESTUDIANTE 1	ESTUDIANTE 2
1. el mejor supermercado		
el peor supermercado		
2. el mejor almacén		
el peor almacén		
3. el mejor restaurante		
el peor restaurante		
4. el mejor aeropuerto		
el peor aeropuerto		
5. el mejor hotel		
el peor hotel		
6. el mejor parque de atracciones		
el peor parque de atracciones		
7. la mejor playa		
la peor playa		
8. el mejor lugar para la luna de miel (*honeymoon*)		
el peor lugar para la luna de miel		
9. la mejor aerolínea (*airline*)		
la peor aerolínea		
10. el mejor coche		
el peor coche		

NOTE FOR 10-26

Have students report their findings, asking them to give reasons for their choices. Then compile classroom opinions as a group, or tally responses for them and present the results during the next class as part of the warm-up.

Suggestion for 10-27 Assign actividad **10-27** for homework so that students come to class prepared to play this guessing game. Have each group choose their best riddle to present to the class.

Suggestion for 10-27 Begin this activity by giving clues about an object you have brought to class.

`8:00`

10·27 Adivina, adivinanza

Trae un objeto personal a la clase y escribe **cuatro** o **cinco** frases sobre él, usando las formas comparativas. No digas el nombre de tu objeto. Lee las frases en grupos de cuatro o cinco estudiantes para ver si los compañeros pueden adivinar (*guess*) lo que es.

Estrategia

One way to approach actividad **10-27** is to arrange your clues from most general to most specific.

MODELO   un bolígrafo

E1:   *1. Es más grande que un anillo.*

2. Es tan importante como un libro.

3. Es menos largo que mi zapato.

4. Seguramente Uds. lo usan tanto como yo.

5. Es tan útil como un lápiz.

E2:   *¡Es un bolígrafo!*

`4:00`

10·28 El transporte

Habla con un/a compañero/a de todos los medios de transporte que usan o han usado (*have used*) y compárenlos, pensando en los aspectos positivos y negativos de cada uno.

MODELO   E1:   *Uso el coche más que el metro pero el metro es más rápido que el coche.*

E2:   *Nunca voy en metro porque no hay metro en mi ciudad. Voy mucho en autobús porque es más barato que un taxi y es más rápido que mi bicicleta.*

10·29 Los mejores regalos (*gifts*)   `5:00`

Escoge uno de los siguientes temas y descríbele la situación a un/a compañero/a. Debes mencionar cuándo y dónde ocurrió, quiénes estaban contigo y qué pasó. Túrnense.

1. el mejor regalo que recibí
2. el mejor regalo que regalé (*gave*)
3. el mejor día de mi vida
4. el peor día de mi vida
5. las mejores vacaciones que tomé
6. las peores vacaciones que tomé

Capítulo 7. El pretérito, pág. 258. Unos verbos irregulares en el pretérito, pág. 266; Capítulo 8. El imperfecto, pág. 306; Capítulo 9. El pretérito y el imperfecto, pág. 334.

ESCUCHA

10-36 to
10-38

ESTRATEGIA   Listening for linguistic cues

You can enhance comprehension by listening for linguistic cues. For example, verb endings can tell you who is participating and whether the incident is taking place now, already took place in the past, or will take place in the future.

10·30   Antes de escuchar

Los amigos de Manolo están en una fiesta. Oyen por casualidad una conversación entre varias personas sobre el viaje y específicamente de algunos viajes que ya tomaron o que quieren tomar en el futuro.

1. ¿Cuáles fueron tus viajes más memorables?
2. ¿Hay un viaje en particular que le puedes recomendar a un/a amigo/a?
3. ¿A dónde quieres ir en tu próximo viaje?

Memo, Cristina, Rosa y sus amigos hablan de unos viajes interesantes.

10·31   A escuchar

CW eBook

CD 4
Track 13

Paso 1   Escucha la conversación entre Memo, Cristina y Rosa para tener una idea general de lo que dicen.

Paso 2   Cristina habla de Venezuela. Escucha otra vez y apunta todos los verbos que puedas que ella usa. ¿Cuál es el tiempo verbal que usa más? Entonces, es un viaje que…

   a. hizo ya.
   b. va a hacer.
   c. quiere hacer.

Paso 3   Escucha una vez más para poder completar la siguiente actividad.

1. ¿Quién sale mañana para Colombia? Escribe los verbos que usa esta persona para hablar de su viaje.   Memo: salgo, tengo, estoy pensando, conocer

2. ¿Habla Rosa de un viaje que hizo ya, va a hacer o quiere hacer? ¿Cómo lo sabes?   Habla de un viaje que hizo ya y también habla de un viaje que quiere hacer. Fue a Uruguay el año pasado pero quiere ir a Bogotá para ver el museo de Botero.

10·32   Después de escuchar

En grupos de tres o cuatro hablen de dos o tres lugares turísticos diferentes que conozcan (*you know*).

(*cont.*)

MEMO: ¿No se los dije? Salgo mañana para Colombia. Tengo una conferencia de trabajo, pero estoy pensando escaparme un par de días para conocer un poco de Venezuela.

ROSA: ¡Qué suerte! Me encantaría ir contigo, Memo. Hace mucho tiempo que quiero ir a Colombia, sobre todo a Bogotá. Como ya saben, mi artista favorito es Fernando Botero y él es colombiano. Me dicen que hay un museo fabuloso…

CRISTINA: Pero, Rosa, ¿no viajaste a Suramérica el año pasado?
ROSA: Sí, pero estuve en Uruguay para visitar a la familia de mi madre. No tuve tiempo de ir a Colombia y, además, Montevideo está muy lejos de Bogotá.
MEMO: Pues, vente conmigo mañana.
ROSA: ¡Ojalá!
[*They laugh*]

SECTION GOALS FOR
Escucha

By the end of the *Escucha* section, students will be able to:

- practice listening for linguistic cues.
- identify key cues that aid comprehension.
- use the pre-listening questions to guide their listening.
- discuss what they heard in the passage.

NATIONAL STANDARDS
Communication, Connections

The new listening strategy, listening for linguistic cues, facilitates communication. The strategy is effective for interpersonal communication (Standard 1.1), as well as for Standard 1.2, being able to understand and interpret spoken Spanish. Students can also apply this strategy when listening to others present information in Spanish (Standard 1.3). The example of listening for verb endings to guide their understanding of the time frame of the story is a skill they are not used to using in English. They have to connect this new strategy to their other listening strategies from learning English because it is extremely beneficial when learning a foreign language (Standard 3.2).

AUDIOSCRIPT FOR 10-31

MEMO: Cristina, ¿adónde fuiste de vacaciones el verano pasado?
CRISTINA: Fui a Venezuela con mi prima. Pasamos una semana en Caracas y cuatro días en la playa.
ROSA: Ah, ¿sí? ¿En qué playa?
CRISTINA: Nos quedamos en La Costa Azul de la Isla de Margarita. Está como a media hora de Caracas en avión, pero nosotras cruzamos en ferry y tardamos dos horas, más o menos.
MEMO: ¿Qué tal el hotel?
CRISTINA: El hotel se llamaba Playa Princesa. Era pequeño, de unos cien cuartos, pero bastante lujoso. Dicen que es famoso porque tiene el mejor restaurante de la isla y la piscina es la más grande de Venezuela. ¿Por qué, Memo? ¿Estás planeando un viaje a Venezuela?

ESCRIBE

10-39 to 10-40

10•33 Antes de escribir

Escoge un lugar turístico de Colombia o Venezuela y búscalo en la Red. Toma apuntes sobre los aspectos que encuentres más interesantes del lugar.

10•34 Un reportaje de un lugar turístico

Organiza tus ideas y escribe un reportaje para una revista turística que incluya como mínimo la siguiente información:

1. dónde está
2. cómo llegar allí
3. qué actividades se pueden hacer
4. dónde uno puede quedarse (hotel de lujo, etc.)
5. el precio del viaje
6. este lugar es más interesante que…
7. este lugar es más/menos barato que…
8. este lugar es el más _____ porque…

10•35 Después de escribir

Presenta tu reportaje a los compañeros de clase. Después de todas las presentaciones deben votar para elegir los **tres** lugares que les gustan más.

¿Cómo andas?

Having completed the second **Comunicación**, I now can…

	Feel Confident	Need to Review
• plan a trip (p. 368)	❏	❏
• describe a past trip (p. 368)	❏	❏
• discuss to whom things belong (p. 372)	❏	❏
• compare people, places, and things (p. 374)	❏	❏
• listen for linguistic cues (p. 379)	❏	❏
• write and present a report on a tourist destination (p. 380)	❏	❏

Rosa María
Gutiérrez Murcia

Colombia

10:00

CW
eBook

CD 4
Track 14

SAM

10-41 to
10-42

DVD/VHS

Vistas
culturales

Les presento mi país

Mi nombre es Rosa María Gutiérrez Murcia y soy de Medellín, la segunda ciudad de Colombia. El setenta y cinco por ciento de la población colombiana se concentra en los centros urbanos y las regiones montañosas del país. En Medellín disfrutamos del único sistema de metro del país que proporciona transporte a la gente que vive en las afueras de la ciudad. ¿Qué tipos de transporte público hay en tu pueblo o ciudad? Bogotá tiene el sistema más extenso de ciclorrutas (caminos para bicicletas) del país; gracias a él, la gente puede circular y disfrutar de los espacios públicos y verdes de la capital. Mi país es muy bello y tiene muchas atracciones para los turistas. Además, es el único país de Suramérica que tiene costa en el Océano Pacífico y en el Mar Caribe.

La catedral de sal de Zipaquirá

El Museo del Oro en Bogotá

ALMANAQUE

Nombre oficial:	República de Colombia
Gobierno:	República
Población:	43.593.035 (2006 est.)
Idiomas:	español
Moneda:	Peso colombiano (COP/$)

¿Sabías que...?

- En Zipaquirá Colombia hay una catedral única. ¡La catedral está situada a 600 pies adentro de una montaña de sal! Es impresionante.

- Simón Bolívar es conocido por ser *El Libertador*. Se considera un héroe en Colombia, Venezuela, Ecuador, Perú, Panamá y Bolivia, entre otros países hispanoamericanos.

PREGUNTAS

1. ¿Qué tiene Colombia que no tiene ningún otro país del continente?

2. ¿Cómo se comparan los medios de transporte de Medellín y Bogotá con los de tu área?

3. ¿Qué tienen en común Colombia, Perú y Chile?

En la Red
Amplía tus conocimientos sobre Colombia en la página web de *¡Anda!*

381

RECURSOS

| T10-7 | T10-7 | Cultural Background Notes |

SECTION GOALS FOR
Cultura

By the end of the *Cultura* section, students will be able to:

- discuss public transportation in Colombia.
- analyze the importance of oil in Venezuela.
- highlight popular cultural places of interest.
- contrast Colombia and Venezuela.

NATIONAL STANDARDS
Communication, Cultures, Comparisons

The readings from *Les presento mi país* require students to understand and interpret written Spanish (Standard 1.2). If they discuss the questions that follow in pairs or small groups, they are engaging in conversations in the interpersonal mode (Standard 1.1). The cultural information presented in the readings provides an in-depth understanding of what makes these countries unique (Standard 2.1), such as the delicacy of eating ants. Students read the information presented and make comparisons about how these countries differ from the United States (Standard 4.2) and how these differences affect the Spanish-speaking people.

CULTURAL BACKGROUND FOR
La catedral de sal de Zipaquirá

The cathedral is constructed approximately 600 feet inside a salt mountain. The salt deposits were formed 200 million years ago. Zipaquirá is a town of approximately 120,000 people. The cathedral was first opened in 1954, and then closed in 1990 due to safety concerns. It was then reopened in 1995.

NOTE FOR
El Museo del Oro

The Museo del Oro de Bogotá is considered one of, if not the premier, gold museum in the world. Located in the Banco de la República, it offers an impressive collection of gold not only from the indigenous empires of western South America, but from around the world.

CULTURAL BACKGROUND FOR
¿Sabías que...?

Simón Bolívar (1782–1830) was born in Caracas, Venezuela. He was a political and military figure credited with leading several independence movements against the Spanish Empire (known as Bolívar's War).

Suggestion for *ciclorrutas* Ask students: Are there bike paths where you live? Why or why not? Do you think a system of bike paths is ecologically sound? Explain.

Víctor Luis
González Martínez

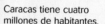

CD 4
Track 15

Vistas
culturales

Les presento mi país

Mi nombre es Víctor Luis González Martínez y soy de Mérida, Venezuela. Actualmente vivo en la capital, Caracas, porque estoy estudiando en la Universidad Central de Venezuela. Mientras estudio, vivo con mis parientes en el centro. Mi tío es ingeniero y trabaja en la industria petrolera. Venezuela es miembro de la Organización de Países Exportadores de Petróleo, conocida como la OPEP. ¿Qué papel tiene Venezuela en la OPEP? Me encanta vivir con mis tíos, pues mi tía es la mejor cocinera de Venezuela; así disfruto de las comidas tradicionales venezolanas como las arepas, las hallacas y el pabellón criollo. ¡Qué ricos! Vivir en la capital, es decir, en la costa, es muy agradable, porque hay mucho que hacer, tanto para nosotros como para los turistas.

Venezuela

La industria petrolera es muy importante para la economía venezolana.

Caracas tiene cuatro millones de habitantes.

ALMANAQUE

Nombre oficial:	República Bolivariana de Venezuela
Gobierno:	República federal
Población:	25.730.435 (2006)
Idiomas:	español (oficial); lenguas indígenas
Moneda:	Bolívar (Bs)

¿Sabías que...?

- El Salto Ángel, a unos 978 metros de altura, es la catarata más alta del mundo. El agua cae desde la cima del Auyan-tepuy, que está en el Parque Nacional Canaima, en el sureste del país.

- En Mérida hay una heladería que ha figurado en el libro Mundial de Récords Guinness por el mayor número de helados: tienen más de 600 sabores. Por costumbre hay 110 sabores disponibles diariamente.

PREGUNTAS

1. ¿Dónde vive Victor? ¿Le gusta? Explica.

2. ¿Cuál es la base principal de la economía venezolana actualmente?

3. La bandera de Venezuela es muy parecida a la de Colombia y a la de Ecuador. ¿Por qué piensas que es así? ¿En qué se diferencian las banderas y a qué se deben estas diferencias?

En la Red
Amplía tus conocimientos sobre Venezuela en la página web de *¡Anda!*

RECURSOS		
T10-8	T10-8	Cultural Background Notes

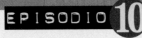

Ambiciones siniestras

EPISODIO 10

lectura

10-36 **Antes de leer.** En preparación para el **Episodio 10,** contesta las siguientes preguntas basadas en el **Episodio 9.**

1. ¿Crees que Manolo, Cisco, Lupe y Marisol van a poder solucionar el nuevo rompecabezas?
2. ¿Crees que van a poder salvar a Eduardo y Alejandra si lo solucionan?
3. ¿Qué le pasa a Marisol? ¿Está enferma?
4. En tu opinión, ¿qué tiene que confesar Cisco?

ESTRATEGIA   Skipping words

If you have attempted to guess the meaning of unfamiliar words from context and are still having problems understanding, you may want to skip the word(s) and follow these steps:

1. Identify the subject and main verb of each sentence.
2. Find descriptions of the subject in the sentence(s).

3. Identify words and phrases that indicate time and place.
4. Look for words that indicate cause and effect.
5. Ignore words set off by commas.
6. Summarize the content of each paragraph and look for information to fill in gaps or to answer any questions you may have.

10-37 **A leer.** Completa las siguientes actividades.

1. Lee superficialmente el episodio y subraya las palabras que no conoces.
2. A continuación hay unas frases de la lectura con posibles palabras problemáticas subrayadas. Léelas y responde.
   a. *Cisco estaba* _destrozado_. *—Me siento responsable por todo— les dijo. —Me pregunto por qué no fui a la policía en seguida. ¡Soy el hombre más tonto del mundo!—*
   - El sujeto de la primera frase es __Cisco__ y el verbo es __estaba__. La palabra _destrozado_ describe a __Cisco__.
   - Por las tres oraciones que siguen sabemos que Cisco se siente:
     1. muy bien
     (2.) muy mal
     3. regular
   b. *En medio de su* _remordimiento_ *Manolo lo interrumpió.*

383

SECTION GOALS FOR
Lectura

By the end of the *Lectura* section, students will be able to:
- apply the new reading strategy, skipping words.
- integrate the new strategy with other reading strategies.
- preview the reading and make predictions.
- comprehend the main idea of the passage.

NATIONAL STANDARDS
Communication

Ambiciones siniestras engages students because they want to know more about this sinister plot. As the readings use more complex Spanish, students may encounter unfamiliar words. The new strategy of skipping unfamiliar words allows them to read for the gist of the passage so they do not miss the plot. This strategy facilitates their communicative skills in reading (Standard 1.2), because they cannot comprehend or interpret a text if they do not have the tools or strategies to help them negotiate meaning. They can apply the strategy of listening for linguistic cues from the *Escucha* section as they listen to the characters in *Ambiciones siniestras* discuss how to proceed with el Sr. Verdugo's puzzle (Standard 1.2). When students can understand what they have read, heard, and seen with others, they can engage in conversations in the interpersonal mode (Standard 1.1).

RECAP OF *AMBICIONES SINIESTRAS:*
Episodio 9

Lectura: At separate times, Cisco and Marisol called Manolo to alert him that they had received another clue from el Sr. Verdugo. Manolo logged on to his e-mail and was frightened to see the next clue. He was supposed to call Marisol back after reading the e-mail, but he did not.

Video: Lupe, Marisol, Cisco, and Manolo organized a videoconference. Lupe and Marisol were in the library working to solve the puzzle that el Sr. Verdugo sent. The four of them discussed possible answers, and tensions were building. Lupe suspected that Cisco knew more than he was letting on, and at the end of the episode he told them he had something to confess.

Si dividimos esa oración en dos partes, «*En medio de su remordimiento*» y «*Manolo lo interrumpió*»:

- ¿cuál es la parte más importante para la comprensión de la lectura?
  la segunda parte

c. *"Cisco, ¿no te dijo nada?"* imploró *Manolo.*

- ¿Por qué *no* es crítico saber lo que significa "imploró" en esta frase?
  Porque explica cómo dijo algo, no lo que dijo.

d. *Aquí les mando como documento adjunto el resto de lo que encontré en la computadora de Eduardo el día que desapareció.*

- La palabra "adjunto" es:
  1. un sustantivo (*noun*).
  2. un verbo.
  ③ un adjetivo.

- Si ignoras la palabra, ¿puedes entender la frase? *sí*

3. Lee el episodio otra vez, empleando esa estrategia con cualquier otra palabra que no comprendas (*you do not understand*).

¿Qué sabía?

CD 4
Track 16

Cisco les confesó todo a Manolo, Marisol y Lupe en la videoconferencia. Les dijo que sabía más del caso de lo que les había dicho°. Les mandó el e-mail de Eduardo el cual descubrió el día que éste desapareció.   *had told them*

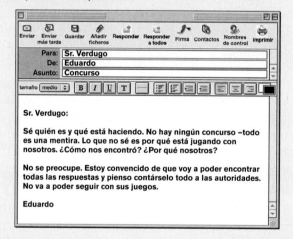

Para: Sr. Verdugo
De: Eduardo
Asunto: Concurso

Sr. Verdugo:

Sé quién es y qué está haciendo. No hay ningún concurso –todo es una mentira. Lo que no sé es por qué está jugando con nosotros. ¿Cómo nos encontró? ¿Por qué nosotros?

No se preocupe. Estoy convencido de que voy a poder encontrar todas las respuestas y pienso contárselo todo a las autoridades. No va a poder seguir con sus juegos.

Eduardo

Cisco estaba destrozado.

—Me siento responsable por todo— les dijo. Me pregunto por qué no fui a la policía en seguida. ¡Soy el hombre más tonto del mundo!

En medio de su remordimiento Manolo lo interrumpió.

—¿Qué sabía Eduardo? Era obvio por su mensaje que sabía que el concurso era fraudulento, pero me pregunto cómo se enteró°. *how he found out* ¿Cómo y dónde descubrió esa información? ¿Cuándo empezó a tener dudas? Cisco, ¿no te dijo nada?— imploró Manolo.

Cisco se quedó mirando la pantalla por varios minutos antes de responder:

—Aquí les mando como documento adjunto el resto de lo que encontré en la computadora de Eduardo el día que desapareció. Les tengo que confesar que yo también tuve dudas e investigué varias ideas que tenía sobre el concurso. Descubrí que era una conspiración Ponzi para estafar° a la gente. El Sr. Verdugo *to defraud* buscaba jóvenes inteligentes que le ayudaran con su malvado° *evil* plan. Eduardo encontró los papeles con mis apuntes que tenía al lado de mi computadora y desapareció con ellos. Yo iba a contactar a las autoridades pero cuando Eduardo se fue con toda mi información, yo tenía que reproducirlo todo. Sin las pruebas°, *proof* ¿quién me iba a creer? Lo siento mucho, perdónenme…

Manolo, Marisol y Lupe escucharon atentamente y recibieron el documento adjunto de Cisco casi al mismo tiempo en sus computadoras y lo leyeron. Marisol fue la primera en responder:

—Me pregunto si Eduardo pudo hablar con las autoridades antes de desaparecer. ¿Se fue en su coche en busca del Sr. Verdugo? ¿Sabía adónde tenía que ir? ¿Qué piensan?

Manolo les respondió:

—Eso es precisamente lo que yo estaba pensando. Y algo más: ¿qué tenía que ver Alejandra con todo esto? No podemos olvidarnos de ella.

La única persona que no respondió fue Lupe. Ella también recibió los mensajes y seguía la teleconferencia entre ellos sin participar. De repente abrió otra ventana en su pantalla y empezó a escribir algo muy detallado. Al mismo tiempo, tomó su teléfono celular y empezó a marcar°… *dial*

10-38 Después de leer.

1. Por fin ¿qué les confesó Cisco a Marisol, Manolo y Lupe?

2. Si no había (*If there wasn't*) ningún concurso, ¿en qué consistía "el juego" del Sr. Verdugo?

3. ¿Cuáles eran las preguntas que tenían Manolo y Marisol ahora?

4. ¿Quién no dijo nada?

5. ¿Qué hacía Lupe al final del episodio?

NOTE FOR *Episodio 10*

In a Ponzi scheme, named for Italian Charles Ponzi, a fraudulent operator offers an unusually high return to investors on an initial investment. The extremely high returns advertised (and paid) necessitate an ever-increasing flow of money from investors to keep the scam going. As investors become greedy, they invest more money. The scheme collapses either by the police being notified or by the Ponzi operator disappearing with the money.

METHODOLOGY • Checking for Comprehension in English

When encouraging students to hypothesize regarding what will happen, it is acceptable to encourage them to brainstorm in English.

Answers to 10-38

1. Les confesó que sabe más de lo que dijo y que Eduardo encontró los papeles de Cisco y le mandó un e-mail al Sr. Verdugo antes de desaparecer.
2. Era una conspiración Ponzi.
3. Quieren saber si Eduardo pudo hablar con las autoridades antes de desaparecer, si salió en busca del Sr. Verdugo y que tiene que ver Alejandra con todo esto.
4. Lupe
5. Miró la pantalla de la computadora, escribió algo y empezó a marcar.

video

10-48 to
10-50

10-39 **Antes del video.** ¿Qué habrá hecho Eduardo (*What must Eduardo have done*) con la información sobre la conspiración Ponzi? ¿Qué escribe Lupe en la computadora y a quién llama? En la segunda parte del episodio vas a saber quién resuelve el rompecabezas y vas a ver una confrontación entre Marisol y Lupe.

¡Marisol, no salgas de tu casa! ¡Estás en peligro!

Chicos, tenemos buenas noticias.

Hace mucho tiempo que descubrí que tú no eres la persona que dices ser.

Episodio 10

«*Falsas apariencias*»

Relájate y disfruta el video.

10-40 **Después del video.** Contesta las siguientes preguntas.

1. ¿Quién resuelve el rompecabezas?
2. ¿Cómo responde Lupe cuando Marisol le dice que va a ir a su casa?
3. ¿Por qué tiene miedo Marisol?
4. ¿Qué hacen Lupe y Marisol con la respuesta del rompecabezas?
5. ¿Qué quiere hacer Cisco?
6. ¿Qué prueba (*proof*) tiene Marisol de que Lupe no es quien dice ser?
7. ¿Cómo termina el episodio?

386

RECURSOS

Video
Script

Y por fin, ¿cómo andas?

Having completed this chapter, I now can...

	Feel Confident	Need to Review
Comunicación		
● talk about modes of transportation (p. 356)	❑	❑
● name the parts of a car (p. 357)	❑	❑
● correctly pronounce **b** and **v** (p. 357)	❑	❑
● influence others by using commands (pp. 360, 364)	❑	❑
● talk about travel (p. 368)	❑	❑
● discuss to whom things belong (p. 372)	❑	❑
● compare people, places, and things (p. 374)	❑	❑
● listen for cues (p. 379)	❑	❑
● write and present a report about a tourist spot (p. 380)	❑	❑
Cultura		
● discuss modes of transportation in the Hispanic world (p. 366)	❑	❑
● discuss travel opportunities in Venezuela (p. 371)	❑	❑
● state three facts about Venezuela and Colombia (pp. 381–382)	❑	❑
Ambiciones siniestras		
● skip words that hinder comprehension (p. 383)	❑	❑
● state what Cisco knows about the contest, provide the answer to the riddle, and give reasons that Lupe may not be what she appears to be (p. 386)	❑	❑

VOCABULARIO ACTIVO

CD 4
Tracks 17-23

El transporte · *Transportation*

el autobús	*bus*
el avión	*airplane*
la bicicleta	*bicycle*
el camión	*truck*
el carro/el coche	*car*
el metro	*subway*
la moto(cicleta)	*motorcycle*
el taxi	*taxi*
el tren	*train*

Unas partes de un vehículo · *Parts of a vehicle*

el aire acondicionado	*air conditioning*
el baúl	*trunk*
la calefacción	*heat*
el limpiaparabrisas	*windshield wiper*
la llanta	*tire*
la llave	*key*
el motor	*motor; engine*
el parabrisas	*windshield*
el tanque	*gas tank*
el volante	*steering wheel*

Otras palabras útiles · *Other useful words*

la autopista	*highway; freeway*
el boleto	*ticket*
la calle	*street*
la cola	*line (of people)*
la estación de servicio	*gas station*
el estacionamiento	*parking*
la licencia (de conducir)	*driver's license*
la multa	*traffic ticket; fine*
la parada	*bus stop*
el peatón	*pedestrian*
el policía	*policeman*
el ruido	*noise*
el semáforo	*traffic light*
el tráfico	*traffic*

388

Unos verbos útiles — *Some useful verbs*

arreglar/hacer la maleta	*to pack a suitcase*
bajar (de)	*to get down (from); to get off (of)*
cambiar	*to change*
caminar, ir a pie	*to walk; to go on foot*
dejar	*to leave*
doblar	*to turn*
entrar	*to enter*
estacionar	*to park*
funcionar	*to work; to function*
ir de vacaciones	*to go on vacation*
ir de viaje	*to go on a trip*
irse del hotel	*to leave the hotel; to check out*
llenar	*to fill*
manejar/conducir	*to drive*
prestar	*to loan; to lend*
registrarse (en el hotel)	*to check in*
revisar	*to check; to overhaul*
sacar la licencia	*to get a driver's license*
salir	*to leave; to go out*
subir (a)	*to go up; to get on*
viajar	*to travel*
visitar	*to visit*
volar (o → ue)	*to fly; to fly away*

El viaje — *The trip*

el aeropuerto	*airport*
la agencia de viajes	*travel agency*
el/la agente de viajes	*travel agent*
el barco	*boat*
el boleto de ida y vuelta	*round-trip ticket*
la estación (de tren, de autobús)	*(train, bus) station*
el extranjero	*abroad*
la maleta	*suitcase*
el pasaporte	*passport*
la reserva	*reservation*
el sello	*postage stamp*
la tarjeta postal	*postcard*
las vacaciones	*vacation*
los viajeros	*travelers*
el vuelo	*flight*

El hotel — *The hotel*

el botones	*bellman*
el cuarto doble	*double room*
el cuarto individual	*single room*
la recepción	*front desk*

Unos lugares — *Some places*

el lago	*lake*
las montañas	*mountains*
el parque de atracciones	*theme park*
la playa	*beach*

11

El mundo actual

¿Qué peligros existen hoy en día para el medio ambiente (*environment*)? Hay más de 5.000 especies de animales en peligro (*danger*) de extinción, 70% del aire en las ciudades está contaminado y las selvas (*jungles*), las cuales contienen más del 50% de todas las especies de plantas y animales existentes, se reducen drásticamente cada año.

OBJETIVOS

CONTENIDOS

Comunicación

- To give your opinion on environmental issues in the United States and in the Spanish-speaking world
- To express what is important or necessary for you and others to do
- To comment on what is possible, probable, and improbable
- To comment on government and current affairs
- To use visual organizers when listening
- To write a public announcement

Cultura

- To describe El Yunque, the rain forest of Puerto Rico
- To list specific facts about politics in the Spanish-speaking world
- To state two interesting facts about this chapter's featured countries: Cuba, Puerto Rico, and the Dominican Republic

Ambiciones siniestras

- To use visual organizers when reading
- To explain who Lupe really is
- To relate what happened to Eduardo and Alejandra

Warm-up for *Chapter Opener* This chapter is about the environment and all aspects related to being responsible citizens in a global village. Start out by asking your students how they contribute to or detract from the well-being of the environment. What changes do they think each person can make to help make the environment cleaner and safer for future generations? Ask your students what endangered animals they can name and where those animals are found.

NOTE FOR *Chapter Opener*

Draw a semantic map or word web on the board and discuss the categories of animals (mammals, reptiles, birds, amphibians) and list the most commonly endangered animals from each group. You could also brainstorm things like ethanol fuels, wind power, cisterns, hybrid cars, bamboo, etc. that students can list as responsible choices that individuals and government could make in the future.

RECURSOS

Lesson Plan

NATIONAL STANDARDS
Communities

Depending on the area in which you live, you might want to consider the following service learning options. If you have a large Hispanic population, you could team up with a local school, zoo, or animal sanctuary and start an environmental campaign about the dangers facing humans and animals and how the Hispanic community can band together to make small changes for big gains (recycling, using less electricity, carpooling, using environmentally friendly products, etc.). Students could partner with the science faculty and other students at your school to make presentations (in Spanish) to the Hispanic community about endangered natural resources and how each community member can do his or her part to preserve nature and the environment. If you do not have a large Hispanic population in your community, students could campaign to have local businesses sell green merchandise and set up recycling projects in your community. You could report the results in Spanish on your school web site. At your university, you could invite the community to a showing of Al Gore's documentary, *An Inconvenient Truth,* as a solo project or as part of Earth Week, or whatever science-themed activities your school does, and discuss the film and its implications in Spanish after the viewing. You might also hold a fundraiser and have your students donate the money to "sponsor" an animal at a local zoo or aquarium (many animals in danger of extinction can be sponsored for as little as $20— check with your local animal welfare agency for details). The animal can be one that is indigenous to a Spanish-speaking country.

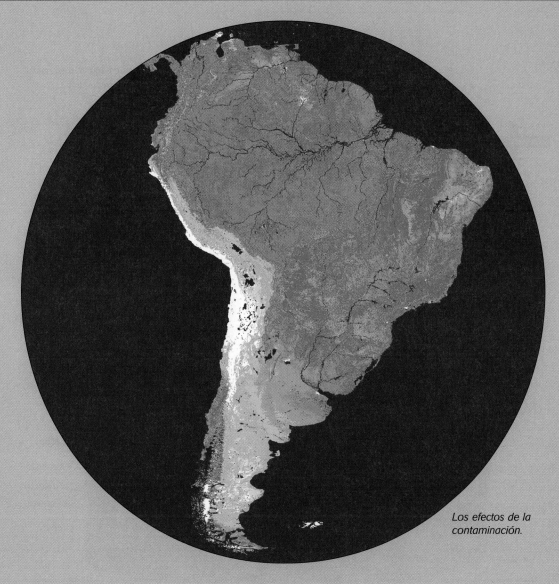

Los efectos de la contaminación.

PREGUNTAS

1 ¿Dónde hay selvas tropicales?

2 ¿Cuántos animales están en peligro de extinción?

3 ¿Dónde está contaminado el aire en los Estados Unidos?

391

Expansion for *Preguntas* These questions are simpler than usual because students do not yet have the vocabulary to respond to higher-level questions on this topic in Spanish. By the end of the chapter you may want to bring them back to the chapter opener and ask:

1. ¿Puedes nombrar algunos animales que estén en peligro de extinción?

2. ¿Qué factores contribuyen a la contaminación del aire?

3. ¿Cómo podemos todos (individuos, ciudades, estados y naciones) contribuir a la mejora del medio ambiente?

Expansion for *Preguntas* Ask students: ¿Por qué es tan importante proteger las selvas?, ¿Por qué es la destrucción de la selva tropical tan peligrosa para el mundo?

CAPÍTULO 11

Comunicación

- Talking about animals
- Discussing environmental issues
- Talking about what is important, probable, and necessary

VOCABULARIO 1 Los animales

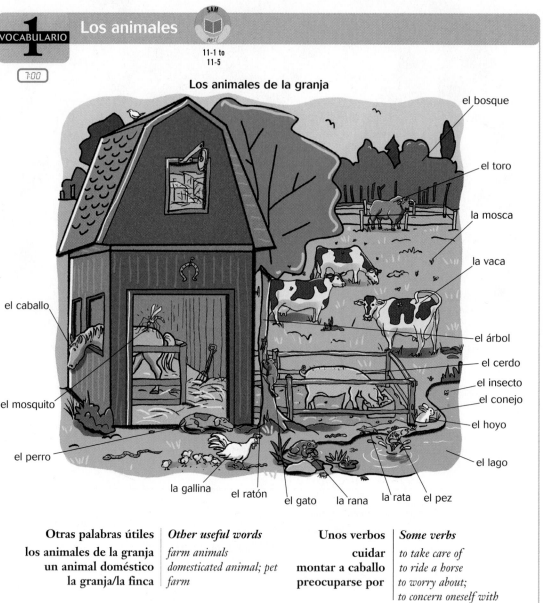

Los animales de la granja

Otras palabras útiles	*Other useful words*	Unos verbos	*Some verbs*
los animales de la granja	*farm animals*	cuidar	*to take care of*
un animal doméstico	*domesticated animal; pet*	montar a caballo	*to ride a horse*
la granja/la finca	*farm*	preocuparse por	*to worry about; to concern oneself with*

Los animales salvajes

la montaña

el elefante

la cueva

el río

el oso

el león

el pájaro

las hormigas

la serpiente

Otras palabras útiles	*Other useful words*	el océano	*ocean*
los animales salvajes	*wild animals*	peligroso/a	*dangerous*
un animal en peligro de extinción	*an endangered species*	la selva	*jungle*
el bosque	*forest*		

CW
eBook

CD 4
Track 24

PRONUNCIACIÓN 5:00

SAM
MSL

11-6 to
11-10

Review of Word Stress and Accent Marks

In **Capítulo 2,** the rules on Spanish word stress and written accent marks were presented. Please review page 63 and complete the following activities.

11•1   Las palabras

Practice pronouncing the following words, focusing on the stress.

1. cerdo	3. árbol	5. río	7. bosque
2. conejo	4. preocuparse	6. montaña	8. cuevas

11•2   Las oraciones

Practice pronouncing the following sentences and pay special attention to the stress.

1. Me preocupo por los animales en peligro de extinción.
2. Mis niños quieren un perro pero sé que no van a cuidarlo.

11•3   Los trabalenguas

Now pronounce the following tongue twister and focus on the stress.

> En el campo hay una cabra (*goat*), ética, perlética, pelapelambrética, pelúa, pelapelambrúa.
>
> Tiene los hijitos éticos, perléticos, pelapelambréticos, pelúos, pelapelambrúos.

3:00

11·4   La fauna

Organiza los animales del vocabulario con un/a compañero/a según las siguientes categorías: **insecto, reptil, mamífero, ave** y **anfibio**.

INSECTO	REPTIL	MAMÍFERO	AVE	ANFIBIO

2:00

11·5   ¿Dónde viven?

Digan en qué lugar viven los siguientes animales.

1. __e__ el conejo
2. __a__ el león
3. __f__ el pájaro
4. __d__ el oso
5. __b__ el pez
6. __c__ la gallina

a. la selva
b. un lago
c. una granja
d. el bosque
e. un hoyo
f. un árbol

5:00

11·6   Las preferencias

Capítulo 8. *Gustar* y verbos como gustar, pág. 294.

Completa los siguientes pasos.

Paso 1   Escribe los nombres de los **tres** animales que más te gustan y de los **tres** que menos te gustan y explica por qué. Usa verbos como **gustar, fascinar, encantar, hacer falta** y **molestar**. Después, comparte tus respuestas con un/a compañero/a.

MODELO   *El animal que más me gusta es el caballo porque es muy fuerte y me encanta montar a caballo. También me gustan los gatos y los perros porque puedo tenerlos en casa. Los tres animales que menos me gustan son… porque…*

Paso 2   Presenten sus respuestas a los compañeros de la clase. ¿Cuál es el animal que más les gusta? ¿El que menos les gusta?

CAPÍTULO 11

Estrategia

Remember that when completing signature search activities like **11-7,** it is important to move quickly around the room, trying to get as many different signatures as possible, while asking and answering all questions in Spanish.

11·7   ¿Qué opinas?

Circula por la clase para hacerles las siguientes preguntas a tres compañeros diferentes. Si alguien contesta afirmativamente, recoge su firma.

Capítulo 7. El pretérito, pág. 258; Unos verbos irregulares en el pretérito pág. 266.

MODELO   ¿Quién… se sacó un conejo de la manga?

E1:   *¿Te sacaste un conejo de la manga?*

E2:   *Sí, me saqué un conejo de la manga en una fiesta.*

E1:   *Pues, firma aquí.*

_____ *Roberto* _____

¿QUIÉN…?		
corrió delante de los toros en los Sanfermines E1: _____ E2: _____ E3: _____	puso una rana en la silla del profesor E1: _____ E2: _____ E3: _____	imitó una vez el ruido del cerdo E1: _____ E2: _____ E3: _____
es alérgico a la picadura de los mosquitos E1: _____ E2: _____ E3: _____	fue de safari y estuvo cerca de un león E1: _____ E2: _____ E3: _____	se sentó encima de un hormiguero (*anthill*) E1: _____ E2: _____ E3: _____

METHODOLOGY • Follow-Up to Group Work

It is important to monitor group work closely for many reasons: to keep students on task, check for understanding, guide and answer questions, and determine how best to follow up the activity. While monitoring group work for actividad **11-6,** note which items students find most amusing or interesting. Have groups present those responses, rather than taking the time to have each group report on all the items.

Additional activity for *Los animales*

   ¿Quién…? Completen los siguientes pasos.

Paso 1 En grupos pequeños, asocien a estudiantes del grupo (o personas que conocen) con la siguiente lista.

MODELO   tener miedo de las serpientes

E1: *Tengo miedo de las serpientes.*

E2: *Mi madre tiene miedo de las serpientes.*

E3: *Yo también tengo miedo de las serpientes.*

E4: *Mis hermanos Mike y Luis tienen miedo de las serpientes.*

1. tener miedo de las serpientes
2. ver un oso el año pasado
3. gustarle los perros
4. tener un animal doméstico
5. gustarle cuidar animales
6. odiar (*to hate*) los insectos, incluyendo moscas y mosquitos
7. saber ordeñar (*to milk*) una vaca
8. ver un elefante o un león

Paso 2 Compartan sus respuestas con los otros grupos.

MODELO   *En nuestro grupo, Mary y yo tenemos miedo de las serpientes. También, la madre de Megan, Tom y el amigo de Chris tienen miedo de las serpientes.*

11-11 to
11-17

VOCABULARIO 2 El medio ambiente

Additional activity for El medio ambiente

Hay que reciclar ¿Qué hacen tu familia, tu comunidad y tu universidad para proteger el medio ambiente? Explícale a un/a compañero/a quién hace qué para mantener nuestro universo. Después, cambien de papel.

MODELO   *Yo voy a la universidad en bicicleta para evitar la contaminación del aire. Mi familia y yo reciclamos el plástico. Mi pueblo ofrece programas de prevención contra incendios. Mi universidad dio un seminario sobre el efecto invernadero y la destrucción de la capa de ozono.*

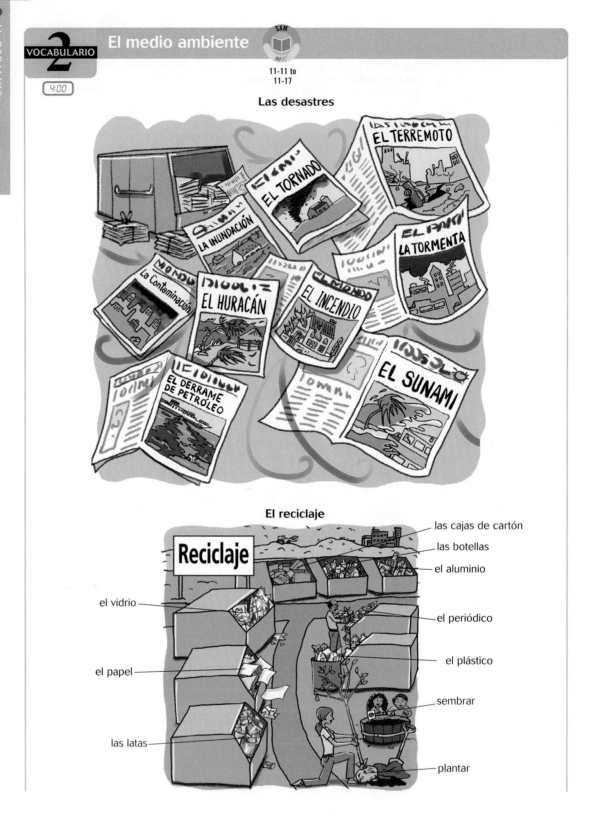

Las desastres

EL TERREMOTO

EL TORNADO

LA INUNDACIÓN

LA TORMENTA

La Contaminación

EL HURACÁN

EL INCENDIO

EL DERRAME DE PETROLEO

EL SUNAMI

El reciclaje

Reciclaje

las cajas de cartón
las botellas
el aluminio
el periódico
el plástico
sembrar
plantar

el vidrio
el papel
las latas

RECURSOS   T11-4   T11-4   Electronic Activity Cache

El planeta	*The planet*		la calidad	*quality*
el cielo	*sky; heaven*		la ecología	*ecology*
la naturaleza	*nature*		puro/a	*pure*
el recurso natural	*natural resource*		el vertedero	*dump*
la selva (tropical)	*jungle; (tropical) rain forest*		vivo/a	*alive; living*
la tierra	*land; soil*			
la Tierra	*Earth*		**Unos verbos**	*Some verbs*
			botar	*to throw away*
Los desastres	*Disasters*		contaminar	*to pollute*
la destrucción	*destruction*		evitar	*to avoid*
el efecto invernadero	*global warming*		hacer daño	*to (do) damage; to harm*
la lluvia ácida	*acid rain*		matar	*to kill*
la tragedia	*tragedy*		proteger	*to protect*
			reciclar	*to recycle*
Otras palabras útiles	*Other useful words*		reforestar	*to reforest*
el aire	*air*		rehusar	*to refuse*
la basura	*garbage*			

3:00

11·8 ¿Qué es...?

Aquí tienen las definiciones. ¿Cuáles son las palabras?

MODELO   E1: lo opuesto de contaminado

         E2: *puro*

> **Fíjate**
>
> Note that *la Tierra* (Earth) is capitalized in Spanish but *la tierra* (land, soil) is not.

1. plantar árboles donde antes los había
2. el estudio de la protección del medio ambiente
3. un lugar designado donde botamos la basura
4. responder de manera negativa a una petición (*request*)
5. estas plantas grandes protegen la Tierra de la potencia del sol
6. ensuciar el agua o el aire, por ejemplo
7. lo opuesto de muerto
8. el posible resultado de la contaminación del aire

12:00

11·9 El reportaje

¿Cómo podemos proteger el medio ambiente?

Paso 1   Escribe un párrafo de **seis** a **ocho** oraciones sobre qué podemos hacer en el futuro para proteger el medio ambiente. Puedes usar la lista de abajo para más ideas.

- sembrar muchas plantas
- reciclar el plástico, el vidrio, el papel y el cartón
- usar carros eléctricos
- proteger los animales en peligro de extinción
- apoyar las instituciones de conservación de los recursos naturales

- proteger la selva tropical
- reforestar los bosques
- usar el carro lo menos posible
- usar energía solar
- no prender (*turn on*) a menudo el aire acondicionado

MODELO *Para evitar la destrucción de los bosques y la selva tropical, no debemos cortar más árboles. En el futuro, debemos plantar más árboles para reforestar el bosque...*

Paso 2   Después, en grupos pequeños, comparen sus oraciones y juntos escriban un reportaje corto con recomendaciones para proteger el medio ambiente.

3:00 11-18 to 11-19

El Yunque: tesoro tropical

1. Es el único bosque lluvioso tropical del sistema de Bosques Nacionales de los EE.UU.
2. Tiene una gran diversidad de flora, sirve de refugio para muchas especies de pájaros como la cotorra y para muchas clases diferentes de coquí.

El Bosque Nacional del Caribe también se conoce como El Bosque Lluvioso de El Yunque, en honor al dios bondadoso (*kind*) indígena Yuquiyú. El Yunque es el único bosque lluvioso tropical que pertenece al Sistema de Bosques Nacionales de los Estados Unidos. Más de 100 billones de galones de agua de lluvia caen anualmente en el bosque sobre el monte El Toro (a 1.076 metros).

El Yunque es el bosque nacional más viejo y pequeño de las Américas. Sin embargo, cuenta con la mayor diversidad de flora. Hay más de 240 especies de árboles en un área de poco más de 11.760 hectáreas (28,000 acres). Además, sirve de refugio a muchas especies de pájaros incluyendo la cotorra o loro (*parrot*) puertorriqueño, el cual está en peligro de extinción. Después del huracán Hugo en 1989 quedaron sólo 20 loros. En esos momentos se empezó un programa para salvarlos y hoy en día existen unos 85. La ranita (rana pequeña) llamada *coquí* es original de Puerto Rico y hay muchas clases diferentes de coquíes en el Yunque.

El Bosque Nacional del Caribe es el lugar de Puerto Rico más frecuentado por los turistas. También lo frecuentan mucho las familias puertorriqueñas durante los fines de semana para pasar el día.

Preguntas

1. ¿Por qué es tan importante El Yunque?

2. ¿Cuáles son algunas de las características del Yunque que lo hacen tan especial?

GRAMÁTICA 3 El subjuntivo

11-20 to 11-24   46, 51

5:00

Es una lástima que no quieran reciclar el plástico, el vidrio, el aluminio y el papel.

In Spanish, *tenses* such as the present, past, and future are grouped under two different moods, the **indicative** mood and the **subjunctive** mood.

Indicative mood	Subjunctive mood
Present	Present
Past	Past
Future	Future

Up to this point you have studied tenses grouped under the *indicative* mood (with the exception of commands) to report what happened, is happening, or will happen. The *subjunctive* mood, on the other hand, is used to express doubt, insecurity, influence, opinion, feelings, hope, wishes, or desires that can be happening now, have happened in the past, or will happen in the future. In this chapter you will learn the present tense of the *subjunctive mood*.

RECURSOS

11-G3 Electronic Activity Cache

Present subjunctive

To form the subjunctive, take the **yo** form of the present indicative, drop the final **-o,** and add the following endings.

> **Fíjate**
>
> You are already somewhat familiar with the subjunctive forms from your practice with *Ud.* (*¡Estudie!*) and negative *tú* (*¡No hables!*) commands.

Present indicative	*yo* form		Present subjunctive
estudiar	estudiø	+ e	**estudie**
comer	comø	+ a	**coma**
vivir	vivø	+ a	**viva**

	estudiar	comer	vivir
yo	estudie	coma	viva
tú	estudies	comas	vivas
él, ella, Ud.	estudie	coma	viva
nosotros/as	estudiemos	comamos	vivamos
vosotros/as	estudiéis	comáis	viváis
ellos/as, Uds.	estudien	coman	vivan

Irregular forms

- Verbs with irregular **yo** forms mantain this irregularity in all forms of the present subjunctive. Note the following examples.

	conocer	hacer	poner	venir
yo	conozca	haga	ponga	venga
tú	conozcas	hagas	pongas	vengas
él, ella, Ud.	conozca	haga	ponga	venga
nosotros/as	conozcamos	hagamos	pongamos	vengamos
vosotros/as	conozcáis	hagáis	pongáis	vengáis
ellos/as, Uds.	conozcan	hagan	pongan	vengan

- Verbs ending in **-car, -gar,** and **-zar** have a spelling change in all present subjunctive forms, in order to maintain the sound of the infinitive.

		Present indicative	Present subjunctive
buscar	c → qu	yo busco	busque
pagar	g → gu	yo pago	pague
empezar	z → c	yo empiezo	empiece

	buscar	pagar	empezar
yo	busque	pague	empiece
tú	busques	pagues	empieces
él, ella, Ud.	busque	pague	empiece
nosotros/as	busquemos	paguemos	empecemos
vosotros/as	busquéis	paguéis	empecéis
ellos/as, Uds.	busquen	paguen	empiecen

NATIONAL STANDARDS

Communication, Communities

The subjunctive affords students the opportunity to express needs, wants, and desires in a linguistically sophisticated way. From an oral and written proficiency standpoint, use of the subjunctive helps elevate the level of an individual's performance in the language.

METHODOLOGY • Chunking

You will note that, yet again, *¡Anda!* is taking a complex concept, the subjunctive, and breaking it down into "bite-size" chunks that make learning possible for students.

Stem-changing verbs

In the present subjunctive, stem-changing **-ar** and **-er** verbs make the same vowel change that they do in the present indicative: **e → ie** and **o → ue**.

	pensar (e → ie)	**poder (o → ue)**
yo	piense	pueda
tú	pienses	puedas
él, ella, Ud.	piense	pueda
nosotros/as	pensemos	podamos
vosotros/as	penséis	podáis
ellos/as, Uds.	piensen	puedan

The pattern is different with the **-ir** stem-changing verbs. In addition to their usual changes of **e → ie**, **e → i**, and **o → ue**, in the **nosotros** and **vosotros** forms the stem vowels change **ie → i** and **ue → u**.

	sentir (e → ie, i)	**dormir (o → ue, u)**
yo	sienta	duerma
tú	sientas	duermas
él, ella, Ud.	sienta	duerma
nosotros/as	sintamos	durmamos
vosotros/as	sintáis	durmáis
ellos/as, Uds.	sientan	duerman

The **e → i** stem-changing verbs keep the change in all forms.

	pedir (e → i, i)
yo	pida
tú	pidas
él, ella, Ud.	pida
nosotros/as	pidamos
vosotros/as	pidáis
ellos/as, Uds.	pidan

Irregular verbs in the present subjunctive

- The following verbs are irregular in the subjunctive.

	dar	**estar**	**saber**	**ser**	**ir**
yo	dé	esté	sepa	sea	vaya
tú	des	estés	sepas	seas	vayas
él, ella, Ud.	dé	esté	sepa	sea	vaya
nosotros/as	demos	estemos	sepamos	seamos	vayamos
vosotros/as	deis	estéis	sepáis	seáis	vayáis
ellos/as, Uds.	den	estén	sepan	sean	vayan

Dar has a written accent on the first- and third-person singular forms **(dé)** to distinguish it from the preposition **de.** All forms of **estar,** except the **nosotros** form, have a written accent in the present subjunctive.

Using the subjunctive

One of the uses of the subjunctive is with fixed expressions that communicate opinion, doubt, probability, and wishes. They are always followed by the subjunctive.

¡Es increíble que este capítulo sea el último!

Opinion

Es bueno/malo/mejor que…	*It's good/bad/better that…*
Es importante que…	*It's important that…*
Es increíble que…	*It's incredible that…*
Es una lástima que…	*It's a pity that…*
Es necesario que…	*It's necessary that…*
Es preferible que…	*It's preferable that…*
Es raro que…	*It's rare that…*

Doubt and probability

Es dudoso que…	*It's doubtful that…*
Es imposible que…	*It's impossible that…*
Es improbable que…	*It's unlikely that…*
Es posible que…	*It's possible that…*
Es probable que…	*It's likely that…*

Wishes and hopes

Ojalá (que)…   *Let's hope that…/Hopefully…*

Es necesario que protejamos los animales en peligro de extinción.

It's necessary that we protect endangered animals.

Es una lástima que algunas personas no quieran reciclar el plástico, el vidrio, el aluminio y el papel.

It's a shame that some people don't want to recycle plastic, glass, aluminum, and paper.

Ojalá (que) haya menos destrucción del medio ambiente en el futuro.

Let's hope that there is less destruction of the environment in the future.

> **Fíjate**
>
> The expression *Ojalá* (*que*) comes from the Arabic expression meaning *May it be Allah's will*. The conjunction *que* is optional in this expression.

> **Fíjate**
>
> The subjunctive of *hay* is *haya*.

1. What is the difference between the subjunctive and the indicative moods?
2. What other verb forms look like the subjunctive?
3. Where does the subjunctive verb come in relation to the word **que?**

Check your answers to the preceding questions in Appendix 1.

NOTE FOR *El subjuntivo*

You may have learned these fixed expressions as impersonal expressions with *ser*. In *¡Anda!,* we have chosen to simply call them, "fixed expressions," under the headings of opinions, doubts, probabilities, wishes, desires, and hopes. This eliminates any confusion between "personal" and "impersonal," because these expressions can be used regardless of the relationship to the speaker.

NOTE FOR *El subjuntivo*

¡Anda! is research-based and coordinated with the National Standards. In addition, hundreds of reviewers were consulted, and they determined that the present subjunctive should at least be introduced in the first year. This chapter's theme lends itself well to expressing opinions, making suggestions and recommendations, and finding solutions to problems. These types of language skills are important to communication, especially in the interpersonal mode (Standard 1.1) and when making presentations (Standard 1.3). Students learned the commands in previous chapters, and therefore already learned how to form subjunctive endings. A more in-depth treatment of the subjunctive continues in *¡Anda! Curso intermedio.*

CAPÍTULO 11

NOTE AND INSTRUCTIONS FOR 11-10

Actividad **11-10** is a fun way of practicing verb forms.

INSTRUCTIONS: Have your students sit in rows. Each row is a team, so each team/row should have an equal number of people. Each person at the head of the row has a piece of paper with as many subject pronouns written on it as there are people in the row. Do not list the pronouns in their conjugation order.

Write any infinitive on the board. The first student writes the subjunctive form of that verb that corresponds to the first pronoun listed. That student then passes the sheet of paper over his/her head. The second student writes the correct form of the subjunctive of the second pronoun and passes the paper to the student sitting behind him/her. The process continues with all of the students in the row. The last student in the row brings the completed sheet to you. The first row to finish with all forms correct wins that round.

Additional rules: 1) Allow any students to correct any forms that came before. 2) After each round, have students move back one seat, with the person in the last seat of the row moving to the front.

Expansion for 11-12 Actividad **11-12** can also be used as a reading comprehension activity that can be done outside of class. You can ask students to complete the following questions for homework or in small groups and check them as a class.

1. *Generalmente, ¿dónde vive la mayoría de los cocodrilos?*
2. *¿Qué tipos de cocodrilos están en peligro de extinción?*
3. *¿En qué lugares se encuentra el cocodrilo americano?*
4. *¿Cuál cocodrilo tiene más peligro de extinción y por qué?*
5. *¿Es peligroso para los humanos el cocodrilo cubano?, ¿por qué?*
6. *¿Qué "talento" tiene el cocodrilo americano que le ayuda a matar?*
7. *¿Cómo podemos proteger los cocodrilos?*
8. *¿Qué sugerencias tienes para vivir en armonía con los cocodrilos?*

⟨5:00⟩ **11·10 ¡Corre!**

Escuchen mientras su profesor/a les explica cómo jugar con las formas de los verbos en el subjuntivo.

⟨4:00⟩ **11·11 Opciones**

Túrnense para crear oraciones completas usando los sujetos indicados en cada frase.

MODELO Es preferible que ella/nosotros/tú (reciclar el vidrio)

E1: *Es preferible que ella recicle el vidrio.*

E2: *Es preferible que nosotros reciclemos el vidrio.*

E3: *Es preferible que tú recicles el vidrio.*

1. Es dudoso que tú/Marta y yo/ella (rehusar reciclar el aluminio) rehuses/rehusemos/rehuse
2. Es necesario que el gobierno/ellos/Uds. (reforestar los bosques) reforeste/reforesten/reforesten
3. Ojalá que ellos/él/nosotros (conservar las selvas tropicales) conserven/conserve/conservemos
4. Es posible que yo/tú/Uds. (poder evitar la lluvia ácida) pueda/puedas/puedan
5. Es importante que mi país/los jóvenes/nosotros (respetar la naturaleza) respete/respeten/respetemos
6. Es una lástima que papá/tú/tus hermanos (botar basura por las calles) bote/botes/boten

---

⟨5:00⟩ **11·12 El cocodrilo**

Completa el siguiente párrafo con la forma correcta del verbo apropiado en el subjuntivo. Después, comparte tus respuestas con un/a compañero/a.

Fíjate

The *yo* form of the present tense (indicative mode) of *proteger* is *protejo*. Therefore the subjunctive of *proteger* is *proteja, protejas,* etc.

El cocodrilo cubano

estar	proteger	haber	matar
poder	existir	ser	vivir

Es raro que los cocodrilos (1) ___vivan/existan___ en el hemisferio occidental. ¡Siempre pienso en el continente de África como hábitat para este animal! Es una lástima que el cocodrilo americano y el cocodrilo cubano (2) ___estén___ en peligro de extinción. Es bueno que el cocodrilo americano (3) ___exista/viva___ en varias partes del hemisferio (Florida, algunas islas del Caribe y varias zonas costeras del Golfo de México y el Océano Pacífico), porque así tiene menos peligro de extinción que el cocodrilo cubano, el cual (*which*) existe solamente en el sureste de Cuba. Es posible que el cocodrilo americano (4) ___sea___ peligroso para los humanos. Son tan grandes que pueden atacar y comer animales de gran tamaño cuando se acercan a beber agua. Es improbable que el cocodrilo cubano (5) ___mate___ a una persona porque es mucho más pequeño y prefiere las aves, pequeños mamíferos, peces y otros animales acuáticos. Es increíble que el cocodrilo americano (6) ___pueda___ galopar distancias cortas, lo que significa que puede matar fuera del agua también. Es necesario que nosotros (7) ___protejamos___ estos reptiles y ojalá que (8) ___haya___ muchos más en el futuro.

COMUNICACIÓN   cuatrocientos tres   403

CAPÍTULO 11

CAPÍTULO 11

11·13 Mis mejores consejos (advice)...

Completa el cuadro con tus mejores consejos. Después, comparte tu información con un/a compañero/a.

PARA PROTEGER LOS RÍOS Y OCÉANOS	PARA EVITAR LA CONTAMINACIÓN DEL AIRE	PARA MANTENER LAS CALLES LIMPIAS
1. *Es importante que no botemos la basura en los ríos.*	1.	1.
2.	2.	2.
3.	3.	3.
4.	4.	4.
5.	5.	5.

11·14 ¿Para quién es necesario que...?

Túrnense para hacer y contestar las preguntas sobre las siguientes situaciones usando una de las expresiones de la pág. 401.

MODELO   estudiar esta noche

E1:   *Es probable que estudie esta noche. ¿Y tú?*

E2:   *Tengo que estudiar pero es posible que vaya al cine.*

1. estudiar este fin de semana
2. comer menos comida rápida
3. arreglar su cuarto
4. gastar menos dinero
5. buscar un nuevo compañero de cuarto
6. dormir más
7. sacar mejores notas
8. comprar un coche nuevo
9. reciclar más

11·15 Posibles determinaciones

¿Cuáles pueden ser tus determinaciones (*resolutions*) para el próximo año? Descríbelas y después compártelas con un/a compañero/a.

Estrategia

Take advantage of activities like **11-15** to challenge yourself to go beyond a simple answer, providing as much pertinent information as you can.

MODELO   *Es mejor que no coma tanto chocolate el próximo año pero es dudoso que pueda evitarlo. ¡Me fascina el chocolate! Es importante que haga más ejercicio. Es una lástima que no me guste hacerlo.*

NOTE FOR 11-14

When practicing these fixed expressions, you may wish to point out to students that if they do not wish to refer to anyone in particular, they should use the infinitive:

Es preferible comer menos.

Additional activity for *El subjuntivo*

 Mis deberes Juntos hagan una lista de por lo menos cinco cosas que deben hacer o que pueden ocurrir este fin de semana.

MODELO   *Es necesario que estudiemos más este fin de semana. También es importante que vayamos al supermercado. Después de ir al supermercado, es necesario que limpiemos la cocina. Es probable que salgamos con nuestros amigos el sábado. Finalmente, es posible que nuestros padres vengan a visitarnos.*

Capítulo 11   **403**

NOTE FOR 11-16

If you prefer, have students write a story rather than a dialogue. You may also want to brainstorm alternate situations with students to tailor the activity to your group.

12:00   **11·16** Es importante que…

Juntos escojan una de las siguientes situaciones para desarrollar en forma de diálogo. Usando las expresiones que acaban de (*have just*) aprender, den consejos según la situación escogida (*chosen*). Después, presenten el diálogo a los compañeros de clase.

Situación A:

La doctora Pérez es especialista en nutrición. María Cecilia es una joven universitaria de dieciocho años que va a hacerle una consulta a la doctora sobre cómo mejorar el cutis (*complexion*).

Situación B:

Bruno quiere comprar un carro usado y le pide a su amigo Manolo, quien trabaja en una agencia de carros, que le ayude.

Situación C:

El sargento López está enamorado de la linda Carolina, pero es tan tímido que nunca la invita a salir con él. Su amiga Carmen trata de ayudarlo.

Situación D:

Patricio se mata estudiando para el examen de matemáticas. Un día antes del examen se da cuenta (*he notices*) de que no tenía un examen de matemáticas, ¡sino de español! Va a su consejero para ver qué le aconseja.

¿Cómo andas?

Having completed the first **Comunicación**, I now can…

	Feel Confident	Need to Review
• talk about certain animals and their habitats (pp. 392–393)	❑	❑
• pronounce words applying appropriate word stress, and know when written accent marks are needed (p. 393)	❑	❑
• discuss the environment and ways to protect it (p. 396)	❑	❑
• form the present subjunctive (p. 398)	❑	❑
• use the subjunctive correctly with fixed expressions to communicate opinion, doubt, probability, and wishes (p. 401)	❑	❑

Comunicación

- Talking about politics
- Specifying location and information using prepositions and prepositional phrases

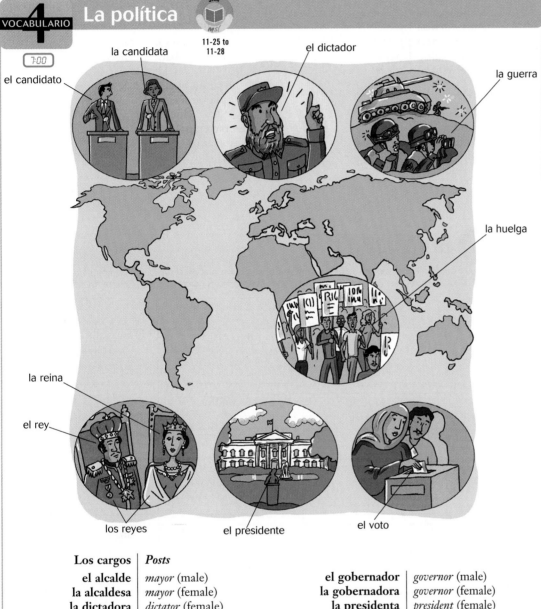

VOCABULARIO 4

La política

7:00

11-25 to
11-28

la candidata

el candidato

el dictador

la guerra

la huelga

la reina

el rey

los reyes

el presidente

el voto

Los cargos	Posts		
el alcalde	*mayor* (male)	**el gobernador**	*governor* (male)
la alcaldesa	*mayor* (female)	**la gobernadora**	*governor* (female)
la dictadora	*dictator* (female)	**la presidenta**	*president* (female)
la diputada	*deputy; representative* (female)	**el senador**	*senator* (male)
el diputado	*deputy; representative* (male)	**la senadora**	*senator* (female)

RECURSOS

T11-5 to T11-6 | T11-5 to T11-6 | Electronic Activity Cache

SECTION GOALS FOR
Comunicación

By the end of the *Comunicación* section, students will be able to:

- discuss how governments are organized and administered.
- debate with others about politics and the environment.
- contrast the political history of the United States with that of Latin America and Spain.
- suggest ways to improve politics in the future.
- identify the uses of *por* and *para*.
- use common prepositions and prepositional phrases.
- form prepositions with the correct pronouns.
- explain where items are located in relation to one another using prepositions.
- use infinitives after prepositions.

NATIONAL STANDARDS
Communication, Cultures, Connections, Comparisons

This final vocabulary presentation in *¡Anda!* provides students with a sophisticated vocabulary that helps them talk and write about current events both in the United States and abroad. Since politics change so rapidly, you may want your students to check the web sites of Spanish-speaking countries to note their current political climates.

The vocabulary for *la política* allows students to talk about current events and reflect on the rapidly changing political policies and leaders. With this vocabulary, students can read news articles from Spanish-language web sites (Standard 1.2) using authentic text to read and interpret written Spanish. They can also engage in conversations with others in the interpersonal mode (Standard 1.1) about what is going on in the world, and they can present to an audience of listeners or readers about their political views (especially interesting during an election year) and debate important issues (Standard 1.3). They can use this information to analyze the cultural differences between the way the United States is governed and its relationship to

other countries (Standards 2.1 and 2.2), and how the government affects the practices, products, and perspectives of the people. Students can make connections between their understanding of U.S. government and diplomatic and economic relationships with Hispanic countries (Standard 3.2). They can compare the government, election process, and rights of the people to see how the culture in the United States differs from Hispanic cultures and how they are governed (Standard 4.2).

Las administraciones y los regímenes	*Administrations and regimes*
el congreso	*congress*
la democracia	*democracy*
la dictadura	*dictatorship*
el estado	*state*
el gobierno	*government*
la ley	*law*
la monarquía	*monarchy*
la presidencia	*presidency*
la provincia	*province*
la región	*region*
el senado	*senate*

Las elecciones	*Elections*
la campaña	*campaign*
el discurso	*speech*
la encuesta	*survey; poll*
el partido político	*political party*

Las cuestiones políticas	*Political matters*
el bienestar	*well-being; welfare*
la defensa	*defense*
la delincuencia	*crime*
el desempleo	*unemployment*
la deuda (externa)	*(foreign) debt*
el impuesto	*tax*
la inflación	*inflation*

Unos verbos	*Some verbs*
apoyar	*to support*
combatir	*to fight; to combat*
elegir	*to elect*
estar en huelga	*to be on strike*
llevar a cabo	*to carry out*
luchar	*to fight; to combat*
meterse en política	*to get involved in politics*
resolver (o → ue)	*to resolve*
votar	*to vote*

5:00   **11·17** Batalla

Completa el cuadro con el nombre de un lugar o una persona. Después, compara tus respuestas con las de un/a compañero/a. Dense un punto por cada acierto (*match*).

1. una reina _____	4. un país con alta inflación _____	7. el nombre del mejor presidente de los EE.UU. _____
2. un estado _____	5. un país con baja inflación _____	8. el nombre de un senador de tu estado _____
3. un país con monarquía _____	6. una ciudad de los EE.UU. con mucha delincuencia (*crime*) _____	9. el nombre de una guerra muy larga _____
10. un rey _____	11. un alcalde _____	12. una senadora _____

11-29

La política en el mundo hispano

Evo Morales, elegido en diciembre de 2005, es el primer presidente indígena de Bolivia.

La historia política de Latinoamérica es la historia de la lucha dramática del ser humano contra fuerzas destructivas como la colonización, el imperialismo, la esclavitud y el genocidio en siglos anteriores y, en épocas más recientes, la pobreza, la corrupción, el nepotismo, la división rígida de clases y el militarismo. Muchos países hispanohablantes han sufrido severas dictaduras o democracias débiles e ineficaces. Esta lucha ahora se traduce en la búsqueda de una relación más justa con el mundo desarrollado y en particular con los Estados Unidos.

En décadas recientes, España ha surgido como un país moderno y avanzado, con un rey progresista y amante de la democracia. América Latina, a su vez, experimentó un periodo de paz y esperanza en la segunda mitad del siglo XX. La guerra que azotó (*whipped*) a Centroamérica en la década de los ochenta acabó y, aunque sus efectos aún se sienten y la recuperación es lenta en algunos países, el estándar de vida en Centroamérica ha aumentado (*has grown*), así como el comercio y el deseo de fortalecer las instituciones democráticas.

Preguntas

Answers to *Preguntas*.
1. Algunos problemas fueron la colonización, el imperialismo, la esclavitud y el genocidio y recientemente la pobreza, la corrupción, el nepotismo, la división rígida de clases y el militarismo.

1. ¿Cuáles fueron algunos de los problemas en la historia política de los países hispanos?

2. ¿Qué cambios han experimentado (*have they experienced*) muchos de los países hispanos en los últimos quince o veinte años?
2. España ha surgido como un país moderno y avanzado, America Latina experimentó un periodo de paz en la segunda mitad del siglo XX y en Centroamérica el comercio y el deseo de fortalecer las instituciones democráticas ha aumentado.

11·18 ¿Qué sabes de...?

Juntos contesten las siguientes preguntas para mostrar sus conocimientos políticos.

1. ¿Cuándo fue la última campaña para la presidencia de los EE.UU.?
2. ¿Cómo se llama el/la gobernador/a de tu estado?
3. ¿Quién fue un/a dictador/a infame? ¿De qué país? ¿Cuándo fue dictador/a?
4. ¿Qué países tiene un rey o una reina? ¿Cómo se llama(n)?
5. ¿Cuántos senadores hay en el senado de los EE.UU.?

11·19 El futuro político

Escribe algunas ideas sobre lo que debe pasar en el futuro en tu ciudad, estado, país o en el mundo. Después, en grupos de tres, escriban un párrafo colectivo para la clase. Usen las expresiones que requieren subjuntivo cuando sea posible.

MODELO   *Es necesario que los partidos políticos no combatan tanto entre sí* (among themselves). *También es importante que el presidente resuelva problemas económicos como la inflación. Es dudoso que podamos bajar la deuda nacional porque todos quieren dinero para sus programas.*

NATIONAL STANDARDS
Communication, Cultures, Connections, Comparisons

By researching and reading about *la política* of Hispanic countries, students are exposed to multiple Goal Areas of the National Standards. They read an authentic text about politics and interpret and understand written Spanish (Standard 1.2). They gain an understanding about how the political history of certain countries in Latin America has shaped their people and cultures, reflected in the practices, perspectives, and products of its people (Standards 2.1 and 2.2). Students can connect what they have learned about the government and history of other countries to how the political leadership and climate has shaped the diplomatic relations between the United States and Hispanic countries; they may have a different viewpoint about how other countries view democracy and the political leaders of the United States (Standard 3.2). Finally, they can compare the Latin American and Spanish dictatorships and military rule to the democracy they have experienced in the United States (Standard 4.2).

NOTE FOR *La política*

Tell students that *el alcalde* has an irregular feminine counterpart, *la alcaldesa*. Another similar pair is *el rey* and *la reina*.

Suggestion for *La política* Have students note how many of the words in this list are cognates. They may want to master these words first, then add those that are unfamiliar to them.

NOTE FOR 11-20

If you find that actividad **11-20** is too challenging for your students, you could start by brainstorming a list of local governmental issues or (non-partisan) problems that the community and/or your state face, and then have students react to the statements. Some ideas include general problems across the United States:

El desempleo en la Compañía X es muy alto.

Los empleados de la Fábrica X están en huelga.

Hay más problemas con el clima y la temperatura alta que en años previos.

En los Estados Unidos hay mucha basura y no hay suficiente reciclaje.

NOTE FOR *Por y para*

Tell students that the reason *por* appears in parentheses in some of the examples is because it is optional.

NOTE FOR *Por y para*

Tell students to note that an infinitive is used when a verb comes immediately after *por* and *para* as well as after all prepositions.

 **11·20** Los partidos políticos

En grupos de cinco o seis estudiantes van a crear un partido político nuevo. Tienen que determinar el nombre del partido y el programa (*platform*). Después, presenten sus partidos a los otros grupos y juntos decidan cuál(es) de los partidos mejor representa(n) las opiniones de la clase.

GRAMÁTICA **5** *Por y para*

11-30 to 11-33

As you have seen, Spanish has two main words to express *for*: **por** and **para.** They have distinct uses and are not interchangeable.

¿Por cuánto tiempo ocupa el presidente la presidencia?

POR is used to express:

1. Duration of time (*during, for*)

El presidente ocupa la presidencia (**por**) cuatro años consecutivos.
The president holds the presidency for four consecutive years.

El alcalde habló (**por**) más de media hora.
The mayor spoke for more than a half hour.

2. Movement or location (*through, along, past, around*)

Los candidatos van **por** la calle hablando con la gente.
The candidates are going through the streets talking with the people.

El rey saluda **por** la ventana.
The king is waving through the window.

PARA is used to express:

1. Point in time or a deadline (*for, by*)

Es dudoso que todos los problemas se solucionen **para** el final de su presidencia.
It is doubtful that all problems will be solved by the end of her presidency.

Es importante que bajemos los impuestos **para** el próximo año.
It is important that we lower taxes by next year.

2. Destination (*for*)

La reina sale hoy **para** Puerto Rico.
The queen leaves for Puerto Rico today.

Los diputados se fueron **para** el Capitolio.
The representatives left for the Capitol.

3. Motive (*on account of, because of, for*)
Decidimos meternos en política **por** nuestros hijos. Queremos asegurarles un futuro mejor.
We decided to get involved in politics because of our children. We want to assure them a better future.
En resumen, nos dijeron que hay que reciclar **por** el futuro de nuestro planeta.
In short, they told us that we must recycle for the future of our planet.

4. Exchange (*in exchange for*)
Gracias **por** su ayuda, señora Presidenta.
Thank you for your help, Madam President.
Limpiaron el vertedero **por** diez mil dólares.
They cleaned the dump for ten thousand dollars.

5. Means (*by*)
Los diputados discutieron los resultados de las elecciones **por** teléfono.
The representatives argued about the election results over the phone.
¿Los reyes van a viajar **por** barco o **por** avión?
Are the king and queen going to travel by ship or by plane?

3. Recipients or intended person or persons (*for*)
Mi hermano escribe discursos **para** la gobernadora.
My brother writes speeches for the governor.
Necesitamos un avión **para** el dictador.
We need a plane for the dictator.

4. Comparison (*for*)
Para un hombre que sabe tanto de la política, no tiene ni idea sobre la delincuencia de nuestras calles.
For a man who knows so much about politics, he has no idea about the crime on our streets.
La taza de desempleo es bastante bajo **para** un país en desarrollo.
The unemployment rate is quite low for a developing country.

5. Purpose or goal (*to, in order to*)
Para recibir más votos, la candidata necesita proponer soluciones **para** los problemas con la deuda externa.
(In order) to receive more votes, the candidate needs to propose solutions for the problems with foreign debt.
Hay que luchar contra la contaminacón **para** proteger el medio ambiente.
One needs to fight pollution to protect the environment.

Suggestion for *Por y para* Some oral questions to practice *por* and *para* are:

¿Por cuánto tiempo estudiaste / hablaste por teléfono / hiciste ejercicio anoche / ayer / anteayer / durante el fin de semana?, ¿Por dónde hay un apartamento / un banco / un mercado / un restaurante?, ¿Para quién compras discos compactos?, ¿Qué tienes que hacer para sacar buenas notas / estar contento/a?

Recycling previous vocabulary works well with these types of directed questions.

Expansion for 11-21 Actividad **11-21** can also be used as a comprehension activity, and you can assign the comprehension questions as homework or for use in small groups.

Contesta cierto (C) o falso (F). Si es falso, corriege las oraciones para que sean ciertas.
1. _____ Leonor pasó todo el verano pasado en la casa de su hermana.
2. _____ Ella vino a pasar sus vacaciones de verano con su hermana.
3. _____ Leonor trajo mucho equipaje a la casa de su hermana.
4. _____ Leonor hizo planes con su hermana por la tarde.
5. _____ Apareció en la casa un grupo de cantantes.
6. _____ Leonor le dio una caja de guitarras a su hermana.
7. _____ La hermana de Leonor vivió en la República Dominicana.
8. _____ Leonor trajo una hamaca a la casa de su hermana.
9. La hermana reaccionó con mucho gusto al ver el paquete.
10. _____ Leonor envió la hamaca desde la República Dominicana a la casa de su hermana.

[7:00] 👥 **11·21** Mi hermana Leonor

Mi hermana Leonor me dio una gran sorpresa para mi cumpleaños.

Paso 1 Para saber qué pasó, completa el siguiente párrafo con **por** o **para**.

Paso 2 Comparte tus respuestas con un/a compañero/a y explícale por qué usaste **por** o **para**.

Leonor, mi hermana, estuvo en mi casa (1) ___por___ un mes el verano pasado. Vino (2) ___para___ mi cumpleaños. Leonor llegó con tres maletas y una enorme caja misteriosa. El día de mi cumpleaños me dijo que (yo) tenía que estar lista (3) ___para___ las cinco de la tarde. Efectivamente, a las cinco en punto estaba sentada en la sala cuando vi (4) ___por___ la ventana a un grupo de amigos. Venían con un trío de guitarras. ¡Era una serenata (5) ___para___ mí! ¡Qué emoción tan grande! La serenata comenzó y Leonor bajó (6) ___por___ la escalera (*staircase*) con una caja. —Es (7) ___para___ ti —me dijo. La abrí y ¡qué sorpresa! Era una hamaca de yute (*jute hammock*) de la República Dominicana, donde Leonor había vivido (*had been*) (8) ___por___ varios meses. —¡Una hamaca (9) ___para___ el patio— exclamé— (10) ___para___ leer y dormir al sol! ¡Qué delicia! Y en seguida pregunté: —Pero, Leonor, ¿cómo trajiste esta hamaca desde Santo Domingo? ¿La trajiste (11) ___por___ avión o la mandaste (12) ___por___ correo? Leonor se rió y me contestó: — (13) ___Para___ ti, querida hermana, soy capaz de hacer muchas cosas. Me la traje en avión. (14) ___Para___ ser una caja tan grande la verdad es que no me causó tantos problemas. ¡Feliz cumpleaños!

Additional activity for *Por y para*
Note that this activity recycles both the present progressive and direct object pronouns.

 ¿Para quién estás comprando...? Túrnense para decir para quiénes están haciendo las siguientes cosas.

MODELO   comprar/libro sobre la inflación

E1:   *¿Para quién estás comprando el libro sobre la inflación?*

E2:   *Estoy comprando el libro para mis padres.*

1. combatir/ desempleo
2. escribir/ discurso
3. pedir/donación (*contribution*)
4. votar/en las elecciones
5. circular/ peticiones
6. meterse/ en política
7. resolver/ problemas del bienestar
8. proteger/ el medio ambiente

TPR activity for *Las preposiciones*
Prepositions lend themselves well to TPR activities. These can be simple, like using classroom objects and giving amusing instructions for the students to follow, e.g., *Pon el lápiz encima de tu cabeza.*

If you want to incorporate world geography with the prepositions, have students work in groups with a map of South America and Central America, with the countries cut out into individual shapes. Create a new map by giving directions such as *Brasil está lejos de Honduras* or *Chile está cerca de Argentina* and have them put their new maps together. See which groups' maps match yours.

5:00 **11·22** Preguntas personales

Túrnense para contestar las siguientes preguntas.

1. ¿Por cuánto tiempo miraste las noticias en la televisión anoche?
2. ¿Por cuánto tiempo estudiaste anoche?
3. ¿Qué ves por la ventana de tu cuarto?
4. ¿Viniste a esta universidad por tus padres o por ti?
5. ¿Para quién votaste la primera vez que pudiste votar?
6. ¿Qué puede hacer un estudiante universitario para ser más activo en la política?
7. ¿Sabes si hay un centro de reciclaje por aquí? ¿Por dónde voy para llegar a él?
8. ¿Qué necesitamos hacer para evitar la contaminación?

GRAMÁTICA 6 — **Las preposiciones y los pronombres preposicionales**

11-34 to 11-36   37

4:00

> Sin duda, su apoyo es esencial. Con ustedes podemos hacer grandes cambios sin dificultades.

Besides the prepositions **por** and **para,** there is a variety of useful prepositions and prepositional phrases, many of which you have already been using throughout *¡Anda!* Study the following list to review the ones you already know and to acquaint yourself with those that may be new to you.

a	*to; at*	**después de**	*after*
a la derecha de	*to the right of*	**detrás de**	*behind*
a la izquierda de	*to the left of*	**en**	*in*
acerca de	*about*	**encima de**	*on top of*
(a)fuera de	*outside of*	**enfrente de**	*across from; facing*
al lado de	*next to*	**entre**	*among; between*
antes de	*before (time/space)*	**hasta**	*until*
cerca de	*near*	**lejos de**	*far from*
con	*with*	**para**	*for; in order to*
de	*of; from; about*	**por**	*for; through; by; because of*
debajo de	*under; underneath*	**según**	*according to*
delante de	*in front of*	**sin**	*without*
dentro de	*inside of*	**sobre**	*over; about*
desde	*from*		

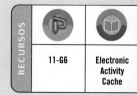

El centro de reciclaje está **a la derecha del** supermercado.

The recycling center is to the right of the supermarket.

La alcadesa va a hablar **acerca de** los problemas que tenemos con la protección del cocodrilo cubano.

The mayor is going to speak about the problems we are having with the protection of the Cuban crocodile.

Vimos un montón de plástico **encima del** papel.

We saw a mountain of plastic on top of the paper.

Quieren sembrar flores **enfrente del** vertedero.

They want to plant flowers in front of the dump.

El proyecto no puede tener éxito **sin** el apoyo del gobierno local.

The project cannot be successful without the support of the local government.

Los pronombres preposicionales

Study the list of pronouns that are used following prepositions.

> **Fíjate**
>
> The list of pronouns that follow prepositions is the same as the list of subject pronouns, except for the first two (*mí* is used instead of *yo*, and *ti* instead of *tú*).

mí	*me*	**nosotros/as**	*us*
ti	*you*	**vosotros/as**	*you*
él	*him*	**ellos**	*them*
ella	*her*	**ellas**	*them*
usted	*you*	**ustedes**	*you*

Para mí, es muy importante resolver el problema de la lluvia ácida.

For me, it's really important to solve the problem of acid rain.

¿Qué candidato está sentado **enfrente de ti**?

Which candidate is seated in front of you?

Se fueron de la huelga **sin nosotros.**

They left the strike without us.

Trabajamos **con ellos** para proteger el medio ambiente.

We work with them to protect the environment.

*Note that **con** has two special forms:

1. con + mí = **conmigo** *with me*
2. con + ti = **contigo**   *with you*

—¿Vienes **conmigo** al discurso?

Are you coming with me to listen to the speech?

—Sí, voy **contigo.**

Yes, I'm going with you.

4:00

11·23 Hablando del candidato

Termina la conversación entre Celia y Manolo sobre el candidato Carlos Arroyo con los pronombres preposicionales apropiados y después comparte tu trabajo con un/a compañero/a.

CELIA: Manolo, ¿qué opinas tú de (1) ___él___?

MANOLO: Pues, te digo que para (2) ___mí___ está muy claro. El señor Arroyo no piensa en (3) ___nosotros___ ni en nuestros problemas.

CELIA: Sí, siempre está con las personas ricas e influyentes (*influential*), tratando de conseguir dinero de (4) ___ellos___ para su campaña.

MANOLO: También creo que vive parte del año aquí y parte en la costa. Para (5) ___mí___ eso significa que quiere ser nuestro líder pero no quiere vivir con (6) ___nosotros___. ¿Y para (7) ___ti___, Celia?

CELIA: Creo que tienes razón. Me gusta hablar con (8) ___tigo (contigo)___ porque me haces pensar en las cosas que no son tan obvias.

CAPÍTULO 11

NOTE FOR
Los pronombres preposicionales
In addition to *conmigo* and *contigo*, you may choose to present the form *consigo*.

Additional activity for *Las preposiciones*

Ahora, dibújenlo ustedes
Pensando en los verbos *ser* y *estar* y en las preposiciones, imaginen seis escenas/situaciones diferentes. Hagan un dibujo simple para ilustrar cada escena/situación y después describan la escena con dos o tres oraciones.

MODELO
Estos gatos están cansados. Son enormes.
Los gatos son enormes. Están cansados y duermen encima de la mesa.

1. Estas tres botellas son de vidrio, son muy pequeñas y están enfrente de una caja de cartón grande.
2. Estas latas son de sopa y atún. Están debajo de la silla.
3. Este hombre es veterinario. El pájaro está enfermo. El veterinario examina el pájaro al lado de una ventana.
4. Hay un peligroso incendio en el bosque, pero está lejos de la ciudad.

Additional activity for
Las preposiciones

La universidad Túrnense para explicar dónde están los siguientes lugares en su universidad.

MODELO *La biblioteca está detrás del centro estudiantil.*

1. la biblioteca
2. el gimnasio
3. el centro estudiantil
4. la librería
5. la capilla (*chapel*)
6. la cafetería
7. tu cuarto o residencia estudiantil
8. el centro de salud
9. el estadio de fútbol

11·24 **Descríbemelo** ⟨3:00⟩

Juntos describan el dibujo usando por lo menos **ocho** preposiciones diferentes.

MODELO *El gato está al lado del árbol.*

1. al lado de	5. debajo de
2. a la derecha de	6. delante de
3. a la izquierda de	7. detrás de
4. cerca de	8. lejos de

⟨5:00⟩ **11·25** **Una política joven**

Completa el párrafo sobre Martina, una candidata nueva en el mundo político, con las preposiciones de la lista. Después compara tu párrafo con el de un compañero.

a	antes de	con (2 veces)	de
después de	entre	sobre	sin

(1) _____Antes de_____ meterse en la política Martina compartió sus ideas (2) _____con_____ mucha gente. (3) _____Entre_____ otras personas se reunió (4) _____con_____ políticos importantes y, (5) _____de_____ ellos, aprendió mucho (6) _____sobre_____ el bienestar, el desempleo y la inflación. (7) _____Después de_____ escuchar todo lo que tenían que decir, ella volvió (8) _____a_____ su casa y empezó a convertir sus ideas en discursos. El próximo paso fue buscar apoyo y dinero. Sabía perfectamente que (9) _____sin_____ ese apoyo no iba a ser posible ganar las elecciones.

11·26 ¿Dónde están? 8:00

Juntos expliquen dónde están los siguientes lugares en El Viejo San Juan, usando siempre las preposiciones apropiadas.

1. La Fortaleza, casa del gobernador
2. El Capitolio, edificio de las oficinas de los senadores y los representantes
3. La Plaza de Armas
4. El Castillo de San Felipe del Morro
5. La Casa Blanca, casa de la familia de Juan Ponce de León
6. La Alcaldía/El Ayuntamiento, edificio donde el alcalde tiene sus oficinas
7. Correos
8. El Banco Popular
9. La puerta de San Juan
10. La catedral de San Juan

11·27 Mi casa   6:00

Capítulo 3. La casa, pág. 100.

Descríbele a un/a compañero/a tu casa (o la casa de tus padres o de un amigo) utilizando las preposiciones apropiadas. Tu compañero/a tiene que dibujar lo que describes. Después, cambien de papel.

Estrategia

Creating visual representations of words and phrases can be a powerful learning tool.

MODELO   *Mi casa tiene cinco habitaciones. Al lado de la puerta principal hay una sala. Detrás de la sala está la cocina. La cocina está a la derecha del comedor…*

11·28 ¿Con quién…?   4:00

Decide quién hace estas actividades contigo y después comparte las respuestas con un/a compañero/a.

MODELO   E1: ¿Quién… habla contigo por teléfono todos los días?

E2: *Mi madre habla conmigo por teléfono todos los días.*

¿Quién…?
1. viene a clase contigo
2. se sienta contigo en la sala de clase
3. hace las actividades de clase contigo
4. estudia contigo fuera de clase
5. almuerza o cena contigo
6. sale contigo por la tarde (para ir al cine/bar/club de baile, etc.)

CULTURAL BACKGROUND FOR 11-26

These buildings are historical sites located in Viejo San Juan, near El Castillo de San Felipe del Morro. Many of them are open to the public and serve as museums or tourist sites, while others are used for government business and officials.

NOTE FOR 11-26

Actividad **11-26** lends itself well to a cultural expansion activity. Students can investigate San Juan web sites such as El Morro on the Internet and present their findings to the class.

Additional activity for *Las preposiciones*

En nuestra clase… Hagan diez oraciones con preposiciones que describan su clase de español.

MODELO   *Ryan se sienta al lado de George./Los libros de mi profesor están encima de su escritorio./Las ventanas están lejos de nosotros.*

Additional activity for *El infinitivo después de preposiciones*

Lo que pasó con el perro
Termina las oraciones de forma lógica según el modelo. Después, comparte las oraciones con un/a compañero/a.

MODELO

E1: Es importante que sepas que el perro se escapó para...

E2: *Es importante que sepas que el perro se escapó para jugar con esa perra bonita del vecino.*

1. Es mejor que busquemos el perro antes de...
2. Es probable que el perro nos evite para...
3. Es posible que el perro tenga hambre después de...
4. Sí, es raro que no venga para...
5. Es dudoso que se vaya con otra persona después de...
6. Ojalá que lo encontremos sin...

GRAMÁTICA 7 — El infinitivo después de preposiciones

11-37 to 11-39

[2:00]

> ¡No me digas que todos tienen que comer antes de salir nosotros!

In Spanish, if you need to use a verb immediately after a preposition, it must always be in the **infinitive** form. Study the following examples:

Antes de reciclar las latas debes limpiarlas.   *Before recycling the cans, you should clean them.*

Después de pisar la hormiga la niña empezó a llorar.   *After stepping on the ant, the little girl began to cry.*

Es fácil decidir **entre reciclar** y **botar.**   *It is easy to decide between recycling and throwing away.*

Necesitamos trabajar con personas de todos los países **para proteger** mejor la Tierra.   *We need to work with people from all countries in order to better protect the Earth.*

Ganaste el premio **por estar** tan interesado en el medio ambiente.   *You won the prize for being so interested in the environment.*

No podemos vivir **sin trabajar** juntos.   *We cannot live without working together.*

[4:00] 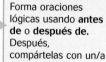 **11·29 De viaje**

Capítulo 10. El viaje, pág. 368.

Fíjate

The sentences for **11-29** can be written two ways. Start the sentence with *antes de + infinitive* or *después de + infinitive* and finish the sentence, as in *Antes de salir necesito hacer la maleta.* Or end the sentence with the prepositional phrase, e.g., *Necesito hacer la maleta antes de salir.*

Forma oraciones lógicas usando **antes de** o **después de.** Después, compártelas con un/a compañero/a.

MODELO

E1: salir/hacer la maleta

E2: *Antes de salir, necesito hacer la maleta. / Antes de salir, tengo que hacer la maleta.*

1. comprar el boleto/ir al banco   Antes de comprar el boleto, tengo que ir al banco.
2. pasar por recepción/subir a la habitación   Después de subir a la habitación, tengo que pasar por recepción.
3. llegar al aeropuerto/mostrar el pasaporte   Después de llegar al aeropuerto, tenemos que mostrar el pasaporte.
4. hacer la maleta/lavar la ropa   Antes de hacer la maleta, necesito lavar la ropa.
5. ir de vacaciones/dejar el gato con mis padres
   Antes de ir de vacaciones, necesito a dejar el gato con mis padres.

RECURSOS | 11-G7 | Electronic Activity Cache

11·30 Mis decisiones [5:00]

Termina estas oraciones y después compártelas con un/a compañero/a.

MODELO   E1: No me voy de aquí sin…
         E2: *No me voy de aquí sin terminar la tarea.*

1. Necesito pensar en el futuro antes de…
2. Quiero hablar con mis padres/mi mejor amigo sobre…
3. Voy a buscar un trabajo después de…
4. Tengo que escoger entre…
5. Me quedo en este lugar hasta…
6. Después pienso ir a _____ para…

ESCUCHA

11-40 to 11-42

ESTRATEGIA   Using visual organizers

Once you know the topic or gist of a passage, it may be helpful to mentally organize what you are about to hear. Determine if a list, chart, or diagram could be useful in helping you keep track of the information.

11·31   Antes de escuchar

Sonia Quiñones tiene un anuncio político en la radio.

1. ¿Qué es un anuncio político?
2. ¿Escuchaste alguna vez un anuncio político de un candidato en la radio o viste uno de estos anuncios en la televisión?
3. ¿Qué información contiene generalmente un anuncio de este tipo?

Sonia Quiñones, candidata

11·32   Al escuchar

CD 4 Track 25

Completa las siguientes actividades.

1. Escucha el anuncio para sacar la idea general.
2. Decide de qué forma quieres organizar la información (*list, chart, diagram,* etc.).
3. Escucha otra vez para completar tu diagrama o lista con la información esencial.
4. Escucha una vez más para añadir algunos detalles.

11·33   Después de escuchar

En grupos de tres o cuatro, compartan su información y juntos decidan si la Dra. Quiñones sería (*would be*) una buena alcaldesa. Expliquen.

SECTION GOALS FOR
Escucha

By the end of the *Escucha* section, students will be able to:

• implement the new strategy, using visual organizers.
• incorporate previously learned listening strategies.
• listen for specific information.
• debate whether they think the candidate in the announcement would be a good mayor.

NATIONAL STANDARDS
Communication

The *Escucha* section introduces the new strategy of using visual organizers. This strategy complements the presentational mode very well (Standard 1.3), because students have a sketch of something they can talk or write about and present to an audience. The students practice their interpretive communication skills (Standard 1.2) as they listen to the passage and understand and interpret its meaning. The post-listening activity requires small group communication (Standard 1.1) as students discuss what they have heard and decide if Sra. Quiñones would make a good mayor.

AUDIOSCRIPT FOR 11-32

Un anuncio de nuestra candidata Sonia Quiñones.

Compañeros y amigos:

Lo que necesitamos es un alcalde honrado y dedicado, o mejor dicho, una alcaldesa honrada y dedicada. Señores, yo quiero ser su alcaldesa. Estoy convencida de que estoy bien calificada para el trabajo. Hace dieciséis años que vivo en este pueblo bello en el corazón de nuestra isla. Mis tres hijos se graduaron de la Escuela Josefina León Zayas y ahora estudian en la Universidad de Puerto Rico en Río Piedras.

Algunos de ustedes me conocen como la doctora Quiñones puesto que soy pediatra. He tratado a casi todos los niños de Jayuya. También sirvo a nuestra comunidad como asesora para la Cruz Roja y presidenta de la organización Ambiente, PR. La salud de nuestros hijos, la protección del medio ambiente y la limpieza del mundo en que vivimos son mis grandes pasiones y van a ser mis prioridades como alcaldesa.

Amigos, votar por mí es votar por el futuro de nuestras familias, nuestro pueblo y nuestra isla.

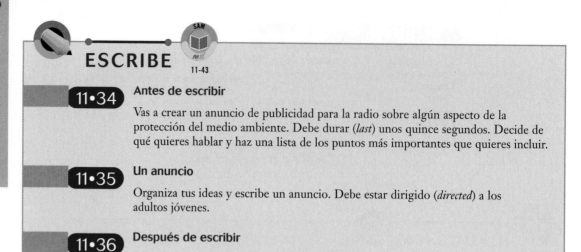

ESCRIBE

11-43

11·34   Antes de escribir

Vas a crear un anuncio de publicidad para la radio sobre algún aspecto de la protección del medio ambiente. Debe durar (*last*) unos quince segundos. Decide de qué quieres hablar y haz una lista de los puntos más importantes que quieres incluir.

11·35   Un anuncio

Organiza tus ideas y escribe un anuncio. Debe estar dirigido (*directed*) a los adultos jóvenes.

11·36   Después de escribir

Presenta tu anuncio a tus compañeros de clase.

¿Cómo andas?

Having completed the second **Comunicación**, I now can…

	Feel Confident	Need to Review
talk about politics (p. 405)	❏	❏
use **por, para,** and other prepositions correctly (p. 408)	❏	❏
use the pronouns that follow prepositions correctly (p. 410)	❏	❏
use infinitives when a verb is needed immediately after prepositions (p. 414)	❏	❏
use visual organizers when listening (p. 415)	❏	❏
write an ad about protecting the environment (p. 416)	❏	❏

Alicia Ortega Mujica

Cuba

Les presento mi país

Mi nombre es Alicia Ortega Mujica y soy de La Habana, la capital de Cuba. La mayoría de los cubanos tenemos herencia española, africana o una mezcla (*mixture*) de las dos. La influencia africana se nota sobre todo en la música cubana, especialmente en la salsa. Celia Cruz, "la reina de la salsa", siempre alababa estas raíces africanas en sus canciones. ¿Qué influencia africana se siente en la música de tu país? Antes, la economía cubana dependía mayormente de la producción de azúcar, pero ahora el turismo es muy importante y el gobierno invierte recursos para desarrollar esa infraestructura a fin de (*in order to*) atraer más visitantes al país.

El Gran Teatro de La Habana y El Ballet Nacional de Cuba

La Plaza de la Revolución

El ajiaco, un plato típico cubano

● ALMANAQUE

Nombre oficial:	República de Cuba
Gobierno:	Estado/Régimen comunista
Población:	11.382.820 (2006 est.)
Idiomas:	español
Moneda:	Peso cubano (CUP) y Peso convertible (CUC)

¿Sabías que…?

● El zunzuncito, el ave más pequeño del mundo, es endémico (*common*) de Cuba. Mide menos de 6 centímetros y pesa menos de 2 gramos. Es una especie de colibrí (*hummingbird*).

PREGUNTAS

1. ¿Cuál es la composición étnica de la población cubana?
2. ¿Cuáles son las bases principales de la economía cubana?
3. ¿Qué tipo de música es popular en Cuba? ¿Es popular en otras partes del mundo?

En la Red
Amplía tus conocimientos sobre Cuba en la página web de *¡Anda!*

417

SECTION GOALS FOR
Cultura

By the end of the *Cultura* section, students will be able to:

• name the cultural influences in Cuba.
• list important agricultural products in Cuba.
• discuss the wildlife common to Cuba.
• identify the natural resources of Puerto Rico.
• state the relationship of Puerto Rico to the United States.
• report about the major products of the Dominican Republic.
• explain how the geography of the Dominican Republic differs from that of other Hispanic countries.
• contrast Cuba, Puerto Rico, and the Dominican Republic with other Hispanic countries.

NATIONAL STANDARDS
Communication, Cultures, Comparisons

Students read about three Hispanic countries: Cuba, Puerto Rico, and the Dominican Republic, in *Les presento mi país*. The reading provides written Spanish and students are able to interpret and understand the cultural information presented (Standard 1.2). They can discuss in pairs or small groups how the three featured countries differ and how they are different from other Hispanic countries they have learned about (Standard 1.1). The information explains how the cultures differ from country to country, and students can compare how the history and geography of these countries affect their products, practices, and perspectives (Standards 2.1 and 2.2). They can then make comparisons between the cultural practices of Cubans, Puerto Ricans, and Dominicans and how they are similar to or different from those of the United States (Standard 4.2).

NOTE FOR *Cultura*

You may live in a part of the country that has a large number of people whose heritage is Puerto Rican, Cuban, or Dominican. At this point in *Capítulo 11*, and as you approach the end of *¡Anda!*, you can include students from these countries in a discussion of their heritage, which will enrich the learning of the entire class.

RECURSOS

T11-7	T11-7	Cultural Background Notes

Suggestion for *La Plaza de la Revolución* Ask students: *¿Qué lugares públicos en los EE.UU. se usan para las demostraciones públicas, tanto políticas como de otro tipo?* (e.g., Times Square in NYC), *¿Cómo se honra en los EE.UU. a los héroes políticos y militares?*

Expansion for *El ajiaco* Ask students: *¿Tenemos una sopa nacional?, ¿un plato nacional?, ¿Cuál es tu sopa favorita?, ¿cómo se prepara?*

Suggestion for *El Ballet Nacional de Cuba* Ask students: *¿Hay alguna compañía de ballet famosa en los EE.UU.? Nombra algún bailarín famoso. ¿Adónde puedes ir a ver una actuación de ballet?*

Víctor Manuel
Báez Montalvo

CD 4
Track 27

Vistas
culturales

Les presento mi país

Mi nombre es Víctor Manuel Baéz Montalvo y soy de San Juan, Puerto Rico. Soy estudiante del Recinto Universitario de Mayagüez, donde han asistido estudiantes muy distinguidos, entre ellos algunos ingenieros de NASA. El Observatorio de Arecibo, sitio del radiotelescopio de un solo plato más grande del mundo, no queda muy lejos. También se puede estudiar una naturaleza muy diversa en la isla: desde un área de cuevas del norte hasta El Yunque, bosque lluvioso del este. Puerto Rico es territorio de los Estados Unidos pero la cuestión de la independencia y la estadidad (*statehood*) se sigue debatiendo. ¿Qué opinas tú de esta cuestión?

Puerto Rico

NOTE FOR
Vista de San Juan

San Juan is located in the northern coastal plains in the Karstic region of Puerto Rico. (Karst contains such features as caves, sinkholes, springs, and sinking streams. These landforms are created by water dissolving the bedrock over many thousands of years.) San Juan is an excellent natural harbor. Founded in 1521, it is technically the oldest city in the United States, founded by Juan Ponce de León five years before he reached St. Augustine, FL. *La ciudad amurallada* is a nickname of San Juan.

Expansion for *Vista de San Juan*
Ask students: ¿Hay alguna ciudad amurallada en los EE.UU.?, ¿Por qué crees que la muralla fue imporante para San Juan en su momento?

NOTE FOR
El coquí

The *coquí* is the "national" frog, or symbol of Puerto Rico. It is a tiny reptile of about 1 inch in length. About 16 different species live on the island, and 13 of those are found in *El Yunque*, the Caribbean National Forest. The *coquí* is so named because of the sound or call made by the male of the species at dusk: co-quí, co-quí.

Expansion for *El coquí* Ask students: ¿Cuál es el símbolo oficial de los EE.UU.?, ¿Había otros posibles "candidatos" cuando fue escogido?, ¿Cuál prefieres tú y por qué?

NOTE FOR
El radiotelescopio de Arecibo

The single-dish radio telescope at the Arecibo Observatory is the largest of its kind in the world. This important scientific facility is open to scientists worldwide on the basis of competitive research proposals and projects. It is located at the National Astronomy and Ionosphere Center in Arecibo, Puerto Rico. It has even appeared in several movies: *GoldenEye* (James Bond), *Contact*, and *Species*. Learn more about this facility at http://www.naic.edu/.

Vista de San Juan, la capital

OCÉANO ATLÁNTICO

Isabela · Arecibo · San Juan
Bayamón · Río Piedras · Isla de Culebra
Mayagüez · PUERTO RICO
Ponce · Isla de Vieques

Mar Caribe

El coquí, el famoso símbolo de Puerto Rico

El radiotelescopio del Observatorio de Arecibo

● ALMANAQUE ●

Nombre oficial: Estado Libre Asociado de Puerto Rico

Gobierno: Territorio de los EE.UU.; Estado Libre Asociado

Población: 3.927.188 (2006 est.)

Idiomas: español e inglés

Moneda: Dólar estadounidense ($)

¿Sabías que...?

● Puerto Rico tiene tres bahías fosforescentes habitadas por millones de microorganismos (dinoflagelados) que emanan (*emanate*) luz cuando son alborotados (*stirred up*). Se puede observar este fenómeno por la noche. ¡Qué maravilla!

PREGUNTAS

1. ¿Qué evidencia del desarrollo avanzado de las ciencias hay en Puerto Rico?
2. Describe la variedad natural de la isla.
3. ¿Hay otros países de Centroamérica que tienen bosques lluviosos?

En la Red
Amplía tus conocimientos sobre Puerto Rico en la página web de *¡Anda!*

Expansion for *El radiotelescopio de Arecibo* Ask students:
¿Qué instalaciones para la investigación científica hay en los EE.UU.?, ¿Dónde están? (e.g., NASA in Texas and NORAD in Colorado)

RECURSOS | T11-8 | T11-8 | Cultural Background Notes

María Carmen
Alcántara Rojas

La República Dominicana

CW
eBook

CD 4
Track 28

DVD/VHS

Vistas
culturales

Les presento mi país

Mi nombre es María Carmen Alcántara Rojas pero mi familia y mis amigos me llaman Mari Carmen. Soy de la República Dominicana, país que ocupa los dos tercios orientales de la isla de La Española. El país es muy montañoso y áspero (*rough*) con cuatro sistemas principales de cordilleras (*mountain ranges*). Un plato típico es *la bandera dominicana*, que consiste en arroz, habichuelas rojas, carne, ensalada y tostones (*plantain chips*)… Si nos visitas, vas a escuchar el merengue y la bachata con sus ritmos contagiosos. Otras aficiones del país son los deportes acuáticos y el béisbol. ¿Sabes qué jugadores dominicanos juegan para equipos estadounidenses?

El merengue, el baile nacional

OCÉANO ATLÁNTICO

Puerto Plata

Santiago

HAITÍ

Samaná

Cotuí

Punta Cana

San Juan

LA REPÚBLICA
DOMINICANA

Santo
Domingo

La Romana

Barahona

San Pedro
de Macoris

Mar Caribe

Vista de
Santo
Domingo,
la capital

El Pico Duarte, en la Cordillera Central, es el pico más alto de las Antillas a unos 3.175 m.s.n.m. (10.417 pies).

● ALMANAQUE ●

Nombre oficial:	La República Dominicana
Gobierno:	Democracia representativa
Población:	9.183.984 (2006 est.)
Idiomas:	español (oficial)
Moneda:	Peso dominicano ($RD)

¿Sabías que…?

- Cristóbal Colón descubrió la isla en su primer viaje y la nombró La Española. Santo Domingo fue la primera ciudad europea fundada en el Nuevo Mundo y hoy en día casi la mitad de la población vive ahí, en la capital.

- La mayoría de los beisbolistas hispanos en las Grandes Ligas son dominicanos.

PREGUNTAS

1. ¿Cómo es la geografía dominicana y qué tiene de especial?
2. ¿Qué es "la bandera dominicana"?
3. ¿Qué tienen en común la República Dominicana y los otros países del Caribe que hemos estudiado?

En la Red
Amplía tus conocimientos sobre la República Dominicana en la página web de *¡Anda!*

419

NOTE FOR

El Pico Duarte

Juan Pablo Duarte is *el padre de la patria dominicana*. This revolutionary led the fight for independence from Spain, obtained in 1844. A monument to him is located at the peak of the mountain.

Expansion for *El Pico Duarte* Ask students: *Levantar un monumento en la cima de una montaña, ¿es un homenaje común en los EE.UU.?, ¿Dónde hay alguno?* (e.g., Mount Rushmore), *¿De qué otra forma se reconoce el heroísmo en los EE.UU.?*

NOTE FOR

El merengue

Merengue means whipped egg whites and sugar in Spanish, similar to the English word meringue. It is unclear as to why this name became the name of a style of music from the Dominican Republic. But, perhaps, we can trace its meaning to a dance move that resembles an egg beater in action.

This style of music was created by Ñico Lora in the 1920s and eventually became the country's national music and dance style. World famous merengue singers include: Los Hermanos Rosario, Juan Luis Guerra, Wilfredo Vargas, Sergio Vargas, Johnny Ventura, Kinito Mendez, Josie Esteban y la Patrulla 15, Pochy y su Cocoband, Fernando Villalona, Cuco Valoy, Elvis Crespo, Miriam Cruz & Las Chicas Del Can, and Conjunto Quisqueya.

Ambiciones siniestras

lectura

11-48

11-37 **Antes de leer.** En el **Episodio 10** tuvimos una confesión de Cisco y surgieron más dudas sobre Lupe. Parece que tiene secretos.

Teniendo esto en cuenta, contesta las siguientes preguntas.

1. ¿Quién es Lupe?
2. ¿Cuáles pueden ser sus secretos?
3. ¿Está en peligro Marisol?

ESTRATEGIA **Using visual organizers**

After you have read a text, it may be useful to create a visual organizer for the information contained therein. In *¡Anda!* you have already worked with timelines, semantic maps (or web diagrams), charts, and Venn diagrams in completing activities. Try these organizers as you read.

11-38 **A leer.** Complete the following steps.

1. Skim the episode and think about which visual organizer(s) would best summarize what you learn about Lupe.
2. Create the visual organizer(s), then read the passage carefully to gather all the information you can to complete your organizer. Finally, share it with your classmates. Did you all create the same type of visual organizer? Which one(s) proved to be most beneficial?

Celia

CD 4
Track 29

Marisol tenía una cara de terror. Lupe se quedó° mirando la pistola que tenía en la mano. Por fin la puso en la mesa y suspiró° lentamente.

stayed there

sighed

—Bueno, —dijo Lupe. —Veo que es necesario que te lo cuente todo ahora. Pensaba hacerlo, pero no en este momento. Creía que te protegía… No quise hacerle daño° a nadie, Marisol. Me mandaron aquí para ayudar.

hurt

—¿Protegerme? ¿Ayudarme? —respondió Marisol. —No sé qué creer. No sé quién eres. No sé qué quieres de mí… de nosotros.

—Marisol, no soy estudiante. Soy agente del FBI.

—¿Cómo? ¿Cómo que eres una agente? No lo comprendo —dijo Marisol. —Te ves tan joven.

—Yo sé que no he sido° honesta —respondió Lupe. —No estoy nada orgullosa de las falsas apariencias y de tantas mentiras°. A veces tengo la sensación de que mi vida es una mentira… pero después pienso en las personas a las que estoy ayudando.

I haven't been
lies

—¿A quiénes estás ayudando? —preguntó Marisol. —Estoy desilusionada… muy desilusionada.

—Escuche —imploró Lupe.

—¿Escuche? —preguntó Marisol, incrédula. —¿Ahora me tratas de «usted»? ¡Éramos amigas! Confiaba en ti.

—Bueno, Marisol. *Te* lo cuento todo pero tienes que dejarme hablar —dijo Lupe.

—Te escucho… ojalá que sea la verdad —respondió Marisol con voz desesperada.

Entonces se sentaron juntas y Lupe empezó a explicárselo todo:

—Mi nombre verdadero es Celia Cortez y soy de Los Ángeles. Me gradué hace ocho años de la Universidad de Georgetown con una especialidad en ciencias políticas. Mientras estaba en el último año, conocí a un hombre increíble y me enamoré de él en seguida. Era el hombre más inteligente, más atractivo, más interesante que había conocido jamás°. Tenía un trabajo muy bueno con el gobierno federal. Era mi mejor amigo… Decidimos casarnos en cuanto me graduara°. Una noche dábamos un paseo por el centro de Washington cuando me dijo que tenía que contarme algo muy importante, que no había sido° totalmente honesto conmigo. Me dijo entonces que trabajaba para el FBI, no para el Departamento del Estado como yo pensaba. Le pregunté por qué decidió contármelo todo aquella noche y me respondió que era porque estaba involucrado° en un trabajo que requería que saliera° de Washington por varias semanas. Me explicó que no iba a poder estar en contacto conmigo mientras tanto. Sin preguntar, imaginaba que iba encubierto°. Nunca pensé en el peligro que le podía esperar. Yo era muy joven y realmente no sabía nada de su trabajo. Dos semanas después recibí la llamada que cambió mi vida por completo— mi amor estaba muerto. Lo mataron. Yo estaba perdida…

that I had ever met

as soon as I graduated

he had not been

involved
required that he leave

undercover

—Ay Lupe… perdón, Celia —respondió Marisol. —Lo siento. ¿Qué hiciste entonces?

—Me gradué y fui a trabajar para la misma agencia para conocer mejor quién era él, para poder saber más de su vida y para sentirme más unida a él. Eso fue, como te dije, hace ocho años.

Sonó el teléfono celular de Celia. Contestó y se quedó escuchando sin decir nada. Cortó y le dijo a Marisol:

—Perdona. Es muy importante que hable con esta persona. Tengo que salir ahora pero después, vuelvo para contestar tus preguntas. Y no te preocupes por Eduardo y Alejandra. Todo eso fue una mentira también.

421

NATIONAL STANDARDS
Communication, Comparisons

The new strategy of creating visual organizers facilitates comprehension of the *Ambiciones siniestras lectura* and *video*. Students are able to read the storyline, organize the new information, and see how it fits with the previous information from other chapters. The reading satisfies one part of Standard 1.2, in which students read to understand and interpret written Spanish. Students work together in pairs to answer the comprehension questions and compare their visual organizers (Standard 1.1), but if they present their visual organizers to the class and explain them in Spanish, they would address Standard 1.3, the presentational mode. The use of visual organizers as a way of preparing for new content and structuring their learning can be applied to whatever other subject they might be studying. This new strategy allows them to make comparisons between their study skills in Spanish and English (Standard 4.1).

Answers to 11-39

1. Celia Cortez
2. Los Ángeles
3. la Universidad de Georgetown; Ciencias políticas
4. Es agente del FBI.
5. Hace ocho años; en la universidad
6. Iba encubierto y lo mataron.
7. Se graduó y consiguió un trabajo en la misma agencia.
8. Celia está hablando por teléfono y después se va.

SECTION GOALS FOR
Video

By the end of the *Video* section, students will be able to:

- brainstorm how they think the episode will end based on the information from the *lectura*.
- reveal the ending of *Ambiciones siniestras*.
- discuss their opinions and feelings about the ending.
- summarize the plot from the first episode to the final episode.

Answers to 11-41

1. en el aeropuerto
2. al centro comercial
3. a nadie
4. Después de que Eduardo contactó al FBI, ellos decidieron ponerlo bajo protección. Después de reconocer Alejandra a Lupe/Celia, el FBI la contactó y ella se infiltró en su organización para mandarle información a Celia.
5. Lupe/El primer rompecabezas vino del Sr. Verdugo. Celia escribió el segundo porque quería distraer a Cisco, Manolo y Marisol para protegerlos.
6. Marisol está viendo las noticias en la televisión. En la televisión hablan del caso y dicen que capturaron al Sr. Verdugo. En ese momento recibe un e-mail sobre otro concurso.

11-39 **Después de leer.** Contesta las preguntas.

1. ¿Cómo se llama Lupe en realidad?
2. ¿De dónde es?
3. ¿Dónde estudió y cuál era su especialidad?
4. ¿Cuál es su trabajo ahora?
5. ¿Cuándo y dónde conoció a su novio?
6. ¿Qué le pasó al novio?
7. ¿Qué hizo ella después?
8. ¿Cómo termina la lectura?

video

SAM
MSL
11-49 to
11-50

11-40 **Antes del video.** ¿Qué crees que sabe Celia del Sr. Verdugo? ¿De Eduardo y Alejandra? ¿Quién llama a Celia? ¿Adónde va ella? En la segunda parte del episodio vas a encontrar todas las respuestas, y más.

Buenas tardes. Soy la agente Celia Cortez.

Llegamos demasiado tarde. Todos se fueron.

Eduardo, ¿estás bien?

Episodio 11

«El desenlace»

Relájate y disfruta el video.

11-41 **Después del video.** Contesta las preguntas.

1. ¿Dónde estaba Celia cuando empezó el episodio del video?
2. ¿Adónde fueron?
3. ¿A quién(es) encontraron allí?
4. ¿Qué les pasó a Eduardo y Alejandra cuando desaparecieron?
5. ¿Quién escribió los rompecabezas? ¿Por qué?
6. ¿Cómo termina **Ambiciones siniestras**?

RECURSOS

IRM

Video Script

Y por fin, ¿cómo andas?

Having completed this chapter, I now can...

	Feel Confident	Need to review

Comunicación
- talk about animals and their habitats (pp. 392–393) ❑ ❑
- pronounce words applying appropriate word stress and know when written accents are needed (p. 393) ❑ ❑
- discuss matters related to the environment (p. 396) ❑ ❑
- use the subjunctive correctly with fixed expressions to communicate opinion, doubt, probability, and wishes (p. 398) ❑ ❑
- talk about politics (p. 405) ❑ ❑
- use **por** and **para** with more accuracy (p. 408) ❑ ❑
- speak and write using a variety of prepositions (p. 410) ❑ ❑
- use visual organizers when listening (p. 415) ❑ ❑
- write an ad about protecting the environment (p. 416) ❑ ❑

Cultura
- talk about El Yunque (p. 398) ❑ ❑
- talk about some aspects of political history and current politics in the Hispanic world (p. 407) ❑ ❑
- share at least two interesting facts about each country: Cuba, Puerto Rico, and the Dominican Republic (pp. 417–419) ❑ ❑

Ambiciones siniestras
- use visual organizers to aid in comprehension of a reading passage (p. 420) ❑ ❑
- explain the truth about Lupe (p. 420) ❑ ❑
- explain what happened to Eduardo and Alejandra and why (p. 422) ❑ ❑

VOCABULARIO ACTIVO

CW
eBook
CD 4
Tracks 30–40

Unos animales — *Some animals*

el caballo	horse
el cerdo	pig
el conejo	rabbit
el elefante	elephant
la gallina	chicken, hen
el gato	cat
la hormiga	ant
el insecto	insect
el león	lion
la mosca	fly
el mosquito	mosquito
el oso	bear
el pájaro	bird
el perro	dog
el pez (*pl.*, los peces)	fish
la rana	frog
la rata	rat
el ratón	mouse
la serpiente	snake
el toro	bull
la vaca	cow

Unos verbos — *Some verbs*

cuidar	to take care of
montar (a caballo)	to ride a horse
preocuparse por	to worry about; to concern oneself with

Las cuestiones políticas — *Political issues*

el bienestar	well-being; welfare
la defensa	defense
la delincuencia	crime
el desempleo	unemployment
la deuda (externa)	(foreign) debt
el impuesto	tax
la inflación	inflation

Otras palabras útiles — *Other useful words*

un animal doméstico	a domesticated animal; pet
un animal en peligro de extinción	an endangered species
un animal salvaje	a wild animal
el árbol	tree
el bosque	forest
la cueva	cave
la finca	farm
la granja	farm
el hoyo	hole
el lago	lake
la montaña	mountain
el océano	ocean
peligroso/a	dangerous
el río	river
la selva	jungle

El medio ambiente — *The environment*

el aluminio	aluminum
la botella	bottle
la caja (de cartón)	(cardboard) box
la contaminación	pollution
el derrame de petróleo	oil spill
el huracán	hurricane
el incendio	fire
la inundación	flood
la lata	can
el papel	paper
el periódico	newspaper
el plástico	plastic
el sunami	tsunami
el terremoto	earthquake
la tormenta	storm
el tornado	tornado
el vidrio	glass

Unos verbos — *Some verbs*

apoyar	to support
botar	to throw away
combatir	to fight; to combat
contaminar	to pollute
cuidar	to take care of
elegir	to elect
estar en huelga	to be on strike
evitar	to avoid
hacer daño	to (do) damage; to harm
llevar a cabo	to carry out
luchar	to fight; to combat
matar	to kill
meterse en política	to get involved in politics
plantar	to plant
preocuparse por	to worry about; to concern oneself with
proteger	to protect
reciclar	to recycle
reforestar	to reforest
rehusar	to refuse
resolver (o → ue)	to resolve
sembrar (e → ie)	to sow
volver	to return
votar	to vote

La política — *Politics*

el alcalde/la alcaldesa	mayor
el/la candidato/a	candidate
el/la dictador/a	dictator
el/la diputado/a	deputy; representative
el/la gobernador/a	governor
la guerra	war
la huelga	strike
el/la presidente/a	president
el rey/la reina	king/queen
el/la senador/a	senator

Las preposiciones — *Prepositions*

See page 410.

Las administraciones y los regímenes — *Administrations and regimes*

el congreso	congress
la democracia	democracy
la dictadura	dictatorship
el estado	state
el gobierno	government
la ley	law
la monarquía	monarchy
la presidencia	presidency
la provincia	province
la región	region
el senado	senate

Las elecciones — *Elections*

la campaña	campaign
el discurso	speech
la encuesta	survey; poll
el partido político	political party
el voto	vote

Otras palabras útiles — *Other useful words*

el aire	air
la basura	garbage
la calidad	quality
la capa de ozono	ozone layer
el cielo	sky; heaven
el desastre	disaster
la destrucción	destruction
la ecología	ecology
el efecto invernadero	global warming
la lluvia ácida	acid rain
la naturaleza	nature
el planeta	planet
puro/a	pure
el recurso natural	natural resource
la selva tropical	jungle; (tropical) rain forest
la Tierra	Earth
la tierra	land; soil
la tragedia	tragedy
el vertedero	dump
vivo/a	alive; living

425

12

Y por fin, ¡lo sé!

NATIONAL STANDARDS

Comunicación

- To convey ideas about past experiences and your daily routine (Communication)
- To share preferences regarding food, clothing, and other topics (Communication)
- To make requests and give advice using commands (Communication)
- To express desires and opinions on a variety of topics (Communication)
- To describe your travel experiences (Communication)
- To express ideas on topics such as health, animals, the environment, and politics (Communication, Connections, Communities)

Cultura

- To share information about Chile, Paraguay, Argentina, Uruguay, Perú, Bolivia, Ecuador, Venezuela, Colombia, Cuba, Puerto Rico, and La República Dominicana. (Cultures, Comparisons, Communication)
- To compare and contrast the countries presented in *Capítulos 7–11* (Cultures, Comparisons)

Ambiciones siniestras

- To go behind the scenes of *Ambiciones siniestras*

OBJETIVOS

Comunicación	
	• To convey ideas about past experiences and your daily routine
	• To share preferences regarding food, clothing, and other topics
	• To make requests and give advice using commands
	• To express desires and opinions on a variety of topics
	• To describe your travel experiences
	• To express ideas on topics such as health, animals, the environment, and politics
Cultura	• To share information about Chile, Paraguay, Argentina, Uruguay, Perú, Bolivia, Ecuador, Venezuela, Colombia, Cuba, Puerto Rico, and La República Dominicana
	• To compare and contrast the countries you learned about in **Capítulos 7–11**
Ambiciones siniestras	• To go behind the scenes of **Ambiciones siniestras**

This final chapter is designed for you to see just how much Spanish you have acquired thus far. The *major points* of **Capítulos 7–11** are recycled in this chapter. No new vocabulary is presented.

All learners are different in terms of what they have mastered and what they still need to practice. Take the time with this chapter to determine what you feel confident with, and what you personally need to work on. And remember, language learning is a process. Like any skill, learning Spanish requires practice, review of the basics, and then more practice!

METHODOLOGY • Philosophy on Recycling

This chapter is unique in *¡Anda!* because it presents an opportunity for instructors and students to have yet another assessment regarding language acquired. In this chapter, *¡Anda!* has synthesized the main points of the final five chapters in a recycled format for students to practice the new skills they are learning. You will note that all of these activities have the students *put it all together;* in other words, *virtually all of the activities in Capítulo 12 are communicative.* There are no discrete point, mechanical activities; some are structured, meaningful activities that help students build towards communicative practice. For mechanical practice, we direct students to make use of the activities in *MySpanishLab™,* or to repeat the activities in their *Student Activities Manual* or in the textbook itself.

Finally, if you have advanced or Heritage language learners, this is an excellent chapter for them, since most of the activities afford them the opportunity to be highly creative.

RECURSOS

IRM

Lesson Plan

METHODOLOGY • Organizing a Review for Students

Researchers and reviewers of *¡Anda!* agree: after giving students strategies on how to conduct an overall review, this chapter is organized by beginning with communicative and engaging activities that focus on grammar and vocabulary from *Capítulo 7*. The recycling continues to move through the chapters, ending with *Capítulo 11*. This is followed by a more comprehensive review, after which students are truly *putting all the chapters together*. Finally, there is a recycling of countries presented in *Capítulos 7–11*.

METHODOLOGY • Recycling vs. Reviewing

In *¡Anda!, recycling* has meant taking previously learned material and recombining it with new material. This concept is supported by Gagné's learning concept of spiraling information. The concept of *review* is revisiting a topic, much like one does before an exam. *Review* is best illustrated in *Capítulo 4* (*Un repaso de ser y estar*), as well as in this chapter. No new information is presented, but rather a review affords students the opportunity to practice in a systematic fashion.

Before we begin revisiting the important grammar concepts, go to the end of each chapter, to the **Vocabulario activo** summary sections, and review the vocabulary that you have learned. Doing so now will help you successfully and creatively complete the following recycling activities. Consult the **Vocabulario activo** pages as needed as you progress through this chapter.

427

12-1 to
12-41

Organizing Your Review

There are processes used by successful language learners for reviewing a world language. What follows are tips that can help you organize your review. There is no one correct way, but these are some suggestions that will best utilize your time and energy.

❶ REVIEWING STRATEGIES

1. Make a list of the *major* topics you have studied and need to review, dividing them into categories: *vocabulary, grammar,* and *culture.* These are the topics where you need to focus the majority of your time and energy.

   Note: The two-page chapter openers can help you determine the *major* topics.

2. Allocate a minimum of an hour each day over a period of days to review. Budget the majority of your time with the major topics. After beginning with the major grammar and vocabulary topics, review the secondary/supporting grammar topics and the culture. Cramming the night before a test is *not* an effective way to review and retain information.

3. Many educational researchers suggest that you start your review with the most recent chapter, or for this review, **Capítulo 11.** The most recent chapter is the freshest in your mind, you tend to remember the concepts better, and you will experience quick success in your review.

4. Spend the most amount of time on concepts where you determine *you* need to improve. Revisit the self-assessment tools from **Y por fin, ¿cómo andas?** in each chapter to see how you rated yourself. Those tools are designed to help you become good at self-assessing what *you* need to work on the most.

❷ REVIEWING GRAMMAR

1. When reviewing grammar, begin with the **major** points, that is, begin with the *preterit, imperfect, pronouns (direct, indirect, and reflexive), commands,* and the *subjunctive.* After feeling confident using the major grammar points correctly, then proceed with the additional grammar points and review them.

2. Good ways to review include redoing activities in your textbook, redoing activities in your **Student Activities Manual**, and (re)doing activities on your *¡Anda!* web site.

❸ REVIEWING VOCABULARY

1. When studying vocabulary, it is usually most helpful to look at the English word, and then say or write the word in Spanish. Make a special list of words that are difficult for you to remember, writing them in a small notebook. Pull out the notebook every time you have a few minutes (in between classes, waiting in line at the grocery store, etc.) to review the words. The **Vocabulario activo** pages at the end of each chapter will help you organize the most important words of each chapter.

2. Saying vocabulary (which includes verbs) out loud helps you retain the words better and incorporate them into your personal active vocabulary.

❹ OVERALL REVIEW TECHNIQUE

1. Get together with someone with whom you can practice speaking Spanish. It is always good to structure the oral practice. One way of doing this is to utilize the composite art pictures from *¡Anda!* and say as many things as you can about each picture. Have a friendly challenge to see who can make more complete sentences or create the longest story about the pictures. You can also structure the practice by speaking solely in the past, for example, or practicing using object pronouns as you speak. This will help you build your confidence and practice stringing sentences together to speak in paragraphs.

2. Yes, it is important for you to know "mechanical" pieces of information such as verb endings, or how to take a sentence and replace the direct object with a pronoun. *But,*

it is *much more important* for you to be able to take those mechanical pieces of information and put them all together, creating meaningful and creative samples of your speaking and writing on the themes of **Capítulos 7–11.** Also remember that **Capítulos 7–11** are built upon previous knowledge that you acquired in the beginning chapters of *¡Anda!*

3. You are on the road to success if you can demonstrate that you can speak and write in paragraphs that express the present, past, and future tenses. Along with expressing ideas in the three major time frames, it is important to demonstrate your richness of language, employing a wide variety of verbs and other words. Keep up the good work!

Comunicación

> **Estrategia**
>
> Before beginning each activity, make sure that you have reviewed carefully the concepts in each given chapter so that you are able to move through the activities seamlessly as you put it all together.

12 1 ¡Fiesta!   Capítulo 7

Decidieron tener una fiesta y tienen que trabajar mucho para prepararlo todo. Organícense siguiendo el modelo.

MODELO

¿Comprar / tú / las bebidas?
E1:   *¿Compraste las bebidas?*
E2:   *Sí, las compré ayer.*

1. ¿Pedir / Uds. / los mariscos?
2. ¿Preparar / tu compañero / los perros calientes?
3. ¿Comprar / tu amigo / el pastel?
4. ¿Limpiar / tú / la sala?

5. ¿Lavar / Uds. / los manteles (*tablecloths*)?
6. ¿Encontrar / Manuel y Manuela / las servilletas?
7. ¿Organizar / Jorge / los CD?
8. ¿Invitar / tú / al profesor?

METHODOLOGY • Tools for Reviewing

If your students choose (or you strongly encourage them) to gain more mechanical practice, prior to beginning the activities in this chapter, repeating the activities they have already done in both the *¡Anda!* textbook and in the *Student Activities Manual* is an excellent start for their review. Re-doing activities is an important review tool that is based on learning theory. This works for the following reasons. First, students are already familiar with the context of the activity, know what they got correct and missed the first time, and hence are able to observe if they have improved. They also are repeating the activities on a different level; since they have already completed the activity, these repetitions go to a meta-analysis level, in which they need to analyze why they continue to miss certain items. The same learning theory concept is similar in music, in which we practice the same scales and arpeggios over and over.

METHODOLOGY • Using this Chapter

Although most of the activities in this chapter utilize the pair icon, you will note that most can be done at home. You can choose whether you want these activities to be oral, written, or a combination of oral and written. You can also choose whether you want the activities to be prepared outside of class or done in class. The decisions are yours to personalize the chapter in a manner that best suits your needs and those of your students.

CAPÍTULO 12

METHODOLOGY • Quantifying Minimum Expectations

You will note that we frequently include the minimum number of sentences expected of the students, either in a speaking or writing activity. If students do not know what these minimum expectations are, many will be happy with mediocre production. Most of us have had bright students who are lazy and unmotivated and are only willing to do the minimum. Hence it is necessary for instructors to let students know what their expectations are and to encourage them to exceed the minimum.

Having provided this rationale, the decision is ultimately yours. You may choose:

1. to use what we have recommended;
2. to require a different minimum level of production;
3. not to state the level of language production. You will notice that some of the directions in this chapter intentionally follow option 3. These are instructional delivery decisions that all of us must make based on a wide variety of differentiated objectives.

12-2 Después de la fiesta

¡La fiesta de la actividad **12-1** fue un éxito! Describan lo que pasó en la fiesta y qué hicieron cuando se fueron los invitados. Sean creativos y usen por lo menos **siete** oraciones.

MODELO *¡Nuestra fiesta fue un éxito! Vinieron muchos invitados. La gente bailó, comió y se divirtió mucho. Escuchamos música latina y rock. Después, tuvimos que pasar la aspiradora…*

12-3 La semana pasada

Túrnense para describir qué hicieron y adónde fueron la semana pasada, usando por lo menos **siete** oraciones en el pretérito con verbos diferentes.

l	m	m	j	v	s	d
estudiar, ver una película	ir al médico	ir al concierto de Juanes			ir al café Chulo	

MODELO *La semana pasada hice muchas cosas. Por ejemplo, vi una película en la televisión. Estudié mucho también. Conduje a la universidad el martes en vez de tomar el autobús porque tuve que ir al médico por la tarde. El miércoles por la noche mi amigo y yo fuimos al concierto de Juanes. Dormí muy poco toda la semana…*

12-4 La boda del siglo

 Capítulo 8

David y Adriana se casan. Tu compañero/a y tú están invitados y están planeando cómo vestirse. Túrnense para hablar del evento siguiendo el modelo.

MODELO tú / prestar / a mí / pantalones / amarillo

E1: *¿Me prestas tus pantalones amarillos?*

E2: *Sí, te los presto. / No, no te los presto.*

1. tú / ponerse / zapatos / negro
2. tú / prestar / a Julieta / blusa / azul / seda
3. ellas / prestar / a Mariela / falda / corto / atrevido
4. Raúl y Rafa / prestar / a Jorge / el cinturón / de cuero / negro
5. Ud. / prestar / a Jaime / coche / nuevo

RECURSOS

T12-1 T12-1

12 5 La recomendación fue...

¿Cuáles fueron sus recomendaciones? Túrnense para formar preguntas y contestar según el modelo.

MODELO   tú / las blusas de Donna Karan (a tus primas)

E1: ¿*Les recomendaste las blusas de Donna Karan a tus primas?*

E2: *No, no se las recomendé.*

1. ellos / los museos de arqueología (a tu profesor/a)
2. tú / el café Starbucks (a tus padres)
3. tu hermano / el hotel Ritz (a su amiga que no tiene dinero)
4. nosotros / la música de Shakira (a unos compañeros)
5. yo / la película *Shrek* (a mis primos de cinco años)
6. Uds. / las novelas de Gabriel García Márquez (a sus tíos)
7. tú / la clase de español (a tu mejor amigo/a)

Estrategia

You can elaborate on your answers as to why you recommended or did not recommend something by adding **porque** and a short explanation. In the model, you could say *No, no se las recomendé porque son muy caras.*

12 6 Una encuesta

Usa las siguientes expresiones para crear una encuesta (*survey*) de **diez** preguntas. Hazles las preguntas a diez personas diferentes y comparte tus resultados con la clase.

PREGUNTA	ME ENCANTA(N)	ME MOLESTA(N)	ME IMPORTA(N)	ME HACE(N) FALTA	ME FASCINA(N)
¿Te gustan los animales salvajes? ¿Cuáles?					Erika: Me fascinan los tigres.
¿Te gusta la ropa elegante?		Alex: Prefiero la ropa informal.			

METHODOLOGY • Reviewing Vocabulary

You will note that students are encouraged to review each chapter's vocabulary on their own. We recommend that they begin their vocabulary review with the two-page list of *Vocabulario* that is found at the end of each chapter.

METHODOLOGY • Recycling

Note that this chapter helps recycle and remind students of concepts learned before *Capítulo 7*. Direct your students to the correct chapter to refresh their memories about concepts presented in the previous semester.

CAPÍTULO 12

Expansion for 12-7 As a follow-up to this activity, ask students to report on what his/her partner read, thus encouraging active listening, summarizing, and reporting back using a different form of the reflexive verbs.

Expansion for 12-8 You may want to collect selected information as students report back in order to compile class statistics (e.g., how many students had a dog, what they wanted to be when they grew up, etc.). You may also want to add additional questions, thus personalizing the activity for your students, regarding other pets they may have had, what they did on weekends, which sports and pastimes were their favorites, etc.

12·7   ¿Qué hiciste ayer?

Escribe un párrafo sobre lo que hiciste ayer. Incluye por lo menos **diez** actividades usando un mínimo de **siete** verbos reflexivos. Después, léeselo a un/a compañero/a.

MODELO   *Ayer me levanté a las seis de la mañana. Me duché en tres minutos. Me puse los pantalones rojos con rayas blancas…*

12·8   A conocerte más aún

Cuando tenías quince años, ¿qué hacías en las siguientes situaciones?

Paso 1   Contesta las preguntas.

MODELO   E1:   ¿Qué hacías por las tardes, después de salir del colegio?

E2:   *Yo jugaba al tenis. ¿Qué hacías tú?*

E1:   *Hacía la tarea y ayudaba a mi madre con los quehaceres de la casa.*

1. ¿Qué te ponías cuando salías con esa "persona especial"?
2. Antes de dormirte, ¿pensabas en tu día?
3. ¿Tenías un perro?
4. ¿Cómo te divertías?
5. ¿Siempre te acordabas de hacer toda la tarea?
6. Si tenías tiempo, ¿con quién(es) te reunías?
7. ¿Dónde te gustaba sentarte en el cine, adelante o atrás?
8. ¿Qué querías ser de mayor?
9. ¿En qué situaciones te ponías nervioso/a?
10. ¿Cuándo te sentías feliz?

> **Estrategia**
>
> Being a good listener is an important life skill. Repeating what your classmate said gives you practice in demonstrating how well you listened.

Paso 2   Escucha las respuestas de tu compañero/a. ¿Cuántas preguntas contestaron Uds. de manera similar? ¿De manera diferente?

RECURSOS   T12-2   T12-2

12 9 Mi primera casa

¿Cómo era tu primera casa o la de un/a amigo/a de tu infancia? Descríbesela a un/a compañero/a en por lo menos **diez** oraciones incluyendo todos los detalles posibles (muebles, colores, etc.).

MODELO   *Mi primera casa estaba en una ciudad pequeña. Tenía dos dormitorios. La cocina era amarilla. El comedor y la sala eran pequeños. Tenía solamente (only) un baño…*

Capítulo 9

12 10 Un diálogo

Imaginen que trabajan como voluntarios con un médico. Creen un diálogo entre el médico y el paciente con respecto a sus síntomas y su tratamiento. Escriban por lo menos **catorce** oraciones.

MODELO   E1 (MÉDICO):   *¿Cómo está? ¿Qué le duele?*

E2 (PACIENTE):   *Creo que tengo catarro o un virus. Me duele todo.*

E1:   *¿Tiene fiebre? ¿Tose? ¿Estornuda?*

E2:   *No, no tengo fiebre pero sí tengo tos. Y sí, estornudo mucho. ¡También me quemé!*

E1:   *¿Se quemó? ¿Cómo?*

E2:   *…*

12 11 ¡Me enfermé!

¿Cuándo fue la última vez que se enfermaron? ¿Qué hicieron? ¿Qué pasó?

Paso 1   Descríbele a un/a compañero/a tu última enfermedad en por lo menos **diez** oraciones.

MODELO   *Hace dos semanas que me enfermé. Tuve la gripe y guardé cama por una semana. Mi madre me llevó al médico porque me dolía el cuerpo y tenía una fiebre…*

Paso 2   Describe en tus propias (own) palabras la enfermedad de tu compañero/a de clase.

Estrategia

It is rare when people remember *everything* that they hear! It is important that you feel comfortable asking someone to repeat information or asking for clarification.

Expansion for 12-10 If time permits, this activity can be done as a class presentation. Students can present their prepared dialogue with their partner, or for an impromptu speaking activity, they can switch partners to simulate a real-life conversational exchange. This activity would be especially good for your Heritage language learners.

CAPÍTULO 12   434   cuatrocientos treinta y cuatro   Y POR FIN, ¡LO SÉ!

CAPÍTULO 12

12 12 Los días de vacaciones   Capítulo 10

¿Qué hiciste durante las últimas vacaciones? Descríbele a tu compañero/a, en por lo menos **diez** oraciones y usando una variedad de verbos y vocabulario, tus últimas vacaciones. Incluye las siguientes palabras:

todos los días	todas las noches	generalmente	normalmente
un día	una vez	una mañana	nunca

MODELO   *Durante las últimas vacaciones nosotros fuimos a Punta Cana. Fue la primera vez que visitamos la República Dominicana. Todos los días íbamos a la playa. Allí nadábamos…*

12 13 Mis vacaciones favoritas

¿Adónde fuiste y cómo fueron tus vacaciones favoritas? Descríbeselas a un/a compañero/a en por lo menos **siete** oraciones usando el pretérito y una variedad de verbos.

MODELO   *Mis vacaciones en Argentina fueron mis mejores vacaciones. Fuimos a la playa, donde mi familia y yo anduvimos muchas horas. Nadé en el océano…*

12 14 Y también...

Imagina que tienes un hijo y que, por primera vez, él va a salir solo con sus amigos y se va a llevar el coche. ¿Qué le aconsejas? Haz mandatos familiares con los siguientes verbos.

MODELO   E1:   leer / el manual

       E2:   *Lee el manual.*

1. conducir/con cuidado   Conduce con cuidado.
2. llevar/el permiso   Lleva el permiso.
3. tener cuidado/los peatones   Ten cuidado con los peatones.
4. llenar el tanque/gasolina   Llena el tanque de gasolina.
5. limpiar/parabrisas   Limpia el parabrisas.

6. no perder/llaves   No pierdas las llaves.
7. no abrir/ventanas/si llueve   No abras las ventanas si llueve.
8. no estacionarse/lugares prohibidos   No te estaciones en lugares prohibidos.
9. no doblar a la izquierda/sin mirar   No dobles a la izquierda sin mirar.
10. no comer ni beber/en el coche   No comas ni bebas en el coche.

12 15 ¡Me molestas!

¿En tu vida hay alguien que te está volviendo loco/a (*is driving you crazy*)? Dile lo que debe y no debe hacer. Puedes usar las palabras y expresiones de la lista y otras también. ¡Sé creativo!

MODELO   *Raúl, por favor, ¡me estás volviendo loca! Primero, guarda tu comida en el refrigerador, no la pongas en el sofá. Segundo, ¡no estornudes encima de la comida! Ponte el abrigo porque hace frío. Cuídate, por favor...*

Estrategia

Organize your thoughts in chronological order, and use transitions in your paragraphs. Consider words like *primero, segundo, tercero, próximo, después*, and *finalmente*.

guardar tu comida	tener más paciencia
no dejar la ropa sucia en el piso	no estornudar
lavar los platos	mejorarte
sacar la basura	cuidarte
no invitar siempre a tus amigos	no ponerte mi ropa

12 16 Estación de servicio

Están en una gasolinera. Túrnense para decirle al empleado (*attendant*) lo que necesitan.

MODELO   *Ponga aire en las llantas, por favor. También, abra el baúl, por favor. Yo no puedo abrirlo...*

Suggestion for reviewing commands You could encourage students to create a list of commands more closely related to their experiences. For example, they could include commands for professors, fellow students, coaches, cafeteria managers, campus police, administrators, politicians, etc.

NOTE FOR 12-18
Encourage students to be creative here and feel free to invent when necessary. Many students may have little travel experience.

Suggestion for 12-19 You may choose to have students write these suggestions for another person rather than for themselves. They could also write the suggestions from the point of view of a parent, friend, physician, therapist, professor, employer, spouse, etc.

12-17 ¡Por fin!

¡Éste es el momento que esperabas! ¡Por fin ustedes son los profesores de español! Túrnense para decirles a sus estudiantes por lo menos **ocho** cosas que deben o no deben hacer. ¡Sean creativos!

MODELO   *Hagan la tarea para mañana. También, hablen en español durante toda la clase…*

12-18 Comparando

Estás planeando unas vacaciones. Dile a tu compañero/a cuáles son, en tu opinión, los mejores y los peores servicios y destinos. Usa comparaciones y superlativos. Crea por lo menos **diez** oraciones.

MODELO   *El aeropuerto de Austin es más pequeño que el aeropuerto de Dallas pero en mi opinión es mejor porque no es muy grande. Para mí, la agencia Travel Experts es la mejor porque saben preparar unos viajes estupendos. Por ejemplo, la playa de Ixtapa en México es tan bonita como la playa de Cancún, y los hoteles no cuestan tanto como los hoteles de Cancún…*

12-19 Mis deberes

Capítulo 11

Siempre hay algo que podemos hacer para mejorarnos. Di por lo menos **diez** cosas que debes hacer ahora o que te propones (*you intend*) hacer en el futuro. Usa el subjuntivo cuando sea necesario.

MODELO   *Primero, es necesario que estudie más en el futuro. También es importante que no coma tanto chocolate pero es dudoso que pueda evitarlo. Entonces, es importante que compre cosas saludables. Pero, ¡qué lástima! ¡Me fascina el chocolate! Pues, como me gusta tanto, es importante que haga más ejercicio. ¡Es una lástima que no me guste hacerlo!*

12 20 Mi casa ideal

¿Cómo esperas que sea tu casa en diez años?

Paso 1 Descríbesela a un/a compañero/a con todo detalle (cuartos, muebles, colores, etc.). Incluye por lo menos **cinco** preposiciones diferentes en la descripción.

MODELO *Espero que mi casa tenga cinco habitaciones. Al lado de la puerta quiero que haya una sala y una cocina detrás de la sala. ¡Ojalá que tenga una cocina muy grande!*

> **Estrategia**
>
> You may want to draw the floor plan of your house and label the rooms. That way, it will be easier to talk about where each room is located in relation to other rooms. When working with a partner, you might want to draw your partner's house as you hear it described, taking note of the prepositions he/she has mentioned.

Paso 2 Repite lo que tu compañero/a te dijo. Es importante que uses y practiques las preposiciones.

Un poco de todo

 12 21 Nuestro medio ambiente y más aún

Creen juntos un reportaje (*report*) para la televisión sobre uno de los siguientes temas.

TEMAS

1. el medio ambiente

2. la política y cuestiones políticas

3. el tiempo

4. el arte, los deportes y otros eventos

NOTE FOR
Un poco de todo

In the *Un poco de todo* section, students put together all the information they have learned thus far. These activities show students how much they have progressed in their competence with Spanish and their ability to communicate. You might decide to film the *entrevistas* and *reportajes* as examples for future students. Additionally, these videos will demonstrate to your current students how much they have learned throughout the course. If you have 'potential' Spanish minors/majors in the course, this would be useful for their language learning portfolio.

Suggestion for 12-21 You may want to ask your students to make a PowerPoint presentation based on this activity.

12 22 ¿Cómo eres?

Conoces un poco a los estudiantes de los países que estudiamos en los capítulos anteriores. ¿Qué más quieres saber de ellos? Escribe por lo menos **diez** preguntas que quieres hacerles. Usa el pretérito, el imperfecto y el subjuntivo.

Gino Breschi Arteaga

Mirta Beatriz
Chávez Villalba

Marina Claudia
Luschini Ojeda

Francisco Tomás
Bacigalupe Bustamante

Milagros Alejandra
Romero Zárate

Raúl Eduardo Loza Arce

María Yolanda
Palacios Mena

Rosa María
Gutiérrez Murcia

Victor Luis
González Martínez

Alicia Ortega Mujica

Victor Manuel
Báez Montalvo

María Carmen
Alcántara Rojas

MODELO
1. *¿Qué estudiaste el semestre pasado?*
2. *¿Adónde fuiste el verano pasado?*
3. *¿Es posible que viajes este verano?*
4. …

12 23 ¿Sabías que...?

Completa estas actividades.

Paso 1 Escribe una o dos cosas interesantes que no sabías antes pero que aprendiste sobre cada uno de los siguientes países.

CHILE	PARAGUAY	ARGENTINA	URUGUAY
1.	1.	1.	1.
2.	2.	2.	2.

PERÚ	BOLIVIA	ECUADOR	COLOMBIA
1.	1.	1.	1.
2.	2.	2.	2.

VENEZUELA	CUBA	LA REPÚBLICA DOMINICANA	PUERTO RICO
1.	1.	1.	1.
2.	2.	2.	2.

Paso 2 Compara la información con el lugar donde tú vives, el estado o el país. ¿Qué cosas son similares? ¿Qué diferencias hay?

Suggestion for 12-23 Have students state the capital of each country in the photos.

Expansion for 12-23 You may choose to collect and expand the information given, turning it into a *Jeopardy!*-type game.

RECURSOS T12-3 T12-3

Suggestion for 12-24 You may wish to make this a class activity where students bring the *platos* to class, along with the recipes. You could compile the recipes to "publish" a class cookbook. Your students could also share the recipes with your school's food service and perhaps have a Hispanic or international foods day.

12 24 ¿Y de postre?

Vas a preparar una cena latina para tus amigos con platos representativos de varios países. Selecciona por lo menos **tres** platos y algo para beber. Indica el país de origen de cada plato y los ingredientes. Si varios países comparten el plato, menciónalos también.

Ropa vieja de Cuba   Una parrillada argentina

12 25 Los símbolos nacionales

Escoge **tres** países distintos y un símbolo para cada uno de ellos. Describe estos símbolos nacionales y habla de cómo y por qué son representativos del país. Después, haz una comparación entre los países y sus símbolos.

12 26 ¿El ecoturismo o una expedición científica?

¡Qué suerte! Recibiste la distinción de ser el/la mejor estudiante de español y puedes elegir entre un viaje de ecoturismo o una expedición antropológica. Piensa en lo que aprendiste de cada país y decide adónde quieres ir para divertirte e investigar más. Después, describe el lugar específico que vas a visitar y di por qué, cómo, cuándo, etc. Si hay dos países con lugares similares, compáralos e indica por qué seleccionaste uno en particular.

Episodio 12

12 27 Tus propias ambiciones siniestras

¡Ahora te toca a ti! Puedes seleccionar entre las siguientes actividades basadas en **Ambiciones siniestras.**

Suggestion for 12-27 Film your students' versions of *Ambiciones siniestras II* and have the class vote on their favorite version.

1. Imagina que eres Oprah o Cristina y que tienes la oportunidad de entrevistar a los actores de **Ambiciones siniestras.** Prepara la entrevista con un/a compañero/a.

2. Escribe tu propia versión reducida de **Ambiciones siniestras.** ¿Termina igual que el original? Compara tu versión con la de un/a compañero/a.

3. Escribe y filma **Ambiciones siniestras II.** Al final, ¿qué pasa con el Sr. Verdugo? Preséntale tu película a la clase.

Y por fin, ¿cómo andas?

Having completed this chapter, I now can...

	Feel Confident	Need to Review
Comunicación		
convey ideas about past experiences and my daily routine	❑	❑
share my preferences regarding food, clothing, and other topics	❑	❑
make requests and give advice using commands	❑	❑
express desires and opinions on a variety of topics	❑	❑
describe my travels and the trips of others	❑	❑
express ideas on topics such as health, animals, the environment, and politics	❑	❑
Cultura		
share information about Chile, Paraguay, Argentina, Uruguay, Perú, Bolivia, Ecuador, Venezuela, Colombia, Cuba, Puerto Rico, and La República Dominicana	❑	❑
compare and contrast many characteristics of the countries I learned about in **Capítulos 7–11**	❑	❑

RECURSOS

PROGRAM

Prepared
Tests A and B

APPENDIX 1

CAPÍTULO PRELIMINAR A

12. Gustar

1. To say you like or dislike one thing, what form of **gustar** do you use?

   gusta

2. To say you like or dislike more than one thing, what form of **gustar** do you use?

   gustan

CAPÍTULO 2

9. El verbo *gustar*

1. To say you like or dislike one thing, what form of **gustar** do you use?

   gusta

2. To say you like or dislike more than one thing, what form of **gustar** do you use?

   gustan

3. Which words in the examples mean *I?* **(Me)** *You?* **(Te)** *He/she?* **(le)**

4. If a verb is needed after gusta/gustan, what form of the verb do you use?

   the infinitive form of the verb

CAPÍTULO 4

4. Los verbos con cambio de raíz

1. Which verb forms look like the infinitive **cerrar**?

   nosotros, vosotros

2. Which verb forms have a spelling change that differs from the infinitive **cerrar**?

   yo, tú, él, ella, usted, ellos, ellas, ustedes.

1. Which verb forms look like the infinitive **pedir**?

   nosotros, vosotros

2. Which verb forms have a spelling change that differs from the infinitive **pedir**?

   yo, tú, él, ella, usted, ellos, ellas, ustedes.

1. Which verb forms look like the infinitive **encontrar**?

   nosotros, vosotros

2. Which verb forms have a spelling change that differs from the infinitive **encontrar**?

   yo, tú, él, ella, usted, ellos, ellas, ustedes.

1. Which verb forms look like the infinitive **jugar**?

   nosotros, vosotros

2. Which verb forms have a spelling change that differs from the infinitive **jugar**?

   yo, tú, él, ella, usted, ellos, ellas, ustedes.

3. Why does **jugar** not belong with the verbs like **encontrar**?

   because the change is *u → ue*, not *o → ue* like *encontrar*.

To summarize...

1. What is a rule that you can make regarding all four groups (e → ie, e → i, o → ue, and u → ue) of stem-changing verbs and their forms?

   Nosotros/vosotros **look like the infinitive. All the other forms have the spelling change.**

2. With what group of stem-changing verbs would you put **querer**?

   e → ie

3. With what group of stem-changing verbs would you put the following verbs:

   demostrar *to demonstrate* **o → ue**
   devolver *to return (an object)* **o → ue**
   encerrar *to enclose* **e → ie**
   perseguir *to chase* **e → i**

6. *Ir + a + infinitivo*

1. When do the actions in these sentences take place: in the past, present, or future?

   future

2. What is the first bold type verb you see in each sentence?

   a form of *ir*

3. In what form is the second bolded verb?

   infinitive

4. What word comes between the two verbs?

   a

   Does this word have an equivalent in English?

   no

5. What is your rule, then, for expressing future actions?

   use a form of *ir + a* + infinitive

8. Las expresiones afirmativas y negativas

1. When you use a negative word (**nadie, nunca,** etc.) in a sentence, does it come before or after the verb?

   The negative word can go before or after the verb.

2. When you use the word **no** and then a negative word in the same sentence, does **no** come before or after the verb? Where does the negative word come in these sentences?

No comes before the verb. The negative word can go before or after the verb.

3. Does the meaning change depending on where you put the negative word? (E.g., **Nadie llama** *versus* **No llama nadie.**)

No, the meaning stays the same.

9. Un repaso de *ser* y *estar*

1. Why do you use a form of **ser** in the first sentence?

because it is a characteristic that remains relatively constant

2. Why do you use a form of **estar** in the second sentence?

because it describes a physical or personality characteristic that can change, or a change in condition

CAPÍTULO 5

2. Los adjetivos demostrativos

1. When do you use **este, ese,** and **aquel**?

when you want to point out *one* masculine person or object

2. When do you use **esta, esa,** and **aquella**?

when you want to point out *one* feminine person or object

3. When do you use **estos, esos,** and **aquellos**?

when you want to point out *two or more* masculine persons or objects, or a mix of masculine and feminine persons or objects

4. When do you use **estas, esas,** and **aquellas**?

when you want to point out *two or more* feminine persons or objects

5. El presente progresivo

1. What is the infinitive of the first verb in each sentence that is in *italics*?

estar

2. What are the infinitives of **haciendo, estudiando, escuchando, tocando, viendo,** and **escribiendo**?

hacer, estudiar, escuchar, tocar, hacer, ver, escribir

3. How do you form the verb forms in **boldface**?

Take the infinitive, drop the *-ar, -er,* or *-ir,* and add *-ando* or *-iendo.*

4. In this new tense, the *present progressive*, do any words come between the two parts of the verb?

no

5. Therefore, your formula for forming the present progressive is:

a form of the verb *estar* + a verb ending in *-ando* or *-iendo*

CAPÍTULO 6

Major grammar points to be reviewed

1. Present tense of:
Regular **ar, er, ir** verbs
Irregular verbs
Stem changing verbs **e → ie, e → i, o → ue, u → ue**

2. Future tense *ir + a + infinitive*

3. Use of direct object pronouns

4. Correctly using *ser* and *estar*

5. Correctly using *gustar*

Major vocabulary to be reviewed

1. The *Vocabulario activo* at the end of each chapter

Major cultural information to be reviewed

1. At least two facts about each of the feature countries

2. At least one point about each of the two culture presentations in each chapter

CAPÍTULO 7

2. Repaso del complemento directo

1. What are direct objects? What are direct object pronouns?

Direct objects receive the action of the verb, answering the questions *what* or *whom.* Direct object pronouns replace direct objects.

2. What are the pronouns (forms)? With what must they agree?

The pronoun forms are *me, te, lo, la, nos, los, las.* They must agree with the direct object.

3. Where are direct object pronouns placed in a sentence?

They are placed either before the verb or attached to the infinitive or *-ando* or *-iendo.*

3. El pretérito

1. What do you notice about the endings for **-er** and **-ir** verbs?

they are the same

2. Where are accent marks needed?

The accent marks are needed on the *yo* and *él/ella/usted* forms.

CAPÍTULO 8

2. Los pronombres de complemento indirecto

1. Who is buying the clothing?
Mi madre.

2. Who is receiving the clothing?

Mi madre **me** compra mucha ropa.
I am receiving the clothes.
Mi madre **te** compra mucha ropa.

You are receiving the clothes.
Mi madre **le** compra mucha ropa a mi hermano.

My brother is receiving the clothes.
Mi madre **nos** compra mucha ropa.
We are receiving the clothes.
Mi madre **os** compra mucha ropa.

You all are receiving the clothes.
Mi madre **les** compra mucha ropa a mis hermanos.
My brothers are receiving the clothes.

¿Me (i.o.) traes la falda de rayas (d.o.)?	*Will you bring me the striped skirt?*
Su novio le (i.o.) regaló la chaqueta de cuero (d.o.).	*Her boyfriend gave her the leather jacket.*
Mi hermana me (i.o.) compró la blusa de seda (d.o.).	*My sister bought me the silk blouse.*
Nuestra compañera de cuarto nos (i.o.) lavó la ropa (d.o.).	*Our roommate washed our clothes for us.*

4. Los pronombres de complemento directo e indirecto usados juntos

1. You know that direct and indirect objects come after the verb. Where do you find the direct and indirect object pronouns?

   before the verb or attached to infinitives or present participles

2. Reading from left to right, which pronoun comes first (direct or indirect)? Which pronoun comes second?

   The indirect object pronoun comes first, and the direct object pronoun comes second.

5. Las construcciones reflexivas

In each drawing:
Who is performing/doing the action?

   a. *La fiesta*   d. *Raúl y Gloria*
   b. *Alberto*   e. *Alberto*
   c. *Beatriz*   f. *Beatriz*

Who or what is receiving the action?

   a. *neighbors*   d. *Raúl and Gloria*
   b. *daughter*   e. *Alberto*
   c. *car*   f. *Beatriz*

Which of the drawings and captions demonstrate reflexive verbs?

   d, e, f (the bottom row.)

CAPÍTULO 10

3. Los mandatos formales

1. Where do the object pronouns appear in affirmative commands? In negative commands? In what order?

   attached to the command; before the command and not attached; IO / DO

2. Why are there written accents on some of the commands and not on others?

   because some commands would change pronunciation without the accent mark

5. Otras formas del posesivo

1. What is the position of each possessive in the left-hand column? in the middle column?

   before the noun; after the noun

2. How do the possessive adjectives and pronouns agree?

   They agree in number and gender with the nouns they describe or replace.

3. What do the sentences mean in the column on the right? What have you removed from the previous sentence?

   Mine works fine; Ours cost a lot; Where are yours? His/hers/yours is $100; the noun

CAPÍTULO 11

3. El subjuntivo

1. What is the difference between the subjunctive and the indicative moods?

   The subjunctive expresses concepts such as doubts, emotions, wishes, and desires. The indicative reports events and happenings.

2. What other verb forms look like the subjunctive?

   The *Usted* and *Ustedes* commands.

3. Where does the subjunctive verb come in relation to the word **que?**

   after the word *que*

CAPÍTULO 12

Major grammar points to be reviewed

1. Past tenses:
   Regular and irregular preterit
   Regular and irregular imperfect
   Uses of the preterit and imperfect

2. Pronouns:
   Direct object
   Indirect object
   Reflexive
   Placement of pronouns

3. Commands:
   Familiar affirmative and negative
   Formal affirmative and negative

4. Subjunctive:
   Formation
   Usage

Major vocabulary to be reviewed

1. The **Vocabulario activo** at the end of each chapter

Major cultural information to be reviewed

1. At least two facts about each of the feature countries

2. At least one point about each of the two culture presentations in each chapter

Regular Verbs: Simple Tenses

Infinitive Present Participle Past Participle	Indicative						Subjunctive		Imperative
	Present	Imperfect	Preterit	Future	Conditional		Present	Imperfect	
hablar	hablo	hablaba	hablé	hablaré	hablaría		hable	hablara	
hablando	hablas	hablabas	hablaste	hablarás	hablarías		hables	hablaras	habla (tú),
hablado	habla	hablaba	habló	hablará	hablaría		hable	hablara	no hables
	hablamos	hablábamos	hablamos	hablaremos	hablaríamos		hablemos	habláramos	hable (usted)
	habláis	hablabais	hablasteis	hablaréis	hablaríais		habléis	hablarais	hablemos
	hablan	hablaban	hablaron	hablarán	hablarían		hablen	hablaran	hablen (Uds.)
comer	como	comía	comí	comeré	comería		coma	comiera	
comiendo	comes	comías	comiste	comerás	comerías		comas	comieras	come (tú),
comido	come	comía	comió	comerá	comería		coma	comiera	no comas
	comemos	comíamos	comimos	comeremos	comeríamos		comamos	comiéramos	coma (usted)
	coméis	comíais	comisteis	comeréis	comeríais		comáis	comierais	comamos
	comen	comían	comieron	comerán	comerían		coman	comieran	coman (Uds.)
vivir	vivo	vivía	viví	viviré	viviría		viva	viviera	
viviendo	vives	vivías	viviste	vivirás	vivirías		vivas	vivieras	vive (tú),
vivido	vive	vivía	vivió	vivirá	viviría		viva	viviera	no vivas
	vivimos	vivíamos	vivimos	viviremos	viviríamos		vivamos	viviéramos	viva (usted)
	vivís	vivíais	vivisteis	viviréis	viviríais		viváis	vivierais	vivamos
	viven	vivían	vivieron	vivirán	vivirían		vivan	vivieran	vivan (Uds.)

Vosotros Commands

hablar	comer	vivir
hablad, no habléis	comed, no comáis	vivid, no viváis

Regular Verbs: Perfect Tenses

Indicative					Subjunctive	
Present Perfect	Past Perfect	Preterit Perfect	Future Perfect	Conditional Perfect	Present Perfect	Past Perfect
he has ha hemos habéis han	había habías había habíamos habíais habían	hube hubiste hubo hubimos hubisteis hubieron	habré habrás habrá habremos habréis habrán	habría habrías habría habríamos habríais habrían	haya hayas haya hayamos hayáis hayan	hubiera hubieras hubiera hubiéramos hubierais hubieran

(+ hablado / comido / vivido in each tense)

Irregular Verbs

Infinitive Present Participle Past Participle	Indicative					Subjunctive		Imperative
	Present	Imperfect	Preterit	Future	Conditional	Present	Imperfect	
andar andando andado	ando andas anda andamos andáis andan	andaba andabas andaba andábamos andabais andaban	anduve anduviste anduvo anduvimos anduvisteis anduvieron	andaré andarás andará andaremos andaréis andarán	andaría andarías andaría andaríamos andaríais andarían	ande andes ande andemos andéis anden	anduviera anduvieras anduviera anduviéramos anduvierais anduvieran	anda (tú), no andes ande (usted) andemos anden (Uds.)
caer cayendo caído	caigo caes cae caemos caéis caen	caía caías caía caíamos caíais caían	caí caíste cayó caímos caísteis cayeron	caeré caerás caerá caeremos caeréis caerán	caería caerías caería caeríamos caeríais caerían	caiga caigas caiga caigamos caigáis caigan	cayera cayeras cayera cayéramos cayerais cayeran	cae (tú), no caigas caiga (usted) caigamos caigan (Uds.)
dar dando dado	doy das da damos dais dan	daba dabas daba dábamos dabais daban	di diste dio dimos disteis dieron	daré darás dará daremos daréis darán	daría darías daría daríamos daríais darían	dé des dé demos deis den	diera dieras diera diéramos dierais dieran	da (tú), no des dé (usted) demos den (Uds.)

Irregular Verbs (continued)

Infinitive / Present Participle / Past Participle	Indicative Present	Imperfect	Preterit	Future	Conditional	Subjunctive Present	Imperfect	Imperative
decir diciendo dicho	digo dices dice decimos decís dicen	decía decías decía decíamos decíais decían	dije dijiste dijo dijimos dijisteis dijeron	diré dirás dirá diremos diréis dirán	diría dirías diría diríamos diríais dirían	diga digas diga digamos digáis digan	dijera dijeras dijera dijéramos dijerais dijeran	di (tú), no digas diga (usted) digamos decid (vosotros), no digáis digan (Uds.)
estar estando estado	estoy estás está estamos estáis están	estaba estabas estaba estábamos estabais estaban	estuve estuviste estuvo estuvimos estuvisteis estuvieron	estaré estarás estará estaremos estaréis estarán	estaría estarías estaría estaríamos estaríais estarían	esté estés esté estemos estéis estén	estuviera estuvieras estuviera estuviéramos estuvierais estuvieran	está (tú), no estés esté (usted) estemos estad (vosotros), no estéis estén (Uds.)
haber habiendo habido	he has ha hemos habéis han	había habías había habíamos habíais habían	hube hubiste hubo hubimos hubisteis hubieron	habré habrás habrá habremos habréis habrán	habría habrías habría habríamos habríais habrían	haya hayas haya hayamos hayáis hayan	hubiera hubieras hubiera hubiéramos hubierais hubieran	
hacer haciendo hecho	hago haces hace hacemos hacéis hacen	hacía hacías hacía hacíamos hacíais hacían	hice hiciste hizo hicimos hicisteis hicieron	haré harás hará haremos haréis harán	haría harías haría haríamos haríais harían	haga hagas haga hagamos hagáis hagan	hiciera hicieras hiciera hiciéramos hicierais hicieran	haz (tú), no hagas haga (usted) hagamos haced (vosotros), no hagáis hagan (Uds.)
ir yendo ido	voy vas va vamos vais van	iba ibas iba íbamos ibais iban	fui fuiste fue fuimos fuisteis fueron	iré irás irá iremos iréis irán	iría irías iría iríamos iríais irían	vaya vayas vaya vayamos vayáis vayan	fuera fueras fuera fuéramos fuerais fueran	ve (tú), no vayas vaya (usted) vamos, no vayamos id (vosotros), no vayáis vayan (Uds.)

Irregular Verbs (continued)

Infinitive Present Participle Past Participle	Indicative					Subjunctive		Imperative
	Present	Imperfect	Preterit	Future	Conditional	Present	Imperfect	
oír oyendo oído	oigo oyes oye oímos oís oyen	oía oías oía oíamos oíais oían	oí oíste oyó oímos oísteis oyeron	oiré oirás oirá oiremos oiréis oirán	oiría oirías oiría oiríamos oiríais oirían	oiga oigas oiga oigamos oigáis oigan	oyera oyeras oyera oyéramos oyerais oyeran	oye (tú), no oigas oiga (usted) oigamos oigan (Uds.)
poder pudiendo podido	puedo puedes puede podemos podéis pueden	podía podías podía podíamos podíais podían	pude pudiste pudo pudimos pudisteis pudieron	podré podrás podrá podremos podréis podrán	podría podrías podría podríamos podríais podrían	pueda puedas pueda podamos podáis puedan	pudiera pudieras pudiera pudiéramos pudierais pudieran	
poner poniendo puesto	pongo pones pone ponemos ponéis ponen	ponía ponías ponía poníamos poníais ponían	puse pusiste puso pusimos pusisteis pusieron	pondré pondrás pondrá pondremos pondréis pondrán	pondría pondrías pondría pondríamos pondríais pondrían	ponga pongas ponga pongamos pongáis pongan	pusiera pusieras pusiera pusiéramos pusierais pusieran	pon (tú), no pongas ponga (usted) pongamos pongan (Uds.)
querer queriendo querido	quiero quieres quiere queremos queréis quieren	quería querías quería queríamos queríais querían	quise quisiste quiso quisimos quisisteis quisieron	querré querrás querrá querremos querréis querrán	querría querrías querría querríamos querríais querrían	quiera quieras quiera queramos queráis quieran	quisiera quisieras quisiera quisiéramos quisierais quisieran	quiere (tú), no quieras quiera (usted) queramos quieran (Uds.)
saber sabiendo sabido	sé sabes sabe sabemos sabéis saben	sabía sabías sabía sabíamos sabíais sabían	supe supiste supo supimos supisteis supieron	sabré sabrás sabrá sabremos sabréis sabrán	sabría sabrías sabría sabríamos sabríais sabrían	sepa sepas sepa sepamos sepáis sepan	supiera supieras supiera supiéramos supierais supieran	sabe (tú), no sepas sepa (usted) sepamos sepan (Uds.)

Irregular Verbs (continued)

Infinitive Present Participle Past Participle	Indicative					Subjunctive		Imperative
	Present	Imperfect	Preterit	Future	Conditional	Present	Imperfect	
salir saliendo salido	salgo sales sale salimos salís salen	salía salías salía salíamos salíais salían	salí saliste salió salimos salisteis salieron	saldré saldrás saldrá saldremos saldréis saldrán	saldría saldrías saldría saldríamos saldríais saldrían	salga salgas salga salgamos salgáis salgan	saliera salieras saliera saliéramos salierais salieran	sal (tú), no salgas salga (usted) salgamos salgan (Uds.)
ser siendo sido	soy eres es somos sois son	era eras era éramos erais eran	fui fuiste fue fuimos fuisteis fueron	seré serás será seremos seréis serán	sería serías sería seríamos seríais serían	sea seas sea seamos seáis sean	fuera fueras fuera fuéramos fuerais fueran	sé (tú), no seas sea (usted) seamos sed (vosotros), no seáis sean (Uds.)
tener teniendo tenido	tengo tienes tiene tenemos tenéis tienen	tenía tenías tenía teníamos teníais tenían	tuve tuviste tuvo tuvimos tuvisteis tuvieron	tendré tendrás tendrá tendremos tendréis tendrán	tendría tendrías tendría tendríamos tendríais tendrían	tenga tengas tenga tengamos tengáis tengan	tuviera tuvieras tuviera tuviéramos tuvierais tuvieran	ten (tú), no tengas tenga (usted) tengamos tened (vosotros), no tengáis tengan (Uds.)
traer trayendo traído	traigo traes trae traemos traéis traen	traía traías traía traíamos traíais traían	traje trajiste trajo trajimos trajisteis trajeron	traeré traerás traerá traeremos traeréis traerán	traería traerías traería traeríamos traeríais traerían	traiga traigas traiga traigamos traigáis traigan	trajera trajeras trajera trajéramos trajerais trajeran	trae (tú), no traigas traiga (usted) traigamos traed (vosotros), no traigáis traigan (Uds.)
venir viniendo venido	vengo vienes viene venimos venís vienen	venía venías venía veníamos veníais venían	vine viniste vino vinimos vinisteis vinieron	vendré vendrás vendrá vendremos vendréis vendrán	vendría vendrías vendría vendríamos vendríais vendrían	venga vengas venga vengamos vengáis vengan	viniera vinieras viniera viniéramos vinierais vinieran	ven (tú), no vengas venga (usted) vengamos venid (vosotros), no vengáis vengan (Uds.)

Irregular Verbs (continued)

Infinitive / Present Participle / Past Participle	Indicative Present	Indicative Imperfect	Indicative Preterit	Indicative Future	Indicative Conditional	Subjunctive Present	Subjunctive Imperfect	Imperative
ver	veo	veía	vi	veré	vería	vea	viera	
viendo	ves	veías	viste	verás	verías	veas	vieras	ve (tú),
visto	ve	veía	vio	verá	vería	vea	viera	no veas
	vemos	veíamos	vimos	veremos	veríamos	veamos	viéramos	vea (usted)
	véis	veíais	visteis	veréis	veríais	veáis	vierais	veamos
	ven	veían	vieron	verán	verían	vean	vieran	ved (vosotros),
								no veáis
								vean (Uds.)

Stem-Changing and Orthographic-Changing Verbs

Infinitive / Present Participle / Past Participle	Indicative Present	Indicative Imperfect	Indicative Preterit	Indicative Future	Indicative Conditional	Subjunctive Present	Subjunctive Imperfect	Imperative
almorzar (z, c)	almuerzo	almorzaba	almorcé	almorzaré	almorzaría	almuerce	almorzara	almuerza (tú)
almorzando	almuerzas	almorzabas	almorzaste	almorzarás	almorzarías	almuerces	almorzaras	no almuerces
almorzado	almuerza	almorzaba	almorzó	almorzará	almorzaría	almuerce	almorzaras	almuerce (usted)
	almorzamos	almorzábamos	almorzamos	almorzaremos	almorzaríamos	almorcemos	almorzáramos	almorcemos
	almorzáis	almorzabais	almorzasteis	almorzaréis	almorzaríais	almorcéis	almorzarais	almorzad
	almuerzan	almorzaban	almorzaron	almorzarán	almorzarían	almuercen	almorzaran	(vosotros)
								no almorcéis
								almuercen (Uds.)
buscar (c, qu)	busco	buscaba	busqué	buscaré	buscaría	busque	buscara	busca (tú)
buscando	buscas	buscabas	buscaste	buscarás	buscarías	busques	buscaras	no busques
buscado	busca	buscaba	buscó	buscará	buscaría	busque	buscara	busque (usted)
	buscamos	buscábamos	buscamos	buscaremos	buscaríamos	busquemos	buscáramos	busquemos
	buscáis	buscabais	buscasteis	buscaréis	buscaríais	busquéis	buscarais	buscad
	buscan	buscaban	buscaron	buscarán	buscarían	busquen	buscaran	(vosotros)
								no busquéis
								busquen (Uds.)

Stem-Changing and Orthographic-Changing Verbs (continued)

Infinitive / Present Participle / Past Participle	Indicative Present	Indicative Imperfect	Indicative Preterit	Indicative Future	Indicative Conditional	Subjunctive Present	Subjunctive Imperfect	Imperative
corregir (g, j) corrigiendo corregido	corrijo corriges corrige corregimos corregís corrigen	corregía corregías corregía corregíamos corregíais corregían	corregí corregiste corrigió corregimos corregisteis corrigieron	corregiré corregirás corregirá corregiremos corregiréis corregirán	corregiría corregirías corregiría corregiríamos corregiríais corregirían	corrija corrijas corrija corrijamos corrijáis corrijan	corrigiera corrigieras corrigiera corrigiéramos corrigierais corrigieran	corrige (tú), no corrijas corrija (usted) corrijamos corregid (vosotros), no corrijáis corrijan (Uds.)
dormir (ue, u) durmiendo dormido	duermo duermes duerme dormimos dormís duermen	dormía dormías dormía dormíamos dormíais dormían	dormí dormiste durmió dormimos dormisteis durmieron	dormiré dormirás dormirá dormiremos dormiréis dormirán	dormiría dormirías dormiría dormiríamos dormiríais dormirían	duerma duermas duerma durmamos durmáis duerman	durmiera durmieras durmiera durmiéramos durmierais durmieran	duerme (tú), no duermas duerma (usted) durmamos dormid (vosotros), no durmáis duerman (Uds.)
incluir (y) incluyendo incluido	incluyo incluyes incluye incluimos incluís incluyen	incluía incluías incluía incluíamos incluíais incluían	incluí incluiste incluyó incluimos incluisteis incluyeron	incluiré incluirás incluirá incluiremos incluiréis incluirán	incluiría incluirías incluiría incluiríamos incluiríais incluirían	incluya incluyas incluya incluyamos incluyáis incluyan	incluyera incluyeras incluyera incluyéramos incluyerais incluyeran	incluye (tú), no incluyas incluya (usted) incluyamos incluid (vosotros), no incluyáis incluyan (Uds.)
llegar (g, gu) llegando llegado	llego llegas llega llegamos llegáis llegan	llegaba llegabas llegaba llegábamos llegabais llegaban	llegué llegaste llegó llegamos llegasteis llegaron	llegaré llegarás llegará llegaremos llegaréis llegarán	llegaría llegarías llegaría llegaríamos llegaríais llegarían	llegue llegues llegue lleguemos lleguéis lleguen	llegara llegaras llegara llegáramos llegareis llegaran	llega (tú), no llegues llegue (usted) lleguemos llegad (vosotros), no lleguéis lleguen (Uds.)
pedir (i, i) pidiendo pedido	pido pides pide pedimos pedís piden	pedía pedías pedía pedíamos pedíais pedían	pedí pediste pidió pedimos pedisteis pidieron	pediré pedirás pedirá pediremos pediréis pedirán	pediría pedirías pediría pediríamos pediríais pedirían	pida pidas pida pidamos pidáis pidan	pidiera pidieras pidiera pidiéramos pidierais pidieran	pide (tú), no pidas pida (usted) pidamos pedid (vosotros), no pidáis pidan (Uds.)

Stem-Changing and Orthographic-Changing Verbs (continued)

Infinitive / Present Participle / Past Participle	Indicative					Subjunctive		Imperative
	Present	Imperfect	Preterit	Future	Conditional	Present	Imperfect	
pensar (ie) pensando pensado	pienso piensas piensa pensamos pensáis piensan	pensaba pensabas pensaba pensábamos pensabais pensaban	pensé pensaste pensó pensamos pensasteis pensaron	pensaré pensarás pensará pensaremos pensaréis pensarán	pensaría pensarías pensaría pensaríamos pensaríais pensarían	piense pienses piense pensemos penséis piensen	pensara pensaras pensara pensáramos pensarais pensaran	piensa (tú), no pienses piense (usted) pensemos pensad (vosotros), no penséis piensen (Uds.)
producir (zc) produciendo producido	produzco produces produce producimos producís producen	producía producías producía producíamos producíais producían	produje produjiste produjo produjimos produjisteis produjeron	produciré producirás producirá produciremos produciréis producirán	produciría producirías produciría produciríamos produciríais producirían	produzca produzcas produzca produzcamos produzcáis produzcan	produjera produjeras produjera produjéramos produjerais produjeran	produce (tú), no produzcas produzca (usted) produzcamos producid (vosotros), no produzcáis produzcan (Uds.)
reír (i, i) riendo reído	río ríes ríe reímos reís ríen	reía reías reía reíamos reíais reían	reí reíste rio reímos reísteis rieron	reiré reirás reirá reiremos reiréis reirán	reiría reirías reiría reiríamos reiríais reirían	ría rías ría riamos riáis rían	riera rieras riera riéramos rierais rieran	ríe (tú), no rías ría (usted) riamos reíd (vosotros), no riáis rían (Uds.)
seguir (i, i) (ga) siguiendo seguido	sigo sigues sigue seguimos seguís siguen	seguía seguías seguía seguíamos seguíais seguían	seguí seguiste siguió seguimos seguisteis siguieron	seguiré seguirás seguirá seguiremos seguiréis seguirán	seguiría seguirías seguiría seguiríamos seguiríais seguirían	siga sigas siga sigamos sigáis sigan	siguiera siguieras siguiera siguiéramos siguierais siguieran	sigue (tú), no sigas siga (usted) sigamos seguid (vosotros), no sigáis sigan (Uds.)
sentir (ie, i) sintiendo sentido	siento sientes siente sentimos sentís sienten	sentía sentías sentía sentíamos sentíais sentían	sentí sentiste sintió sentimos sentisteis sintieron	sentiré sentirás sentirá sentiremos sentiréis sentirán	sentiría sentirías sentiría sentiríamos sentiríais sentirían	sienta sientas sienta sintamos sintáis sientan	sintiera sintieras sintiera sintiéramos sintierais sintieran	siente (tú), no sientas sienta (usted) sintamos sentid (vosotros), no sintáis sientan (Uds.)

Stem-Changing and Orthographic-Changing Verbs (continued)

Infinitive Present Participle Past Participle	Indicative					Subjunctive		Imperative
	Present	Imperfect	Preterit	Future	Conditional	Present	Imperfect	
volver (ue) volviendo vuelto	vuelvo vuelves vuelve volvemos volvéis vuelven	volvía volvías volvía volvíamos volvíais volvían	volví volviste volvió volvimos volvisteis volvieron	volveré volverás volverá volveremos volveréis volverán	volvería volverías volvería volveríamos volveríais volverían	vuelva vuelvas vuelva volvamos volváis vuelvan	volviera volvieras volviera volviéramos volvierais volvieran	vuelve (tú), no vuelvas vuelva (usted) volvamos volved (vosotros), no volváis vuelvan (Uds.)

APPENDIX 3

CAPÍTULO PRELIMINAR A

Los saludos/*Greetings*

¿Cómo andas? *How are you doing?*
¿Cómo vas? *How are you doing?*
El gusto es mío. *Pleased to meet you; The pleasure is all mine.*
Hasta entonces. *Until then.*
¿Qué hubo? *How's it going? What's happening? What's new?*
¿Qué pasa? *How's it going? What's happening? What's new?*
¿Qué pasó? *How's it going? What's happening? What's new?*

Las despedidas/*Farewells*

Nos vemos. *See you.*
Que te vaya bien. *Hope everything goes well.*
Que tenga(s) un buen día. *Have a nice day.*
Vaya con Dios. *Go with God.*

Las presentaciones/*Introductions*

Me gustaría presentarle a... *I would like to introduce you to... (formal)*
Me gustaría presentarte a... *I would like to introduce you to... (familiar)*

Expresiones útiles para la clase/*Useful classroom expressions*

Preguntas y respuestas/*Questions and answers*

(No) entiendo. *I (don't) understand.*
¿Puede repetir, por favor? *Could you repeat, please?*

Expresiones de cortesía/*Polite expressions*

Muchas gracias. *Thank you very much.*
No hay de qué. *Not at all.*

Mandatos para la clase/*Instructions for class*

Saque(n) un bolígrafo/papel/lápiz. *Take out a pen/a piece of paper/pencil.*

Las nacionalidades/*Nationalities*

argentino/a *Argentinian*
boliviano/a *Bolivian*
chileno/a *Chilean*
colombiano/a *Colombian*
costarricense *Costa Rican*
dominicano/a *Dominican*
ecuatoriano/a *Ecuadorian*
guatemalteco/a *Guatemalan*
hondureño/a *Honduran*
nicaragüense *Nicaraguan*
panameño/a *Panamanian*
peruano/a *Peruvian*
uruguayo/a *Uruguayan*
venezolano/a *Venezuelan*

Expresiones del tiempo/*Weather expressions*

el arco iris *rainbow*
el chirimiri *drizzle (Spain)*
Está despejado. *It's clear.*
Hace fresco. *It's cool.*
Hay neblina/niebla. *It's foggy.*
la humedad *humidity*
los copos de nieve *snowflakes*
las gotas de lluvia *raindrops*
el granizo *hail*
el hielo *ice*
el huracán *hurricane*
la llovizna *drizzle*
el pronóstico *weather forecast*
el/los rayo/s, el relámpago *lightning*
la tormenta *storm*
el tornado *tornado*
el/los trueno/s *thunder*

CAPÍTULO 1

La familia/*Family*

el/la ahijado/a *godchild*
el bisabuelo *great-grandfather*
la bisabuela *great-grandmother*
el/la cuñado/a *brother-in-law/sister-in-law*
la familia política *in-laws*
el/la hermanastro/a *stepbrother/stepsister*
el/la hijastro/a *stepson/stepdaughter*
el/la hijo/a único/a *only child*
la madrina *godmother*
el/la medio/a hermano/a *half brother/half sister*
los medios hermanos *half brothers and sisters*
la mami *Mommy; Mom (Latin America)*
el marido *husband*
la mujer *wife*
el/la nieto/a *grandson/granddaughter*
los nietos *grandchildren*
la nuera *daughter-in-law*
el padrino *godfather*
el papi *Daddy; Dad (Latin America)*
el pariente *relative*
el/la prometido/a *fiancé(e)*
los sobrinos *nieces and nephews*
el/la suegro/a *father-in-law/mother-in-law*
los suegros *in-laws*
la tatarabuela *great-great-grandmother*
el tatarabuelo *great-great-grandfather*
la tía abuela *great-aunt*
el tío abuelo *great-uncle*
el/la viudo/a *widower/widow*
el yerno *son-in-law*

Otra palabra útil/*Another useful word*

divorciado/a *divorced*

La gente/*People*

el bato *friend; guy (in SE USA slang)*
el/la chaval/a *young man/young woman (Spain)*
el chamaco *young man (Cuba, Honduras, Mexico, El Salvador)*
el/la fulano/a *unknown man/woman*

Los adjetivos/*Adjectives*

La personalidad y otros rasgos/*Personality and other characteristics*

amable *nice; kind*
bobo/a *stupid; silly*
el/la bromista *person who likes to play jokes*
cariñoso/a *loving; affectionate*
chistoso/a *funny*
cursi *pretentious; affected*
divertido/a *funny*
educado/a *well-mannered; polite*
elegante *elegant*
empollón/ona *bookworm; nerd*
encantador/a *charming; lovely*
espabilado/a *smart; vivacious; alert (Latin America)*
frustrado/a *frustrated*
gracioso/a *funny*
grosero/a *unpleasant*
histérico/a *crazed*
impaciente *impatient*
indiferente *indifferent*
irresponsable *irresponsible*
malvado/a *evil; wicked*
majo/a *pretty; nice (Spain)*
mono/a *pretty; nice (Spain, Caribbean)*
odioso/a *unpleasant*
pesado/a *annoying person*
pijo/a *posh; snooty (Spain)*
progre *liberal; progressive (Spain)*
sabelotodo/a *know-it-all*
viejo/a *old*

Las características físicas/*Physical characteristics*

atlético/a *athletic*
bello/a *beautiful (Latin America)*
blando/a *soft*
esbelto/a *slender*
flaco/a *thin*
frágil *fragile*
hermoso/a *beautiful; lovely*
musculoso/a *muscular*
robusto/a *sturdy*

Otras palabras útiles/*Other useful words*

demasiado/a *too much*
suficiente *enough*

CAPÍTULO 2

Las materias y las especialidades/*Subjects and majors*

la agronomía *agriculture*
la antropología *anthropology*
el cálculo *calculus*
las ciencias políticas *political sciences*
las comunicaciones *communications*
la contabilidad *accounting*
la economía *economics*
la educación física *physical education*
la enfermería *nursing*

la filosofía *philosophy*
la física *physics*
la geografía *geography*
la geología *geology*
la historia *history*
la ingeniería *engineering*
la literatura comparada *comparative literature*
el mercadeo *marketing (Latin America)*
la mercadotecnia (el márketing) *marketing (Spain)*
la medicina del deporte *sports medicine*
la química *chemistry*
los servicios sociales *social work*
la sociología *sociology*
la terapia física *physical therapy*

En la sala de clase/*In the classroom*

el aula *classroom*
el/la alumno/a *student*
la bombilla *light bulb*
la cámara proyectora *overhead camera*
el cielorraso *ceiling*
el enchufe *wall socket*
el interruptor *light switch*
las luces *lights*
el ordenador *computer (Spain)*
la pantalla *screen*
el proyector *projector*
la prueba *test*
el pupitre *student desk*
el rotulador *marker*
el sacapuntas *pencil sharpener*
el suelo *floor*
la tarima *dais; platform*

Los verbos/*Verbs*

apuntar *to point*
asistir a clase *to attend class*
beber *to drink*
entrar *to enter*
entregar *to hand in*
mirar *to look; observe*
prestar atención *to pay attention*
repasar *to review*
responder *to answer*
sacar *to take out*
sacar buenas/malas notas *to get good/bad grades*
tomar apuntes *to take notes*

Las palabras interrogativas/*Interrogative words*

¿Con cuánto/a/os/as? *With how many...?*
¿Con qué? *With what...?*
¿Con quién? *With whom...?*
¿De dónde? *From where...?*
¿De qué? *About what...?*
¿De quién? *Of whom...?*

Emociones y estados/*Emotions and states of being*

agotado/a *exhausted*
agradable *nice*
alegre *happy*
asombrado/a *amazed; astonished*

asqueado/a *disgusted*
asustado/a *scared*
deprimido/a *depressed*
desanimado/a *discouraged; disheartened*
disgustado/a *upset*
dormido/a *sleepy*
emocionado/a *moved; touched*
entusiasmado/a *delighted*
fastidiado/a *annoyed; bothered*
ilusionado/a *thrilled*
optimista *optimistic*
pesimista *pessimistic*
retrasado/a *late*
sonriente *smiling*
soñoliento/a *sleepy (Spain)*

Los lugares/*Places*

el apartamento estudiantil *student apartment*
el campo de fútbol *football field*
el campus *campus*
la cancha de tenis/baloncesto *tennis/basketball court*
la/s casa/s de hermandad/es *fraternity and sorority housing*
el centro comercial *mall*
el comedor estudiantil *student dining hall*
la habitación *room*
la matrícula *registration*
el museo *museum*
la oficina de consejeros *guidance/advising office*
el supermercado *supermarket*
el teatro *theater*

La residencia/*The dorm*

los bafles *speakers (Spain)*
el calendario *calendar*
la cama *bed*
el iPod *iPod*
el Internet *Web*
las literas *bunkbeds*
la llave *memory stick*
la mesita de noche *nightstand*
el móvil *cell phone (Spain)*
la redacción/la composición *essay*
la tarjeta de crédito *credit card*
la tarjeta de identidad; el carnet *ID card*
los videojuegos *video games*

Los deportes y los pasatiempos/*Sports and pastimes*

cazar *to hunt*
conversar con amigos *to talk with friends*
escalar *to go mountain climbing*
esquiar *to ski*
estar en forma *to be in shape*
hablar por teléfono *to talk on the phone*
hacer alpinismo *to go hiking*
hacer el footing *to go jogging (Spain)*
hacer gimnasia *to exercise*
hacer senderismo *to hike*
hacer yoga *to do yoga*
ir al centro comercial *to go the mall; to go downtown*
ir a fiestas *to go to parties*
ir a un partido de... *to go to a ... (game)*

jugar al ajedrez *to play chess*
jugar al boliche *to bowl*
jugar al ráquetbol *to play racquetball*
jugar juegos electrónicos *to play video games*
levantar pesas *to lift weights*
mirar videos *to watch videos*
montar a caballo *to go horseback riding*
pasear *to go out for a ride; to take a walk*
pasear en barco *to sail*
ir a navegar *to sail*
pescar *to fish*
practicar boxeo *to box*
practicar ciclismo *to cycle*
practicar lucha libre *to wrestle*
practicar las artes marciales *to do martial arts*
salir a cenar/comer *to go out to dinner/eat*
tirar un platillo volador *to throw a Frisbee*

Palabras asociadas con los deportes y los pasatiempos/*Words associated with sports and pastimes*

el/la aficionado/a *fan*
el bate *bat*
el campo *field*
los libros de...
   acción *action books*
   aventura *adventure books*
   cuentos cortos *short stories*
   ficción (ciencia-ficción) *fiction (science fiction)*
   horror *horror books*
   misterio *mystery books*
   romance *romance books*
   espías *spy books*
el palo de golf *golf club*
la pista *track*
la pista y el campo *track and field (Spain)*
la raqueta *racket*

CAPÍTULO 3

La casa/*The house*

la alcoba *bedroom*
el armario empotrado *closet (Spain)*
el ático *attic*
la bodega *cellar*
la buhardilla *attic*
el clóset *closet (Latin America)*
el corredor *hall*
el cuarto *bedroom*
el despacho *office*
el desván *attic*
el pasillo *hallway*
el patio *patio; yard*
el placar *closet (Argentina)*
el portal *porch*
el porche *porch*
la recámara *bedroom (Mexico)*
el salón *salon; lounge; living room*
el tejado *roof*
la terraza *terrace; porch*
el vestíbulo *entrance hall*

En la sala y el comedor/*In the living room and dining room*

la banqueta/el banquillo *small seating stool*
la estantería *bookcase*
la mecedora *rocking chair*
la moqueta *carpet (Spain)*

En la cocina/*In the kitchen*

el congelador *deep freezer*
el friegaplatos *diswasher*
el frigorífico *refrigerator (Spain)*
el horno *oven*
el lavavajillas *dishwasher (Spain)*
el taburete *bar stool*

Otras palabras/*Other words*

el aparato eléctrico *electric appliance*
la chimenea *chimney*
la cómoda *dresser*
las cortinas *curtains*
el espejo *mirror*
el fregadero *sink*
los gabinetes *cabinets*
la lavadora *washer*
la secadora *dryer*
el librero *bookcase (Mexico)*
la nevera *refrigerator*
las persianas *shutters; window blinds*

En el baño/*In the bathroom*

la cisterna *toilet water tank*
el espejo *mirror*
los grifos *faucets*
la jabonera *soap dish*
el toallero *towel rack*

En el dormitorio/*In the bedroom*

el edredón *comforter*
la frazada *blanket (Latin America)*

Los quehaceres de la casa/*Household chores*

barrer *to sweep*
cortar el césped *to cut the grass*
fregar los platos *to wash the dishes*
fregar los suelos *to clean the floors*
guardar la ropa *to put away clothes*
lavar la ropa *to do laundry*
ordenar *to put in order*
planchar la ropa *to iron*
recoger *to clean up in general*
recoger la mesa *to clean up after a meal*
regar las plantas *to water the plants*
sacudir las alfombras *to shake out the rugs*

Expresiones con *tener/Expressions with* **tener**

tener celos *to be jealous*
tener novio/a *to have a boyfriend/girlfriend*

Los colores/*Colors*

púrpura *purple (Spain)*
azul/verde claro *light blue/green*
azul/verde oscuro *dark blue/green*
rosa *pink (Spain)*

CAPÍTULO 4

Lugares en una ciudad o pueblo/*Places in a city or town*

la alberca *swimming pool—sports complex (Mexico)*
el ambulatorio *medical center—(not a hospital) (Spain)*
el aseo *public restroom*
la catedral *cathedral*
el campo de golf *golf course*
la capilla *chapel*
la clínica *clinic*
el consultorio *doctor's office*
el convento *convent*
la cuadra *block (Latin America)*
la ferretería *hardware store*
la fogata *bonfire*
la frutería *fruit store*
la fuente *fountain*
la gasolinera *gas station*
la heladería *ice cream shop*
la manzana *block (Spain)*
el mercadillo *open-air market*
la mezquita *mosque*
la papelería *stationary store*
la panadería *bread store*
la pastelería *pastry shop*
la pescadería *fish shop; fishmonger*
la piscina *pool*
el polideportivo *sports center*
el quiosco *newsstand*
los servicios *public restrooms*
la sinagoga *synagogue*
la tienda de juguetes *toy store*
la tienda de ropa *clothing store*
el zócalo *plaza (Mexico)*

CAPÍTULO 5

El mundo de la música/*The world of music*

la musica...alternativa *alternative*
          ...bluegrass *bluegrass*
el coro *the choir*
el cuarteto *quartet*
el equipo de cámara/sonido *camera/sound crew*
el/la mánager *manager*
el merengue *merengue*
la música popular *popular music*
el/la organista *organist*
la pandilla *gang; posse*
los seguidores *groupies*
el teclado *keyboard*

El mundo del cine/The world of film

Gente/*People*

el/la cinematógrafo/a *cinematographer*
el/la director/a *director*
el/la guionista *scriptwriter*

Las películas/*Movies*

el cortometraje *short (film)*
los dibujos animados *cartoons*
el guión *script*
el montaje *montage*

CAPÍTULO 7

Las carnes y las aves/*Meats and poultry*

las aves de corral *poultry*
la carne de cerdo *pork*
la carne de cordero *lamb*
la carne de res *beef*
la carne molida *ground beef*
la carne picada *ground beef (Spain)*
el chorizo *highly seasoned pork sausage*
la chuleta *chop*
el chuletón *T-bone (Spain)*
el jamón serrano *prosciutto ham (Spain)*
el pavo *turkey*
la salchicha *sausage; hot dog*
el salchichón *spiced sausage (Spain)*
la ternera *veal*
el tocino *bacon*

El pescado y los mariscos/*Fish and seafood*

las almejas *clams*
las anchoas *anchovies*
los calamares *squid*
el cangrejo *crab*
el chillo *red snapper (Puerto Rico)*
las gambas *shrimp*
el huachinango *red snapper (Mexico)*
la langosta *lobster*
el lenguado *flounder*
la ostra *oyster*
el pulpo *octopus*
la sardina *sardines*

Las frutas/*Fruits*

el aguacate *avocado*
el albaricoque *apricot*
el ananá *pineapple (Latin America)*
el banano *banana; banana tree*
la cereza *cherry*
la china *orange (Puerto Rico)*
la ciruela *plum*
el durazno *peach*
la fresa *strawberry*
el melocotón *peach*
la papaya *papaya*
la piña *pineapple*
el pomelo *grapefruit*

la sandía *watermelon*
la toronja *grapefruit*

Las verduras/*Vegetables*

la aceituna *olive*
la alcaparra *caper*
el apio *celery*
la berza *cabbage (Spain)*
el calabacín *zucchini*
la calabaza *squash; pumpkin*
los champiñones *mushrooms*
la col *cabbage*
la coliflor *cauliflower*
los espárragos *asparagus*
las espinacas *spinach*
los guisantes *peas*
las habichuelas *kidney beans (Puerto Rico)*
los hongos *mushrooms (Latin America)*
las judías verdes *green beans*
el pepinillo *pickle*
el pepino *cucumber*
el pimiento *pepper*
el repollo *cabbage*
la salsa *sauce*
las setas *wild mushrooms (Spain)*
la zanahoria *carrot*

Los postres/*Desserts*

el arroz con leche *rice pudding*
la batida *milkshake*
el batido *milkshake (Spain)*
los bocaditos *bite-size sandwiches*
los bollos *sweet bread*
el bombón *sweets; candy*
el caramelo *sweets; candy*
los chocolates *chocolates*
los chuches *candies in general (Spain)*
la dona *donut*
el dónut *donut (Spain)*
el flan *caramel custard*
la natilla *custard*
los pastelitos *turnover, pastry, finger cakes*
la tarta *cake*

Las bebidas/*Beverages*

el champán *champagne*
la sidra *cider*
el zumo *juice (Spain)*

Más comidas/*More foods*

el ajo *garlic*
la avena *oatmeal*
el caldo *broth*
el consomé *clear soup*
los fideos *noodles (in soup)*
la harina *flour*
la jalea *jelly; marmalade (Spain, Puerto Rico)*
la mantequilla *butter*
la margarina *margarine*
la miel *honey*
el pan dulce *sweet roll*

el panqueque *pancake*
las tortas americanas *pancakes (Spain)*

Las comidas/*Meals*

el aperitivo *appetizer*
las tapas *hors d'oeuvres*

Los condimentos y las especias/*Condiments and spices*

el aderezo *seasoning; dressing*
el aliño *seasoning; dressing (Spain)*

Unos términos de la cocina/*Some cooking terms*

agregar *to add*
asar *to roast; broil*
aumentar libras/kilos *to gain weight*
batir *to beat*
calentar *to heat*
derretir *to melt*
espesarse *to thicken*
freír *to fry*
mezclar *to mix*
revolver *to stir*
servir *to serve*
unir *to combine*
verter *to pour*

Otras palabras/*Other words*

aclararse *to thin*
añadir *to add*
el batidor *beater*
la batidora *hand-held mixer*
la cacerola *saucepan*
cocer *to cook*
la copa *goblet; wine glass*
el cuenco *bowl; mixing bowl*
echar (algo) *to add*
el fuego (lento, mediano, alto) *(low, medium, high) heat*
la fuente *serving platter/dish*
el ingrediente *ingredient*
el kilogramo *kilogram (or 2.2 pounds)*
el nivel *level*
la olla *pot*
el pedazo *piece*
el platillo *saucer*
el plato hondo *bowl*
el plato sopero *soup bowl*
la receta *recipe*
recalentar *to reheat*
remover *to stir (Spain)*
la sartén *frying pan*
el/la sopero/a *soup serving bowl*

En el restaurante/*In the restaurant*

la cucharilla *teaspoon (Spain)*
el friegaplatos *dishwasher (person)*
el/la mesero/a *waiter/waitress (Latin America)*
el/la pinche *kitchen assistant*

CAPÍTULO 8

La ropa y la joyería/*Clothing and jewelry*

el albornoz *bathrobe (Spain)*
las alpargatas *espadrille shoes (Spain)*
el anorak *rain-proof coat*
los aretes *earrings*
la bolsa *bag*
la bufanda *scarf*
la capa de agua *raincoat (Puerto Rico)*
la cartera *pocketbook, purse*
el chubasquero *raincoat (Spain)*
el collar *necklace*
la correa *belt*
el gorro *wool cap; hat*
los mahones *jeans (Puerto Rico)*
las pantallas *earrings (Puerto Rico)*
el peine *comb*
la peinilla *comb (Latin America)*
los pendientes *earrings*
la prenda *piece of clothing*
la pulsera *bracelet*
la sombrilla *parasol*
los vaqueros *jeans*
las zapatillas de tenis *sneakers; tennis shoes (Spain)*

Más palabras útiles/*More useful words*

de buena/mala calidad *good/poor quality*
de goma *(made of) rubber*
de lino *(made of) linen*
de manga corta/larga/media *short/long/half sleeve*
de nilón *nylon*
de oro *(made) of gold*
de plata *(made) of silver*
de platino *platinum*
de puntitos *polka dotted*

Para comprar ropa/*To go clothes shopping*

el escaparate *store window*
el/la dependiente/a *clerk*
la ganga *bargain*
la liquidación *clearance sale*
el maniquí *mannequin*
el mostrador *counter*
la oferta *offer; sale*
la rebaja *sale; discount*
el tacón alto/bajo *high/low heel*
la venta *clearance sale*
la vitrina *store window*
los zapatos planos/de cuña *flat/wedge shoes*

Unos adjetivos/*Some adjectives*

amplio/a *wide*
apretado/a *tight*

Unos verbos reflexivos/*Some reflexive verbs*

desvestirse (e → i → i) *to get undressed*

CAPÍTULO 9

El cuerpo humano/*The human body*

la arteria *artery*
el cabello *hair*
la cadera *hip*
la ceja *eyebrow*
el cerebelo *cerebellum*
el cerebro *brain*
la cintura *waist*
el codo *elbow*
la costilla *rib*
la frente *forehead*
el hombro *shoulder*
el hueso *bone*
el labio *lip*
la lengua *tongue*
las mejillas *cheeks*
la muñeca *wrist*
el músculo *muscle*
el muslo *thigh*
los nervios *nerves*
la pestaña *eyelash*
la piel *skin*
el pulmón *lung*
la rodilla *knee*
el talón *heel*
el trasero *buttocks (Spain)*
el tobillo *ankle*
la uña *nail*
las venas *veins*

Unas enfermedades y unos tratamientos médicos/*Some illnesses and medical treatments*

el alcoholismo *alcoholism*
la alta tensión *high blood pressure*
el ataque del corazón *heart attack*
la baja tensión *low blood pressure*
el cáncer *cancer*
la depresión *depression*
la diabetes *diabetes*
el dolor de cabeza *headache*
el/la drogadicto/a *drug addict*
la hipertensión *high blood pressure*
el infarto *heart attack*
la inflamación *inflammation*
el mareo *dizziness*
la narcomanía *drug addiction*
la presión alta/baja *high/low blood pressure*
la quemadura *burn*
el sarampión *measles*
el sida *AIDS*
la tirita *bandage*
la varicela *chicken pox*

Otros verbos útiles/*Other useful verbs*

contagiarse de *to catch (an illness)*
desmayarse *to faint*
desvanecerse *to faint*
doblarse *to sprain*
enyesar *to put on a cast*
fracturar(se) *to break; to fracture*
hacer gárgaras *to gargle*
hinchar *to swell*
pegársele *to catch something*
recetar *to prescribe*
respirar *to breathe*
sacar la sangre *to draw blood*
tomarle la presión *to take someone's blood pressure*
tomarle el pulso *to take someone's pulse*
tomarle la temperatura *to check someone's temperature*
torcerse *to sprain*
vomitar *to vomit*

Otras palabras útiles/*Other useful words*

las alergias *allergies*
el antihistamínico *antihistamine*
la camilla *stretcher*
la cura *cure*
la dosis *dosage*
la enfermedad *illness*
las gotas para los ojos *eyedrops*
los medicamentos *medicines*
las muletas *crutches*
operar *to operate*
el/la paciente *patient*
la penicilina *penicillin*
el pulso *pulse*
las pruebas médicas *medical tests*
la radiografía *X-ray*
el resultado *result*
retorcerse *to sprain*
el termómetro *thermometer*
la vacuna *vaccination*

CAPÍTULO 10

El transporte y otras palabras/*Transportation and other words*

el aparcamiento *parking lot*
el atasco *traffic jam*
el billete *ticket*
el camino *dirt road*
el camión *bus (Mexico)*
la camioneta *pickup truck; van; station wagon*
el carnet *driver's license (Spain)*
la carretera *highway*
enviar *to send; to dispatch*
la goma *tire (Latin America)*
la guagua *bus (Caribbean)*
el guía *steering wheel (Puerto Rico)*
el paso de peatones *crosswalk*
el seguro del coche *car insurance*
el tiquete *ticket*
la velocidad *speed*

Unas partes de un vehículo/*Some parts of a car*

el acelerador *accelerator; gas pedal*
el cinturón de seguridad *seat belt*
el claxon *horn*
el espejo retrovisor *rearview mirror*
los frenos *brakes*
las luces *lights*
el maletero *car trunk (Spain)*
el parachoques *bumper*
la transmisión *transmission*

Un verbo útil/*A useful verb*

perderse *to get lost*

El viaje/*Travel*

los cheques de viajero *traveler's checks*
la dirección *address*
el equipaje *luggage*
la estampilla *(postage) stamp*
la oficina de turismo *tourist office*
el paquete *package*
el pasaje de ida y vuelta *round-trip ticket*
los pasajes *(travel) tickets*
el sobre *the envelope*

El hotel/*The hotel*

el/la camarero/a *service maid*
el/la guardia de seguridad *security guard*
el/la portero/a *doorman/woman*
el/la recepcionista *receptionist*
el servicio *room service (cleaning)*
el/la telefonista *telephone operator*

CAPÍTULO 11

Unos animales/*Some animals*

la abeja *bee*
la ardilla *squirrel*
la ballena *whale*
la cabra *goat*
el cangrejo *crab*
el ciervo *deer*
el cochino *pig*
la culebra *snake*
el dinosaurio *dinosaur*
la foca *seal*
el gallo *rooster*
el gorila *gorilla*
la iguana *iguana*
la jirafa *giraffe*
el lobo *wolf*
el loro *parrot*
la mariposa *butterfly*
el marrano *pig*
el mono *monkey*
el nido *nest*
la oveja *sheep*
la paloma *pigeon; dove*
el pato *duck*

el puerco *pig*
el pulpo *octopus*
el puma *puma*
el rinoceronte *rhinoceros*
el saltamontes *grasshopper*
el tiburón *shark*
el tigre *tiger*
la tortuga *turtle*
el venado *deer*
el zorro *fox*

El medio ambiente/*The environment*

el aerosol *aerosol*
el agua subterránea *ground water*
la Antártida *Antarctica*
el Ártico *the Arctic*
la atmósfera *atmosphere*
el aumento *increase*
el bióxido de carbono *carbon dioxide*
el carbón *coal*
el central nuclear *nuclear plant*
el clorofluorocarbono *chlorofluorocarbon*
el combustible fósil *fossil fuel*
la cosecha *crop; harvest*
la descomposición *decomposition*
el desperdicio de patio *yard waste*
el ecosistema *ecosystem*
la energía *energy*
la energía eólica (molinos de viento) *wind power (windmills)*
la industria *industry*
insoportable *unbearable; unsustainable*
el medio ambiente *environment*
el oxígeno *oxygen*
el país *country*
el pesticida *pesticide*
el petróleo *petroleum*
la piedra *rock; stone*
las placas solares *solar panels*
la planta eléctrica *power plant*
el plomo *lead*
el polvo *dust*
el rayo de sol *ray of sunlight*
el rayo ultravioleta *ultraviolet ray*
el riesgo *risk*

Unos verbos/*Some verbs*

atrapar *to trap*
conseguir *to achieve*
corroer *to corrode*
dañar *to damage*
desarrollar *to evolve; to develop*
descongelarse *to melt; melt down*
destruir *to destroy*
hacer huelga *to go on strike*
hundirse *to sink*
luchar en contra *to fight against*
prevenir *to prevent*
realizar *to achieve*
tirar *to throw away (Spain)*

La política/*Politics*

la constitución *constitution*
la ciudadanía *citizenship*
el/la ciudadano/a *citizen*
el/la congresista *congressman/woman*
el gobierno *the government*
la monarquía constitucional *constitutional monarchy*
el paro general *general strike*
el/la primer/a ministro/a *prime minister*
el/la secretario/a de estado *secretary of state*

Las cuestiones políticas/*Political issues*

el aborto *abortion*
el abuso de menores *child abuse*
el derecho de trabajadores *workers' rights*
la eutanasia *euthanasia*
el genocidio *genocide*
la inmigración ilegal *illegal immigration*
la pena capital *death penalty*
la seguridad social *social security*
la violencia doméstica *domestic violence*

A

a to; at (5, **11**); **~ cambio** in exchange (4); **~ causa de** as a result of (5); **~ continuación** following (10); **~ eso de** around (7); **~ fin de** in order to (**11**); **~ fines de** at the end of (8); **~ la derecha de** to the right of (**3, 7, 11**); **~ la izquierda de** to the left of (**3, 7, 11**); **~ la parrilla** grilled (7); **~ la vez** at the same time (4); **~ la.../~ las...** at... o'clock (**PA**); **~ lo mejor** maybe (5); **~ mano** on hand (10); **~ menudo** often (**2, 8**); **~ principios de** at the beginning of (7); **¿~ qué hora?** at what time? (**PA**); **~ través de** through (**11**); **~ veces** sometimes; from time to time (**2, 4**); **~ ver** let's see (2)

abajo below (9)
abarcar to encompass (5)
abolir to revoke; to repeal, to abolish (5)
Abra(n) el libro en la página... Open your book to page... (**PA**)
abrazo, el hug (**PA**)
abrigo, el overcoat (8)
abril April (**PA**)
abrir to open (2)
abuelo/a, el/la grandfather/ grandmother (**1**)
abuelos, los grandparents (**1**)
aburrido/a boring; bored (with **estar**) (**PB, 1, 2, 5**)
acabar con to end (4)
acabar de to have just (1, 9)
acción, una película de action film (5)
aceite, el oil (7)
acerca de about (4, **11**)
acercarse to approach; to move near (4)
acierto, el match (**11**)
acompañar to accompany (6)
aconsejar to advise (12)
acontecimiento, el event (9)
acordarse de (ue) to remember (8)
acostarse (ue) to go to bed (8)
actor, el actor (5)
actriz, la actress (5)
adecuado/a suitable (10)
además in addition (1)
adentro inside (10)
Adiós. Good-bye. (**PA**)
adivinar to guess (4)

adjunto/a attached (10)
administración de empresas, la business administration (2)
¿Adónde? To where? (2)
advertir (ie, i) to warn (8)
aeropuerto, el airport (**10**)
afeitarse to shave (8)
afición, la interest (2)
aficionado/a, el/la fan (3, 5)
afuera de outside of (**11**)
afueras, las outskirts (3)
agencia de viajes, la travel agency (6, **10**)
agente de viajes, el/la travel agent (**10**)
agosto August (**PA**)
agradable agreeable; pleasant (5)
agua, el water; **~ (con hielo)** water (with ice) (5, 7); **~ dulce** fresh water (5)
ahora now (4)
aire, el air (**11**); **~ acondicionado** air conditioning (10)
ajo, el garlic (7)
al (contraction of **a** and **el**) to the; **~ aire libre** in the open air (8); **~ horno** baked (7); **~ igual** the same as (3); **~ lado de** beside; next to (3, 7, **11**); **~ revés** in reverse (8)
alabar to praise (11)
alborotado/a stirred up (11)
alcalde, el mayor (*masc.*) (**11**)
alcaldesa, la mayor (*fem.*) (**11**)
alegrarse to be happy (10)
alegre happy (5)
alemán/alemana German (**PA**)
alergia, tener to be allergic (9)
alfabetización, la literacy (8)
alfombra, la rug; carpet (3)
algo something (3, **4**)
algodón, el cotton (8)
alguien someone (4)
algún some/any (4)
alguno/a some/any (1, **4**)
alimento, el food (7)
aliviarse to alleviate (5)
allá over there (6)
allí there (4, **6**)
almacén, el department store (4)
almohada, la pillow (3)
almorzar (ue) to have lunch (4, **7**)
almuerzo, el lunch (5, **7**)
alquilar to rent; to sublet (3)
alrededor around (9)
altillo, el attic (3)
altiplano, el high plateau (9)
alto/a tall (**1**)

altura, la altitud; height (9); **el mal de altura** altitude sickness (9)
aluminio, el aluminum (**11**)
amante, el/la lover (11)
amarillo/a yellow (3)
ambulante roving (4)
amenaza, la threat (8)
amigo/a, el/la friend (**1**)
amor, el love (4)
ampliar to increase (2)
amueblado/a furnished (3)
analizar to analyze (9)
ancho/a wide (7, **8**)
andar to walk (7)
anfibio, el amphibian (11)
anillo, el ring (5)
animado/a animated (5)
animal, el animal (**11**); **~ doméstico** domesticated animal, pet (**11**); **~ en peligro de extinción** endangered species (**11**); **~ salvaje** wild animal (**11**)
anoche last night (7)
anotar to note; to jot down (5)
anteayer the day before yesterday (7)
antepasado/a, el/la ancestor (9)
antes de before (time/space) (2, **11**)
antiácido, el antacid (9)
antibiótico, el antibiotic (9)
antiguo/a old; ancient (2, **3**)
antipático/a unpleasant (**1**)
anuncio, el advertisement; flyer (1)
añadir to add (5)
año, el year (**PA**); **~ pasado** last year (4, 7); **tener... años** to be... years old (3)
aparato doméstico, el appliance (8)
apariencia, la appearance (11)
apartado, el section (8)
apartamento, el apartment (2)
apartarse to move away (11)
apasionado/a passionate (5)
apellido, el last name (8)
apodo, el nickname (5)
apoyar to support (5, **11**); **~ a un/a candidato/a** to support a candidate (4)
apoyo, el support (11)
aprender to learn (2)
aprobado/a approved (10)
aprobar (ue) to pass (a test) (10)
apropiado/a appropriate (5)
apuntes, los notes (**2**)
aquel/la that (way over there) (**5**)
aquél/la that one (way over there) (**5**)

aquellos/as those (way over there) (**5**)
aquéllos/as those ones (way over there) (**5**)
aquí here (1, **6**)
araña, la spider (5)
árbol, el tree (2,**11**)
arco iris, el rainbow (4)
armario, el armoire; closet; cabinet (3)
arquitectura, la architecture (2)
arreglar to straighten up; to arrange; to fix (**3**)
arreglar/hacer la maleta to pack a suitcase (**10**)
arreglarse to get ready (**8**)
arriesgado/a adventurous (**10**)
arroz, el rice (7)
arte, el art (2)
artesanía, la arts and crafts (2, **4**)
artículo, el article (5)
artista, el/la artist (**5**)
asado/a roasted; grilled (**7**)
asegurar to assure (10)
asesinar to murder (11)
asesor/a, el/la advisor (11)
asiento, el seat (10)
asignar to assign (4)
asistir to attend (11)
asociado/a associated (5)
asociar to associate (4)
áspero/a rough (11)
aspiradora, la vacuum cleaner (3); **pasar ~** to vacuum (**3**)
aspirina, la aspirin (9)
asunto, el subject; matter (1, **6**)
asustado/a frightened (7)
asustar to scare (9)
atacar to attack (11)
atender (ie) to attend to; to assist (8)
aterrador/a frightening (9)
atletismo, el track and field (2)
atractivo/a appealing (**10**)
atraer to attract (8)
atravesado/a crossed (9)
atrevido/a daring (**8**)
atún, el tuna (5, **7**)
aumentar to grow (increase) (11)
aunque although; though (5)
autobús, el bus (**10**)
autopista, la freeway (**10**)
autoridad, la authority (5)
ave, el bird (11)
aventura, la adventure (2)
aventurero/a, el/la adventurer (**10**)
averiguar to find out (3)
aves, las poultry (7)
avión, el airplane (**10**)
ayer yesterday (**2, 7**)
ayuda, la help (1)
ayudante, el/la assistant (5)
ayudar to help (3)

azotar to whip (11)
azúcar, el sugar (7)
azul blue (**3**)

B

bahía, la bay (4)
bailar to dance (2)
baile, el dance (5)
bajar (de) to get down (from); to get off (of) (**10**)
bajo below; under (7)
bajo/a short (in stature) (**1**)
balcón, el balcony (3)
banana, la banana (7)
banco, el bank (4)
bandera, la flag (10)
bañarse to bathe (8)
bañera, la bathtub (3)
baño, el bathroom (3); **el traje de baño** swimsuit, bathing suit (8)
bar, el bar (4)
barato/a cheap (4, 7)
barco, el boat (**10**)
barrio, el neighborhood (8)
barro, el clay (2)
basarse en to base one's judgment on (5)
básquetbol, jugar al to play basketball (2)
bastante rather; enough (3)
Bastante bien. Just fine. (**PA**)
bastar to be enough (8)
basura, la garbage (**11**); **sacar ~** to take out the garbage (**3**)
bata, la robe (8)
batata, la yam (7)
batería, la drums (5)
baterista, el/la drummer (5)
baúl, el trunk (10)
bebida, la beverage (7)
beige beige (3)
béisbol, jugar al to play baseball (2)
bello/a beautiful (10)
besito, el little kiss (PA)
beso, el kiss (1)
biblioteca, la library (2)
bicicleta, la bicycle (10)
bidet, el bidet (3)
bien good; well; **bastante ~** just fine (**PA**); **~ cocido/a** well done; well cooked (7); **~ hecho/a** well done; well cooked (7); **~ puesto** well set (7); **~, gracias.** Fine, thanks. (**PA**)
bienestar, el well-being; welfare (11)
bilingüe bilingual (1)
biología, la biology (2)
bistec, el steak (7)
blanco/a white (3)
bloque, el block (11)
blusa, la blouse (8)

boca, la mouth (**9**)
boda, la wedding (4)
boleto, el ticket (8, **10**); **~ de ida y vuelta** round-trip ticket (**10**)
bolígrafo, el ballpoint pen (2)
bolso, el bag; purse (7, **8**)
bondadoso/a kind (11)
bonito/a pretty (**1**)
borrador, el eraser (2)
bosque, el forest (4, **11**)
botar to throw away (11)
botas, las boots (8)
bote, el boat (4)
botella, la bottle (5,**11**)
botones, el bellman (10)
brazo, el arm (9)
broma, la joke (3)
¡Buen provecho! Enjoy your meal! (7)
Buenas: ~ noches. Good evening.; Good night. (**PA**); **~ tardes.** Good afternoon. (**PA**)
bueno/a good (**1**); **¡Qué ~!** That's great! (2)
Buenos días. Good morning. (**PA**)
bullicio, el hubbub (4)
buscar to look for (1, **4**)
búsqueda, la search (11)

C

caballo, el horse (**11**)
cabeza, la head (**9**); **tener dolor de cabeza** to have a headache (**9**)
cacique, el chief (9)
cada each; every (1)
cadena, la chain (3)
caer to fall (9)
café brown (3); **el ~** coffee (4, 7)
cafetería, la cafeteria (2)
caja (de cartón), la (cardboard) box (**11**)
cajero automático, el ATM machine (**4**)
calcetines, los socks (8)
calculadora, la calculator (2)
calefacción, la heater (**10**)
calidad, la quality (8, **11**)
caliente hot (temperature) (7)
calificado/a qualified (11)
callarse to get/keep quiet (8)
calle, la street (**3, 10**)
calor, tener to be hot (3)
cama, la bed (3); **hacer ~** to make the bed (3)
camarero/a, el/la waiter/waitress (7)
camarones, los shrimp (7)
cambiar to change (7, **10**); **~ de papel** to change roles (3)
caminar to walk; to go on foot (2, **10**)
caminata, hacer una to take a walk (4)
camión, el truck (**10**)

camisa, la shirt (**8**)

camiseta, la T-shirt (**8**)

campamento de niños, el summer camp (**4**)

campaña, la campaign (**11**); ~ **política** political campaign (**4**)

campesino/a, el/la farmer (**11**)

campo, el country (rural) (**3**)

canadiense Canadian (**PA**)

canción, la song (**5**)

candidato/a, el/la candidate (**11**)

canoa, la canoe (**4**)

cansado/a tired (**2**)

cantante, el/la singer (**5**)

cantar to sing (**5**)

capa de ozono, la ozone layer (**11**)

capaz capable (**8**)

capítulo, el chapter (**6**)

cara, la face (**5**, **9**)

característica física, la physical characteristic (**1**)

caracterizar to characterize (**9**)

carne, la meat (**7**)

caro/a expensive (**3**, **7**)

carrera, la career (**1**)

carreta, la cart (**5**)

carretera, la highway (**10**)

carro, el car (**10**)

carta, la letter (**4**)

casa, la house (**1**, **3**)

casado/a, estar to be married (**1**)

casarse to marry (**7**)

casi almost (**4**); ~ **siempre** almost always (**8**)

caso, el case (**10**)

castillo, el castle (**3**)

catarata, la waterfall (**8**)

catarro, el cold (**9**); **tener (un) catarro** to have a cold (**9**)

catorce fourteen (**PA**)

CD, el compact disk (**2**)

cebolla, la onion (**7**)

cena, la dinner (**7**)

cenar to have dinner (**7**)

centavo, el cent (**5**)

centro, el downtown (**4**); ~ **comercial** mall; business/shopping district (**4**); ~ **estudiantil** student center; student union (**2**)

cepillarse (el pelo, los dientes) to brush (one's hair, teeth) (**8**)

cerámica, la ceramics (**2**)

cerca (de) close; near (**2**, **7**, **11**)

cerdo, el pork; pig (**7**, **11**)

cereal, el cereal (**7**)

cerebro, el brain (**9**)

cero zero (**PA**)

cerrado/a closed (**3**)

cerrar (ie) to close (**4**)

cerveza, la beer (**PB**, **7**)

cestería, la basket making (**2**)

chamán, el shaman (**9**)

Chao. Bye. (**PA**)

chaqueta, la jacket (**8**)

cheque, el bank check (**4**)

chicle, el gum (**2**)

chico/a, el/la boy/girl (**1**)

chile, el chili pepper (**7**)

chino/a Chinese (**PA**)

chisme, el gossip (**7**)

cibercafé, el Internet café (**4**)

ciclorruta, la bicycle path (**10**)

ciego/a blind (**3**)

cielo, el sky; heaven (**11**)

cien one hundred (**1**, **2**); ~ **mil** one hundred thousand (**3**); ~ **millones** one hundred million (**3**)

ciencia ficción, una película de science fiction film (**5**)

ciencias, las science (**2**); ~ **políticas** political science (**2**)

Cierre(n) el libro/los libros. Close your book/s. (**PA**)

cierto/a true (**4**)

cima, la top; summit (**10**)

cinco five (**PA**)

cincuenta fifty (**1**)

cine, el movie theater (**4**)

cintura, la waist (**9**)

cinturón, el belt (**8**)

circular to circulate (**8**); ~ **una petición** to circulate a petition (**4**)

círculo, el circle (**8**)

cita, la appointment; date (**4**, **8**)

ciudad, la city (**1**, **3**, **4**)

claro of course (**3**)

claro/a light (colored) (**8**)

clase, la class; **la sala de clase** classroom (**2**)

clasificar to classify (**5**)

cliente/a, el/la customer (**7**)

clima, el climate (**7**)

club, el club (**4**); ~ **campestre** country club (**4**)

coche, el car (**10**)

cocido/a boiled; baked (**7**)

cocina, la kitchen (**3**)

cocinar to cook (**3**, **7**)

cocinero/a, el/la chef; cook (**4**, **7**)

cocodrilo, el crocodile (**11**)

código, el code (**2**)

cognado, el cognate (**PA**)

cola, la line (of people) (**10**)

colcha, la bedspread; comforter (**3**)

colegio, el high school (**8**)

colgar (ue) to hang up (**7**)

colibrí, el hummingbird (**11**)

colocar to place (**11**)

color, el color (**3**)

combatir to fight, to combat (**11**)

comedor, el dining room (**3**)

comentario, el comment (**5**)

comenzar (ie) to begin (**2**, **4**)

comer to eat (**2**)

cómico/a funny (**1**)

comida, la dinner; meal; food (**PB**, **7**); **repartir comidas** to hand out/deliver food (**4**)

como like (**1**); **tan... como** as... as (**1**)

¿Cómo? What?; How? (**PA**, **2**); ¿~ **andas?** How are you doing? (**PA**); ¿~ **está usted?** How are you? (*for.*) (**PA**); ¿~ **estás?** How are you? (*fam.*) (**PA**); ¿~ **se dice... en español?** How do you say... in Spanish? (**PA**); ¿~ **se escribe... en español?** How do you write... in Spanish? (**PA**); ¿~ **se llama usted?** What is your name? (*for.*) (**PA**); ¿~ **te llamas?** What is your name? (*fam.*) (**PA**)

cómodo/a comfortable (**8**)

compañero/a, el/la companion, colleague; ~ **de clase** classmate (**2**); ~ **de cuarto** roommate (**2**)

compañía, la company (**8**)

comparación, la comparison (**10**)

compartir to share (**3**)

competencia, la competition (**7**)

compilar to compile (**11**)

complejo, el complex (**3**)

composición, la composition (**2**)

comprar to buy (**2**)

compras, las shopping (**4**); **hacer ~** to go shopping (**7**); **ir de compras** to go shopping (**2**)

comprender to understand (**1**, **2**)

comprobar (ue) to check (**3**)

computadora, la computer (**2**)

común common (**4**)

con with (**2**, **11**)

concierto, el concert (**5**); **dar un concierto** to give/perform a concert (**5**)

concursante, el/la contestant (**8**)

concurso, el contest (**3**)

condimento, el seasoning; condiment (**7**)

conducción, la driving (**10**)

conducir to drive (**7**, **10**); **la licencia de ~** driver's license (**10**)

conejo, el rabbit (**11**)

confiar to trust (**8**)

congreso, el congress (**11**)

conjunto, el group; band; outfit (**5**, **8**)

conmigo with me (**8**)

conmovedor/a moving, emotional (**5**)

conocer to know (**3**)

conocido/a known (**4**)

conocimiento, el knowledge (**2**)

conseguir (i, i) to get (**7**)

consejero/a, el/la counselor (**4**)

consejo, el advice (**5**)

conspiración, la conspiracy (**7**)

construir to construct (**9**)

consultorio, el doctor's office (**9**)

contagioso/a contagious (11)
contaminación, la pollution (11)
contaminar to pollute (11)
contar (ue) to tell (a story) (5)
contemporáneo/a contemporary (3)
contener (ie) to contain (7)
contenido, el content (9)
contento/a content, happy (2)
contestador automático, el answering machine (7)
contestar to answer (1, 2)
Conteste(n). Answer. (PA)
contigo with you (7)
convencer to convince (5)
corazón, el heart (9)
corbata, la tie (8)
cordillera, la chain of mountains (7)
coro, el chorus (7)
corregir (i) to correct (3)
correo, el post office (4); ~ **electrónico** e-mail (3); **la oficina de correos** post office (4)
correr to run (2)
cortar(se) to cut (oneself) (9)
cortejo, el courting (7)
cortesía, la courtesy, politeness (PA)
corto/a short (length) (8, 10)
cosa, la thing (3)
cosecha, la crop (7)
costa, la coast (4)
costar (ue) to cost (2, 4)
costumbre, la custom (7)
costurera, la seamstress (8)
cotidiano/a daily (4)
crear to create (3)
creativo/a creative (5)
crecer to grow (8)
creer to believe (2)
crudo/a rare (meat); raw (7)
cruzar to cross (5)
cuaderno, el notebook (2)
cuadro, el square; picture; painting (3)
cuadros, de checked (8)
¿Cuál/es? Which (one/s)? (2)
¿Cuándo? When? (2)
¿Cuánto/a/os/as? How much?; How many? (2)
cuarenta forty (1)
cuarto, el room (2, 3); ~ **doble** double room (10); ~ **individual** single room (10)
cuarto/a fourth (5)
cuatro four (PA)
cuatrocientos four hundred (2)
cubano/a Cuban (PA)
cubrir to cover (7)
cuchara, la soup spoon; tablespoon (7)
cucharada, la spoonful (7)
cucharita, la teaspoon (7)
cuchillo, el knife (7)

cuello, el neck (9)
cuenta, la bill; account (4); ~, **por favor.** The check, please. (7); **darse cuenta** to realize (9); **tener en cuenta** to keep in mind (5)
cuento, el story (5)
cuero, el leather (8)
cuerpo, el body (9)
cuestiones políticas, las political issues (11)
cueva, la cave (11)
cuidado, tener to be careful (3)
cuidadoso/a careful (5)
cuidar to take care of (9, 11)
culpable guilty (8)
cumpleaños, el birthday (8)
cura, la cure (4)
curandero/a, el/la folk healer (4)
curar to cure (9)
curita, la adhesive bandage (9)
curso, el course (2)
cuyo/a/os/as whose (5)

D

daño, hacer to (do) damage (11)
dar to give (3); ~ **con** to find (2); ~ **un concierto** to give/perform a concert (5); ~ **vida** to give life (5)
darse cuenta to realize (9)
dato, el data; information (9)
de of; from (1, 11); ~ **cuadros** checked (8); ~ **la mañana** in the morning (PA); ~ **la noche** in the evening (PA); ~ **la tarde** in the afternoon (PA); ~ **lunares** polka-dotted (8); ~ **mal gusto** in poor taste (8); ~ **manga larga** long sleeved (8); ~ **nada.** You're welcome. (PA); ~ **nuevo** again (4); ~ **pronto** suddenly (4); ~ **rayas** striped (8); ~ **repente** suddenly (PB); ~ **vez en cuando** once in a while (9)
debajo de under (7, 11)
deber ought to, should (1, 4)
deber, el obligation; duty (4)
debido a owing to (8)
débil weak (1)
décimo/a tenth (5)
decir (i) to say (3)
decisión, la resolution (9)
dedicar to devote (3)
dedo, el finger (9); ~ **del pie** toe (9)
defensa, la defense (11)
dejar to leave (7, 10)
delante de in front of (7, 11)
delgado/a thin (1)
delicia, la delight (11)
delincuencia, la crime (11)
demás, los the others (4)

demasiado too; too much (2)
democracia, la democracy (11)
demostrar (ue) to demonstrate (4)
dentro de inside of (3, 11)
dependiente/a, el/la clerk (8)
deporte, el sport (2)
derecha de, a la to the right of (3, 7, 11)
derecho, el law; right (legal) (2)
derrame de petróleo, el oil spill (11)
desaparecer to disappear (5)
desaparecido/a missing (9)
desaparición, la disappearance (7)
desarrollado/a developed (7)
desarrollar to develop (11)
desastre, el disaster (4, 11)
desayunar to have breakfast (7)
desayuno, el breakfast (7)
descansar to rest (7)
descifrar to decipher (9)
describir to describe (1)
descubrir to discover (4)
descuento, el discount (8)
desde from; since (3, 7, 11)
desear to wish, to want (2)
desempleo, el unemployment (11)
desesperado/a desperate (11)
deshidratar to dehydrate (9)
desierto, el desert (9)
desigualdad, la inequality (10)
desordenado/a messy (3)
desorientador/a disorienting (9)
despedida, la farewell (PA)
despertador, el alarm clock (2)
despertarse (ie) to wake up; to awaken (8)
después de after (5, 6, 11)
destacar to stand out (5)
destinatario, el addressee (5)
destino, el destination (8)
destrozado/a shattered; destroyed (10)
destrucción, la destruction (11)
detalle, el detail (6)
determinación, la resolution (11)
detrás de behind (4, 11)
deuda (externa), la (foreign) debt (11)
devolver (ue) to return (an object) (4)
día, el day (PA)
diálogo, el dialogue (4)
diario/a daily (4)
dibujar to draw (4)
dibujo, el drawing (3)
dicho, el saying (1)
diciembre December (PA)
dictador/a, el/la dictator (11)
dictadura, la dictatorship (11)
diecinueve nineteen (PA)
dieciocho eighteen (PA)
dieciséis sixteen (PA)
diecisiete seventeen (PA)

diente, el tooth (**9**); **cepillarse los dientes** to brush one's teeth (**8**)
diez ten (**PA**)
difícil difficult (**1, 2, PB, 10**)
dinero, el money (**2**)
diputado/a, el/la representative (**11**)
dirección, la address (**8**)
dirigir to conduct; to direct (**3, 11**)
discapacitado/a, el/la handicapped person (**3**)
disco compacto, el compact disk (**2**)
disculpa, la apology (**10**)
discurso, el speech (**11**)
discutir to discuss (**4**)
diseñador/a, el/la designer (**8**)
diseño, el design (**4**)
disfrutar to enjoy (**5**)
disponible available (**10**)
distraer to entertain; distract (**5**)
divertirse (ie, i) to enjoy oneself; to have fun (**5, 8**)
dividido por divided by (**1**)
doblar to turn (**10**)
doce twelve (**PA**)
docena, la dozen (**7**)
doctor/a, el/la doctor (**9**)
documental, una película documentary film (**5**)
doler (ue) to hurt (**9**)
dolor, el pain (**9**); **~ de cabeza** headache (**9**); **~ de espalda** backache (**9**); **~ de estómago** stomachache (**9**); **~ de garganta** sore throat (**9**)
domingo, el Sunday (**PA**)
¿Dónde? Where? (**2**)
dormir (ue) to sleep (**4**)
dormirse (ue, u) to fall asleep (**8**)
dormitorio, el bedroom (**3**)
dos two (**PA**)
doscientos two hundred (**2**)
dramática, una película drama film (**5**)
ducha, la shower (**3**)
ducharse to shower (**8**)
duda, la doubt (**5**)
dulces, los candy; sweets (**7**)
duplicar to duplicate (**10**)
durante during (**3**)
durar to last (**11**)
duro/a hard; hard-boiled (**7**)
DVD, el DVD (**2**)

E

echar una siesta to take a nap (**PB**)
ecología, la ecology (**11**)
edad, la age (**3**)
edificio, el building (**2**)
efecto invernadero, el global warming (**11**)
ejemplo, el example (**4**)

ejercicio, el exercise (**3**); **hacer ejercicio** to exercise (**2**)
ejército, el army (**5**)
el the (**1, 2**)
él he (**PA, 2**)
elefante, el elephant (**11**)
elegante elegant (**8**)
elegir (i, i) to elect (**9, 11**)
ella she (**PA**)
ellos/as they (**PA**)
emanar to emanate (**11**)
embarazada pregnant (**9**)
embriaguez, la intoxication (**10**)
emitido/a issued (**10**)
emoción, la emotion (**2**)
emocionado/a excited (**4**)
emocionante moving, emotional; exciting (**5, 10**)
empezar (ie) to begin (**4**)
empleado/a, el/la attendant; employee (**12**)
emplear to employ (**10**)
empleo, el employment (**3**)
empresa, la company; firm (**8**)
empresario/a, el/la agent; manager (**5**)
en in (**11**); **~ punto** on the dot (**1**); **~ seguida** immediately (**9**); **~ vez de** instead of (**8**)
enamorarse to fall in love (**11**)
Encantado/a. Pleased to meet you. (**PA**)
encantar to love; to delight (**8**)
encender (ie) to turn on (light) (**9**)
encerrar (ie) to enclose (**4**)
encima (de) on top (of) (**3, 7, 11**)
encontrar (ue) to find; to meet (**2, 4**)
encubierto/a undercover (**11**)
encuesta, la survey; poll (**11**)
endémico/a common (to a region) (**11**)
enero January (**PA**)
enfermar(se) to get sick (**9**)
enfermedad, la illness (**9**)
enfermero/a, el/la nurse (**9**)
enfermo/a ill; sick (**2**); **estar ~** to be sick (**5, 9**)
enfocarse to focus (**9**)
enfrente (de) in front (of); across from; facing (**2, 4, 11**)
enhorabuena, la congratulations (**11**)
enojado/a angry (**2**)
enorme enormous (**3**)
ensalada, la salad (**7**)
ensayar to practice/rehearse (**5**)
ensayo, el essay (**2**)
enseñar to teach; to show (**2**)
ensuciar to dirty (**11**)
entender (ie) to understand (**4**)
enterarse to find out (**8**)
entero/a entire (**3**)

entonces then (**5, 6**)
entrada, la ticket (**5**)
entrar to enter (**2, 10**); **~ ganas** to get an urge (**9**)
entre among; between (**2, 11**)
entregar to hand in (**7**)
entrenador/a, el/la trainer (**4**)
entretenerse (ie) to entertain oneself (**8**)
entretenido/a entertaining (**5**)
entrevista, la interview (**3**)
entrevistador/a, el/la interviewer (**3**)
enviar to send (**8**)
envolver (ue) to wrap (**7**)
épico/a epic (**5**)
episodio, el episode (**3**)
época, la epoch (**4**)
equilibrado/a balanced (**7**)
equipaje, el luggage (**10**)
equipo, el team (**2**)
equivocarse to be mistaken (**9**)
Es la.../Son las... It's... o'clock. (**PA**)
escalera, la staircase (**3**)
escaparse to escape (**10**)
escena, la scene (**7**)
esclavitud, la slavery (**11**)
escoger to choose (**4**)
esconder to hide (**8**)
Escriba(n). Write. (**PA**)
escribir to write (**1, 2**)
escritor/a, el/la writer (**6**)
escritorio, el desk (**2**)
escuchar música to listen to music (**2**)
Escuche(n). Listen. (**PA**)
escudo, el coat of arms (**3**)
escuela, la school (**4**)
ese/a that (**5**)
ése/a that one (**5**)
esos/as that; those (**3, 5**)
ésos/as those ones (**5**)
espacio, el space (**3**)
espalda, la back (**9**); **tener dolor de espalda** to have a backache (**9**)
espantoso/a scary (**5**)
español/a Spanish (**PA**)
especia, la spice (**7**)
especialidad, la major (**1, 2**); **~ de la casa** specialty of the house (**7**)
especie, la species (**11**)
esperanza, la hope (**11**)
esperar to wait for; to hope (**2**)
esposo/a, el/la husband/wife (**1**)
Está nublado. It's cloudy. (**PA**)
estación, la season (**PA**); station (**10**); **~ (de tren, de autobús)** (train, bus) station (**10**); **~ de servicio/de gasolina** gas station (**10**)
estacionamiento, el parking (**10**)
estacionarse to park (**10**)
estadidad, la statehood (**11**)
estadio, el stadium (**2**)

estado, el state of being (**2, 11**)

estadounidense (norteamericano/a) American (**PA**)

estafar to defraud (**10**)

estampado/a print; with a pattern or design (**8**)

estándar, el standard (**11**)

estante de libros, el bookcase (**3**)

estar to be (**2**); ~ **casado/a** to be married (**1**); ~ **de acuerdo** to agree (**4**); ~ **enfermo/a** to be sick (**5, 9**); ~ **en huelga** to be on strike (**11**); ~ **listo/a** to be ready (**5**); ~ **nublado** to be cloudy (**PA**); ~ **saludable** to be healthy (**9**); ~ **sano/a** to be healthy (**9**)

este, el east (**4**)

este/a this (**5**)

éste/a this one (**5**)

estereotipo, el stereotype (**2**)

estilo, el style (**5**)

estimulante challenging (**10**)

esto this (**3**); **¿Qué es ~?** What's this? (**PA**)

estómago, el stomach (**9**); **tener dolor de estómago** to have a stomachache (**9**)

estornudar to sneeze (**9**)

estornudo, el sneeze (**9**)

estos/as these (**5**)

éstos/as these ones (**5**)

estrategia, la strategy (**10**)

estrecho/a narrow; tight (**7, 8**)

estrella, la star (**5**)

estrenar una película to release a film/movie (**5**)

estreno, el opening (**5**)

estrés, el stress (**4**)

estudiante, el/la student (**1, 2**)

estudiar to study (**1, 2**)

estudio, el study (**8**)

estufa, la stove (**3**)

estupendo/a stupendous (**5**)

etapa, la stage (**4**)

evitar to avoid (**9, 11**)

evolucionar to evolve (**5**)

examen, el exam (**2**); ~ **físico** physical exam (**9**)

excursión, ir de to take a short trip (**4**)

exige más/menos more/less demanding (**10**)

exigente demanding (**9**)

éxito, tener to be successful (**3**)

expedido/a por completed by (**10**)

experimentar to experience (**11**)

explicar to explain (**1**)

expresión, la expression (**PA**)

extranjero, el abroad (**10**)

extraño/a strange (**3**)

F

fábrica, la factory (**8**)

fácil easy (**2, PB**)

falda, la skirt (**8**)

falso/a false (**7**)

faltar to miss (**4**)

fama, la fame (**5**)

familia, la family (**1**)

farmacéutico/a, el/la pharmacist (**9**)

farmacia, la pharmacy (**9**); ~ **de turno/guardia** 24-hour pharmacy (**9**)

fascinar to fascinate (**8**)

febrero February (**PA**)

fecha, la date (**5**)

feliz happy (**2**)

feo/a ugly (**1**)

fiar to trust (**10**)

fiebre, la fever (**9**)

fiesta, la party (**PB**)

fila, la row (**5**)

fin, el end (**11**); ~ **de semana** weekend (**3**); ~ **de semana pasado** last weekend (**7**)

finalista, el/la finalist (**3**)

finalmente finally (**6**)

finca, la farm (**11**)

fino/a fine; delicate (**5**)

firma, la signature (**3**)

firmar to sign (**3**)

flor, la flower (**8**)

floreciente flourishing (**8**)

formal formal (**8**)

foto(grafía), la photograph (**1**)

francés/francesa French (**PA**)

frase, la sentence (**4**)

fraude, el fraud (**6**)

frecuencia, la frequency (**4**)

frecuentemente frequently (**8**)

fresco/a fresh (**7**)

frijoles, los beans (**7**)

frío, tener to be cold (**3**)

frito/a fried (**7**)

fruta, la fruit (**7**)

fuente, la source; fountain (**3**)

fuera de outside (**4**)

fuerte strong; loud (**1**)

fuerza, la force, strength (**7**)

fumar to smoke (**10**)

funcionar to work; to function (**10**)

fundado/a founded (**11**)

fútbol, el soccer (**2**); ~ **americano** football (**2**)

futuro, el future (**4**)

G

galleta, la cookie (**7**)

gallina, la chicken, hen (**7, 11**)

gallo, el rooster (**7**)

galopar to gallop (**11**)

ganar to win (**3**)

garaje, el garage (**3**)

garganta, la throat (**9**); **tener dolor de garganta** to have a sore throat (**9**)

gastar to spend (**7**)

gasto, el expense (**10**)

gato, el cat (**10, 11**)

generalmente generally (**8**)

género, el genre (**5**)

gente, la people (**1**)

gimnasio, el gymnasium (**2**)

gira, la tour (**5**); **hacer una gira** to tour (**5**)

gobernador/a, el/la governor (**11**)

gobierno, el government (**1, 11**)

golf, jugar al to play golf (**2**)

gordo/a fat (**1**)

gorra, la cap (**8**)

grabaciones, las recordings (**5**)

grabar to record (**5**)

Gracias. Thank you. (**PA**)

graduarse to graduate (**4**)

gramo, el gram (**7**)

grande big; large (**1**)

granja, la farm (**11**)

grano, el bean (**4**)

grasa, la fat (**7**)

gratis free (**5**)

gripe, la flu (**9**); **tener ~** to have the flu (**9**)

gris gray (**3**)

gritar to yell; to scream (**8**)

guantes, los gloves (**8**)

guapo/a handsome/pretty (**1**)

guardar to put away; to keep (**3**); ~ **cama** to stay in bed (**9**)

guerra, la war (**11**); **una película de guerra** war film (**5**)

guía, la guide (**4**)

guitarra, la guitar (**5**)

guitarrista, el/la guitarist (**5**)

gustar to like (**PA**)

H

hábil skillful; capable (**5**)

habilidad, la ability (**5**)

habitación, la room (**5**)

hablar to speak (**1, 2**)

Hace: ~ **buen tiempo.** The weather is nice. (**PA**); ~ **calor.** It's hot. (**PA**); ~ **frío.** It's cold. (**PA**); ~ **mal tiempo.** The weather is bad. (**PA**); ~ **sol.** It's sunny. (**PA**); ~ **viento.** It's windy. (**PA**)

hacer to do; to make (**3**); ~ **daño** to (do) damage (**11**); ~ **falta** to need; to be lacking (**8**); ~ **la cama** to make the bed (**3**); ~ **las compras** to go shopping (**7**); ~ **mímica** to play charades (**8**); ~ **una caminata** to take a walk (**4**)

hambre, tener to be hungry (**3**)

hamburguesa, la hamburger (**7**)

hasta until (**2**, **11**); ~ **luego.** See you later. (**PA**); ~ **mañana.** See you tomorrow. (**PA**); ~ **pronto.** See you soon. (**PA**)

hay there is; there are (**2**)

hecho/a de made from (**9**)

heladería, la ice cream shop (**10**)

helado, el ice cream (**7**)

helado/a iced (**7**)

herencia, la heritage (**1**)

herida, la wound (**9**)

hermano/a, el/la brother/sister (**1**)

hermanos, los brothers and sisters, siblings (**1**)

hermoso/a beautiful (**4**)

hervido/a boiled (**7**)

hielo, el ice (**7**); **el agua con hielo** ice water (**5**, **7**)

hijo/a, el/la son/daughter (**1**)

hijos, los sons and daughters, children (**1**)

hispano/a Hispanic (**PA**)

hispanohablante, el/la Spanish speaker (**1**)

historia, la story (**PB**)

hogar, el home (**8**)

hoguera, la campfire (**4**)

hoja, la leaf (**4**)

hojalatería, la tin work (**2**)

¡Hola! Hi!; Hello! (**PA**)

hombre, el man (**1**)

honrado/a honorable (**11**)

hora, la hour (**1**); **¿Qué hora es?** What time is it? (**PA**)

horario (de clases), el (class) schedule (**2**)

hormiga, la ant (**11**)

hormiguero, el anthill (**11**)

hospital, el hospital (**9**)

hotel, el hotel (**10**)

hoy today (**2**); ~ **(en) día** today; nowadays (**5**)

hoyo, el hole (**11**)

huelga, la strike (**11**); **estar en huelga** to be on strike (**11**)

huevo, el egg (**7**)

humilde humble (**3**)

humor, una película de funny/comedy film (**5**)

huracán, el hurricane (**11**)

I

idioma, el language (**2**)

iglesia, la church (**4**)

igual que the same as (**7**)

igualdad, la equality (**10**)

Igualmente. Likewise. (**PA**)

imagen, la image (**8**)

imaginativo/a imaginative (**5**)

imitar to imitate (**11**)

imperio, el empire (**9**)

impermeable, el raincoat (**8**)

importar to matter; to be important (**4**, **8**)

impresionante impressive (**3**, **5**)

impuesto, el tax (**11**)

incendio, el fire (**11**)

incluir to include (**4**)

incluso including (**4**)

incómodo/a uncomfortable (**9**)

increíble incredible (**8**)

incumbir to concern (**8**)

indicar to indicate (**4**)

indígena indigenous (**7**)

ineficaz ineffectual (**11**)

infame infamous (**11**)

infancia, la childhood (**12**)

infección, tener una to have an infection (**9**)

inflación, la inflation (**11**)

influyente influential (**11**)

informal casual (**8**)

informática, la computer science (**2**)

informe, el report (**9**)

ingeniero/a, el/la engineer (**10**)

inglés/inglesa English (**PA**)

inodoro, el toilet (**3**)

insecto, el insect (**11**)

inteligente intelligent (**1**)

intentar to try (**7**)

intercambio, el exchange (**4**)

interesante interesting (**1**, **10**)

interesar to interest (**2**)

intérprete, el/la interpreter (**5**)

intervenir (ie) to intervene (**11**)

inundación, la flood (**11**)

invertir (ie, i) to invest (**11**)

invierno, el winter (**PA**)

involucrado/a involved (**11**)

inyección, la shot (**9**)

ir to go (**4**); ~ **a pie** to walk; go on foot (**10**); ~ **de excursión** to take a short trip (**4**); ~ **de vacaciones** to go on vacation (**7**, **10**)

irse to go away; to leave (**8**); ~ **del hotel** to leave the hotel; to check out (**10**)

isla, la island (**7**)

izquierda de, a la to the left of (**3**, **7**, **11**)

J

jamás never (emphatic) (**4**)

jamón, el ham (**7**)

japonés/japonesa Japanese (**PA**)

jarabe, el cough syrup (**9**)

jardín, el garden (**3**)

jazz, el jazz (**5**)

jeans, los jeans (**8**)

jefe, el boss (**9**)

jerga, la jargon (**8**)

joven young (**1**)

joven, el/la young man/young woman (**1**)

joya, la jewel (**9**)

juego, el game (**4**)

jueves, el Thursday (**PA**)

jugador/a, el/la player (**3**)

jugar (ue) to play (**4**); ~ **al básquetbol** to play basketball (**2**); ~ **al béisbol** to play baseball (**2**); ~ **al fútbol** to play soccer (**2**); ~ **al fútbol americano** to play football (**2**); ~ **al golf** to play golf (**2**); ~ **al tenis** to play tennis (**2**)

jugo, el juice (**7**)

julio July (**PA**)

junio June (**PA**)

junto con along with, together with (**2**)

juntos/as together (**3**)

L

la the (**1**)

laboratorio, el laboratory (**2**)

lado, el side (**2**)

lago, el lake (**5**, **10**, **11**)

lámpara, la lamp (**3**)

lana, la wool (**8**)

lápiz, el pencil (**2**)

largo/a long (**7**, **8**, **10**)

las the (**1**)

lástima, la pity (**11**)

lastimar(se) to injure someone; (to get hurt; to hurt oneself) (**9**)

lata, la can (**11**)

latir to beat (heart) (**9**)

lavabo, el sink (**3**)

lavaplatos, el dishwasher (**3**)

lavar to wash (**7**); ~ **los platos** to wash the dishes (**3**)

lavarse to wash oneself (**8**)

Lea(n). Read. (**PA**)

lección, la lesson (**5**)

leche, la milk (**4**, **7**)

lechuga, la lettuce (**7**)

lectura, la reading (**1**)

leer to read (**2**)

lejos (de) far (from); far away (**2**, **11**)

lengua, la language (**5**)

lento/a slow (**3**, **5**)

león, el lion (**11**)

letra, la lyrics; letter (alphabet) (**5**)

levantarse to get up; to stand up (**8**)

ley, la law (**2**, **11**)

leyenda, la legend (**9**)

libre free (**2**)

librería, la bookstore (**2**)
libro, el book (**1**, **2**); **Cierre(n)** ~. Close your book. (**PA**); **el estante de libros** bookcase (**3**)
licencia (de conducir), la driver's license (**10**); **sacar** ~ to get a driver's license (**10**)
ligero/a light (weight) (**5**)
limón, el lemon (**7**)
limpiaparabrisas, el windshield wiper (**10**)
limpiar to clean (**3**)
limpio/a clean (**3**)
lío, el mess (muddle) (**9**)
liso/a solid-colored (**8**)
listo/a ready; **estar** ~ to be ready (**5**)
literatura, la literature (**2**)
llamada, la phone call (**7**)
llamar to call (**2**)
llamarse to be called (**8**)
llanta, la tire (**10**)
llave, la key (**7**, **10**)
llegar to arrive (**2**)
llenar to fill (**9**, **10**)
llevar to wear; to take; to carry (**5**, **8**); ~ **a alguien al médico** to take someone to the doctor (**4**); ~ **a cabo** to carry out (**11**); ~ **puesto** to wear; to have on (**8**)
llorar to cry (**8**)
Llueve. It's raining. (**PA**)
lluvia, la rain (**PA**); ~ **ácida** acid rain (**11**)
lluvioso/a rainy (**11**)
lo: ¡~ **odio!** I hate it! (**2**); ~ **que** what; that which (**3**); ~ **sé.** I know. (**PA**); ~ **siento** I'm sorry (**10**)
localizar to locate (**5**)
loco/a crazy (**9**)
loro, el parrot (**11**)
los the (**1**)
lucha libre, la wrestling (**2**)
luchar to fight; to combat (**11**)
luego later; then (**3**, **6**); **hasta** ~ see you later (**PA**)
lugar, el place (**2**); **tener lugar** to take place (**2**)
lugareño/a, el local person; villager (**4**)
lujo, el luxury (**10**)
luna de miel, la honeymoon (**10**)
lunares, de polka-dotted (**8**)
lunes, el Monday (**PA**)
luz, la light (**11**)

M

madrastra, la stepmother (**1**)
madre, la mother (**1**)
maíz, el corn (**7**)
mal de altura, el altitude sickness (**9**)

mala suerte, la bad luck (**4**)
maleta, la suitcase (**10**); **arreglar/hacer** ~ to pack a suitcase (**10**)
malo/a bad (**1**)
malvado/a evil (**10**)
mamá, la mom (**1**)
mamífero, el mammal (**11**)
mancha, la stain (**9**)
mandar to send (**2**); ~ **una carta** to send/mail a letter (**4**)
mandato, el command (**PA**)
mandioca, la yucca (**7**)
manejar to drive (**8**, **10**)
manga larga, de long sleeved (**8**)
mano, la hand (**1**, **9**)
manta, la blanket (**3**)
mantel, el tablecloth (**7**)
mantener (ie) to maintain (**9**)
mantequilla, la butter (**7**)
manzana, la apple (**4**, **7**)
manzanilla, la chamomile (**9**)
mañana tomorrow (**1**, **2**); **de la** ~ in the morning (**PA**); **hasta** ~ see you tomorrow (**PA**)
mapa, el map (**2**)
maquillarse to put on make up (**8**)
mar, el sea (**9**)
maravilloso/a marvelous (**7**)
marcar to dial (**9**)
mareado/a nauseous (**9**)
mariscos, los seafood (**7**)
marrón brown (**3**)
martes, el Tuesday (**PA**)
marzo March (**PA**)
más plus; more (**1**, **2**); ~ **o menos.** So, so. (**PA**); ~ **tarde que** later than (**7**); ~ **temprano que** earlier than (**7**)
mascota, la pet (**10**)
matar to kill (**10**, **11**)
matemáticas, las mathematics (**2**)
materia, la subject (**2**)
mayo May (**PA**)
mayonesa, la mayonnaise (**7**)
mayor older; bigger (**1**, **10**); **el/la** ~ the biggest (**1**, **10**)
mayordomo, el butler (**10**)
mayores, los elderly men/women (**4**); **las personas mayores** elderly men/women (**4**)
mayoría, la majority (**7**)
Me llamo... My name is... (**PA**)
medianoche, la midnight (**PA**)
medias, las stockings; hose (**8**)
medicamento, el medication (**9**)
medicina, la medicine (**2**)
médico/a, el/la doctor (**9**)
medio ambiente, el environment (**11**)
medio de transporte, el means of transportation (**10**)
mediodía, el noon (**PA**)
medir (i, i) to measure (**11**)

mejor better (**5**, **10**); **el/la** ~ the best (**1**, **4**, **10**)
mejorar(se) to get better; to improve (**9**)
melón, el melon (**7**)
mencionar to mention (**4**)
menor smaller (**10**); **el/la** ~ the smallest (**10**)
menos minus; less (**1**, **2**); **más o** ~ so-so (**PA**); **por lo** ~ at least (**3**)
mensaje, el message (**3**)
mentir (ie, i) to lie (**4**)
mentira, la lie (**5**)
menú, el menu (**7**)
mercado, el market (**4**)
merecer to deserve (**11**)
merendar (ie) to have a snack (**7**)
merienda, la snack (**7**)
mermelada, la jam; marmalade (**7**)
mes, el month (**PA**)
mesa, la table (**2**); **poner** ~ to set the table (**3**)
meterse en política to get involved in politics (**11**)
metido/a en involved in (**11**)
método, el method (**4**)
metro, el subway (**10**)
mexicano/a Mexican (**PA**)
mezcla, la mixture (**7**)
mí me (**2**)
microondas, el microwave (**3**)
miedo, el fear (**5**); **tener miedo** to be afraid (**3**)
miembro, el member (**4**)
mientras while (**2**)
miércoles, el Wednesday (**PA**)
mil one thousand (**2**, **3**)
milla, la mile (**2**)
millón one million (**3**)
mínimo, el minimum (**5**)
mío/a/os/as mine (**10**)
mirar to look at (**3**)
mi/s my (**1**, **2**)
mismo/a/os/as, el/la/los/las same (**1**)
misterio, una película de mystery film (**5**)
mitad, la half (**11**)
mochila, la book bag; knapsack (**2**)
moda, la style; fashion (**8**)
modelo, el/la model (**8**)
moderno/a modern (**3**)
molestar to bother (**8**)
monarquía, la monarchy (**11**)
moneda, la money (**1**)
monstruo, el monster (**9**)
montaña, la mountain (**8**, **10**, **11**)
montañoso/a mountainous (**4**)
montar: ~ **a caballo** to ride a horse (**11**); ~ **en bicicleta** to ride a bike (**2**)

monte, el mountain (11)
montón, el pile (7)
morado/a purple (3)
morir (ue, u) to die (4)
mosca, la fly (11)
mosquito, el mosquito (11)
mostaza, la mustard (7)
mostrar (ue) to show (4)
moto(cicleta), la motorcycle (1, **10**)
motor, el motor; engine (**10**)
mover (ue) to move (10)
muchacho/a, el/la boy/girl (**1**)
muchas veces many times (**8**)
mucho a lot (2, **8**); ~ **gusto.** Nice to meet you. (**PA**)
mueble, el piece of furniture (3)
muerto/a dead (11)
mujer, la woman (**1**)
multa, la traffic ticket; fine (**10**)
mundo, el world (PA)
muñeca, la doll (8)
músculo, el muscle (9)
museo, el museum (4)
música, la music (2, **5**); ~ **clásica** classical music (**5**); ~ **popular** pop music (**5**)
musical, una película musical film (5)
músico/a, el/la musician (5)
muy very (**1**); ~ **bien.** Really well. (**PA**); ~ **poco** very little (2)

N

nacer to be born (8)
nacido/a born (2)
nacionalidad, la nationality (**PA**)
nada nothing (3, **4**)
nadar to swim (2)
nadie no one, nobody (**4**)
naranja orange (*color*) (**3**); **la ~** orange (*fruit*) (7)
nariz, la nose (**9**)
narrar to narrate (6)
natación, la swimming (2)
natal native (3)
naturaleza, la nature (3, **11**)
náusea, la nausea (**9**)
necesitar to need (2)
negocio, el business (8)
negro/a black (3)
nervioso/a upset; nervous (2); **ponerse ~** to get nervous (8)
ni... ni neither... nor (3, **4**)
Nieva. It's snowing. (**PA**)
nieve, la snow (**PA**)
nigeriano/a Nigerian (**PA**)
ningún none (**4**)
ninguno/a none (**4**)
niño/a, el/la little boy/little girl (**1**); **el campamento de niños** summer camp (4)

nivel, el level (9)
No. No. (**PA**); ~ **cabe duda** there is no doubt (9); (~) **comprendo.** I (don't) understand. (**PA**); (~) **es verdad.** It's (not) true. (1); (~) **lo sé.** I (don't) know. (**PA**); ~ **obstante** however (11)
noche, de la in the evening (**PA**)
nombre, el name (1)
noreste, el northeast (2)
normalmente normally (**8**)
norte, el north (7)
norteamericano/a, el/la American (**PA**)
nosotros/as we (**PA**)
nota, la grade (4)
noticia, la news item (11)
novecientos nine hundred (2)
noveno/a ninth (5)
noventa ninety (1)
noviembre November (**PA**)
novio/a, el/la boyfriend/girlfriend (**1**)
nube, la cloud (**PA**)
nublado/a cloudy (**PA**); **está ~** it's cloudy (**PA**)
nuestro/a/os/as our/s (**1**, **10**)
nueve nine (**PA**)
nuevo/a new (3)
número, el number (**PA**)
nunca never (2, **4**)

O

o... o either... or (**4**)
objeto, el object (3)
obra, la work (3)
obtener (ie) to obtain (4)
occidental western (8)
océano, el ocean (**11**)
ochenta eighty (**1**)
ocho eight (**PA**)
ochocientos eight hundred (2)
octavo/a eighth (**5**)
octubre October (**PA**)
ocultar to hide (5)
ocupar to occupy (4)
ocurrir to occur (4, **9**)
oeste, el west (2)
oficina, la office (3); ~ **de correos** post office (4)
ofrecer to offer (1)
oído, el inner ear (**9**)
oír to hear (3)
ojalá let's hope that; hopefully (11)
ojear las vitrinas to window-shop (8)
ojo, el eye (9)
olvidar to forget (7)
once eleven (**PA**)
ópera, la opera (5)
opinar to think, to express an opinion (1)

opinión, la opinion (4)
oportunidad, la opportunity (3)
opuesto, el opposite (4, 11)
oración, la sentence (3)
orden, el order (5)
oreja, la ear (**9**)
organizar to organize (**4**)
orgulloso/a proud (4)
origen, el origen (1)
orquesta, la orchestra (5)
oscuro/a dark (8)
oso, el bear (9, **11**)
otoño, el autumn, fall (**PA**)
otra vez again (4)
otro/a other (4)

P

paciente patient (**1**)
paciente, el/la patient (9)
padrastro, el stepfather (**1**)
padre, el father (**1**)
padres, los parents (**1**)
pagar to pay (7)
página, la page (2)
país, el country (1)
paisaje, el landscape (8)
pájaro, el bird (**11**)
palabra, la word (1)
pan, el bread (7)
pantalla, la screen (5)
pantalones, los pants (8); ~ **cortos** shorts (8); ~ **vaqueros** jeans (8)
papá, el dad (**1**)
papa, la potato (7); **las papas fritas** french fries; potato chips (7)
papel, el paper; role (**2**, **11**); **hacer ~** to play the role (3)
paquete, el package (10)
par, el pair; couple (9)
para for; in order to (5, **11**)
parabrisas, el windshield (**10**)
parada, la bus stop (**10**)
paraguas, el umbrella (8)
parar to stop (PB)
pararse to stand (10)
parecer to seem (2)
parecido/a similar (7)
pared, la wall (2)
pareja, la pair (9)
pariente, el/la relative (PB)
parque, el park (4); ~ **de atracciones** theme park (**10**)
párrafo, el paragraph (4)
partido, el game (9); ~ **político** political party (**11**)
pasado/a last (7)
pasado, el past (4)
pasaje, el passage (9)
pasajero/a, el/la passenger (10)

pasaporte, el passport (**10**)
pasar: ~ **la aspiradora** to vacuum (**3**); ~ **(por)** to pass (through); to happen (**2, 3**)
pasatiempo, el pastime (**2**)
pasear to take a walk (**4**)
paso, el step (**3**)
pastel, el pastry; pie (**7**)
pastilla, la pill (**9**)
patata, la potato (**7**)
patinar to skate (**2**)
paz, la peace (**5**)
peatón, el pedestrian (**10**)
pecho, el chest (**9**)
pedagogía, la education (**2**)
pedir (i) to ask for; to order (**4, 7**)
peinarse to comb one's hair (**8**)
película, la film; movie (3, 4, 5); ~ **de acción** action film (**5**); ~ **de ciencia ficción** science fiction film (**5**); ~ **documental** documentary (**5**); ~ **dramática** drama film (**5**); ~ **de guerra** war film (**5**); ~ **de humor** funny/comedy film (**5**); ~ **de misterio** mystery film (**5**); ~ **musical** musical film (**5**); ~ **romántica** romantic film (**5**); ~ **de terror** horror film (**5**)
peligro, el danger (**4**)
peligroso/a dangerous (5, **10, 11**)
pelo, el hair (**9**); **cepillarse** ~ to brush one's hair (**8**)
pelota, la ball (**2**)
pensar (ie) to think (**4**)
peor worse (**10**)
peor, el/la the worst (**4, 10**)
pequeño/a small (**1**)
pera, la pear (**7**)
perder (ie) to lose; to miss; to waste (**4, 10**)
perdido/a lost (**4**)
perezoso/a lazy (**1**)
periódico, el newspaper (7, **11**)
periodismo, el journalism (**2**)
periodista, el/la journalist (**3**)
pero but (**2**)
perro, el dog (8, **11**); ~ **caliente** hot dog (4, **7**)
perseguir (i) to chase (**4**)
personaje, el character (**PB**)
personalidad, la personality (**1**)
personas mayores, las elderly men/women (**4**)
pertenecer to pertain (**4**)
pesadilla, la nightmare (**8**)
pesar to weigh (11)
pescado, el fish (**7**)
pésimo/a heavy, depressing (**5**)
peso, el weight (**9**)
petición, la request (**11**)
petróleo oil (**11**); **el derrame de petróleo** oil spill (**11**)

pez, el fish (**11**)
pianista, el/la pianist (**5**)
piano, el piano (**5**)
picadura, la bite (**11**)
picante spicy (**7**)
pie, el foot (**9**); **ir a pie** to go on foot (**10**)
pierna, la leg (**9**)
pijama, el pajamas (**8**)
pimienta, la pepper (**7**)
pintar to paint (**2**)
pintarse to dye (**9**)
pintura, la painting (**8**)
piscina, la pool (**2**)
pisco, el Peruvian brandy (**7**)
piso, el floor; story (in a building) (**3**); **el primer piso** second floor (**3**); **el segundo piso** third floor (**3**); **el tercer piso** fourth floor (**3**)
pista, la clue (**5**)
pistola, la pistol (**8**)
pizarra, la chalkboard (**2**); **Vayan a ~.** Go to the board. (**PA**)
placer, el pleasure (**7**)
plan, el plan (**4**)
planear to plan (**6**)
planeta, el planet (**11**)
planta, la plant (**3**); ~ **baja** ground floor (**3**)
plantar to plant (**11**)
plástico, el plastic (**11**)
plátano, el banana (**7**)
plato, el plate; dish (4, **7**); **lavar los platos** to wash the dishes (**3**)
playa, la beach (4, **10**)
plaza, la town square (**4**)
población, la population (**1**)
pobre poor (**1**)
pobreza, la poverty (**11**)
poco, (un) a little; few (**1, 2**);
poco hecho/a rare (meat) (**7**)
poder to be able to (**3**); **el** ~ power (**9**)
policía, el/la policeman/woman (**10**)
poliéster, el polyester (**8**)
política, la politics (**11**); **meterse en política** to get involved in politics (**11**)
pollo, el chicken (**7**)
poner to put; to place (**3**); ~ **la mesa** to set the table (**3**)
ponerse: ~ **la ropa** to get dressed (**8**); ~ **nervioso/a** to get nervous (**8**)
por times; by; for; through; because of (**1, 11**); ~ **casualidad** by chance (**10**); ~ **ciento** percent (**1**); ~ **favor.** Please. (**PA**); ~ **fin** finally (**PA**); ~ **lo menos** at least (**3**); ¿~ **qué?** Why? (**2**); ~ **su cuenta** on their own (**7**); ~ **supuesto** of course (**3**)

porcentaje, el percentage (**7**)
porque because (**1**)
portarse to behave (**8**)
portátil portable (**4**)
porteño/a person from Buenos Aires (**8**)
postre, el dessert (**7**)
potencia, la potency (**11**)
precio, el price (**3**)
predecir (i) to predict (**4**)
preferencia, la preference (**4**)
preferir (ie, i) to prefer (**4**)
pregunta, la question (**PA**)
preguntar to ask (**2**)
premio, el prize; award (**3**)
prenda, la garment (**8**)
prender to turn on (**11**)
preocupado/a worried (**2**)
preocuparse por to worry about; to concern oneself with (3, **11**)
preparar to prepare; to get ready (**2**); ~ **la comida** to cook (**3**)
preparativo, el preparation (**5**)
presentación, la presentation (**PA**)
presentar una película to show a film/movie (**5**)
presentarse al juicio to go to court (**10**)
presentimiento, el premonition (**4**)
presidencia, la presidency (**11**)
presidente/a, el/la president (**PB, 11**)
prestar to loan; to lend (8, **10**)
presupuesto, el budget (**8**)
previo/a previous (**10**)
primavera, la spring (**PA**)
primer piso, el second floor (**3**)
primer/o/a first (4, **5**)
primo/a, el/la cousin (**1**)
principal main (**4**)
prisa, la haste (**7**); **tener prisa** to be in a hurry (**3**)
profesor/a, el/la professor (**2**)
profundo/a deep (**9**)
programa, el platform (political) (**11**)
promedio average (**5**)
prometedor/a promising (**5**)
pronto soon (**5**); **hasta** ~ see you soon (**PA**)
propina, la tip (7, **10**)
propio/a own (**6**)
proponer to propose (**5**)
proporcionar to provide (**8**)
propósito, el purpose (**7**)
proteger to protect (7, **11**)
provincia, la province (**11**)
próximo/a next (**PB**)
prueba, la proof (**10**)
psicología, la psychology (**2**)
pueblo, el town (3, **4**)
puerta, la door (**2**)
puertorriqueño/a Puerto Rican (**PA**)

punto, el point (8)
puntual punctual (4)
puro/a pure (11)

Q

¿Qué? What? (2); **¡~ bueno!** That's great! (2); **¿~ es esto?** What is this? (PA); **¿~ hora es?** What time is it? (PA); **¿~ significa?** What does it mean? (PA); **¿~ tal?** How's it going? (PA); **¿~ tiempo hace?** What's the weather like? (PA)
quedar bien/mal to fit well/poorly (8)
quedarse to stay; to remain (8)
quehaceres, los chores (3)
quemar(se) to burn (oneself) (9)
querer (ie) to want; to love (2, 3)
querido/a dear (1)
queso, el cheese (7)
¿Quién/es? Who? (PA, 2)
Quiero: ~ presentarle a... I would like to introduce you to...(for.) (PA); **~ presentarte a...** I would like to introduce you to...(fam.) (PA)
quince fifteen (PA)
quinientos five hundred (2)
quinto/a fifth (5)
quitarse (la ropa) to take off (one's clothes) (8)
quizás maybe (9)

R

radio, el/la radio (2)
raíz, la root (11)
rana, la frog (11)
rápido/a rapid (2)
raro/a strange; rare (7, 11)
rasgo, el characteristic (1)
rata, la rat (11)
ratón, el mouse (11)
rayas, de striped (8)
razón, la reason (3)
razón, tener to be right (3)
realizar to act out; to fulfill (7, 11)
recepción, la front desk (10)
receta, la recipe; prescription (7, 9)
recetar to prescribe (9)
recibir to receive (1, 2)
reciclar to recycle (11)
reclutar to recruit (10)
recoger to pick up; collect (3)
recomendar (ie) to recommend (4)
recompensa, la reward (11)
reconocer to recognize (8)
recordar (ue) to remember (4)
recuerdo, el memento; memory (3, 7)
recurso, el resource (11)
reforestar to reforest (11)

refrán, el saying (1)
refresco, el soft drink (7)
refrigerador, el refrigerator (3)
refugio, el refuge (11)
refutar to refute (8)
regalar to give (8)
regalo, el gift (7)
regatear to bargain; negotiate the price (7)
región, la region (11)
registrarse (en el hotel) to check in (10)
regla, la rule (8)
regresar to return (2)
Regular. So-so. (PA)
rehusar to refuse (11)
reina, la queen (11)
reír (i, i) to laugh (4)
relajante relaxing (10)
relajarse to relax (5)
reloj, el clock; watch (2)
remedio casero, el household remedy (7)
remordimiento, el remorse (10)
renombrar to rename (4)
renovar to renew (8)
repartir comidas to hand out/deliver food (4)
repasar to review (5)
repetir (i) to repeat (4)
Repita(n). Repeat. (PA)
reponer to replace (9)
reportaje, el report (10)
represa, la dam (7)
representar to perform (8)
reproductor de CD/DVD, el CD/DVD player (2)
requerir (ie) to require (11)
reseña, la review (5)
reserva, la reservation (10)
reservar una mesa to reserve a table (7)
resfriado, el cold (9); **tener un resfriado** to have a cold (9)
residencia, la residence; **~ de ancianos** nursing home/assisted living facility (4); **~ estudiantil** dormitory (2)
resolver (ue) to resolve (8, 11)
respetar to respect (5)
respetuoso/a respectful (9)
respirar to breathe (9)
responsable responsible (1)
respuesta, la answer (PA)
restaurante, el restaurant (4)
resuelto/a resolved (10)
resultado, el result (4)
resumir to summarize (9)
resumen, el summary (9)
reunión, la meeting (2)
reunirse to get together; to meet (8)
reutilizar to reuse (11)

revisar to check; to overhaul (10)
revista, la magazine (5)
rey, el king (11)
rico/a rich (1)
riesgo, el risk (9)
río, el river (11)
ritmo, el rhythm (5)
rito, el rite (7)
robo, el robbery (7)
rock, el rock (music) (5)
rojo/a red (3)
romántica, una película romantic film (5)
rompecabezas, el riddle (7)
romper(se) to break (9)
ropa, la clothes (3); **~ interior** underwear (8); **ponerse ~** to get dressed (8); **quitarse ~** to take off one's clothes (8)
rosado/a pink (3)
roto/a broken (9)
rueda, la wheel (10)
ruido, el noise (3, 10)
ruina, la ruin (9)

S

sábado, el Saturday (PA)
sábanas, las sheets (3)
saber to know (4)
sabor, el flavor (5)
sacar to get (a grade); to take out (2, 10); **~ la basura** to take out the garbage (3); **~ la licencia** to get a driver's license (10); **~ un CD** to release a CD (5)
sacudir el polvo to dust (3)
sal, la salt (7)
sala, la living room (3); **~ de clase** classroom (2); **~ de urgencias** emergency room (9)
salida, la exit (9)
salir to leave; to go out (3, 10)
salsa, la salsa (5); **~ de tomate** ketchup (7)
salud, la health (9)
saludable, estar to be healthy (9)
saludo, el greeting (PA)
salvar to save (8)
sandalias, las sandals (8)
sangre, la blood (9)
sano/a, estar to be healthy (9)
secarse to dry off (8)
sed, tener to be thirsty (3)
seda, la silk (8)
sede, la seat (of government) (9)
seguir (i) to follow; to continue (doing something) (4)
según according to (3, 11)
segundo/a second (5)
segundo piso, el third floor (3)

seguramente surely (2)
seguridad, la security (2)
seguro/a sure (9)
seguro médico, el medical insurance (9)
seis six (**PA**)
seiscientos six hundred (2)
seleccionar to select (5)
sello, el postage stamp (**10**)
selva, la jungle (9, 11); **~ tropical** (tropical) rain forest; jungle (**11**)
semáforo, el traffic light (**10**)
semana, la week (7); **~ pasada** last week (**7**)
sembrar (ie) to sow (**11**)
semejanza, la similarity (6)
semestre, el semester (2)
senado, el senate (**11**)
senador/a, el/la senator (**11**)
sencillo/a simple (10)
sentado/a seated (5)
sentarse (ie) to sit (8)
sentirse (ie, i) to feel (3, **8**)
señor (Sr.), el man, gentleman (1)
señora (Sra.), la woman; lady (1)
señorita (Srta.), la young woman; Miss (**1**)
septiembre September (**PA**)
séptimo/a seventh (5)
ser to be (**PA**); **~ alérgico/a** to be allergic (9); **el ~ humano** human being (**11**)
serenata, la serenade (11)
serio/a serious (9)
serpiente, la snake (**11**)
servilleta, la napkin (7)
servir (i) to serve (4)
sesenta sixty (1)
setecientos seven hundred (2)
setenta seventy (**1**)
sexto/a sixth (**5**)
si if (2)
sí yes (**PA, 2**)
siempre always (2, **3, 4, 8**)
sierra, la mountain range (9)
siete seven (**PA**)
siglo, el century (3)
significado, el meaning (8)
significar to mean (4)
siguiente following (3)
silla, la chair (2)
sillón, el armchair (3)
símbolo, el symbol (12)
simpático/a nice (1)
sin without (4, **11**); **~ embargo** nevertheless (2, **6**)
sino but rather (4)
síntoma, el symptom (9)
sitio, el site (11)
sobre over; about (5, **11**); **~ todo** above all (**5**)
sociedad, la society (8)

sofá, el sofa (3)
sol, el sun (**PA**)
solamente only (8)
soler (ue) to be accustomed to (10)
solicitar to solicit (11)
solicitud, la application (2)
sólo only (3)
solo/a only one; alone (7)
soltero, el bachelor (7)
solucionar to solve (5)
sombrero, el hat (8)
son equals (1)
sonar to ring (7)
sonido, el sound (5)
sopa, la soup (7)
soroche, el altitude (mountain) sickness (9)
sorprendente surprising (5)
sorpresa, la surprise (8)
sospechoso/a suspicious (2)
sótano, el basement (3)
Soy... I'm... (**PA**)
su/s his, her, its, your, their (**1**)
suave smooth (5)
subir (a) to go up; to get on (**10**)
subrayar to underline (7)
sucio/a dirty (3)
sudadera, la sweatshirt (8)
sudar to sweat (9)
suelo, el floor (3)
sueño, tener to be sleepy (3)
suerte, la luck (5); **la mala suerte** bad luck (4); **tener suerte** to be lucky (**3**)
suéter, el sweater (**8**)
sugerencia, la suggestion (10)
sujeto, el subject (8)
sunami, el tsunami (**11**)
supermercado, el supermarket (**4**)
sur, el south (7)
sureño/a southern (8)
surgir to emerge (8)
suspirar to sigh (11)
suspiro, el sigh (9)
sustituir to substitute (5)
suyo/a, el/la theirs (7)
suyo/a/os/as his, her/s, your/s (*for.*), their/s (3, **10**)

T

tacha, la mark (7)
tal vez perhaps (3)
tamaño, el size (9)
también too; also (1,2)
tambor, el drum (5)
tamborista, el/la drummer (5)
tampoco nor/neither (7)
tan... como as... as (1)
tanque, el gas tank (**10**)
tanto/a so much (9)

tantos/as so many (2)
tapas, las appetizers (3)
tardar en to take (time) (8)
tarde late (3); **de la ~** in the afternoon (**PA**); **más ~ que** later than (7)
tarea, la homework (2)
tarifa, la tariff; toll (5)
tarjeta, la card (4); **~ de crédito** credit card (7); **~ postal** postcard (**10**)
taxi, el taxi (**10**)
taza, la cup (7)
té (helado/caliente), el tea (iced/hot) (**7**)
teatro, el theater (**4**)
techo, el roof (3)
tela, la fabric (8)
televisión, la TV; **ver ~** to watch TV (**2**)
televisor, el TV set (**2**)
tema, el theme; topic (3)
temblar (ie) to tremble (7)
temer to fear (8)
temperatura, la temperature (**PA**)
templado/a temperate (8)
templo, el temple (4)
temprano early (3); **más ~ que** earlier than (7)
tenedor, el fork (7)
tener (ie) to have (1); **~ alergia** to be allergic (9); **~... años** to be... years old (3); **~ calor** to be hot (3); **~ un catarro** to have a cold (9); **~ cuidado** to be careful (3); **~ dolor de cabeza** to have a headache (9); **~ dolor de espalda** to have a backache (9); **~ dolor de estómago** to have a stomachache (9); **~ dolor de garganta** to have a sore throat (9); **~ en cuenta** to keep in mind (5); **~ éxito** to be successful (3); **~ frío** to be cold (3); **~ ganas de + (infinitive)** to feel like + (verb) (3); **~ (la/una) gripe** to have the flu (9); **~ hambre** to be hungry (3); **~ lugar** to take place (2); **~ miedo** to be afraid (3); **~ prisa** to be in a hurry (3); **~ que + (infinitive)** to have to + (verb) (3); **~ que ver con** to be related to (4); **~ razón** to be right (3); **~ suerte** to be lucky (3); **~ sueño** to be sleepy (3); **~ sed** to be thirsty (3); **~ tos** to have a cough (9); **~ vergüenza** to be embarrassed (3); **~ un virus** to have a virus (9); **~ una infección** to have an infection (9)
tenis, jugar al to play tennis (2)
tercer piso, el fourth floor (3)
tercer/o/a third (2, **5**)
terminar to finish; to end (2)
término medio medium (7)

terremoto, el earthquake (5, **11**)

terror, una película de horror film (**5**)

tesoro, el treasure (**10**)

tiburón, el shark (**5**)

tiempo, el weather; time (**PA**, **4**); **¿Qué tiempo hace?** What's the weather like? (**PA**)

tienda, la store (**2**); **~ de campaña** tent (**4**)

tierra, la land; soil (5, **11**); **la Tierra** Earth (**11**)

tío/a, el/la uncle/aunt (**1**)

tirar to throw (**8**)

título, el title (**7**)

tiza, la chalk (**2**)

tocador, el dresser (**3**)

tocar to touch (**5**); **~ un instrumento** to play an instrument (**2**)

todavía still (**3**)

todo everything (**2**); **sobre ~** above all (**5**)

todos los días every day (**8**)

tomar to take; to drink (**2**); **~ el sol** to sunbathe (**2**)

tomate, el tomato (**7**); **la salsa de tomate** ketchup (**7**)

tónico/a stressed, emphasized (syllable) (**10**)

tonto/a silly; dumb (**1**)

tormenta, la storm (**11**)

tornado, el tornado (**11**)

torneo, el tournament (**4**)

toro, el bull (**11**)

torre, la tower (**3**)

torta, la cake (**7**)

tos, la cough (**9**);

tener tos to have a cough (**9**)

toser to cough (**9**)

tostada, la toast (**7**)

trabajador/a hard-working (**1**)

trabajar to work (**2**); **~ como voluntario/a** to volunteer (**4**)

trabajo, el work (**1**); **~ en prácticas** internship (**8**); **~ remunerado** job with a salary (**4**)

trabalenguas, el tongue twister (**4**)

tradicional traditional (**3**)

traducir to translate (**11**)

traer to bring (**3**)

tráfico, el traffic (**10**)

tragedia, la tragedy (**11**)

trágico/a tragic (**5**)

traje, el suit (5, **8**); **~ de baño** swimsuit; bathing suit (**8**)

tranquilizarse to calm down (**9**)

tranquilo/a calm; peaceful (5, **10**)

transitar to enter/exit (**10**)

transporte, el transportation (**10**); **el medio de transporte** means of transportation (**10**)

tratamiento, el treatment (**9**)

tratar to treat (**9**); **~ de** to try to (5, **9**)

tratarse de to deal with; to be about (**8**)

trece thirteen (**PA**)

treinta thirty (**PA**)

tren, el train (**10**)

tres three (**PA**)

trescientos three hundred (**2**)

tribu, la tribe (**2**)

triste sad (**2**)

trompeta, la trumpet (**5**)

trompetista, el/la trumpet player (**5**)

tú you (*fam.*) (**PA**, **2**)

tu/s your (*fam.*) (**1**, **2**)

turnarse to take turns (**3**)

tuyo/a/os/as yours (*fam.*) (**10**)

U

último/a last (**5**)

un/a a; one (**1**)

únicamente only (**9**)

único/a only (sole) (**4**)

unido/a close-knit (**7**)

uno one (**PA**)

unos/as some (**1**)

usar to use (**2**)

usted/es you (*for.*) (**PA**)

útil useful (**PA**)

V

vaca, la cow (**11**)

vacaciones, las vacation (**10**); **ir de vacaciones** to go on vacation (7, **10**)

valor, el value (**6**)

vaqueros, los jeans (**8**)

vaso, el glass (**7**)

Vaya(n) a la pizarra. Go to the board. (**PA**)

vecino/a, el/la neighbor (**8**)

vehículo, el vehicle (**10**)

veinte twenty (**PA**)

veinticinco twenty-five (**PA**)

veinticuatro twenty-four (**PA**)

veintidós twenty-two (**PA**)

veintinueve twenty-nine (**PA**)

veintiocho twenty-eight (**PA**)

veintiséis twenty-six (**PA**)

veintisiete twenty-seven (**PA**)

veintitrés twenty-three (**PA**)

veintiuno twenty-one (**PA**)

venda, la bandage (**9**)

vendaje, el bandage (**9**)

vendar(se) to bandage (oneself); to dress (a wound) (**9**)

vendedor/a, el/la seller; vendor (**3**)

vender to sell (**7**)

venir (ie) to come (**3**)

ventana, la window (**2**)

ver to see (**3**); **~ la televisión** to watch TV (**2**)

verano, el summer (**PA**)

verdad, la truth (**3**)

verdadero/a true (**7**)

verde green (**3**)

verdura, la vegetable (**7**)

vergüenza, tener to be embarrassed (**3**)

vertedero, el dump (**11**)

vestido, el dress (**8**)

vestirse (i, i) to get dressed (**8**)

vez, la time (**5**); **muchas veces** many times (**8**); **otra vez** again (**4**); **tal vez** perhaps (**3**)

viajar to travel (2, **10**)

viaje, el trip (8, **10**); **la agencia de viajes** travel agency (6, **10**); **el/la agente de viajes** travel agent (**10**); **ir de viaje** to go on a trip (**10**)

viajeros, los travelers (**10**)

vida, la life (**2**)

vidrio, el glass (**11**)

viejo/a old (**3**)

viento, el wind (**PA**)

viernes, el Friday (**PA**)

vigilar to watch (**9**)

vinagre, el vinegar (**7**)

vino, el wine (**7**)

virus, tener un to have a virus (**9**)

visitar to visit (**10**)

vivienda, la housing (**3**)

vivir to live (**2**)

vivo/a alive; living (**11**)

vocabulario, el vocabulary (**1**)

volante, el steering wheel (**10**)

volar (ue) to fly; to fly away (**10**)

volcán, el volcano (**4**)

voluntariado, el volunteerism (**4**)

volver (ue) to return (4, **11**)

vosotros/as you (*fam. pl. Spain*) (**PA**)

votar to vote (**11**)

voto, el ballot (**11**)

voz, la voice (**5**)

vuelo, el flight (**10**)

vuestro/a/os/as your/s (*fam. pl. Spain*) (**1**, **10**)

Y

y and (**2**); **¿~ tú?** And you? (*fam.*) (**PA**); **¿~ usted?** And you? (*for.*) (**PA**)

ya already (**4**); **~ no** no longer (**5**); **~ que** since (**1**)

yo I (**PA**)

Z

zapatillas, las slippers (**8**)

zapatos, los shoes (**8**); **~ de tenis** tennis shoes (**8**)

A

a un/a (**1**)
a little (un) poco (**1, 2**)
a lot mucho (**2, 8**)
ability la habilidad (**5**)
able to, to be poder (**3**)
abolish, to abolir (**5**)
about acerca de; sobre (4, 5, **11**);
  to be ~ tratarse de (8)
above all sobre todo (**5**)
abroad el extranjero (**10**)
accompany, to acompañar (6)
according to según (3, **11**)
account la cuenta (**4**)
accustomed to, to be soler (ue) (10)
acid rain la lluvia ácida (**11**)
across from enfrente de (**11**)
act out, to realizar (7)
action film la película de acción (**5**)
actor el actor (**5**)
actress la actriz (**5**)
add, to añadir (5)
address la dirección (8)
addressee el destinatario (5)
adhesive bandage la curita (**9**)
adventure la aventura (2)
adventurer el/la aventurero/a (10)
adventurous arriesgado/a (**10**)
advertisement el anuncio (1)
advice el consejo (5)
advise, to aconsejar (12)
advisor el/la asesor/a (**11**)
afraid, to be tener miedo (3)
after después de (5, **6, 11**)
afternoon: Good ~. Buenas tardes.
  (**PA**); **in the ~** de la tarde (**PA**)
again otra vez; de nuevo (4)
age la edad (3)
agency, travel la agencia de viajes (6,
  10)
agent el/la empresario/a (**5**); **travel
  ~** el/la agente de viajes (**10**)
agree, to estar de acuerdo (4)
agreeable agradable (5)
air el aire (**11**); **in the open ~** al aire
  libre (**8**)
air conditioning el aire
  acondicionado (**10**)
airplane el avión (**10**)
airport el aeropuerto (**10**)
alarm clock el despertador (**2**)
alive vivo/a (**11**)
allergic, to be ser alérgico/a; tener
  alergia (**9**)
alleviate, to aliviarse (5)
almost casi (4); **~ always** casi
  siempre (**8**)

alone solo/a (7)
along with junto con (2)
already ya (4)
also también (1, **2**)
although aunque (5)
altitude la altura (9); **~ (mountain)
  sickness** el soroche; el mal de
  altura (9)
aluminum el aluminio (**11**)
always siempre (2, **4, 8**)
American estadounidense
  (norteamericano/a) (**PA**)
among entre (2,**11**)
amphibian el anfibio (**11**)
analyze, to analizar (9)
ancestor el/la antepasado/a (9)
ancient antiguo/a (2)
and y (2); **~ you?** ¿Y usted? (*for.*);
  ¿Y tú? (*fam.*) (**PA**)
angry enojado/a (2)
animal el animal (**11**); **domesticated
  ~** el animal doméstico (**11**); **wild
  ~** el animal salvaje (**11**)
animated animado/a (**5**)
answer la respuesta (**PA**); **~.**
  Conteste(n). (**PA**); **to ~** contestar
  (1, **2**)
answering machine el contestador
  automático (7)
ant la hormiga (**11**)
antacid el antiácido (**9**)
anthill el hormiguero (11)
antibiotic el antibiótico (**9**)
apartment el apartamento (2)
apology la disculpa (10)
appealing atractivo/a (**10**)
appearance la apariencia (11)
appetizers las tapas (3)
apple la manzana (4, **7**)
appliance el aparato doméstico (8)
application la solicitud (2)
appointment la cita (4)
approach, to acercarse (4)
appropriate apropiado/a (5)
approved aprobado/a (10)
April abril (**PA**)
architecture la arquitectura (2)
arm el brazo (**9**)
armchair el sillón (**3**)
armoire el armario (**3**)
army el ejército (5)
around a eso de; alrededor (7, 9)
arrange, to arreglar (5)
arrive, to llegar (2)
art el arte (2)
article el artículo (5)
artist el/la artista (**5**)
arts and crafts la artesanía (2, **4**)

as: ~ a result of a causa de (5); **~ ...
  ~** tan... como (1)
ask, to preguntar (**2**); **~ for** pedir (i)
  (**4**)
aspirin la aspirina (9)
assign, to asignar (4)
assist, to atender (ie) (8)
assistant el/la ayudante (5)
assisted living facility la residencia
  de ancianos (**4**)
associate, to asociar (4)
associated asociado/a (5)
assure, to asegurar (10)
at a (5, **11**); **~ least** por lo menos (3);
  ~ the beginning a principios de
  (7); **~ the end of** a fines de (8); **~
  the same time** a la vez (4); **~
  what time?** ¿A qué hora? (**PA**); **~
  ... o'clock.** A la.../A las... (**PA**)
ATM machine el cajero automático
  (**4**)
attached adjunto/a (10)
attack, to atacar (11)
attend, to asistir (11); **~ to** atender
  (ie) (8)
attendant el/la empleado/a (12)
attic el altillo (**3**)
attract, to atraer (8)
August agosto (**PA**)
aunt la tía (**1**)
authority la autoridad (5)
autumn el otoño (**PA**)
available disponible (10)
average promedio (5)
avoid, to evitar (**9, 11**)
awaken, to despertarse (ie) (**8**)
award el premio (3)

B

bachelor el soltero (7)
back la espalda (**9**)
backache, to have a tener dolor de
  espalda (**9**)
bad malo/a (**1**); **~ luck** la mala suerte
  (4)
bag el bolso (7); **book ~** la mochila
  (**2**)
baked al horno; cocido/a (**7**)
balanced equilibrado/a (7)
balcony el balcón (**3**)
ball la pelota (**2**)
ballot el voto (**11**)
ballpoint pen el bolígrafo (**2**)
banana la banana; plátano (**7**)
band el conjunto (**5**)

bandage la venda; el vendaje (**9**); **adhesive ~** la curita (**9**); **to ~ (oneself)** vendar(se) (**9**)

bank el banco (**4**); **~ check** el cheque (**4**)

bar el bar (**4**)

bargain, to regatear (**7**)

base one's judgment on, to basarse en (**5**)

baseball, to play jugar al béisbol (**2**)

basement el sótano (**3**)

basket making la cestería (**2**)

basketball, to play jugar al básquetbol (**2**)

bathe, to bañarse (**8**)

bathing suit el traje de baño (**8**)

bathroom el baño (**3**)

bathtub la bañera (**3**)

bay la bahía (**4**)

be, to ser, estar (**PA, 2**)

beach la playa (**4, 10**)

beans los frijoles (**7**)

bear el oso (**9, 11**)

beat (heart), to latir (**9**)

beautiful hermoso/a; bello/a (**4, 10**)

because porque (**1**); **~ of** por (**2, 11**)

bed la cama (**3**); **to go to ~** acostarse (ue) (**8**); **to make the ~** hacer la cama (**3**)

bedroom el dormitorio (**3**)

bedspread la colcha (**3**)

beer la cerveza (**PB, 7**)

before (time/space) antes de (**2, 11**)

begin, to comenzar (ie); empezar (ie) (**2, 4**)

behave, to portarse (**8**)

behind detrás (de) (**4, 11**)

beige beige (**3**)

believe, to creer (**2**)

bellman el botones (**10**)

below bajo; abajo (**7, 9**)

belt el cinturón (**8**)

beside al lado de (**3, 7**)

better mejor (**5, 10**)

between entre (**2, 11**)

beverage la bebida (**7**)

bicycle la bicicleta (**10**); **~ path** la ciclorruta (**10**); **to ride a ~** montar en bicicleta (**2**)

bidet el bidet (**3**)

big grande (**1**)

bigger mayor (**1, 10**)

bilingual bilingüe (**1**)

bill la cuenta (**4**)

biology la biología (**2**)

bird el pájaro; el ave (**11**)

birthday el cumpleaños (**8**)

bite la picadura (**11**)

black negro/a (**3**)

blanket la manta (**3**)

blind ciego/a (**3**)

block el bloque (**11**)

blood la sangre (**9**)

blouse la blusa (**8**)

blue azul (**3**)

boat el bote; el barco (**4, 10**)

body el cuerpo (**9**)

boiled cocido/a; hervido/a (**7**)

book el libro (**1, 2**); **~ bag** la mochila (**2**); **Close your ~.** Cierre(n) el libro. (**PA**); **Open your ~ to page …** Abra(n) el libro en la página… (**PA**)

bookcase el estante de libros (**3**)

bookstore la librería (**2**)

boots las botas (**8**)

bored aburrido/a (**2**)

boring aburrido/a (**PB, 1, 5**)

born nacido/a (**2**); **to be ~** nacer (**8**)

boss el jefe (**9**)

bother, to molestar (**8**)

bottle la botella (**5, 11**)

box (cardboard) la caja (de cartón) (**11**)

boy el chico; el muchacho (**1**); **little ~** el niño (**1**)

boyfriend el novio (**1**)

brain el cerebro (**9**)

brandy, Peruvian el pisco (**7**)

bread el pan (**7**)

break, to romper(se) (**9**)

breakfast el desayuno (**7**); **to have ~** desayunar (**7**)

breathe, to respirar (**9**)

bring, to traer (**3**)

broken roto/a (**9**)

brother el hermano (**1**)

brown café; marrón (**3**)

brush (one's hair, teeth), to cepillarse (el pelo, los dientes) (**8**)

budget el presupuesto (**8**)

building el edificio (**2**)

bull el toro (**11**)

burn (oneself), to quemar(se) (**9**)

bus el autobús (**10**); **~ stop** la parada (**10**)

business el negocio (**8**); **~ administration** la administración de empresas (**2**); **~/shopping district** el centro comercial (**4**)

but pero (**2**); **~ rather** sino (**4**)

butler el mayordomo (**10**)

butter la mantequilla (**7**)

buy, to comprar (**2**)

by por (**1, 11**); **~ chance** por casualidad (**10**)

Bye. Chao. (**PA**)

C

cabinet el armario (**3**)

cafe el café (**4**); **Internet ~** el cibercafé (**4**)

cafeteria la cafetería (**2**)

cake la torta (**7**)

calculator la calculadora (**2**)

call: phone ~ la llamada (**7**); **to ~** llamar (**2**)

called, to be llamarse (**8**)

calm tranquilo/a (**5, 10**); **to ~ down** tranquilizarse (**9**)

camp: summer ~ el campamento de niños (**4**)

campaign la campaña (**11**); **political ~** la campaña política (**4**)

can la lata (**11**)

Canadian canadiense (**PA**)

candidate el/la candidato/a (**11**); **to support a ~** apoyar a un/a candidato/a (**4**)

candy los dulces (**7**)

canoe la canoa (**4**)

cap la gorra (**8**)

capable hábil; capaz (**5, 8**)

car el coche; el carro (**10**)

card la tarjeta (**4**); **credit ~** la tarjeta de crédito (**7**)

career la carrera (**1**)

careful cuidadoso/a (**5**); **to be ~** tener cuidado (**3**)

carpet la alfombra (**3**)

carry, to llevar (**5**); **~ out** llevar a cabo (**11**)

cart la carreta (**5**)

case el caso (**10**)

castle el castillo (**3**)

casual informal (**8**)

cat el gato (**10, 11**)

cave la cueva (**11**)

CD/DVD player el reproductor de CD/DVD (**2**)

cent el centavo (**5**)

century el siglo (**3**)

ceramics la cerámica (**2**)

cereal el cereal (**7**)

chain la cadena (**3**); **~ of mountains** la cordillera (**7**)

chair la silla (**2**)

chalk la tiza (**2**)

chalkboard la pizarra (**2**)

challenging estimulante (**10**)

chamomile la manzanilla (**9**)

change, to cambiar (**7, 10**); **~ roles** cambiar de papel (**3**)

chapter el capítulo (**6**)

character el personaje (**PB**)

characteristic el rasgo (**1**); **physical ~** la característica física (**1**)

characterize, to caracterizar (**9**)

charades, to play hacer mímica (**8**)

chase, to perseguir (i) (**4**)

cheap barato/a (**4**, **7**)

check, to revisar; comprobar (ue) (**3**, **10**); **bank ~** el cheque (**4**); **The ~, please.** La cuenta, por favor. (**7**); **to ~ in** registrarse (en el hotel) (**10**); **to ~ out** irse del hotel (**10**)

checked de cuadros (**8**)

cheese el queso (**7**)

chef el/la cocinero/a (**4**)

chest el pecho (**9**)

chicken el pollo (meat); gallina (bird) (**7**)

chief el cacique (**9**)

childhood la infancia (**12**)

children los hijos (**1**)

chili pepper el chile (**7**)

Chinese chino/a (**PA**)

choose, to escoger; elegir (i, i) (**4**, **9**)

chores los quehaceres (**3**)

chorus el coro (**8**)

church la iglesia (**4**)

circle el círculo (**8**)

circulate, to circular (**8**); **~ a petition** circular una petición (**4**)

city la ciudad (**1**, **3**, **4**)

classical music la música clásica (**5**)

classify, to clasificar (**5**)

classmate el/la compañero/a de clase (**2**)

classroom la sala de clase (**2**)

clay el barro (**2**)

clean limpio/a (**3**); **to ~** limpiar (**3**)

clerk el/la dependiente/a (**8**)

climate el clima (**7**)

clock el reloj (**2**); **alarm ~** el despertador (**2**)

close cerca (de) (**2**); **to ~** cerrar (ie) (**4**); **~ your book/s.** Cierre(n) el libro/los libros. (**PA**)

closed cerrado/a (**3**)

close-knit unido/a (**7**)

closet el armario (**3**)

clothes la ropa (**3**)

cloud la nube (**PA**)

cloudy, it's está nublado (**PA**)

club el club (**4**); **country ~** el club campestre (**9**)

clue la pista (**5**)

coast la costa (**4**)

coat of arms el escudo (**3**)

cocoa bean el grano de cacao (**4**)

code el código (**2**)

coffee el café (**7**)

cognate el cognado (**PA**)

cold el catarro; el resfriado (**9**); **it's ~** hace frío (**PA**); **to be ~** tener frío (**3**); **to have a ~** tener (un) catarro; tener un resfriado (**9**)

collect recoger (**3**)

color el color (**3**)

comb one's hair, to peinarse (**8**)

combat, to luchar; combatir (**11**)

come, to venir (ie) (**3**)

comfortable cómodo/a (**8**)

comforter la colcha (**3**)

command el mandato (**PA**)

comment el comentario (**5**)

common común (**4**); **~ (to a region)** endémico/a (**11**)

compact disk el disco compacto (el CD) (**2**)

company la compañía; la empresa (**8**)

comparison la comparación (**10**)

competition la competencia (**7**)

compile, to compilar (**11**)

completed by expedido/a por (**10**)

complex el complejo (**3**)

composition la composición (**2**)

computer la computadora (**2**); **~ science** la informática (**2**)

concern, to incumbir (**8**); **~ oneself with** preocuparse por (**3**, **11**)

concert el concierto (**5**); **to give/perform a ~** dar un concierto (**5**)

condiment el condimento (**7**)

conduct, to dirigir (**3**)

congratulations la enhorabuena (**11**)

congress el congreso (**11**)

conspiracy la conspiración (**7**)

construct, to construir (**9**)

contagious contagioso/a (**11**)

contain, to contener (ie) (**7**)

contemporary contemporáneo/a (**3**)

content contento/a (state of being); el contenido (**2**, **9**)

contest el concurso (**3**)

contestant el/la concursante (**8**)

continue (doing something), to seguir (i) (**4**)

convince, to convencer (**5**)

cook el/la cocinero/a (**7**); **to ~** cocinar, preparar la comida (**3**, **7**)

cookie la galleta (**7**)

corn el maíz (**7**)

correct, to corregir (i) (**3**)

cost, to costar (ue) (**2**, **4**)

cotton el algodón (**8**)

cough la tos (**9**); **~ syrup** el jarabe (**9**); **to ~** toser (**9**); **to have a ~** tener tos (**9**)

counselor el/la consejero/a (**4**)

country el país (nation); el campo (rural area) (**1**, **3**); **~ club** el club campestre (**4**)

couple el par (**9**)

course el curso (**2**)

courtesy la cortesía (**PA**)

courting el cortejo (**7**)

cousin el/la primo/a (**1**)

cover, to cubrir (**7**)

cow la vaca (**11**)

crazy loco/a (**9**)

create, to crear (**3**)

creative creativo/a (**5**)

credit card la tarjeta de crédito (**7**)

crime la delincuencia (**11**)

crocodile el cocodrilo (**11**)

crop la cosecha (**7**)

cross, to cruzar (**5**)

crossed atravesado/a (**9**)

cry, to llorar (**8**)

Cuban cubano/a (**PA**)

cup la taza (**7**)

cure la cura (**4**); **to ~** curar (**9**)

custom la costumbre (**7**)

customer el/la cliente/a (**7**)

cut (oneself), to cortar(se) (**9**)

D

dad el papá (**1**)

daily cotidiano/a; diario/a (**4**)

dam la represa (**7**)

damage, to (do) hacer daño (**11**)

dance el baile (**5**); **to ~** bailar (**2**)

danger el peligro (**4**)

dangerous peligroso/a (**5**, **10**, **11**)

daring atrevido/a (**8**)

dark oscuro/a (**8**)

data el dato (**9**)

date la fecha; la cita (**5**, **8**)

daughter la hija (**1**)

day el día (**PA**); **the ~ before yesterday** anteayer (**7**)

dead muerto/a (**11**)

deal with, to tratarse de (**8**)

dear querido/a (**1**)

debt (foreign) la deuda (externa) (**11**)

December diciembre (**PA**)

decipher, to descifrar (**9**)

deep profundo/a (**9**)

defense la defensa (**11**)

defraud, to estafar (**10**)

dehydrate, to deshidratar (**9**)

delicate fino/a (**5**)

delight la delicia (**11**); **to ~** encantar (**8**)

demanding exigente (**9**); **more/less ~** exige más/menos (**10**)

democracy la democracia (**11**)

demonstrate, to demostrar (ue) (**4**)

department store el almacén (**4**)

depressing pésimo/a (**5**)

describe, to describir (**1**)

desert el desierto (**9**)

deserve, to merecer (**11**)

design el diseño (**4**)

designer el/la diseñador/a (**8**)

desk el escritorio (**2**); **front ~** la recepción (**10**)
desperate desesperado/a (11)
dessert el postre (**7**)
destination el destino (8)
destroyed destrozado/a (10)
destruction la destrucción (**11**)
detail el detalle (**6**)
develop, to desarrollar (11)
developed desarrollado/a (**7**)
devote, to dedicar (3)
dial, to marcar (9)
dialogue el diálogo (4)
dictator el/la dictador/a (**11**)
dictatorship la dictadura (**11**)
die, to morir (ue, u) (**4**)
difficult difícil (**2, PB, 10**)
dining room el comedor (**3**)
dinner la cena; la comida (PB, **7**); **to have ~** cenar (**7**)
direct, to dirigir (11)
dirty sucio/a (**3**); **to ~** ensuciar (11)
disappear, to desaparecer (5)
disappearance la desaparición (**7**)
disaster el desastre (4, **11**)
discount el descuento (8)
discover, to descubrir (4)
discuss, to discutir (4)
dish el plato (4, **7**); **to wash the dishes** lavar los platos (**3**)
dishwasher el lavaplatos (**3**)
disorienting desorientador/a (9)
distract, to distraer (5)
divided by dividido por (**1**)
do, to hacer (**3**)
doctor el/la doctor/a; el/la médico/a (**9**); **~'s office** el consultorio (9)
documentary film el documental (**5**)
dog el perro (8, **11**)
doll la muñeca (8)
domesticated animal el animal doméstico (**11**)
door la puerta (**2**)
dormitory la residencia estudiantil (**2**)
double room el cuarto doble (**10**)
doubt la duda (**5**); **there is no ~** no cabe duda (**9**)
downtown el centro (**4**)
dozen la docena (**7**)
drama film la película dramática (**5**)
draw, to dibujar (**4**)
drawing el dibujo (3)
dress el vestido (**8**); **to ~ (a wound)** vendar(se) (**9**)
dresser el tocador (**3**)
drink, to tomar (**2**)
drive, to conducir; manejar (**7, 10**)
driver's license la licencia (de conducir) (**10**)
driving la conducción (10)

drum el tambor (**5**)
drummer el/la baterista; el/la tamborista (**5**)
drums la batería (**5**)
dry off, to secarse (**8**)
dumb tonto/a (**1**)
dump el vertedero (**11**)
duplicate, to duplicar (10)
during durante (**3**)
dust, to sacudir el polvo (**3**)
duty el deber (**4**)
DVD el DVD (**2**)
dye, to pintarse (9)

E

each cada (1)
ear la oreja (**9**); **inner ~** el oído (**9**)
earlier than más temprano que (**7**)
early temprano (3)
Earth la Tierra (**11**)
earthquake el terremoto (5, **11**)
east el este (**4**)
easy fácil (**2, PB**)
eat, to comer (**2**)
ecology la ecología (**11**)
education la pedagogía (**2**)
egg el huevo (**7**)
eight ocho (**PA**); **~ hundred** ochocientos (**2**)
eighteen dieciocho (**PA**)
eighth octavo/a (**5**)
eighty ochenta (**1**)
either ... or o... o (**4**)
elderly men/women las personas mayores; los mayores (**4**)
elect, to elegir (i, i) (**11**)
elegant elegante (**8**)
elephant el elefante (**11**)
eleven once (**PA**)
e-mail el correo electrónico (**3**)
emanate, to emanar (11)
embarrassed, to be tener vergüenza (**3**)
emerge, to surgir (8)
emergency room la sala de urgencias (**9**)
emotion la emoción (**2**)
emotional emocionante; conmovedor/a (**5**)
empire el imperio (9)
employ, to emplear (10)
employee el empleado (12)
employment el empleo (3)
enclose, to encerrar (ie) (**4**)
encompass, to abarcar (5)
end el fin (11); **to ~** terminar; acabar con (2, 4)
endangered species el animal en peligro de extinción (**11**)

engine el motor (**10**)
engineer el/la ingeniero/a (10)
English inglés/inglesa (**PA**)
enjoy: ~ your meal! ¡Buen provecho! (**7**); **to ~** disfrutar (**5**); **to ~ oneself** divertirse (ie, i) (**5, 8**)
enormous enorme (3)
enough bastante (3); **to be ~** bastar (8)
enter, to entrar (2, **10**); **~/exit** transitar (10)
entertain, to distraer (5); **~ oneself** entretenerse (ie) (8)
entertaining entretenido/a (**5**)
entire entero/a (3)
environment el medio ambiente (**11**)
epic épico/a (**5**)
episode el episodio (3)
epoch la época (4)
equality la igualdad (10)
equals son (**1**)
eraser el borrador (**2**)
escape, to escaparse (10)
essay el ensayo (**2**)
evening: Good ~. Buenas noches. (**PA**); **in the ~** de la noche (**PA**)
event el acontecimiento (9)
every cada (1); **~ day** todos los días (**8**)
everything todo (**2**)
evil malvado/a (10)
evolve, to evolucionar (5)
exam el examen (**2**); **physical ~** el examen físico (**9**)
example el ejemplo (4)
exchange el intercambio (4)
excited emocionado/a (**4**)
exciting emocionante (**10**)
exercise el ejercicio (**3**); **to ~** hacer ejercicio (**2**)
exit la salida (9)
expense el gasto (10)
expensive caro/a (3, **7**)
experience, to experimentar (11)
explain, to explicar (1)
express an opinion, to opinar (1)
expression la expresión (**PA**)
eye el ojo (**9**)

F

fabric la tela (**8**)
face la cara (5, **9**)
facing enfrente de (**11**)
factory la fábrica (**8**)
fall (season) el otoño (**PA**); **to ~** caer (9); **to ~ asleep** dormirse (ue, u) (**8**); **to ~ in love** enamorarse (11)
false falso/a (**7**)
fame la fama (**5**)

family la familia (**1**)

fan el/la aficionado/a (**3**, **5**)

far (from) lejos (de) (**2**,**11**)

farewell la despedida (**PA**)

farm la finca; la granja (**11**)

farmer el/la campesino/a (**11**)

fascinate, to fascinar (**8**)

fashion la moda (**8**)

fat gordo/a; la grasa (**1**, **7**)

father el padre (**1**)

fear el miedo (**5**); **to ~** temer (**8**)

February febrero (**PA**)

feel, to sentirse (ie, i) (**3**, **8**); **~ like +** *(verb)* tener ganas de + *(infinitive)* (**3**)

fever la fiebre (**9**)

few poco (**2**)

fifteen quince (**PA**)

fifth quinto/a (**5**)

fifty cincuenta (**1**)

fight, to luchar; combatir (**11**)

fill, to llenar (**9**, **10**)

film la película (**5**); **action ~** la película de acción (**5**); **documentary ~** el documental (**5**); **drama ~** la película dramática (**5**); **funny/comedy ~** la película de humor (**5**); **horror ~** la película de terror (**5**); **musical ~** la película musical (**5**); **mystery ~** la película de misterio (**5**); **romantic ~** la película romántica (**5**); **science fiction ~** la película de ciencia ficción (**5**); **to release a ~** estrenar una película (**5**); **to show a ~/movie** presentar una película (**5**); **war ~** la película de guerra (**5**)

finalist el/la finalista (**3**)

finally por fin; finalmente (**PA**, **6**)

find, to dar con; encontrar (ue) (**2**, **4**); **~ out** averiguar; enterarse (**3**, **8**)

fine fino/a; la multa (**5**, **10**); **~, thanks.** Bien, gracias. (**PA**)

finger el dedo (**9**)

finish, to terminar (**2**)

fire el incendio (**11**)

first primer/o/a (**4**, **5**)

fish el pescado; el pez (**7**, **11**)

fit well/poorly, to quedar bien/mal (**8**)

five cinco (**PA**); **~ hundred** quinientos (**2**)

fix, to arreglar (**5**)

flag la bandera (**10**)

flavor el sabor (**5**)

flight el vuelo (**10**)

flood la inundación (**11**)

floor el piso; el suelo (**3**); **fourth ~** el tercer piso (**3**); **ground ~** la planta baja (**3**); **second ~** el primer piso (**3**); **third ~** el segundo piso (**3**)

flourishing floreciente (**8**)

flower la flor (**8**)

flu la gripe (**9**); **to have the ~** tener (la/una) gripe (**9**)

fly la mosca (**11**); **to ~** volar (ue) (**10**)

flyer el anuncio (**3**)

focus, to enfocarse (**9**)

folk healer el/la curandero/a (**4**)

follow, to seguir (i) (**4**)

following siguiente; a continuación (**3**, **10**)

food la comida; el alimento (**PB**, **7**)

foot el pie (**9**); **to go on ~** caminar; ir a pie (**10**)

football, to play jugar al fútbol americano (**2**)

for para; por (**2**, **5**, **11**)

force la fuerza (**7**)

forest el bosque (**4**, **11**); **rain (tropical) ~** la selva tropical (**11**)

forget, to olvidar (**7**)

fork el tenedor (**7**)

formal formal (**8**)

forty cuarenta (**1**)

fountain la fuente (**3**)

four cuatro (**PA**); **~ hundred** cuatrocientos (**2**)

fourteen catorce (**PA**)

fourth cuarto/a (**5**); **~ floor** el tercer piso (**3**)

fraud el fraude (**6**)

free libre; gratis (**2**, **5**)

freeway la autopista (**10**)

French francés/francesa (**PA**); **~ fries** las papas fritas (**7**)

frequency la frecuencia (**4**)

frequently frecuentemente (**8**)

fresh fresco/a (**7**); **~ water** el agua dulce (**5**)

Friday el viernes (**PA**)

fried frito/a (**7**)

friend el/la amigo/a (**1**)

frightened asustado/a (**7**)

frightening atterador/a (**9**)

frog la rana (**11**)

from de, desde (**3**, **11**)

from time to time a veces (**2**)

front desk la recepción (**10**)

fruit la fruta (**7**)

fulfill, to realizar (**11**)

fun, to have divertirse (ie, i) (**5**, **8**)

function, to funcionar (**10**)

funny cómico/a (**1**); **~/comedy film** la película de humor (**5**)

furnished amueblado/a (**3**)

furniture los muebles; **piece of ~** el mueble (**3**)

future el futuro (**4**)

G

gallop, to galopar (**11**)

game el juego; el partido (**4**, **9**)

garage el garaje (**3**)

garbage la basura (**11**); **to take out the ~** sacar la basura (**3**)

garden el jardín (**3**)

garlic el ajo (**7**)

garment la prenda (**8**)

gas: ~ station la estación de servicio/de gasolina (**10**); **~ tank** el tanque (**10**)

generally generalmente (**8**)

genre el género (**5**)

gentleman el señor (Sr.) (**1**)

German alemán/alemana (**PA**)

get, to conseguir (i, i) (**7**); **~ (a grade)** sacar (**2**); **~ (dressed)** ponerse (la ropa); vestirse (i, i) (**8**); **~ (nervous)** ponerse (nervioso/a) (**8**); **~ a driver's license** sacar la licencia (**10**); **~ an urge** entrar ganas (**9**); **~ better** mejorar(se) (**9**); **~ down (from)** bajar (de) (**10**); **~ involved in politics** meterse en política (**11**); **~ off (of)** bajar (de) (**10**); **~ on** subir (a) (**10**); **~ ready** preparar; arreglarse (**2**, **8**); **~ sick** enfermar(se) (**9**); **~ together** reunirse (**8**); **~ up** levantarse (**8**); **~/keep quiet** callarse (**8**)

gift el regalo (**7**)

girl la chica, la muchacha (**1**); **little ~** la niña (**1**)

girlfriend la novia (**1**)

give, to dar; regalar (**3**, **8**); **~ life** dar vida (**5**); **~/perform a concert** dar un concierto (**5**)

glass el vaso; el vidrio (**7**, **11**)

global warming el efecto invernadero (**11**)

gloves los guantes (**8**)

go, to ir (**4**); **Go to the board.** Vaya(n) a la pizarra. (**PA**); **to ~ away** irse (**8**); **to ~ on a trip** ir de viaje (**10**); **to ~ on foot** caminar; ir a pie (**10**); **to ~ on vacation** ir de vacaciones (**7**, **10**); **to ~ out** salir (**3**); **to ~ shopping** ir de compras; hacer las compras (**2**); **to ~ to bed** acostarse (ue) (**8**); **to ~ to court** presentarse al juicio (**10**); **to ~ up** subir (a) (**10**)

golf, to play jugar al golf (**2**)

good bueno/a (**1**); **~ afternoon.** Buenas tardes. (**PA**); **~ evening/night.** Buenas noches. (**PA**); **~ morning.** Buenos días. (**PA**); **~-bye.** Adiós. (**PA**)

gossip el chisme (**7**)

government el gobierno (1, **11**)
governor el/la gobernador/a (**11**)
grade la nota (4)
graduate, to graduarse (4)
gram el gramo (7)
grandfather el abuelo (**1**)
grandmother la abuela (**1**)
grandparents los abuelos (**1**)
gray gris (3)
green verde (3)
greeting el saludo (**PA**)
grilled a la parrilla; asado/a (7)
ground floor la planta baja (3)
group el conjunto (5)
grow, to crecer; aumentar (8, 11)
guess, to adivinar (4)
guide la guía (4)
guilty culpable (8)
guitar la guitarra (5)
guitarist el/la guitarrista (**5**)
gum el chicle (2)
gymnasium el gimnasio (2)

H

hair el pelo (9)
half la mitad (11)
ham el jamón (7)
hamburger la hamburguesa (7)
hand la mano (1, 9); **on ~** a mano
   (10); **to ~ in** entregar (7)
hand out/deliver food, to repartir
   comidas (4)
handicapped person el/la
   discapacitado/a (3)
handsome guapo/a (**1**)
hang up, to colgar (ue) (7)
happen, to pasar (3)
happy contento/a; feliz; alegre (2, 5);
   to be ~ alegrarse (10)
hard: ~-boiled duro/a (7);
   ~-working trabajador/a (**1**)
haste prisa (7)
hat el sombrero (8)
have, to tener (**1**); **~ a backache** tener
   dolor de espalda (9); **~ a cold** tener
   (un) catarro; tener un resfriado (9);
   ~ a cough tener tos (9); **~ a
   headache** tener dolor de cabeza (9);
   ~ a snack merendar (ie) (7); **~ a
   sore throat** tener dolor de garganta
   (9); **~ a stomachache** tener dolor
   de estómago (9); **~ a virus** tener un
   virus (9); **~ an infection** tener una
   infección (9); **~ breakfast**
   desayunar (7); **~ dinner** cenar (7);
   ~ fun divertirse (ie, i) (5, 8); **~ just**
   acabar de (1, 9); **~ lunch** almorzar
   (ue) (4, 7); **~ the flu** tener (la/una)
   gripe (9); **~ to + (verb)** tener que +
   (infinitive) (3)

he él (**PA, 2**)
head la cabeza (9)
headache, to have a tener dolor de
   cabeza (9)
health la salud (9)
healthy, to be estar saludable; estar
   sano/a (9)
hear, to oír (3)
heart el corazón (9)
heater la calefacción (**10**)
heaven el cielo (**11**)
height la altura (9)
Hello! ¡Hola! (**PA**)
help la ayuda (1); **to ~** ayudar (3)
hen la gallina (7, **11**)
her su/s (1); **~/s** suyo/a/os/as (**10**)
here aquí (1, 6)
heritage la herencia (1)
Hi! ¡Hola! (**PA**)
hide, to ocultar; esconder (5, 8)
high: ~ plateau el altiplano (9); **~
   school** el colegio (8)
highway la carretera (10)
his su/s; suyo/a/os/as (1, 10)
Hispanic hispano (PA)
hole el hoyo (**11**)
home el hogar (8); **nursing ~** la
   residencia de ancianos (4)
homework la tarea (2)
honeymoon la luna de miel (10)
honorable honrado/a (11)
hope la esperanza (11); **let's ~ that**
   ojalá (11); **to ~** esperar (2)
hopefully ojalá (11)
horror film la película de terror (5)
horse el caballo (11); **to ride a ~**
   montar a caballo (11)
hospital el hospital (9)
hot (temperature) caliente (7); **~
   dog** el perro caliente (4, 7); **It's ~.**
   Hace calor. (**PA**); **to be ~** tener
   calor (3)
hotel el hotel (**10**); **to leave the ~**
   irse del hotel (**10**)
hour la hora (1)
house la casa (1, 3)
household remedy el remedio casero
   (7)
housing la vivienda (3)
How? ¿Cómo? (**PA, 2**); **~ are you
   doing?** ¿Cómo andas? (**PA**); **~ are
   you?** ¿Cómo está usted? (for.);
   ¿Cómo estás? (fam.) (**PA**); **~ do
   you say... in Spanish?** ¿Cómo se
   dice... en español? (**PA**); **~ do you
   write... in Spanish?** ¿Cómo se
   escribe... en español? (**PA**); **~
   much/many?** ¿Cuánto/a/os/as?
   (2); **~'s it going?** ¿Qué tal? (**PA**)
however no obstante (11)
hubbub el bullicio (4)

hug el abrazo (PA)
human being el ser humano (11)
humble humilde (3)
hummingbird el colibrí (11)
hungry, to be tener hambre (3)
hurricane el huracán (**11**)
hurry, to be in a tener prisa (3)
hurt, to doler (ue) (9); **~ oneself**
   lastimar(se) (9)
husband el esposo (**1**)

I

I yo (**PA**); **~ (don't) understand.**
   (No) comprendo. (**PA**); **~ don't
   know.** No lo sé. (**PA**); **~ hate it!**
   ¡Lo odio! (2); **~ know.** Lo sé. (**PA**);
   **~ would like to introduce you
   to...** Quiero presentarle a... (for.);
   Quiero presentarte a... (fam.) (**PA**);
   ~'m... Soy... (**PA**); **~'m sorry** lo
   siento (10)
ice el hielo (7); **~ cream** el helado (7);
   ~ cream shop la heladería (10)
iced helado/a (7)
if si (2)
ill enfermo/a (2)
illness la enfermedad (9)
image la imagen (8)
imaginative imaginativo/a (5)
imitate, to imitar (11)
immediately en seguida (9)
important, to be importar (4, 8)
impressive impresionante (3, **5**)
improve, to mejorar(se) (9)
in en (11); **~ addition** además (1); **~
   exchange** a cambio (4); **~ front
   (of)** enfrente (de); delante de (2, 4,
   11); **~ order to** para, a fin de
   (5,11); **~ poor taste** de mal gusto
   (8); **~ reverse** al revés (8); **~ the
   afternoon** de la tarde (**PA**); **~ the
   evening** de la noche (**PA**); **~ the
   morning** de la mañana (**PA**); **~ the
   open air** al aire libre (8)
include, to incluir (4)
including incluso (4)
increase, to ampliar (2)
incredible increíble (8)
indicate, to indicar (4)
indigenous indígena (7)
ineffectual ineficaz (11)
inequality la desigualdad (10)
infamous infame (11)
infection, to have an tener una
   infección (9)
inflation la inflación (**11**)
influential influyente (11)
information el dato (9)
injure someone, to lastimar (9)
inner ear el oído (9)

insect el insecto (**11**)

inside adentro (10); **~ of** dentro de (3, **11**)

instead of en vez de (8)

instrument, to play an tocar; tocar un instrumento (**2, 5**)

insurance, medical el seguro médico (9)

intelligent inteligente (**1**)

interest la afición (2)

interest, to interesar (2)

interesting interesante (**1, 10**)

Internet café el cibercafé (**4**)

internship el trabajo en prácticas (8)

interpreter el/la intérprete (5)

intervene, to intervenir (ie) (**11**)

interview la entrevista (3)

interviewer el/la entrevistador/a (3)

intoxication la embriaguez (10)

invest, to invertir (ie, i) (**11**)

involved involucrado/a (**11**); **~ in** metido/a en (**11**)

island la isla (7)

issued emitido/a (10)

issues, political las cuestiones políticas (**11**)

It's: ~ (not) true. (No) es verdad. (1); **~ cloudy.** Está nublado. (**PA**); **~ cold.** Hace frío. (**PA**); **~ hot.** Hace calor. (**PA**); **~ raining.** Llueve. (**PA**); **~ snowing.** Nieva. (**PA**); **~ sunny.** Hace sol. (**PA**); **~ windy.** Hace viento. (**PA**); **~ ... o'clock.** Es la…/Son las… (**PA**)

its su/s

J

jacket la chaqueta (**8**)

jam la mermelada (7)

January enero (**PA**)

Japanese japonés/japonesa (**PA**)

jargon la jerga (8)

jazz el jazz (**5**)

jeans los jeans; los (pantalones) vaqueros (**8**)

jewel la joya (9)

job with a salary el trabajo remunerado (4)

joke la broma (3)

jot down, to anotar (5)

journalism el periodismo (**2**)

journalist el/la periodista (3)

juice el jugo (7)

July julio (**PA**)

June junio (**PA**)

jungle la selva, la selva tropical (9, **11**)

Just fine. Bastante bien. (**PA**)

K

keep, to guardar (**3**); **~ in mind** tener en cuenta (5)

ketchup la salsa de tomate (**7**)

key la llave (7, **10**)

kill, to matar (10, **11**)

kind bondadoso/a (**11**)

king el rey (**11**)

kiss el beso (1); **little ~** el besito (PA)

kitchen la cocina (3)

knapsack la mochila (2)

knife el cuchillo (7)

know, to conocer; saber (**3, 4**)

knowledge el conocimiento (2)

known conocido/a (4)

L

laboratory el laboratorio (2)

lacking, to be hacer falta (8)

lady la señora (Sra.) (**1**)

lake el lago (5, **10, 11**)

lamp la lámpara (**3**)

land la tierra (5, **11**)

landscape el paisaje (8)

language el idioma; la lengua (**2, 5**); **languages** los idiomas (2)

large grande (**1**)

last último/a; pasado/a (5, 7); **~ name** el apellido (8); **~ night** anoche (7); **~ week** la semana pasada (7); **~ weekend** el fin de semana pasado (7); **~ year** el año pasado (4, 7); **to ~** durar (**11**)

late tarde (3)

later luego (3); **~ than** más tarde que (7)

laugh, to reír (i, i) (4)

law el derecho; la ley (**2, 11**)

lazy perezoso/a (**1**)

leaf la hoja (4)

learn, to aprender (2)

leather el cuero (**8**)

leave, to salir; irse; salir; dejar (3, **8, 10**); **~ the hotel** irse del hotel (10)

left of, to the a la izquierda de (3, 7, **11**)

leg la pierna (**9**)

legend la leyenda (9)

lemon el limón (7)

lend, to prestar (8, **10**)

less menos (2)

lesson la lección (5)

let's: ~ see a ver (2); **~ hope that** ojalá (**11**)

letter la carta; la letra (alphabet) (**4, 5**); **to mail/send a ~** mandar una carta (**4**)

lettuce la lechuga (7)

level el nivel (9)

library la biblioteca (**2**)

license: driver's ~ la licencia (de conducir) (**10**)

lie la mentira (5); **to ~** mentir (ie) (**4**)

life la vida (2)

light claro/a (light in color); ligero/a (light in weight); la luz (5, **8, 11**); **traffic ~** el semáforo (**10**)

like como (1); **to ~** gustar (**PA**)

Likewise. Igualmente. (**PA**)

line (of people) la cola (**10**)

lion el león (**11**)

Listen. Escuche(n). (**PA**); **to ~ to music** escuchar música (**2**)

literacy la alfabetización (8)

literature la literatura (2)

little: ~ boy/girl el/la niño/a (**1**); **~ kiss** el besito (PA)

live, to vivir (**2**)

living vivo/a (**11**); **~ room** la sala (3)

loan, to prestar (8, **10**)

local person el lugareño/a (4)

locate, to localizar (5)

long largo/a (7, **8, 10**); **~ sleeved** de manga larga (8)

look: to ~ at mirar (1); **to ~ for** buscar (1, **4**)

lose, to perder (ie) (**4, 10**)

lost perdido/a (4)

loud fuerte (3)

love el amor (4); **to ~** querer (ie); encantar (**3, 8**); **to fall in ~** enamorarse (**11**)

lover el/la amante (**11**)

luck la suerte (5)

lucky, to be tener suerte (3)

luggage el equipaje (10)

lunch el almuerzo (5, 7); **to have ~** almorzar (ue) (**4, 7**)

luxury el lujo (10)

lyrics la letra (5)

M

machine, answering el contestador automático (7)

made from hecho/a de (9)

magazine la revista (5)

mail/send a letter, to mandar una carta (**4**)

main principal (4)

maintain, to mantener (ie) (9)

major la especialidad (**1, 2**)

majority la mayoría (7)

make, to hacer (3); **~ the bed** hacer la cama (3)

make up el maquillaje; **to put on ~** maquillarse (8)

mall el centro comercial (**4**)

mammal el mamífero (11)

man el hombre; el señor (Sr.) (**1**); **elderly men/women** las personas mayores; los mayores (**4**); **young ~/woman** el/la joven (**1**)

manager el/la empresario/a (**5**)

many: ~ times muchas veces (**8**); **so ~/much** tanto/a/os/as (**2**, **9**)

map el mapa (**2**)

March marzo (**PA**)

mark la tacha (**7**)

market el mercado (**4**)

marmalade la mermelada (**7**)

married, to be estar casado/a (**1**)

marry, to casarse (**7**)

marvelous maravilloso/a (**7**)

match el acierto (**11**)

mathematics las matemáticas (**2**)

matter el asunto (**6**); **to ~** importar (**4**, **8**)

May mayo (**PA**)

maybe quizás; a lo mejor (**5**, **9**)

mayonnaise la mayonesa (**7**)

mayor el alcalde; la alcadesa (**11**)

me mí (**2**)

meal la comida (**PB**, **7**)

mean, to significar (**4**)

meaning el significado (**8**)

means of transportation el medio de transporte (**10**)

measure, to medir (i, i) (**11**)

meat la carne (**7**)

medical insurance el seguro médico (**9**)

medication el medicamento (**9**)

medicine la medicina (**2**)

medium término medio (**7**)

meet, to encontrar (ue); reunirse (**4**, **8**)

meeting la reunión (**2**)

melon el melón (**7**)

member el miembro (**4**)

memento el recuerdo (**3**)

memory el recuerdo (**7**)

mention, to mencionar (**4**)

menu el menú (**7**)

mess (muddle) el lío (**9**)

message el mensaje (**3**)

messy desordenado/a (**3**)

method el método (**4**)

Mexican mexicano/a (**PA**)

microwave el microondas (**3**)

midnight la medianoche (**PA**)

mile la milla (**2**)

milk la leche (**4**, **7**)

mine mío/a/os/as (**10**)

minimum el mínimo (**5**)

minus menos (**1**)

Miss la señorita (Srta.) (**1**)

miss, to faltar; perder (ie) (**4**, **7**, **10**)

missing desaparecido/a (**9**)

mistaken, to be equivocarse (**9**)

mixture la mezcla (**7**)

model el/la modelo (**8**)

modern moderno/a (**3**)

mom la mamá (**1**)

monarchy la monarquía (**11**)

Monday el lunes (**PA**)

money el dinero; la moneda (**1**, **2**)

monster el monstruo (**9**)

month el mes (**PA**)

more más (**2**); **~/less demanding** exige más/menos (**10**)

morning: Good ~. Buenos días. (**PA**); **in the ~** de la mañana (**PA**)

mosquito el mosquito (**11**)

mother la madre (**1**)

motor el motor (**10**)

motorcycle la moto(cicleta) (**1**, **10**)

mountain la montaña; el monte (**8**, **10**, **11**); **~ range** la sierra (**9**)

mountainous montañoso/a (**4**)

mouse el ratón (**11**)

mouth la boca (**9**)

move, to mover (ue) (**10**); **~ away** apartarse (**11**); **~ near** acercarse (**4**)

movie la película (**3**,**4**, **5**); **~ theater** el cine (**4**)

moving conmovedor/a; emocionante (**5**)

murder, to asesinar (**11**)

muscle el músculo (**9**)

museum el museo (**4**)

music la música (**2**, **5**); **classical ~** la música clásica (**5**); **listen to ~** escuchar música (**2**); **pop ~** la música popular (**5**)

musical film la película musical (**5**)

musician el/la músico/a (**5**)

mustard la mostaza (**7**)

my mi/s (**1**, **2**); **~ name is...** me llamo... (**PA**)

mystery film la película de misterio (**5**)

N

name el nombre (**1**); **last ~** apellido (**8**); **What is your ~?** ¿Cómo se llama usted? (*for.*); ¿Cómo te llamas? (*fam.*) (**PA**)

nap, to take a echar una siesta (**PB**)

napkin la servilleta (**7**)

narrate, to narrar (**6**)

narrow estrecho/a (**7**, **8**)

nationality la nacionalidad (**PA**)

native natal (**3**)

nature la naturaleza (**3**, **11**)

nausea la náusea (**9**)

nauseous mareado/a (**9**)

near cerca (de) (**2**, **7**, **11**)

neck el cuello (**9**)

need, to necesitar; hacer falta (**2**, **8**)

negotiate the price, to regatear (**7**)

neighbor el/la vecino/a (**8**)

neighborhood el barrio (**8**)

neither... nor ni... ni (**3**, **4**)

nervous nervioso/a (**2**)

never nunca; jamás (emphatic) (**2**, **4**)

nevertheless sin embargo (**2**, **6**)

new nuevo/a (**3**)

news item la noticia (**11**)

newspaper el periódico (**7**, **11**)

next próximo/a (**PB**); **~ to** al lado de (**3**, **7**, **11**)

nice simpático/a (**1**); **~ to meet you.** Mucho gusto. (**PA**)

nickname el apodo (**5**)

Nigerian nigeriano/a (**PA**)

night: Good ~. Buenas noches. (**PA**); **last ~** anoche (**7**)

nightmare la pesadilla (**8**)

nine nueve (**PA**); **~ hundred** novecientos (**2**)

nineteen diecinueve (**PA**)

ninety noventa (**1**)

ninth noveno/a (**5**)

no no (**PA**); **~ longer** ya no (**5**); **~ one** nadie (**4**)

nobody nadie (**4**)

noise el ruido (**3**, **10**)

none ningún; ninguno/a (**4**)

noon el mediodía (**PA**)

nor/neither tampoco (**7**)

normally normalmente (**8**)

north el norte (**7**)

northeast el noreste (**2**)

nose la nariz (**9**)

note, to anotar (**5**)

notebook el cuaderno (**2**)

notes los apuntes (**2**)

nothing nada (**3**, **4**)

November noviembre (**PA**)

now ahora (**4**)

nowadays hoy (en) día (**5**)

number el número (**PA**)

nurse el/la enfermero/a (**9**)

nursing home la residencia de ancianos (**4**)

O

object el objeto (**3**)

obligation el deber (**4**)

obtain, to obtener (ie) (**4**)

occupy, to ocupar (**4**)

occur, to ocurrir (**4**, **9**)

ocean el océano (**11**)

October octubre (**PA**)

of de (**1**, **11**); **~ course** por supuesto; claro (**3**)

offer, to ofrecer (**1**)

office la oficina (**3**); **post ~** la oficina de correos; correos (**4**)

often a menudo (**2, 8**)

oil el aceite (**7**); **~ spill** el derrame de petróleo (**11**)

old antiguo/a; viejo/a (**2, 3**)

older mayor (**1, 10**)

on: ~ hand a mano (**10**); **~ the dot** en punto (**1**); **~ their own** por su cuenta (**7**); **~ top (of)** encima (de) (**3, 7, 11**)

once in a while de vez en cuando (**9**)

one uno; un/a (**PA, 1**); **~ hundred** cien (**1, 2**); **~ hundred million** cien millones (**3**); **~ hundred thousand** cien mil (**3**); **~ million** un millón (**3**); **~ thousand** mil (**2, 3**)

onion la cebolla (**7**)

only sólo; único/a; solamente; únicamente (**3, 4, 8, 9**); **~ one** solo/a (**7**)

open, to abrir (**2**); **Open your book to page…** Abra(n) el libro en la página… (**PA**)

opening el estreno (**5**)

opera la ópera (**5**)

opinion la opinión (**4**)

opportunity la oportunidad (**3**)

opposite opuesto/a; el opuesto (**4, 11**)

orange naranja (color); la naranja (fruit) (**3, 7**)

orchestra la orquesta (**5**)

order el orden (**5**); **to ~** pedir (**7**)

organize, to organizar (**4**)

origen el origen (**1**)

other otro/a (**4**)

others, the los demás (**4**)

ought to/should deber (**1, 4**)

our/s nuestro/a/os/as (**1, 10**)

outfit el conjunto (**8**)

outside of (a)fuera de (**4, 11**)

outskirts las afueras (**3**)

over sobre (**5, 11**); **~ there** allá (**6**)

overcoat el abrigo (**8**)

overhaul, to revisar (**10**)

owing to debido a (**8**)

own propio/a (**6**); **on their ~** por su cuenta (**7**)

ozone layer la capa de ozono (**11**)

P

pack a suitcase, to arreglar/hacer la maleta (**10**)

package el paquete (10)

page la página (2)

pain el dolor (9)

paint, to pintar (2)

painting el cuadro; la pintura (3, 8)

pair la pareja; el par (9)

pajamas el pijama (8)

pants los pantalones (8)

pantyhose las medias (**8**)

paper el papel (**2, 11**)

paragraph el párrafo (4)

parents los padres (**1**)

park el parque (**4**); **theme ~** el parque de atracciones (**10**); **to ~** estacionarse (**10**)

parking el estacionamiento (**10**)

parrot el loro (11)

party la fiesta (**PB**); **political ~** el partido político (**11**)

pass: to ~ (a test) aprobar (ue) (10); **to ~ (through)** pasar (por) (2)

passage el pasaje (9)

passenger el/la pasajero/a (10)

passionate apasionado/a (**5**)

passport el pasaporte (**10**)

past el pasado (4)

pastime el pasatiempo (2)

pastry el pastel (7)

patient paciente; el/la paciente (**1, 9**)

pay, to pagar (7)

peace la paz (5)

peaceful tranquilo/a (5, 10)

pear la pera (7)

pedestrian el peatón (**10**)

pen, ballpoint el bolígrafo (**2**)

pencil el lápiz (**2**)

people la gente (**1**)

pepper la pimienta (**7**); **chili ~** el chile (**7**)

percent por ciento (**1**)

percentage el porcentaje (7)

perform, to representar (8)

perhaps tal vez (3)

person: handicapped ~ el/la discapacitado/a (3); **local ~** el lugareño (4); **~ from Buenos Aires** porteño/a (8)

personality la personalidad (**1**)

pertain, to pertenecer (4)

Peruvian brandy el pisco (7)

pet la mascota; el animal doméstico (**10, 11**)

pharmacist el/la farmacéutico/a (9)

pharmacy la farmacia (**9**); **24-hour ~** la farmacia de turno/guardia (9)

phone call la llamada (**1**)

photograph la foto(grafía) (1)

physical: ~ characteristic la característica física (**1**); **~ exam** el examen físico (**9**)

pianist el/la pianista (5)

piano el piano (5)

pick up, to recoger (3)

picture el cuadro (3)

pie el pastel (7)

piece of furniture el mueble (3)

pig el cerdo (**11**)

pile el montón (7)

pill la pastilla (9)

pillow la almohada (**3**)

pink rosado/a (**3**)

pistol la pistola (8)

pity la lástima (11)

place el lugar (**2**); **to ~** poner; colocar (**3, 11**)

plan el plan (**4**); **to ~** planear (6)

planet el planeta (**11**)

plant la planta (**3**); **to ~** plantar (**11**)

plastic el plástico (**11**)

plate el plato (7)

platform (political) el programa (**11**)

play, to jugar (ue) (**4**); **~ an instrument** tocar; tocar un instrumento (**2, 5**); **~ baseball** jugar al béisbol (**2**); **~ basketball** jugar al básquetbol (**2**); **~ charades** hacer mímica (**8**); **~ football** jugar al fútbol americano (**2**); **~ soccer** jugar al fútbol (**2**); **~ tennis** jugar al tenis (**2**); **~ the role** hacer el papel (**3**)

player el/la jugador/a (**3**); **CD/DVD ~** el reproductor de CD/DVD (**2**); **trumpet ~** el/la trompetista (**5**)

pleasant agradable (5)

Please. Por favor. (**PA**)

Pleased to meet you. Encantado/a. (**PA**)

pleasure el placer (7)

plus más (**1**)

point el punto (8)

policeman/woman el/la policía (**10**)

politeness la cortesía (**PA**)

political: ~ campaign la campaña política (**4**); **~ issues** las cuestiones políticas (**11**); **~ party** el partido político (**11**); **~ platform** el programa (**11**); **~ science** las ciencias políticas (**2**)

politics la política (**11**)

polka-dotted de lunares (**8**)

poll la encuesta (**11**)

pollute, to contaminar (**11**)

pollution la contaminación (**11**)

polyester el poliéster (**8**)

pool la piscina (**2**)

poor pobre (**1**)

pop music la música popular (**5**)

population la población (**1**)

pork el cerdo (**7**)

portable portátil (**4**)

post office la oficina de correos; correos (**4**)

postage stamp el sello (**10**)

postcard la tarjeta postal (**10**)

potato la papa; la patata (**7**); **~ chips** las papas fritas (**7**)

potency la potencia (**11**)

poultry las aves (**7**)

poverty la pobreza (**11**)

power el poder (9)
practice/rehearse, to ensayar (5)
praise, to alabar (11)
predict, to predecir (i) (4)
prefer, to preferir (ie) (4)
preference la preferencia (4)
pregnant embarazada (9)
premonition el presentimiento (4)
preparation el preparativo (5)
prepare, to preparar (2)
prescribe, to recetar (9)
prescription la receta (9)
presentation la presentación (PA)
presidency la presidencia (11)
president el/la presidente/a (PB, 11)
pretty bonito/a; guapo/a (1)
previous previo/a (10)
price el precio (3); **to negotiate the ~** regatear (7)
print (with a pattern or design) estampado/a (8)
prize el premio (3)
professor el/la profesor/a (2)
promising prometedor/a (5)
proof la prueba (10)
propose, to proponer (5)
protect, to proteger (7, 11)
proud orgulloso/a (4)
provide, to proporcionar (8)
province la provincia (11)
psychology la psicología (2)
Puerto Rican puertorriqueño/a (PA)
punctual puntual (4)
pure puro/a (11)
purple morado/a (3)
purpose el propósito (7)
purse el bolso (8)
put, to poner (3); **~ away** guardar (3); **~ on make up** maquillarse (8)

Q

qualified calificado/a (11)
quality la calidad (8, 11)
queen la reina (11)
question la pregunta (PA)

R

rabbit el conejo (11)
radio el/la radio (2)
rain la lluvia (PA); **acid ~** la lluvia ácida (11); **(tropical) ~ forest** la selva tropical (11)
rainbow el arco iris (4)
raincoat el impermeable (8)
raining, it's llueve (PA)
rainy lluvioso/a (11)
raise, to subir (11)
rapid rápido (2)

rare poco hecho/a, crudo/a (meat); raro/a (7, 11)
rat la rata (11)
rather bastante (3)
raw crudo/a (7)
read, to leer (2); **Read.** Lea(n). (PA)
reading la lectura (1)
ready, to be estar listo/a (5)
realize, to darse cuenta (9)
Really well. Muy bien. (PA)
reason la razón (3)
receive, to recibir (1, 2)
recipe la receta (7)
recognize, to reconocer (8)
recommend, to recomendar (ie) (4)
record, to grabar (5)
recordings las grabaciones (5)
recruit, to reclutar (10)
recycle, to reciclar (11)
red rojo/a (3)
reforest, to reforestar (11)
refrigerator el refrigerador (3)
refuge el refugio (11)
refuse, to rehusar (11)
refute, to refutar (8)
region la región (11)
rehearse, to ensayar (5)
related to, to be tener que ver con (4)
relative el/la pariente (PB)
relax, to relajarse (5)
relaxing relajante (10)
release: to ~ a CD sacar un CD (5); **to ~ a film/movie** estrenar una película (5)
remain, to quedarse (8)
remedy, household el remedio casero (7)
remember, to recordar (ue); acordarse de (ue) (4, 8)
remorse el remordimiento (10)
rename, to renombrar (4)
renew, to renovar (8)
rent, to alquilar (3)
repeal, to abolir (5)
repeat, to repetir (i) (4); **Repeat.** Repita(n). (PA)
replace, to reponer (9)
report el informe; el reportaje (9, 10)
representative el/la diputado/a (11)
request la petición (11)
require, to requerir (ie) (11)
reservation la reserva (10)
reserve a table, to reservar una mesa (7)
resolution la decisión; la determinación (9, 11)
resolve, to resolver (ue) (8, 11)
resolved resuelto/a (10)
resource el recurso (11)
respect, to respetar (5)

respectful respetuoso/a (9)
responsible responsable (1)
rest, to descansar (7)
restaurant el restaurante (4)
result el resultado (4)
return, to regresar; devolver (an object); volver (ue) (2, 4, 11)
reuse, to reutilizar (11)
review la reseña (5); **to ~** repasar (5)
revoke, to abolir (5)
reward la recompensa (11)
rhythm el ritmo (5)
rice el arroz (7)
rich rico/a (1)
riddle el rompecabezas (7)
ride, to montar; **~ a bike** montar en bicicleta (2); **~ a horse** montar a caballo (11)
right (legal) el derecho (2); **to be ~** tener razón (3); **to the ~ of** a la derecha de (3, 7, 11)
ring el anillo (5); **to ~** sonar (7)
risk el riesgo (9)
rite el rito (7)
river el río (11)
roasted asado/a (7)
robbery el robo (7)
robe la bata (8)
rock (music) el rock (5)
role el papel (3)
romantic film la película romántica (5)
roof el techo (3)
room el cuarto; la habitación (2, 3, 5); **dining ~** el comedor (3); **double ~** el cuarto doble (10); **emergency ~** la sala de urgencias (9); **single ~** el cuarto individual (10)
roommate el/la compañero/a de cuarto (2)
rooster el gallo (7)
root la raíz (11)
rough áspero/a (11)
round-trip ticket el boleto de ida y vuelta (10)
roving ambulante (4)
row la fila (5)
rug la alfombra (3)
ruin la ruina (9)
rule la regla (8)
run, to correr (2)

S

sad triste (2)
salad la ensalada (7)
salsa la salsa (5)
salt la sal (7)
same el/la/los/las mismo/a/os/as (1); **the ~ as** al igual; igual que (3, 7)

sandals las sandalias (**8**)
Saturday el sábado (**PA**)
save, to salvar (**8**)
say, to decir (i) (**3**)
saying el dicho; el refrán (**1**)
scare, to asustar (**9**)
scary espantoso/a (**5**)
scene la escena (**7**)
schedule el horario (de clases) (**2**)
school la escuela (**4**)
science las ciencias (**2**); ~ **fiction film** la película de ciencia ficción (**5**); **computer** ~ la informática (**2**); **political** ~ las ciencias políticas (**2**)
scream, to gritar (**8**)
screen la pantalla (**5**)
sea el mar (**9**)
seafood los mariscos (**7**)
seamstress la costurera (**8**)
search la búsqueda (**11**)
season la estación (**PA**)
seasoning el condimento (**7**)
seat la sede (of government); el asiento (**9, 10**)
seated sentado/a (**5**)
second segundo/a (**5**); ~ **floor** el primer piso (**3**)
section el apartado (**8**)
security la seguridad (**2**)
see: ~ **you later.** Hasta luego. (**PA**); ~ **you soon.** Hasta pronto. (**PA**); ~ **you tomorrow.** Hasta mañana. (**PA**); **to** ~ ver (**3**)
seem, to parecer (**2**)
select, to seleccionar (**5**)
sell, to vender (**7**)
seller el/la vendedor/a (**3**)
semester el semestre (**2**)
senate el senado (**11**)
senator el/la senador/a (**11**)
send, to mandar; enviar (**2, 8**); ~**/mail a letter** mandar una carta (**4**)
sentence la oración; la frase (**3, 4**)
September septiembre (**PA**)
serenade la serenata (**11**)
serious serio/a (**9**)
serve, to servir (i) (**4**)
set the table, to poner la mesa (**3**)
seven siete (**PA**); ~ **hundred** setecientos (**2**)
seventeen diecisiete (**PA**)
seventh séptimo/a (**5**)
seventy setenta (**1**)
shaman el chamán (**9**)
share, to compartir (**3**)
shark el tiburón (**5**)
shattered destrozado/a (**10**)
shave, to afeitarse (**8**)
she ella (**PA**)
sheets las sábanas (**3**)

shirt la camisa (**8**)
shoe el zapato (**8**); **tennis shoes** los zapatos de tenis (**8**)
shop, to comprar; **to window-shop** ojear las vitrinas (**8**)
shopping las compras (**4**); ~ **district** el centro comercial (**4**); **to go** ~ ir de compras, hacer las compras (**2**)
short bajo/a (in stature); corto/a (in length) (**1, 8, 10**)
shorts los pantalones cortos (**8**)
shot la inyección (**9**)
should (ought to) deber (**1, 4**)
show, to enseñar; mostrar (ue) (**2, 4**); ~ **a film/movie** presentar una película (**5**)
shower la ducha (**3**); **to** ~ ducharse (**8**)
shrimp los camarones (**7**)
siblings los hermanos (**1**)
sick enfermo/a (**2**); **to be** ~ estar enfermo/a (**5, 9**)
side el lado (**2**)
sigh el suspiro (**9**) suspirar (**9, 11**)
sign, to firmar (**3**)
signature la firma (**3**)
silk la seda (**8**)
silly tonto/a (**1**)
similar parecido/a (**7**)
similarity la semejanza (**6**)
simple sencillo/a (**10**)
since ya que; desde (**1, 7**)
sing, to cantar (**5**)
singer el/la cantante (**5**)
single room el cuarto individual (**10**)
sink el lavabo (**3**)
sister la hermana (**1**)
sit, to sentarse (ie) (**8**)
site el sitio (**11**)
six seis (**PA**); ~ **hundred** seiscientos (**2**)
sixteen dieciséis (**PA**)
sixth sexto/a (**5**)
sixty sesenta (**1**)
size el tamaño (**9**)
skate, to patinar (**2**)
skillful hábil (**5**)
skirt la falda (**8**)
sky el cielo (**11**)
slavery la esclavitud (**11**)
sleep, to dormir (ue) (**4**)
sleepy, to be tener sueño (**3**)
slippers las zapatillas (**8**)
slow lento/a (**3, 5**)
small pequeño/a (**1**)
smaller menor (**10**)
smallest, the el/la menor (**10**)
smoke, to fumar (**10**)
smooth suave (**5**)
snack la merienda (**7**); **to have a** ~ merendar (ie) (**7**)

snake la serpiente (**11**)
sneeze el estornudo (**9**); **to** ~ estornudar (**9**)
snow la nieve (**PA**)
snowing, it's nieva (**PA**)
so: ~ **many/much** tanto/a/os/as (**2, 9**); ~~**.** Más o menos.; Regular. (**PA**)
soccer, to play jugar al fútbol (**2**)
society la sociedad (**8**)
socks los calcetines (**8**)
sofa el sofá (**3**)
soft drink el refresco (**7**)
soil la tierra (**5, 11**)
solicit, to solicitar (**11**)
solid-colored liso/a (**8**)
solve, to solucionar (**5**)
some unos/as (**1**)
some/any algún; alguno/a (**1, 4**)
someone alguien (**4**)
something algo (**3, 4**)
sometimes a veces (**2, 4**)
son el hijo (**1**)
song la canción (**5**)
soon pronto (**5**)
sore throat, to have a tener dolor de garganta (**9**)
sound el sonido (**5**)
soup la sopa (**7**); ~ **spoon** la cuchara (**7**)
source la fuente (**3**)
south el sur (**7**)
southern sureño/a (**8**)
sow, to sembrar (ie) (**11**)
space el espacio (**3**)
Spanish español/a (**PA**); ~ **speaker** el/la hispanohablante (**1**)
speak, to hablar (**1, 2**)
specialty of the house la especialidad de la casa (**7**)
species la especie (**11**); **endangered** ~ el animal en peligro de extinción (**11**)
speech el discurso (**11**)
spend, to gastar (**7**)
spice la especia (**7**)
spicy picante (**7**)
spider la araña (**5**)
spill, oil el derrame de petróleo (**11**)
spoon la cuchara (**7**); **soup** ~ la cuchara (**7**)
spoonful la cucharada (**7**)
sport el deporte (**2**)
spring la primavera (**PA**)
square el cuadro (**3**)
stadium el estadio (**2**)
stage la etapa (**4**)
stain la mancha (**9**)
staircase la escalera (**3**)
stamp, postage el sello (**10**)
stand, to pararse (**10**); ~ **out** destacar (**5**); ~ **up** levantarse (**8**)

standard el estándar (11)

star la estrella (**5**)

state el estado (9, **11**); ~ **of being** el estado (2)

statehood la estadidad (11)

station (train, bus) la estación (de tren, de autobús) (**10**); **gas ~** la estación de servicio/de gasolina (**10**)

stay, to quedarse (**8**); ~ **in bed** guardar cama (**9**)

steak el bistec (**7**)

steering wheel el volante (**10**)

step el paso (3)

stepfather el padrastro (**1**)

stepmother la madrastra (**1**)

stereotype el estereotipo (2)

still todavía (3)

stirred up alborotado/a (11)

stockings las medias (**8**)

stomach el estómago (**9**)

stomachache, to have a tener dolor de estómago (**9**)

stop: bus ~ la parada (**10**); **to ~** parar (**PB**)

store la tienda (2); **department ~** el almacén (**4**)

storm la tormenta (**11**)

story la historia; el cuento; el piso (in a building) (**PB**, 3, 5)

stove la estufa (3)

straighten up, to arreglar (3)

strange extraño/a; raro/a (3, 7)

strategy la estrategia (10)

street la calle (3, **10**)

strength la fuerza (7)

stress el estrés (4)

stressed (emphasized) tónico/a (10)

strike la huelga (**11**); **to be on ~** estar en huelga (**11**)

striped de rayas (8)

strong fuerte (**1**)

student el/la estudiante (1, 2); ~ **center/union** el centro estudiantil (**2**)

study el estudio (8); **to ~** estudiar (1, **2**)

stupendous estupendo/a (**5**)

stupid tonto/a (3)

style el estilo; la moda (5, **8**)

subject el asunto; la materia; el sujeto (1, 2, 8)

sublet, to alquilar (3)

substitute, to sustituir (5)

subway el metro (**10**)

successful, to be tener éxito (3)

suddenly de repente; de pronto (**PB**, 4)

sugar el azúcar (7)

suggestion la sugerencia (10)

suit el traje (5, **8**); **bathing ~** el traje de baño (**8**)

suitable adecuado/a (10)

suitcase la maleta (**10**); **to pack a ~** arreglar/hacer la maleta (**10**)

summarize, to resumir (9)

summary el resumen (9)

summer el verano (**PA**); ~ **camp** el campamento de niños (**4**)

summit la cima (10)

sun el sol (**PA**)

sunbathe, to tomar el sol (2)

Sunday el domingo (**PA**)

sunny, it's hace sol (**PA**)

supermarket el supermercado (**4**)

support el apoyo (11); **to ~** apoyar (5, **11**); **to ~ a candidate** apoyar a un/a candidato/a (**4**)

sure seguro/a (9)

surely seguramente (2)

surprise la sorpresa (8)

surprising sorprendente (5)

survey la encuesta (11)

suspicious sospechoso (2)

sweat, to sudar (9)

sweater el suéter (**8**)

sweatshirt la sudadera (**8**)

sweets los dulces (7)

swim, to nadar (2)

swimming la natación (2)

swimsuit el traje de baño (8)

symbol el símbolo (12)

symptom el síntoma (9)

T

table la mesa (2); **to reserve a ~** reservar una mesa (7); **to set the ~** poner la mesa (3)

tablecloth el mantel (7)

tablespoon la cuchara (7)

take, to tomar; llevar (2, 5); ~ **a nap** echar una siesta (**PB**); ~ **a short trip** ir de excursión (**4**); ~ **a walk** hacer una caminata; pasear (**4**); ~ **care of** cuidar (9, **11**); ~ **off (one's clothes)** quitarse (la ropa) (**8**); ~ **out the garbage** sacar la basura (3); ~ **out** sacar (10); ~ **place** tener lugar (2); ~ **someone to the doctor** llevar a alguien al médico (**4**); ~ **(time)** tardar en (8); ~ **turns** turnarse (3)

tall alto/a (**1**)

tariff la tarifa (5)

tax el impuesto (11)

taxi el taxi (10)

tea (iced/hot) el té (helado/caliente) (7)

teach, to enseñar (2)

team el equipo (2)

teaspoon la cucharita (7)

tell (a story), to contar (ue) (5)

temperate templado/a (8)

temperature la temperatura (**PA**)

temple el templo (4)

ten diez (**PA**)

tennis: ~ **shoes** los zapatos de tenis (**8**); **to play ~** jugar al tenis (2)

tent la tienda de campaña (4)

tenth décimo/a (**5**)

Thank you. Gracias. (**PA**)

that ese/a (**5**); ~ **(way over there)** aquel/la (**5**); ~ **one** ése/a (**5**); ~ **one (way over there)** aquél/la (**5**); ~ **which** lo que (3); ~**'s great!** ¡Qué bueno! (2)

the el, los, la, las (**1**, 2); ~ **best** el/la mejor (1, **4**, **10**); ~ **biggest** el/la mayor (1, **10**); ~ **check, please.** La cuenta, por favor. (**7**); ~ **day before yesterday** anteayer (7); ~ **same as** al igual; igual que (3, 7); ~ **smallest** el/la menor (**10**); ~ **weather is bad.** Hace mal tiempo. (**PA**); ~ **weather is nice.** Hace buen tiempo. (**PA**); ~ **worst** el/la peor (**4**, **10**)

theater el teatro (**4**); **movie ~** el cine (**4**)

their su/s (**1**)

theirs suyo/a/os/as (7, **10**)

theme el tema (3); ~ **park** el parque de atracciones (**10**)

then entonces; luego (5, 6)

there allí (**4**, **6**); ~ **is no doubt** no cabe duda (9); ~ **is/are** hay (2); **over ~** allá (**6**)

these estos/as (**5**); ~ **ones** éstos/as (**5**)

they ellos/as (**PA**)

thin delgado/a (**1**)

thing la cosa (3)

think, to opinar; pensar (ie) (1, **4**)

third tercer/o/a (2, **5**); ~ **floor** el segundo piso (3)

thirsty, to be tener sed (3)

thirteen trece (**PA**)

thirty treinta (**PA**)

this (one) esto (neuter); este/a; éste/a (this one) (3, **5**)

those esos/as; ésos/as (those); aquellos/as; aquéllos/as (those way over there) (3, **5**)

though aunque (5)

threat la amenaza (8)

three tres (**PA**); ~ **hundred** trescientos (2)

throat la garganta (**9**); **to have a sore ~** tener dolor de garganta (**9**)

through por, a través de (2, **11**)

throw, to tirar (8); ~ **away** botar (**11**)

Thursday el jueves (**PA**)

ticket la entrada, el boleto (**5, 10**); **round-trip ~** el boleto de ida y vuelta (**10**); **traffic ~** la multa (**10**)

tie la corbata (**8**)

tight estrecho/a (**7, 8**)

time el tiempo; la vez (**4, 5**); **from ~ to ~** a veces (**2**); **many times** muchas veces (**8**); **What ~ is it?** ¿Qué hora es? (**PA**)

times por (**1**)

tin work la hojalatería (**2**)

tip la propina (**7, 10**)

tire la llanta (**10**)

tired cansado/a (**2**)

title el título (**7**)

to a (**11**); **~ where?** ¿Adónde? (**2**)

toast la tostada (**7**)

today hoy (**2**)

toe el dedo del pie (**9**)

together juntos/as (**3**); **~ with** junto con (**2**)

toilet el inodoro (**3**)

toll la tarifa (**5**)

tomato el tomate (**7**)

tomorrow mañana (**1, 2**)

tongue twister el trabalenguas (**4**)

too también; demasiado (**1, 2**); **~ much** demasiado (**2**)

tooth el diente (**9**)

top la cima (10); **on ~ (of)** encima (de) (**3, 7, 11**)

topic el tema (**3**)

tornado el tornado (**11**)

tour la gira (**5**); **to ~** hacer una gira (**5**)

tournament el torneo (**4**)

tower la torre (**3**)

town el pueblo (**3, 4**); **~ square** la plaza (**4**)

track and field el atletismo (**2**)

traditional tradicional (**3**)

traffic el tráfico (**10**); **~ light** el semáforo (**10**); **~ ticket** la multa (**10**)

tragedy la tragedia (**11**)

tragic trágico/a (**5**)

train el tren (**10**)

trainer el/la entrenador/a (**4**)

translate, to traducir (**11**)

transportation el transporte (**10**); **means of ~** el medio de transporte (**10**)

travel: ~ agency la agencia de viajes (**6, 10**); **~ agent** el/la agente de viajes (**10**); **to ~** viajar (**2, 10**)

travelers los viajeros (**10**)

treasure el tesoro (**10**)

treat, to tratar (**9**)

treatment el tratamiento (**9**)

tree el árbol (**2, 11**)

tremble, to temblar (ie) (**7**)

tribe la tribu (**2**)

trip el viaje (**8, 10**); **to go on a ~** ir de viaje (**10**); **to take a (short) ~** ir de excursión (**4**)

truck el camión (**10**)

true cierto/a; verdadero/a (**4, 7**); **It's (not) ~.** (No) es verdad. (**1**)

trumpet la trompeta (**5**); **~ player** el/la trompetista (**5**)

trunk el baúl (**10**)

trust, to confiar; fiar (**8, 10**)

truth la verdad (**3**)

try, to intentar; tratar de (to try to) (**5, 7, 9**)

T-shirt la camiseta (**8**)

tsunami el sunami (**11**)

Tuesday el martes (**PA**)

tuna el atún 5, 7

turn, to doblar (**10**); **~ on** encender (ie); prender (**9, 11**)

TV set el televisor (**2**)

twelve doce (**PA**)

twenty veinte (**PA**); **~-eight** veintiocho (**PA**); **~-five** veinticinco (**PA**); **~-four** veinticuatro (**PA**); **~-nine** veintinueve (**PA**); **~-one** veintiuno (**PA**); **~-seven** veintisiete (**PA**); **~-six** veintiséis (**PA**); **~-three** veintitrés (**PA**); **~-two** veintidós (**PA**)

two dos (**PA**); **~ hundred** doscientos (**2**)

u

ugly feo/a (**1**)

umbrella el paraguas (**8**)

uncle el tío (**1**)

uncomfortable incómodo/a (**9**)

under bajo; debajo de (**7, 11**)

undercover encubierto/a (**11**)

underline, to subrayar (**7**)

understand, to comprender; entender (ie) (**1, 2, 4**)

underwear la ropa interior (**8**)

unemployment el desempleo (**11**)

unpleasant antipático/a (**1**)

until hasta (**2, 11**)

upset nervioso/a (**2**)

use, to usar (**2**)

useful útil (**PA**)

V

vacation las vacaciones (**10**); **to go on ~** ir de vacaciones (**7, 10**)

vacuum, to pasar la aspiradora (**3**)

value el valor (**6**)

vegetable la verdura (**7**)

vehicle el vehículo (**10**)

vendor el/la vendedor/a (**3**)

very muy (**1**); **~ little** muy poco (**2**)

villager el lugareño/a (**4**)

vinegar el vinagre (**7**)

virus, to have a tener un virus (**9**)

visit, to visitar (**10**)

vocabulary el vocabulario (**1**)

voice la voz (**5**)

volcano el volcán (**4**)

volunteer, to trabajar como voluntario/a (**4**)

volunteerism el voluntariado (**4**)

vote, to votar (**11**)

W

waist la cintura (**9**)

wait for esperar (**2**)

waiter el camarero (**7**)

waitress la camarera (**7**)

wake up, to despertarse (ie) (**8**)

walk: to take a ~ hacer una caminata; pasear (**4**); **to ~** caminar; andar; ir a pie (**2, 7, 10**)

wall la pared (**2**)

want, to desear; querer (ie) (**2, 3**)

war la guerra (**11**); **~ film** la película de guerra (**5**)

warn, to advertir (ie, i) (**8**)

wash, to lavar (**7**); **~ oneself** lavarse (**8**); **~ the dishes** lavar los platos (**3**)

waste, to perder (ie) (**4**)

watch el reloj (**2**); **to ~** vigilar (**9**); **to ~ TV** ver la televisión (**2**)

water: ~ with ice el agua con hielo (**5, 7**); **fresh ~** el agua dulce (**5**)

waterfall la catarata (**8**)

we nosotros/as (**PA**)

weak débil (**1**)

wear, to llevar; llevar puesto (**5, 8**)

weather el tiempo (**PA**); **The ~ is nice/bad.** Hace buen/mal tiempo. (**PA**); **What's the ~ like?** ¿Qué tiempo hace? (**PA**)

wedding la boda (**4**)

Wednesday el miércoles (**PA**)

week la semana (**7**); **last ~** la semana pasada (**7**)

weekend el fin de semana (**3**); **last ~** el fin de semana pasado (**7**)

weigh, to pesar (**11**)

weight el peso (**9**)

welfare el bienestar (**11**)

well: Really ~. Muy bien. (**PA**); **~ done/cooked** bien cocido/a; bien hecho/a (**7**); **~ set** bien puesto (**7**); **~-being** el bienestar (**11**)

west el oeste (**2**)

western occidental (**8**)

what lo que (**3**)

What? ¿Qué? (**2**); ¿Cómo? (**PA, 2**); **~ does it mean?** ¿Qué significa? (**PA**); **~ is this?** ¿Qué es esto? (**PA**); **~ is your name?** ¿Cómo se llama usted? (*for.*); ¿Cómo te llamas? (*fam.*) (**PA**); **~ time is it?** ¿Qué hora es? (**PA**); **~'s the weather like?** ¿Qué tiempo hace? (**PA**)

wheel la rueda (**10**); **steering ~** el volante (**10**)

When? ¿Cuándo? (**2**)

Where? ¿Dónde? (**2**); **to ~?** ¿adónde? (**2**)

Which (one/s)? ¿Cuál/es? (**2**)

while mientras (**2**); **once in a ~** de vez en cuando (**9**)

whip, to azotar (**11**)

white blanco/a (**3**)

Who? ¿Quién? ¿Quiénes? (**PA, 2**)

whose cuyo/a/os/as (**5**)

Why? ¿Por qué? (**2**)

wide ancho/a (**7**, **8**)

wife la esposa (**1**)

wild animal el animal salvaje (**11**)

win, to ganar (**3**)

wind el viento (**PA**)

window la ventana (**2**); **to ~-shop** ojear las vitrinas (**8**)

windshield el parabrisas (**10**); **~ wiper** el limpiaparabrisas (**10**)

windy, it's hace viento. (**PA**)

wine el vino (**7**)

winter el invierno (**PA**)

wish, to desear (**2**)

with con (**2, 11**); **~ me** conmigo (**8**); **~ you** contigo (**7**)

without sin (**4, 11**)

woman la mujer; la señora (Sra.) (**1**); **young ~** la joven (**1**); la señorita (Srta.) (**1**)

wool la lana (**8**)

word la palabra (**1**)

work el trabajo; la obra (**1, 3**); **to ~** trabajar; funcionar (**2, 10**)

world el mundo (**PA**)

worried preocupado/a (**2**)

worry about, to preocuparse por (**3, 11**)

worse peor (**10**)

worst, the el/la peor (**4, 10**)

wound la herida (**9**)

wrap, to envolver (ue) (**7**)

wrestling la lucha libre (**2**)

write, to escribir (**1, 2**); **Write.** Escriba(n). (**PA**)

writer el/la escritor/a (**6**)

Y

yam la batata (**7**)

year el año (**PA**); **last ~** el año pasado (**4, 7**); **to be... years old** tener... años (**3**)

yell, to gritar (**8**)

yellow amarillo/a (**3**)

Yes. Sí. (**PA, 2**)

yesterday ayer (**2, 7**)

you usted/es (*for.*); tú (*fam.*); vosotros/as (*fam. pl. Spain*) (**PA, 2**)

You're welcome. De nada. (**PA**)

young joven (**1**); **~ man** el joven (**1**); **~ woman** la joven, la señorita (Srta.) (**1**)

your tu/s (*fam.*); su/s (*for.*); vuestro/a/os/as (*fam. pl. Spain*) (**1, 2**)

yours tuyo/a/os/as (*fam.*); suyo/a/os/as (*for.*); vuestro/a/os/as (*fam. pl. Spain*) (**10**)

yucca la mandioca (**7**)

Z

zero cero (**PA**)

INDEX